Frommer's®
Peru

My Peru

by Neil Edward Schlecht

I REMEMBER THE FIRST TIME I HAPPENED UPON MACHU PICCHU, LONG

 before I was aware of a country named Peru. In the first grade, I saw a photograph of the ruins, dreamily secluded in clouds and the Andes, and was mesmerized. Peru exerts that kind of hold on people, even 6-year-olds. My first visit to Machu Picchu did the trick, prompting more than 20 years of travel to Peru. I quickly learned that, for all the Incas' incredible achievements—including building a continent-spanning empire and leaving behind the exquisite, enigmatic work of landscape art that is their famous "lost city"—there is much, much more to this unique country.

I could rhapsodize about Peru's astonishing variety of regions and places to experience. But what most comes to mind is an explosion of color. I think of the bright oranges, yellows, and reds of textiles in mountain markets. The blood red *chullos* (stocking caps) with neon-colored pompoms that reveal men's marital status on Taquile Island. Colors really erupt during the country's flamboyant festivals: the flowing robes, headgear, and pageantry of Inti Raymi, the Festival of the Sun in Cusco; the sinister costumes in the Dance of the Devils in Puno; the mad and monstrous masks of Paucartambo's Virgen del Carmen. I'm betting the extraordinary colors of Peru will stick with you, too. There's little doubt Machu Picchu will.

© Neil Schlecht

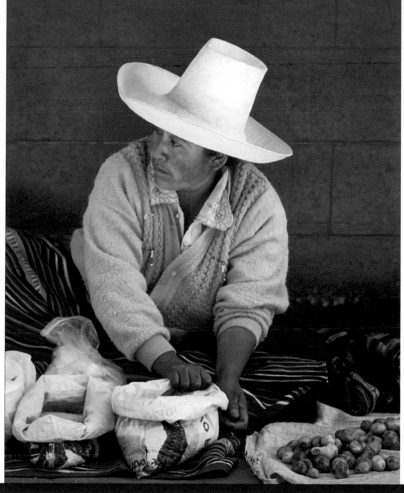

THE ISLANDS OF LAKE TITICACA (left) Seen from its banks, the azure expanse of Lake Titicaca, the world's highest navigable body of water at 3,800m (13,000 ft.), is one of Peru's most remarkable sights. But even more incredible is experiencing the lake and its series of unique islands up close. Though the floating Uros, Taquile, and Amantaní are all worthwhile visits, my favorite destination is tiny Isla Suasi, a pristine, remote place that's the only privately owned island in all of Titicaca.

CAJAMARCA'S MERCADO CENTRAL (above) The sprawling open-air food market in this jewel of an unsung town in northern Peru offers everything from wheelbarrows of fresh strawberries and stacks of salted cod to large rice sacks stuffed with live guinea pigs. You can even pick up one of those towering *sombreros de paja* (straw hats) that locals wear. The highest-quality hats take a month to weave, and can cost as much as $400—what most farmers make in a year.

CUSCO'S PLAZA DE ARMAS AT DUSK (above)
Cusco's old central square remains the hub of this vibrant city, the 600-year-old capital of the Incas. When dusk falls, amber streetlights and colonial churches and arcades glow against a darkening blue-black Andean sky.

CEVICHE (right) One must-eat in Peru is *ceviche*, raw fish and shellfish that's marinated, or "cooked," in lime juice and chile peppers and served with toasted corn, sweet potato, and raw onion. Lima is ground zero for ceviche crawls; there are 2,000 *cevicherías* in the capital alone.

One of the strangest sights in Peru is the **NASCA LINES,** enormous drawings in the desert sands that cover an area of nearly 200 square miles and can only be appreciated from the window of a small plane. So peculiar are the hundreds of figures, some as large as 1,000 feet long and mysteriously etched into the earth more than a millennium ago, that some theorists have invoked extraterrestrials to explain their origins. Though most experts now agree they were constructed by the Nasca (pre-Inca) culture, no one can definitively state their exact purpose.

© Derrick Francis Furlong/Alamy

© Neil Schlecht

AMAZON CANOPY WALKWAY (above) A growing number of lodges in the Amazon Basin—which covers nearly two-thirds of Peru—have erected canopy walkways, aerial pathways of ladders, cables and netting, more than 30m (100 ft.) above the forest floor. It's the closest you're likely to come to seeing the jungle from the perspective of its bird and monkey inhabitants.

MONASTERIO DE SANTA CATALINA (right) Behind thick *sillar* (white volcanic stone) walls, the glorious 16th-century Dominican convent is the centerpiece of Arequipa, Peru's elegant "white city." The sun-baked maze of narrow, cobalt blue and terra-cotta passageways, plant-filled patios, and secret niches conjures a southern Spain dreamscape. For a few hours at least, you, like the few cloistered nuns who remain here, may find it tough to leave.

NIÑOS HOTEL, CUSCO (right) The amazing "Children's Hotel" in the old center of Cusco is a steal—stylish and immaculate for the price—and it's the anchor of a nonprofit foundation that supports street kids in Cusco (in addition to three hotels, it operates a school, hospital, restaurants, and athletic facilities, all serving disadvantaged youths). It's the kind of place you almost wish charged more.

INCA STONEMASONRY, CUSCO (below) The Incas were master engineers and stonemasons, and their remarkable handiwork can be seen all over Cusco, from the smooth, angled niches and curved walls of the Temple of the Sun to the massive blocks of ruins from Sacsayhuamán to Ollantaytambo (and, of course, Machu Picchu).

© Neil Schlecht

© Frans Lemmens/zefa/Corbis

Cruz del Cóndor, a lookout at the edge of incredibly deep **COLCA CANYON,** is a mecca for viewing giant Andean condors, the largest birds in the world (their wingspans reach 11 ft. or more). Every morning, crowds gather, giddy at the anticipation of seeing the great birds appear over the immense canyon. As if on cue, condors emerge and begin to swirl slowly, gaining altitude before taking off down the river for feeding. © *Johan Elzenga/Alamy*

ABOUT THE AUTHOR

Neil Edward Schlecht first trekked to Machu Picchu in 1983 during his junior year abroad in Quito, Ecuador, and he has continued making pilgrimages to Peru ever since. He is the author and co-author of a dozen travel guides (including *Frommer's Barcelona Day by Day, Frommer's New York State,* and *Spain For Dummies*), and his articles on travel, art, wine, and tennis have appeared in *Galeria Antiqvaria, The Irish Times,* CNN.com, and USOpen.com. After long stints in Spain and Brazil, he currently resides in Litchfield County, Connecticut.

Published by:

WILEY PUBLISHING, INC.

111 River St.
Hoboken, NJ 07030-5774

ISBN 978-0-470-60223-2

Editor: Chris Summers, with Maureen Clarke
Production Editor: Jonathan Scott
Cartographer: Guy Ruggiero
Photo Editor: Richard H. Fox
Production by Wiley Indianapolis Composition Services

Front cover photo: Machu Picchu: detail of window with ruins and clouds beyond
Back cover photo: Ollantaytambo: woman seen from behind, walking down cobblestone street

For information on our other products and services or to obtain technical support, please contact our Customer Care Department within the U.S. at 877/762-2974, outside the U.S. at 317/572-3993 or fax 317/572-4002.

Wiley also publishes its books in a variety of electronic formats. Some content that appears in print may not be available in electronic formats.

Manufactured in the United States of America

5 4 3 2 1

Frommer's®

Peru

5th Edition

by Neil E. Schlecht

WILEY
Wiley Publishing, Inc.

CONTENTS

4 SUGGESTED PERU ITINERARIES   75

5 THE ACTIVE VACATION PLANNER   85

6 LIMA   105

7 THE CENTRAL COAST & HIGHLANDS   149

8 CUSCO   184

9 MACHU PICCHU & THE SACRED VALLEY OF THE INCAS   238

10 SOUTHERN PERU   290

PERU

CONTENTS

LIST OF MAPS

HOW TO CONTACT US

In researching this book, we discovered many wonderful places—hotels, restaurants, shops, and more. We're sure you'll find others. Please tell us about them, so we can share the information with your fellow travelers in upcoming editions. If you were disappointed with a recommendation, we'd love to know that, too. Please write to:

Frommer's Peru, 5th Edition
Wiley Publishing, Inc. • 111 River St. • Hoboken, NJ 07030-5774

AN ADDITIONAL NOTE

Please be advised that travel information is subject to change at any time—and this is especially true of prices. We therefore suggest that you write or call ahead for confirmation when making your travel plans. The authors, editors, and publisher cannot be held responsible for the experiences of readers while traveling. Your safety is important to us, however, so we encourage you to stay alert and be aware of your surroundings. Keep a close eye on cameras, purses, and wallets, all favorite targets of thieves and pickpockets.

FROMMER'S STAR RATINGS, ICONS & ABBREVIATIONS

Every hotel, restaurant, and attraction listing in this guide has been ranked for quality, value, service, amenities, and special features using a **star-rating system.** In country, state, and regional guides, we also rate towns and regions to help you narrow down your choices and budget your time accordingly. Hotels and restaurants are rated on a scale of zero (recommended) to three stars (exceptional). Attractions, shopping, nightlife, towns, and regions are rated according to the following scale: zero stars (recommended), one star (highly recommended), two stars (very highly recommended), and three stars (must-see).

In addition to the star-rating system, we also use **six feature icons** that point you to the great deals, in-the-know advice, and unique experiences that separate travelers from tourists. Throughout the book, look for:

(Finds	Special finds—those places only insiders know about
(Fun Facts	Fun facts—details that make travelers more informed and their trips more fun
(Moments	Special moments—those experiences that memories are made of
(Overrated	Places or experiences not worth your time or money
(Tips	Insider tips—great ways to save time and money
(Value	Great values—where to get the best deals

The following **abbreviations** are used for credit cards:

AE	American Express	**DISC**	Discover	**V**	Visa
DC	Diners Club	**MC**	MasterCard		

TRAVEL RESOURCES AT FROMMERS.COM

Frommer's travel resources don't end with this guide. Frommer's website, **Frommers.com,** has travel information on more than 4,000 destinations. We update features regularly, giving you access to the most current trip-planning information and the best airfare, lodging, and car-rental bargains. You can also listen to podcasts, connect with other Frommers.com members through our active-reader forums, share your travel photos, read blogs from guidebook editors and fellow travelers, and much more.

The Best of Peru

Peru is legendary among world travelers looking for exciting new experiences. Stunningly endowed in both natural and man-made attractions, the country offers much more than most trips can even hope to take in: charming Andean highland towns with colonial architecture, remote jungle lodges in the Amazon basin, soaring snowcapped mountains and volcanoes, a 3,220km (2,000-mile) Pacific coastline, and, of course, Machu Picchu and the stunning legacies of the Incas and other sophisticated pre-Columbian civilizations. Peru is a place of brilliant hand-woven textiles and exuberant celebrations, exotic animals, and fascinating peoples. It is a country bursting with opportunities for memorable travel experiences and outdoor adventure. The following lists describe some of my favorite places and activities, from hotels and restaurants to outdoor experiences and festivals. But the fun of traveling to a fascinatingly diverse country such as Peru is compiling your own unforgettable list.

1 THE MOST UNFORGETTABLE TRAVEL EXPERIENCES

- **Soaring over the Nasca Lines:** One of South America's great enigmas, these ancient, baffling lines are etched into the desert sands along Peru's southern coast. There are giant trapezoids and triangles, the identifiable shapes of animal and plant figures, and more than 10,000 lines that can only really be seen from the air. Variously thought to be signs from the gods, agricultural and astronomical calendars, or even extraterrestrial airports, the Nasca Lines were constructed between 300 B.C. and A.D. 700. Small-craft overflights dip and glide, and passengers strain their necks against the window to see mysterious figures such as "the Astronaut." See "Nasca," in chapter 7.

- **Gazing at Machu Picchu:** However you get to it—whether you hike the fabled Inca Trail or hop aboard one of the prettiest train rides in South America—Machu Picchu more than lives up to its reputation as one of the most

spectacular sites on earth. The ruins of the legendary "lost city of the Incas" sit majestically among the massive Andes, swathed in clouds. The ceremonial and agricultural center, never discovered or looted by the Spaniards, dates to the mid-1400s but seems even more ancient. Despite its enormous popularity, exploring the site remains a thrilling experience, especially at sunrise, when dramatic rays of light creep over the mountaintops. For the classic, panoramic postcard views, see the ruins from the Sun Gate or the top of Huayna Picchu. See "Machu Picchu & the Inca Trail," in chapter 9.

- **Hiking the Inca Trail:** The legendary trail to Machu Picchu, the Camino del Inca, is one of the world's most rewarding ecoadventures. The arduous 4-day trek leads across astonishing Andean mountain passes and through some of the greatest attractions in Peru, including dozens of Inca ruins, dense cloud

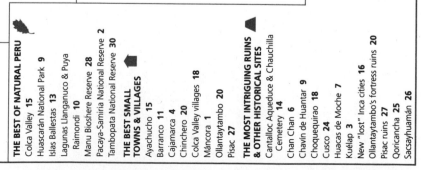

THE BEST OF NATURAL PERU
Colca Valley 15
Huascarán National Park 9
Islas Ballestas 13
Lagunas Llanganuco & Puya Raimondi 10
Manu Biosphere Reserve 28
Pacaya-Samiria National Reserve 2
Tambopata National Reserve 30

THE BEST SMALL TOWNS & VILLAGES
Ayachucho 15
Barranco 11
Cajamarca 4
Chinchero 20
Colca Valley villages 18
Máncora 1
Ollantaytambo 20
Pisac 27

THE MOST INTRIGUING RUINS & OTHER HISTORICAL SITES
Cantalloc Aqueduce & Chauchilla Cemetery 14
Chan Chan 6
Chavín de Huantar 9
Choquequirao 18
Cusco 24
Huacas de Moche 7
Kuélap 3
New "lost" Inca cities 16
Ollantaytambo's fortress ruins 20
Pisac ruins 27
Qoricancha 25
Sacsayhuamán 26

THE BEST OUTDOOR EXPERIENCES
Exploring Calco Canyon 17
Mountain & volcano climbing new Arequipa 14
Mountain biking in the Callejón de Huaylas 7
Running big-time white water 16, 17
Spotting birds & wildlife in the Amazon 29
Surfing the waves of Peru's Pacific Coast 5, 12
Trekking & climbing in the Cordillera Blanca 8
Trekking in the Sacred Valley 19

forest, and breathtaking mountain scenery. The trek has a superlative pay-off: a sunset arrival at the glorious ruins of Machu Picchu, shrouded in mist at your feet. The Inca Trail has become extraordinarily popular and heavily regulated, however; for those looking for more off-the-beaten-track and per-haps more "authentic" ruins treks, Cho-quequirao, Salcantay, and other alternatives to the Inca Trail await, as do new luxury versions of the trail (that still wind up at Machu Picchu). See "Machu Picchu & the Inca Trail" in chapter 9.

- **Floating on Lake Titicaca:** Lake Titi-caca, the world's highest navigable body of water, straddles the border between Peru and Bolivia. To locals, it is a mys-terious and sacred place. An hour's boat ride from Puno takes you to the Uros floating islands, where communities dwell upon soft patches of reeds. Visi-tors have a rare opportunity to experi-ence the ancient cultures of two inhabited natural islands, Amantaní and Taquile, by staying with a local family. The views of the oceanlike lake, at more than 3,600m (12,000 ft.) above sea level, and the star-littered night sky are worth the trip. Even better for those with an adventuresome spirit and extra time are kayaking on Titicaca and spending the night on private Suasi

Island. See "Puno & Lake Titicaca" in chapter 10.

- **Marveling as Condors Soar over Colca Canyon:** The world's second-deepest canyon (twice as deep as the Grand Canyon), Colca is the best place in South America to see giant Andean condors, majestic birds with wingspans of up to 3.5m (11 ft.). From a stunning lookout point nearly 1,200m (4,000 ft.) above the canyon river, you can watch as the condors appear, slowly circle, and gradually gain altitude with each pass until they soar silently above your head and journey down the river. A truly spine-tingling spectacle, the flight of the big birds might make you feel quite small and insignificant—and certainly less graceful. See "Colca Val-ley" in chapter 10.

- **Plunging Deep into the Jungle:** How-ever you do it, and in whichever part of the Amazon-basin rainforest you do it, Peru's massive tracts of jungle are not to be missed. The northern jungle is most accessible from Iquitos, and the south-ern Amazon, which features two phe-nomenal national reserves, Manu and Tambopata, is approachable from Cusco and Puerto Maldonado. You can take a river cruise, stay at a rustic jungle lodge, or lose yourself with a private guide, making camp and catching din-ner along the way. See chapter 11.

2 THE BEST RUINS & HISTORICAL SIGHTS

- **Cantalloc Aqueduct & Chauchilla Cemetery:** An incredible necropolis dating to around A.D. 1000 and a sophisticated irrigation system in the area around Nasca are two of the south's most interesting archaeological sites. Of the thousands of graves at Chauchilla, 12 underground tombs have been exposed. What they hold is fascinating: the bleached bones of children and

adults with dreadlocks, and some of the garments and goodies they were buried with. Close to town, nearly three dozen aqueducts represent a spectacular engi-neering feat of the Incas and their pre-decessors. The canals have air vents forming spirals descending to the water current and are still in use today by local farmers. See "Nasca" in chapter 7.

- **Colonial and Inca Cusco:** Vibrant Cusco, the ancient Inca capital, is a living museum of Peruvian history, with Spanish colonial churches and mansions sitting atop perfectly constructed Inca walls of exquisitely carved granite blocks that fit together without mortar. Streets still have evocative Quechua-language names that date back to Inca times, such as Saqracalle ("Where the demons dwell") and Pumaphaqcha ("Puma's tail"). See "What to See & Do" in chapter 8.
- **Qoricancha–Templo del Sol:** The Inca Temple of the Sun is an exceptional example of the Incas' masterful masonry. Dedicated to sun worship, the greatest temple in the Inca Empire was a gleaming palace of gold before the Spaniards raided it. During the summer solstice, the sun still magically illuminates a niche where the Inca chieftain held court. See p. 218.
- **Sacsayhuamán:** On a hill overlooking Cusco, the monumental stonework at Sacsayhuamán forms massive zigzagged defensive walls of three tiers. Built by the Inca emperor Pachacútec in the mid-15th century, some blocks weigh as much as 300 tons, and they fit together seamlessly without mortar. The main pageant of the splendid Inti Raymi festival, one of the greatest expressions of Inca and Quechua culture, is celebrated every June 24 at Sacsayhuamán. See "What to See & Do" in chapter 8.
- **Pisac Ruins:** At the beginning of the Sacred Valley, just 45 minutes from Cusco, are some of the most spectacular Inca ruins in Peru. Equal parts city, religious temple, and military complex—and perhaps a royal estate of the Inca emperor—the ruins enjoy stunning views of the valley. A hike up the steep hillside to the ruins, beginning at Pisac's main square, is one of the most rewarding climbs you're likely to take. See "Pisac" in chapter 9.
- **Ollantaytambo's Fortress Ruins:** Even though the Incas never finished this temple for worship and astronomical observation, it is still extraordinary, one of the greatest examples of their unparalleled engineering and craftsmanship. On a rocky outcrop perched above the valley, dozens of rows of incredibly steep stone terraces are carved into the hillside; high above are elegant examples of classic Inca masonry in pink granite. If that weren't enough, the charming little town of "Ollanta" is a perfect grid of Inca-laid streets with rushing canals. See "Ollantaytambo" in chapter 9.
- **New "Lost" Inca Cities:** Archaeologists keep unearthing fantastic Inca ruins in and around Machu Picchu (which obviously qualifies as the most fascinating ruins of all). Most are still being excavated and documented, but Choquequirao, to which hard-core trekkers put off by the crowds and regulations of the Inca Trail are now hiking, and the recent discoveries of Qorihuayrachina, Cota Coca, and Llactapata are all envisioned as new Machu Picchus. See "On the Trail of 'New' Inca Cities: The Discovery Continues" on p. 276.
- **Huacas de Moche:** On the outskirts of Trujillo, this complex of mysterious Moche adobe pyramids, the Temple of the Sun and Temple of the Moon, dates to A.D. 500. The Temple of the Sun (Huaca del Sol), today sadly eroded, is still mammoth—it was once probably the largest man-made structure in the Americas. The smaller Temple of the Moon (Huaca de la Luna) has been excavated; revealed inside are cool polychromatic friezes of a scary figure, the decapitator god. See "Trujillo" in chapter 12.
- **Chan Chan:** A sprawling city of adobe in the Moche Valley, just beyond Trujillo, Chan Chan was the capital of the

formidable Chimú Empire. Begun around A.D. 1300, it is the largest adobe complex of pre-Columbian America. Among the nine royal palaces, the partially restored Tschudi Palace has unusual friezes and is evocative enough to spur thoughts of the unequaled size and sophistication of this compound of the Chimú kingdom, which reached its apogee in the 15th century before succumbing to the Incas. Chan Chan includes three other sites, all quite spread out, including a modern museum. See "Trujillo" in chapter 12.

- **The Ruins of Kuélap & Choquequirao:** The remote site of Kuélap, hidden by thick cloud forest and more than 800 years old, is one of the manmade wonders of Peru waiting to be discovered by visitors. The ruins are still tough and time-consuming to get to, but the fortress complex of 400 round buildings, surrounded by a massive defensive wall, rewards the efforts of adventurous amateur archaeologists.

The same can be said about Choquequirao, an extraordinary and massive Inca construction that is only 30% uncovered; it takes 4 or 5 difficult days on foot to get there and back, but it's a superb alternative to overcrowded Machu Picchu. See "The Road Less (or More Comfortably) Traveled" in chapter 9 and "The Ruins of Kuélap" on p. 402.

- **Chavín de Huántar:** About 110km (68 miles) from Huaraz and the Cordillera Blanca are the 3,000-year-old ruins of Chavín de Huántar, a fortress-temple with excellent stonework, constructed by the Chavín culture from about 1200 to 300 B.C. These are the best-preserved ruins of one of Peru's most sophisticated and influential ancient civilizations. In a subterranean tunnel is the Lanzón, a huge and handsome stone carving and cult object shaped like a dagger. See "Huaraz & the Cordillera Blanca" in chapter 12.

3 THE BEST MUSEUMS

- **Museo Arqueológico Rafael Larco Herrera,** Lima: The world's largest private collection of pre-Columbian art focuses on the Moche dynasty (A.D. 200–700) and its extraordinary ceramics. Packed shelves in this 18th-century colonial building hold an incredible 45,000 pieces. And it wouldn't be a proper presentation of the Moche culture without a Sala Erótica, dedicated to the culture's shockingly explicit ceramic sexual depictions. See p. 136.
- **Museo de la Nación,** Lima: The National Museum traces the art and history of the earliest inhabitants to the Inca Empire. It's sprawling but very well designed, with scale models of major archaeological sites and great carved totems and textiles. See p. 136.

- **Convento y Museo de San Francisco,** Lima: The capital's best colonial-era church, the Convent of St. Francis is a striking 17th-century baroque complex with gorgeous glazed ceramic tiles and carved ceilings. The museum holds excellent examples of religious art and a splendid library, but deep beneath the church are some creepy catacombs, dug in the 16th century to house the remains of tens of thousands of priests and parishioners. See p. 132.
- **Museo Antonini,** Nasca: A private archaeology museum with a mission, this Italian initiative presents artifacts from the sophisticated Nasca culture and details the process of the excavations. In the museum's backyard is the Bisambra aqueduct, an ancient Nasca

stone irrigation canal. The museum is in possession of the world's greatest collection of painted textiles, from the huge adobe city of Cahuachi nearby, but as of yet has no place to display them. See p. 172.

- **Convento y Museo de Santa Catalina,** Cusco: This handsome, early-17th-century convent was constructed on top of the Acllawasi, where the Inca emperor sequestered his chosen Virgins of the Sun. The museum's collection of colonial and religious art is terrific. It's the best place in Peru to study the painters of the famed Escuela Cusqueña, which forged a unique style of Amerindian art by combining indigenous and Spanish styles. See p. 213.

- **Museo de Arte Precolombino,** Cusco: This handsomely designed museum of pre-Columbian art possesses some pristine pieces representing the whole of Peru's history, all taken from Lima's overwhelming Larco Herrera museum. Housed in a colonial mansion on one of Cusco's prettiest squares, the museum is small enough to be engaging rather than exhausting. See p. 217.

- **Monasterio de Santa Catalina,** Arequipa: The Convent of Santa Catalina, founded in 1579, is hands-down the greatest religious monument in Peru. More than a convent, it's an extraordinary architectural complex, with Spanish-style cobblestone streets, passageways, plazas, and cloisters, where more than 200 sequestered nuns once lived (only a handful remain). Spending a sunny afternoon here is like being transported

to another world: a small village in Andalucía, Spain. See p. 312.

- **Museo Santuarios Andinos,** Arequipa: The Museum of Andean Sanctuaries focuses on a singular exhibit, one of the most important recent archaeological finds in Peru: Juanita, the Ice Maiden of Ampato. A 13- or 14-year-old girl sacrificed in the 1500s by Inca priests on a volcano at more than 6,000m (20,000 ft.), "Juanita" was discovered in almost perfect condition in 1995. Her frozen remains, kept inside a high-tech chamber, have been studied by scientific teams from the U.S. and Peru to elicit clues from her DNA. See p. 316.

- **Museo Tumbas Reales de Sipán,** Lambayeque: Peru's newest major museum is stunningly modern on the outside, echoing the north's ancient Moche pyramids, and it holds the spectacular tomb of the Lord of Sipán within. One of Peru's most important archaeological discoveries, El Señor de Sipán is a Moche royal figure, buried 1,700 years ago with a wealth of ceremonial ornaments and treasures. This museum is perhaps the best expression of Peru's ancient grandeur. See p. 398.

- **Conjunto Monumental de Belén,** Cajamarca: A historic architectural complex of carved volcanic stone, Belén comprises an extraordinary colonial church and two former hospitals housing medical and archaeological exhibits, including textiles and ceramics dating back to 1500 B.C. and interesting ethnographic displays. See p. 409.

4 THE BEST OF NATURAL PERU

- **Islas Ballestas:** The Ballestas Islands, considered the "Peruvian Galápagos," are home to an amazing roster of protected species, including huge colonies of sea lions, endangered turtles, Humboldt penguins, red boobies, pelicans, turkey vultures, and red-footed cormorants. The islands are so covered with migratory and resident seabirds that they are known for their production of *guano,* or bird droppings. The Ballestas are part of the Paracas National Reserve, two-thirds of which is ocean. Sadly, the Reserve was affected by the 2007 earthquake, losing one of its iconic stone formations, known as the "Cathedral." See "Pisco & the Reserva Nacional de Paracas" in chapter 7.

- **Colca Valley:** The Colca Canyon is an awe-inspiring site and the best place in South America to witness giant condors, but the entire area, which Mario Vargas Llosa called the "Valley of Wonders," is extraordinarily scenic. From snowcapped volcanoes to patchwork valleys of green, narrow gorges, and beautiful desert landscapes, Colca has it all. On the way to Colca Canyon, you pass the Salinas and Aguada Blanca Nature Reserve, where you can glimpse vicuñas, llamas, and alpacas from the road. See "Colca Valley," in chapter 10.

- **Tambopata National Reserve:** A huge reserve of rainforest in the *departamento* (province) of Madre de Dios, Tambopata has outstanding biodiversity: more species of birds (nearly 600) and butterflies (1,200) than any place of similar size on earth, as well as a dozen different types of forest and gorgeous oxbow lakes, and at least 13 endangered animal species. The famous Tambopata macaw clay lick, where thousands of brilliantly colored macaws and parrots gather daily for feedings, ranks as one of the wildlife highlights of Peru. See "The Southern Amazon Jungle" in chapter 11.

- **Manu Biosphere Reserve:** Remote Manu—about as close as you're likely to come to virgin rainforest anywhere—is the second-largest protected area in Peru. Its incredibly varied habitats include Andes highlands, cloud forests, and lowland tropical rainforests. One hectare (2½ acres) of forest in Manu could have 10 times the number of species of trees found in a hectare of temperate forest in Europe or North America, and Manu has the highest bird, mammal, and plant diversity of any park on the planet. The reserve is one of the world's finest for birding (greater even than all of Costa Rica); other wildlife includes giant river otters, cocks-of-the-rock, and perhaps 15,000 animal species, as well as native Amerindian tribes that remain untouched by the modern world. See "The Southern Amazon Jungle" in chapter 11.

- **Pacaya-Samiria National Reserve:** This reserve, nearly 322km (200 miles) south of Iquitos, is the largest protected area in Peru and one of the best conserved in the world. Its dense, pristine rainforest and wetlands comprise 1.5% of Peru's total surface area and contain some of the Amazon's greatest wildlife, including pink dolphins, macaws, black caimans, spider monkeys, and giant river turtles. Found in the reserve (at last count) are 539 species of birds, 101 species of mammals, 256 kinds of fish, and 22 species of orchids. See "Into the Wild: Farther Afield from Iquitos" on p. 100.

- **Huascarán National Park:** For trekkers and climbers, the soaring peaks of the longest tropical mountain range in the world are a South American mecca. It's a visual feast, with 200 alpine lakes, 600 glaciers, and incomparable mountain vistas. The park, a UNESCO Biosphere Reserve and World Heritage Trust site, contains nearly the whole of the 161km (100-mile) Cordillera Blanca. See "Huaraz & the Cordillera Blanca," in chapter 12.

- **Lagunas de Llanganuco & Puya Raimondi:** Near Huaraz, the snowcapped peaks of the Cordillera Blanca are the biggest natural draw for trekkers, but the area is replete with all kinds of natural wonders. The two Llanganuco lakes are turquoise, glacier-fed alpine lakes that reflect the snowy summits of several 6,000m (20,000-ft.) mountains. In the valley of Pachacoto, 56km (35 miles) from Huaraz, are the famous Puya Raimondi plants: trippy bromeliad plants that soar up to 12m (39 ft.), flower just once in 100 years, and immediately die. The colorful flowers, against the backdrop of the Cordillera Blanca mountains, make for one of the prettiest pictures in Peru. See "Huaraz & the Cordillera Blanca" in chapter 12.

5 THE BEST SMALL TOWNS & VILLAGES

- **Barranco:** Technically a suburb of Lima and not a proper small town, Barranco feels like an independent village, worlds removed from the chaotic capital city. Overlooking the sea, this most bohemian part of Lima has great old architecture, cool bars, and restaurants, and a relaxed, artsy vibe. See chapter 6.

- **Ayacucho:** A pristine colonial gem of a small city nestled in the Central Highlands, Ayacucho, until the mid-1990s, was prisoner to a homegrown guerrilla movement that precluded almost all visitors from being able to relish its collection of stunning colonial-era churches. Ayacucho feels like a small town, at least outside of its Easter and Carnaval celebrations, and is also ground zero for Peru's best handicrafts—the best place in the country to pick up treasures direct from artisans. See "A Gem in the Central Highlands: Ayacucho" in chapter 7.

- **Pisac:** The first of the Sacred Valley settlements outside Cusco, Pisac has a great colorful and lively artisans' market and some of the most splendid Inca ruins this side of Machu Picchu. A massive fortress complex clings to a cliff high above town, affording sensational views of the valley. See "Pisac" in chapter 9.

- **Chinchero:** Just beyond Cusco, but not technically part of the Sacred Valley, Chinchero is best known for its bustling Sunday artisans' market, one of the best in Peru. But the graceful, traditional Andean town, higher even than Cusco, has mesmerizing views of snowy mountain ranges, a lovely colonial church, and its own Inca ruins. In the pretty main square, you can still see the huge stones and 10 trapezoidal niches of an Inca wall, originally part of a royal palace. See "Urubamba & Environs" in chapter 9.

- **Ollantaytambo:** One of the principal villages of the Sacred Valley of the Incas, "Ollanta" (as the locals call it) is a spectacularly beautiful place along the Urubamba River; the gorge is lined by agricultural terraces, and snowcapped peaks rise in the distance. The ruins of a formidable temple-fortress overlook the old town, a perfect grid of streets built by the Incas, the only such layout remaining in Peru. See "Ollantaytambo" in chapter 9.

- **Colca Valley Villages:** Chivay, on the edge of Colca Canyon, is the valley's main town, but it isn't much more than a laid-back market town with fantastic hot springs on its outskirts. Dotting the Colca Valley and its extraordinary agricultural terracing are 14 charming colonial villages dating to the 16th century, each marked by a centerpiece church. Yanque, Coporaque, Maca, and Lari are among the most attractive towns, but these villages are best appreciated for their adherence to tradition. Natives in the valley are descendants of the pre-Inca ethnic communities Collaguas and Cabanas, and they maintain the vibrant style of traditional dress, highlighted by fantastically embroidered and sequined hats. See "A Typical Guided Tour of Colca Valley" on p. 334.

- **Cajamarca:** A mini-Cusco in the northern highlands, delightful Cajamarca surprisingly doesn't get much tourist traffic—yet. Beautifully framed by the Andes and sumptuous green countryside, with a historic core of colonial buildings where an important Inca city once stood, Cajamarca—a city with the feel of a small town—is elegant and easygoing. It's also very well positioned for day trips into the country and to fascinating archaeological sites; indeed, several of Peru's nicest and most relaxing country hotels are located here. See "Cajamarca" in chapter 12.

- **Máncora:** A funky little town, long popular with surfing addicts and hippie travelers who passed through and never left, Máncora, sandwiched between Peru's beautiful Pacific coast and the amazingly arid desert of the north, is now gaining a reputation for more than its waves and bars. New hotels and restaurants are luring a whole new breed of traveler. See "Máncora and Peru's Northern Beaches," on p. 418.

6 THE BEST OUTDOOR EXPERIENCES

- **Trekking in the Sacred Valley:** The most famous trek outside Cusco is, of course, the Inca Trail to Machu Picchu. But if you're not up to 4 strenuous days with a group along a highly structured trail, there are plenty of additional hiking options in the Sacred Valley. Other trails are much less crowded and share some of the same extraordinary scenery. Ollantaytambo and Yucay are the best bases for walks in the pretty countryside of the Urubamba Valley. The trek from the Inca site Moray to the Salineras salt mines is particularly stunning. See chapter 9.

- **Running Big-Time White Water:** Just beyond Cusco in the Urubamba Valley are some excellent river runs, ranging from mild to world-class. Novices can do 1-day trips to get a taste of this thrilling sport, while more experienced rafters can take multiday trips and even hard-core rafting journeys along the Tambopata River in the Amazon jungle. The area around Arequipa and the Colca Canyon in southern Peru is even better for rafting. The easiest and most convenient runs from Arequipa are on the Río Chili. More advanced rafting, ranging up to Class VI, beckons on the Río Majes, Río Colca, and Río Cotahuasi. See "Extreme Sacred Valley: Outdoor Adventure Sports" on p. 244, and "Colca Valley," in chapter 10.

- **Exploring Colca Canyon:** Perhaps second only to the Callejón de Huaylas Valley in northern Peru for quality independent hiking is Colca Canyon. One of the most celebrated hikes is the descent into the canyon itself, from the Cruz del Cóndor lookout. There are others that are even longer and more demanding, but more accessible hikes are also possible; walking from one village to another, or bicycling around the valley should satisfy most peoples' outdoors urges. Excursions on horseback throughout the valley and into the canyon are also possible. Hard-core sports enthusiasts might take on remote Cotahuasi Canyon, deeper and more rugged even than Colca. See "Colca Valley," in chapter 10.

- **Mountain & Volcano Climbing Near Arequipa:** For mountaineers (and fit, adventurous travelers), the volcanoes just beyond Arequipa are perfect for some of Peru's best ascents. Several don't demand technical skills. Towering El Misti, which forms part of the Arequipa skyline, is an extremely popular climb, and the city's other major volcano, Chachani, also presents an accessible ascent. Peaks in the Colca Valley are great for serious climbers; these include the Ampato Volcano and Coropuna, which, at more than 6,425m (21,079 ft.), is perhaps the most stunning mountain in the Cotahuasi Valley and is for specialists only. See "Colca Valley," in chapter 10.

- **Spotting Birds & Wildlife in the Peruvian Amazon:** Peru's Amazon rainforest is some of the most biologically diverse on the planet. The southeastern jungle and its two principal protected areas, the Tambopata National Reserve and the Manu Biosphere Reserve, are terrific for viewing wildlife and more than 1,000 species of birds. One of the great birding spectacles is the sight of thousands of macaws and parrots feeding at a clay lick. Keep your eyes peeled for more elusive wildlife, such as caimans, river otters, and even jaguars and tapirs. See "The Southern Amazon Jungle," in chapter 11.

- **Surfing the Waves of Peru's Pacific Coast:** Brazil might be more popularly known as a surfing destination, but wave connoisseurs dig Peru, with 2,000km (1,200 miles) of Pacific coastline and a great variety of left and right reef breaks, point breaks, and big-time waves. Beaches are mostly uncrowded, but the water is cold, and most surfers wear wet suits year-round. More than two dozen beaches attract *surfistas*. Northern Peru, best from October to March, is the top choice of most, and surfers hang out in the easygoing fishing villages of Huanchaco and Máncora; the biggest and best waves in Peru

are found at Puerto Chicama, Lobitos, Cabo Blanco, and Los Órganos. Though it can't compete with the north, the best beaches in southern Peru, where surfing is best from April to December, are Punta Hermosa, Punta Rocas, Cerro Azul, and Pico Alto. See "Side Trips from Lima" in chapter 6, and "Trujillo" in chapter 12.

- **Trekking & Climbing in the Cordillera Blanca:** The Cordillera Blanca, the highest tropical mountain chain in the world, is almost wholly contained in the protected Huascarán National Park. For walkers and mountaineers, the scenery of snowcapped peaks, glaciers, lakes, and rivers is unrivaled in Peru. Fifty summits soar between 4,800 and 6,662m (15,748–21,857 ft.) high, so naturally, expert mountaineers are drawn to the Cordillera, but trekking and climbing opportunities abound for less-experienced outdoors types. The classic trek is the 4- to 5-day Santa Cruz–Llanganuco route, one of the most beautiful in South America. See "Huaraz & the Cordillera Blanca," in chapter 12.

- **Mountain Biking in the Callejón de Huaylas:** Mountain biking is developing some legs in Peru. The top spot is the valley near the Cordillera Blanca, the pristine mountain range in central Peru. Hundreds of mountain and valley horse trails lace lush fields and push past picturesque Andean villages and alpine lakes. Hard-core peddlers can test their lung capacity climbing to 5,000m (16,400-ft.) mountain passes. For cycling camaraderie, check out the Semana del Andinismo in Huaraz, which features a mountain-bike competition. See "Huaraz & the Cordillera Blanca" in chapter 12.

7 THE BEST ARCHITECTURE

- **Colonial Lima:** The old center of Lima Centro preserves a wealth of fine colonial-era buildings that have survived fires, earthquakes, and decades of inattention. Churches include San Pedro (the best-preserved example of early colonial religious architecture in the city), La Merced, and San Agustín. Equally interesting are the historic quarter's few remaining *casas coloniales,* such as Casa Riva-Agüero, Casa Aliaga, and Casa de Osambela Oquendo. Though the capital's unruliness makes appreciating its colonial core a bit daunting, it's worth the effort. See "What to See & Do" in chapter 6.

- **Cusco's Inca Masonry:** Everywhere in Cusco's old center are stunning Inca walls, made of giant granite blocks so amazingly carved that they fit together without mortar, like jigsaw puzzle pieces. For the most part, the colonial architecture has not stood up nearly as well as the Incas' bold structures, which are virtually earthquake proof. The best examples are the curved stones at the Sun Temple, Qoricancha; along Hatunrumiyoc, an alleyway lined with polygonal stones and featuring a 12-angled stone; and another pedestrian-only alleyway, Inca Roca, which has a series of stones that forms the shape of a puma. See "The Magic of Inca Stones: A Walking Tour" on p. 220.

- **The Mystery of Moray:** A peculiar Inca site with a mystical reputation, Moray isn't the Inca version of the Nasca Lines, although it sure looks like it could be. A series of inscrutable ringed terraces sculpted in the earth, the deep-set bowls formed an experimental agricultural center to test new crops and conditions. The different levels produce microclimates, with remarkable differences in temperature from top to bottom. See "Urubamba & Environs," in chapter 9.

- **Ollantaytambo's Old Town:** Though "Ollanta" is best known for its Inca ruins perched on an outcrop, equally spectacular is the grid of perfectly constructed *canchas,* or city blocks, that reveal the Incas as masterful urban planners as well as stonemasons. The 15th-century *canchas,* amazingly preserved, each had a single entrance opening onto a main courtyard. Rippling alongside the lovely stone streets, canals carry water down from the mountains. See "Ollantaytambo" in chapter 9.

- **Machu Picchu's Temple of the Sun:** Even as ruins, Machu Picchu rises to the stature of great architecture. Brilliant elements of design and stonemasonry can be found around every corner, but perhaps the greatest example of architectural prowess is the Temple of the Sun. A tapered tower, it has the finest stonework in Machu Picchu. A perfectly positioned window allows the sun's rays to come streaming through at dawn on the South American winter solstice in June, illuminating the stone at the center of the temple. A cave below the temple, carved out of the rock, has a beautifully sculpted altar and series of niches that create mesmerizing morning shadows. See "Machu Picchu & the Inca Trail" in chapter 9.

- **Colonial Arequipa:** The colonial core of Arequipa, Peru's second city, is the most graceful and harmonious in the country. Most of its elegant mansions and churches are carved from *sillar,* or white volcanic stone. The Plaza de Armas is one of the prettiest main squares in Peru, even though the cathedral was recently damaged by a major earthquake. Other colonial churches of note are La Compañía, San Francisco,

San Agustín, and the Monasterio de la Recoleta. Arequipa also has some of Peru's finest colonial seigniorial homes, which feature beautiful courtyards, elaborately carved stone facades, and period furnishings. Don't miss Casa del Moral, Casa Ricketts, and Casa Arróspide. See "Arequipa" in chapter 10.

- **The River Architecture of Iquitos:** A humid Amazon river city, Iquitos might not be a place you'd expect to find distinguished architecture, but the rubber barons who made fortunes in the 19th century lined the Malecón Tarapacá riverfront with handsome mansions covered in colorful Portuguese glazed tiles, or *azulejos*. The best are Casa Hernández, Casa Cohen, Casa Morey, and the Logia Unión Amazónica. Also check out the Casa de Fierro, designed by Gustave Eiffel and entirely constructed of iron in Paris and shipped to Peru, or the wild wooden houses on stilts in the often-flooded shantytown district of Belén. See "Iquitos & the Northern Amazon" in chapter 11.
- **Trujillo's Casas Antiguas:** The colorful pastel facades and unique iron window grilles of Trujillo's colonial- and Republican-era houses represent one of Peru's finest architectural ensembles. Several have splendid interior courtyards and *mudéjar*-style (Moorish-Christian) details. Fine homes grace the lovely Plaza de Armas and the streets that radiate out from it. Among those outfitted with historic furnishings and open to the public are Palacio Iturregui, Casa Urquiaga (where Simón Bolívar once lived), Casa de la Emancipación, Casa Ganoza Chopitea, and Casa Orbegoso. See "Trujillo" in chapter 12.
- **Cumbe Mayo's Aqueduct:** This weird and wonderful spot near Cajamarca draws visitors for its strange rock formations that mimic a stone forest. But the structure that was engineered by man, a pre-Inca aqueduct constructed around 1000 B.C., is most extraordinary. The 8km (5-mile) canal is carved from volcanic stone in perfect lines to collect and redirect water on its way to the Pacific Ocean. Right angles slow the flow of water and ease the effects of erosion. The aqueduct is likely the oldest man-made structure in South America. See "Cajamarca" in chapter 12.

8 THE BEST FESTIVALS & CELEBRATIONS

- **Fiesta de la Cruz** (across Peru): The Festival of the Cross isn't as solemnly Catholic as it might sound. Best in Lima, Cusco, and Ica, the festival does feature cross processions (although the decorated crosses are vibrant), but it also displays a surfeit of folk music and dance, the highlight being the daring "scissors dancers," who once performed on top of churches.
- **El Señor de los Milagros** (Lima): The Artist Once Again Known as Prince would love this highly religious procession, with tens of thousands of participants all clad in bright purple. The Lord of Miracles, the largest procession in South America, lasts a full 24 hours. It venerates a miraculous painting of Jesus Christ, which was created by an Angolan slave and survived the devastating 1746 earthquake, even though almost everything around it was felled.
- **Inti Raymi** (Cusco): The Festival of the Sun, one of the greatest pageants in South America, celebrates the winter solstice and honors the Inca sun god with a bounty of colorful Andean parades, music, and dance. It takes over Cusco and transforms the Sacsayhuamán ruins overlooking the city into a majestic stage.

- **Virgen del Carmen** (Paucartambo): The tiny, remote Andean colonial village of Paucartambo is about 4 hours from Cusco, but it hosts one of Peru's wildest festivals. Its 3 days of dance, revelry, drinking, and outlandish, scary costumes pack in thousands who camp all over town (there's almost nowhere to stay) and then wind up (temporarily) at the cemetery.
- **Virgen de la Candelaria** (Puno): Puno, perhaps the epicenter of Peruvian folklore, imbues its festivals with a unique vibrancy. Candlemas (or Virgen de la Candelaria), which is spread over 2 weeks, is one of the greatest folk religious festivals in South America, with an explosion of music, dance, and some of the most fantastic costumes and masks seen anywhere.
- **Puno Week** (Puno): Puno, the fiesta capital of Peru, rises to the occasion for a full week every November to mark its Amerindian roots. A huge procession from Lake Titicaca into town remembers the legend of the first Inca emperor, who emerged from the world's highest navigable lake to establish the Inca Empire. The procession deviates into dance, music, and oblivion. Day of the Dead, early in the week, is a joyous celebration that prompts picnics at cemeteries.

9 THE BEST HOTELS

- **Casa Andina Private Collection Miraflores,** Lima (✆ 01/213-9739): Resurrected from Lima's first and fondly remembered, but long abandoned, five-star hotel, this well-located Miraflores property has taken on new life and is now one of the top places to stay both for business and leisure travelers. Rooms are smart, and amenities include an indoor/outdoor pool, excellent restaurant, and cool little traveler's cafe. See p. 116.
- **Miraflores Park Hotel,** Lima (✆ 01/610-4000): The top business traveler's hotel in Lima, this oasis of refinement and luxury is still small enough to cater to your every whim. The Park Hotel is the height of style, with handsome, spacious rooms; huge bathrooms; and an elegant restaurant and bar. There's a small pool and a gym with sauna on the top floor, overlooking the *malecón,* parks, and the coastline. See p. 116
- **Country Club Lima Hotel,** Lima (✆ 01/611-9000): A revived, supremely elegant hacienda-style hotel from the 1920s, this grand estate is full of antiques and has plenty of character, but it remains a relaxed place that's good for families. Given its high standards, it's not a bad deal, either. At this excellent retreat from the stress of modern Lima, the country club aspect isn't neglected: Golf and tennis are both available. See p. 120
- **Hotel Paracas, Paracas National Reserve,** Pisco (✆ 056/581-333): Few makeovers are as successful as the one given this longtime favorite of families visiting Paracas. Now a Starwood Luxury Collection property, it glistens with contemporary style, while retaining its open and airy, waterfront feel. A spectacular new infinity pool leads to a strikingly modern lounge and restaurant, a dose of style never before seen in the southern Peruvian desert. See p. 158.
- **La Casona,** Cusco (✆ 01/610-0400): This extraordinary boutique hotel has just 11 rooms but is one of the most luxurious places in Peru. Right on

pretty Plazoleta Nazarenas, it inhabits a beautiful old colonial house and is teeming with art and antiques; the rooms built around the courtyard, as well as the sumptuous bathrooms, are jaw-droppingly immense. See p. 181.

- **Hotel Monasterio,** Cusco (℃ **084/ 241-777**): Extraordinarily carved out of a 16th-century monastery, itself built over the foundations of an Inca palace, this Orient-Express hotel is the most dignified and historic place to stay in Peru. With its own gilded chapel and 18th-century Cusco School art collection, it's an attraction in its own right. Rooms are gracefully decorated with colonial touches, particularly the rooms off the serene first courtyard. See p. 194.

- **Aranwa Sacred Valley,** Huayllabamba (℃ **084/205-080**): The Sacred Valley has been trending upscale for a few years, but this luxury retreat takes it to a new level. It is, simply, one of the most sybaritic places to stay in Peru. The country estate is a small village built around a colonial hacienda, with a surfeit of services, including one of the finest spas in Peru. See p. 248.

- **Inkaterra Machu Picchu,** Aguas Calientes (℃ **084/211-122**): It's not next to the ruins, but this rustic hotel, a compound of bungalows ensconced in lush tropical gardens and cloud forest, is full of character and by far the nicest place in Aguas Calientes. With loads of nature trails and guided activities, it's a superb retreat for naturalists. And after a day at Machu Picchu, the spring-fed pool is a great alternative to the thermal baths in town. Junior suites, with fireplaces and small terraces, are the most coveted rooms. See p. 284.

- **Casa Andina Private Collection Arequipa,** Arequipa (℃ **866/220-4434**): Brilliantly carved out of a stately colonial building—a national historic monument that was once the Mint House—this stunning property feels like a chic boutique hotel, but with the superb services, including an excellent restaurant, of a much larger hotel. Its location just a block from the famed Santa Catalina monastery couldn't be better. See p. 249.

- **Hotel Libertador Plaza Mayor Trujillo,** Trujillo (℃ **044/232-741**): One of the finest hotels in northern Peru, the Libertador boasts a coveted location overlooking Trujillo's lovely Plaza de Armas. It inhabits a striking colonial mansion and features nice extras, such as a courtyard patio, good restaurant, outdoor pool, and both dry and steam saunas. Best of all, it's a very good value. See p. 390.

- **Hotel Costa del Sol,** Cajamarca (℃ **076/343-434**): It's not flashy, but this modern, business-oriented hotel has the finest location in Cajamarca— next to the cathedral and overlooking the gorgeous Plaza de Armas. Rooms are nicely outfitted, there's a nice spa and rooftop pool, and the glass-enclosed restaurant is perfect for gazing out over the square, where Cajamarca comes to life. See p. 414.

- **Vichayito Bungalows & Carpas,** Vichayito, Máncora (℃ **01/435-4173**): This former ecolodge, right on a wide and long stretch of one of the finest beaches in northern Peru, has been given an extreme makeover. Now part of the burgeoning Peruvian luxury hotel group Aranwa, it proposes a very novel idea: African safari–like (but exceedingly well-equipped) tents. If you like the idea of acting like a modern adventurer, but with five-star comforts, this is your kind of place. See p. 120.

- **Second Home Peru,** Lima (© 01/477-5021): This small inn takes the B&B to a new level. Occupying the home of one of Peru's best-known artists, Victor Delfín, it hugs the coastline in bohemian Barranco. Rooms are elegant and airy, and the entire house is a small museum of Delfín's work. See p. 123.
- **Fallen Angel: The Guest House,** Cusco (© 084/258-184: One of the wildest places you're likely to stay, certainly in Peru, is this boutique artist's den, upstairs from the celebrated restaurant of the same name. The immense and painstakingly baroque rooms carry the unique vision of Andrés Zuniga. I suppose some people might be a tad uncomfortable in something so "out there," but anyone with a creative or adventurous streak should be in heaven. See p. 193.
- **Niños Hotel,** Cusco (© 084/231-424): Even if this great little inn had no redeeming social and moral value, it would still be one of the best informal places to stay in Peru. The fact that it operates as part of a foundation that dedicates its profits to helping and housing Cusco's street children is a welcome bonus. The small Dutch-owned hotel, located in a restored and nicely if simply decorated colonial house, is charming, immaculate, and a great value. The trick is getting a reservation—try many months in advance of your arrival. See p. 199.
- **Torre Dorada,** Cusco (© 084/241-698): Even though it's outside the city center, this exceptional and extremely friendly family-run boutique hotel, in a quiet residential neighborhood 5 minutes from downtown Cusco, more than makes up for the inconvenience with superb service and a warm ambience. The inn isn't luxurious, but you won't

find a friendlier place in Peru, and the breakfast buffet is better than those at most top-flight hotels. See p. 205.
- **Hotel Pisaq,** Pisac (©/fax 084/203-062): On the main square of Pisac, which is overrun on market days, this friendly little inn has neat features for a budget hostel: hand-painted murals, a sauna, an attractive courtyard, and a little cafe serving home-cooked meals and great pizza from a wood-burning oven. See p. 243.
- **Ticllabamba Maison d'Hôtes,** Yucay (© 01/999-352-664): This tiny, secluded luxury guesthouse (with just two accommodations) is the kind of getaway that delivers all the beauty and serenity the Sacred Valley is famous for. Its foundation as a 16th-century Royal Inca estate makes its exclusivity perfectly natural. See p. 248.
- **El Albergue,** Ollantaytambo (©/fax 084/204-014): An American-owned hostel right next to the railroad tracks—but much quieter than that would indicate—this comfortable little place has just a few rooms and shared bathrooms. Beds are excellent, and the vibe, with relaxing gardens and Labrador retrievers running around, is great. There's also a cool wood-fired sauna. See p. 260.
- **Amazon Yarapa River Lodge,** Northern Amazon (© 315/952-6771 or 065/993-1172): A splendid, award-winning conservationist lodge good enough to be partnered with Cornell University and host its faculty and students at its field lab, this place is also perfect for amateur botanists and biologists. Though it's hidden away in the Reserva Nacional Pacaya-Samiria, the largest of Peru's protected areas and one of the top spots for wildlife viewing, the lodge is unexpectedly comfortable and

attractive, with huge private bungalows, a lounge, and a hammock house overlooking the river.

- **Reserva Amazónica Rainforest Lodge,** Tambopata (✆ **800/442-5042** or 01/610-0400): The swankest lodge in the Peruvian Amazon, this is the place for a comfortable jungle experience. You'll still get plenty of jungle, whether spotting birds on a canopy walk, watching for caimans along the river, or stalking monkeys on a small island. But when it comes time to relax, you'll do it in style with cocktails and dinner in the stylish main house before retiring to your plush African-style bungalow. See p. 350.

- **Explorer's Inn,** Tambopata (✆ **01/ 447-8888**): One of the most renowned and respected ecolodges in the Peruvian Amazon is this 30-year-old pioneer that hosts both ecotourists and scientists. About 3 hours upriver from Puerto Maldonado, the inn—featuring thatched-roof bungalows—is superb for viewing otters, monkeys, and jungle birds. See p. 351.

- **Tahuayo Lodge,** northern Amazon (✆ **800/262-9669**): The top lodge in Peru's northern Amazon, about 4 hours from Iquitos and associated with the Rainforest Conservation Fund, is the only lodge with access to the terrific Tamshiyacu-Tahuayo Reserve. It's remote and small, but features excellent jungle programs, including zip-line canopy ropes for treetop nature viewing. See p. 369.

- **Intiqa Hotel,** Puno (✆ **051/366-900**): A new, midsize hotel in Puno (which could use a drastic injection of style), this exceptionally friendly and clean place, with nicely decorated rooms and great service, is a value traveler's dream. There are more luxurious hotels along the banks of Lake Titicaca, but this is by far the best bet in town. See p. 305.

- **Casa Andina Private Collection,** Isla Suasi (✆ **01/213-9739**): This incredibly remote and private ecolodge, sequestered on the only private island in the middle of majestic Lake Titicaca, is one of Peru's most unique lodgings. If it's solitude, stunning scenery, and utter serenity you're after, this is your place. Although it's all-solar powered and fits in handsomely with the natural surroundings, this isn't some thatched-roof hut; it's actually quite luxurious. A perfect, unexpected retreat. See p. 320.

- **Casa Arequipa,** Arequipa (✆ **054/284- 219**): This elite 1950s mansion on the outskirts of Arequipa feels like a European boutique hotel, with luxury linens, furnishings, and bathrooms that rival the finest upscale hotels in the country, but for a fraction of the price. Though it's in a residential neighborhood that's a nice walk or short taxi ride from the colonial downtown of Arequipa, that minor inconvenience is a very small price to pay. The breakfast buffet and personal attention will make you think you're in a large five-star hotel. See p. 322.

- **La Casa de Melgar Hostal,** Arequipa (✆/fax **054/222-459**): In a pretty colonial house made of *sillar* stone, this small inn exudes style and charm. With thick walls, multiple interior courtyards, and gardens, it's much nicer than most inexpensive hotels. The ground-floor rooms, with vaulted brick ceilings, look like they're straight out of a movie shoot. See p. 323.

- **Colca Lodge,** Coporaque (✆ **054/531- 191**): A handsome Colca Valley ecolodge that hugs the banks of the river, this rustic hotel is large enough to accommodate groups but sensitively designed enough to ensure privacy and serenity. That's especially true if you find your way to the beautiful stone thermal pools, which no other hotel in the zone can match. See p. 339.

- **Las Casitas del Colca,** Yanque (© 01/610-8300): A favorite of sophisticated travelers venturing into the rustic Colca Canyon, the parador, owned by Orient-Express, has a unique country charm and elegance. It has recently been transformed into one of the most luxurious country hotels anywhere. The spacious and private bungalows have their own plunge pools and patios. The excellent dining room serves fresh country meals, and guests can choose from lots of hiking and horseback-riding opportunities. What was once a bargain, though, has become a refuge for the wealthy. See p. 339.

- **Hotel Posada del Puruay,** Cajamarca (© 01/336-7869): In the gorgeous highland countryside just outside Cajamarca, this country hotel rests in a restored 1830 farmhouse. The grounds, with gardens, horses, and amenities such as a barbecue pit, are surefire selling points, but the inn also has huge rooms, friendly personal service, a very good restaurant, and an extensive video library. See p. 415.

- **Hotel DCO Suites, Lounge & Spa,** Las Pocitas, Máncora (© 01/242-3961): It may be saddled with a cumbersome name, but this stellar boutique hotel sets new standards in Peru for beachside chicness, a harbinger of things to come in pretty but rough-and-tumble Máncora. Right on top of a gorgeous stretch of beach, this strikingly modern, multilevel, seven-suite hotel has style to burn, including a superb restaurant, infinity pool and an open-air rooftop spa, making it one of the swankiest places I've seen in Peru. See p. 419.

11 THE BEST LOCAL DINING EXPERIENCES

- **Barbecuing Peruvian-Style:** The Peruvian version of a barbecue get-together is called a *pachamanca;* it's basically cooking meat and veggies over coals or hot stones in a hole in the ground. On weekends in the countryside, mostly in the mountains, you'll see families gathered around smoky subterranean grills, cooking up pork or beef and potatoes and vegetables. (You can also get *pachamanca*-style dishes in some traditional restaurants.)

- **Savoring a Pisco Sour:** Peru's national drink is the pisco sour, a delicious concoction made from the white-grape brandy called pisco. Made frothy when mixed with egg whites, lemon juice, sugar, and bitters, it's cold and complex—the closest thing to a Peruvian margarita. Try one with ceviche or a robust Andean meal—or just knock 'em back late at night at a gringo-filled bar.

- **Going Native with Jungle Cuisine:** Peru's vast Amazon is full of exotic critters and plants, so it's logical that it would produce its own unique cuisine. Some of what restaurateurs deal in is endangered animals, though, so I don't advise satisfying your curiosity to try sea-turtle soup or caiman, even if the locals do it. Local jungle dishes that you don't have to feel bad about trying include *patarashca,* a steamed river fish wrapped in banana leaves; *juanes,* a kind of rice tamale; *timbuche,* a thick soup made with local fish; *paiche,* an Amazon-size local fish; and *chonta,* a hearts of palm salad. If you don't make it to the jungle, another way of going native (in the highlands and along the coast) is to eat *cuy,* or guinea pig. See chapters 2 and 11.

- **Slurping Ceviche:** One of the classic dishes of Peruvian coastal cooking is ceviche—raw fish and shellfish marinated in lime or lemon juice and hot chili peppers, and served with raw onion, sweet potato, and toasted corn. It's wonderfully refreshing and spicy. The best place to try one? A seaside *cevichería*, specializing in umpteen varieties of deliciously fresh ceviche.

- **Relaxing at a *Quinta*:** There are elegant restaurants in Lima, Cusco, Arequipa, and Iquitos, but there's nothing quite like an informal *quinta*—an open-air restaurant specializing in Andean home-cooking. It's an Andean tradition perhaps best explored in the crisp air of Cusco, which has a trio of *quintas* that are especially popular with locals on weekends. Look for informal garden or courtyard settings, large portions of Peruvian cooking, and reasonable prices. Most *quintas* are open only for lunch, so plan on it as your main meal of the day. Not only will you eat well, but it's also a great way to spend a sunny afternoon. See "Cusco's *Quintas*" on p. 210.

- **Chugging *Chicha*:** An ancient Andean tradition is the brewing of *chicha,* beer made from fermented maize. You can find it at a few traditional restaurants, but for an authentic Andean experience, the best place to get it is at a simple bar or home that flies the *chicha* flag—a long pole with a red flag or, often, balloon—which is the local way of advertising that there's home-brewed *chicha* available inside. Served warm, in monstrous tumblers for a few pennies,

it's not to many foreigners' liking, but it's one of the best ways to go native. *Chicha morada,* a refreshment made from blue corn, is something altogether different: It's sweet and nonalcoholic, and it actually tastes good (especially with ceviche).

- **Self-Medicating with *Mate de Coca*:** Coca-leaf tea, a perfectly legal local drink that has been a tradition in the Andes for centuries, is a great way to deal with the high altitude of the mountains, which can make your head spin and your body reel. As soon as you hit Cusco or Puno, head straight for the *mate de coca*—most hotels have it at the ready for their guests. And if that doesn't work, strap on the oxygen tank (many hotels supply that for their guests, too).

- **Touring Ica's Bodegas:** Peru, one of the great winemaking countries of the world? Probably not, but the southern desert coast does have a thriving wine industry. The most famous product is pisco, but the many traditional bodegas (wineries) throughout the Ica countryside also make regular table wines. A few bodegas give tours and tastings. Ica hosts a hopping Wine Festival in March, which is a good time to tour the region if you're into wine and general merriment. Harvest time, late February through April, is the other time to visit, when you can see people crushing grapes the old-fashioned way—with their feet. See "Ica" in chapter 7.

12 THE BEST RESTAURANTS

- **Astrid y Gastón,** Lima (© 01/242-4422): Still one of the coolest restaurants in the country is this stylish modern place serving a creative and sophisticated brand of Creole-Mediterranean fare. Behind a nondescript

facade in the Miraflores district is the restaurant that catapulted Gastón Acurio to stardom, and it's still probably his best. See p. 125.

- **La Mar Cebichería,** Lima (© 01/421-3365): A designer and celebrity-chef take on the neighborhood *cevichería* at this hottest restaurant in Lima. It's only open for lunch, though, and doesn't take reservations, so it's a bit of a challenge to get a seat at the stylish hot spot. The focus is on moderately priced, delicious ceviche, and traditional Limeño fare served up with hip twists. See p. 126.

- **Chala,** Lima (✆ 01/252-8515): A chic but laid-back lounge and restaurant—perfect for the artsy Barranco neighborhood, this spot serves *"costa fusion,"* adapting Peruvian coastal and Limeño dishes with Mediterranean touches. The place to be is out on the deck, under the tall trees. You won't believe you're in Lima. See p. 129.

- **Restaurant Huaca Pucllana,** Lima (✆ 01/445-4042): One of the best places for dining in the capital has the most unique location: within the compound of an over 1,500-year-old adobe pyramid. The restaurant is both hip and relaxed, with a covered terrace looking out over the low pyramid and illuminated excavation walkways. The creative Peruvian menu offers new twists on classic *comida criolla* (Creole cooking). See p. 126.

- **Cicciolina,** Cusco (✆ 084/239-510): Cusco's newly creative restaurant scene is still spearheaded by this warm and consistently great upstairs spot, which serves stylish novo Andino cuisine. You might think you've landed in a chic Tuscan country eatery, but the menu is eclectic, with a soft spot for unusual spices. The hopping bar is a smart haunt for predinner drinks and a terrific selection of tapas, though the sexy, hushed dining room is one of the sleekest in Cusco. See p. 206.

- **Chi Cha,** Cusco (✆ 084/240-520): Gastón Acurio's talented hands have either transformed modern Peruvian cooking or simply displayed a knack for promoting its delectable diversity,

beginning in Lima and expanding outward. Whatever you think, his new minichain of restaurants, which combine some of the chef's standard dishes with his take on regional cuisine, have been automatic hits. His versions of Cusco highlander cuisine in a sophisticated, secluded space, is a fine addition to the city's formerly ho-hum dining scene. See p. 206.

- **Limo,** Cusco (✆ 084/240-668): Though it overlooks the gorgeous Plaza de Armas, the travelers' hub in Cusco, this brilliant new restaurant is anything but a tourist trap. If fact, it's one of my favorite new restaurants in Peru. Stylish but welcoming and fun, it brings great sushi and *tiraditos* to Cusco; and it's a bargain, given the chic surroundings, attention to detail, splendid cocktails and the city's best views. See p. 208.

- **MAP Café,** Cusco (✆ 084/242-476): Cusco's most surprisingly modern restaurant is tucked into the colonial patio of the city's great pre-Columbian art museum. It quietly makes a dramatic statement with its minimalist design: a glass and steel box. The Novo Andino dishes are every bit as elegant and cleanly presented. With a super wine list and the opportunity to stroll through the museum after dinner, it makes a perfect, sophisticated date spot, but keep in mind that it's Cusco's most expensive restaurant. See p. 206.

- **Jack's Café Bar,** Cusco (✆ 084/806-960): The first place many gringos hit when they arrive in Cusco, and one that they understandably return to time and time again, is this amiable, casual and bustling cafe on the way up the hill to the San Blas district. It's anything but fancy, but it is a great spot for any meal, a terrific deal, and perfect for bonding with fellow travelers over a few drinks. See p. 212.

- **El Huacatay,** Urubamba (Sacred Valley; ✆ 084/201-790): Most visitors to the Sacred Valley eat either at nondescript cafes or hotel restaurants. This new place is a welcome addition, a chef-owned restaurant that's elegant and relaxed, serving very nice versions of Andean standards. It's perfect for a long, lingering lunch in the garden or a more elegant dinner by candlelight in the small dining room. Refreshingly, it's a favorite of both gringos and (upscale) locals. See "Urubamba & Environs" in chapter 9.

- **Indio Feliz,** Aguas Calientes (© 084/211-090): The town at the bottom of Machu Picchu is a little scrappy, so this Peruvian-French restaurant really stands out. In an attractive and popular two-level dining room, it offers a great-value three-course menu. If by chance you just completed the 4-day Inca Trail trek, treat yourself to a meal here. See p. 288.
- **Chi Cha,** Arequipa (© 054/287-360): Famed Lima chef Gastón Acurio takes on equally celebrated Arequipeño cuisine in a sprawling and handsome colonial manor house in the heart of historic Arequipa. This incarnation of Chi Cha seems even more felicitous than the Cusco version, a result both of the emblematic building and the spicy and unique local dishes that inspired Acurio. See p. 324.
- **Sol de Mayo,** Arequipa (© 054/254-148): This is the best place in town for traditional Arequipeño cooking, which has quite a reputation in Peru. The setting, around a courtyard garden where strolling musicians play, is delightful. It's a perfect place to sink your teeth into local Peruvian specialties and is a great place to splurge. See p. 325.
- **La Trattoria del Monasterio,** Arequipa (© 054/204-062): A stylishly reserved restaurant carved out of the city's most distinguished walls, belonging to the

Santa Catalina monastery, this laid-back Italian spot is a real find. With a menu designed by Peru's hottest chef, a nice wine list, a trio of quiet dining rooms, and accessible prices, it's a welcome change from noisier and more solicitous restaurants populating Arequipa's highly trafficked restaurant rows.

- **Zig Zag,** Arequipa (© 054/206-020): This chic and inviting restaurant has a unique specialty: stone-grilled ostrich. Healthier than other meats, ostrich is really good, as is another popular dish served here: alpaca (which is also healthier than red meat). In this two-level space with *sillar* walls and vaulted ceilings, the grilled meat is not the only thing that makes this a memorable dining experience. See p. 325.
- **Club Colonial,** Huanchaco (© 044/761-639): An unexpectedly chic and stylish restaurant in the low-key beach resort of Huanchaco, this Belgian-French place has the kind of ambience you'd look to find in Barranco in Lima, not the north coast. The candlelit dining room is like a cool expatriate's house, and the menu is a tantalizing mix of Peruvian and Franco-Belgian items. Whether you order meat or fresh fish, or even a Belgian standard, you're in for a treat. See p. 393.
- **Fiesta Restaurant Gourmet,** Chiclayo (© 074/201-970): Chiclayo might not be widely known as a dining capital, but cognoscenti are aware that its northern Peruvian cuisine can hold its own against any regional cooking in the country. And Fiesta, which has been promoting it for a couple of decades now, is its top ambassador. This handsome restaurant, full of regulars and good cheer, is a superb place to get in on the secret. See p. 126.

- **Miraflores,** Lima: The Peruvian capital has the biggest number of shops and selection of goods from across the country, as might be expected. The Miraflores district has dozens of shops stocked to the rafters with handicrafts from around Peru. For one-stop shopping, there are mini-malls of many stalls selling ceramics, textiles, and other souvenirs. The best silver jewelry and antiques shops are also in Miraflores. See "Shopping" in chapter 6.

- **Barrio de San Blas,** Cusco: Galleries around the Plaza de Armas of the old Inca capital are wonderful for all kinds of wool and alpaca fashions and silver jewelry. But especially flavorful is the picturesque and bohemian neighborhood of San Blas, which rises into the hills above Cusco, bursting with the studios and workshops of artists and artisans, as well as art galleries and ceramics shops. You can pop into several studios and see artists at work. See "Shopping" in chapter 8.

- **Pisac's Crafts Market:** Thousands of tourists descend each Sunday morning on Pisac's liveliest handicrafts market, which takes over the central plaza and spills across adjoining streets. Many sellers, decked out in the dress typical of their villages, come from remote populations high in the mountains. Pisac is one of the best spots for colorful Andean textiles, including rugs, alpaca sweaters, and ponchos. See "Pisac," in chapter 9.

- **Pablo Seminario,** Urubamba: Urubamba leaves the Sunday tourist handicrafts markets to other towns in the Sacred Valley, but it's home to one of the coolest ceramics shops in Peru. Pablo Seminario, originally from the north of the country, now operates out of a lovely place that is equal parts home, workshop, storefront, and zoo. His work features funky pre-Columbian motifs. See "Urubamba & Environs," in chapter 9.

- **Chinchero's Handicrafts Market:** It's not as popular as Pisac's market, but in many ways, Chinchero's is even more authentic, and the setting is just as spectacular. The big one is on Sunday, when the tourist buses come through, but less-hectic Tuesday and Thursday are probably better for making a deal. The quality of handicrafts is usually quite excellent. Take your camera; the sellers still wear traditional garments. See "Urubamba & Environs" in chapter 9.

- **Isla Taquile,** Lake Titicaca: The Taquile islanders are famous for their dress and exquisite textiles. Travelers can pick up some of the finest woven and embroidered waistbands and wool stocking caps in Peru, including some that are normally reserved for community authorities. Because they're so finely made, Taquile textiles are more expensive than the mass-produced handicrafts you'll find elsewhere in Peru. Islanders operate a co-op on the main plaza and sell from stalls during festivals. See "Puno & Lake Titicaca," in chapter 10.

- **Arequipa:** Alpaca sweaters, ponchos, and hats are classic Peruvian souvenirs, and you can score them across the Andes and in Lima, but Arequipa is the top spot for really excellent export-quality goods. You'll find great designs in baby alpaca, vicuña, and wool. Visit any of the shops near the Plaza de Armas, including the alpaca boutiques that now inhabit the old cloisters of the La Compañía church. Another good spot, for slightly less swank goods, is the general handicrafts market *(mercado de artesanía),* whose stalls are in what used to be the old town jail. See "Arequipa," in chapter 10.

- **Barrio Belén,** Iquitos: Handicrafts, particularly textiles and other items from the Shipibo tribe in the Amazon, are available at the large artisans' market out by the airport, but shopping of a very different sort is pursued at the popular market in the waterfront Barrio de Belén. The wildly colorful market, which spreads over several long blocks and is a riot of activity, sells everything under the Amazon sun; let your senses be the judge. Look for unusual Amazon fish and fruits, and exotic jungle meats, such as monkey and caiman. When it becomes too much, take a breather at the fresh juice stands. See "Iquitos & the Northern Amazon" in chapter 11.

---

14 THE BEST REASONS FOR BRAGGING RIGHTS

- **Singing Protest Songs 'Til the Sun Comes Up:** A musical highlight of a visit to Peru is visiting an authentic *peña,* a small, informal club featuring musicians and patrons singing the songs of *música criolla* or *música folclórica.* The best are in Lima, but one of my favorites is **Peña Usha Usha,** in the northern town of Cajamarca. See chapters 6 and 12.

- **Checking Off a Gourmet Tour:** If you've discovered Peruvian cuisine, you'll have an inkling of how wonderfully diverse, creative, and accomplished it is. Trying ceviche in Lima or along the north coast is a must, but go beyond that and hit restaurants serving some of the finest regional cuisines in Peru (Arequipeña, Chiclayana, Cusqueña). Or knock off a tour of all the restaurants of Gastón Acurio, Peru's best known chef and a global ambassador for Peruvian cooking. See "Eating & Drinking in Peru" on p. 41.

- **Taking the High Road:** The Ferrocarril Central Andino, called the "Tren Macho," is the highest railway in the world, climbing to more than 4,500m (15,000 ft.) on the way from Lima to Huancayo in the Central Highlands. Unfortunately, the passenger railway has experienced all kinds of problems in recent years; even when it's on, it travels only once a month from July to October. If it is running, though, it's a truly thrilling and occasionally vertigo-inducing ride. If you're one of the lucky few to ride it, you've got plenty to brag about. See chapter 7.

- **Surfing Big Sand:** The southern desert of Peru is a strange, unrelenting landscape, but it has the highest sand dunes in South America. An extreme sport quickly gaining in popularity is surfing the dunes on sand boards and *areneros* (dune buggies). The biggest are near Nasca, but probably the prettiest spot is the dunes that ring the Huacachina Lagoon outside of Ica. See "Ica" in chapter 7.

- **Gazing at the Stars at Sacsayhuamán:** The Sacsayhuamán ruins are amazing enough by day; imagine those immense, elegantly laid stones at night, high above Cusco. At night, it won't be hard to perceive the Incas' worship of the natural world, in which the moon was a deity. If your visit coincides with a full moon in that gargantuan sky, you'll be talking about it back home for months. A similar experience would be hiking along the Inca Trail and spending that last night before pushing on to Machu Picchu under a full moon. See "What to See & Do" in chapter 8.

1

- **Lighting It Up at Tres Cruces:** Beyond the remote Andean village of Paucartambo, known for its Virgen de Carmen festival, is Tres Cruces, perched on a mountain ridge on the edge of the Amazon basin. Famous for its almost hallucinogenic, multihued sunrise, the spot was held sacred by the Incas, and it's not hard to see why. During the winter months (May–July), the special effects are beyond belief. To enhance your bragging rights, note that Tres Cruces is a royal pain to reach. See "Side Trips from Cusco" in chapter 8.

- **Hopping the Hiram Bingham Train to Machu Picchu:** Once upon a time, you could zip to the most famous Inca ruins by helicopter, but for my money, the new old-world luxury train named for the discoverer of Machu Picchu is even better. With wood-paneled cars, full white-glove meal and cocktail service, on-board Peruvian musicians, and an included tour of the ruins, it's definitely traveling in style. Sure, it costs several times the regular tourist train, but this is Machu Picchu, right? See "Machu Picchu & the Inca Trail," in chapter 9.

- **Scaling Huayna Picchu in Record Time:** Huayna Picchu hovers above Machu Picchu in the classic postcard shot of the ruins. People of all ages and decent physical condition can climb to the summit; to properly boast, you've got to race the steep stone path in close to record time (about 15 min. at last report). Even if you don't beat the record, you can savor the stunning, indescribable view as you wait for your heart rate to return to normal. See "Machu Picchu & the Inca Trail," in chapter 9.

- **Completing a 5-Day Andes Trek:** Hiking the Inca Trail to Machu Picchu may get all the attention, and though it's still one of the greatest ecoadventures on the planet, it's gotten a little popular for true adventurers. Trekkers in search of more solitude and hardcore authenticity are instead heading to Choquequirao and other sites in the southern highlands, where the Incas once roamed but few tourists do. See "Machu Picchu & the Inca Trail," in chapter 9.

- **Running a Class VI in Colca Canyon:** Extremely technical white-water rafting in the Colca (as well as Cotahuasi) Canyon is the stuff for which bragging was made. Imagine telling your friends that you hurtled down the river at the bottom of a canyon more than twice as deep as the Grand Canyon! This is for hard-core runners only; trips are expensive and lengthy. See "Colca Valley," in chapter 10.

- **Rumbling by Truck to Puerto Maldonado:** If you like tests of sheer perseverance, travel by truck from Cusco to Puerto Maldonado, the gateway to the Tambopata Reserve in the southern Amazon. It'll take between 3 and 10 days on a road that's 95% unpaved, but what's time (and a sore body) to a good story? See "The Southern Amazon Jungle," in chapter 11.

- **Trippin' Jungle Style:** If spotting wildlife and trekking through primary rainforest isn't stimulating enough, you can do your best to imitate the ancient ways of Amazon tribes and shamans by taking part in an authentic *ayahuasca* ceremony (there are lots of hucksters, so you have to find a real practitioner, or shaman). The natural hallucinogenic potion, made of herbs, roots, and other plants, is supposed to mess with your mind. But for locals, it's a deeply respected ritual. See "Iquitos & the Northern Amazon," in chapter 11.

- **Fishing for Piranha:** If you visit a jungle lodge, you might have the opportunity to head out on the Amazon or its tributaries in a dugout canoe to fish for piranha. Most are surprisingly small, but their famous teeth are very much present. For a special dinner, have the lodge cook fry 'em up for you that night. For extra credit, do it from a swanky Amazon river cruise boat, such as the ultrastylish **Aqua Expeditions.** See "Iquitos & the Northern Amazon" in chapter 11.

- **Bagging 6,000m (20,000 ft.) Peaks in the Cordillera Blanca:** For expert climbers, the Cordillera Blanca is a mountaineering mecca. From May to September, fit climbers can score several 6,000m (20,000-ft.) summits in the Parque Nacional Huascarán in just a couple weeks. Huascarán, at 6,768m (22,205 ft.), is the big one, the highest mountain in the Peruvian Andes and the tallest tropical mountain in the world. See "Huaraz & the Cordillera Blanca" in chapter 12.

15 THE BEST OF PERU ONLINE

- **www.peru.info:** The most comprehensive official Peru site is the website of Promperú. It has detailed sections on Peruvian history, festivals, trip-planning, and outdoor "adrenaline rushes," all with extensive pull-down menus, as well as a stock of photo and video images and audio files.
- **www.saexplorers.org:** The website of the rightly famous South American Explorers (based in Ithaca, New York, with clubhouses in Lima, Cusco, and Quito, Ecuador) has vital information such as travel advisories and links to websites on specific Peruvian destinations. You can also order the club's "Information Packet" of fact sheets and member tips.
- **www.andeantravelweb.com/peru:** The Andean Travel Web, a private website run by gringos in Peru, is a mini-guide to the country, with information on all the major destinations and activities, transportation, the latest in Inca Trail regulations, local tour operators, and helpful things such as ecotourism links. It doesn't cover northern Peru, however, sticking to the most well-trod regions.
- **www.livinginperu.com:** An English-language site directed toward foreign residents of Peru, this is the best place to get the latest news on Peru, including transportation issues, political info, and other practical matters that affect not only residents but also visitors. It also contains up-to-date cultural and event information.
- **www.traficoperu.com:** This online travel agent has details on practical matters—domestic airlines, bus transportation, and hotels—plus a few cheap domestic packages, and a good selection of regional and city maps.

2

Peru in Depth

Peru has a habit of turning virtually every visitor into an amateur archaeologist or outdoors enthusiast. Intriguing ruins from the Incas and even more ancient cultures fire the imagination, and outstanding museum collections of ceramics, spectacular textiles, and remarkably preserved mummies weave a complex tale of some of the world's most advanced cultures. And yet—Cusco and Machu Picchu's immense popularity notwithstanding—with so many temples and burial sites still being excavated, and ruins almost continually discovered in remote jungle regions, Peru still has the rare feeling of a country in the 21st century that hasn't been exhaustively explored.

The third-largest country in South America (after Brazil and Argentina), Peru has grown rapidly as a travel destination over the past decade, though it still seems comparatively undervalued given all it has to offer. With spectacular Andes mountains and highland culture, a swath of Amazon rainforest second only to Brazil, one of the richest arrays of wildlife in the world, and some of the Americas' greatest ruins of pre-Columbian cultures, Peru deserves to be experienced by so many more people.

Most know it only as the land of the Incas, symbolized by the mysteries of Machu Picchu, the famous lost city tucked high in the Andes. Yet Peru is littered with archaeological discoveries of many civilizations, from one end to another, highland to coast. Just 2 decades ago, a *National Geographic* team discovered Juanita the Ice Maiden, an Inca princess sacrificed on Mount Ampato more than 500 years ago. (Her frozen corpse is now exhibited in Arequipa.) In the last decade, archaeologists unearthed more than 2,000 extraordinarily well-preserved mummies from one of Peru's largest Inca burial sites, which was found under a shantytown on the outskirts of Lima. Researchers now describe Caral, a site in central Peru, north of Lima, believed to date to 2600 B.C., as the oldest city in the Americas, and, in late 2007, archaeologists celebrated the discovery of a 4,000-year-old temple on the northern coast.

It's not surprising, then, that when Francisco Pizarro, the Spanish conquistador, and his fortune-hunting cronies descended on Peru in 1528, they found not only vast riches, but also a highly sophisticated culture. The Spaniards soon overpowered the awed and politically weakened Inca Empire, but they didn't discover the Incas' greatest secret: the imperial city of Machu Picchu, hidden high in the Andes. Machu Picchu, finally revealed to the world in 1911 by a Yale historian, is acclaimed as the pinnacle achievement of the continent's pre-Columbian societies.

The Incas left behind numerous examples of their exquisite stone architecture and eye for unparalleled natural settings, but a long line of equally advanced cultures preceded the relatively short-lived Inca Empire. Over several thousand years, civilizations up and down the south Pacific coast and deep in the highlands developed ingenious irrigation systems, created sophisticated pottery and weaving techniques, and built great pyramids, temples, fortresses, and cities of adobe. Early peoples constructed mysterious cylindrical towers and the even more enigmatic Nasca Lines, giant drawings of animals and symbols somehow etched into the desert plains for eternity. Peru's fascinating history is in evidence everywhere: in open graves with bits and pieces of ancient textiles; in mortarless

Inca stones that serve as foundations for colonial churches; and in traditional dress, foods, and festivals, as well as Andean customs and beliefs that reveal a country and a people very much rooted in its past.

1 PERU TODAY

Modern Peru is no less complicated than its past. The country's recent history of suffering—2 decades of political mayhem and corruption, surprise attacks from homegrown Maoist "Shining Path" terrorists, cocaine trafficking, and violent street crime—is well documented. Throughout the 1980s and early '90s, Peruvians fled the capital and the countryside, fearful of attack; few travelers were brave enough to plan vacations in the troubled nation.

Though Peru is rich in artifacts and culture, it remains very poor, a society thoroughly dominated by elites. Half the population lives at or below the poverty line. The horrendous violence of 2 decades ago has now almost completely abated, and outside of areas deep in the jungle, there are no areas where visitors should not feel welcome to travel. Indeed, rumors of a Shining Path revival have not been borne out, even though at least two major attacks in the last decade, including a bombing near the U.S. embassy in Lima, have been attributed to the group.

The disgraced former president Alberto Fujimori, who fled the country to live in exile in Japan, was arrested in Chile in 2005 attempting to return to Peru in a surprise bid to run for president. Extradited to Peru and jailed in 2006, Fujimori stood trial at the end of 2007 on charges of ordering the murders of suspected Shining Path guerrillas and their collaborators by death squad (he remains in a jail in Lima, sentenced to 25 years for his role in ordering death squads, along with three other concurrent sentences, including for abuse of power, bribery and illegal wiretapping of phones). The trial marked the first time in Peruvian history that a former

president has been tried for crimes committed during his administration.

With the 2001 election of Alejandro Toledo, the country's first president of native Indian origin, many Peruvians believed that the country had finally turned a corner and that the 21st century would bring stability, progress, and prosperity. But although the economy grew at an impressive rate and Peru is now safer and more stable than it has been in recent memory, it remains a country beset by widespread poverty and unpredictability. A former president, Alan García—who himself had also fled Peru after a disastrous term in the 1980s—returned from exile and, improbably, captured the 2006 presidential election.

The Peruvian economy has expanded steadily in the last decade, but much of that growth has been stimulated by foreign investment in mining and other sectors, from which few Peruvians benefit. Like previous governments, Toledo's administration was plagued by instability, abuse of power, and poor management, opening the door for García, a one-time populist, who positioned himself as a centrist, seeking to put a clamp on inflation and pursuing free-market policies. Most notably, he pushed aggressively for a free-trade agreement with the United States, a treaty that was ratified by the U.S. Congress in December 2007 and which entered into force in February 2009 (Peru is seeking similar agreements with Mexico and Canada). The Peruvian economy recorded a robust growth rate of 9.2% in 2008, a 15-year high and one of the most impressive in the world, and to date the García presidency—which runs until 2011—has been largely stable and peaceful. The pace of growth dropped by half in 2009, though.

Despite those recent economic successes, fears remain that continued peasant uprisings in neighboring Bolivia, triggered in part by U.S. military efforts to eradicate coca growing, could still spread to Peru. The move of Bolivia's president, the leftist Evo Morales, to nationalize energy concerns and legalize coca farming speaks to a growing influence of disenfranchised Amerindian populations in Andean countries. And as proof that past sins are easily forgotten in Peru, one of the leading contenders for the presidential election in 2011 is Keiko Fujimori, the daughter of the jailed former president and a right-wing lawmaker whose candidacy is apparently largely based on her desire to free her father from incarceration

In Peru, the divide between rich and poor, coastal elites and indigenous highlanders, and modern and traditional, continues to loom large. Even against that backdrop, though, Peru is more welcoming than ever for visitors. Too many unfortunate years of corrupt politicians, lawlessness, and economic disarray succeeded in clouding but never eclipsing the beauty and complexity of this fascinating Andean nation.

PERUVIAN PEOPLE & CULTURE

Peru's nearly 30 million people are predominantly *mestizo* (of mixed Spanish and indigenous heritage) and Andean Indian, but the population is a true melting pot of ethnic groups. Significant minority groups of Afro-Peruvians (descendants of African slaves, living mainly in the coastal area south of Lima), immigrant Japanese and Chinese populations among the largest in South America, and smaller groups of European immigrants, including Italians and Germans, help make up Peru's population of 28 million. In the early days of the colony, Peruvian-born offspring of Spaniards were called *criollos*, though that term today refers mainly to coastal residents and Peruvian cuisine.

After Bolivia and Guatemala, Peru has the largest population by percentage of Amerindians in Latin America. Perhaps half the country lives in the *sierra*, or highlands, and most of these people, commonly called *campesinos* (peasants), live in either small villages or rural areas. Descendants of Peru's many Andean indigenous groups in remote rural areas continue to speak the native languages Quechua (made an official language in 1975) and Aymara

---

Tips Watch Your Language

The term cholo is often used to describe Peruvians of color and obvious Amerindian descent, usually those who have migrated from the highlands to the city. It is frequently employed as a derogatory and racist term by the Limeño population of European descent, but former President Alejandro Toledo has claimed the term for himself and all mestizos (those of mixed race) of Peru, in an attempt to demonstrate pride in their common culture and to take the sting out of the term. Afro-Peruvians are more commonly called morenos(as) or negros(as). Using any of these terms can potentially be a complicated and charged matter for foreigners, especially those who have little experience in the country or fluency in the language. At any rate, it's best for gringos (foreigners; almost always not a derogatory term) simply to steer clear of such linguistic territory. It's better to refrain from making distinctions among races and colors than to risk offending someone.

or other Amerindian tongues, and for the most part, they adhere to traditional regional dress. However, massive peasant migration to cities from rural highland villages has contributed to a dramatic weakening of indigenous traditions and culture across Peru. (The government of Alejandro Toledo, himself a proud *cholo,* or person of direct Andean Indian roots, committed itself to a valorization and preservation of native language and traditions, though.)

RELIGION

Peruvians are a predominantly Roman Catholic people (more than 90% claim to be Catholic), although Protestant evangelical churches have been winning converts, a fact that is worrisome to the Catholic Church. Animistic religious practices (worship of deities representing nature), inherited from the Incas and others, have been incorporated into the daily lives of many Peruvians and can be seen in festivals and small individual rituals such as offerings of food and beverage to Pachamama, or Mother Earth.

2 LOOKING BACK AT PERU

First inhabited as many as 20,000 years ago, Peru was the cradle of several of the most ancient and sophisticated pre-Columbian civilizations in the Americas. The Chavín, Paracas, Nasca, Huari, Moche, and Incas, among others, form a long line of complicated, occasionally overlapping, and frequently warring cultures stretching back to 2000 B.C. Before the Incas, two other civilizations, the Chavín and the Huari-Tiahuanaco, achieved pan-Andean empires. Most of what is known about pre-Columbian cultures is based on the unearthing of temples and tombs because none possessed a written language. Further complicating matters is the fact that, as one culture succeeded a previous one, it imposed its values and social structure on the vanquished but also assimilated features useful to it, making distinction among some early cultures exceedingly difficult.

Early societies were located mainly in the coastal areas and highlands. Many fell victim to warfare, cyclical floods, extended drought, and earthquakes. Evidence of pivotal pre-Columbian cultures—including ruined temples; spectacular collections of ceramics, masks, and jewelry; and tombs found with well-preserved mummies—is everywhere in Peru, and some sites are only now being excavated and combed for clues.

The first inhabitants are thought by most historians to have crossed the Bering Strait in Asia during the last ice age, worked their way across the Americas, and settled the region around 20,000 B.C. (although this migratory pattern has been disputed by some scholars). They were nomadic hunter-gatherers who lived along the central and northern coasts. The Pikimachay cave, which dates to 12,000 B.C., is the oldest site in Peru. The earliest human remains, discovered near Huánaco in highland Peru, are from around 7000 B.C. Early Peruvians were responsible for cave paintings at Toquepala (Tacna, 7000 B.C.) and houses in Chillca (Lima, 5000 B.C.). Experts say that recent analysis of findings at the coastal site Caral, in the Supe Valley, demonstrates the existence of the earliest complex civilization in the Americas. The city was inhabited as many as 4,700 years ago, 1,000 years earlier than once believed.

PRE-INCA CULTURES

Over the course of nearly 15 centuries, pre-Inca cultures settled principally along the Peruvian coast and highlands. Around 6000 B.C., the Chinchero people along the southern desert coast mummified their dead, long before the ancient Egyptians had thought of it. By the 1st century B.C., during what is known as the Formative, or Initial, period, Andean society had designed sophisticated irrigation canals and produced the first textiles and decorative ceramics. Another important advance was the specialization of labor, aided in large part by the development of a hierarchical society.

The earliest known Peruvian civilization was the **Chavín culture** (1200–400 B.C.), a theocracy that worshiped a feline, jaguarlike god and settled in present-day Huántar, Ancash (central Peru). Over 8 centuries, the Chavín, who never developed into a military or mercantilistic empire, unified groups of peoples across Peru. The most spectacular remnant of this culture, known for its advances in stone carving, pottery, weaving, and metallurgy, is the Chavín de Huántar temple, 40km (25 miles) east of Huaraz. The ceremonial center, a place of pilgrimage, contained wondrous examples of religious carving, such as the Tello Obelisk and the Raimondi Stella. The temple demonstrates evidence of sophisticated engineering and division of labor.

A subsequent society, the **Paracas** culture (700 B.C.–A.D. 200), took hold along the southern coast. It is renowned today for its superior textile weaving, considered perhaps the finest example of pre-Columbian textiles in the Americas. The Paracas peoples were sophisticated enough to dare to practice trepanation, a form of brain surgery that consisted of drilling holes in the skull to cure various ailments and correct cranial deformation.

The Classical period (A.D. 200–1100) was one of significant social and technological development. Likely descendants of the Paracas, the Moche and Nasca cultures are among the best studied in pre-Columbian Peru. The **Moche** (or **Mochica**) civilization (A.D. 200–700), one of the first true urban societies, dominated the valleys of the north coast near Trujillo and conquered a number of smaller groups in building their widespread empire. The Moche were a highly organized hierarchical civilization that created extraordinary adobe platform complexes, such as the Temples of the Sun and Moon near Trujillo (the former was the largest man-made structure of its day in the Americas), and the burial site of Sipán, near Chiclayo, where the remains and riches of the famous Lord of Sipán, a religious and military authority, were unearthed in remarkably preserved royal tombs. Moche pottery, produced from molds, contains vital clues to their way of life, down to very explicit sexual representations. Its frank depictions of phalluses, labia, and nontraditional bedroom practices might strike some visitors as pre-Columbian pornography.

The **Nasca** culture (A.D. 300–800) established itself along the coastal desert south of Lima. Nasca engineers created outstanding underground aqueducts, which permitted agriculture in one of the most arid regions on earth, and its artisans introduced polychrome techniques in pottery. But the civilization is internationally known for the enigmatic **Nasca Lines,** geometric and animal symbols etched indelibly into the desert, elements of an agricultural and astronomical calendar that are so vast that they can only really be appreciated from the window of an airplane.

The **Huari** (also spelled **Wari**) culture (A.D. 600–1100), an urban society that was the first in Peru to pursue explicitly expansionist goals through military conquest, settled the south-central *sierra* near Ayacucho. Along with the **Tiahuanaco** people, with whom they shared a central god figure, they came to dominate the Andes, with an empire spreading all the way to Chile and Bolivia. Both cultures achieved superior agricultural technology, in the form of canal irrigation and terraces.

Separate regional cultures, the best known of which is the **Chimú** culture (A.D. 700), developed and thrived over the next 4 centuries. The Chimú, adroit metallurgists and architects, built the citadel of Chan Chan, a compound of royal palaces and the largest adobe city in the world, near the northern coastal city Trujillo. The Chimú were the dominant culture in Peru before the arrival and expansion of the Incas, and they initially represented a great northern and coastal rivalry to the Incas. Other cultures that thrived during the same period were the **Chachapoyas,** who constructed the impressive Kuélap fortress in the northern highlands; the **Ica** (or **Chincha**), south of Lima; and the *altiplano* (high plains) groups that built the finely crafted *chullpa* towers near Puno and Lake Titicaca. The Sicán (or Lambayeque) culture, which built great temple sites and buried its dead with extraordinary riches, fell to the Chimú near the end of the 14th century. The Chimú themselves were, in turn, conquered by the Incas.

THE INCA EMPIRE

Though Peru is likely to be forever synonymous with the Incas, who built the spectacular city of Machu Picchu high in the Andes and countless other great palaces and temples, the society was merely the last in a long line of pre-Columbian cultures. The Inca Empire (1200–1532) was relatively short-lived, but it remains the best documented of all Peruvian civilizations. Though the height of its power lasted for little more than a century, the Inca Empire extended throughout the Andes, all the way from present-day Colombia down to Chile—a stretch of more than 5,635km (3,500 miles). At its apex, the Inca Empire's reach was longer than even that of the Romans.

The Incas were a naturalistic and ritualistic people who worshiped the sun god Inti and the earth goddess Pachamama, as well as the moon, thunder, lightning, and the rainbow, all regarded as deities. The Inca emperors were believed to be direct descendants of the sun god. The bold Andes Mountains were at least as important in their system of beliefs: The dwelling places of respected spirits, the 7,000m (22,960-ft.) peaks were the sites of human sacrifices. The Incas founded Cusco, the sacred city and capital of the Inca Empire (which they called Tahuantinsuyo, or Land of Four Quarters). The ruling sovereign was properly called the Inca, but today the term also refers to the people and the empire.

The Incas' Andean dominance was achieved through formidable organization and a highly developed economic system. The Incas rapidly expanded their empire first through political alliances and absorption, and then by swift military conquest. Though the Incas imposed their social structure and way of life, they also assimilated useful skills and practices, even granting administrative positions to defeated nobles of the Chimú and other cultures. The Incas thus succeeded in achieving political and religious unification across most of their domain.

The Incas recorded an astounding level of achievement. They never developed a system of writing, but they kept extraordinary records with an accounting system of knots on strings, called *quipus.* They laid a vast network of roadways, nearly 32,200km (20,000 miles) total across the difficult territory of the Andes, connecting cities, farming communities, and religious sites. A network of runners, called *chasquis,* operated on the roads, relaying messages and even transporting foodstuffs from the coast to the Andes. *Tambos,* or way stations, dotted the highways, serving as inspection points and shelters for relay runners. The Inca Trail was a sacred

Chakana, the Inca Cross

The ever-present Inca cross, the **Chakana** (consisting of four symmetrical sides of three steps each and a hole in the middle) is the very symbol of Inca civilization and its complex cosmology. Represented in it are three levels of existence or worlds (*Hana Pacha,* the higher world of the *apus,* or gods; *Kay Pacha,* the middle world of man's everyday existence; and *Ucu Pacha,* the lower world inhabited by spirits of the dead and ancestors). The hole in the center of the cross is both the axis through which a shaman might travel to other worlds and states of consciousness, and representative of Cusco, the center of the Incan empire. Some believe the chakana to be a compass or calendar. The familiar motif of three steps is seen repeatedly in Inca constructions, from Machu Picchu to the Temple of the Sun in Cusco.

highway, connecting the settlements in the Urubamba Valley to the ceremonial center, Machu Picchu.

The Incas' agricultural techniques were exceedingly skilled and efficient, with advanced irrigation systems and soil conservation. The Incas were also extraordinary architects and unparalleled stonemasons. Inca ruins reveal splendid landscaping and graceful construction of perfectly cut stones and terraces on inaccessible sites with extraordinary views of valleys and mountains.

A rigid hierarchy and division of labor ruled Inca society. At the top, just below the Inca sovereign (who was also the chief military and religious figure and considered a descendant of the sun), was the ruling elite: nobles and priests. Tens of thousands of manual laborers provided the massive manpower necessary to construct temples and palaces throughout the empire. The Inca kept chosen maidens, or Virgins of the Sun *(acllas),* who serviced him and Inca nobles.

Extraordinarily tight community organization was replicated across the empire. At the heart of the structure was the Inca's clan, the *panaca,* composed of relatives and descendants. Spanish conquistadors chronicled a dynasty that extended to 12 rulers, from **Manco Cápac,** the empire's

founder in 1200 who was said to have risen out of Lake Titicaca, to **Atahualpa,** whose murder in Cajamarca by Spanish conquerors spelled the end of the great power.

The Inca **Pachacútec** ruled from 1438 to 1463, and he is considered the great builder of Inca civilization. Under his rule, Cusco was rebuilt, and some of the most brilliant examples of Inca architecture were erected, including Cusco's Qoricancha (Temple of the Sun), the Ollantaytambo and Sacsayhuamán fortresses, and, of course, the famed religious city of Machu Picchu. Pachacútec also initiated the empire's expansion. It was Pachacútec's successor, **Tupac Yupanqui** (1463–93), however, who achieved dominance from Ecuador to Chile. A great conqueror, he defeated his Chimú rivals in northern Peru.

After the death of the Inca **Huayna Cápac** in 1525, civil war ensued, brought on by the empire splitting between his two sons, Atahualpa and Huáscar. The Spaniards, arriving in northern Peru in 1532, found a severely weakened empire—a pivotal reason the Incas so swiftly succumbed to a small band of invading Spaniards. Another key was the Spaniards' superior military technology. Against cannons and cavalry, the Incas' slings, battle-axes, and cotton-padded armor stood little chance. But their defeat remains puzzling to most visitors to Peru, not to mention many scholars.

SPANISH CONQUEST & COLONIALISM

Columbus and his cohorts landed in the Americas in 1492, and by the 1520s, the Spanish conquistadors had reached South America. Francisco Pizarro led an expedition along Peru's coast in 1528. Impressed with the riches of the Inca Empire, he returned to Spain and succeeded in raising money and recruiting men for a return expedition. In 1532, Pizarro made his return to Peru over land from Ecuador. After founding the first Spanish city in Peru, San Miguel de Piura, near the Ecuadorian border, he advanced upon the northern highland city of Cajamarca, an Inca stronghold. There, a small number of Spanish troops—about 180 men and 30 horses—cunningly captured the Inca emperor Atahualpa. The emperor promised to pay a king's ransom of gold and silver for his release, offering to fill his cell several times over, but the Spaniards, having received warning of an advancing Inca army, executed the emperor in 1533. It was a catastrophic blow to an already weakened empire.

Pizarro and his men massacred the Inca army, estimated at between 5,000 and 6,000 warriors. The Spaniards installed a puppet Inca, Tupac Huallpa, the brother of Huáscar, who had died while Atahualpa was being held. They then marched on Cusco, capturing the capital city on November 15, 1533, and emptying the Sun Temple of its golden treasures. After the death of Tupac Huallpa en route, a new puppet was appointed, Manco Inca.

Pizarro founded the coastal city of Lima 2 years later, which became the capital of the new colony, the Viceroyalty of Peru. The Spanish crown appointed Spanish-born viceroys the rulers of Peru, but

Spaniards battled among themselves for control of Peru's riches, and the remaining Incas continued to battle the conquistadors. A great siege was laid to Cusco in 1536, with Manco Inca and his brothers directing the rebellion from Sacsayhuamán. Pizarro was assassinated in 1541, and the indigenous insurrection ended with the beheading of Manco Inca, who had escaped to Vilcabamba, deep in the jungle, in 1544. Inca Tupac Amaru led a rebellion in 1572 but also failed and was killed.

Over the next 2 centuries, Lima gained in power and prestige at the expense of the old Inca capital and became the foremost colonial city of the Andean nations. The Peruvian viceroyalty stretched all the way from Panama to Tierra del Fuego. Cusco focused on cultural pursuits and became the epicenter of the Cusco School of painting (Escuela Cusqueña), which incorporated indigenous elements into Spanish styles, in the 16th and 17th centuries.

INDEPENDENT PERU

By the 19th century, grumbling over high taxes and burdensome Spanish controls grew in Peru, as it did in most colonies in the Americas. After liberating Chile and Argentina, José de San Martín set his sights north on Lima in 1821 and declared it an independent nation the same year. Simón Bolívar, the other hero of independence on the continent, came from the other direction. His successful campaigns in Venezuela and Colombia led him south to Ecuador and finally Peru. Peru won its independence from Spain after crucial battles in late 1824. Though Peru mounted its first civilian government, defeat by Chile in the War of the Pacific (1879–83) left Peru in a dire economic position.

Several military regimes ensued, and Peru finally returned to civilian rule in 1895. Land-owning elites dominated this new "Aristocratic Republic." In 1911, the Yale historian Hiram Bingham happened upon the ruins of the imperial city Machu

Picchu—a discovery that would begin to unravel the greatness of the Incas and forever associate Peru with the last of its pre-Columbian civilizations.

Peru launched war with Ecuador over a border dispute—just one of several long-running border conflicts—in 1941. Though the 1942 Treaty of Río de Janeiro granted the area north of the River Marañon to Peru, Ecuador would continue to claim the territory until the end of the 20th century.

3 PERU'S ARTS & CULTURE

PERUVIAN DANCE

Dances associated with Afro-Peruvian music include lively and sensual **festejo** dances, in which participants respond to the striking of the cajón, one of the Afro-Peruvian music's essential instruments. The *alcatraz* is an extremely erotic dance. Females enter the dance floor with tissue on their posteriors. The men, meanwhile, dance with lit candles. The not-so-subtle goal on the dance floor is for the man to light the woman's tissue (and thus become her partner).

Peruvian tourism authorities produce a guide to festivities, music, and folk art, and it features a diagram of native dances in Peru. Especially up and down the coast, and in the central corridor of the Andes, the map is a bewildering maze of numbers indicating the indigenous dances practiced in given regions. Two dances, though, have become synonymous with Peru, the huayno and marinera.

The **huayno** is the essential dance in the Andes, with pre-Columbian origins fused with Western influences. Couples dancing the huayno perform sharp turns, hops, and taplike *zapateos* to keep time. Huayno music is played on quena, charango, harp, and violin. The **marinera,** a sleek, sexy, and complex dance of highly coordinated choreography, is derivative of other folkloric dances in Peru, dating back to the 19th century. There are regional variations of the dance, which differ most from the south coast to the northern highlands. Dancers keep time with a handkerchief in one hand. Marinera music in Lima is performed by guitar and cajón, while a marching band is de rigueur in the north. Marinera festivals are held across Peru, but the most celebrated one is in Trujillo in January.

One of the most attention-getting dances in Peru, though, is that performed by **scissors dancers.** Their *danza de las tijeras* is an exercise in athleticism and balance. Dancers perform gymnastic leaps and daring stunts to the sounds of harp and violin. The main instrument played to accompany the dance is the pair of scissors, made up of two independent sheets of metal around 25 centimeters long. The best places to see scissors dancers are Ayacucho, Arequipa, and Lima.

PERUVIAN MUSIC

There is evidence of music in Peru dating back 10,000 years, and musical historians have identified more than 1,000 genres of music in the country. Traditional instruments include *pututos* (trumpets made from seashells) and many other wind instruments crafted from cane, bone, horns, and precious metals, as well as a wide range of percussion instruments. Exposure to Western cultures has introduced new instruments such as the harp, violin, and guitar to Peruvian music. But Peruvian music can still be identified by its distinctive instruments, and there are many besides the basics of highland music.

The *cajón* is a classic percussion instrument, typical in *música criolla* and *música negra,* as well as *marinera.* A simple wooden box with a sound hole in the back, the cajón is played by a musician who sits on top and pounds the front like a bongo. The cajón has been introduced into flamenco music by none other than the legendary flamenco guitarist Paco de Lucía. Another popular instrument is the **zampoña,** which belongs to the panpipe family and varies greatly in size. The zampoña is never absent at festivals in southern Peru, particularly Puno.

For additional information on Peruvian music, see the section below, "Peru in Popular Culture."

PERUVIAN TEXTILES

Woven textiles have to be considered among the great traditional arts of Peru. Peru has one of the most ancient and richest weaving traditions in the world; for more than 5,000 years, Peruvian artisans have used fine natural fibers for hand weaving, and the wool produced by alpacas, llamas, and vicuñas is some of the finest in the world, rarer even than cashmere. The most ancient textiles that have been found in Peru come from the Huaca Prieta temple in Chicama and are more than 4,000 years old. In pre-Columbian times, hand-woven textiles, which required extraordinary patience and skill, were prized and extremely valuable; distinctive textiles were indicators of social status and power. They were traded as commodities. Paracas, Huari, and Inca weavings are among the most sophisticated and artful ever produced in Peru. The Paracas designs were stunningly intricate, with detailed animals, human figures, and deities against dark backgrounds. Huari weaving features abstract figures and bold graphics. The Incas favored more minimalist designs, without embroidery. The finest Inca textiles were typically part of ritualistic ceremonies—many were burned as offerings to spirits.

Whereas pre-Columbian civilizations in Peru had no written language, textiles were loaded with symbolic images that serve as indelible clues to the cultures and beliefs of textile artists. Worship of nature and spiritual clues are frequently represented by motifs in textiles. Many of the finest textiles unearthed were sacred and elaborately embroidered blankets that enveloped mummies in burial sites. Found in tombs in the arid coastal desert, one of the world's driest climates, the textiles are remarkably preserved in many cases.

Contemporary Peruvian artisans continue the traditions, sophisticated designs, and techniques of intricate weaving inherited from pre-Columbian civilizations, often employing the very same instruments used hundreds of years ago and still favoring natural dyes. The drop spindle (weaving done with a stick and spinning wooden wheel), for example, is still used in many regions, and it's not uncommon to see women and young girls spinning the wheel as they tend to animals in the fields. Excellent-quality woven items, the best of which are much more than mere souvenirs, include typical Andean *chullo* wool or alpaca hats with earflaps, ponchos, scarves, sweaters, and blankets.

4 THE LAY OF THE LAND

ECOSYSTEMS

Peruvians are fond of pointing out that their country consists of three distinct geological components: coast, *sierra* (highlands), and *selva* (jungle). Although the largest cities are situated along the coast, the Amazon rainforest, which makes up nearly two-thirds of Peru, and the bold Andes mountain range dominate the country. The Pacific coastal region is a narrow strip that runs from one end of the country to the other (a distance of some

2,200km/1,400 miles) and is made up almost entirely of desert. The Andes, South America's longest mountain range, is the most significant feature of the Peruvian landscape. The mountain ranges in the center of Peru, north of Lima, are among the highest in Peru. Within Huascarán National Park, the Cordillera Blanca stretches 200km (124 miles) and contains a dozen peaks more than 5,000m (16,400 ft.) tall; the highest is Huascarán, at 6,768m (22,205 ft.). In extreme southern Peru, near Puno and Lake Titicaca, the Andes yield to the *altiplano,* the arid high plains, with altitudes of 3,300 meters (11,000 ft.). The *selva* ranges from cloud forest in the south to low-lying flatlands in the north. Although 60% of Peru is Amazon rainforest, only about 5% of the country's human inhabitants reside there. Massive Lake Titicaca, shared with Bolivia, is the largest lake in South America and the world's highest navigable body of water (at 3,830m/12,566 ft.).

FLORA AND FAUNA

Nearly two-thirds of Peru is jungle, and many naturalists and biologists believe that Peru's Amazon rainforest holds the greatest diversity in the world. It teems with a staggering roster of wildlife: 400 species of mammals, 2,000 species of fish, 300 reptiles, 1,800 birds, and more than 50,000 plants. The country counts 84 of 103 existing ecosystems and 28 of the 32 climates on the planet among its remarkable statistics. Recent studies have shown that a region just south of Iquitos has the highest concentration of mammals anywhere in the world. Peru's other significant fauna are the great Andean condors, found principally in Colca Canyon, near Arequipa, and the rich marine life of the Paracas National Reserve and Islas Ballestas (Peru's version of the Galápagos Islands), home to communities of endangered Humboldt penguins and sea turtles, sea lions, red boobies and flamingoes. Coastal Peru south of Lima is also home to one of the greatest population densities of dolphins in the world, with one-third of the world's species identified.

ENVIRONMENTAL THREATS

The vast Amazon basin that pertains to Peru holds a phenomenal wealth of flora and fauna but a dwindling human presence. Indigenous Amazonian tribes have been greatly reduced by centuries of disease, deforestation, and assimilation. There were once some six million people, 2,000 tribes and/or ethnic groups, and innumerable languages in the Amazon basin; today the indigenous population is less than two million. Still, many traditions and languages have yet to be extinguished, especially deep in the jungle—though most visitors are unlikely to come into contact with groups of unadulterated, non-Spanish-speaking native peoples.

Peru is losing nearly 300,000 hectares (740,000 acres) of rainforest annually. The primary threats to Peru's tropical forests are deforestation caused by agricultural expansion, cattle ranching, logging, oil extraction and spills, mining, illegal coca farming, and colonization initiatives. Deforestation has shrunk territories belonging to indigenous peoples and wiped out more than 90% of the population.

Peru has 72 million hectares (178 million acres) of natural-growth forests—70% in the Amazon jungle region—that comprise nearly 60% of the national territory. Peru has done a slightly better job of setting aside tracts of rainforest as national park reserves and regulating industry than have some other Latin American and Asian countries. The Manu Biosphere Reserve, the Tambopata National Reserve, and the Pacaya-Samiria National Reserve are three of the largest protected rainforest areas in the world, and the government regulates entry of tour groups. Peru augmented the Bahuaja-Sonene National Park, which was created in 1996, by 809,000 hectares (nearly 2 million acres) in 2001. INRENA, Peru's Institute for Natural Resource Management, enforces logging regulations and reseeds Peru's Amazon forests, and in 2008, President García created the country's first Ministry of the Environment. A handful of Peruvian and international environmental and conservation groups, such as ProNaturaleza and Conservation International are active in Peru, working on reforestation and sustainable forestry projects.

Jungle ecotourism has exploded in Peru, and rainforest regions are now much more accessible than they once were, with more lodges and eco-options than ever. Many are taking leading roles in sustainable tourism even as they introduce protected regions to more travelers.

5 PERU IN POPULAR CULTURE

BOOKS
Nonfiction

The classic work on Inca history and the Spanish conquistadors is *The Conquest of the Incas* (Harvest Books, 2003), by John Hemming, a very readable narrative of the fall of a short-lived but uniquely accomplished empire. *Lost City of the Incas* (Phoenix Press, 2003), is the travelogue and still-amazing story of Hiram Bingham, the Yale academic who brought the "lost city" to the world's attention in 1911. Bingham's book makes for a very interesting read, especially after so many years of speculation and theory about the site. Also available by Bingham is *Inca Land: Explorations in the Highlands of Peru* (National Geographic, 2003), detailing four expeditions into the Peruvian Andes, originally published in 1922.

The Incas and their Ancestors (Thames and Hudson, 2001), by Michael Moseley, is a good account of the Inca Empire and, importantly, its lesser-known predecessors. For most readers, it serves as a good introduction to Peru's archaeology and the sites they will visit, although some people find that it reads too much like a textbook. Illustrations include black-and-white photographs of Inca drawings and a few color photos. A terrific story of a recent archaeological find is *Discovering the Ice Maiden: My Adventures on Ampato* (National Geographic Society, 1998), by Johan Reinhard. The account of Reinhard's discovery of a mummified Inca princess sacrificed 500 years ago on a volcano summit in southern Peru details the team's search and its race to save what is considered one of the most important archaeological discoveries in recent decades. The book contains excellent color photographs of the maiden who can now be viewed in Arequipa. Reinhard's *The Ice Maiden: Inca Mummies, Mountain Gods, and Sacred Sites in the Andes* (National Geographic, 2005) is a memoir of archaeological adventures and the impact of his discovery of Juanita (both on him personally and the interpretation of Peruvian history).

The Peru Reader: History, Culture, Politics (Duke University Press, 1995), edited by Orin Starn, is one of the finest primers on Peru's recent history and political culture. It includes essays by several distinguished voices, including Mario Vargas Llosa.

The Madness of Things Peruvian, Democracy Under Siege, by Alvaro Vargas Llosa (Transaction Publishers, 1994), isn't easy to find, and it only chronicles up to the mid-'90s, but it is a well-rendered analysis of the failings of Peruvian democracy. Robin Kirk's *The Monkey's Paw: New Chronicles from Peru* (University of

Massachusetts Press, 1997) is a story of the impact of social and economic upheaval in Peru on marginalized peoples, with the homegrown guerrilla movements taking center stage.

Naturalists and birders might want to pick up *A Field Guide to the Birds of Peru* (Ibis Pub Co., 2001), by James F. Clements, although it is perhaps not the comprehensive field guide that a country as biologically diverse as Peru deserves. Many serious birders prefer *A Guide to the Birds of Colombia* (Princeton University Press, 1986), by Steven Hilty and William Brown, probably the definitive regional guide (and covering many of the birds also found in Peru). Also of interest is *A Parrot Without a Name: The Search for the Last Unknown Birds on Earth* (University of Texas Press, 1991), by Don Stap, an account of John O'Neill and LSU scientists documenting new species in the jungles of Peru.

Peru: The Ecotravellers' Wildlife Guide (Academic Press, 2000), by biologists David Pearson and Les Beletsky, is a 500-page handbook survey of Peruvian flora and fauna, including information about conservation, habitats, national parks, and reserves. It's a good introduction for readers ready to explore the Peruvian outdoors, from the Andes to the Amazon and other repositories of Peru's magnificent animal and plant life. The book is nicely illustrated and useful for identification purposes.

Peter Frost's *Exploring Cusco* (Nuevas Imágenes, 1999) is one of the best-detailed local guides, with excellent historical information and frank commentary by the author, a longtime Cusco resident, on the ancient Inca capital, the Sacred Valley, and, of course, Machu Picchu. *Peru & Bolivia: Backpacking and Trekking* (Bradt Publications, 1999), by Hilary Bradt, is a trusty guide, now in its third decade, of classic treks in Peru and Bolivia. Although it's in its seventh edition, with several new walks and treks added, some readers find it

outdated. Still, it's a good all-around guide for trekkers and walkers.

The Cloud Forest: A Chronicle of the South American Wilderness (Ingram, 1996) is a travelogue by Peter Matthiessen, who trekked some 10,000 miles through South America, including the Amazon and Machu Picchu. Matthiessen found larger-than-life characters and ancient trails deep in the jungle, experiences that led to the author's fictional novel *At Play in the Fields of the Lord* (Vintage Books, 1991). Set in the unnamed Peruvian jungle, it's a thriller about the travails of the missionary Martin Quarrier and an outsider, Lewis Moon, a mercenary who takes a much different tack while immersing himself in a foreign culture. Both are displaced outsiders whose lives have an irreversible impact on native Amerindian communities deep in the Amazon.

Another good travelogue on Peru is *The White Rock* (Overlook, 2003), by Hugh Thomson, an absorbing account of Thomson's 20 years traveling throughout the Andes of Peru, Bolivia, and Ecuador in search of lost Inca cities.

Fiction

The towering figure in contemporary Peruvian fiction is Mario Vargas Llosa, Peru's most famous novelist and a perennial candidate for the Nobel Prize, who was nearly elected the country's president back in 1990. It's difficult to choose from among his oeuvre of thoroughly praised works; *Aunt Julia and the Scriptwriter* (Penguin, 1995) is one of his most popular works, but it's without the heft of others, such as *The Real Life of Alejandro Mayta* (Noonday Press, 1998), a dense meditation on Peruvian and South American revolutionary politics that blurs the lines between truth and fiction, or *Death in the Andes* (Penguin, 1997), a deep penetration into the contemporary psyche and politics of Peru. Another side of the author is evident in the small erotic gem *In Praise of the*

Stepmother (Penguin, 1991), a surprising and beautifully illustrated book. His powerful book *The Feast of the Goat* (Farrar Straus & Giroux, 2001), about the Dominican dictator Rafael Trujillo, made the year-end best lists of many critics in 2001. Vargas Llosa might be a difficult and "heavy" writer, but he is an unusually engaging one.

Alonso Cueto is one of the next generation's most ballyhooed novelists; he won several international awards for *La Hora Azul* (*The Blue Hour;* Editorial Anagrama, 2005). *El Susurro de la Mujer Ballena* (*The Whisper of the Whale Woman;* Planeta, 2007) is his latest.

César Vallejo, born in Peru in 1892, is one of the great poets of Latin America and the Spanish language. *Complete Posthumous Poetry* (University of California Press, 1980), in translation, and *Trilce* (Wesleyan University Press, 2000), a bilingual publication, are the best places to start with this great poet. Vallejo wrote some of the poems in *Trilce,* a wildly creative and innovative avant-garde work that today is considered a masterpiece of modernism, while in prison. Vallejo later fled to Europe and immersed himself in the Spanish Civil War.

FILMS

Peru's film industry trails far behind those of its neighbors Argentina and Brazil, though a recent Oscar nomination may begin to change that. In a historic achievement for Peruvian film *La Teta Asustada* ("The Milk of Sorrow"), by Claudia Llosa, was nominated for an Academy Award for Best Foreign Language Film in 2010 (it also received the Golden Bear award at the Berlin International Film Festival in 2009). Less exalted but also reaching an international audience was *Máncora* (Maya Entertainment Group, 2009), a sexy Peruvian road movie set in part in the Pacific surfing resort along the northern coast, which debuted at the Sundance Film Festival in 2009.

The best-known films about or featuring Peru are still foreign. Two recent documentaries try to untangle the lasting impact of disgraced former president Alberto Fujimori. *The Fall of Fujimori: When Democracy and Terrorism Collide* (Stardust Productions, 2006) is a portrait of the eccentric ex-President and his controversial war against guerrilla movements in Peru. *State of Fear* (Skylight Pictures, 2006), based on the findings of the Peruvian Truth Commission, chronicles the 2-decade-long reign of terror by Shining Path. It doesn't shy away from documenting the abuses of the government in fighting terrorism.

Touching the Void (IFC Films 2004), available on DVD, is the harrowing dramatic reenactment (based on the book by Joe Simpson) of a climber's disastrous and near-fatal accident climbing in the Andes mountains near Huaraz. It is gripping, but may derail any mountaineering plans you had.

The Dancer Upstairs (Fox Searchlight 2003), a drama directed by John Malkovich and starring Javier Bardem, is a political thriller loosely based on the hunt for Abimael Guzman, the Shining Path leader, and the complicated story of the American Lori Benson, implicated and imprisoned as a terrorist collaborator in Peru (though the movie is set in an unnamed South American nation). *The Motorcycle Diaries* (MCA Home Video, 2005), an excellent 2004 film by Walter Salles about the young Che Guevara, is in large part a travelogue of Argentina, Chile, Colombia, and Venezuela, but Machu Picchu plays a scene-stealing role.

On a slightly lesser artistic note, the last installment in the Indiana Jones series, *Indiana Jones and the Kingdom of the Crystal Skull* (Paramount Home Entertainment, 2008), takes place in part in Peru, including the Nasca Lines and (ostensibly) the Peruvian jungle (actually filmed in Hawaii).

Peter Matthiessen's novel *At Play in the Fields of the Lord* (1991) was later made by Hector Babenco into an occasionally pretty but silly movie starring John Lithgow, Daryl Hannah, and Tom Beringer with a bowl-cut and face paint, and relocated from the Amazon Basin of Peru to Brazil.

MUSIC

Many travelers may be at least superficially familiar with the dominant strains of Peruvian music. Anyone who has traveled in Europe, South America, or even Asia is likely to have seen and heard roving bands of street musicians decked out in highlander garb (ponchos and *chullo* hats) playing the *música folclórica* that emanates from high in the Andes mountains. Known for its use of the **quena** (pan flute), played like a recorder, **charango** (from the lute family), and mandolin, the distinctive sounds of this Peruvian music—similar to that heard in other Andean countries, such as Bolivia and Ecuador—were widely sampled in the Simon and Garfunkel song "El Cóndor Pasa." That song was based on a melody by a Peruvian composer, Daniel Alomía Robles, who himself had appropriated a traditional Quechua *huayno* folk melody.

I'd point adventurous ears with an interest in ethnomusicology toward a handful of Andean *música folclórica* recordings released by the Smithsonian Folkways Series. "Mountain Music of Peru," a 2-volume series released in the early 1990s, includes recordings, celebratory and religious in nature, that were made in mountain villages in the 1960s. As such, they are raw and lack studio polish. Smithsonian also issues other volumes covering the traditional regional music of Peru, from "Cajamarca and the Colca Valley" (Vol. 3) to "The Region of Ayacucho" (Vol. 6). Though its song selections aren't specifically Peruvian, listeners may also enjoy the "Rough Guide to the Music of the Andes" compilation.

Just as there is a notable divide in Peruvian cuisine, with radically different takes in the *sierra* (mountains) and *costa* (coast), so too is Peruvian music divided along these lines. In coastal areas, principally Lima and communities just south, such as El Carmen, the most distinctive music came from the Afro-Peruvian population, descendants of slaves. Black Peruvians created a unique mix of African rhythms and Spanish and other European influences, called *música criolla*. Percussion is fundamental, in addition to strings and vocals, but the music is frequently bluesier than its jazz-inflected Afro counterparts that developed in Brazil and Cuba. A great place to start exploring is the compilation, selected by David Byrne and released on his Luaka Bop label, "Afro-Peruvian Classics: The Soul of Black Peru," featuring the influential singers and groups Eva Ayllón, Susana Baca, Perú Negro, Chabuca Granda, Nicomedes Santa Cruz, and others. Those same stars (but no repeat songs) are also featured on "The Rough Guide to Afro Peru."

Chicha is a relatively new addition to the list of musical genres. A hybrid of sorts of the *huayno* (see above) and Colombian *cumbia, chicha* is an extremely popular urban dance, especially among the working class. It has spread rapidly across Peru and throughout Latin America.

Susan Baca, with her recordings on the Luaka Bop label, has reached an audience of American and international ears. Look for her eponymous album or "Ecos de Sombra." Both are superb. In Peru, Eva Ayllón is even more of a megastar. A good recording available worldwide is "Eva! Leyenda Peruana." Another longtime female Afro-Peruvian performer is Chabuca Granda; a greatest hits collection of her work is called "Latinoamericana." Perú Negro's albums "Sangre de un Don" and "Jogorio," recorded after the death of the group's founder Ronaldo Campos in 2001, are both widely available.

A taste of Peruvian music serves either as great preparation for a trip to Peru or as a fond souvenir after the fact. But nothing equals grooving to live Peruvian coastal *música criolla* in a nightclub, at a stylish Lima jazz bar, or *peña*—a one-time social club now frequented by locals and tourists for live music—or hearing highlands' *música folclórica* during an Andean festival or stumbling upon it in a town square. The renaissance of Peru's indigenous musical forms is a hugely welcome development in this culturally rich country.

6 EATING & DRINKING IN PERU

FOOD & DRINK

Peruvian cuisine is among the finest and most diverse cuisines found in Latin America-and, indeed, the world. It is one of the most important contributors to the wave of Pan-Latino restaurants gaining popularity across the globe. As knowledge of Peruvian food spreads, more and more travelers are even making focused gastronomic pilgrimages to Peru—for many travelers, the cuisine will rank among the highlights of their visit.

Peruvian cooking differs significantly by region, and subcategories mirror exactly the country's geographical variety: coastal, highlands, and tropical. The common denominator among them is a blend of indigenous and Spanish (or broader European) influences, which has evolved over the past 4 centuries. Traditional Peruvian coastal cooking is often referred to as *comida criolla*, and it's found across Peru. The other main types of cuisine are *andino,* or *Andean* (highlands), and *novo andino* (creative or haute twists on and updates of traditional highlander cooking). Several celebrity chefs, including Gastón Acurio and Pedro Miguel Schiaffino, are leading the charge of contemporary Peruvian cuisine, often offering their creative takes on traditional dishes.

Coastal preparations concentrate on seafood and shellfish, as might be expected. The star dish, and the most exported example of Peruvian cuisine, is *ceviche,* a classic preparation of raw fish and shellfish marinated (not cooked) in lime or lemon juice and hot chili peppers, served with raw onion, sweet potato, and toasted corn. Ceviche has been around since the time of some of Peru's earliest civilizations, although a traditional Andean argument over whether Peruvians or Ecuadorians should be credited with creating it persists. *Cevicherías,* traditionally open only for lunch, usually serve several types of ceviche as well as a good roster of other seafood. *Tiradito* is finely sliced fish marinated with lime juice and *ají* peppers, essentially Peruvian sashimi or carpaccio. Other coastal favorites include *escabeche* (a tasty fish concoction served with peppers, eggs, olives, onions, and prawns), *conchitas* (scallops), and *corvina* (sea bass). Land-based favorites are *cabrito* (roast kid) and *ají de gallina* (a tangy creamed chicken and chili dish).

Highlanders favor a more substantial style of cooking. Corn and potatoes were staples of the Incas and other mountain civilizations before them. Meat, served with rice and potatoes, is a mainstay of the diet, as is trout *(trucha). Lomo saltado,* strips of beef mixed with onions, tomatoes, peppers, and french-fried potatoes and served with rice, seems to be on every menu. *Rocoto relleno,* a hot bell pepper stuffed with vegetables and meat, and *papa rellena,* a potato stuffed with veggies and then fried, are just as common (but are occasionally extremely spicy). Soups are excellent.

In the countryside, you might see people in the fields digging small cooking holes in the ground. They are preparing *pachamanca,* a roast cooked over stones. It's the Peruvian version of a picnic; on weekends, you'll often see families outside Cusco and other places stirring smoking fires in the ground while the kids play soccer nearby. *Cuy* (guinea pig) is considered a delicacy in many parts of Peru, including the *sierra,* but its elevated status was never much apparent to me. It comes roasted or fried, with head and feet upturned on the plate.

In the Amazon jungle regions, most people fish for their food, and their diets consist almost entirely of fish such as river trout and *paiche* (a huge river fish). Restaurants feature both of these, with accompaniments including *yuca* (a root), *palmitos* (palm hearts) and *chonta* (palm-heart salad), bananas and plantains, and rice tamales known as *juanes.* Common menu items such as chicken and game are complemented by exotic fare such as caiman, wild boar, turtle, monkey, and piranha fish.

In addition to Peruvian cooking, visitors will find plenty of international restaurants, including a particularly Peruvian variation, *chifas* (restaurants serving Peruvian-influenced Chinese food, developed by the large immigrant Chinese population), a mainstay among many non-Chinese Peruvians. *Chifas* are nearly as common as restaurants serving *pollo a la brasa* (spit-roasted chicken), which are everywhere in Peru.

Drinking is less of an event in Peru. While Peruvian wines from the coastal desert south and local beers are improving, they still can't really compare with superior examples found elsewhere on the continent (Chile and Argentina, predominantly). Most wines in better restaurants come from these three countries, along with Spain. Yet one indigenous drink stands out: *pisco,* a powerful white-grape brandy. The pisco sour (a cocktail mixed with pisco, egg whites, lemon juice, sugar,

and bitters) is effectively Peru's margarita: tasty, refreshing, and ubiquitous. New takes on the pisco sour have sprung up at sophisticated mixology bars: maracuyá (passion fruit) sours, coca sours (made with macerated coca leaves), and other sours highlighting indigenous tropical fruits, such as lúcuma. Pisco is also taken straight.

Peruvians everywhere (but especially in the highlands) drink *chicha,* a tangy, fermented brew made from maize and inherited from the Incas. Often served warm in huge glasses, it is unlikely to please the palates of most foreign visitors, although it's certainly worth a try if you come upon a small, informal place with the *chicha* flag flying in a rural village (it means something akin to "fresh *chicha* available inside"). *Chicha morada,* on the other hand, is nothing to be afraid of. It is a delicious nonalcoholic beverage, deep purple in color, prepared with blue corn and served chilled, the perfect accompaniment to ceviche. *Masato* is a beer made from *yuca,* typical of the Amazon region.

DINING CUSTOMS

Among the more interesting dining customs—beyond the eating of guinea pig—is the lovely habit of offering a sip of beer or *chicha* before the meal to Pachamama, or Mother Earth. Many Peruvians still ritualistically thank the earth for its bounty, and they show their appreciation by spilling just a bit before raising the drink to their own mouths.

Restaurants range from the rustic and incredibly inexpensive to polished places with impeccable service and international menus. Set three-course meals are referred to by a variety of terms: *menu del día, menu económico, menu ejecutivo, menu de la casa,* and *menu turístico.* They are all essentially the same thing and can sometimes be had for as little as S/10. In general, you should ask about the preparation of many Peruvian dishes because many are quite spicy. Informal eateries serving Peruvian cooking are frequently called *picanterías* and *chicherías*.

Fixed-price lunch deals are referred to as *menus del día* (or simply *menu*). The majority of restaurants include taxes and services in their prices, and your bill will reflect the menu prices. Others (including some upscale restaurants), however, separate taxes and services, and the bill can get pretty byzantine, especially when it comes to imported wine. You might see a subtotal, followed by a 10% service charge, a 20% "selectivo" wine tax, and a 19% IGV (general sales tax). It's crazy. Fortunately, the restaurants that do this are rare.

Note: Some upscale restaurants will place a couple of small plates of cheese, sausage, olives, or other tidbits on your table to nibble on as you wait for your meal. In almost all cases, you will be charged for these items, called a *cubierto,* or cover. Usually, it'll add S/5 to S/15 to your bill. If you don't touch the stuff, in theory you shouldn't have to pay for it because you didn't order it, but many restaurants automatically tack on the charge—and few are the customers who don't consider the *cubierto* part of the cost of eating out.

Dining hours are not much different from typical mealtimes in cities in North America or Great Britain, except that dinner *(cena)* is generally eaten after 8pm in restaurants. Peruvians do not eat nearly as late as Spaniards. Although lunch *(almuerzo)* is the main meal of the day, for most visitors, it generally is not the grand midday affair it is in Spain, unless you are dining at an outdoor *quinta,* where most locals linger over lunch for a couple hours.

If you invite a Peruvian to have a drink or to dine with you, it is expected that you will pay (the Spanish verb *invitar* literally connotes this as an invitation). Do not suggest that a Peruvian acquaintance join you in what will certainly be an expensive restaurant or cafe for him or her, and then pony up only half the tab.

Planning Your Trip to Peru

Mesmerizing Peru—a land of pre-Columbian ruins and lost cities, Andes Mountains and Amazon jungle—is a destination that many first-time travelers may know little about, beyond the famed Machu Picchu. This chapter details everything you need to know to make planning your trip to Peru less daunting, from the lay of the land and how to get there to money and health concerns. It also covers other critical information for planning your trip, such as tour operators and travel packages, and tips on Peruvian accommodations, dining, and shopping.

For additional help in planning your trip and for more on-the-ground resources in Peru, please turn to "Fast Facts," on p. 445.

1 WHEN TO GO

PEAK SEASON

Peak travel season for foreigners is in great part determined by weather. Peru experiences two very distinct seasons, wet and dry—terms that are much more relevant than "summer" and "winter." Peru's high season for travel coincides with the driest months: May through October, with by far the greatest number of visitors in July and August. May and September are particularly fine months to visit much of the country. Airlines and hotels also consider the period from mid-December through mid-January as peak season.

From June to September (winter in the Southern Hemisphere) in the highlands, days are clear and often spectacularly sunny, with chilly or downright cold nights, especially at high elevations. For trekking in the mountains, including the Inca Trail, these are by far the best months. This is also the best time of the year to visit the Amazon basin: Mosquitoes are fewer, and many fauna stay close to the rivers (although some people prefer to

travel in the jungle during the wet season, when higher water levels allow for more river penetration). Note that Peruvians travel in huge numbers around July 28, the national holiday, and finding accommodations in popular destinations around this time can be difficult.

CLIMATE

Generally, May through October is the dry season; November through April is the rainy season, and the wettest months are January through April. In mountain areas, roads and trek paths can become impassable. Peru's climate, though, is markedly different among its three regions. The coast is predominantly arid and mild, the Andean region is temperate to cold, and the eastern lowlands are tropically warm and humid.

On the desert **coast,** summer (Dec–Apr) is hot and dry, with temperatures reaching 77°F to 95°F (25°C–35°C) or more along the north coast. In winter (May–Oct), temperatures are much milder, though with high humidity. Much

Lima's Average Temperatures & Precipitation

	Jan	Feb	Mar	Apr	May	June	July	Aug	Sept	Oct	Nov	Dec
Avg. High (°F)	77	79	79	75	70	66	63	63	63	66	68	73
Avg. High (°C)	25	26	26	24	21	19	17	17	17	19	20	23
Avg. Low (°F)	66	68	66	65	61	59	57	56	56	57	61	63
Avg. Low (°C)	19	20	19	18	16	15	14	13	13	14	16	17
Wet Days	1	0	0	0	1	1	1	2	1	0	0	0

Cusco's Average Temperatures & Precipitation

	Jan	Feb	Mar	Apr	May	June	July	Aug	Sept	Oct	Nov	Dec
Avg. High (°F)	66	66	67	68	68	67	67	68	68	70	69	68
Avg. High (°C)	19	19	19	20	20	19	19	20	20	21	21	20
Avg. Low (°F)	44	44	44	41	37	34	34	34	39	42	43	43
Avg. Low (°C)	7	7	7	5	3	1	1	1	4	6	6	6
Wet Days	12	11	10	6	4	3	4	3	2	2	1	5

of the coast, including Lima, is shrouded in a gray mist called *garúa*. Only extreme northern beaches are warm enough for swimming.

In the **highlands** from May to October, rain is scarce. Daytime temperatures reach a warm 68°F to 77°F (20°C–25°C), and nights are often quite cold (near freezing), especially in June and July. Rainfall is very abundant from December to March, when temperatures are slightly milder—64°F to 68°F (18°C–20°C) dropping only to 59°F (15°C) at night. The wettest months are January and February. Most mornings are dry, but clouds move in during the afternoon and produce heavy downpours.

Although the Amazon **jungle** is consistently humid and tropical, with significant rainfall year-round, it, too, experiences two clearly different seasons. During the dry season (May–Oct), temperatures reach 86°F to 100°F (30°C–38°C) during the day. From November to April, there are frequent rain showers (which last only a few hours at a time), causing the rivers to swell; temperatures are similarly steamy.

PUBLIC HOLIDAYS

National public holidays in Peru include New Year's Day (Jan 1), Three Kings Day (Jan 6), Maundy Thursday and Good Friday (Easter week, Mar or Apr), Labor Day (May 1), Fiestas Patrias (July 28–29), Battle of Angamos (Oct 8), All Saints' Day (Nov 1), Feast of the Immaculate Conception (Dec 8), and Christmas (Dec 24–25).

For additional information about regional festivals, see individual destination chapters. Also check http://events. frommers.com, where you'll find a searchable, up-to-the-minute roster of what's happening in cities all over the world.

PERU CALENDAR OF EVENTS

JANUARY

Entrega de Varas, Cusco. Community elders *(yayas)* designate the highest authorities of their villages in this pre-Columbian festival, which is celebrated with *chicha* (fermented maize beer) and *llonque* (sugar-cane alcohol); elders give the mayor the *vara* (a staff, or scepter) as a symbol of his position of authority. January 1.

Fiesta de la Santa Tierra, Lake Titicaca. The main festival on Isla Amantaní sees the population split in two—half at the Temple of Pachamama and the other half at the Temple of Pachatata, symbolizing the islanders' ancient dualistic belief system. Third Thursday in January.

Marinera Dance Festival, Trujillo. One of the stateliest dances in Peru, the flirtatious marinera involves a couple, each partner with a handkerchief in his or her right hand. The man wears a wide-brimmed hat and poncho, and the woman wears a lace Moche dress. For 10 days, the festival, which draws couples from all over the country, is held in the Gran Chimú soccer stadium. There are also float processions throughout the city and dancing in the Plaza de Armas. January 20 to January 30.

FEBRUARY

Virgen de la Candelaria (Candlemas), Puno. Puno lives up to its billing as Folk Capital of the Americas with this festival, which gathers more than 200 musicians and dance troupes. On the festival's main day, February 2, the Virgen is led through the city in a colorful procession of priests and pagans carefully maintaining the hierarchy. Especially thrilling is the dance of the demons, or *la diablada.* Dancers in wild costumes and masks blow panpipes and make offerings to the earth goddess Pachamama. February 1 to February 14.

Carnaval. Lively pre-Lenten festivities. (Look out for balloons filled with water—or worse.) Cajamarca is reputed to have the best and wildest parties; Puno and Cusco are also good. The weekend before Ash Wednesday.

MARCH

Festival Internacional de la Vendimia (Wine Festival), Ica. A celebration of the grape harvest and the region's wine and pisco brandy, with fairs, beauty contests, floats, and musical festivals, including Afro-Peruvian dance. Second week of March.

Las Cruces de Porcón, Porcón. Near Cajamarca, a dawn procession of massive decorated wooden crosses through the valley of Porcón re-creates the entry of Christ into Jerusalem. The main day of the festival, Palm Sunday, presents four separate ceremonies. Ultimately, the crosses are decorated with mirrors (symbolizing the souls of the dead), and locals hang metal bells to announce the arrival of the crosses to the community. Mid-March to first week of April.

Semana Santa. Handsome and spectacularly reverent processions mark Easter Week. The finest are in Cusco and Ayacucho. Late March/early April.

Lord of the Earthquakes, Cusco. Representing a 17th-century painting of Christ on the cross that is said to have saved the city from a devastating earthquake, the image of the Lord of Earthquakes *(El Señor de los Temblores)* is carried through the streets of Cusco in a reverential procession, much like the Incas once paraded the mummies of their chieftains and high priests. Easter Monday, late March or early April.

APRIL

Peruvian Paso Horse Festival, Pachacámac. The Peruvian Paso horse, one of the world's most beautiful breeds, is celebrated with the most important annual national competition at the Mamacona stables near Pachacámac, 30km (19 miles) south of Lima. April 15 to April 20.

MAY

Fiesta de la Cruz. The Festival of the Cross features folk music and dance, including "scissors dancers," and processions in which communities decorate crosses and prepare them for the procession to neighboring churches. The *danzantes de tijeras* (scissors dancers) rc-create old times, when they performed on top of church bell towers. Today the objective is still to outdo one another with daring feats. Celebrations are especially lively in Lima, Cusco, and Ica. May 2 and 3.

Qoyllur Rit'i, Quispicanchis, near Cusco. A massive indigenous pilgrimage marks this ritual, which is tied to the fertility of the land and the worship of Apus, the spirits of the mountains. It forms part of the greatest festival of native Indian nations in the hemisphere: Qoyllur Rit'i. The main ceremony is held at the foot of Mount Ausangate, with 10,000 pilgrims climbing to the snowline along with dancers in full costume representing mythical characters. Others head to the summit, in search of the Snow Star, and take huge blocks of ice back down on their backs—holy water for irrigation purposes. First week in May.

Fiesta de Mayo, Huaraz. Also known as *El Señor de la Soledad,* this festival is celebrated with traditional dances, ski races, and a lantern procession. May 2 to May 10.

JUNE

Corpus Christi, Cusco. A procession of saints and virgins arrives at the Catedral to "greet" the body of Christ. Members of nearby churches also take their patron saints in a procession. An overnight vigil is followed by a new procession around the Plaza de Armas, with images of five virgins clad in embroidered tunics and the images of four saints: Sebastian, Blas, Joseph, and the Apostle Santiago (St. James). Early June.

Virgen del Carmen, Paucartambo. In a remote highland village 4 hours from Cusco, thousands come to honor the Virgen del Carmen, or Mamacha Carmen, patron saint of the *mestizo*

population, with 4 days of splendidly festive music and dance, as well as some of the wildest costumes in Peru. Dancers even perform daring moves on rooftops. The festival ends in the cemetery in a show of respect for the souls of the dead. Pisac also celebrates the Virgen del Carmen festival, almost as colorfully. June 15 to June 18.

Semana del Andinismo, Huaraz and Callejón de Huaylas. For outdoors fanatics, this celebration of outdoor adventure includes opportunities to partake in trekking, skiing, mountain biking, rafting, rock climbing, and hang gliding—and plenty of parties to accompany them. Mid- to late June.

Inti Raymi, Cusco. The Inca Festival of the Sun—the mother of all pre-Columbian festivals—celebrates the winter solstice and honors the sun god with traditional pageantry, parades, and dances. One of the most vibrant and exciting of all Andean festivals, it draws thousands of visitors who fill Cusco's hotels. The principal event takes place at the Sacsayhuamán ruins and includes the sacrifice of a pair of llamas. General celebrations last several days. June 24.

San Juan, Cusco and Iquitos. The feast day of St. John the Baptist, a symbol of fertility and sensuality, is the most important date on the festival calendar in the entire Peruvian jungle. John the Baptist has taken on a major symbolic significance because of the importance of water as a vital element in the entire Amazon region. Events include fiestas with lots of music and regional cuisine. In Iquitos, don't miss the aphrodisiac potions with suggestive names. June 24 in Cusco; June 25 in Iquitos.

San Pedro/San Pablo, near fishing villages in Lima and Chiclayo. The patron saints of fishermen and farmers, Saint Peter and Saint Paul, are honored at this festival; figures of the saints are carried with incense, prayers, and hymns down to the sea and are taken by launch around the bay to bless the waters. June 29.

JULY

Fiesta de Santiago, Isla Taquile. This celebration of St. James is a festive and very traditional pageant of color, with exuberant dances and women in layered, multicolored skirts. July 25 and August 1 and 2.

Fiestas Patrias. A series of patriotic parties mark Peru's independence from Spain in 1821. Official parades and functions are augmented by cockfighting, bullfighting, and Peruvian Paso horse exhibitions in other towns. The best celebrations are in Cusco, Puno, Isla Taquile, and Lima. July 28 and 29.

AUGUST

Santa Rosa de Lima, Lima. Major devotional processions honor the patron saint of Lima. August 30.

SEPTEMBER

International Spring Festival, Trujillo. Trujillo celebrates the festival of spring with marinera dance, decorated streets and houses, floats, and schoolchildren dancing in the streets—led, of course, by the pageant beauty queen. Last week in September.

OCTOBER

El Señor de los Milagros, Lima. The Lord of Miracles is the largest procession in South America, and it dates from colonial times. Lasting nearly 24

hours and involving tens of thousands of purple-clad participants, it celebrates a Christ image (painted by an Angolan slave) that survived the 1746 earthquake and has since become the most venerated image in the capital. October 18.

NOVEMBER

Todos Santos and **Día de los Muertos.** Peruvians salute the dead by visiting cemeteries carrying flowers and food. Families hold candlelight vigils in the cemetery until dawn. The holiday is most vibrantly celebrated in the highlands. November 1 and 2.

Puno Week, Puno. A major procession from the shores of the lake to the town stadium celebrates Manco Cápac, who, according to legend, rose from the waters of Lake Titicaca to establish the Inca Empire. Dances and music take over Puno, with events often taking a turn for the inebriated. Spectacular "Day of the Dead" celebrations coincide with Puno Week. First week of November.

DECEMBER

Santuranticuy Fair, Cusco. One of the largest arts-and-crafts fairs in Peru—literally, "saints for sale"—is held in the Plaza de Armas. Artisans lay out blankets around the square, as in traditional Andean markets, and sell figurines and Nativity scenes as well as ceramics, carvings, pottery, and *retablos* (altars). Vendors sell hot rum punch called *ponche.* December 24.

2 ENTRY REQUIREMENTS

PASSPORTS

For information on obtaining a Visa, please visit "Fast Facts," on p. 445.

Citizens of the United States, Canada, Great Britain, South Africa, New Zealand, and Australia do not require visas to enter Peru as tourists—only valid passports. Citizens of any of these countries conducting business or enrolled in formal educational programs in Peru do require visas;

contact the embassy or consulate in your home country for more information. For information on children's passports and travel, see "Specialized Travel Resources: Family Travelers," later in this chapter, and the "Fast Facts: Peru" section in chapter 13.

Tourist (or landing) cards, distributed on arriving international flights or at border crossings, are good for stays of up to 90 days. Keep a copy of the tourist card for presentation upon departure from Peru. (If you lose it, you'll have to pay a $4 fine.) A maximum of three extensions, at 30 days each for a total of 180 days, is allowed.

No immunizations are required for entry, although if you plan to travel to jungle regions, read "Medical Requirements," below.

IN THE US The **Embassy of Peru** is located at 1700 Massachusetts Ave. NW, Washington, DC 20036 (© **202/833-9860;** www.peruvianembassy.us). There are Peruvian consulates in Atlanta, Boston, Chicago, Dallas, Denver, Hartford, Houston, Los Angeles, Miami, New York, Paterson (N.J.), and San Francisco (and honorary consulates in several other cities). For their contact information, visit the **Peruvian Ministry of Foreign Relations** website (Ministerio de Relaciones Exteriores del Perú) at www.rree.gob.pe.

IN CANADA The **Embassy of Peru** is at 130 Albert St., Ste. 1901, Ottawa, Ontario K1P 5G4 (© **613/238 1777;** www.embassyofperu.ca). Peruvian consulates are in Montreal (© **514/844-5123**), Toronto (© **416/963-9696**), and Vancouver (© **604/662-8880**).

IN THE UK The **Peruvian Embassy** is located at 52 Sloane St., London SW1X 9SP (© **020/7235-1917;** www.peru-embassy.co.uk).

IN AUSTRALIA The **Embassy of Peru** in Canberra is located at 40 Brisbane Ave., Level 2, Barton ACT 2600 (© **02/6273-7351;** www.embaperu.org.au). The

Peruvian consulate has an office in Sydney at 30 Clarence St., 3rd Floor, NSW 2000 (© **02/9262-6464**).

IN NEW ZEALAND The **Embassy of Peru** is located at Level 8, Cigna House, 40 Mercer St., Wellington (© 04/499-8087; www.embassyofperu.org.nz).

CUSTOMS
What You Can Take Home from Peru

For information on what you're allowed to bring home, contact one of the following agencies:

U.S. Citizens: U.S. Customs & Border Protection (CBP), 1300 Pennsylvania Ave., NW, Washington, DC 20229 (© **877/287-8667;** www.cbp.gov).

Canadian Citizens: Canada Border Services Agency (© **800/461-9999** in Canada, or 204/983-3500; www.cbsa-asfc.gc.ca).

U.K. Citizens: HM Revenue & Customs at © 0845/010-9000 (from outside the U.K., 020/8929-0152), or consult their website at **www.hmce.gov.uk.**

Australian Citizens: Australian Customs and Border Protection Service at © **1300/363-263,** or log on to **www.customs.gov.au.**

New Zealand Citizens: New Zealand Customs Service, The Customhouse, 17–21 Whitmore St., Box 2218, Wellington (© **04/473-6099** or 0800/428-786; www.customs.govt.nz).

Exports of protected plant and endangered animal species—live or dead—are strictly prohibited by Peruvian law and should not be purchased. This includes headpieces and necklaces made with macaw feathers, and even common "rain sticks," unless authorized by the Natural Resources Institute (INRENA). Vendors in jungle cities and airports sell live animals and birds, as well as handicrafts made from insects, feathers, or other natural products. Travelers have been detained and arrested by the Ecology Police for carrying such items.

It is also illegal to take pre-Columbian archaeological items and antiques, including ceramics and textiles, and colonial-era art out of Peru. Reproductions of many such items are available, but even their export could cause difficulties at Customs or with overly cautious international courier services if you attempt to send them home. To be safe, look for the word "reproduction" or an artist's name stamped on reproduction ceramics, and keep business cards and receipts from shops where you have purchased them. Particularly fine items might require documentation from Peru's National Institute of Culture (INC) verifying that the object is a reproduction and may be exported. You might be able to obtain a certificate of authorization from the INC kiosk at Lima's Jorge Chávez International Airport or the **INC** office at the National Museum Building, Av. Javier Prado Este 2465, 6th Floor, San Borja (② 01/476-9900).

MEDICAL REQUIREMENTS

No vaccinations are officially required of travelers to Peru, but you are wise to take certain precautions, especially if you are planning to travel to jungle regions. See "Staying Healthy," (p. 56) for additional information.

3 GETTING THERE & GETTING AROUND

GETTING TO PERU
By Plane
All overseas flights from North America and Europe arrive at Lima's **Jorge Chávez International Airport** (② **01/517-3502;** www.lap.com.pe; airport code LIM). Major international airlines from North and South America, Europe and Asia all fly to Lima. For more information on which airlines travel to Peru, please see "Airline, Hotel & Car Rental Websites," p. 450.

In Peru, it's very important to reconfirm airline tickets in advance. For local flights, reconfirm 48 hours in advance; for international flights, reconfirm 72 hours before traveling (and be sure to arrive at the airport a minimum of 2 hr. in advance). The airport tax on domestic flights is $6, and $31 on international flights. The tax must be paid—in cash only (either in U.S. or Peruvian Nuevos Soles)—before boarding.

By Bus
You can travel overland to Peru through Ecuador, Bolivia, or Chile. Although the journey isn't short, Lima can be reached from major neighboring cities. If traveling from Quito or Guayaquil, you'll pass through the major northern coastal cities on the way to Lima. From Bolivia, there is frequent service from La Paz and Copacabana to Puno and then on to Cusco. From Chile, most buses travel from Arica to Tacna, making connections to either Arequipa or Lima.

The most common overland trip to Peru from a neighboring country is from La Paz, Bolivia, to Puno, on the banks of Lake Titicaca (which is partly in Peru and partly in Bolivia). The trip is about a 5-hour direct ride. **Ormeño** (② **01/472-5000;** www.grupo-ormeno.com.pe) travels to La Paz as well as Venezuela, Colombia, Ecuador, Chile, and Argentina.

GETTING AROUND
Because of its size and natural barriers, including difficult mountain terrain, long stretches of desert coast, and extensive rainforest, Peru is complicated to navigate. Train service is very limited, covering only a few principal tourist routes, and many trips take several days by land. Visitors

with limited time tend to fly everywhere they can. Travel overland, though very inexpensive, can be extremely time-consuming and uncomfortable. However, for certain routes, inter-city buses are your only real option.

By Plane

Flying to major destinations within Peru is the only practical way around the country if you want to see several places in a couple weeks or less. Peru is a deceptively large country, and natural barriers make getting around rather difficult. Most major Peruvian cities can be reached by air, although not always directly. Some places in the jungle, such as Iquitos, can be reached only by airplane (or a very long and arduous boat ride). Flying to major destinations, such as Lima, Cusco, Arequipa, Puerto Maldonado, and Iquitos, is simple and relatively inexpensive. One-way flights to most destinations are between $89 and $219. Prices fluctuate according to the season. Puno (and Lake Titicaca), however, require passengers to fly first to Juliaca before continuing by land the rest of the way (45km/28 miles)—a reality that prompts many to take a direct train or bus from Cusco to Puno.

Peru's carriers, some of which are small airlines with limited flight schedules, include **LAN** (© **866/435-9526** or 305/670-9999 in the U.S., **01/213-8200** in Lima; www.lan.com), **LC Busre** (© **01/619-1313;** www.lcbusre.com.pe), **Star Perú** (© **01/705-9000;** www.star peru.com); **TACA Airlines** (© **800/400-TACA** [8222] in the U.S., or 01/511-8222 in Lima; www.taca.com); and the new carrier, **Peruvian Airlines** (© **01/716-6000;** www.peruvianairlines.pe).

All airlines fly in and out of Lima. LAN is the only domestic airline that flies to most major destinations. LC Busre flies to Cajamarca, Huaraz, and Ayacucho, while Star Perú goes to Trujillo, Chiclayo, Iquitos, and Cusco; Taca flies to Arequipa and Cusco.

Connections through Lima are often necessary, although many destinations are accessible directly from Arequipa and Cusco, and some routes might be limited to only several days a week. Both flight schedules and fares are apt to change frequently and without notice. One-way fares are generally half the round-trip fare. Flights should be booked several days in advance, especially in high season, and you should also make sure that you get to the airport at least 45 minutes in advance to avoid being bumped from a flight.

LAN has a somewhat complicated and inconvenient air pass program for those who fly to Peru on its airline; passengers may purchase a minimum of three flight coupons (purchase must be made prior to landing in Peru). Depending on your flight schedule, however, this program may not save you much money over purchasing flights once in Peru.

By Train

The four tourist or passenger train routes operated by **PeruRail** (a private company owned by Orient-Express) are all very popular and scenic journeys. Because luggage theft has long been a problem on Peruvian trains, you should (if possible) purchase a premium-class ticket that limits access to ticketed passengers.

By far the most popular train routes in Peru connect Cusco, the Sacred Valley, and Machu Picchu. The train to Machu Picchu from Cusco is a truly spectacular journey. Two new tourist train companies, **Inca Rail** and **Andean Railways,** now travel from the Sacred Valley (Ollantaytambo) to Machu Picchu. For prices and schedules of these and all Cusco and Sacred Valley trains, see chapter 8.

The PeruRail **Titicaca Route** journey from Cusco to Puno is one of the most scenic and popular in Peru, although it is rather slow and pricey. Trains stop in Juliaca en route.

There are no PeruRail train passes. For additional information, contact **PeruRail**

Combi or Carro? Getting Around in and out of Town

Getting around Peru demands a mastery of terms that designate varied modes of transportation and a bewildering array of vehicles that aren't always easy to distinguish.

Within cities, travelers have several options. The most convenient and expensive are **taxis,** which function, for the most part, like taxis elsewhere in the world. However, taxis in Peru are wholly unregulated; in addition to registered, licensed taxis, you'll find "taxi" drivers who are merely folks with access to a two-bit car—usually rented for the purpose—and a taxi sticker to plunk inside the windshield. In Lima, this is overwhelmingly the case, and unregistered taxi drivers can be difficult to negotiate with for a fair price. There are no meters, meaning that you have to negotiate a price before (not after) accepting a ride. In other cities, such as Cusco, taxis conform to standard pricing (S/3–S/4 within town), so taking cabs outside of Lima is a considerably less daunting proposition for most travelers.

Combis are vans that function as private bus services. They often race from one end of town to another, with fare collectors hanging out the door barking the name of the route. Combis also cover routes between towns. *Colectivos* are essentially indistinguishable from combis—they are vans that cover regular routes (such as between Cusco and Pisac), and they usually depart when they're full. Routes are often so popular, though, that colectivos leave regularly, as often as every 15 minutes, throughout the day. For inter-city transport, there is a similar slate of options. *Micros* are small buses, often old and quite colorful, that travel between cities. Both colectivos and micros are quite crowded, have a reputation for pickpockets, and can be hailed at any place along the street without regard for bus stops. You pay a *cobrador* (money collector), who usually hangs out at the door barking destinations at would-be travelers, rather than the driver.

Autobuses (also called *buses* or *omnibuses*) are large coaches for long-distance travel on scheduled inter-city routes. Classes of buses are distinguished by price and comfort: *Económico* is a bare-bones bus with little more than a driver and an assigned seat; classes designated *especial* (or sometimes "Inka") have reclining seats, videos, refreshments, and bathrooms.

As if that complex web of terms wasn't enough to get a handle on, there's an additional warning to heed: It's not uncommon to hear locals refer—loosely and confusingly—to buses as *carros* (which normally just means "car") and to colectivos as *taxis.*

(© 01/612-6700 in Lima, 084/581-414 in Cusco); **Inca Rail** (© **084/233-030;** www.incarail.com); or **Machu Picchu Train** (© **084/221-199;** www.machu picchutrain.com).

The **Ferrocarril Central Andino S.A.,** the spectacular high-altitude journey from Lima to Huancayo in the Central Highlands—the world's highest passenger line—is again in service for passenger travel after being shut down until a few years ago, though its notoriously problematic history makes it very difficult to plan a trip around riding the train. As of this writing, it runs once a month between July and November. For additional information, see chapter 7, and check for updates before you arrive in Peru (✆ 01/226-6363; www.ferrocarrilcentral.com.pe).

By Bus

Buses are the cheapest and most popular form of transportation in Peru—for many Peruvians, they are the only means of getting around—and they have by far the greatest reach. A complex network of private bus companies crisscrosses Peru, with many competing lines covering the most popular routes. Many companies operate their own bus stations, and their locations, dispersed across many cities, can be endlessly frustrating to travelers. Luggage theft is an issue on many buses; passengers should keep a watchful eye on carry-on items and pay close attention when bags are unloaded. Only a few long-distance companies have luxury buses comparable in comforts to European models (bathrooms, reclining seats, and movies). These premium-class ("Royal" or "Imperial" class) buses cost up to twice as much as regular-service buses, although for many travelers, the additional comfort and services are worth the difference in cost (which remains inexpensive).

For many short distances (such as Cusco to Pisac), colectivos (smaller buses without assigned seats) are the fastest and cheapest option.

Ormeño (✆ 01/472-5000; www. grupo-ormeno.com.pe), **Cruz del Sur** (✆ 01/311-5050; www.cruzdelsur.com. pe), **Oltursa** (01/708-5000; www.oltursa. com.pe), and **Civa** (✆ 01/418-1111; www.civa.com.pe) are among the bus companies with the best reputations for long-distance treks. Given the extremely confusing nature of bus companies, terminals, and destinations—which makes it

impossible to even begin to list every possible option here—it is best to approach a local tourism information office or travel agency (most of which sell long-distance bus tickets) with a destination in mind and let the office direct you to the terminal for the best service (and, if possible, book the ticket for you).

By Car

Getting around Peru by means of a rental car isn't the easiest or best option for the great majority of travelers. It is also far from the cheapest. Distances are long, the terrain is either difficult or unrelentingly boring for long stretches along the desert coast, roads are often not in very good condition, Peruvian drivers are aggressive, and accident rates are very high. The U.S. State Department warns against driving in Peru, particularly at night or alone on rural roads at any time of day. A four-wheel-drive vehicle is the best option in many places, but trucks and jeeps are exceedingly expensive for most travelers.

However, if you want maximum flexibility and independence for travels in a particular region (say, to get around the Sacred Valley outside of Cusco, or to visit Colca Canyon beyond Arequipa) and you have several people to share the cost with you, a rental car could be a decent option. By no means should you plan to rent a car in Lima and head off for the major sights across the country; you'll spend all your time in the car. It is much more feasible to fly or take a bus to a given destination and rent a car there. The major international rental agencies are found in Lima, and a handful of international and local companies operate in other cities, such as Cusco and Arequipa. Costs average between $40 and $70 per day, plus 18% insurance, for an economy-size vehicle.

To rent a car, you need to be at least 25 years old and have a valid driver's license and passport. Deposit by credit card is usually required. Driving under the influence of alcohol or drugs is a criminal offense.

Major rental companies in Peru include **Avis** (✆ 01/575-0912, ext. 4155; www. avis.com); **Budget** (✆ 01/575-1674; www.budget.com); **Dollar** (✆ 01/444-3050; www.dollar.com); **Hertz** (✆ 01/575-1390; www.hertz.com); **InterService Rent a Car** (✆ 01/442-2256); **National Car Rental** (✆ 01/433-3750; www. nationalcar.com); and **Paz Rent a Car** (✆ 01/436-3941).

For mechanical assistance, contact the **Touring Automóvil Club del Perú (Touring Club of Peru)** in Lima at ✆ **01/221-3225** (www.touringperu.com. pe), or in Cusco at ✆ **084/224-561.**

4 MONEY & COSTS

The Value of the Peruvian Nuevos Sol (S/) vs. Other Popular Currencies

S/	US$	Can$	UK£	Euro (€)	Aus$	NZ$
S/1	$0.35	C$0.36	£0.22	€0.26	A$0.39	NZ$0.50

At press time, US$1 equals S/2.8. Frommer's lists exact prices in the local currency. The currency conversions quoted above were correct at press time. However, rates fluctuate, so before departing consult a currency exchange website such as **www. oanda.com/convert/classic** to check up-to-the-minute rates.

On the whole, though prices have risen in the past couple of years and it is slightly more expensive than its Andean neighbors, Ecuador and Bolivia, Peru remains inexpensive by North American and European standards. To those with strong currencies—European and British citizens—Peru is likely to seem comparatively cheap. Peruvians tend to haggle over prices and accept and even expect that others will (politely) haggle, except of course in major stores and restaurants. In the bigger cities, prices for virtually everything—but especially hotels and restaurants—are higher, particularly in Lima. In addition, prices can rise in the high season, such as the Independence Day holidays (late July), Easter week (Mar or Apr), or Christmas, due to heavy demand, especially for hotel rooms and bus and plane tickets.

CURRENCY

Peru's official currency is the **nuevos sol (S/),** divided into 100 *centavos.* Coins are issued in denominations of 5, 10, 20, and 50 centavos, and bank notes in denominations of 10, 20, 50, 100, and 200 soles. At press time, the rate of exchange had dipped to just under 3 soles to the U.S. dollar (from a high of about 3.5). The U.S. dollar is the second currency; many hotels post their rates in dollars, and plenty of shops, taxi drivers, restaurants, and hotels across Peru accept U.S. dollars for payment. *Note:* Because many Peruvian hotels, tour operators, and transportation vendors charge prices solely in dollars, U.S. dollar rates are often listed in this book.

EXCHANGING MONEY

You'll avoid lines at airport ATMs by exchanging at least some money—just enough to cover airport incidentals and transportation to your hotel—before you leave home (though don't expect the exchange rate to be ideal). You can exchange money at your local American Express or Thomas Cook office or at your bank.

What Things Cost in Peru	S/.
Short taxi ride	S/3–S/6
Double room at an inexpensive hotel	S/30–S/50
Double room at a moderate hotel	S/50–S/120
Double room at an expensive hotel	S/120–S/200
Cup of coffee or bottle of water	S/3
Movie	S/10
Lunch	S/15–S/50
Dinner	S/45–S/125

3

American Express also dispenses traveler's checks and foreign currency via **www.americanexpress.com** or © **800/807-6233,** but they'll charge a $15 order fee and shipping costs.

Peru is still very much a cash society. In villages and small towns, it could be impossible to cash traveler's checks or use credit cards. Make sure that you have cash (both soles and U.S. dollars) on hand. If you pay in dollars, you will likely receive change in soles, so be aware of the correct exchange rate. U.S. dollars are by far the easiest foreign currency to exchange. Currencies other than U.S. dollars receive very poor exchange rates.

Banks are no longer the place of choice in Peru for exchanging money: Lines are too long, the task is too time-consuming, and rates are often lower at *casas de cambio* (exchange houses) or by using credit or debit card ATMs or money-changers, which are legal in Peru. If you can't avoid banks, all cities and towns have branches of major international and local banks; see "Fast Facts" in individual destination chapters for locations. Money-changers, often wearing colored smocks with "$" insignias, can be found on the street. They offer current rates of exchange, but count your money carefully (you can simplify this by exchanging easily calculable amounts, such as $10 or $100), and make sure you have not received any counterfeit bills.

Counterfeit bank notes and even coins are common, and merchants and consumers across Peru vigorously check the authenticity of money before accepting payment or change. (The simplest way: Hold the bank note up to the light to see the watermark.) Many people also refuse to accept bank notes that are not in good condition (including those with small tears, that have been written on, and even that are simply well worn), and visitors are wise to do the same when receiving change, to avoid problems with other payments. Do not accept bills with tears (no matter how small) or taped bills.

Making change in Peru is often a problem. You should carry small bills and even then be prepared to wait for change. At one bar in Iquitos, I once paid with a S/20 note (less than $7) and the waiter said, "Hold on, I'm going to get change"—and he hopped on a bicycle and took off, not reappearing with correct change for nearly a half-hour.

Automated teller machines (ATMs) are the best way of getting cash in Peru; they're found in most towns and cities, although not on every street corner. ATMs allow customers to withdraw money in either Peruvian soles or U.S. dollars. Screen instructions are in English as well as Spanish. Some bank ATMs dispense money only to those who hold accounts there. Most ATMs in Peru accept only one type of credit/debit card and international money network, either **Cirrus** (℃ **800/424-7787;** www.mastercard. com) or **PLUS** (℃ **800/843-7587;** www. visa.com). Visa and MasterCard ATM cards are the most widely accepted; Visa/PLUS is the most common.

Be sure you know your personal identification number (PIN) and daily withdrawal limit before you depart. At some ATMs, your personal identification number (PIN) must contain four digits. *Note:* Remember that many banks impose a fee every time you use a card at another bank's ATM, and that fee can be higher for international transactions (up to $5 or more) than for domestic ones (where they're rarely more than $2). In addition, the bank from which you withdraw cash may charge its own fee. For international withdrawal fees, ask your bank.

Also, note that many credit and debit cards now assess a 1% to 3% "transaction fee" on **all** charges you incur abroad (whether you're using the local currency or your native currency).

5 HEALTH

STAYING HEALTHY

Contact the **International Association for Medical Assistance to Travelers** (IAMAT; ℃ **716/754-4883,** or 416/652-0137 in Canada; www.iamat.org) for tips on travel and health concerns, and for lists of local, English-speaking doctors. The United States **Centers for Disease Control and Prevention** (℃ **800/311-3435;** www.cdc.gov) provides up-to-date information on health hazards by region or country and offers tips on food safety. Travel Health Online (www.tripprep. com), a consortium of travel medicine practitioners, may also offer helpful advice on traveling abroad. You can find listings of reliable clinics overseas at the **International Society of Travel Medicine** (www. istm.org).

No vaccinations are officially required of travelers to Peru, but you are wise to take certain precautions, especially if you are planning to travel to jungle regions.

A yellow-fever vaccine is strongly recommended for trips to the Amazon. Peruvian authorities confirmed an outbreak of yellow fever in the northeastern Department of Amazonas in December 2005. The Pan American Health Organization reported an outbreak and 52 total cases of yellow fever in Peru during the first 6 months of 2004, with slightly more than half of those resulting in death. (However, just two of those occurred in areas covered in this book, Loreto and Madre de Dios.)

The **Centers for Disease Control and Prevention** (℃ **800/311-3435;** www.cdc. gov) warns that there is a risk of malaria and yellow fever in all areas except Arequipa, Moquegua, Puno, and Tacna; Lima and the highland tourist areas (Cusco, Machu Picchu, and Lake Titicaca) are also not at risk.

The Centers for Disease Control and Prevention also recommend taking antimalarial drugs at least 1 week before arriving in the jungle, during your stay there, and for at least 4 weeks afterward.

In addition, the CDC recommends vaccines for hepatitis A and B and typhoid, as well as booster doses for tetanus, diphtheria, and measles, although you might want to weigh your potential exposure before getting all these shots.

For additional information on travel to tropical South America, including World Health Organization news of disease outbreaks in particular areas, see the CDC website at www.cdc.gov/travel/tropsam. htm. Also of interest is the World Health Organization's informational page on Peru, www.who.int/countries/per/en.

Remember to carry your vaccination records with you if you are traveling to the jungle.

GENERAL AVAILABILITY OF HEALTH CARE

Prescriptions can be filled at *farmacias* and *boticas;* it's best to know the generic name of your drug. For most health matters that are not serious, a pharmacist will be able to help and prescribe something. In the case of more serious health issues, contact your hotel, the tourist information office, or, in the most extreme case, your consulate or embassy for a doctor referral. Hospitals with English-speaking doctors are listed in individual destination chapters.

It's wise to get all vaccinations and obtain malarial pills before arriving in Peru, but if you decide at the last minute to go to the jungle and need to get a vaccine in the country, you can go to the following **Oficinas de Vacunación** in Lima: Av. del Ejército 1756, San Isidro (© **01/264-6889**); Jorge Chávez International Airport, second floor; and the International Vaccination Center, Dos de Mayo National Hospital, Avenida Grau, Block 13. In the airport at Puerto Maldonado, in the southern jungle, public nurses are also frequently on hand to administer yellow-fever shots to travelers who have not received the vaccination.

COMMON AILMENTS

As a tropical South American country, Peru presents certain health risks and issues, but major concerns are limited to those traveling outside urban areas and to the Amazon jungle. The most common ailments for visitors to Peru are common traveler's diarrhea and altitude sickness, or **acute mountain sickness (AMS),** called *soroche* locally.

ALTITUDE SICKNESS Cusco sits at an elevation of about 3,400m (11,000 ft.), and Lake Titicaca sits at 3,830m (12,566 ft.). At these altitudes, shortness of breath and heart pounding are normal, given the paucity of oxygen. Some people experience intense headaches, loss of appetite, extreme fatigue, and nausea. Most symptoms develop the first day at high altitude, although occasionally travelers have delayed reactions. The best advice is to rest on your first day in the highlands. Drink plenty of liquids, including the local remedy *mate de coca,* or coca-leaf tea. (Coca, as opposed to cocaine, is a mild sedative, and it's perfectly legal to consume coca tea or chew coca leaves in Peru, though it's not legal to bring back coca leaves.) Avoid alcohol and heavy food intake. Give yourself at least a day or two to acclimatize before launching into strenuous activities. Many hotels in Cusco offer oxygen for those severely affected with headaches and shortness of breath. If symptoms persist or become more severe, seek medical attention. People with heart or lung problems and persons with the sickle cell trait could develop serious health complications at high altitudes, or even die from medical conditions exacerbated by high altitude.

SUN EXPOSURE Limit your exposure to the sun, especially during the first few days of your trip and at high altitudes, from 11am to 2pm. Even though it can be chilly or cold in the Andes, the sun is a killer (the higher the altitude and thinner the air, the more dangerous the sun's harmful rays are). Along Peru's desert coast, the sun is also extremely potent and likely to burn visitors who don't take adequate precautions. Wear a hat and use a sunscreen with a high protection factor (SPF 30 or higher), and apply it liberally. Remember that children require more protection than do adults. Heat exhaustion and heat stroke are serious maladies and are not difficult to get if you don't take proper precautions in Peru.

DIETARY DISTRESS Visitors should drink only bottled water, which is widely available. Do not drink tap water, even in major hotels, and try to avoid drinks with ice. If you're trekking in the mountains or visiting remote rural areas where bottled water is not available, boil water to purify it or use water-purification tablets. Carry bottled water with you at all times (especially on long bus or train rides); the heat of the desert and the high altitudes of the Andes will dehydrate you very quickly.

You're safer eating fruits that you can peel or salads and fruits washed with purified water, as well as foods that have been thoroughly cooked. Shellfish should be avoided by most; although ceviche is one of Peru's classic dishes, travelers should at least know that the fish and shellfish in it are not cooked, but marinated. That said, many, if not most, travelers eat it with few or no problems. (Your best bet is to eat ceviche only at clean, upscale places.) Vegetarian restaurants can be found in most cities (look for branches of the chain Govinda in the largest cities). If no vegetarian restaurant is available, most others will be able to accommodate you with salads, fruits, and vegetables such as *papas* (potatoes) and *palta* (avocado), although *palta rellena* is usually stuffed with chicken or tuna.

What To Do If You Get Sick Away From Home

Any foreign consulate can provide a list of area doctors who speak English. If you get sick, consider asking your hotel concierge to recommend a local doctor—even his or her own. You can also try the emergency room at a local hospital. Many hospitals also have walk-in clinics for emergency cases that are not life-threatening; you may not get immediate attention, but you won't pay the high price of an emergency room visit. We list additional **emergency numbers** in the "Fast Facts" section in chapter 13.

If you suffer from a chronic illness, consult your doctor before your departure. Pack **prescription medications** in your carry-on luggage, and carry prescription medications in their original containers, with pharmacy labels—otherwise they won't make it through airport security. Also carry copies of your prescriptions in case you lose your pills or run out. (Carry the generic name of prescription medicines, in case a local pharmacist is unfamiliar with the brand name.) Don't forget an extra pair of contact lenses or prescription glasses.

For travel abroad, you may have to pay all medical costs up front and be reimbursed later.

6 SAFETY

STAYING SAFE

Peru has not earned a great reputation for safety among some travelers, although the situation is no longer as dangerous as during the violent crime wave and terrorist threats of the late 1980s and early 1990s. Personal safety is an issue to be taken seriously in most large Peruvian cities, especially Lima, Cusco, Arequipa, and Huaraz. Simple theft and pickpocketing are fairly common; most thieves look for moments when travelers, laden with bags and struggling with maps, are distracted. Assaults and robbery are rare, but have been reported in many cities. In most heavily touristed places in Peru, a heightened police presence is noticeable, however.

Although most visitors travel freely throughout Peru without incident, warnings must be heeded seriously. In downtown Lima and the city's residential and hotel areas, the risk of street crime, including theft and muggings, remains high. Carjackings, assaults, and armed robberies are not unheard of in Lima. Occasional armed attacks at ATMs occur. Be especially vigilant at Lima's international airport, where a number of robberies and attacks have been reported. Street crime is prevalent in Cusco, Arequipa, and Puno, and pickpockets are known to patrol public markets. In Cusco, "strangle" muggings (in which victims are choked unconscious and then relieved of all belongings) were reported in recent years, particularly on the streets leading off the Plaza de Armas, in the San Blas neighborhood, and near the train station. You should still not walk alone late at night on deserted streets. There were at least three reports of rape in Cusco in the last 5 years, one by a gang. In rural areas outside Cusco, trekkers should travel in groups. But while hiking with others is essential, it doesn't guarantee one's safety; indeed, in recent years, a couple of groups of hikers along the Inca Trail were attacked and robbed.

In major cities, taxis hailed on the street can lead to assaults—I highly recommend using telephone-dispatched radio taxis, especially at night. Ask your hotel or restaurant to call a cab, or you can call one yourself from the list of recommended taxi companies in the individual city chapters.

Travelers should exercise extreme caution on public city transportation, where pickpockets are rife, and on long-distance buses and trains (especially at night), where thieves employ any number of strategies to relieve passengers of their bags. You need to be supremely vigilant, even to the extreme of locking your backpack and suitcases to luggage racks. Be extremely careful in all train and bus stations, too. Several provincial and inter-city buses and combis traveling from cities to villages have been attacked and passengers robbed.

In general, do not wear expensive jewelry, keep expensive camera equipment out of view as much as possible, and use a money belt inside your pants or shirt to safeguard your cash, credit cards, and passport. Wear your daypack on your chest rather than your back when walking in crowded areas. The time to be most careful is when you have most of your belongings

on your person—for example, when going from the airport or train or bus station to your hotel. At airports, it's best to spend a little more for official airport taxis; if in doubt, request the driver's official ID. Don't venture beyond airport grounds for a street taxi. Have your hotel call a taxi for your trip to the airport or bus station.

Report any criminal activity to the nearest police station or tourism police office; contact information is listed in the "Fast Facts" section in individual destination chapters.

In addition to safety and health concerns, travelers planning a trip to Peru should keep a close watch on current events. Although the large-scale terrorist activities of the local groups Sendero Luminoso and MRTA were largely stamped out in the early 1990s, the U.S. State Department reported a resurfacing of the long-dormant Maoist terrorist network Sendero Luminoso in remote parts of the central highlands in late 2001. In March 2002, a radical offshoot of the Sendero Luminoso was blamed for a car bomb attack that killed 10 near the U.S. embassy in Lima. Two more isolated attacks in 2003 were attributed to Sendero Luminoso. Neither group, however, is currently considered to be active in any of the areas covered in this book.

Since the election of Alan García in 2006, there has been considerably greater political stability, but in a country where half the population remains below the poverty line, worker strikes and a return to instability are never out of the question. At present, stability concerns should not deter anyone from traveling to the country, but it's always wise to check for travel advisories before you depart.

Women traveling alone in Peru, as in most Latin American countries, may attract unwanted attention and harassment from local men, who may be very insistent and persistent. Their advances can usually be warded off with a forceful

Staying Safe

Most travelers visit Peru without any problems. But as in any foreign destination, you should always keep your wits about you. Before you depart, check for travel advisories from the **U.S. State Department** (www.travel.state.gov), **Foreign Affairs and International Trade Canada** (www.voyage.gc.ca), the (www.fco.gov.uk/travel), and the **Australian Department of Foreign Affairs and Trade** (www.dfat.gov.au/consular/advice).

Once you're there, keep some common-sense safety advice in mind: Stay alert and be aware of your surroundings; don't walk down dark, deserted streets; and always keep an eye on your personal belongings. Theft at airports and bus stations is not unheard of, so be sure to put a lock on your luggage.

See "Fast Facts: Safety" in chapter 13 for information on country-specific safety concerns and numbers to call in case of an emergency.

"No!", simple *"Déjame en paz"* ("Leave me alone"), or claim that one is married and traveling with her husband *("Estoy casada. Ya viene mi marido.")*. Though one hopes the stereotype is dying out, some Peruvian men may still assume that foreign women are more sexually permissive than local women.

Gays and travelers of color may also be subjected to discrimination and very unwelcoming behavior, either on the street or occasionally at bars and nightclubs. See the sections below on "Specialized Travel Resources" for more information about attitudes toward minority groups in Peru.

For information about legal drinking and drug use, see p. 445. Anyone interested in obtaining cocaine locally or participating in *ayahuasca* (plant-based hallucinogens) ceremonies should be aware that there are frequently safety considerations involved, both in terms of personal health and potential robbery.

7 SPECIALIZED TRAVEL RESOURCES

GAY & LESBIAN TRAVELERS

Although the Inca nation flag looks remarkably similar to the gay rainbow flag, Peru, a predominantly Catholic and socially conservative country, could not be considered among the world's most progressive in terms of societal freedoms for gays and lesbians. It remains a male-dominated, macho society where homosexuality is considered deviant. Across Peru, there is still considerable prejudice exhibited toward gays and lesbians who are out, or men—be they straight or gay—who are thought to be effeminate. The word *maricón* is, sadly, a commonly used derogatory term for homosexuals.

In the larger cities, especially Lima and Cusco, there are a number of establishments—bars, discos, inns, and restaurants—that are either gay-friendly or predominantly gay. Outside those areas, and in the small towns and villages of rural Peru, openly gay behavior is unlikely to be tolerated by the general population.

There are a number of helpful websites for gay and lesbian travelers to Peru. **Gay Peru** (www.gayperu.com) includes gay-oriented package tours, news items, and nightclubs and hotels (with versions in both English and Spanish). **Purple Roofs** (www.purpleroofs.com/southamerica/peru.html) has a decent listing of gay and lesbian lodgings, restaurants, and nightclubs throughout Peru. **Gay Lima** (http://lima.queercity.info) covers Lima and other parts of Peru, with English-language information on nightclubs and gay-friendly establishments and activities. If you can read Spanish, **www.deambiente.com** also has detailed listings and articles about gay life in Peru. **GlobalGayz** (www.globalgayz.com) includes a very interesting article on gay life in Peru. Among other things, it details the former Fujimori government's dismissal of homosexual diplomats and other public servants. The site also covers gay news, with insiders' perspectives on being gay in Peru, and gay lodging listings.

For more gay and lesbian travel resources visit www.frommers.com.

TRAVELERS WITH DISABILITIES

Most disabilities shouldn't stop anyone from traveling. However, Peru is considerably less equipped for accessible travel than are most parts of North America and Europe. Comparatively few hotels are outfitted for travelers with disabilities, and only a few restaurants, museums, and means of public transportation make special accommodations for such patrons. There are few ramps, very few wheelchair-accessible bathrooms, and almost no telephones for the hearing-impaired.

Though it continues to lag behind Europe and North America, Peru has been a perhaps unlikely leader in South America in terms of seeking to make its tourist infrastructure more accessible to people with disabilities. In 1998, Peru initiated a countrywide project targeting tourism establishments to improve facilities, and in the last decade, Peru was the only country in South America to attend a Society for Accessible Travel & Hospitality conference.

Request a copy of "Tourism for the People with Disabilities: The First Evaluation of Accessibility to Peru's Tourist Infrastructure," available from the Peruvian embassy in your home country, before your visit to Peru. The 99-page report features evaluations of hotels, restaurants, museums, attractions, airports, and other services in Lima, Cusco, Aguas Calientes, Iquitos, and Trujillo.

A helpful website for accessible travel in Peru is **Access-Able Travel Source** (www.access-able.com), which offers detailed destination articles on accessible travel in Peru and a wealth of specific information about Aguas Calientes, Chiclayo, Cusco, Huanchaco, Iquitos, Lima, the Chicama and Moche valleys, Pisac, Trujillo, and Yucay. Within individual reviews, you'll find information on ramps, door sizes, room sizes, bathrooms, and wheelchair availability.

One Peruvian hotel chain, **Posadas del Inca** (www.sonesta.com), stands out in a country where few places are equipped for accessible travel. With properties in Lima, Cusco, Yucay, and Puno, it maintains rooms in every hotel that are accessible for travelers with disabilities. See individual destination chapters for full reviews.

Many travel agencies offer customized tours and itineraries for travelers with disabilities. **Apumayo Expediciones** (© 054/246-018; www.apumayo.com) is way out in front in Peru, offering tours specifically designed for travelers with physical disabilities. **Accessible Journeys** (© 800/846-4537 or 610/521-0339; www.disabilitytravel.com) caters specifically to slow walkers and wheelchair travelers and their families and friends; the organization offers a 10-day "Peru Explorer" trip to Lima, Paracas, Cusco, the Sacred Valley, and Machu Picchu. **Inka-Natura Travel** (www.inkanatura.com) is also particularly well equipped to deal with travelers with disabilities: Beyond the website's specifics on Peru, it is an excellent resource with all kinds of general information and answers to frequently asked questions about traveling with disabilities.

Organizations that offer assistance to travelers with disabilities include **MossRehab** (www.mossresourcenet.org), the **American Foundation for the Blind** (**AFB**; 🕾 **800/232-5463**; www.afb.org), and **SATH** (Society for Accessible Travel & Hospitality; 🕾 **212/447-7284**; www. sath.org). **AirAmbulanceCard.com** is now partnered with SATH and allows you to preselect top-notch hospitals in case of an emergency.

For more on organizations that offer resources to travelers with disabilities, go to www.frommers.com.

FAMILY TRAVELERS

Peruvians are extremely family-oriented, and children arouse friendly interest in locals. Although there aren't many established conventions, accommodations, or discounts for families traveling with children, Peru can be an excellent country in which to travel, as long as families remain flexible and are able to surmount difficulties in transportation, food, and accommodations.

Few hotels automatically offer discounts for children or allow children to stay free with their parents. Negotiation with hotels is required. On buses, children have to pay full fare if they occupy a seat (which is why you'll see most kids sitting on their parent's or sibling's lap). Many museums and other attractions offer discounts for children 5 and under. Children's meals are rarely found at restaurants in Peru, but sometimes it's possible to specially order smaller portions. Peruvian food might be very foreign to many children—how many kids, or adults, for that matter, will be keen on tasting roasted guinea pig?—but familiar foods, such as fried chicken, pizza, and spaghetti, are easy to find in almost all Peruvian towns.

Throughout this guide, look for the icons designating kid-friendly attractions, hotels, and restaurants.

For a list of family-friendly travel resources, turn to the experts at www. frommers.com.

WOMEN TRAVELERS

Peru continues to be a very macho, male-dominated society. Although women are a growing part of the professional workforce and a relatively recent feminist movement is evident in urban areas, women do not yet occupy the (still unequal) position they do in many Western societies. Still, women should not encounter any insurmountable difficulties traveling in Peru.

However, women should not be surprised to encounter perhaps unwelcome attention from men, especially if traveling alone. Many Peruvian men consider *gringas*—essentially, any foreign women—to be more sexually open than Peruvian women; thus, foreigners are frequently the targets of their advances. Blonde women are frequently singled out. *Piropos,* come-ons that are usually meant as innocuous compliments rather than as crude assessments of a woman's physical attractiveness or sexuality, are common in Latin America. However, comments can occasionally be crude and demeaning, and groping is not unheard of in public places (such as on crowded buses). Sexual assaults are rare, but the threat felt by some women, especially if they do not comprehend the Spanish slang employed in come-ons, is understandable.

Many men, as well as Peruvian women, might be curious about why a woman isn't married or traveling with a boyfriend. A woman traveling alone could elicit comments of sympathy or even pity. Wearing a ring on your wedding finger and deflecting comments and advances with a story about your husband working in Lima and meeting you in 2 days (or something to that effect) could be a useful tactic. In general, the problem is much more pronounced in large cities than in small towns and the countryside. Amerindian populations are conservative and even shy in dealing with foreigners, including women.

Women on the receiving end of catcalls and aggressive come-ons should do what Peruvian women do: Ignore them. If that doesn't succeed, contact the tourist police (offices are listed in the "Fast Facts" section of individual destination chapters). Although some Peruvian men might be innocently interested in meeting a foreign woman, it is not a good idea to accept an invitation to go anywhere alone with a man.

Women traveling in a group with other females, or especially with a man, are less likely to attract unwanted attention from men. Although I would hesitate to tell a woman friend that she should not travel alone in Peru, traveling with even one other woman might feel like a safer situation for many women, at least psychologically. If you are traveling alone, never walk alone at night anywhere—always call for a registered taxi. It's also a good idea to have a whistle handy; a piercing sound blast will deter almost any aggressor.

For general travel resources for women, go to www.frommers.com.

SENIOR TRAVEL

Peru as a nation greatly respects the contributions and wisdom of society's elders, but that consideration doesn't necessarily translate into automatic deferential treatment of senior tourists. Discounts for seniors are not automatic across Peru. Still, you should mention the fact that you're a senior when you first make your travel reservations; although almost all airlines have canceled their senior discount and coupon book programs, many hotels still offer lower rates for seniors.

Members of **AARP,** 601 E St. NW, Washington, DC 20049 (© **888/687-2277;** www.aarp.org), get discounts on hotels, airfares, and car rentals. AARP offers members a wide range of benefits, including *AARP*

The Magazine and a monthly newsletter. Anyone 50 and older can join.

Many reliable agencies and organizations target the 50-plus market. **Elderhostel** (© **877/426-8056;** www.elderhostel. org) arranges study programs for people 55 and older (and a spouse or companion of any age) in more than 80 countries, including Peru. Most courses last 2 to 4 weeks, and many include airfare, accommodations in university dormitories or modest inns, meals, and tuition. **Elder-Treks** (© **800/741-7956;** www.elder treks.com) offers small-group tours to off-the-beaten-path or adventure-travel locations, restricted to travelers 50 and older; it currently offers a 19-day trip to Peru and Bolivia.

Frommers.com offers more information and resources on travel for seniors.

STUDENT TRAVEL

If you're a student, you'd be wise to arm yourself with an **International Student Identity Card (ISIC),** which offers substantial savings on rail passes, plane tickets, and entrance fees throughout Peru (though the card may not be as immediately recognized in Peru as it is, say, in Europe). It also provides you with basic health and life insurance and a 24-hour help line. The card is available from **STA Travel** (© **800/781-4040** in North America; www.sta.com or www.statravel. com; or www.statravel.co.uk in the U.K.), the biggest student travel agency in the world. If you're no longer a student but are still under 26, you can get an **International Youth Travel Card (IYTC)** from the same group, which entitles you to some discounts (but not on museum admissions). **Travel CUTS** (© **800/667-2887** or 416/614-2887; www.travelcuts. com) offers similar services for both Canadians and U.S. residents. Irish students may prefer to turn to **USIT** (© **01/602-1600;** www.usitnow.ie), an Ireland-based specialist in student, youth, and independent travel.

Many reputable tour companies offer singles-only trips to Peru. Two to try are **Singles Travel International** (© 877/ 765-6874; www.singlestravelintl.com)

and **Backroads** (© 800/462-2848; www. backroads.com).

For more information on traveling single, go to www.frommers.com.

8 SUSTAINABLE TOURISM

Sustainable tourism means conscientious travel. It means being careful with the environments you explore, and it means respecting the communities you visit. Two overlapping components of sustainable travel are ecotourism and ethical tourism. Peru is an ecotourism paradise, and many of the companies organizing good, sustainable travel initiatives can be found in chapter 5, "The Active Vacation Planner."

The **International Ecotourism Society (TIES)** defines ecotourism as responsible travel to natural areas that conserves the environment and improves the well-being of local people. TIES suggests that ecotourists follow these principles:

- Minimize environmental impact.
- Build environmental and cultural awareness and respect.
- Provide positive experiences for both visitors and hosts.
- Provide direct financial benefits for conservation and for local people.
- Raise sensitivity to host countries' political, environmental, and social climates.
- Support international human rights and labor agreements.

You can find some eco-friendly travel tips, statistics, and touring companies and associations—listed by destination under "Travel Choice"—at the **TIES** website, www.ecotourism.org.

While much of the focus of ecotourism is about reducing impacts on the natural environment, ethical tourism concentrates on ways to preserve and enhance local economies and communities, regardless of location. You can embrace ethical tourism by staying at a locally owned hotel or

shopping at a store that employs local workers and sells locally produced goods.

Volunteer travel has become increasingly popular among those who want to venture beyond the standard group-tour experience to learn languages, interact with locals, and make a positive difference while on vacation in Peru. Volunteer options are listed under "Resources for Green Travel," below.

Deforestation is the main threat to Peru's fragile ecosystem. Farming has virtually wiped out most of the region's rainforests, and logging is a major threat. Such destruction has been devastating to many species, including man himself, in the form of displaced indigenous tribes, and has led to drinking-water shortages, flash flooding, and mud slides. Though environmental awareness is growing, solving the region's huge environmental problems, including not just deforestation but the effects of overpopulation and industrial pollution, clearly remains an uphill struggle.

Peru has 72 million hectares (178 million acres) of natural-growth forests—70% in the Amazon jungle region—that comprise nearly 60% of the national territory. Peru has done a slightly better job of setting aside tracts of rainforest as national park reserves and regulating industry than have some other Latin American and Asian countries. The Manu Biosphere Reserve, the Tambopata National Reserve, and the Pacaya-Samiria National Reserve are three of the largest protected rainforest areas in the world, and the government regulates entry of tour groups. Peru augmented the Bahuaja-Sonene National

General Resources for Green Travel

In addition to the resources for Peru listed above, the following websites provide valuable wide-ranging information on sustainable travel. For a list of even more sustainable resources, as well as tips and explanations on how to travel greener, visit www.frommers.com/planning.

- **Responsible Travel** (www.responsibletravel.com) is a great source of sustainable travel ideas; the site is run by a spokesperson for ethical tourism in the travel industry. **Sustainable Travel International** (www.sustainable travelinternational.org) promotes ethical tourism practices, and manages an extensive directory of sustainable properties and tour operators around the world.
- In the U.K., **Tourism Concern** (www.tourismconcern.org.uk) works to reduce social and environmental problems connected to tourism. The **Association of Independent Tour Operators** (**AITO;** www.aito.co.uk) is a group of specialist operators leading the field in making holidays sustainable.
- In Canada, **www.greenlivingonline.com** offers extensive content on how to travel sustainably, including a travel and transport section and profiles of the best green shops and services in Toronto, Vancouver, and Calgary.
- In Australia, the national body which sets guidelines and standards for ecotourism is **Ecotourism Australia** (www.ecotourism.org.au). **The Green Directory** (www.thegreendirectory.com.au), **Green Pages** (www.thegreen pages.com.au), and **EcoDirectory** (www.ecodirectory.com.au) offer sustainable travel tips and directories of green businesses.
- **Carbonfund** (www.carbonfund.org), **TerraPass** (www.terrapass.org), and **Cool Climate**(http://coolclimate.berkeley.edu) provide info on "carbon offsetting," or offsetting the greenhouse gas emitted during flights.
- The **"Green" Hotels Association** (www.greenhotels.com) recommends green-rated member hotels around the world that fulfill the company's stringent environmental requirements. **Environmentally Friendly Hotels** (www.environmentallyfriendlyhotels.com) offers more green accommodation ratings. The **Hotel Association of Canada** (www.hacgreenhotels.com) has a Green Key Eco-Rating Program that audits the environmental performance of Canadian hotels, motels, and resorts.
- **Sustain Lane** (www.sustainlane.com) lists sustainable eating and drinking choices around the U.S.; also visit **www.eatwellguide.org** for tips on eating sustainably in the U.S. and Canada.
- For information on animal-friendly issues throughout the world, visit **Tread Lightly** (www.treadlightly.org). For information about the ethics of swimming with dolphins, visit the **Whale and Dolphin Conservation Society** (www.wdcs.org).
- **International Volunteer Programs Association** (www.volunteer international.org) has a list of questions to help you determine the intentions and the nature of a volunteer program. For general info on volunteer travel, visit **http://volunteer.goabroad.com** and **www.idealist.org**.

Park, which was created in 1996, by 809,000 hectares (nearly 2 million acres) in 2001. INRENA, Peru's Institute for Natural Resource Management, enforces logging regulations and reseeds Peru's Amazon forests, and, in 2008, President García created the country's first Ministry of the Environment. A handful of Peruvian and international environmental and conservation groups, such as ProNaturaleza and Conservation International are active in Peru, working on reforestation and sustainable forestry projects.

Yet Peru is losing nearly 300,000 hectares (740,000 acres) of rainforest annually. The primary threats to Peru's tropical forests are deforestation caused by agricultural expansion, cattle ranching, logging, oil extraction and spills, mining, illegal coca farming, and colonization initiatives. Deforestation has shrunk territories belonging to indigenous peoples and wiped out more than 90% of the population. (There were once some six million people, 2,000 tribes and/or ethnic groups, and innumerable languages in the Amazon basin; today the indigenous population is less than two million.) Jungle ecotourism has exploded in Peru, and rainforest regions are now much more accessible than they once were, with more lodges and eco-options than ever. Many are taking leading roles in sustainable tourism even as they introduce protected regions to more travelers.

9 SPECIAL- AND GENERAL-INTEREST TOURS

For additional agencies specializing in soft adventure, outdoors-oriented adventure travel, and specialized programs including volunteering, culinary, and cooking trips, and language classes in Peru, be sure to see chapter 5, "The Active Vacation Planner."

For more information on escorted general-interest tours, including questions to ask before booking your trip, see www.frommers.com/planning.

SPECIAL-INTEREST TRIPS
North America- and Europe-Based Companies

- **Abercrombie & Kent** ★★ (© 800/554-7016; www.abercrombiekent.com) calls itself the "original luxury travel company." It runs an extensive lineup of high-end luxury trips, all of which are well managed and pampered, with stays in many of the finest hotels available. The tours aren't cheap, but if you want to go in style, A&K is the way to go. Group size is generally limited to 16 people. About a dozen Peru itineraries are available (such as the 9-day "Wonders of Peru," a family adventure, and combo trips with Bolivia and the Galápagos); check the website for occasional discounts on selected tours and dates.

- **Adventure Life** ★★ (© 800/344-6118; www.adventure-life.com), based in Missoula, Montana, is an Andean specialist with a roster of a couple dozen interesting Peru trips that focus mainly on ecotours and adventure trips, including some to off-the-beaten-path destinations and a group service trip, although it also offers some cushy "hotel-based trips."

- **Adventures Abroad Group** (© 800/665-3998; www.adventures-abroad.com), with offices in Washington state as well as the U.K., Canada, Australia, and New Zealand, has a massive database of trips. The tour operator prides itself on small group travel, from 4 to 21 participants. Peruvian offerings are highlights tours, ranging from 7 to 21 days, but longer trips include features such as hiking the Inca Trail.

Several trips combine either Ecuador or Bolivia with Peruvian attractions.

- **Butterfield & Robinson** ★ (① **866/ 551-9090** or 800/6781-1477 in Europe; www.butterfield.com) is a top upscale tour company that promotes biking and walking trips. You'll stay at some of the country's finest hotels and will get full van support for any light adventure trips. To Peru, it offers an 8-day "Peru Walking" tour. Trips are top-of-the-line (with commensurate pricing).
- **Exito Latin American Travel Specialists** ★ (① **800/655-4053**; www.exito travel.com) has a limited number of Peru packages, including the Inca Trail to Machu Picchu and jungle lodge tours. It's also a very good source for finding discounted airfares to Peru and elsewhere in Latin America, as well as language programs.
- **Gap Adventures** (① **800/708-7761** or 0870/999-0144 in the U.K.; www. gapadventures.com), the "Great Adventure People," focuses on adventure-oriented "independent travel with the security of a group" in Central and South America. It offers a huge number and variety of Peru trips (190 or more with stops in Peru). Some trips are more comfortable; others are a bit edgier. Most group trips have a maximum of 12 travelers.
- **Yampu Latin American Tours** has offices in New York (① **888/YAMPU-01** [926-7801]; www.yampu.com), Stowe (VT), and London. These South American travel specialists offer a variety of Peru trips, including rainforest expeditions, spiritual sojourns, trekking and adventure-sports tours, and targeted cultural programs.
- **Ladatco Tours** (① **800/327-6162;** www.ladatco.com) has specialized in tours to Central and South America for 3 decades. Its Explorer Tours are locally hosted and include hotels, sightseeing

with an English-speaking guide, and all land, cruise, and air transportation. There are "Pampered Adventure" programs and custom-designed tours—in all, more than two dozen trips to Peru throughout high season. Tours are a bit pricey but are well designed, and prices include airfare from Miami.

- **Latin America Escapes, Inc.** (① **800/510-5999**; www.latinamerican escapes.com) is a California-based company that offers fully escorted trekking and adventure trips, cultural tours, and natural history programs in Peru, as well as customized trips with your own private guide and driver and fully hosted independent tours with all major details (transportation, hotels, and tours) included. Check the website for current specials.
- **Nature Expeditions International** (① **800/869-0639**; www.naturexp. com) has a good reputation for package tours and has been in business since 1973. It offers a 10-day highlights trip to Lima, Cusco, the Sacred Valley, and Arequipa, as well as a 7-day trip to Lima, Cusco, and Machu Picchu. All trips have interesting, educational lecture options.
- **Overseas Adventure Travel** ★ (① **800/493-6824**; www.oattravel. com) is an English outfit with economical small-group (10–16 people) tours, such as its 11-day "Real Affordable Peru" trip. Another tour combines Machu Picchu and the Galápagos Islands.
- **Peru for Less** ★★ (① **877/269-0309** or 203/002-0571 in the U.K.; www. peruforless.com), originally a company based in Texas and now headquartered in Lima, lives up to its plainspoken name, guaranteeing "the lowest prices outside Peru." It has a great roster of affordable Peru tour packages, such as "Historical Peru," which visits Lima, Paracas, Nasca, Arequipa, Cusco, and

Machu Picchu, and very competent teams on the ground. It has recently branched out with alternative trekking tours in the Cusco region, including small-group treks to Choquequirao and Vilcabamba and a dozen more. Tours include guides, hotels, all visits and transfers, plus daily breakfast.

- **Southwind Adventures** ★ (© 800/377-9463; www.southwindadventures. com) plans distinctive and high-end adventure trips with a cultural emphasis in South America. Among them are 16 Peruvian trips, from mountain biking to specialty tours such as the "Urubamba Weaver's Trek." Custom trips include a 21-day Grand Andean Traverse trekking expedition, with possibilities for bird-watching, rafting, and family adventure.

- **Tambo Tours** (Value (© 888/2GO-PERU [246-7378]; www.tambotours. com), based in Houston, is a Peru specialist and one of the best spots to shop for a package deal to Peru. It offers a huge array of great-value trips to most parts of the country, including off-the-beaten path destinations and culturally oriented tours, as well as customized tours and discounted airfares.

- **Tico Travel** (© 800/493-8426; www. ticotravel.com), an established expert on Costa Rica and Central America, with an office in Ft. Lauderdale, Florida, now offers packages to Peru and discounted airfares. Its good-value 4- to 9-day packages cover Cusco, Lima, and Lake Titicaca.

Peru-Based Companies

- **Amazing Peru** ★ (© 800/704-2915 in the U.S. and Canada, 0808/520-0309 in the U.K.; www.amazingperu. com) is a well-run multipurpose agency, with several offices in Peru and an extensive roster of trips, offering everything from family and honeymoon

tours to luxury trips and adventure and jungle tours, for virtually any budget.

- **Aracari** ★★★ (© 312/239-8726 in the U.S., 020/3287-5262 in the U.K.; www.aracari.com) is something different in the world of Peruvian travel agencies, focusing on handcrafted, upscale, private-access tours. Run by a Peruvian-born woman and ex-banker who calls their customized itineraries "intelligent travel design," Aracari offers minimum 3-night itineraries in the top locations across Peru, along with carefully chosen, often small luxury boutique hotels as bases (by and large, the hotels I most highly recommend in this guide). Trips range from cuisine-oriented itineraries to outdoors adventure and archaeology, including specialized themes such as "Peru for Art Lovers and Foodies" and "Family Adventure in the Andes." Most impressive is the roster of exclusive private houses and haciendas offered for private luncheons, cocktails, and art-collection tours. If you're looking for unique, select adventure in Peru, it's tough to best Aracari.

- **Chaska Tours** ★ (© 084/240-424; www.chaskatours.com) is a professional, multipurpose Cusco-based company offering a large menu of travel itineraries both in groups and tailored for individuals (you can go right on the website and fill out a custom request form), especially ecotourism and adventure trips. It has everything from day tours in Cusco and jungle tours to off-the-beaten path trekking and mountain-biking excursions and jampacked 11-day trips that take in Cusco, the Sacred Valley, Titicaca, and the Amazon.

- **Class Adventure Travel (CAT)** ★ (© 877/240-4770 in the U.S., 0207/096-1259 in the U.K.; www.cat-travel.com) is a very professional and dependable Dutch-owned and -operated firm with offices in Lima and Cusco, as well as Argentina, Bolivia, and Brazil. It offers adventure (rafting and trekking) and jungle tours, long trips (a 17-day "Ancient Cultures of Peru" trip), short trips (a 7-day Cusco and Puno trip), and design-your-own tours. If you arrive in Peru and then decide to book a tour, CAT is without doubt one of the best general agencies to contact.

- **Fiesta Tours International** (© 01/ 225-1336; www.fiestatoursperu.com) has a multitude of trips within Peru, such as its 6-day "Discover Peru" tour. It also deals in airfares from Miami or Los Angeles.
- **Peru Gateway Travel** (© 888/671- 2852; www.peru-explorer.com) also has an extensive roster of Peru tours and a good selection of hotels.

One good source of package deals—airfare, accommodations, and other elements of your trip—is the airlines themselves. Most major airlines offer air/land packages, including **American Airlines Vacations** (© 800/321-2121; www.aavacations.com), **Delta Vacations** (© 800/ 221-6666; www.deltavacations.com), **Continental Airlines Vacations** (© 800/ 301-3800; www.covacations.com), and **United Vacations** (© 888/854-3899; www.unitedvacations.com). Several big

online travel agencies—Expedia, Travelocity, Orbitz, and Lastminute.com—also do a brisk business in packages.

Miami is usually the jumping-off point for package deals to Peru. The following are just a few among the longtime packagers to Peru and other destinations in Central and South America. A recommended tour operator and travel agency long specializing in South America packages, including some to Peru, is **Exito Latin American Travel Specialists** (see above). **Tara Tours** (© 800/327-0080; www. taratours.com), based in Miami, is also worth a look; it usually offers several air/ land packages to Peru, as well as tours such as the 9-day "Tara's Inka Journey" (Cusco, Machu Picchu, Lima, and the Amazon), and more adventurous tours to Kuelap and Sipán in northern Peru.

Fly Latin America, based in Costa Rica (© 800/788-7857; www.flylatinamerica. net/peru) has good airfares to Peru from North America and all over, as well as air/ hotel and tour packages. For more information on escorted general-interest tours, including questions to ask before booking your trip, see www.frommers.com/ planning.

---

10 STAYING CONNECTED

CELLPHONES

The three letters that define much of the world's wireless capabilities are GSM (Global System for Mobiles), a big, seamless network that makes for easy cross-border use. In the U.S., T-Mobile, AT&T Wireless, and Cingular use this quasi-universal system; in Canada, Microcell and some Rogers customers are GSM, and all Europeans and most Australians use GSM. If your cellphone is on a GSM system, and you have a world-capable multiband phone such as many Sony Ericsson,

Motorola, and Samsung models, you can make and receive calls throughout much of Peru. Just call your wireless operator and ask for "international roaming" to be activated on your account. Unfortunately, per-minute charges can be high.

For many, **renting** a phone is a better idea. While you can rent a phone from any number of sites in Peru, including kiosks at airports and at car-rental agencies, I suggest renting the phone before you leave home. North Americans can rent one before leaving home from **InTouch**

Global (*☏* 800/872-7626; www.intouch global.com) or **RoadPost** (*☏* 888/290-1606 or 905/272-5665; www.roadpost. com). InTouch will also, for free, advise you on whether your existing phone will work overseas; simply call *☏* 703/222-7161 between 9am and 4pm EST, or go to www.intouchglobal.com/travel.htm.

If you decide to wait to rent a phone once you land, **Peru Rent-a-Cell** (*☏* 01/517-1856) has representatives and a booth awaiting flights in baggage claim at the Lima and Cusco airports and rents small Nokia cellphones for just $10 per month. Incoming calls are free. If you use your phone only to receive incoming calls, either from within Peru or from any other country, you only pay that one-time activation fee. Otherwise, domestic calls cost 70¢ per minute, and calls placed to other countries cost $1.50 per minute.

Anyone headed to more remote parts of Peru might consider renting a **satellite phone** ("satphone"). It's different from a cellphone in that it connects to satellites and works where there's no cellular signal or ground-based tower. You can rent satellite phones from RoadPost (see above). InTouch USA (see above) offers a wider range of satphones but at higher rates. Per-minute call charges can be even cheaper than roaming charges with a regular cellphone, but the phone itself is more expensive. As of this writing, satphones were outrageously expensive to buy, so don't even think about it.

TELEPHONES

Peru's telephone system has been much improved since it was privatized and acquired by Spain's Telefónica in the mid-1990s. (There are now several additional players in the market, including Bell South.) It is relatively simple to make local and long-distance domestic and international calls from pay phones, which accept coins and phone cards (*tarjetas telefónicas*). Most phone booths display country and city codes, and contain instructions in English and Spanish.

For tips on calling Peru from abroad and calling within Peru, see the inside front cover of this book.

Your best, cheapest bet for making international calls from Peru is to head to any Internet cafe with an international calling option. These cafes have connections to Skype, Net2Phone, or some other **VoIP service**. International calls made this way can range anywhere from 5¢ to $1 per minute—much cheaper than making direct international calls or using a phone card. If you have your own Skype or similar account, you just need to find an Internet cafe that provides a computer with a headset.

The easiest way to make a long-distance call within the country is to purchase a phone card (maximum S/30). Many of these cards, purchased at newspaper kiosks and street vendors who sell nothing else, are called **Tarjeta 147.** To use such a card, first rub off the secret number. Dial the numbers 1-4-7 and then dial the 12-digit number on your card. A voice recording will tell you (in Spanish only) the value remaining on the card and instruct you to dial the desired telephone number. It will then tell you how many minutes you can expect to talk with the amount remaining. You can also make international calls from Telefónica offices and hotels, although surcharges levied at the latter can be extraordinarily expensive.

Toll-free numbers: Numbers beginning with 0800 within Peru are toll-free when called from a private phone (not from a public pay phone), but calling an 800 number in the States from Peru is not toll-free. In fact, it costs the same as an overseas call.

INTERNET ACCESS

More and more hotels, resorts, airports, cafes, and retailers are going **Wi-Fi** (wireless fidelity), becoming "hotspots" that

ⓘ Tips Where Are You @?

The @ symbol is hard to find on a Latin American keyboard. You must keep your finger on the "Alt" key, and then press "6" and "4" on the number pad to the right. If you're still unsuccessful and at an Internet cafe, ask the assistant to help you type an *arroba*.

offer free high-speed Wi-Fi access or charge a small fee for usage. Most laptops sold today have built-in wireless capability. To find public Wi-Fi hotspots in Peru and throughout South America, go to **www. jiwire.com**; its Hotspot Finder holds the world's largest directory of public wireless hotspots.

For dial-up access, most business-class hotels throughout Peru offer dataports for laptop modems, and a growing number offer free high-speed Internet access. Wherever you go, bring a **connection kit** of the right power and phone adapters, a spare phone cord, and a spare Ethernet network cable—or find out whether your hotel supplies them to guests.

In Peru, by far the easiest way to check your e-mail and surf the Web is to drop in at the Internet *cabinas* (booths) that can be found in virtually every city and even small towns. Connections are usually fast, and the service is as little as S/2 per hour.

Although there's no definitive directory for cybercafes, two places to start looking are **www.cybercaptive.com** and **www.cyber cafe.com**. I've also included specific recommendations in the "Fast Facts" section of most destinations.

Aside from formal cybercafes, most **youth hostels** and many hotels nowadays have at least one computer with Internet access. In Peru, many **nightclubs** and **bars** offer Web hookups. Some **hotel business centers** charge exorbitant rates; be sure to ask before assuming computer usage is free. Most major airports now have **Internet kiosks** scattered throughout their gates. These kiosks, which you'll also see in shopping malls, hotel lobbies, and tourist information offices around the world, give you basic Web access for a per-minute fee that's usually higher than cybercafe prices. The kiosks' clunkiness and high price mean they should be avoided whenever possible.

11 TIPS ON ACCOMMODATIONS

A wide range of accommodations— including world-class luxury hotels in modern high-rise buildings and 16th-century monasteries, affordable small hotels in colonial houses, rustic rainforest lodges, and inexpensive budget inns—can be found in Peru. Midrange options have expanded in recent years, but the large majority of accommodations still court budget travelers and backpackers (outside Lima's hosting of international business travelers).

Accommodations go by many names in Peru. *Hotel* generally refers only to comfortable hotels with a range of services, but *hostal* (or *hostales,* plural) is used for a wide variety of smaller hotels, inns, and pensions. (Note that *hostal* is distinct from the English-language term "hostel.") At the lower end are mostly *hospedajes, pensiones,* and *residenciales.* However, these terms are often poor indicators—if they are indicators at all—of an establishment's quality or services. Required signs outside reflect

Shopping in Peru

Peru is one of the top shopping destinations in Latin America, with some of the finest and best-priced crafts anywhere. Its long traditions of textile weaving and colorful markets bursting with tourists have produced a dazzling display of alpaca-wool sweaters, blankets, ponchos, shawls, scarves, typical Peruvian hats, and other woven items. Peru's ancient indigenous civilizations were some of the world's greatest potters, and reproductions of Moche, Nasca, Paracas, and other ceramics are available. (Until recently, it was surprisingly easy to get your hands on the real thing, but that's no longer the case.) In some cities—especially Lima, Cusco, and Arequipa—antique textiles and ceramics are still available. Some dealers handle pieces that are 1,000 years old or more (and others simply claim their pieces are that old). However, exporting such pre-Columbian artifacts from Peru is illegal.

Lima and Cusco have the lion's share of tourist-oriented shops and markets—particularly in Lima, you can find items produced all over the country—but other places might be just as good for shopping. Locals in Puno and Taquile Island on Lake Titicaca produce spectacular textiles, and Arequipa is perhaps the best place in Peru to purchase very fine, extremely soft baby-alpaca items. Handcrafted *retablos* (altars) from Ayacucho, depicting weddings and other domestic scenes, are famous throughout Peru and are available across the country. The Shipibo tribe of the northern Amazon produces excellent hand-painted textiles and decorative pottery. You'll also see items in the jungle made from endangered species—alligator skins, turtle shells, and the like. Purchasing these items is illegal, and it only encourages locals to further harm the natural environment and its inhabitants.

Baby alpaca and very rare vicuña are the finest woolens and are amazingly soft. Although many merchants are happy to claim that every woven wool item in their possession is alpaca or baby alpaca, much of what is sold in many

these categories: H (hotel), HS *(hostal),* HR *(hotel residencial),* and P *(pensión).* As in most countries, the government's hotel-rating system means that establishments are awarded stars for the presence of certain criteria—a pool, restaurant, elevator, and so on—more than for standards of luxury. Thus, it is not always true that the hotel with the most stars is necessarily the most comfortable or elegant. Luxury hotels are rare outside Lima and Cusco; budget accommodations are plentiful across the country, and many of them are quite good for the price. Some represent amazing values at less than $50 a night for

a double—with a dose of local character and breakfast, to boot.

The great majority of hotels in Peru are small and midsize independent inns; few international hotel chains operate in Peru. You'll find a Holiday Inn here and a Marriott, Best Western, or Orient-Express hotel there, but, by and large, the chains you'll come into contact with are Peruvian chains. The most prominent, although they have only a handful of hotels each, are Casa Andina, Sonesta, and Libertador. Casa Andina and Sonesta hotels are comfortable, decorated similarly, and generally good values. Casa Andina also has an tourist centers is anything but. Most, if not all, of the inexpensive, lookalike (S/15–S/60) sweaters, shawls, hats, and gloves you'll see in countless markets and stalls are made of acrylic or acrylic blends, and some even are blends of natural fibers and fiberglass. (A trekking guide in Cusco recently told me only partly in jest that you have to listen closely to people hawking cheap alpaca goods; they aren't saying "baby alpaca," but "may be alpaca.") If your new "alpaca" sweater stinks when it gets wet, it's llama wool. If you want the real thing—which is not nearly as cheap but still much less expensive than what you'd pay for alpaca of such fine quality in other countries—visit one of the established chain stores in large cities (most have "alpaca" in the name). Arequipa is one of the finest centers for alpaca goods, though Cusco and Lima are also excellent places to shop for alpaca.

The *artesanía* (popular arts) center par excellence of Peru is the highlands city of Ayacucho. The distinctive ceramic churches and *retablos* that are mainstays of handicrafts shops across Peru all come from Ayacucho (and a couple of small towns nearby), although a number of artisans have relocated to larger cities to more effectively market their wares.

In Lima, Cusco, and most tourist centers, there are scores of general, lookalike *artesanía* shops, and prices might not be any higher than what you'd find at street markets. At stores and in open markets, bargaining—gentle, good-natured haggling over prices—is accepted and even expected. However, when it gets down to ridiculously small amounts of money, it's best to recognize that you are already getting a great deal on probably handmade goods and you should relinquish the fight over a few *soles*.

Many prices for goods include a 19% sales tax, which, unfortunately, is refundable only on purchases made at the international departure lounge of Jorge Chávez International Airport.

upscale line of Private Collection hotels in a few choice spots. The Libertador hotels are elegant four- and five-star establishments, largely in historic buildings.

In-room air-conditioning isn't as common, especially in lower-priced and moderately priced inns and hotels, as it is in many countries. In highland towns, such as Cusco and Puno, that's not usually a problem, as even in warmer months it gets pretty cool at night. In coastal and jungle towns (and at jungle lodges), it gets considerably warmer, though most hotels that don't offer air-conditioning units have ceiling or other fans. If you're concerned about having air-conditioning in your room in a warmer destination, it may be necessary to bump up to a more expensive hotel.

Advance reservations are strongly recommended during high season (June–Oct) and during national holidays and important festivals. This is especially true of hotels in the middle and upper categories in popular places such as Cusco and Machu Picchu. Many hotels quote their rates in U.S. dollars. If you pay in cash, the price will be converted into soles at the going rate. Note that at most budget and many midrange hotels, credit cards are not accepted. Most published rates can be negotiated and travelers can often get greatly reduced rates outside of peak season simply by asking. This is especially true of jungle lodges, where published international prices differ greatly from the rate one might obtain on-site.

Hotel taxes and service charges are an issue that has caused some confusion in recent years. Most upper-level hotels add a 19% general sales tax (IGV) and a 10% service charge to the bill. However, foreigners who can demonstrate they live outside of Peru are not charged the 19% tax (though they are responsible for the 10% service charge). In practice, hotels sometimes either mistakenly or purposely include the IGV on everyone's bill; presentation of a passport is sufficient to have the tax deducted from your tab. Many hotels—usually those at the midlevel and lower ranges—simplify matters by including the tax in their rates; at these establishments, you cannot expect to have the tax removed from your charges. At high-end hotels, be sure to review your bill and ask for an explanation of additional taxes and charges. Prices in this book do not include taxes and service charges unless otherwise noted.

Safety is an issue at many hotels, especially at the lower end, and extreme care should be taken with regard to personal belongings left in the hotel. Leaving valuables lying around is asking for trouble. Except for hotels at the lowest levels, all have safety deposit boxes. (Only luxury hotels have room safes.) Place your belongings in a carefully sealed envelope. If you arrive in a town without previously arranged accommodations, you should be at least minimally wary of taxi drivers and others who insist on showing you to a hotel. Occasionally, these will provide excellent tips, but, in general, they will merely be taking you to a place where they are confident they can earn a commission.

A final precaution worth mentioning is the electric heater found on many showerheads. These can be dangerous, and touching them while functioning can prompt an unwelcome electric jolt.

For tips on surfing for hotel deals online, visit www.frommers.com.

Suggested Peru Itineraries

Unless you have at least 3 weeks or a month to spend in vast Peru, you probably won't get to see as much of the country as you'd like, at least on a first trip. Peru is deceptively large, and at least as important are the considerable geographic and transportation barriers that make zipping around the country complicated. Some regions require difficult travel by land, with no air access. A real danger is trying to do too much in too short a period. Even on relatively short trips of 2 weeks or less, you have to take into account those hefty distances and transportation routes, not to mention natural factors—such as jet lag and acclimatization to high altitude—that require most visitors to slow down.

1 THE REGIONS IN BRIEF

Peru shares borders with Ecuador and Colombia to the north, Brazil and Bolivia to the east, and Chile to the south. It lies just below the Equator and is the third-largest country in South America—larger than France and Spain combined, covering an area of nearly 1,300,000 sq. km (500,000 sq. miles).

Peruvians like to say that their country consists of three distinct geological components: coast, *sierra* (highlands), and *selva* (jungle). The capital, Lima, lies on the coast, but the Amazon rainforest, which makes up nearly two-thirds of Peru, and the bold Andes mountain range dominate the country. Peru's considerable size, natural barriers, and a lack of efficient transportation alternatives make it a somewhat difficult and time-consuming place to get around.

THE CENTRAL COAST & HIGHLANDS   The Pacific coastal region is a narrow strip that runs from one end of the country to the other (a distance of some 2,200km/1,400 miles) and is almost entirely desert. Lima, the capital, lies about halfway down the coast. To the south, in one of the driest areas on earth, are Pisco, Ica, and Nasca, the cradle of several of Peru's most important ancient civilizations, as well as the famously mysterious Nasca Lines and the Ballestas Islands, promoted locally as "Peru's Galápagos" for their diverse indigenous fauna. The area is especially prone to earthquakes, such as the devastating one that struck the region in August 2007. Inland and tucked high in the Central Andes, Ayacucho is one of Peru's most fascinating cities, known for its colonial churches and artisanship but less felicitously associated with the Shining Path terrorist group.

CUSCO & THE SACRED VALLEY   The dramatic Andes mountains in south-central Peru contain the country's most famous sights, including the former Inca capital of Cusco and scenic highland villages that run the length of the beautiful Sacred Valley. The valley is dotted with singularly impressive Inca ruins, of which Machu Picchu (and the Inca Trail leading to it) is undoubtedly the star. Cusco sits at an elevation of some 3,400m (11,000 ft.). Indigenous culture is particularly strong in the region.

Peru's UNESCO World Heritage Sites

- Cusco city (designated in 1983)
- Machu Picchu Historic Sanctuary (1983)
- Archaeological Site of Chavín (1985)
- Huascarán National Park (1985)
- Manu National Park (1987)
- Chan Chan Archaeological Zone (1988)
- Río Abiseo National Park (1990)
- Historic Center of Lima (1991)
- Nasca Lines (1994)
- Historic Center of Arequipa (2000)

SOUTHERN PERU   Massive Lake Titicaca, shared with Bolivia, is the largest lake in South America and the world's highest navigable body of water (at 3,830m/12,566 ft.). Indigenous peoples inhabit ancient villages on islands (some of them man-made) in the middle of this huge body of water. Puno, at the edge of Lake Titicaca, is a rough-and-tumble town that hosts some of Peru's liveliest festivals. The elegant colonial city of Arequipa is one of Peru's most gorgeously situated, at the base of three snowcapped volcanoes. Nearby is Colca Canyon, twice as deep as the Grand Canyon and site of perhaps the best place in all South America to view the regal condor.

AMAZONIA   Although about 60% of Peru is Amazon rainforest, only about 5% of the country's human inhabitants reside there. One of the world's most dazzling arrays of wildlife—more than 1,700 species of birds (more than the population found in the continental U.S.) and 2,000 species of fish—make it their home. For the visitor, there are two primary jungle destinations. The northern jungle, of which Iquitos is the principal gateway (but accessible only by plane or boat), is the most explored and has the most facilities. Much less trafficked and more controlled is the Madre de Dios department, in the south, which contains Manu Biosphere Reserve, Puerto Maldonado, and Tambopata National Reserve. These can be reached by land or air from Cusco.

NORTHERN PERU   Peru's north is much less visited than the south, even though it possesses some of the country's most outstanding archaeological sights. Trujillo, Chiclayo, and Cajamarca (a lovely small city in the highlands) are the main colonial towns of interest. Near Trujillo and Chiclayo are Chan Chan, Túcume, and Sipán, extraordinary adobe cities, pyramids, and royal tombs and treasures that predate the Incas.

The mountain ranges in the center of Peru, north of Lima, are among the highest in Peru. Within Huascarán National Park, the Cordillera Blanca stretches 200km (124 miles) and contains a dozen peaks more than 5,000m (16,400 ft.) tall; the highest is Huascarán, at 6,768m (22,205 ft.). The region is a favorite of trekkers and outdoor-adventure travelers who come to Peru with white-water rafting, ice climbing, and other sports in mind. The main jumping-off point for these activities is the town of Huaraz. In valleys east of the capital is the important archaeological site Chavín de Huántar.

Also in Northern Peru are unassuming beach towns where the waves attract surfers from across the globe; Máncora, Órganos, and Punta Sal are among the most popular among a 25km (15-mile) stretch of coast. They are getting increasingly built up into low-key resorts with hotels and second home owners from Lima.

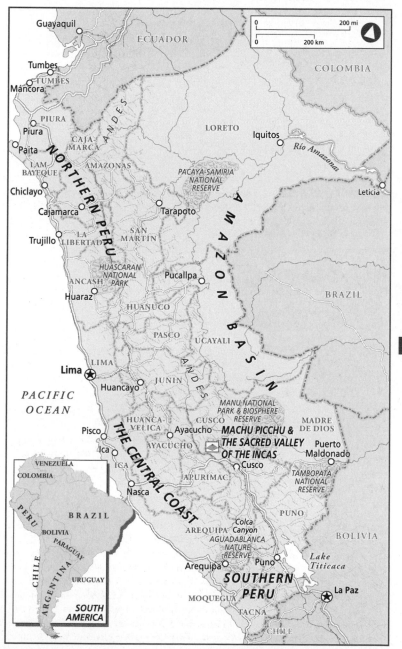

2 THE BEST OF PERU IN 1 WEEK

Though Peru boasts astounding variety, most people don't have time to experience the range of its offerings (of course, that's what return trips are for). For first-timers, there's one place almost everyone has absolutely got to see: Machu Picchu. I certainly have no problem with that: It's where I was determined to go before I'd ever stepped foot on the South American continent. In a single week, there's really just enough time to see the best of Cusco and Incan Peru (and it won't involve crazed travel from one place to the next all over Peru). This itinerary will give you an idea of how to best experience the ancient Inca capital, the empire's alluring, once-thought-lost imperial city, and the Urubamba Valley that the Incas held sacred.

Day ❶: Arrive in Lima; Transfer to Cusco

All international flights arrive in Lima, but try to arrange it so that an overnight flight gets you there very early in the morning, with time enough to get an 8am or 9am flight to Cusco (note that flights are occasionally delayed by weather in Cusco, though, so the earlier the flight, the better). With only a week in Peru, there's little need to linger in Lima unless you want a day to take it easy and see Colonial Lima and have lunch at a *cevichería*.

Take it easy in Cusco on your first day. Drink a lot of water (and perhaps some coca-leaf tea) and get a good night's rest. The altitude (more than 3,400m/11,000 ft.) combined with an overnight international flight will prove very taxing. Have a light, relaxing lunch at **Jack's Café Bar** (p. 212), a popular gringo hangout serving excellent sandwiches, salads and fruit shakes. Limit yourself to taking a stroll around the delightful **Plaza de Armas** (p. 213), popping into the tourist information office to pick up your *boleto turístico* (tourist ticket for the main sights in Cusco and the Sacred Valley), and choosing a spot for dinner. I'd suggest **Cicciolina** (p. 206) or, for superb sushi and views of the Plaza de Armas, **Limo** (p. 208).

Day ❷: Colonial Cusco

Sticking to the area near the Plaza de Armas, visit the **Cathedral** (p. 214) and the **Convento y Museo de Santa Catalina** (p. 213) in the morning. After lunch, see the stunning **Qoricancha (Temple of the Sun;** p. 218) to get an idea of the Incas' incredible masonry and the clash of native and Spanish culture. Take a walk along the **Calles Loreto** and **Hatunrumiyoc** to see some more magnificent Inca stonework. In Plaza Nazarenas, check out the beautifully designed **Museo de Arte Precolombino (MAP;** p. 217) and some of the upscale alpaca goods shops on the square. Then stop at **MAP Café** (p. 206), the chic restaurant in the museum's courtyard, for a celebratory dinner, or visit **Chi Cha,** a star chef's take on Cusqueña cuisine (p. 206). Have a pisco sour at one of the lively cafes or bars near the Plaza de Armas afterward.

Day ❸: Sacred Valley: Pisac

With luck your third day in Peru will be a Tuesday, Thursday, or (better yet) Sunday—those are market days in the Urubamba Valley (the **Valle Sagrado de los Incas**). Take a *combi* or taxi to Pisac and check out the popular and lively **artisans' market.** Have lunch at **Ulrike's Café** (p. 246) right on the main square. After lunch, either hike up to or grab a taxi to the **Inca ruins** (p. 242) looming above town. Pisac's ruins will give you a taste of what you're about to see in Ollantaytambo and Machu Picchu. Head a little farther along in the valley (again by taxi or combi) to a rustic country hotel near **Urubamba**

1 Lima
2 Cusco
3 Pisac
4 Ollantaytambo
5 Machu Picchu
6 Cusco
7 Lima

or **Yucay,** where you'll have dinner and spend the night.

Day **4**: Sacred Valley: Ollantaytambo

Wake early and take a taxi to **Ollantaytambo** (p. 255), where you'll want to arrive as close to opening as possible to explore the **Fortress Ruins** (p. 257) before the busloads arrive. Then grab lunch at **Café Mayu** (p. 260) by the train station and take a walk around Ollanta's **Old Town** (p. 258). Very energetic types who can manage a few hours after lunch should go for a hike in the Valley, perhaps to **Salineras de Maras** (p. 253), the ancient salt mines near Urubamba.

If you don't mind moving around, you could transfer to a hotel in Ollanta to enjoy it at night when there are few tourists (and be there for the train the next morning to Machu Picchu). Otherwise head back to your hotel near Urubamba.

Day **5**: What You Came For: Machu Picchu

Catch an early morning train from Ollantaytambo to **Aguas Calientes** (p. 283), the rough-edged town that sits below **Machu Picchu** (p. 266). Catch the bus up to the ruins and spend the day exploring them (hiking up to the **Huayna Picchu peak** for panoramic views if you're in shape; p. 271). Have lunch at the Machu Picchu

Sanctuary Lodge next to the ruins and stay until late in the afternoon, after the large tour groups have left. Spend the night either next to the ruins (if you've got very deep pockets) or back down in Aguas Calientes (which is actually more fun). Hit the bars along the railroad tracks to share stories with some of the backpackers who've survived the Inca Trail.

Day ❻: Back to Cusco

Now that you've acclimatized to the Andes and seen some of the greatest legacies of the Incas, head back by train to the old Inca capital, Cusco. In the afternoon, stroll around the hilly **San Blas** (p. 217) neighborhood, site of dozens of cool shops and art galleries. Do some shopping for handicrafts, souvenirs, and art. If Machu Picchu and Ollantaytambo have intensified your interest in Inca architecture, catch a cab (or walk) up to the fantastic ruins, **Sacsayhuamán** (p. 222), overlooking the city. If you

have any energy left, get a taste of Cusco's hopping nightlife at one of the pubs or nightclubs around the Plaza de Armas. Then make your way up bustling **Calle Procuradores,** Cusco's gringo alley and restaurant row. If you're dining on a budget, pick an informal restaurant along Calle Plateros, just off the Plaza de Armas, such as **Chez Maggy** (p. 211); if you're looking for something more refined, with an emphasis on organic and vegetarian cuisine, try **Greens** (p. 208).

Day ❼: Back to Lima and Back Home

Do some final shopping in Cusco before catching a flight to Lima. You'll probably have an evening flight back home, so you may have enough time for a ceviche lunch in Lima and, if you're ambitious, a short tour of colonial **Lima Centro** (p. 109) in the late afternoon.

3 THE BEST OF PERU IN 2 WEEKS

This 2-week itinerary will allow you to experience the greatest of southern Peru, from its historic colonial cities to its natural wonders. First on everyone's list, of course, are the lively ancient Inca capital Cusco and that empire's legendary lost city, Machu Picchu. But in a relatively short amount of time you can also delve into dense Amazonian jungle; Lake Titicaca, the world's highest navigable body of water; and one of the world's deepest canyons, Colca (but keep in mind, this is a very full itinerary, and you may need to cut either the jungle or Colca Canyon). Plenty of people find it irresistible and linger in Cusco and the Sacred Valley of the Incas (especially if they want to hike the Inca Trail to Machu Picchu or do another highland trek), or don't have a full 2 weeks for travel in Peru. In that case, it's probably best to concentrate on a particular region so that you don't lose too much time traveling. Of course, if your primary interest is wildlife viewing in the great Amazon, you'll want to plan everything around a 4- to 7-day jungle expedition deep into Tambopata National Reserve, Manu Biosphere Reserve, or the jungle around Iquitos in northern Peru.

Day ❶: Arrive in Lima

All international flights arrive into the rather chaotic capital, Lima, and even though most people are headed elsewhere, you may find yourself obligated to spend

at least a day in Lima. Make the most of it by touring the colonial quarter, or perhaps visiting one of the country's great museums, such as the **Museo Larco** or **Museo de la Nación,** and hitting either a great

Map legend:
1. Lima
2. Cusco
3. Machu Picchu
4. Puerto Maldonado
5. Tambopata National Reserve
6. Puno
7. Lake Titicaca
8. Arequipa
9. Colca Canyon
10. Lima

Area of detail — PERU — Lima

SUGGESTED PERU ITINERARIES

4

THE BEST OF PERU IN 2 WEEKS

---

cevichería or a cutting-edge *novo andino* restaurant. See chapter 6.

Then get out of Lima and on your way to Peru's greatest attractions. (If you're able to get an overnight flight that puts you into Lima early in the morning, you may want to consider flying immediately to Cusco to save time and avoid the hassles of Lima.)

Days ❷–❸: On to Cusco, Old Inca Capital

Although you may want to hit Cusco running, the city's altitude, more than 3,400m (11,000 ft.), is daunting to most travelers. Spend a couple of days seeing the old Inca

capital at a relaxed pace, making sure to hang out around the **Plaza de Armas** and visit the **La Catedral (Cathedral), Convento de Santa Catalina (Santa Catalina Convent),** and **Qoricancha (Temple of the Sun).** Cusco is one of the best places in Peru to shop, eat, and party, so make sure to squeeze those vital activities in with sightseeing. See chapter 8.

Day ❹: The Stuff of Legend: Machu Picchu

Though I think Machu Picchu deserves an overnight stay (and even 2 days exploring the ruins), if you're trying to see the best of Peru in 2 weeks, you can't afford the time.

So take the morning train from Cusco to Machu Picchu **(Aguas Calientes),** South America's number-one attraction. Spend the middle part of the day exploring the ruins here (p. 283) and then head back to Cusco on the train.

Day ❺: Cusco

If you weren't able to catch an archaeology museum in Lima, or even if you did, check out the beautifully designed **Museo de Arte Precolombino (MAP;** p. 217). Enjoy some of the lively cafes, bars, and restaurants of Cusco; you'll find plenty while strolling around the **Barrio de San Blas** (p. 217). If you have time and plenty of energy, catch a cab (or walk up to) the fantastic ruins, **Sacsayhuamán** (p. 222), overlooking the city.

Days ❻–❽: Into the Jungle

Take an early morning, half-hour flight from Cusco to **Puerto Maldonado,** the gateway to the southern Peruvian Amazon jungle of **Tambopata National Reserve** (p. 98). Board a boat for a 2-day, 1-night trip to one of the jungle lodges along the Río Madre de Dios. A 3-day, 2-night adventure, either within 1 hour of Puerto Maldonado or 4 to 5 hours away along the Río Tambopata, is even better, if you have the time. On the third day, head back to Puerto and then catch a flight to Cusco. Spend the night in Cusco; see chapter 8 for options.

Day ❾: South to Lake Titicaca

From Cusco, take the extraordinarily scenic train to **Puno** and **Lake Titicaca** (or if you want to visit some of the Inca ruins en route, take one of the premium tour bus services that make a day of the journey). Spend the night in Puno and rest up (and get accustomed to the even higher altitude) for the next day's boat trip out on the lake. See chapter 10.

Day ❿: Lake Titicaca and Isla Taquile

While an overnight trip that allows you to spend a night with a family either on Isla Taquile or Amantaní is the best way to experience the people and customs of Titicaca, you can also do a 1-day trip that lets you to visit the **Uros floating islands** and the fascinating culture of **Isla Taquile.** If you have an extra couple days, an unforgettable Titicaca experience is the **Suasi Island** ecolodge. See chapter 10.

Day ⓫: Arequipa

Catch an early morning flight from Juliaca (the nearest airport, an hour from Puno) to Arequipa, the elegant southern city known as "La Ciudad Blanca" for its beautiful colonial buildings made of *sillar,* or white volcanic stone. Stay close to the gorgeous **Plaza de Armas** and spend the afternoon at the wondrous **Monasterio de Santa Catalina,** one of the finest examples of colonial religious architecture in the Americas. See chapter 10.

Days ⓬–⓭: Colca Valley

From Arequipa, set off on a 2-day, 1-night exploration of **Colca Canyon,** the best spot in South America to observe giant Andean condors, which soar overhead at **Cruz del Cóndor.** Explore some of the villages of the valley, as well as the thermal baths, on the first day and spend the night at a rustic hotel in Colca before marveling at the condors the next morning. For those with less time, it's possible, though brutal, to "do" Colca on a 1-day adventure, leaving very early in the morning (practically the middle of the night) to get there in time for the condors' lift-off at 9am. See chapter 10.

Day ⓮: Morning in Arequipa, Then Back to Lima

Spend the morning shopping for alpaca goods before flying to **Lima,** where you'll catch your flight back home.

Traveling to Peru with small children will be a challenge; though Peruvians are very family-oriented, transportation difficulties and the rugged appeal of many of Peru's primary attractions may test parents' resourcefulness and patience, as well as that of the children. Slightly older and adventurous children, however, should revel in the archaeological grandeur of Machu Picchu, the indigenous peoples of Lake Titicaca, and the phenomenal flora and fauna of the Amazon jungle. A trip with children may not differ much with respect to the places one chooses to visit, though there are some specific things to do and ways to do them in those places that may appeal more to kids. Families should approach Peru as an excellent learning experience about South American history, ecology, and Peruvian culture.

Days ❶–❷: The Sacred Valley of the Incas

Families will probably want to stick to the tried-and-true highlights of Peru, beginning with Cusco and Machu Picchu. Instead of beginning in the old Inca capital, however, it might make more sense to head straight to the **Sacred Valley of the Incas,** where the altitude is lower (requiring less acclimatization) and there is more open space. Stay at one of the area's rustic country hotels, where kids can go horseback riding and teenagers can go whitewater rafting or mountain biking in the Valley. Athletic kids should like climbing the Inca ruins of **Ollantaytambo** and **Pisac,** where they can admire not only Inca ingenuity but also the stunning mountain views. See chapter 9.

Day ❸: Machu Picchu

Children will greatly enjoy the **scenic train** to Machu Picchu. It's a good idea to consider spending the night in Aguas Calientes, as seeing the ruins of Machu Picchu involves a lot of climbing and you'll require a lot of stamina to see it thoroughly. The **Inkaterra Machu Picchu Hotel** (p. 284), though expensive, has great grounds, birding walks, and a swimming pool.

Very athletic children will eat up the hike to **Huayna Picchu** (p. 271), which provides some of the most dramatic panoramic views you're likely to stumble

across. Nearly as good, and less challenging, are routes from the **Intipunku** (the Sun Gate, where hikers come upon the site from the Inca Trail; p. 274). See chapter 9.

Days ❹–❻: From Cusco to the Jungle

A short flight from Cusco to Puerto Maldonado and a drive to the pier is all it takes to plunge into the Amazon jungle. Two good lodges that don't require too much river travel time are **Reserva Amazónica** (for families that may enjoy a bit of pampering) and **Sandoval Lake Lodge** (for those who prefer to rough it a bit); see p. 350 and 349. The first has a private treetop canopy walk, which kids should love, and a small island that is a private refuge for several types of monkeys; boats take guests out at night to look for caimans on the river. A 3-day, 2-night stay is a good option. See chapter 11.

Day ❼: A Breather in Cusco

Fly back to Cusco and spend the day getting to know the city. The city is full of fun and funky restaurants, such as **Chez Maggy** (p. 211), that will appeal to young ones, and kids should like spotting the dressed-up llamas that wander Cusco's streets.

Kids should also appreciate the blocks of **Inca stone masonry** that fit together like a giant jigsaw puzzle; have them try to locate the puma stone on Calle Inca Roca and the 12-angled stone on Calle Hatun-rumiyoc. At the ruins of **Sacsayhuamán** (p. 222), on a hill overlooking Cusco, are huge rocks with slick grooves—kids of all ages use them as slides. See chapter 8.

Days ❽–❿: Lake Titicaca
The long but terrifically **scenic train** ride from Cusco to Lake Titicaca is one of the best in South America. Stay in a hotel perched on the edge of the lake, and head out on a **boat tour** of Titicaca (either day-long or with an overnight stay). Kids

should marvel at the natives who live on the floating islands, and older kids who like to rough it will enjoy visiting the communities on **Isla Taquile** (p. 298) and staying overnight with a family on **Isla Amantaní** (p. 300). The next day fly from Puno (Juliaca, actually) to Lima for your flight home. If you have extra time in Lima, which isn't exactly a family-friendly city, take older kids to the **Museo Larco** (p. 136) to survey the sometimes eye-popping ceramics of ancient Peruvian civilizations.

The Active Vacation Planner

"Peru" is derived from a word in Quechua signifying "land of abundance," a remarkable apt name for this diverse country. There is little question that, in its distinct *costa, sierra,* and *selva* (coast, highlands, and jungle) regions, Peru is blessed with an enormous variety of wilderness and some of the world's greatest and most diverse plant and animal species. It has been reported that Peru contains 84 of the known 104 biosystems in the world; more than 400 species of mammals and 300 species of reptiles; 50,000 plant species (among them the world's highest count of orchids, more than 3,000 kinds); and nearly 2,000 bird species, about 10% of the world's total. With desert sands, dense Amazon rainforest canopy, amazing Andean peaks, and the world's deepest canyons, Peru is a country that inspires travelers to get active and get outdoors. Everything from soft adventure and easy walks to extreme sports is available and easily arranged either on your own (for the former) or with top-notch agencies and guides.

Indeed, Peru is perhaps the most diverse and best-equipped outdoors destination in South America. It is now rare to see visitors from abroad come to Peru with the intention of staying clean and dry in pressed slacks and loafers. Almost every gringo who sets foot beyond Lima is more properly outfitted in fleece pullovers, hiking boots, daypacks, and Gore-Tex water-repellent gear. In the minds of many nonspecialists, getting outdoors in Peru is still limited to easily reached jungle treks and lodges, day hikes in the valleys, and—if you're really adventurous—treks along ancient Inca trails. Whether that's your speed or you want to go hard-core, plunging deep into the jungle or mountains, it isn't hard to come up with a plan to experience the best of natural Peru.

Amazingly, given its natural abundance, Peru is still relatively new to the ecotourism game. Its infrastructure to receive large groups of ecotourists is not quite as developed as that of some other countries, such as Costa Rica. But Peru is quickly catching up, and tour operators, guides, and agencies, both local and international, are increasingly specializing in outdoor and active travel. The oldest jungle lodges in the Peruvian Amazon have been around for more than 3 decades. Lodges, climbing and rafting expeditions, and birding and hiking trips all cater to environmentally aware travelers with deep interests in nature and seeing "the real Peru."

Other active trips focus on culinary Peru—the diverse national cuisine is one of the world's finest, even if until recently it flew under the radar of many foodie types—voluntcering, and language classes.

Whether you want to make active and outdoor travel the sole focus of your trip or treat it as just an add-on, there are many different ways to approach it. This chapter lays out your options, from tour operators who run multiactivity package tours (and frequently include stays at ecolodges) to the best spots in Peru to get outdoors (with listings of tour operators, guides, and outfitters that specialize in each), and it provides an overview of the country's national parks and nature reserves. You'll also find a handful of tips on health and safety in the wilderness, what to bring, and educational and volunteer travel options for those with the time and desire to work toward the maintenance and preservation of Peru's natural wonders and gain a more in-depth understanding of Peru's culture and people.

1 ORGANIZED ADVENTURE TRIPS

Because most travelers have limited time and resources, organized ecotourism or adventure travel packages, arranged by tour operators abroad or in Peru, are popular ways of combining cultural and outdoor activities. Bird-watching, horseback riding, rafting, and hiking can be teamed with visits to destinations such as Cusco, the Sacred (Urubamba) Valley and Machu Picchu, or Arequipa and Lake Titicaca.

Traveling with a group has several advantages over traveling independently. Your accommodations and transportation are arranged, and most (if not all) of your meals are included in the cost of a package. If your tour operator has a reasonable amount of experience and a decent track record, you should proceed to each of your destinations quickly without the snags and long delays that you might face if you're traveling on your own. You'll also have the opportunity to meet like-minded travelers who are interested in nature and active sports. Some group trekking trips include *porteros* or *arrieros* (porters or muleteers) who carry extra equipment. On some luxury treks of the Inca Trail, porters will even carry your backpack, so all you have to do is hike your lazy self up and over the mountain passes.

In the best cases of organized outdoors travel, group size is kept small (10–15 people), and tours are escorted by knowledgeable guides who are either naturalists or biologists. Be sure to inquire about difficulty levels when you're choosing a tour. While most companies offer "soft adventure" packages that those in decent but not overly athletic shape can handle, others focus on more hard-core activities geared toward very fit and seasoned adventure travelers.

See also the escorted tour operators listed under "Special-Interest Trips" in chapter 3. Several operators offer adventure and outdoors components to their more standard Peru packages.

U.S. & INTERNATIONAL ADVENTURE TOUR OPERATORS

These agencies and operators specialize in well-organized and coordinated tours that cover your entire stay. Many travelers prefer to have everything arranged and confirmed before arriving in Peru—a good idea for first-timers and during high season (especially for travel to Cusco and its immediate environs, including the Inca Trail). Many of these operators provide great service but are not cheap; 10-day tours generally cost upwards of $2,500 or more per person, and do not include airfare to Peru.

Adventure Life ★★ (© 800/344-6118; www.adventure-life.com), based in Missoula, Montana, and specializing in Central and South America, has an interesting roster of rugged Peru trips, frequently with a community focus, including a 12-day multi-sport tour (mountain biking, hiking, rafting, jungle tour, and Machu Picchu), rainforest ecolodge tours, and a 10-day "Cachiccata Trek: The Inca Trail Less Traveled," as well as plenty of tour extensions. One Peru trip is specifically designed to raise money (40% of

> **Tips Inca Trail Regulations**
>
> Trekkers once could embark on the Inca Trail on their own, but new regulations imposed by the Peruvian government to limit environmental degradation and damage to the trail itself now require all trekkers to go with officially sanctioned groups, guides and porters. See the "Inca Trail Regulations" box and "Inca Trail Tour Agencies," both in chapter 9, for more information.

trip cost) for the organization's nonprofit fund (which aims to give back to local communities).

Adventure Specialists ★ (℃ 719/783-2086; www.adventurespecialists.org) travels only to the Copper Canyon (Mexico), Colorado, and Peru. In Peru, it specializes in treks, horse trips, and archaeology expeditions, as well as wildlife and birding adventures by dugout canoe in the Manu Biosphere Reserve. The founder is one of the archaeologists credited with the November 2003 rediscovery of Llactapata, a "lost" Inca city.

Amazonia Expeditions (℃ 800/262-9669; www.perujungle.com or www.peruandes.com) has offered good-value, personalized, and flexible ecotourism trips to the Peruvian jungle and the Andes since 1981. Trips of up to 7 days are all-inclusive (even laundry and tips are included). Jungle trips are to the Tahauyo Lodge (4 hr. from Iquitos) and the Tamshiyacu-Tahuayo Reserve (they are the only licensed tour operator to the latter). The two websites focus on the group's jungle adventures and Inca ruins/Andes treks respectively.

Andean Treks ★★ (℃ 800/683-8148; www.andeantreks.com) is a personalized, high-quality Latin American adventure-tour operator that focuses on trekking in the Andes and exploring the jungle throughout Peru. The Massachusetts-based group's roster of reasonably priced trips for all levels includes cloud-forest treks, llama trekking, trips to Manu and Tambopata, and highlands treks that combine white-water rafting or Amazon lodge stays. Trips range from easy to hard-core.

Backroads ★ (℃ 800/462-2848; www.backroads.com) is a luxury-tour company that offers upscale, light-adventure trips around the globe, and it has several tours of Peru on its menu. It specializes in walking, hiking and biking tours from Cusco to Machu Picchu, some of which incorporate stays at the Mountain Lodges of Peru (p. 90). Service is personalized and the guides are top-notch.

Condor Journeys and Adventures ★ (℃ 01700/741-318 in the U.K. or 318/775 0190 in the U.S.; www.condorjourneys-adventures.com) is one of the top U.K. agencies organizing package tours to Latin America. Condor offers a huge number of varied trips to Peru, including archaeology tours and lots of soft- and hard-core adventure and outdoor travel: hiking programs along Inca roads, horseback treks to Machu Picchu, rainforest and white-water rafting in canyons and along the Apurímac and Urubamba, mountain-biking expeditions, and special, unusual programs such as "Mystical Peru" and hikes to Salcantay and Vilcabamba by llama.

GorpTravel (℃ 877/440-GORP [4677]; www.gorptravel.com), a self-styled "Guide to Outdoor Travel," is a wholesaler with a vast range of options for adventure and more general travel throughout Peru and the world offered by outfitters across the globe. It recently offered more than 150 outdoor-oriented vacations to Peru (including a "Peru Top 20" list). A few are basic highlights trips, while others are cultural and language vacations or specialist adventures for very active and adventurous sorts.

International Expeditions (℃ 800/633-4734; www.internationalexpeditions.com) features Amazon cruises and jungle-lodge tours (including luxurious river cruises run by Jungle Expeditions). The main tours to Peru are an Amazon Explorer "Jungles of Peru" and a 9-day Amazon Voyage. Visitors help with reforestation projects and participate in conservation programs and tree planting with local naturalists. Extensions to Cusco, Machu Picchu, Lima, and the Nasca Lines are available.

Journeys International ★ (℃ 800/255-8735; www.journeys.travel), based in Ann Arbor, Michigan, offers small-group (4–12 people) natural history tours guided by naturalists. Trips include the 9-day "Amazon & Andes Odyssey," which includes the Tambopata National Reserve along with Cusco, Machu Picchu, and the Sacred Valley; and special Amazon and Inca trips for families.

Mountain Travel Sobek ★★★ (℃ 888/831-7526, or 0808/234-2243 in the U.K.; www.mtsobek.com) offers seven itineraries to Peru, including the 8-day "Andean Explorer," with day hikes and rafting. Options for mountaineers and committed trekkers include 13 days of strenuous trekking in Cordillera Blanca (mostly camping); a shorter 5-day (but still hard-core) trekking option in the same area; and a challenging 15-day rafting trip along the Tambopata River (half camping, half inns). A unique trip is the off-the-beaten path "Other Inca Trail"—the company also arranges luxury treks to Machu Picchu with stays at the cool inns owned and operated by **Mountain Lodges of Peru** (see below). Trips are helpfully rated for difficulty. The company was named one of *National Geographic Adventure*'s "Best Outfitters on Earth" in 2007.

Overseas Adventure Travel ★ (℃ 800/493-6824; www.oattravel.com) offers natural history and "soft adventure" itineraries, with optional add-on excursions. Tours are limited to 16 people and are guided by naturalists. All accommodations are in small hotels, lodges, or tent camps. The 11-day "Real Affordable Peru" includes rafting on the Urubamba and a *curandero* healing ceremony. The 16-day "Machu Picchu & Galápagos" tour features a good bit of walking. Amazon River cruises and rainforest trips are also featured.

Tropical Nature Travel ★★★ (℃ 877/827-8350; www.tropicalnaturetravel.com) is known as one of the most sophisticated conservation groups organizing travel to jungle wildlife lodges in Manu and Tambopata. In tandem with its local conservation partner, InkaNatura, it operates four lodges, including Manu Wildlife Center, Cock of the Rock Lodge, Sandoval Lake Lodge, and the new Heath River Wildlife Center; and its Amazon jungle trips can't be beat. The outfit has expanded its itineraries to include trekking, rafting, and archaeology culture trips to places such as Chachapoyas and Colca Canyon.

Wilderness Travel ★★★ (℃ 800/368-2794; www.wildernesstravel.com) is a Berkeley-based outfitter specializing in cultural, wildlife, and hiking group tours that are arranged with tiered pricing (the cost of the trip varies according to group size). There are 13 different tours to Peru, including a 17-day Trekking in the Cordillera Huayhuash Blanca, Choquequirao trail to Machu Picchu, and a unique "Peru Festivals Trek." Wilderness Travel also offers soft, luxury treks to Machu Picchu with stays at the cool inns owned and operated by **Mountain Lodges of Peru** (see below). Trips are helpfully graded according to difficulty.

Wildland Adventures ★★★ (℃ 800/345-4453; www.wildland.com), based in Seattle, is one of the top international outdoor-tour companies with operations in Peru. It offers excellent special-interest trekking and rainforest expedition programs, with customizing options. There are lodge-based programs, primarily in the jungle; trekking expeditions, such as the Machu Picchu Mountain lodges trek; and special adventures focusing on photographing Peru's "Ancient Lands and Native Spirits." Wildland's programs are well designed, guides are very professional, and the organization is focused on authentic travel experiences—all reasons *National Geographic Adventure* named it one of "Best Outfitters on Earth" in 2007.

In addition to these companies, many extremely well-regarded environmental organizations regularly offer organized trips to Peru. **The Nature Conservancy** ★★ (© 800/628-6860; www.nature.org/aboutus/travel/travel) offers "conservation journeys" with members; the trips change from year to year, but past trips to Peru have included a riverboat Amazon voyage that visits the Nature Conservancy project in the Pacaya-Samiria National Reserve. The **Smithsonian Institution** ★★ (© 877/338-8687; www.si.edu) offers "Smithsonian Journeys," study tours for members, which have included a river cruise of the northern Amazon and a long (and expensive) trip down the Amazon from Belém, Brazil, to Pevas, Peru. The **National Audubon Society** (© 800/967-7425; http://travel.audubon.org) also offers "Nature Odysseys," which focus on birding and natural history arranged through carefully selected travel partners. An excellent resource for information on ecotravel is **Sacred Earth** (www.sacredearth.com), a loose consortium of "ethnobotanists" and ecotravelers that publishes an e-zine and has links to a half-dozen featured trips and workshops in Peru, including Manu camping journeys and shamanistic "Listening to the Plants" tours of the northern Amazon.

PERUVIAN TOUR AGENCIES

Many tour companies based in the United States and elsewhere subcontract portions of their tours to established Peruvian companies on the ground in Lima, Cusco, and across the country. Though it's often simpler to go with international tour companies, in some cases, independent travelers can benefit by organizing their tours directly with local agencies. Prices on the ground can be cheaper than contracting a tour from abroad, but there are risks of not getting what you want when you want it. Also, the world of subcontracting can be byzantine, and even Peruvian travel agencies hire out adventure and outdoor specialists.

Local agencies offering adventure options abound, especially in Cusco, Arequipa, Huaraz, and Iquitos. These agencies can arrange everything from white-water rafting to day treks to horseback riding. Some tours might be held only when there are enough interested people or on fixed dates, so it's worthwhile to contact a few of the companies before you leave for Peru to find out what they might be doing when you arrive. See the sections on local tour and adventure agencies in each of the destination chapters; for travel in the Sacred Valley, Amazon Basin, Lake Titicaca, Colca Canyon, and the Huaraz area, these are pretty much indispensable unless you contract with an international operator prior to your trip.

Class Adventure Travel (CAT) ★ (© 877/240-4770 in the U.S. and Canada, 0207/0906-1259 in the U.K.; www.cat-travel.com) is a fine all-purpose agency with offices in Lima and Cusco (it also has offices in Bolivia, Chile, and Argentina). In addition to professionally organizing virtually any kind of travel detail in Peru, its adventure offerings include rafting, trekking, and jungle tours.

Explorandes Peru ★★ (© 01/715-2323; www.explorandes.com) has been doing trekking and river expeditions in Peru for nearly 3 decades, and has regional offices in Lima, Cusco, Huaraz, and Puno. One of the top high-end agencies for treks and mountaineering in Peru, it's reasonably priced and especially good for forming very small private groups. It offers a number of soft adventure trips (with stays in hotels and full- and half-day river trips) and an even more impressive lineup of real adventure, including cool, unique trips such as llama trekking to Chavín, a festival trek, rafting on the Apurímac River, treks on southern peaks around Cusco, and hard-core trekking in the Cordillera Blanca and Huayhuash. Amazon extensions are available.

Mountain Lodges of Peru ★★ (*©* 01/421-7777; www.mountainlodgesofperu. com), a Peruvian trekking company, has built a series of small, spectacular lodges on private lands in the Vilcabamba mountain range west of the Sacred Valley. The sleek inns have whirlpools, fireplaces, and nice dining rooms. The company offers its own 6-day treks to Machu Picchu and also contracts with a handful of international adventure tour operators, including **Backroads, Mountain Travel Sobek,** and **Wilderness Travel** (see above).

Peru Expeditions ★ (*©* 01/447-2057; www.peru-expeditions.com) is a Lima-based company run by Rafael Belmonte, an amiable fellow and dedicated cyclist. His company runs all kinds of cool trips across Peru, including treks, four-wheel-drive vehicle tours, and mountain biking, as well as Andean festivities tours, and more standard tours to destinations such as Arequipa, Cusco, and Colca Canyon.

Peru for Less ★★ (*©* 877/269-0309, or 203/002-0571 in the U.K.; www.perufor less.com), which began in Texas and is now based in Lima, has added a whole roster of well-designed and personalized alternative trekking tours in the Cusco region, including small-group treks to Choquequirao and Vilcabamba, to its slate of more standard travel packages.

SAS Travel Peru ★ (*©* 084/249-194; www.sastravelperu.com), based in Cusco, is one of the most popular agencies organizing outdoor travel for backpackers and budget-minded travelers. Its roster includes the Inca Trail, a number of short treks in the Cusco area and a couple of longer, more challenging mountain treks lasting up to a week. Jungle treks are to Manu and Tambopata. SAS also offers white-water rafting, paragliding, climbing, mountain biking, and horseback riding.

---

2 ACTIVITIES A TO Z

The listings in this section describe the best places to practice particular sports and activities and include the top tour operators and outfitters. If you want to focus on only one active sport during your trip to Peru, these companies are your best bets for quality equipment and knowledgeable service—but almost all of them will allow you to combine one activity with another or engage in general cultural sightseeing.

BALLOONING & HANG GLIDING

In the mid-1970s, two foreigners constructed a balloon out of cotton and reed in an effort to prove that ancient cultures could have used balloons to design the mysterious Nasca Line drawings in the southern desert sands. Too bad that didn't spark a wild interest in ballooning and hang gliding in Peru. So many parts of the country would be absolutely glorious to fly silently over: the Sacred Valley, the Nasca Lines, the valleys of the Callejón de Huaylas, the magnificent pre-Columbian ruins, and the great canyons near Arequipa. Alas, the only outfitter operating balloon flights in Peru is a U.S.-owned company, **Aero Sports Club of the Sacred Valley,** Av. de la Cultura 220, Ste. 36, Cusco (*©* 084/232-352; www.globosperu.com), and even it offers flights on an inconsistent basis, mainly in the Urubamba Valley. If you're interested, contact the company before

---

Fun Facts **Butterflies**

Peru has become famous among bird-watchers, but naturalists who are fans of butterflies are in for an equal treat. Peru has the greatest diversity of butterflies in the world and the largest number of species: 3,700 (more than those found in all of subequatorial Africa).

---

your trip to Peru (and have other backup plans). Flights are generally May through August only.

BIRD-WATCHING

Peru is one of the greatest countries on earth for birders. The bird population in Peru is, incredibly, about 10% of the world's total. With nearly 2,000 species of resident and migrant birds identified throughout Peru, great bird-watching sites abound.

Manu Biosphere Reserve, believed to have the highest concentration of bird life on the planet, is legendary among birders. It boasts more than 1,000 species of birds. Cocks-of-the-rock, quetzals, toucanets, tanagers, and seven species of colorful macaws await patient birders. Some visitors have spotted as many as 500 species in relatively short visits to Manu. For specialists, the **Manu Wildlife Center** has the best reputation among birders, although **Pantiacolla Lodge** is highly recommended, too.

The **Tambopata National Reserve** is also extraordinary for birding and more accessible than Manu. The reserve, about a third the size of Costa Rica, claims more species of birds (around 600) and butterflies (more than 1,200) than any place of similar size. Both Tambopata and Manu are famous for their *collpas,* or salt licks, where hundreds of macaws, parrots, and other birds appear daily to feed. Nearer to Puerto Maldonado, good birding areas include the Sandoval and Valencia lakes, but they cannot compare to either of the major reserves. **Explorer's Inn** is renowned as one of the top birding lodges in South America.

In the northern Amazon, the **Pacaya-Samiria National Reserve** is home to more than 500 species of birds. The northern Amazon doesn't have quite the reputation that the varied cloud forests leading to Manu and the rest of the southeastern jungle do, although there is excellent birding in and around the protected Machu Picchu Sanctuary. **Inkaterra Machu Picchu** (p. 284) organizes birding tours and has more than 100 species of birds on its property in Aguas Calientes.

A handful of jungle lodges and river-cruise operators offer specialized birding options, but none is as complete as the trips offered by the specialist tour operators below. Birding sites worth visiting are **Ornifolks,** a network of birding enthusiasts (www.ornifolks.org), and **WorldTwitch** (www.worldtwitch.com), which has links to birding lodges, tour operators, and organizations throughout Peru, as well as the Americas and the Caribbean. A portal with good information on birding in Peru is **Birding Peru** (www.birding-peru.com); it features birding forums, information about specialized tour operators, and birding news.

Although Peru is one of the top birding destinations in the world, specialists complain about the lack of an essential field guide. See "Peru in Popular Culture" in chapter 2, for a discussion on books about birding in Peru.

Birding Peru (www.birdingperu.com) is a Peru-based tour operator that links to birding trips offered by major outfitters to all regions of the country, including the highlands, coasts, and rainforest, and provides good general information on birding throughout Peru.

Field Guides ★★ (© 800/728-4953; www.fieldguides.com) is an Austin, Texas-based specialty bird-watching travel operator with trips worldwide. It features six birding trips to Peru, including the Manu Biosphere Reserve, Tambopata, Machu Picchu and the eastern slope of the Andes, the Amazon, and a 24-day tour of the endemic-rich region of northern Peru. Group size is limited to 14 participants.

Kolibri Expeditions ★ (© 01/273-7246; www.kolibriexpeditions.com), based in Lima, offers birding tours across Peru and South America, including condor-watching trips. Most are no-frills, budget camping trips, but the outfit now also offers a few pampered, high-end trips (such as the "Marvelous Spatuletail Tours").

Tanager Tours ★ (© 01/9858-3660; www.tanagertours.com) is a Dutch-owned specialist bird-watching tour operator based in Trujillo. It organizes birding trips to Manu, Puerto Maldonado, and many other spots in Peru.

WINGS ★ (© 888/293-6443; www.wingsbirds.com) is a specialty bird-watching travel operator with 3 decades of experience in the field. It promotes three trips to Peru, including an 18-day trip to Machu Picchu and the Manu Biosphere Reserve and one to the north and Andes in search of the long-whiskered owlet. Group size is usually between 6 and 18 people.

HORSEBACK RIDING

Lovers of horseback riding will find several areas in Peru to pursue their interest, as well as hotels and operators that can arrange everything from a couple hours in a saddle to 2-week trips on horseback. The best areas for treks on horseback are the Colca Canyon, near Arequipa, and the Callejón de Huaylas, the valley near the peaks of the Cordillera Blanca; a couple of local and international tour operators offer horse trekking in those areas. Otherwise, your options are mostly limited to a few country hotels in Cajamarca, the Sacred Valley, and Colca Valley.

In the area around Pisco, horseback riding is available in Ica at **Hotel Las Dunas** (p. 165). For riding on the outskirts of Cusco, the **Casa Andina** hotel group (www.casa-andina.com) arranges excellent day-long trips, available for walking between the ruins (Sacsayhuamán, Q'enko, Puca Pucara, and Tambomachay) just beyond Cusco and in the countryside. In the Sacred Valley, check out **Sonesta Posadas del Inca** (p. 250) and **Sol y Luna Lodge & Spa** (p. 249); in Ollantaytambo, you can usually arrange horseback riding along valley trails by asking around the main square. The **Las Casitas del Colca** (p. 339) has horses for treks in the Colca Valley and Canyon; local agencies in Arequipa that arrange horseback treks through the Colca Canyon include **Colca Trek** (© 054/202-461; www.colcatrek.com) and **Peru Trekking** (© 054/223-404). In Huaraz, try **Andino Club Hotel** (p. 429) or **Monttrek** (below), which arranges good horseback mountain and valley treks. A number of country hotels just outside Cajamarca have horses for riding, including **Hotel & Spa Laguna Seca, Hotel Posada del Puruay,** and **Hostal Portada del Sol Hacienda;** see chapter 12 for details. Finally, most people go to the jungle for bird-watching or canoe trips, but **Manu Expeditions** (© 084/226-671; www.manuexpeditions.com) organizes horseback riding from the Manu Wildlife Center.

Tour Operators

Adventure Specialists (© 719/630-2086; www.adventurespecialists.org) organizes horse-supported Machu Picchu treks, including the unique 8-day "Machu Picchu Pony Express."

Monttrek (© 043/421-124), based in Huaraz, offers horseback riding and other adventure sports in the area around the Cordillera Blanca.

Perol Chico ★★ (© 084/9846-24475; www.perolchico.com), in Urubamba, operates a ranch and is one of the top horseback-riding agencies in Peru, offering full riding vacations with Peruvian Paso horses and stays at the ranch, as well as 1- and 2-day day rides (and up to 12-day horseback adventures in the Sacred Valley).

Southwind Adventures (© 800/377-9463; www.southwindadventures.com) offers horse-packing among its roster of adventure trips in Peru.

Sol y Luna Lodge & Spa (p. 249) in Urubamba also organizes horseback-riding programs that range from a half-day trip to 14-day trips in the Sacred Valley on Peruvian Paso horses.

JUNGLE LODGES & TOURS

Nearly two-thirds of Peru is rainforest, and options for exploring it are myriad, from jungle lodges to independently guided treks, to river cruises. The most important issue is choosing which major jungle destination fits best with your interest, time, and budget. Nearly all the international and Peruvian tour operators and wholesalers that do outdoor and adventure travel—for that matter, almost all agencies that handle travel to Peru—have some sort of jungle packages available. Some, of course, are more immersion-oriented than others. You can do a jungle add-on to a trip to Cusco or a full-scale jungle trek and cruise lasting 2 weeks or more. See the earlier tour operators listed in "Organized Adventure Trips," the packagers listed in "Special-Interest Trips" (in chapter 3), and, of course, the individual lodges and companies in chapter 11.

MOUNTAIN BIKING

Mountain biking is still in its infancy in Peru, although fat-tire options are growing fast. **Colca Valley** and **Canyon, Huaraz** and the **Callejón de Huaylas,** and the **Sacred Valley** are the major areas for off-road cycling. The **Manu jungle** is also good for hard-core biking. Several tour companies in those places rent bikes, and the quality of the equipment is continually being upgraded. If you plan to do a lot of biking and are very attached to your rig, bring your own. See individual destination chapters for rental listings.

My favorite mountain-biking spots are horse and mountain trails in the spectacular Callejón de Huaylas, which provide the kind of amazing climbing found in the Rockies of the western United States and mountain views that are second to none. Mountain bikers, along with other adventure-sports fans, descend on Huaraz and the valley every June for its celebrated Semana del Andinismo. The Colca Valley is also an outstanding region for hard-core mountain biking, though there are fewer tour outfitters targeting the area. For gentler but also incredibly scenic trail riding, you can't beat the Sacred Valley.

Tour Operators & Outfitters

In Huaraz and the Callejón de Huaylas, the top two agencies for mountain biking are **Mountain Bike Adventures** ★★ (© 043/424-259; www.chakinaniperu.com), run by Julio Olaza, and **Pony Expeditions** ★ (© 043/391-642; www.ponyexpeditions.com), run by Alberto Cafferata.

THE ACTIVE VACATION PLANNER

ACTIVITIES A TO Z

Which Jungle? Comparing Piranhas and Monkeys

Choosing where to go in the Peruvian jungle is complicated. To begin, you need to define how much time and money you can spend, how you want to get there, and how much immersion—expeditions range from light to hard-core—you're interested in once there.

Cusco is the best base for excursions to the southern jungle, while ecolodges and cruise trips in the northern jungle are accessible from Iquitos, to which most visitors fly. For many, the relative proximity of the southern Amazon basin to Cusco and the Sacred Valley makes a jungle experience in that part of the country all the more appealing.

Of the major jungle regions, the Manu Biosphere Reserve is the least touched by man. It is the most inaccessible zone and, therefore, also the most expensive for expeditions. Most visits require close to a week. But Manu also provides perhaps the best opportunities for viewing Amazon wildlife (especially birds). The Tambopata National Reserve also offers excellent jungle experiences and wildlife, including easy access to the splendid macaw clay lick, with less expenditure of time and money.

Peru's northeastern jungle near Iquitos has suffered the most penetration by man and tour operators, having been accessible to travelers for much longer than other parts of the Peruvian jungle. For travelers, though, the region is more convenient, with many more expeditions and lodges operating there, and prices are generally more affordable. Note, however, that the chances of phenomenal large mammal sightings—which are remote anywhere—are even slimmer in the northern Amazon. Travelers with limited time and budgets often fly to Iquitos (by far the most interesting jungle city in Peru) and hop on an inexpensive jungle lodge tour from there, although similarly reasonably priced tours are available from Puerto Maldonado in the south.

Peru Bike ★ (© **01/260-8225;** www.perubike.com), based in Lima, has a great schedule of Andes mountain-biking trips across Peru, including Huascarán and Lake Titicaca loops, and cool day trips, on GT bikes. **Monttrek** (© **043/421-124**) also offers organized mountain-biking tours. **Peru Expeditions ★** (© **01/447-2057;** www.peru-expeditions.com), based in Lima, is run by a former top cyclist and runs mountain-biking trips in the Sacred Valley to Machu Picchu.

In Cusco, **Peru Discovery ★** , Triunfo (Sunturwasi) 392, Of. 113 (© **054/274-541;** www.perudiscovery.com/english) is the top specialist, with a half-dozen bike trips that include hard-core excursions. The local outfitters **Amazonas Explorer** (© **084/252-846;** www.amazonas-explorer.com), **Apumayo Expediciones ★** (© **084/9847-66732;** www.apumayo.com), **Eric Adventures ★★** (© **084/234-764;** www.ericadventures.com), and **Instinct Travel** (© **084/233-451;** www.instinct-travel.com) offer 1- to 5-day organized mountain-biking excursions for novices and experienced single-trackers. In the Sacred Valley, **Ecomontana** (www.ecomontana.com), run by the mountain biker Omar Zarzar, rents good mountain bikes and organizes extended as well as shorter cyclotourism

rides around Urubamba, with top equipment. **Manu Adventures** (© 084/261-640;
www.manuadventures.com) and **Manu Nature Tours** (© 084/252-721; www.manu
peru.com) offer mountain-biking add-ons to lodge stays and jungle treks. In Arequipa,
Colca Trek (© 054/202-461; www.colcatrek.com) and **Peru Trekking** (© 054/223-
404) feature mountain biking in the Colca Canyon.

RIVER CRUISES

River cruises along the Amazon and its tributaries are one of the best ways to experience
the Peruvian jungle. Cruises give travelers the option of floating luxury and good meals,
as well as the ability to stop in and see several different environments and river and
jungle communities. The huge and remote **Pacaya-Samiria National Reserve** is one of
the best and most up-and-coming zones for cruises into pristine jungle and wetlands; see
chapter 11 for details. Iquitos-based **Jungle Expeditions** ★ (© 065/262-340; www.
junglex.com) and **Green Tracks Amazon Tours & Cruises** (© 800/892-1035; www.
amazontours.net) offer a variety of river cruises in the northern Amazon, and **International Expeditions** ★ (© 800/633-4734; www.internationalexpeditions.com) is one of
the most experienced tour operators organizing luxurious river cruises from the United
States. But by far the coolest thing in cruises is the newest entry in the Peruvian water,
upscale **Aqua Expeditions** ★★★ (© 866/603-3687; www.aquaexpeditions.com), a
sleek modern ship with haute cuisine by a famous Peruvian chef that's far from your
typical boat or cruise fare.

SURFING

Though it remains somewhat under the general public's radar, Peru has recently become
one of the world's top surfing destinations among surfing aficionados. It has 2,000km
(1,200 miles) of Pacific coastline and huge possibilities for left and right reef breaks,
point breaks, and monster waves, and boarders can hit the surf year-round. Northern
beaches, especially Puerto Chicama north of Trujillo, and Cabo Blanco and other spots
near Máncora, even farther north, draw surfers to some of the best waves in South
America. There are also good surfing beaches south of Lima, though they aren't as spectacular as in the north, where the waters are also much warmer. The north is better from
October to March, while the surfing in the south is good April through December and
tops in May. The best surfing site, with webcams and reports on water conditions and
the best beaches up and down Peru, is **www.peruazul.com**. Check out **www.wannasurf.
com/spot/South_America/Peru** for basic surfing information and maps, as well as **Wave
Hunters** (below) for good information and surf tours to Peru. For more details, see
"Outdoor Activities & Spectator Sports" and "Side Trips from Lima" in chapter 6.

(**Fun Facts** **Whose Board Came First?**

Surfing is generally thought to have its origins in Polynesia or the South Sea
Islands, but several historians claim that men first hopped aboard things not so
dissimilar to modern surfboards in ancient Peru some 2,000 years ago. Textiles
and pottery of pre-Columbian, north-coast civilizations depict men cruising
waves on totora-reed rafts (although they were more likely fishermen in search
of dinner than rad dudes out looking for point breaks).

Wave Hunters (© 760/494-7392; www.wavehunters.com/peru-surfing/peru.asp), a California-based organization, offers a surfeit of good information on Peru's coastline and celebrated waves, as well as different, inexpensive small-group surfing tours in central and northern Peru, including stays at Pico Alto International Surf Camp in Punta Hermosa. They work with a group called Octopus Surf Tours in northern Peru.

Pure Vacations (© 0845/229-0045; www.purevacations.com/south-america/peru/), based in the U.K., has organized surf travel since 1999 and combines northern Peru with Ecuador for 14-day surf trips.

TREKKING & MOUNTAIN CLIMBING

Peru is one of the world's great trekking and mountain-climbing destinations, and its mountains and gorgeous valleys, ideal for everything from hard-core climbs to 6,000m (19,700-ft.) peaks to gentle walks through green valleys, are one of the country's calling cards. Experienced mountaineers, ice climbers, trekkers, and regular old athletic types and hikers beeline to Peru to experience the grandeur of the great Cordillera Blanca, the volcanoes and canyons around Arequipa, and, of course, the Andes mountains in and around Cusco. The most celebrated trek, of course, is the Inca Trail to Machu Picchu— truly one of the world's most rewarding treks, provided that the crowds don't get you down in high season. Many agencies in Cusco offer guided treks to Machu Picchu; so do larger international operators, some of whom are now offering newer alternatives to the Inca Trail. See chapter 9 for additional information on recommended tour operators.

Trekking circuits of varying degrees of difficulty lace the valleys and mountain ridges of Peru's *sierra*. Yet only a few have become popular, commercial trekking routes. Independent trekkers who like to blaze their own trail (metaphorically speaking—you should always stick to existing trails) have a surfeit of options in Peru for uncrowded treks.

For adventure tourism, trekking and climbing rank with expeditions into the Amazon jungle as the biggest outdoor draws in Peru. Scores of outfitters, both international and local, organize a full run of mountain-climbing and trekking package tours. If you do outdoor travel in Peru, you should include soft trekking, at a minimum, and many agencies specialize in trekking and climbing. Independent travelers can hook up with local agencies for tailored experiences. And travelers of all stripes can set out on easy treks in any of the areas above. There are details on accessible trekking in the destination chapters; see especially chapters 9, 10, and 12.

The best months for climbing are during the dry season, between May and September (June–Aug is perhaps best). In Huaraz, the Semana de Andinismo, held annually in June, attracts mountain climbers from around the world.

One of the best independent resources for hiking and climbing information in Peru is the **South American Explorers** clubhouses in Lima and Cusco (© 01/445-3306 in Lima, or 084/245-484 in Cusco; www.saexplorers.org). You have to become a member first ($50 per year) for full access to their trail reports and other information, but if you're serious about trails and climbs in Peru, it's money well spent. You can join via the website or on the spot at a clubhouse.

Tour Operators

There are numerous candidates to organize trekking tours of Peru from abroad. See "Organized Adventure Trips," earlier in this chapter, for complete listings. Among the best are **Adventure Specialists, Andean Treks, Mountain Travel Sobek, Southwind**

Adventures, **Wildland Adventures,** and **Wilderness Travel.** All have plenty of options, good guides, and high levels of professionalism. One of the top Peruvian operators with a national reach is **Explorandes;** it and all the agencies authorized to lead Inca Trail treks offer many options in Cusco and across Peru. Other full-purpose travel agencies, such as **Peru for Less,** are also jumping in to offer their clients a series of alternative treks in the Cusco highlands and elsewhere.

The local agencies listed in the chapters 9, 10, and 12 are the best places to turn if you want to organize some trekking or climbing once on the ground in Peru. There are also excellent local agencies specializing in experienced mountain-climbing expeditions in Arequipa, Huaraz, and Caraz. The best groups arrange a large number of area climbs and have equipment rental. Several have a 24-hour mountain-rescue service.

WHITE-WATER RAFTING

Peru, home to the origin of the mighty Amazon and great canyon rivers, has some stunning opportunities for white-water rafting. Whether you're a total novice or a world-class river runner, Peru has fantastic white water suited to your abilities. The rivers flowing through the **Colca** and **Cotahuasi canyons,** other rivers nearer to Arequipa, and the Andean rivers of the **Urubamba Valley** stand out. A good adventurous experience is rafting in the Amazon jungle on the **Tambopata River.** There's also good white water on the **Río Santa** in the Callejón de Huaylas.

If you're just experimenting with river rafting, stick to Class II and III rivers. If you already know your way around a raft and a paddle, there are plenty of Class IV and V sections to run. Hard-core runners come to Peru for some fantastic, multiday rafting trips to Class V and even Class VI rivers in remote canyons. The best months for rafting are May through September, when water levels are low. (During the rainy season, canyon rivers can be extremely dangerous.)

Tour Operators

A half-dozen agencies in Arequipa, Cusco, and the Sacred Valley organize a range of local white-water opportunities. See chapters 9 and 10 for more information. Specialists include **Amazonas Explorer ★** (✆ **084/252-846;** www.amazonas-explorer.com), which offers white-water rafting tours that can be combined with Inca Trail treks. Trips, which feature small groups, can be booked from abroad. Among its Peru trips are rafting on the Río Apurímac, inflatable canoeing on the source of the Amazon (combined with trekking the Inca Trail), rainforest rafting, and extreme Class IV to VI in Cotahuasi, the world's deepest canyon. **SwissRaft Peru ★★** , Plateros 369 (✆ **084/264-124;** www.swissraft-peru.com), based in Cusco, organizes 1-day rafting trips year-round on the Apurímac, Cusipata, and Chuquicahuana, as well as 4-day trips on the Apurímac.

---

3 PERU'S NATIONAL PARKS & NATURE RESERVES

Peru's extraordinary natural environment features a wealth of protected areas, wildlife reserves, and archaeological zones. Dozens of national parks and nature preserves make up a bit more than 10% of Peru. The majority of these national parks and nature reserves are undeveloped tropical forests, with few services or facilities available for tourism. Others, however, offer easier access to their wealth of natural wonders. The discussion below is not a complete listing of all of Peru's national parks and protected areas. Rather, it details the ones that are the most accessible and most rewarding for visitors, including several of the largest and most biodiverse on the planet.

Many of them require visitor's permits, for a small fee. If you go with an organized tour, the tour operators almost always take care of the bureaucratic details and include the fees in their package price. See the listings of specialty tour operators in "Organized Adventure Trips," earlier in this chapter.

Peru's protected natural areas go by several names in Spanish, according to distinct legal statutes and protections: *parques nacionales* (national parks), *reserves nacionales* (national reserves), *sanctuarios nacionales/históricos* (national or historic sanctuaries), and *zonas reservadas* (reserve zones), among others.

MANU NATIONAL PARK & BIOSPHERE RESERVE ★★★

Manu is probably the most famous national park in Peru. Covering nearly a million hectares, Manu National Park & Biosphere Reserve is the second-largest protected area in the country and one of the largest in South America. It is also thought to be the most biodiverse zone on earth. Created in 1973, the park reserve is on the eastern slopes of the Andes within the Amazon basin and comprises an extraordinary variety of habitats, including tropical lowland forest, mountain forest, and grasslands. The reserve zone contains the lower Manu River, the Río Alto Madre de Dios, and a number of beautiful oxbow lakes. About 1,000 bird species—about a quarter of all birds known in South America and 10% of all species in the world—and more than 200 species of mammals have been identified. Also found in the park are at least 13 endangered wildlife species, including black caimans, giant river otters, and ocelots. Botanists have claimed that Manu has a greater number of plant species than any other protected area on earth.

Manu is superb for observing wildlife, but trips to Manu are lengthy and costly. Most trips bus travelers in and fly them out by light aircraft. There are very few lodges within the designated reserve and cultural zones, and access to the reserve zone is by organized tour. Independent visits are possible in the cultural zone only.

TAMBOPATA NATIONAL RESERVE ★★★

The Tambopata National Reserve is more accessible and less restrictive than Manu. The park is made up principally of lowland forest along the Tambopata River. A number of lodges are in and around the reserve, accessible from Puerto Maldonado. The lodges offer shorter stays but usually include naturalist-led expeditions to remote areas. Independent travel with a guide can also be arranged in Puerto Maldonado. Although Manu is more celebrated and probably more pristine, with greater species diversity, the flora and fauna that can be observed by most visitors at Tambopata are remarkably similar.

HUASCARAN NATIONAL PARK ★★★

Home to a chain of snowcapped mountains that comprise the longest tropical range in the world, the 161km (100-mile) Cordillera Blanca in the central Andes, Huascarán is a mecca for climbers and a host of outdoor and adventure travelers. Its scenery and offerings—mountain climbing, trekking, horseback riding, white-water rafting, fishing, and mountain biking, among others—are perhaps unequaled in the Americas. With 200 alpine lakes, 600 glaciers, spectacular mountain vistas, and nearby ancient pre-Columbian ruins, though, Huascarán is also a magnet for travelers who want to appreciate the scenery with just their eyes, not necessarily their legs and lungs.

Fun Facts Giant Otters

One of the most fascinating creatures that visitors have a chance of spotting in the southeastern Amazon basin in Peru is the giant otter *(Pteronura brasiliensis)*, the largest of the 13 otter species in the world. Hunted for its pelt, it has landed on the World Conservation Union ignominious Red List of Endangered Species and has probably been eliminated in Argentina and Uruguay. It has recovered in Peru, but fewer than a couple hundred probably exist.

Giant otters today are primarily "hunted" by tourists and photographers. The large and very active animals are found in lakes and rivers of tropical lowlands, where they can rather easily be observed. Conservationists are concerned that otters in Manu and Tambopata, among other places, have suffered from human interference in the form of tourist canoes, which leads to long-term changes in behavior and decreases in reproduction. Less invasive observation towers and viewing platforms have been constructed in Cochas Otorongo and Salvador in the Manu Biosphere Reserve. The Giant Otter Project of the Frankfurt Zoological Society (www.giantotterperu.org) is overseeing monitoring and protection of the species in the Pacaya-Samiria National Reserve and the Manu and Bahuaja-Sonene national parks in southeastern Peru.

Named for the highest peak in Peru, the park's altitude ranges from 2,500m to 6,768m (8,202 ft.–22,205 ft.) and includes more than two dozen snowcapped peaks above 6,000m (19,700 ft.). Huascarán is the second-highest park in the South American Andes. Climbing and trekking opportunities range from expert to moderate, with the latter easily managed by anyone in good shape. Arrangements for manageable 2-day walks and 2-week camping hikes crisscrossing the formidable passes of the Cordillera can be easily arranged in Huaraz and Caraz.

For independent treks in the park, a permit must be obtained from the park office in Huaraz. Some locals and foreign visitors have complained that the national park is not being managed as well as it might be, and that trash has accumulated along the major trails.

MACHU PICCHU HISTORICAL SANCTUARY ★★

Machu Picchu is much more than the famous Inca ruins carved into a mountainside. The Machu Picchu Historical Sanctuary, named a UNESCO natural and cultural World Heritage Site in 1983, is a designated archaeological zone and 33,000-hectare (81,545-acre) preserve. International concern over environmental damage to Machu Picchu and the Inca Trail led the Peruvian government to introduce more stringent measures to protect the zone's natural heritage, including limits on the number of people allowed on the trail. Proposals that would severely compromise the natural environment, such as the building of cable cars to the ruins, have been defeated, at least for now.

International environmental and conservation groups, such as World Parks Endowment, have been lobbying the Peruvian government to create a large Inca National Park and expand the protected area around Machu Picchu into the neighboring Vilcanota and Vilcabamba mountains, which would establish a major protected area.

THE ACTIVE VACATION PLANNER

5

PERU'S NATIONAL PARKS & NATURE RESERVES

PACAYA-SAMIRIA NATIONAL RESERVE ★★★

The largest natural reserve in Peru, Pacaya-Samiria is one of the Amazon's (and the world's) richest wildlife habitats. Covering more than 2 million hectares (5 million acres) of pristine rainforest and wetlands in the north-central Amazon region (about 322km/200 miles south of Iquitos), the reserve is difficult to penetrate during the rainy season (Dec–Mar). The reserve is full of rivers and lakes, and it boasts some of the Amazon's most abundant species of flora and fauna.

Pacaya-Samiria is considerably less accessible than the jungle farther north and is much less visited than Manu or Tambopata. Several tour operators now organize river cruises, canoe trips, and camping expeditions, and a couple of native communities are promoting camping trips and immersion experiences. A permit from INRENA, the Peruvian parks authority, is required to enter the preserve.

PARACAS NATIONAL RESERVE ★

South of Lima, in the department of Ica on the southern coast, this peninsula is blessed with an abundance of marine wildlife and seabirds. About two-thirds of the 335,000-hectare (827,800-acre) reserve is ocean; the desert landscape is barren and rather absent of most plant life. The Ballestas Islands, contained within the nature preserve, are rich in bird and sea lion life, and present excellent and very accessible opportunities for viewing wildlife up close.

---

4 SAFETY & ETIQUETTE IN WILD PERU

Although many outdoor travel itineraries in Peru require no special medications or vaccinations, there are special considerations for jungle travel. Additionally, acclimatization to the high altitude of the Andes is essential for anyone seeking to do trekking or climbing in the mountains.

For tropical travel in Peru, the Centers for Disease Control and Prevention recommends vaccinations against yellow fever, hepatitis A or immunoglobulin (IG), hepatitis B, typhoid, and booster doses for tetanus-diphtheria and measles, as well as pills for malaria. For more detailed information, see "Health," in chapter 3.

Most tours and activities are extremely safe, but there are risks involved in any adventure activity. The risks involved in mountain climbing, ice climbing, and white-water rafting are considerable. Know and respect your own physical limits and skills (or lack thereof) before undertaking any high-risk activity.

Be prepared for extremes in temperature and rainfall, and wide fluctuations in weather. A sunny morning hike can quickly become a cold and wet ordeal, so it's a good idea to carry some form of rain gear when hiking in the rainforest, bring sufficient protection against the cold at high altitudes, and have a dry change of clothing waiting at the end of the trail. Be sure to bring plenty of sunscreen, no matter where you travel. See "What to Bring," below, for more suggestions.

If you do any trekking or camping, exercise caution with the native species that live in natural habitats. Don't go poking under rocks or fallen branches: Snakebites are very rare, but don't do anything to increase the odds. If you do encounter a snake, stay calm, don't make any sudden movements, and *do not* try to handle it. The chance of getting bitten by a venomous snake is small; however, if you're bitten, wash out the bite and surrounding area very thoroughly (don't go Hollywood and try to suck out the venom). Because the bite might cause swelling, remove your jewelry. If symptoms persist, seek medical attention; the best way to demonstrate to a doctor what kind of snake bit you, of course, is to hand over the dead snake—certainly not always possible. Also beware of centipedes, scorpions, and spiders, including tarantulas, brown recluses, and black widows. If you are bitten by a dog or another creature, such as a bat, there is a risk of rabies. Wash out the wound thoroughly with soap and water, and seek medical attention. For a detailed "disease risk analysis" and other precautions, take a look at **Travel Medicine**'s website at **www.travmed.com**.

Avoid swimming in jungle rivers unless a guide or local operator can vouch for their safety. Although white-water sections and stretches in mountainous areas are generally pretty safe, many rivers in the Amazon basin are home to contingents of crocodile and caiman populations.

Bugs and bug bites (and blisters) will probably be your greatest health concern in the Peruvian wilderness. For the most part, bugs are merely an inconvenience, although mosquitoes can carry malaria or dengue (see "Health" in chapter 3 for more information). Strong repellent and proper clothing will minimize both the danger and the inconvenience. On beaches, you might be bitten by sand fleas. These nearly invisible insects leave an irritating welt. Try not to scratch because this can lead to open sores and infections.

However, in all probability, Peru's bounteous nature needs to be protected from visitors more than visitors need to be protected from it. A fundamental component of enjoying nature is leaving the natural environment undisturbed. The responsible outdoor traveler's maxim is: Take nothing but memories (and photos); leave nothing but footprints. Do not cut or uproot plants or flowers. Pack out everything you pack in, and *never* litter. Leave places the way you found them. If you see garbage lying around in protected areas, pack it out, along with your own trash. Don't scratch your name or any other graffiti on trees or ancient monuments. On trails, bury your excrement as far as possible from the trail. Over the years, too many insensitive trekkers along the Inca Trail, among other spots, did not follow this common-sense advice and did so much damage that international organizations, such as UNESCO, worried about the trail's survival.

To support local communities and appreciate what you have the rare opportunity to experience, it's a great idea to use (and adequately tip or pay) local guides and porters, and support locally owned businesses and artisans.

5 WHAT TO BRING

Outdoor and adventure travel in Peru requires some special gear, and it's a good idea to come prepared; you're more likely to find a better selection of equipment, apparel, and other outdoor gear at home than you are in Peru. You can rent some equipment, such as crampons for ice climbing, but you'd be wise to bring most nontechnical items with you.

The most basic items for travelers to Peru who are doing any sort of light adventure, such as trekking or jungle lodge stays, are (already broken-in and preferably waterproof) **hiking boots** (it's not a bad idea to take them in a carry-on or wear them on the plane, to avoid their loss), outdoor apparel such as **fleece pullovers,** and a **daypack.**

Essential gear for almost all travelers to Peru includes

- a sun hat
- sunscreen
- cold-weather and water-repellent clothing
- light trekking shoes or boots
- several pairs of thick socks

Additional items for light adventure include

- good backpacking or climbing boots
- a base layer (thermal underwear or wicking-quality shirt)
- malarial pills (if traveling to jungle regions)
- insect repellent
- a pocketknife
- toilet paper
- a flashlight or headlamp
- a mosquito net
- a sleeping bag
- diarrhea medicine
- energy bars or other trail snack foods
- sports sandals or comfortable slides for post-climbing and trekking, or for river and wet-weather wear
- a water bottle or other portable hydration system
- a good internal-frame backpack

Stuff to bring for hard-core adventure travel includes

- food supplies and cooking equipment
- a filter and/or water-purification tablets
- a first-aid kit
- a compass and whistle
- a tent, camping stove, and cookware
- adequate fuel
- topographical maps of trails

6 VOLUNTEER & STUDY PROGRAMS

Study and volunteer programs, including Spanish-language programs, are often a great way to travel in and experience a country with greater depth than most independent and package travel allows. Cultural immersion and integration with locals are the aims of many such programs, leading to a richer and more unique experience for many travelers.

Volunteering, in particular, often leads to greater culture sensitivity and cross-cultural learning experiences. Especially in a developing, largely poor country such as Peru, volunteers see up-close the realities of the lack of running water and electricity, the relative absence of luxuries, and simple, home-cooked foods—not to mention local customs and traditions. And, at least for a short time, volunteers get the rewarding opportunity to lend their abilities and sweat toward addressing some of the challenges Peruvians face. Such aspects of Peruvian life might be considerably more difficult to apprehend if staying in nice hotels and dining at upscale restaurants.

Most volunteer organizations are not-for-profit entities that charge participants to go abroad (to cover administrative and other costs), so volunteering isn't usually a way to get a free vacation. If you're concerned, though, ask about the cost breakdown for costs and field expenses. Any established, reputable volunteer organization should be willing to do this. Then you could always compare those costs to what traveling on your own would amount to.

Below are several institutions and organizations that work on humanitarian and sustainable development projects in Peru. Some international relief organizations, such as **Doctors Without Borders** (www.doctorswithoutborders.org) and **CARE** (www.care.org), accept volunteers to work crises and relief efforts. The devastating earthquakes in southern Peru in 2001 and 2007 brought hundreds of volunteers to Peru.

VOLUNTEER PROGRAMS

Cross-Cultural Solutions★★★ (② 800/380-4777; www.crossculturalsolutions.org), with offices in New Rochelle, New York, and Brighton, U.K., offers weeklong volunteer programs in Peru (in Lima's Villa El Salvador shantytown and Ayacucho, formerly a stronghold of the guerilla organization the Shining Path). The "Volunteer Abroad" section lists a number of opportunities for volunteering in Peru, including teaching and environmental research. **Projects Abroad** ★★ (② 888/839-3535; www.projects-abroad.org), with headquarters in New York and a local field office in Urubamba (in the Sacred Valley), organizes several unique volunteer and internship opportunities in Peru, including Inca restoration projects (such as the Sacsayhuamán ruins on the outskirts of Cusco), rainforest conservation, teaching, and nursing. **ProWorld**★ (② 877/429-6753 in the U.S. and Canada, or 0870/750-7202 in the U.K.; www.myproworld.org) has its headquarters in Bellingham, Washington, and it offers work, study and internship programs in Peru in the fields of health, environmental conservation, and social and economic development are based in Cusco and Urubamba. The organization has built schools, irrigation systems, and fish farms. **World Leadership School**★★ (② 888/831-8109; www.worldleadershipschool.com) is a Colorado-based organization that operates 3- to 4-week programs, concentrating on infrastructure and natural disaster prevention in El Carmen on the desert coast; cultural preservation in Ollantaytambo, in the Sacred Valley; and climate change and ecosystem preservation in Puerto Maldonado, the gateway to the southern Amazon jungle. **Mundo Azul** ★★ (② 01/99410-4206; www.mundoazul.org), based in Lima, takes volunteers on environmental conservation and sustainable development programs along the coast (marine biology research) and in the rainforest (threatened species). Trips off the coast south of Lima to view and photographically document the large population of playful dolphins may be the most fun you can have doing an environmentally conscious volunteer program.

Other volunteer programs include **Habitat for Humanity** ★★★ (② 800/422-4828; www.habitat.org), with a base in Arequipa (Comité Nacional Hábitat para la Humanidad Perú; ② 054/422-724), and **Volunteers for Peace** (② 802/259-2759; www.vfp.org), based in Vermont.

RESEARCH OPPORTUNITIES

Earthwatch Institute (② 800/776-0188; www.earthwatch.org) has a unique mission: It sends travelers out to work in the field alongside scientists involved in archaeology and environmental conservation. There are three Peru research and education trips: You can join a 13-day excavation of a pre-Inca site, assist with research of Peruvian macaws, or document the biology of Andean rivers. But the trips are not all work; they're a way to see a fascinating slice of the country from an insider's—academic or conservationist—perspective.

SPANISH-LANGUAGE PROGRAMS

Local language schools, primarily located in Cusco as well as Lima and Arequipa, and offering both short- and long-term study programs, often with home stays, are listed in chapter 8. **International Partners for Study Abroad** (www.studyabroadinternational.com/file/schools_Peru.html) lists a number of Spanish-study programs in Cusco. **Gorp-Travel** (© 877/440-GORP [4677]; www.gorptravel.com) occasionally lists Spanish-study programs of short duration in Peru and other South American countries; follow the "Learning Vacations" link on the website for options.

One standout school in Cusco is the **Amigos Spanish School,** Zaguan del Cielo B-23 (© 084/242-292; www.spanishcusco.com); it's a nonprofit school that assists disadvantaged children through its Amigos Foundation. In Lima, **El Sol Escuela de Español,** Grimaldo de Solar 469, Miraflores (© 800/381-1806; http://elsol.idiomasperu.com), marries language classes to cooking workshops, dance classes, and other activities. Other schools to try in Lima are the **Instituto Cultural Peruano Norteamericano,** Angamos Oeste 160, Miraflores (© 01/241-1940; www.icpna.edu.pe) and **Instituto de Idiomas,** Camino Real 1037, San Isidro (© 01/442-8761). In **Arequipa,** classes are on offer via the **Centro de Intercambio Cultural,** Cercado Urbanización Universitaria (© 054/221-165; www.ceicaperu.com); **Centro de Idiomas UNSA,** San Agustín 106 (© 054/247-524); and **Centro Cultural Peruano Norteamericano,** Melgar 209 (© 054/801-022).

CULINARY VACATIONS & COOKING CLASSES

Peru's sophisticated, diverse cuisine has attracted a great deal of worldwide attention in the past decade, and gastronomic tourism is beginning to take hold in Peru. Two companies offer food-centric vacations. **A Taste of Peru** ★ (© 01/247-5208; www.atasteofperu.com) is run by two young Peruvian sisters—one now based in Northern California, the other in Madrid—with impressive resumes in the culinary world, in the U.S., Europe, Peru, and Asia. They offer half- and full-day culinary experiences, as well as 8-day foodie trips to Lima, Cusco, and Machu Picchu. Their upscale gourmet trips take in food markets and restaurants in Lima and Cusco, and participants attend pisco tastings and ceviche demonstrations.

Pica Peru ★★ (© 866/440-2561; www.peruculinaryvacations.com), based in Denver, Colorado, is run by Kazia Jankowski, a food writer and author of the *Moon Peru* travel guide. Her new company offers culinary tours that include cooking classes, beginning in Lima restaurants and then traveling to Cusco, the Sacred Valley, and Machu Picchu, or instead venture to the north coast and the surfing capital Máncora. Trips last 9 to 10 days, with a maximum of 8 travelers, and includes four cooking classes.

Aracari ★★★ (© 312/239-8726 in the U.S., or 020/3287-5262 in the U.K.; www.aracari.com), an upscale Peruvian agency that designs excellent custom tours, offers a "Peru for Art Lovers and Foodies" trip and creates personalized culinary tours with exclusive visits to private houses and haciendas offered for private luncheons and cocktails, as well as cooking classes, visits to food markets and dining at some of the finest restaurants in Peru.

Lima

Lima once ranked as the richest and most important city in the Americas and was considered to be the most beautiful colonial settlement in the region. Founded in 1535 by the conquistador Francisco Pizarro, the Spanish Crown's "City of Kings" quickly became the center of power and trade for the entire American vice regency that stretched from Quito to Santiago. Lima was home to some of the Americas' finest baroque and Renaissance churches, palaces, and mansions, as well as the continent's first university, founded in 1551. For 2 centuries, the capital also served as the headquarters of the Spanish Inquisition.

When Spain created a rival vice regency in Río de la Plata, which subsequently grew rich from silver mines, Lima quickly fell into decline. An earthquake decimated the city in 1746, leaving more than 4,000 dead and few buildings standing. Today the capital of Peru is a sprawling, chaotic, and mostly unlovely metropolis, and many visitors dart through it rather quickly—or they bypass it altogether. Peru's blistering poverty is more apparent here than perhaps anywhere else: Depressing shantytowns called *pueblos jóvenes* lacerate the outer rings of the city. The despair of a large segment of the capital's largely migrant and *mestizo* population contrasts uncomfortably with the ritzy apartment and office buildings in the residential suburbs. And as if that weren't enough, for most of the year, an unrelenting gray cloud called the *garúa* hangs heavily overhead, obscuring the coastline and dulling the city's appearance. Although it virtually never rains in Lima, the sun comes out only from December to April; the rest of the time, Lima makes London look almost like Lisbon.

Lima has calmed down a bit since the chaotic 1980s and 1990s, when the city was the scene of carjackings, kidnappings, embassy takeovers, and strong-arm political maneuvers. But much of the city still feels schizophrenic; outer suburbs such as Barranco are welcome, relatively gentle oases, worlds apart from the congestion and grime of the rest of the city. Although middle-class Limeños from residential *barrios* are again venturing downtown along with foreign visitors, there are still plenty of locals who consider central Lima off-limits.

Lima demands some effort to sift beneath the soot and uncover the city's rewards, especially when such extraordinary treasures hover over the horizon in the Andes Mountains and in the Amazon jungle. So why come to Lima except to beeline it to Cusco or elsewhere? If you skip Lima altogether, you'll miss a vital part of what Peru is today. With a population of more than eight million—about one-third of Peru's population—and as the seat of the national government and the headquarters of most industry, Lima thoroughly dominates Peru's political and commercial life. The old *centro* is slowly being spruced up, and the refurbishing of classic colonial buildings and a greater police presence have made the historic part of the city more welcoming to visitors. Spread across the capital are the country's finest museums, as well as its most creative restaurants and most vibrant nightlife. In addition, Peruvian (and specifically, Limeño) cuisine is the subject of a growing international buzz, and foodies bent on a gastronomic tour of Peru are flocking to Lima's diverse restaurant scene.

Even if you have only a day or two for Lima, the city's art and archaeology museums serve as perfect introductions to the rich history and culture you'll encounter elsewhere in the country. Not to be missed are the Museo de la Nación, which traces the history of Peru's ancient civilizations, and the Rafael Larco Herrera Museum, the world's largest private collection of pre-Columbian art. If you also squeeze in a tour of colonial Lima, dine at a great *criollo* (Creole) restaurant or *cevichería*, soak up some energetic nightlife, and browse the country's best shops, you might just come away from Lima pleasantly surprised, if not wholly enamored of the city.

1 ORIENTATION

ARRIVING

Lima is the gateway for most international arrivals to Peru; see "Getting There & Getting Around" in chapter 3 for more detailed information.

By Plane

All flights from North America and Europe arrive at Lima's **Aeropuerto Internacional Jorge Chávez** (✆ 01/511-6055), located 16km (10 miles) west of the city center. Lima is connected by air with all major cities in Peru; there are regular flights to Ayacucho, Cusco, Puerto Maldonado, Juliaca, Arequipa, Tacna, Cajamarca, Chiclayo, Trujillo, Pucallpa, Iquitos, Tarapoto, and Piura. The major domestic airlines are **LAN** (✆ 212/582-3250 in the U.S., or 01/213-8200; www.lan.com), **LC Busre** (✆ 01/619-1313; www.lcbusre.com.pe), **Star Perú** (✆ 01/705-9000; www.starperu.com), and **Taca** (✆ 01/511-8222; www.taca.com). A new company that sounds like it should have been around for decades, **Peruvian Airlines** (✆ 01/716-6000; www.peruvianairlines.pe) recently entered the airspace with flights from Lima to Iquitos and Arequipa (with more destinations to come).

The airport has a tourist information booth (in the international terminal only), two 24-hour currency-exchange windows, three banks, ATMs, a post office, and car-rental desks, including **Avis** (✆ 01/575-1637, ext. 4155; www.avis.com), **Budget** (✆ 01/575-1674; www.budget.com), and **Hertz** (✆ 01/575-1390; www.hertz.com). The tourist information booth can help with hotel reservations. The arrival and departure terminals can be very congested, especially when long lines form to pay departure taxes, when a number of flights arrive at once, and early in the morning when many flights depart Lima for Cusco. Be very mindful of your luggage and other belongings at all times. To get through large groups of travelers and relatives all hovering about, you might need to forget about being polite and simply push your way through the crowd.

Domestic departures require payment of $6 exit tax; for international departures, the tax is $31. You must take your boarding pass to one of the booths in either terminal and stand in line to pay and receive a stamp indicating payment (in cash only) before proceeding to the departures area. Remember to reconfirm your flight at least 48 hours in advance and arrive at the airport with ample time before your flight. Flights are frequently overbooked, and passengers who have not reconfirmed their flights or who arrive later than (usually) 45 minutes before scheduled departure risk being bumped from the flight. Flights to Cusco are especially popular; make your reservations as far in advance as possible. Also check to be sure that you will have enough time to make your connecting

La Molina

La Encalada

Panamericana Sur

Carretera Central

Los Frutales

CHINATOWN

🔟

Av. Abancay

Circunvalacion

SAN BORJA

Aramburu

PLAZA RAIMONDI

🔟7️⃣

⓰ ⓯ ⓮ ⓭

OVALO BALTA

Benavides

Angamos

MIRAFLORES

La Paz

BARRANCO

Egurren

⓬

ALAMEDA DE LOS DESCALZOS

9️⃣

Panamericana Norte

Jr. de la Union

PLAZA DE ARMAS

Junin

Huallaga

Cusco

Carabaya

Av. Grau

PLAZA DE SAN MARTIN

paseo de la Republica

OVALO GUTIERREZ

3️⃣

EL OLIVAR

Larco

Diagonal

Pardo

28 de Julio

6️⃣

C. de Superunda

Callao

PLAZA UNION

Tacna

Emancipacion

Nicolas de Pierola

CENTRO

Av. de la Vega

PLAZA BOLOGNESI

PLAZA 2 DE MAYO

Av. Colonial

Av. Arica

A. Ugarte

Av. Bolivar

CAMPO DE MARTE

Av. 28 de Julio

Av. Arequipa

7️⃣ 1️⃣1️⃣

8️⃣

Camino Real

SAN ISIDRO

Santa Cruz

5️⃣

4️⃣

Comandante Espinar

Alcantores

See also the Miraflores and San Isidro maps

See also the Lima Centro maps

Av. Javier Prado

Av. Salaverry

1️⃣

2️⃣

Av. Brasil

Universitaria

Elmer Faucett

Av. Venezuela

Av. Argentina

Av. La Marina

Av. Saenz Peña

Av. Marina

NOTE: MAP NOT DRAWN TO SCALE

Aeropuerto Internacional Jorge Chávez

CALLAO

Malecon Figueredo

PERU
Lima

LIMA

6

ORIENTATION

ACCOMMODATIONS ■
La Posada del Parque Hostal **7**
Second Home Peru **12**

DINING ◆
Antica Trattoria **15**
Café del Museo **1**
Café Tostado **16**
Canta Rana **15**
Chala **14**
Costa Verde **6**
El Rincón Que No Conoces **11**
Manos Morenas **15**

ATTRACTIONS ●
Barrio Chino (Chinatown) **10**
Fundación Museo Amano **4**
Huaca Pucllana **3**
Museo Arqueológico Rafael Larco Herrera **1**
Museo de Arte Colonial Pedro do Osma **13**
Museo de la Nación **8**
Museo de Oro del Perú **17**
Museo Nacional de Arqueología,
  Antropología e Historia del Perú **2**
Parque del Amor **5**
Plaza de Acho/Museo Taurino **9**

flight if coming from overseas, and that you haven't been sold a charter flight inadvertently (American Airlines did this to me, and I was forced to stay over a day in Lima until I could get a regular flight the next day).

The airport is the best place to rent a cellphone for use in Peru. Representatives of **Peru Rent-a-Cell** (✆ 01/517-1856) are in the arrivals terminal offering inexpensive cell phone use (just $10 for the phone, and incoming calls are free).

To get from the airport to Lima—either downtown or to suburbs such as Miraflores, San Isidro, and Barranco (the sites of most tourist hotels)—you can take a taxi or private bus. When you exit with your luggage, you will immediately be besieged with taxi offers; the ones nearest the door are invariably the most expensive. **Taxis** (who have plenty of representatives hawking their services) inside the security area at the international arrivals terminal charge around $15 to Miraflores (about 30 minutes to 1 hour from the airport) and $12 to downtown Lima (Lima Centro)—though they'll almost certainly begin by asking for more.

The **Urbanito Airport shuttle service** (✆ 01/814-6932 or 01/517-1893) delivers passengers to the doors of their hotels. Stop by the desk in the international terminal for information about buses to downtown, costing $6, and Miraflores and San Isidro, costing $8, which leave every half-hour or so. The shuttle stops at the hotel of each passenger; at peak hours, if there are many passengers, this might not be the fastest way from the airport. Unless you're alone, it's also probably not the cheapest. Call a day ahead to arrange a pickup for your return to the airport. Private **limousine taxis** (*taxis ejecutivos,* or *remises*) also have desks in the airport; their fares are about S/150 one-way. One to try is **MitsuTaxi** (✆ 01/261-7788).

By Bus

Lima is connected by bus to neighboring countries and all major cities in Peru. No central bus terminal exists, however; the multitude of bus companies serving various regions of the country all have terminals in Lima, making bus arrivals and departures exceedingly confusing for most travelers. Many terminals are located downtown, although several companies have their bases in the suburbs. Most bus terminals have nasty reputations for thievery and general unpleasantness; your best bet is to grab your things and hop into a cab pronto.

Of the dozens of bus companies servicing the capital and points around the country, the largest with frequent service in and out of Lima are **Ormeño** (✆ 01/472-5000; www.grupo-ormeno.com.pe), Av. Javier Prado Este 1059, San Isidro; Av. Carlos Zavala 177 (✆ 01/427-5679), and reservations (✆ 01/472-5000; www.grupo-ormeno.com); **Cruz del Sur,** Av. Javier Prado Este 1101, La Victoria (✆ 01/311-5050; www.cruz delsur.com.pe), and Jirón Quilca (✆ 01/424-1005; www.cruzdelsur.com.pe); **Transportes Civa,** Av. Paseo de la República 575 (✆ 01/418-1111; www.civa.com.pe); and **Oltursa,** Av. Aramburú 1160, San Isidro (✆ 01/708-5000; www.oltursa.com.pe).

By Train

For information on one of South America's most spectacular rail journeys, from Lima to Huancayo in the Central Highlands, see "Highest Railroad in the World" box on p. 177.

VISITOR INFORMATION

A 24-hour tourist information booth, **iPerú** (✆ 01/574-8000), operates in the international terminal at the Jorge Chávez International Airport. The most helpful **iPerú** office is in Miraflores, at the **Larcomar** shopping mall, Módulo 10, Av. Malecón de la Reserva

610 (© **01/445-9400**), open Monday through Friday from 11am to 1pm and 2 to 8pm.
Another office is in San Isidro at Jorge Basadre 610 (© **01/421-1627**), open Monday
through Friday from 8:30am to 6:30pm. The **Oficina de Información Turística** in Lima
Centro is at Pasaje Los Escribanos 145, just off the Plaza de Armas, in Lima Centro
(© **01/427-6080**); it's open Monday through Saturday from 9am to 6pm.

One of the best private agencies for arrangements and city tours, as well as general
information, is **Fertur Perú,** Jr. Junín 211 (© **01/427-2626;** www.fertur-travel.com),
with an office in the Hotel España and a branch at Calle Schell 485 in Miraflores
(© 01/445-1760). Another excellent spot for information and advice, particularly on
outdoor and adventure travel in Peru, such as trekking, mountaineering, and rafting, is
the office of **South American Explorers,** Piura 135, Miraflores (© **01/445-3306;** www.
saexplorers.org). The organization is legendary among veteran South American travelers,
and it's not a bad idea to become a member ($50) before traveling so that you can take
advantage of its resources (you can also join on the spot). The clubhouse in Lima maintains a great library of maps, books, trail information, trip reports, and storage facilities.
It's open Monday through Friday from 9:30am to 5pm (Wed until 8pm), and Saturday
from 9:30am to 1pm. There are also clubhouses in Cusco and Quito, Ecuador.

CITY LAYOUT
Lima is an exceedingly diffuse city, so it's complicated to get around. The city center,
known as Lima Centro, abuts the Río Rímac and the Rímac district across the river. The
city beyond central Lima is a warren of ill-defined neighborhoods; most visitors are likely
to set foot in only San Isidro, Miraflores, and Barranco, which hug the coast and the
circuit of urban beaches leading to the so-called "Costa Verde." Major thoroughfares
leading from the city center to outer neighborhoods are Avenida Benavides (to Callao);
Avenida Brasil (to Pueblo Libre); Avenida Arequipa, Avenida Tacna, and Avenida Garcilaso de la Vega (to San Isidro and Miraflores); Paseo de la República (also known as Vía
Expresa) and Avenida Panamá (to Miraflores and Barranco); and Avenida Panamericana
Sur (to San Borja and south of Lima).

THE NEIGHBORHOODS IN BRIEF

LIMA CENTRO Lima Centro is the
historic heart of the city, where the
Spaniards built the country's capital in
colonial fashion. It has repeatedly suffered from earthquakes, fires, and
neglect, so although it was once the
continent's most important colonial
city, stunning examples of the original
town are less prevalent than one might
expect. Much of Lima Centro is dirty,
unsafe, crowded, and chaotic, although
city officials are finally getting to much-
needed restoration of the remaining
historic buildings and have drastically
upgraded police presence in the city
center (making it just about as safe as
anywhere in the city during the day).

The great majority of visitors stay in
outer suburbs rather than Lima Centro;
most hotels are small *hostales* (inns)
aimed at budget travelers and backpackers. The absolute heart of the Lima
Centro is the Plaza de Armas, site of La
Catedral (cathedral) and government
palaces, and nearly all the colonial mansions and churches of interest are within
walking distance of the square. Several
of Lima's top museums are in **Pueblo
Libre,** a couple kilometers southwest of
Lima Centro, while **San Borja,** a couple kilometers directly south of Lima
Centro, holds two of the finest collections in all of Peru.

MIRAFLORES & SAN ISIDRO   San Isidro and Miraflores, the city's most exclusive residential and commercial neighborhoods, are farther south (5–8km/3–5 miles) toward the coast. These districts are now the commercial heart of the city, having usurped that title from Lima Centro some years ago. San Isidro holds many of the city's top luxury hotels and a slew of offices and shopping malls. Miraflores is the focus of most travelers' visits to Lima; it contains the greatest number and variety of hotels, bars, and restaurants, as well as shopping outlets. A number of the city's finest hotels are along the *malecón* (boulevard) in Miraflores. Although San Isidro and Miraflores are middle-class neighborhoods, both are congested and not entirely free of crime.

BARRANCO   Barranco, several kilometers farther out along the ocean, is a tranquil former seaside village that is the city's coolest and most relaxed district, now known primarily for its nightlife. It is where you'll find many of Lima's best restaurants and especially bars, and live-music spots, frequented by Limeños and visitors alike. Though there are only a few boutique hotels and hostels in Barranco, increasingly it's becoming a cool place to stay, especially for young people. The next district along the beach is **Chorrillos,** a residential neighborhood known primarily for its *Pantanos de Villa,* or swamps that are rich with flora and fauna.

2 GETTING AROUND

Navigating Lima is a complicated and time-consuming task, made difficult by the city's sprawling character (many of the best hotels and restaurants are far from downtown, spread among three or more residential neighborhoods), heavy traffic and pollution, and a chaotic network of confusing and crowded *colectivos* and unregulated taxis.

BY TAXI

Taxis hailed on the street are a reasonable and relatively quick way to get around in Lima. However, taxis are wholly unregulated by the government: All anyone has to do to become a taxi driver is get his hands on a vehicle—of any size and condition, although most are tiny Daewoo "Ticos"—and plunk a cheap TAXI sticker inside the windshield. Then he is free to charge whatever he thinks he can get—with no meters, no laws, and nobody to answer to except the free market. One has to counsel visitors to be a bit wary of taking taxis in Lima, even though I personally have never had problems greater than a dispute over a fare. (If you're not fluent in Spanish, and even if you are but you have an obviously non-Peruvian appearance, be prepared to negotiate fares.) Limeños tell enough stories of theft and even the occasional violent crime in unregistered cabs to make hailing one on the street inadvisable for older visitors or for those with little command of Spanish or experience traveling in Latin America. If you hail a taxi on the street, taxi drivers themselves have told me, try to pick out older drivers; many contend that young punks are almost wholly responsible for taxi crime. If the issue of getting into quasi-official cabs makes you nervous, by all means call a registered company from your hotel or restaurant—especially at night (even though the fare can be twice as much).

Registered, reputable taxi companies—the safest option—include **Taxi Amigo** (© 01/349-0177), **Taxi Móvil** (© 01/422-6890), **Taxi Line** (© 01/330-2795), and

Lima Taxis: The Runaround

Besides the issue of safety, there's another cause for concern when getting in a taxi in Lima: The drivers very often don't know where the heck they're going. Many are notoriously ignorant of the city they drive in. I once tried to get one in Miraflores to take me to Barranco, the next neighborhood along the coast (5 miles away) and the most popular nightlife destination in Lima. The driver looked at me blankly. "You've never heard of Barranco?" I asked, incredulous. "Perhaps you can lead me?" he asked. Yeah, and perhaps you can pay me. Time and time again in Lima, I, a resident of New York, have had to give taxi drivers directions. The reason for such unfamiliarity is that many taxi drivers are newly arrived immigrants from mountain villages and other cities across Peru, and they're about as unfamiliar with the city as you are. They come to Lima, rent someone's vehicle and a TAXI sticker, and become taxi drivers without so much as a glance at a map. Yet another reason to have your hotel or restaurant call an official cab.

Taxi Seguro (© 01/275-2020). Whether you call or hail a taxi, you'll need to establish a price beforehand—so be prepared to bargain. Most fares range from S/8 to S/15. From Miraflores to downtown, expect to pay S/10; from Miraflores to San Isidro or from San Isidro to downtown, about S/8; and from Miraflores to Barranco, S/10. Note that when you hail a taxi on the street, the fare requested will surely be a bit higher; it makes sense to try to haggle.

BY BUS

Micros and *combis* are very inexpensive means of transportation in the city (see the "*Combi* or Carro? Getting Around in and out of Town" box in chapter 3 for more info). Routes are more or less identified by signs with street names placed in the windshield, making many trips confusing for those unfamiliar with Lima. Some do nothing more than race up and down long avenues (for example, the bus labeled TODO AREQUIPA travels the length of Avenida Arequipa). For assistance, ask a local for help; most Limeños know the incredibly complex bus system surprisingly well. Although they sometimes seem to hurtle down the street, because they make so many stops, trips from the outer suburbs to downtown can be quite slow. Most micros and combis cost S/3, and slightly more after midnight and on Sunday and holidays. When you want to get off, shout *baja* (getting off) or *esquina* (at the corner).

From Lima Centro to Miraflores, look for buses with signs in the windows indicating LARCO–SCHELL–MIRAFLORES (or some combination thereof). From Miraflores to downtown Lima, you should hop on a bus headed along WILSON/TACNA. Buses to Barranco have signs that read CHORILLOS/HUAYLAS.

BY FOOT

Lima can be navigated by foot only a neighborhood at a time (and even then, congestion and pollution strongly discourage much walking). Lima Centro and Barranco are best seen by foot, and, although large, Miraflores is also walkable. Between neighborhoods, however, a taxi is essential.

(*Fast Facts* **Lima**

Airport See "Arriving," earlier in this chapter.

American Express There's an office in Lima at Av. Santa Cruz 621, Miraflores (℃ **01/710-3900**); it's open Monday through Friday from 9am to 5pm. There are other offices at Jr. Rio de Janeiro 216, Miraflores, Lima (℃ 610-6000); in Cusco, Av. del Sol 864, Cusco (℃ **84/243-918**); and in Arequipa, Santa Catalina 105B (℃ 54/281-800). They will replace stolen or lost travelers' checks and sell American Express checks with an Amex card, but they do not cash their own checks.

Banks & Currency Exchange Peruvian and international banks with currency-exchange bureaus and ATMs are plentiful throughout Lima Centro, especially in the outer neighborhoods such as Miraflores, San Isidro, and Barranco, which are full of shopping centers, hotels, and restaurants. Money-changers, usually wearing colored smocks (sometimes with obvious "$" insignias), patrol the main streets off Parque Central in Miraflores and central Lima with calculators and dollars in hand.

Principal banks include **Banco Central,** Jr. Antonio Miró Quesada 441 (℃ 01/427-6250); **Banco Continental,** Av. Los Paracas s/n (℃ 01/436-1469); **Banco de Comercio,** Jr. Lampa 560 (℃ 01/428-9400); **Banco Wiese,** Jr. Cusco 245 (℃ 01/428-6000); and **Citibank,** Miguel Dasso 121, San Isidro (℃ 01/442-5146).

Car Rentals See "Arriving," earlier in this chapter.

Dentists & Doctors The U.S. and British embassies (see "Embassies & Consulates," below) provide lists of English-speaking doctors, dentists, and other healthcare personnel in Lima. An organization called **Doctor Más** (℃ **01/444-9377**) sends English-speaking doctors to hotels for emergencies and prescriptions. For dentists, you might also try contacting the **International Academy of Integrated Dentistry,** Centauro 177, Urbanización Los Granados, Monterrico, Surco (℃ **01/435-2153**). Additionally, see "Hospitals," below.

Drugstores Two huge, multiservice pharmacies *(farmacias)* open 24 hours a day are **Farmacia Deza,** Av. Conquistadores 1140, San Isidro (℃ **01/440-3798**); and **Pharmax,** Av. Salaverry 3100, San Isidro, in the Centro Comercio El Polo (℃ **01/264-2282**). A chain with a number of storefronts across Lima is **Superfarma,** at Av. Benavides 2849 (℃ **01/222-1575**) and Avenida Armendariz, Miraflores (℃ **01/446-3333**). These and other pharmacies have 24-hour delivery service. For additional locations, consult the Yellow Pages under "Farmacias" and "Boticas."

Embassies & Consulates **U.S.,** Avenida La Encalada, Block 17, Surco (℃ **01/434-3000**); **Australia,** Víctor A. Belaúnde 147/Vía Principal 155, office 1301, San Isidro (℃ **01/222-8281**); **Canada,** Calle Bolognesi 228, Miraflores (℃ **01/319-3200**); **U.K.** and **New Zealand,** Av. Jose Larco 1301, Miraflores (℃ **01/617-3000**).

Emergencies In case of an emergency, call the 24-hour **traveler's hot line** (℃ **01/574-8000**) or the **tourist police,** or POLTUR (℃ **01/460-1060** in Lima, or 01/460-0965). The **INDECOPI** 24-hour hot line can also assist in contacting police to report a crime (℃ **01/224-7888** in Lima, 01/224-8600, or toll-free 0800/42579 from any private phone).The general **police** emergency number is ℃ **105;** for **fire,** dial ℃ **116.**

Hospitals English-speaking medical personnel and 24-hour emergency services are available at the following hospitals and clinics: **Clínica Anglo-Americana,** Alfredo Salazar, Block 3, San Isidro (℡ 01/712-3000); **Clínica San Borja,** Guardia Civil 337, San Borja (℡ 01/475-4000); **Maison de Sante,** Calle Miguel Adgouin 01/208–222, near the Palacio de Justicia (℡ 01/428-3000, emergency 01/427-2941); and **Clínica Ricardo Palma,** Av. Javier Prado Este 1066, San Isidro (℡ 01/224-2224). For an ambulance, call **Alerta Médica,** at ℡ 01/470-5000, or **San Cristóbal,** at ℡ 01/440-0200.

Internet Access Internet *cabinas* (booths) are everywhere in Lima. Rates are about S/2 to S/3 per hour, and most are open daily from 9am to 10pm or later. Try **Telnet,** Jr. Camaná 315; **Internet Pardo,** Av. José Pardo 620; **Cybersandeg,** Jr. de la Unión 853, Of. 112; **Wamnet,** corner of Diez Canseco and Alcanfores, Mezzanine, Miraflores; or **C@bin@s de Internet,** Diez Canseco 380, Miraflores.

Maps Tourist-information booths give out free maps, but in a sprawling, confusing city such as Lima, they are inadequate for more than basic directions. Probably the best street map available is the "Lima 2000" map sold at bookstores and kiosks. Good topographical maps are available from the **Instituto Geográfico Nacional (IGN),** located at Av. Aramburú 1190, San Isidro (℡ **01/475-9960**). Hiking maps are available from the **South American Explorers,** Piura 135, Miraflores (℡ **01/445-3306**).

Newspapers & Magazines In Lima, you will find copies (although rarely same-day publications) of the *International Herald Tribune* and the *Miami Herald,* as well as *Time, Newsweek,* and other special-interest publications. Top-flight hotels sometimes offer free daily fax summaries of the *New York Times* to their guests. Among local publications, look for *Rumbos,* a glossy Peruvian travel magazine in English and Spanish with excellent photography. *El Comercio* and *La República* are two of the best daily Spanish newspapers.

Police The **Policía Nacional de Turismo (National Tourism Police)** has staff members that speak English and are specifically trained to handle the needs of foreign visitors. The main office in Lima is at Av. Javier Prado Este 2465, 5th Floor, San Borja (next to the Museo de la Nación); the 24-hour tourist police line is ℡ **01/574-8000.** Also see "Emergencies" above.

Post Office & Mail Lima's main post office *(Central de Correos)* is on the Plaza de Armas at Camaná 195 (℡ **01/427-0370**) in central Lima. The Miraflores branch is at Petit Thouars 5201 (℡ **01/445-0697**); the San Isidro branch is at Calle Las Palmeras 205 (℡ **01/422-0981**). A **DHL/Western Union** office is at Nicolás de Piérola 808 (℡ **01/424-5820**).

Restrooms The only public restrooms you're likely to find will be in airport and bus terminals, bars and restaurants, museums, and hotels. Sometimes it's easier to duck into a large hotel than into a restaurant.

Safety In downtown Lima and the city's residential and hotel areas, the risk of street crime remains high. Although carjackings, assaults, and armed robberies are not routine, they're not unheard of, either. Armed attacks at ATMs have also occurred. Use ATMs during the day, with other people present. Most thefts occur on public transportation, such as buses and combis. There have been several reports of thieves who've boarded buses in and out of Lima to cities both north and south of the capital, relieving passengers at gunpoint of their valuables. Be very careful with your belongings; leave your passport and other valuables in the hotel safe, and use a money belt. Public street markets are also frequented by thieves, as are parks (especially at night) and the beaches in and around Lima.

Although the large-scale terrorist activities of the local groups Sendero Luminoso and MRTA were largely stamped out in the early 1990s, there have been reports of a possible resurgence. Neither group, however, is currently active in any of the areas covered in this book.

Also see "Getting Around" above.

Taxis See "Getting Around," above.

Telephone Lima's area code is 01. It need not be dialed when making local calls within Lima, but it must be dialed when calling Lima from another city. Telephone booths are found throughout the city; the principal Telefónica del Perú office, where you can make long-distance and international calls, is on Plaza San Martín (Carabaya 937) in Lima Centro (© **01/224-9355**). It's open Monday through Saturday from 8am to 6pm and Sunday 8am to 1pm.

3 WHERE TO STAY

Lima Centro has its share of hotels and budget inns, but most people head out to the residential neighborhoods of Miraflores, San Isidro, and, to a lesser extent, Barranco. These barrios have little in the way of official sights, but they are more convenient for nightlife and shopping, and probably safer, if not necessarily much quieter.

Hotel rates in Lima are the highest in the country, especially at the top end. There are plenty of midrange and budget choices, although few have the charm of affordable *hostales* in other cities. Particularly at the top echelon, hotels tack on taxes and service charges to quoted rates, whereas most moderate and less-expensive inns quote rates that already include all taxes and service charges. Be on the lookout for any hotel that tries to charge you the 19% IGV (sales tax) on the basic room rate in addition to a 10% service charge; foreigners and nonresidents with the passport to prove it should be exempt from the IGV (but not the service charge). Unless otherwise noted, prices do not include taxes, service charges, or breakfast. Most *hostales* in Lima—unlike in Cusco, Arequipa, and a few other highland towns—do feature 24-hour hot water.

LIMA CENTRO
Inexpensive
Hostal de las Artes ★ (Value) Well located on the southern fringes of Lima Centro, a block from Plaza Bolognesi, this small Dutch-owned *hostal* is very friendly and well run—and one of the best budget bargains in town. It occupies an attractive, restored 19th-century colonial-style house and has a pretty patio. It's safe, clean, and understandably very popular with backpackers and other value-conscious travelers. Some rooms could afford to be spruced up a bit, so if several are available, ask to see a couple on different floors. The *hostal* is also very gay-friendly, and it features solar heating. In case this one's full, the owners also operate a second, more basic *hostal* around the corner.

ACCOMMODATIONS■
Hostal de las Artes **1**
Hotel España **7**
La Posada del Parque Hostal **2**

DINING◆
Cocolat Café **5**
L'Eau Vive **6**
Los Escribanos **4**
T'anta **3**
Wa Lok **8**

Map labels: Viru · Puente Santa Rosa · Ayabaca · RIMAC · Chiclayo · Viru · Trujillo · Casma · Cañete · Chancay · Callao · Tacna · Ica · Torrico · Huancavelica · Caillloma · Camana · Train Station · PLAZA DE ARMAS · Junin · Ancash · Lampa · Huallaga · PLAZA 2 DE MAYO · Emancipacion · Moquegua · Carabaya · Jirón de la Unión · CENTRO · Ucayali · Andahuaylas · Nicolas de Piérola · Ocoña · Cusco · Miró Quesada · Paruro · Alfonso Ugarte · Quilca · Puno · Azángaro · Abancay · Casma Ayacucho · Torrico · PLAZA SAN MARTIN · Apurimac · PLAZA FRANCIA · Lampa · Nicolas de Piérola · Uruguay · Washington · Canana · Inca Garcilaso de la Vega · Jirón de la Unión · Roosevelt · Cotabambas · Sandia · Leticia · Inambari · To Chinatown · Bolivia · Jiron Chota · Paseo de la República · Aljovin · Zavala · Ayacucho · Montevideo · España · Cuadros · 9 de Diciembre · PLAZA GRAU · Grau · CALLAO · Map Area · CENTRO · PLAZA BOLOGNESI · Arequipa · Via Expresa · LIMA · MIRAFLORES · To Miraflores, San Isidro & Barranco · *(i)* Information

Scale: 0 – 1/4 mi · 0 – 0.25 km

*Sidebar:* LIMA · 6 · WHERE TO STAY

Jr. Chota 1460, Lima. ℂ **01/433-0031.** Fax 01/428-5546. www.hostaldelasartes.net. 18 units. $18–$20 double with private bathroom; $5 per person dormitory-style. Rates include airport transfer (by prior arrangement). No credit cards. *In room:* No phone.

Hotel España ★ Value Near the Convento de San Francisco and just 4 blocks from the Plaza de Armas, this extremely popular budget *hostal* has a funky flair and communal atmosphere. If you're looking to hook up with backpackers from around the globe and set off to explore Peru, you can't do better than Hotel España. It occupies a rambling colonial building chock-full of paintings, ceramics, faux Roman busts, plants, and even the occasional mummy and skull. A maze of rooms, most with shared bathrooms and some with odd numbers such as D3 and G2, is located up a winding staircase. The rooms themselves are simple, with concrete floors but brightly colored walls; they're well-kept, but with cheesy bedspreads. The leafy rooftop garden terrace, with views of San Francisco, is a good place to hang out and trade travel tales. Security is said to be a little lax, so store your stuff in the lockers. Hot water goes to the early bird. The place can be noisy and even a little nuts, but that's part of its charm.

Azángaro 105, Lima. Ⓒ/fax **01/428-5546.** www.hotelespanaperu.com. 30 units. $11 double without bathroom; $15 with bathroom. No credit cards. **Amenities:** Cafe. *In room:* No phone.

La Posada del Parque Hostal ★ (Finds) Monica Moreno runs this safe, great-value, and delightful guesthouse, which occupies a lovely 1920s *casona* on what has to be one of the most peaceful streets near the center of Lima—it's a long cul-de-sac lined with gardens and other stately homes. Her house, in the Santa Beatriz district, is full of Peruvian popular art and offers unusual amenities at such an economical rate, such as Internet access, satellite TV, and homemade pizzas and beer upon request. Monica is more than willing to help travelers with all their needs. The rooms are spacious and impeccable, with excellent bathrooms and hot water. The owner also has a one-bedroom suite (Suite del Parque) nearby, which is perfect for longer stays.

Parque Hernán Velarde 60, Santa Beatriz, Lima. Ⓒ **01/433-2412.** Fax 01/332-6927. www.incacountry. com. 9 units. $45–$48 double. MC, V. **Amenities:** Free Internet (in lobby); safe (in lobby). *In room:* TV, no phone.

MIRAFLORES
Very Expensive

Miraflores Park Hotel ★★★ The exceedingly elegant Miraflores Park Hotel bathes business executives and upscale tourists in unsurpassed luxury. It hugs the *malecón,* the park-lined avenue that traces the Lima coastline. From the cozy, library-like lobby and handsome restaurant to the tastefully appointed, plush rooms (including marble and granite bathrooms most New Yorkers would give their left arms to have), the hotel is a distinguished address from head to foot. All rooms are suites with comfortable king-size beds and sitting areas. Many rooms have ocean views—at least for the few days of the year when you can see the coast in Lima. Special promotional rates are often available online.

Av. Malecón de la Reserva 1035, Miraflores, Lima. Ⓒ **01/610-4000.** Fax 01/242-3393. www.mira-park. com. 81 units. $655–$680 deluxe double; from $795 and up suite. AE, DC, MC, V. **Amenities:** Restaurant; bar; cafe; concierge; exercise room; small outdoor rooftop pool; sauna; squash court. *In room:* A/C, TV/ DVD, fridge, hair dryer, Wi-Fi ($15/day).

Expensive
Casa Andina Private Collection Miraflores ★★ (Kids) Casa Andina, the fast-growing Peruvian hotel chain, took over this high-rise hotel, which had been Lima's first five-star hotel but was then abandoned for a number of years, and completely gutted it, turning it into its showcase property in 2008. The result is sure to become a favorite of business travelers: It has all the amenities and services of the city's top luxury business hotels, but without the exorbitant prices of many of its competitors. But it's also great for leisure travelers and families, and is considerably less expensive than most big-city, five-star hotels. The well-designed accommodations are sleeker and more luxurious than at most of the group's other hotels, and many feature nice views over the city. The sleek, modern restaurant is very good, and the spa and heated swimming pool are excellent bonuses.

ACCOMMODATIONS ■
Casa Andina Classic Miraflores
San Antonio **19**
Casa Andina Private Collection
Miraflores **15**
Hostal El Patio Miraflores **14**
Hostal José Luis **18**
Hotel Antigua Miraflores **6**
Inka Lodge **4**
JW Marriott Hotel & Casino **21**
Miraflores Park Hotel **22**
Pariwana Hostel Lima **9**
San Antonio Abad **17**
Sonesta Posadas del Inca
Miraflores **16**

DINING ◆
Antico Ristorante Italiano
di Porto Rotondo **5**
Astric y Gastón **11**
Café Café **8**
La Mar Cebicheria **1**
Fiesta Restaurant Gourmet **20**
Las Brujas de Cachinche **7**
Pescados Capitales **2**
Restaurant Huaca Pucllana **3**
Segundo Muelle **10**

La Paz 463, Miraflores, Lima. For reservations in the U.S. ℂ **866/220-4434;** Lima ℂ 01/213-9739. Fax 01/213-9790. www.casa-andina.com. 148 units. $190–$317 double; $350 and up suite. Rates include breakfast buffet. AE, DC, MC, V. **Amenities:** 2 restaurants; bar; concierge; gym; heated swimming pool; spa; smoke-free rooms. *In room:* A/C, TV, fridge, hair dryer, Wi-Fi.

JW Marriott Hotel Lima ★★   This upscale business traveler's hotel isn't as luxurious as the exclusive Swissôtel, but it's more affordable, making it a very good value given the overall quality and dependability of the Marriott chain. It's a gleaming, ultramodern 25-story high-rise building hugging the coast and parks along the *malecón*, replete with glitzy ground-floor shops and a much-frequented casino. It seems to serve mostly short- and long-term business travelers from North and South America, but it's perfectly fine for leisure travelers and families. Children can be easily entertained at the outdoor pool or on the tennis court. Rooms are very well equipped and comfortable, with nice bathrooms, if without a whole lot of individual character. Inexpensive weekend rates are frequently available, making the Marriott one of the best values in Lima.

Av. Malecón de la Reserva 615, Miraflores, Lima. ℂ **800/228-9290** in the U.S. and Canada, or 01/217-7000. Fax 01/217-7100. www.marriott.com/hotels/travel/limdt-jw-marriott-hotel-lima. 300 units. $320–$380 double; $420 suite. AE, DC, MC, V. Valet parking. **Amenities:** 2 restaurants; cafe; concierge; health club; outdoor pool; sauna. *In room:* A/C, TV, fridge, hair dryer, Wi-Fi.

Moderate

Casa Andina Classic Miraflores San Antonio ★ (**Value**)   Well located, and well executed, like all Casa Andina properties, this midsize hotel—one of three the chain operates in the capital—has ample bedrooms that are cheerfully decorated, with brightly striped bedspreads and sunburned yellow walls. Marble bathrooms are large, and the breakfast buffet is a winner. Casa Andina is perfect for the traveler who seeks comfort, good value, and no unpleasant surprises. A second Casa Andina Classic is located nearby, at Av. Petit Thouars 5444.

Av. 28 de Julio 1088, Miraflores, Lima. For reservations in the U.S. ℂ **866/220-4434;** Lima ℂ 01/213-9739. Fax 01/241-4051. www.casa-andina.com. 49 units. $98–$131double. Rates include breakfast buffet. AE, DC, MC, V. **Amenities:** Babysitting; concierge; room service; smoke-free rooms. *In room:* A/C, TV, fridge, hair dryer on request, Wi-Fi.

Hotel Antigua Miraflores ★ (**Finds**)   This charming early-20th-century mansion, full of authentic Peruvian touches and color, calls itself "a hidden treasure in the heart of Miraflores." As many return visitors know, that's not just hype. The hotel is owned and operated by a North American who's a longtime Lima resident. The house is elegant and tasteful, lined with colonial Peruvian art, and built around a leafy courtyard. The staff is exceptionally helpful and friendly. Rooms range from huge suites with large Jacuzzis and kitchenettes to comfortable double rooms with handcrafted furniture and good-quality beds. Most bathrooms are quite luxurious, with colonial tiles, brass fixtures, and bathtubs. The public rooms look more like an art gallery than a hotel lobby (the paintings are for sale).

Av. Grau 350, Miraflores, Lima. ℂ **01/241-6116.** Fax 01/241-6115. www.peru-hotels-inns.com. 35 units. $94–$109 double; $129 suite. Rates include a nice selection of breakfasts. AE, DC, MC, V. Free parking. **Amenities:** Restaurant; bar; small gym; Jacuzzi. *In room:* A/C, TV, fridge, hair dryer.

Sonesta Posada del Inca Miraflores ★ (**Value**)   The Miraflores branch of a chain with a handful of hotels across Peru, this small modern hotel has an excellent location and is efficient and professionally run. Centrally located just 2 blocks from Parque Central (Parque Kennedy), it's within easy walking distance of Miraflores' many nightclubs, restaurants, and shops. The well-appointed rooms aren't huge, but they come with very comfortable beds, good-size bathrooms, and an ocher-and-deep-green color scheme with plaid bedspreads.

Alcanfores 329, Miraflores, Lima. © **800/SONESTA** (766-3782) or 01/241-7688. Fax 01/447-1164. www. sonesta.com/miraflores. 28 units. $91–$200 double. Rates include breakfast buffet. AE, DC, MC, V. Free parking. **Amenities:** 24-hr. cafe and bar; concierge; fitness center (¹/₂ block from hotel); smoke-free rooms. In room: A/C, TV, fridge, hair dryer on request.

Inexpensive

B&B Jose Luis   This youth-hostel-like B&B—which keeps itself hidden away by not posting a sign out front—has operated on word of mouth for two decades. Deceptively large, with a capacity for nearly 60 guests, it's one of the cheapest places in Miraflores. It's secluded in a quiet residential part of the district, a 10-minute walk from Parque Central and its hubbub of nightlife and shops. There's a definite family feeling here, with cooking and laundry facilities. The common rooms are busy with furnishings and patterned wallpaper, but many rooms have bunk beds, set up in dorm-room style. All have private bathrooms.

Francisco de Paula Ugarriza 727, Miraflores, Lima. © **01/444-1015.** Fax 01/446-7177. www.hoteljoseluis. com. 20 units. $12 per person. Rates include breakfast. No credit cards. In room: No phone.

Hostal El Patio Miraflores ★ (Finds   Set back from the street, behind an iron gate and built around a flower-filled Andalusian-style patio, this friendly, good-value inn has real personality. It's an unexpected but welcome respite from the grime and chaos of Lima. The comfortable, if not luxurious, rooms in the rambling colonial mansion feature good natural light and are cozy and brightly colored. Though a relatively small hotel, it's run very efficiently, and the staff goes out of its way to help visitors find their way in Lima.

Calle Ernesto Diez Canseco 341, Miraflores, Lima. © **01/444-2107.** Fax 01/444-1663. www.hostalelpatio. net. 25 units. S/150–S/180 double; S/195–S/225 suite. Rates include continental breakfast. AE, DC, MC, V. In room: A/C, TV, fridge, Wi-Fi.

Inka Lodge ★ (Value   The best new budget inn in Lima is this modern, spotless and well-run small *hostal* with very good facilities, such as a roof terrace, computers with Internet access, kitchen use, and storage lockers. Rooms aren't large, but they're tastefully decorated for the price, and the location, on a quiet street just 5 blocks from Parque Kennedy in the heart of Miraflores, is safe and convenient. Choose from doubles with shared bathrooms or rooms for three or more, or dorm rooms with bunk beds. Bathrooms are very well maintained. Though the inn's website claims it has a "homely atmosphere," I think what they mean is that, for a budget inn, it actually has character, and quite a bit at that. Thoughtful touches, many of which are uncommon among budget *hostales*, include free bottled water and round-the-clock coffee.

Elias Aguirre 278, Miraflores, Lima. © **01/242-6989.** www.inkalodge.com. 7 units. $28 double with shared bathroom; $14 per person in shared dorm rooms. Rates include taxes and continental breakfast. MC, V. **Amenities:** High-speed Internet (in lobby); kitchen use; storage lockers. In room: A/C, TV, no phone.

Pariwana Hostel Lima (Value   Related to the terrific new hostel in Cusco (p. 199), this Lima incarnation boasts a convenient location facing Parque Kennedy, but doesn't benefit from the lovely colonial manor house of its sister property. Then again, Lima can hardly compete with Cusco on aesthetic grounds, either. Still, this is a good choice for students and backpackers (and single women, for whom there are sex-segregated dorm rooms) who are looking more for inexpensive digs and bonhomie than anything else. And there's plenty of the latter, with lots of group activities, a bar/restaurant, games, breakfast until 1pm and more. Though it has a lovely central staircase, rooms aren't quite as sparkling as in Cusco, but with the clean provided towels, rooftop terrace, locker and storage services, and cheap meals (not to mention drinks), that may not matter much for a couple of nights, as the price is right.

Av. Larco 189, Miraflores, Lima. (C) **01/242-4350.** www.pariwana-hostel.com. 60 units. S/90 double; S/27–S/36 per person in dorm room with shared bathroom. Rates include breakfast. No credit cards. **Amenities:** Restaurant/bar; lockers, TV room. *In room:* No phone; Wi-Fi.

San Antonio Abad Hotel (Value)   Named for a saint, this clean and very friendly neighborhood hotel aims high. Its goal is to be welcoming and comfortable, and it succeeds. The colonial building, near the commercial center of Miraflores and several parks, has a garden terrace, fireplace, and sitting room. Rooms, which are simply decorated but ample, have private bathrooms with round-the-clock hot water. Because of street noise (ever present in Lima), you might ask for a room with an interior courtyard view.

Av. Ramón Ribeyro 301, Miraflores, Lima. (C) **01/447-6766.** Fax 01/446-4208. www.hotelsanantonioabad. com. 24 units. $70 double. Rates include breakfast buffet and airport pickup. AE, DC, MC, V. Free parking. **Amenities:** Restaurant; bar. *In room:* A/C, TV, fridge, hair dryer on request.

SAN ISIDRO
Very Expensive
Country Club Lima Hotel ★★★ (Kids)   This incredibly grand, lovely, and sprawling hacienda-style hotel, built in 1927, is a swank and character-filled place to rest your head. It's simply the most elegant hotel in Lima. Although it appears large, the hotel is actually very cozy, friendly, and low-key. Rooms—all of which are suites, with separate work areas—are large and very luxurious, with tons of antiques and old-world appeal (although they don't skimp on modern conveniences). Many of the huge, stunning marble bathrooms have large Jacuzzis and separate showers. A member of the Leading Hotels of the World, it is ideal for just about anyone, including families, but it is especially perfect for stressed-out business travelers who've seen one too many blandly elegant hotels. Public rooms are very refined and inviting, with chandeliers and high wood-beam ceilings, a close approximation of a local nobleman's estate. It's not surprising that the hotel hosts frequent social functions. There's live music Friday and Saturday evenings in the elegant restaurant, and afternoon tea is served to the accompaniment of live piano music. Appropriately enough, the Country Club Hotel sits next to a golf course and tennis club (guest privileges included). The hotel is actually pretty fairly priced for this elevated luxury and service, especially if you're able to get one of the excellent corporate rates or special offers frequently available on the website.

Los Eucaliptos 590, San Isidro, Lima. (C) **800/745-8883** in the U.S. and Canada, or **01/611-9000.** Fax 01/611-9002. www.hotelcountry.com. 75 units. $345–$455 double; $490–$1,650 suite. AE, DC, MC, V. Valet parking. **Amenities:** 3 restaurants; bar; concierge; fitness center; access to nearby Lima Golf Club; outdoor pool; sauna. *In room:* A/C, TV, fridge, Wi-Fi.

Swissôtel Lima ★★   One of Lima's most exclusive and sophisticated properties is this sparkling high-rise hotel. Formerly the Peruvian-owned Oro Verde, it takes its pedigree as part of the international Swissôtel chain very seriously: The hotel is very Continental classy. The lobby is awash in fine carpets, corridors are curiously lined with giant neoclassical columns, restaurants serve Swiss and Italian as well as Peruvian fare, and

LIMA

6

WHERE TO STAY

ACCOMMODATIONS ■
Casa Bella B&B 3
Country Club Lima Hotel 2
Libertador Lima Hotel 1
Sonesta Hotel El Olivar Lima 7
Swissôtel Lima 4

DINING ◆
Dánica 9
Segundo Muelle 6, 8
T'anta 5

service is, of course, eminently efficient. Rooms are spacious and well-appointed. Executive rooms include a work desk, two telephone lines, a coffee machine, a private executive lounge/boardroom, and cocktails (!). For business facilities, this property rivals the Marriott and Miraflores Park Hotel, although I find the last the most distinguished of the three. Value rates and packages are often available.

Vía Central 150 (Centro Empresarial Real), San Isidro, Lima. ✆ **01/421-4400.** Fax 01/421-4422. www. swissotel.com. 244 units. $250–$550 double; $650 and up suite. AE, DC, MC, V. Valet parking. **Amenities:** 3 restaurants; cafeteria; bar/lounge; concierge; fitness center; small heated outdoor pool; sauna; spa. *In room:* A/C, TV.

Expensive

Libertador Lima Hotel ★ Ⓥⓐⓛⓤⓔ Smack in the middle of the San Isidro financial district, the Libertador—which overlooks the private Lima Golf Club—is relatively unassuming and tranquil, especially considering the more imposing and flashier hotels nearby. Still, that's its charm. It doesn't try too hard, but it gets the job done for guests who are both business travelers and tourists. Part of a five-member well-run Peruvian chain of upscale hotels, this midsize offering is handsomely decorated with modern art, Kilim rugs, and bold colors, eschewing the typical blandness of business hotels. It also has a nice top-floor restaurant and bar with good views. It's quite a good value, especially if you can get an upgrade to a junior suite or reserve online.

Los Eucaliptos 550, San Isidro, Lima. ✆ **877/778-2281** in the U.S. and Canada, or 01/518-6500. Fax 01/518-6290. www.libertador.com.pe. 43 units. $160 double; $285 suite. AE, DC, MC, V. Valet parking. **Amenities:** Restaurant; bar; concierge; gym; Jacuzzi; sauna. *In room:* A/C, TV, fridge.

Sonesta Hotel El Olivar Lima ★★ Ⓥⓐⓛⓤⓔ The Sonesta chain's top-of-the-line property, aimed squarely at visiting business travelers, is named for the historic Olive Grove Park, which it faces. This seven-story hotel is well located for its clientele, in a peaceful section of the San Isidro business district of the city. The rooms, a step up from the more rustic decor in the chain's Posadas del Inca, are quite large, with boldly colored fabrics and beige marble bathrooms. Service is friendly and efficient, and the amenities outdo those of most hotels in the city. The recently revamped restaurant is winning accolades in the Peruvian press, and is an excellent spot for lunch or dinner.

Pancho Fierro 194, San Isidro, Lima. ✆ **800/SONESTA** (766-3782) or 01/712-6000. Fax 01/712-6099. www.sonesta.com/lima. 134 units. $170–$200 double; $220–$400 suite. Rates include breakfast buffet. Children 7 and under stay free in parent's room. AE, DC, MC, V. Free parking. **Amenities:** 2 restaurants; cafe; cocktail lounge; bar; concierge; fitness center w/rooftop outdoor pool; Jacuzzi; sauna. *In room:* A/C, TV/DVD, fridge, hair dryer, Wi-Fi.

Moderate

Casa Bella B&B ★ Ⓥⓐⓛⓤⓔ A very pleasant midrange choice in an area better known for its business-oriented luxury hotels, this safe and modern, exceptionally clean inn, 1 block from the swank Country Club, offers private and quiet accommodations. While a little larger than the typical B&B, with 12 rooms, this nicely furnished, slick contemporary home gives travelers a nice impression of staying at a friend's home. The spacious and airy nonsmoking rooms are attractively decorated, with good bedding, and several have backyard garden views. Whether for a few days or a longer stay, Casa Bella is tough to beat for the price.

Las Flores 459 San Isidro. ✆ **720/470-7237** in the U.S., or 01/421-7354. www.casabellaperu.net. 12 units. $65–$75 double; $85–$175 suite. Rates include continental breakfast. MC, V. Free parking. **Amenities:** Kitchen. *In room:* Wi-Fi.

Second Home Peru ★★★ (Finds   Lilian Delfín runs this extraordinary, and unique, small inn in the longtime, coast-hugging home of her father, the well-known Peruvian painter and sculptor Victor Delfín. The place is perfect for the relaxed and still slightly bohemian neighborhood of Barranco. This is no bland B&B; the idiosyncratic 1913 home is replete with artistic flavor—and multiple works by Delfín, who recently turned 80 and continues to paint every day (the artist's studio and living quarters are apart from the main house, tumbling down the cliff). Though the house overlooks the ocean and the rooms are exceedingly spacious and elegant, the rambling two-story house—something like a Tudor-Craftsman—is probably not for everyone. But many, especially those interested in the arts or spending a few days in town, will find it a magical home away from home in Lima. To my mind, it's one of the coolest and best-value places to stay in all of Peru. My large room had a beautiful wood floor and beams, a huge picture window framing the misty gray Pacific, deep claw-foot tub, and what felt like the most luxurious linens in Lima. If you ask politely, Lilian may take you to visit her father's fascinating studio, where a giant puma-head fountain spouts water into the swimming pool (open to guests). But at a minimum, you'll get to have breakfast at Delfín's funky, Gaudí-style, neo-medieval kitchen. If you're headed to Cusco, check out Lilian's brother's place, **Second Home Cusco** (p. 204).

Domeyer 366, Barranco, Lima. ℂ **01/477-5021.** Fax 01/247-1042. www.secondhomeperu.com. 5 units. $95–$100 double; $120 suite. Rates include breakfast. AE, DC, MC, V. Free parking. *In room:* A/C, TV, hair dryer.

---

4 WHERE TO DINE

Lima is the most cosmopolitan dining city in all of Peru, and perhaps the greatest food city in South America, with restaurants of all budgets and a wide range of cuisines—from upscale seafood restaurants and *comida criolla* (coastal Peruvian cooking), to Chinese and plenty of Italian, French, and other international restaurants. Lima is also the top spot in the country to sample truly creative gastronomy, as well as the dish Peru is perhaps best known for: ceviche.

Sometimes entire streets and neighborhoods specialize in a single type of food. In Lima Centro, you can visit the *chifas* of Chinatown, and Miraflores, a pedestrian street off Parque Central (Boulevard San Remo) is referred to as "Little Italy" for its scores of lookalike pizzerias and Italian restaurants, which draw scores of tourists looking for cheap eats and plentiful beer. Museum goers–slash-foodies can kill two birds with one stone at the Museo Arqueológico Rafael Larco Herrera, which now features a handsome restaurant, **Café del Museo** (p. 136), with a menu by Gastón Acurio, the celebrated chef and man behind the restaurants Astrid y Gastón, Cebichería La Mar, and T'anta.

Restaurants here, predictably, are most crowded in the early evening, especially Thursday through Saturday. In the business districts of Miraflores and San Isidro, lunch can also get quite busy—at least in the nicer restaurants that are popular with local and international businessmen. To locate restaurants in Lima Centro, Miraflores, and San Isidro, see the maps "Where to Stay & Dine in Lima Centro" (p. 115), "Where to Stay & Dine in Miraflores" (p. 117), and "Where to Stay & Dine in San Isidro" (p. 121).

Moderate

El Rincón Que No Conoces ★★ (**Finds**) CREOLE/PERUVIAN Although stuck in a bit of a no-man's land (at least for tourists)—at the edge of the Centro—this authentic, amiable, old-school Peruvian *criollo* restaurant, helmed by Teresa Izquierdo Gonzáles, a 70-something institution of a chef, is worth the trek. Doña Teresa has been cooking here for more than 30 years, and her neighborhood eatery may have gotten a little more polished and popular (it's even welcomed Rachel Ray of Food Network through its doors), but it hasn't deviated from its mission: classic Creole cooking. A good place to start is with a *causa* (a yellow potato torta stuffed with chicken, shrimp or tuna), or perhaps a *palta rellena* (stuffed avocado). A similarly classic main dish is the *tacu-tacu* (rice and beans) with *asado a la tira* (short ribs). The menu is long, portions are large, and you can hardly take a wrong turn. If you really want to sample a variety of Creole cooking, show up on Wednesday, when there's a buffet that includes a pisco sour for S/35. With a name like "The Corner Joint You've Never Heard of," one might expect this to be a modest little hut with no sign out front. Instead, it's a rather handsome and cozy two-story restaurant with high ceilings and a warm atmosphere—reflective of the woman in the kitchen.

Bernardo Alcedo 363, alt. cuadra 20 de Petit Thouars, Lince. (©) **01/471-2171.** Reservations recommended. Main courses S/20–S/32. No credit cards. Tues–Sun noon–4:30pm.

L'Eau Vive (**Finds**) FRENCH/PERUVIAN If you're feeling obscenely rich in this impoverished country, you'll do a tiny bit of good and feel better by eating here. The restaurant, run by a French order of nuns, donates its proceeds to charity. In a colonial palace 2 blocks from the Plaza de Armas and across the street from one of Lima's most important mansions, Torre Tagle, it features several large dining rooms with high ceilings. If you come for the cheap lunch *menu*, though, you'll have to sit in the simpler front rooms. The "a la carte" dining rooms are considerably more elegant. The lunch menu is a deal, and at night you get a pious show free with dinner: The nuns sing "Ave Maria" promptly at 9:30pm. The French menu includes items such as prawn bisque, trout baked in cognac, and grilled meats; it also incorporates some international dishes from around the globe—chiefly, the many countries from which the order's nuns come. The restaurant's heyday was clearly a few years ago, and some have complained that the food and service aren't up to snuff anymore, but this is still an old favorite you can feel good about patronizing, even if it's not the finest meal you can have in Lima.

Ucayali 370. (©) **01/427-5612.** Reservations recommended on Fri–Sat nights. Main courses S/10–S/43. AE, MC, V. Mon–Sat 12:30–3pm and 7:30–9:30pm.

Los Escribanos PERUVIAN On one of Lima Centro's more appealing streets, a tiny pedestrian passageway near the Plaza de Armas, this unassumingly elegant two-story eatery has an attractive terrace with outdoor tables. Popular with local businessmen and travelers who trickle out of the tourism information office next door, it offers particularly good deals at lunch (with bargain *platos únicos* and a fixed-price menu that's served until 9pm). The evening menu lists plenty of *criollo* and seafood plates from the Peruvian coast, including gourmet dishes with pre-Columbian influences. At lunch, though, most people sit down to more standard fare, such as grilled trout and fettuccine Alfredo, served with a salad and beverage.

Pasaje Nicolás de Ribera El Viejo (Los Escribanos) 137–141. (©) **01/427-9102.** Reservations recommended on Fri–Sat nights. Main courses S/12–S/30. MC, V. Mon–Thurs 9am–9pm; Fri–Sat 9am–midnight.

Tips **Peruvian Chifas**

Chinatown (Barrio Chino), southeast of the Plaza de Armas and next to the Mercado Central (beyond the Chinese arch on Jirón Ucayali), is a good place to sample the Peruvian take on Chinese food. These *chifas,* inexpensive restaurants with similar menus, are everywhere in the small but dense neighborhood. Among those worth visiting (generally open daily 9am–10pm or later) are **Wa Lok** ★★, Jr. Paruro 864 (✆ **01/427-2750**), probably the best known in the neighborhood; and **Salón China,** Jr. Ucayali 727 (✆ **01/428-8350**), which serves a good lunch buffet for S/30.

Inexpensive

Cocolat Café BISTRO A good and quick spot for lunch or dinner is this simple little bistro on the popular pedestrian passageway, near the Plaza de Armas, that's lined with restaurants. It serves sandwiches, salads, and sides such as empanadas; the midday menu is a particularly good deal for an appetizer and main course. Top it off with a great selection of homemade chocolates and good coffee, and you might just want to linger for a while on the sidewalk terrace. It's also a good spot for breakfast.

Pasaje Nicolás de Ribera El Viejo (Los Escribanos) 121. ✆ **01/427-4471.** Reservations not accepted. Main courses S/9–S/15. No credit cards. Mon–Sat 8am–6:30pm.

MIRAFLORES & SAN ISIDRO

Very Expensive

Astrid y Gastón ★★★ INTERNATIONAL/PERUVIAN Hidden discreetly behind a nonchalant facade (though one of an antique colonial house), on a busy side street leading to Parque Kennedy, is this warm and chic modern colonial dining room and cozy bar. It continues to be my favorite restaurant in Lima, even though it now has some high-end challengers. Gastón Acurio has been Peru's celebrity chef for at least a decade, with a burgeoning empire of fine-dining restaurants not only in Lima but also a handful of other cities in both North and South America (including San Francisco) and a cooking show on TV. His signature restaurant in the capital is warm and elegant, with high white peaked ceilings and orange walls decorated with colorful modern art. In back is an open kitchen and a secluded wine-salon dining room. The place is sophisticated and hip but low-key, a description that could fit most of its clients, who all seem to be regulars. The menu might be called *criollo*-Mediterranean: Peruvian with a light touch. Try spicy roasted kid or the excellent fish called *noble robado,* served in miso sauce with crunchy oysters. The list of desserts—the work of Astrid, the other half of the husband-wife team—is nearly as long as the main course menu, and they are spectacular. Fans of Acurio should check out **La Mar Cebichería** (p. 126) and his latest Lima restaurant, Panchita (Av. Dos de Mayo 298, Miraflores; ✆ **01/447-8272**), his take on traditional anticuchos, or kebabs.

Cantuarias 175, Miraflores. ✆ **01/242-4422.** www.astridygaston.com. Reservations recommended. Main courses S/38–S/79. AE, DC, MC, V. Mon–Sat 12:30–3:30pm and 7:30pm–midnight.

Brujas de Cachiche ★ CRIOLLO The "Witches of Cachiche" celebrates 2,000 years of local culture with a menu that's a tour of the "magical" cuisines of pre-Columbian Peru. The chef even uses ancient recipes and ingredients. The extensive menu

includes classic Peruvian dishes, such as *ají de gallina,* but concentrates on fresh fish and shellfish and fine cuts of meat with interesting twists and unusual accompaniments. Brujas de Cachiche sole is prepared with Asian and *criollo* spices, and served with peas and bell peppers sautéed in soybean sauce. A steak in pisco-butter sauce comes with braised mushrooms. Among the excellent desserts, several continue the indigenous theme, such as *mazamorra morada* (purple corn pudding and dried fruit). The restaurant, in a sprawling old house with several warmly decorated dining rooms, is popular both night and day with well-heeled Limeños, expat businessmen and foreign government officials, and tourists; it's exclusive and it's expensive, but it's worth the splurge. A lunch buffet is served Tuesday through Friday and Sunday from 11am to 4pm, and gastronomic festivals are frequent.

Jr. Bolognesi 460, Miraflores. ℂ **01/447-1883.** www.brujasdecachiche.com.pe. Reservations recommended. Main courses S/32–S/65. AE, DC, MC, V. Mon–Sat 1pm–midnight; Sun noon–5pm.

Fiesta Chiclayo Gourmet ★★ NORTHERN PERUVIAN I'm sure few visitors probably know much if anything about the cuisine of Chiclayo, a city in northern Peru, but it's famous among Peruvians for its unique contributions to their nation's kitchen. And the name of the restaurant probably doesn't entice foreigners much, conjuring a Cancun bar with wet t-shirt contests, but this gourmet restaurant in rather laidback digs for an upscale Miraflores restaurant serves some of the best hearty fare in the capital; in fact, it's the favorite restaurant of a Limeño friend who's quite the gourmand. The surroundings are pretty simple, even if the food is not. Try the charcoal-grilled ceviche, *tacu-tacu con medallones de mero* (rice and beans with medallions of grouper), or the Chiclayana specialties baby goat and *arroz con pato* (rice with duck). Be warned that this can be fairly heavy food; you may need a siesta after a visit to Fiesta.

Av. Reducto 1278, Miraflores. ℂ **01/242-9009.** www.restaurantfiestagourmet.com. Reservations recommended. Main courses S/39–S/59. AE, DC, MC, V. Daily 12:30–5pm and 8–11pm.

Restaurant Huaca Pucllana ★★ NOUVEAU PERUVIAN Located in an unparalleled setting—within the compound of a 1,500-year-old adobe pyramid built by the original inhabitants of Lima—is one of the city's greatest dining surprises. This beautiful and serene upscale restaurant, with knockout views of the pyramid and secluded in the midst of Lima's chaotic jumble, makes for a remarkable night out. The low hump of adobe bricks and excavation walkways are illuminated at night, and diners can take a tour of the construction and digs after dinner. The restaurant is handsomely designed in a rustic colonial style; you can dine indoors or out, but the best spot is surely the covered terrace. The menu is creative Peruvian, with fusion touches spicing up classic *criollo* cooking. Excellent appetizers include *humitas verdes* (tamales) and *causitas pucllana* (balls of mashed potatoes with shrimp and avocado). Main courses are focused on meats, such as rack of lamb, but I had an excellent marinated grouper with an interesting Asian twist. Desserts are worth saving room for; the napoleon, with chocolate mousse and passion fruit sorbet between chocolate cookies, is heavenly.

General Borgoño, Block 8 (Huaca Pucllana), Miraflores. ℂ **01/445-4042.** Reservations recommended. Main courses S/32–S/60. AE, DC, MC, V. Mon–Sat 12:30pm–midnight; Sun 12:30–4pm.

Expensive
La Mar Cebichería ★★ CEVICHE/SEAFOOD The restaurant everyone in Lima seems to be lining up to get in—no reservations are accepted, so get there early or sneak in late in the afternoon—is this upscale *cevichería,* courtesy of hot chef Gastón Acurio.

Fashionable, stylishly designed, and moderately priced, it represents the best of traditional Limeño cooking, but with an edge. Some ceviche purists will tell you that you don't need to go to a hip, expensive spot for ceviche, and while it's true the most authentic ceviche spots are no-frills neighborhood joints, there's nothing wrong with jazzing up the formula in my book. The airy, plant-filled space has a chic, modern touch, with an angular, poured concrete facade, bamboo roof, turquoise chairs, and cement floors. The fish—choose from a couple dozen types of ceviche, as well as rice-based seafood dishes and whole fish—is always fresh and carefully prepared. The restaurant even features a cool cocktail bar with great pisco-based drinks, like the "Cholopolitan," that would surely be a hit late into the night were it to stay open. But owing to *cevichería* tradition, it's strictly a daytime affair.

Av. La Mar 770, Miraflores. ℂ **01/421-3365.** www.lamarcebicheria.com. Reservations not accepted. Main courses S/19–S/49. AE, DC, MC, V. Mon–Fri noon–5pm; Sat–Sun 11:30am–5:30pm.

Pescados Capitales ★★ CEVICHE/SEAFOOD With an easygoing, hip style that's similar to Cebichería La Mar's, this upscale ceviche and seafood restaurant is popular with Lima's *gente bella* (beautiful people). The name is a sly riff on the phrase for "original sin" (*pescado*, or fish, being just one letter removed from *pecado*, or sin); the dishes have names like "ire," "envy," and "avarice," and the menu declares that a few larger dishes are for the "vain or gluttonous." The restaurant has a large open-air terrace where overflow crowds sip pisco sours and beers on weekend afternoons, and a big, airy, and busy dining room under a high bamboo and glass roof. A terrific starter is Lujuria Freudiana (grilled baby squid), while the ceviche capital is a yummy mix of sole, salmon, and tuna.

Av. La Mar 1370, Miraflores. ℂ **01/421-8808.** Reservations not accepted. Main courses S/28–S/48. AE, DC, MC, V. Daily 12:30–5pm and 8–11pm.

Moderate
Antico Ristorante Italiano di Porto Rotondo ★ ITALIAN
A pretty yellow colonial house with an inviting library-like club bar off to one side, Porto Rotondo is a sophisticated retreat in the midst of Miraflores's hustle and bustle. Inside you'll find deep red walls, black-and-white tile floors, and large mirrors. The menu focuses on classic and well-prepared Italian dishes: ravioli, risotto, gnocchi, and *osso buco*, as well as fresh fish. Some nights, there are many more people sitting at the bar than around the dining tables in the next room.

Recavarren 265, Miraflores. ℂ **01/447-9575.** Reservations recommended. Main courses S/25–S/38. MC, V. Daily noon–4pm and 8pm–midnight.

Dánica ★★ (Finds) ITALIAN/MEDITERRANEAN/PERUVIAN
This new favorite of Limeños, helmed by a hot young female chef, is what might be called a gourmet neighborhood eatery. The interior is casual, looking more like an upscale café than a fine-dining destination, and though you can get Italian comfort food, Vanessa Siragusa also turns out some very creative and elaborate fusion dishes. If there's one dish (besides the scrumptious desserts) to highlight, it might be the stir-fried beef risotto, a cross between Peru's mainstay lomo saltado and risotto (though the *raviolis de asado*, or roast meat ravioli with mustard sauce, comes in a close second). But in keeping with the neighborhood theme, it's one of the friendliest (not to mention, best-value) restaurants in town—there's little doubt why friends of mine return nearly every week to visit Dánica.

Av. Emilio Cavenecia 170, San Isidro. ℂ **01/421-1891.** Reservations recommended. Main courses S/22–S/35. AE, DC, MC, V. Mon–Sat 12:30pm–12:30am; Sun 12:30–10:30pm.

Segundo Muelle ★ (Kids) CEVICHE/SEAFOOD   At the top of most people's lists of favorite Peruvian dishes is ceviche, and you won't have trouble finding a *cevichería* anywhere along the coast. Often you have to choose between either upscale or down-and-dirty versions. This informal lunch-only place in Miraflores, across from the cheesy Parque del Amor and oceanfront *malecón,* is one of the most reasonable options in Lima for excellent fresh fish and ceviche plates without any fuss. Choose between a simple, almost cafeteria-style interior and an upstairs outdoor deck with sea views. If you're new to ceviche, you can't go wrong with the *mixto* (white fish, octopus, prawns, snails, scallops, and squid). A long list of other fish dishes is offered, including sole, salmon, and seafood pastas. Top off your meal with *chicha morada,* a purple corn beverage made with pineapple and lemon—it's sweet and delicious. Kids' plates are available for S/15. Another branch is in San Isidro at Av. Conquistadores 490.

Av. Carnaval y Moreyra 605, San Isidro. (✆) **01/241-5040.** www.segundomuelle.com. Reservations not accepted. Main courses S/18–S/40. MC, V. Daily noon–5pm.

T'anta ★★ (Kids) CAFE/PERUVIAN   Like a Peruvian Dean & Deluca (an upscale deli/market in New York City), T'anta (which means "bread" in Quechua) serves delicious, casual eats in its cafe or prepared foods to go. It now has a complete menu, with a full range of creative snack foods and small meals, including classic Peruvian dishes. From fresh salads and panini to Peruvian sandwiches called *sánguches* and homemade pastas and terrific desserts, this stylish but informal place, the brainchild of Astrid (the dessert wizard of Astrid y Gastón fame) hits the spot no matter what you're in the mood for, or when. It's very chic and modern, with poured concrete and an angled glass wall. With its full list of cool cocktails (such as the *maricucha* or *aguaymanto* sour), it's also a great spot for drinks. You may come for a coffee or a cocktail, but I guarantee that you'll end up at least having dessert. One dessert that had me coming back for more was the *tartita de maracuyá* (passion-fruit tart). There are now three other locations in Lima, including one in the Centro on Pasaje Nicolás de Rivera del Viejo 142.

Av. 28 de Julio 888, Miraflores. (✆) **01/421-9708.** Reservations not accepted. Main courses S/19–S/42. AE, DC, MC, V. Daily 8am–midnight.

Inexpensive

Café Café CAFE/COFFEE   A tried-and-true people-watching spot with a menu of 100-plus drinks and dozens of gourmet coffees, this agreeable two-story cafe, located just off the main park in Miraflores, is also ideal for a quick lunch or simple dinner. The predominantly young crowd drops by not only to meet up with friends and hang out at the outdoor tables, but also to sample inexpensive pizzas, salads, or one of the 26 sandwiches. For folks in need of a real meal, there are also larger plates, including a fish of the day. It's also a good spot to have a quick and inexpensive breakfast. This spot is just one of several branches in town.

Mártir Olaya 250, Miraflores. (✆) **01/445-1165.** Main courses S/9–S/34. AE, DC, MC, V. Daily 8:30am–1:30am.

BARRANCO

To locate the following restaurants, see the "Lima at a Glance" map on p. 107.

Very Expensive

Costa Verde (Overrated) SEAFOOD   Any time a restaurant in Peru lists all prices in dollars, you know it's not going to be cheap. Costa Verde, perched on a promontory

Cevicherías

You can't really go to Peru—especially Lima—without sitting down for an irresistibly fresh plate of ceviche (also written *cebiche*), the tantalizing plate of raw fish and shellfish that's marinated in lime or lemon juice and chili peppers and served with toasted corn, sweet potato, and raw onion. The citrus juices "cook" the fish, so it's not really raw the way sushi is. Plenty of restaurants of all stripes—from lowly neighborhood joints to snooty fine-dining spots popular with government bureaucrats and visiting businessmen—offer ceviche, but you really have to go to an authentic *cevichería* for the true experience. In addition to **Segundo Muelle** (p. 128) and **Canta Rana** (p. 130), another worth checking out is **Punta Sal,** Malecón Cisneros, block 3, at the corner of Trípoli in Miraflores (© **01/242-4524**), one of a small chain of informal *cevicherías* pretty similar to Segundo Muelle. Hip takes on the *cevichería* include Gastón Acurio's La Mar **Cebichería** (p. 126) and **Pescados Capitales** (p. 127). Peruvians view ceviche as a daytime dish, and most *cevicherías* aren't even open for dinner (the high acidity makes for difficult nighttime digestion for many); for the full experience, go at lunchtime and order a classic pisco sour to start, followed by *chicha morada* (or, if you're feeling kinky, a bottle of curiously neon-yellow Inka Cola).

jutting out into the ocean along the "green coast" south of Miraflores, is probably as expensive a meal as you'll have in Peru, but it's also good enough to draw a decent number of Limeños celebrating special occasions. It draws a bigger share of foreigners, as evidenced by the touristy little national flags the hostess places on everyone's table. The big-time seafood buffet is what makes everyone's eyes bulge. There's a daily lunch buffet and also a huge gourmet dinner buffet ($60 a head), which the restaurant claims is registered in the *Guinness Book of Records.* The regular menu seems not to have changed in more than 3 decades of business, but you can't really argue with sea bass with wild mushrooms and morel sauce with scallop mousse, or basil and ricotta gnocchi with river shrimp in saffron sauce. Sit in the glass-enclosed atrium—although it's rather devoid of character, you'll get to hear the sound of waves crashing against the shore. Then again, that could be the sound of your bank account groaning.

Circuito de Playas (Playa Barranquito), Barranco. © **01/227-1244.** Reservations recommended. Main courses $15–$36. AE, DC, MC, V. Daily noon–midnight.

Expensive

Chala ★★ FUSION/PERUVIAN This sleek restaurant and lounge down by the "bridge of sighs" in Barranco was one of my new faves in Lima a couple of years ago; although it now has a new chef and isn't quite the revelation it once was, it's still very good. The restaurant serves imaginative fare it calls *"costa fusion,"* meaning adaptations of Peruvian coastal and Limeño dishes with largely Mediterranean influences. While the chic, colorful interior is coolly international, the gorgeous long deck outdoors, under an old wooden ceiling, tall trees, and squawking birds, has a great tropical, and sexy, feel. Start by sipping a *maracuyá* (passion-fruit) sour and munching on banana chips, before moving on to an extremely fresh salad with mushrooms, avocado, and tomatoes. A tasty entree, identified by the esoteric name "Oleaje Espirituoso," is a terrific dish of grouper served on a bed of zucchini gnocchi and a crème of *huacatay* (a local herb).

Bajada de Baños 343, Barranco. ℂ **01/252-8515.** Reservations recommended. Main courses S/28–S/55. AE, DC, MC, V. Tues–Sat noon–3pm and 5–11pm; Sun 11am–5pm.

Moderate

Antica Trattoria ★ ⒱alue ⒦ids ITALIAN This charming and laid-back Italian restaurant perfectly suits the surrounding neighborhood, which has large doses of both qualities. It has a number of small, separate dining rooms decorated with a warm, rustic and minimalist masculinity: stucco walls, dark wood-beamed ceilings, country-style wood tables, and simple, solid chairs. The house specialty is gourmet pizza from the wood-fired ovens, but the menu has several tempting ideas to lure you away from pizza, such as homemade pastas and *osso buco*, or delicious *lomo fino a la tagliata* (beef buried under a mound of arugula). The relaxed environment makes this a great date place, as well as the perfect spot for dinner before stepping out to one of Barranco's live music or dance clubs.

San Martín 201, Barranco. ℂ **01/247-5752.** Reservations recommended. Main courses S/19–S/42. AE, DC, MC, V. Daily noon–midnight.

Canta Rana ★★ ⒻindsⓈ CEVICHE/SEAFOOD A relaxed and informal place (in local lingo, a *huarique*) that looks almost like the interior of a garage and is immensely popular with locals, "the Singing Frog" is the very definition of a neighborhood *cevichería.* You might not guess it from the outside, but it's one of the best spots in town for ceviche and fresh seafood in a classic coastal manner. The menu lists 15 types of sea bass, including one stuffed with langoustines, as well as infinite varieties of ceviche. The traditional ceviche (big enough for two) is served on a flat plate with heaps of purple onions, some *choclo* (maize), and a wedge of *camote* (sweet potato). The best way to wash it down is with a chilled pitcher of *chicha morada.* The shacklike interior is decorated with simple wood tables, and the walls are festooned with *fútbol* (soccer) paraphernalia. For a high dose of local color and excellent seafood, Canta Rana's a perfect lunch spot.

Génova 101, Barranco. ℂ **01/247-7274.** Reservations recommended. Main courses S/18–S/40. AE, MC, V. Tues–Sat 11am–11pm; Sun–Mon 11am–6pm.

Inexpensive

Café Tostado ★ ⒻindsⓈ HOME COOKING/PERUVIAN It's hard to call this amazingly authentic little lunch (and early dinner, I suppose) spot a restaurant, even. It's something akin to a country eating club in the midst of the big city, an extraordinarily rustic dining hall that looks like the kind of place a bunch of Argentine gauchos would chow down after a long morning working the herds on the pampas. But it's popular with Limeños of all stripes, from laborers, retired guys, business folks in stylish suits, and hipsters, who gather at communal tables and choose one of two dishes on offer. There's no menu, just the daily dish. Tuesday, for example, is hearty pastas, such as tallarines with homemade pesto. The cook, Pepe, who's found every day stirring myriad pots and pans at the open kitchen in back, is best known for his rabbit a la orange (served only by advance order). No alcohol or beer is served; just sodas and water. For some visitors to Lima, this may be a stretch; others will be pleased to find something wholly unique and local in an increasingly homogenized world.

Nicolás de Pierola 232, Barranco. ℂ **01/247-7133.** Reservations recommended. Main courses S/10–S/25. No credit cards. Daily 11am–7pm.

Many visitors to Lima are merely on their way to other places in Peru, and few spend more than a couple of days in the capital. But because nearly all transport goes through Lima, most people take advantage of layovers to see what distinguishes the city: its colonial old quarter—once the finest in the Americas—and several of the finest museums in Peru, all of which serve as magnificent introductions to Peruvian history and culture.

Much of the historic center has suffered from sad neglect; the municipal government is committed to restoring the aesthetic value, but, with limited funds, it faces a daunting task. Today central Lima has a noticeable police presence and is considerably safer than it was just a few years ago. A full day in Lima Centro should suffice; depending on your interests, you could spend several days traipsing through Lima's many museum collections, many of which are dispersed in otherwise unremarkable neighborhoods. But for those with a couple extra days in the city, when Lima's traffic and grit get to you, head to the artsy coastal neighborhood, Barranco, home to Lima's best nightlife and the site of a handful of excellent small museums. It will likely greatly improve your impressions of the capital.

LIMA CENTRO: COLONIAL LIMA

Lima's grand **Plaza de Armas** ★ (also called the **Plaza Mayor,** or **Main Square**), the original center of the city and the site where Francisco Pizarro founded the city in 1535, is essentially a modern reconstruction. The disastrous 1746 earthquake that initiated the city's decline leveled most of the 16th- and 17th-century buildings in the old center. The plaza has witnessed everything from bullfights to Inquisition-related executions. The oldest surviving element of the square is the central bronze fountain, which dates from 1651. Today the square, although perhaps not the most beautiful or languid in South America, is still rather distinguished beneath a surface level of grime and bustle (and it has been named a UNESCO World Heritage Site). The major palaces and cathedral are mostly harmonious in architectural style and color. (The facades are a mix of natural stone and a once-bold yellow color now dulled by smog and mist.) On the north side of the square is the early-20th-century **Palacio del Gobierno (Presidential Palace),** where a changing of the guard takes place daily at noon; free guided visits of the palace are offered Monday through Friday from 10am to 12:30pm. The **Municipalidad de Lima (City Hall)** is on the west side of the plaza. Across the square is **La Catedral (Cathedral),** rebuilt after the earthquake, making it by far the oldest building on the square, and, next to the cathedral, the **Palacio Episcopal (Archbishop's Palace),** distinguished by an extraordinary wooden balcony.

A block north of the Plaza de Armas, behind the Presidential Palace, is the Río Rímac and a 17th-century Roman-style bridge, the **Puente de Piedra** (literally, "stone bridge"). It leads to the once-fashionable **Rímac** district, today considerably less chic—some would say downright dangerous—although it is the location of a few of Lima's best *peñas,* or live *criollo* (Creole/coastal) music clubs. The **Plaza de Acho bullring,** once the largest in the world, and the decent **Museo Taurino (Bullfighting Museum)** are near the river at Hualgayoc 332 (© **01/482-3360**). The museum is open Monday through Friday from 9am to 3pm, and Saturday from 9am to 2pm, and admission is S/6. The ring is in full swing during the Fiestas Patrias (national holidays) at the end of July; the regular season runs October through December.

Five blocks southwest of Plaza de Armas is Lima Centro's other grand square, **Plaza San Martín.** Inaugurated in 1921, this stately square with handsome gardens was recently renovated. At its center is a large monument to the South American liberator, José de San Martín.

Lima's **Barrio Chino,** the largest Chinese community in South America (200,000 plus), is the best place to get a taste of the Peruvian twist on traditional Chinese cooking in the neighborhood's *chifas*. For recommendations, see the "Peruvian *Chifas*" box on p. 125. The official boundary of Chinatown is the large gate on Jirón Ucayali.

The Top Attractions

La Catedral ★ Lima's baroque cathedral, an enlargement of an earlier one from 1555, was completed in 1625. It suffered damages in earthquakes in 1687 and was decimated by the big one in 1746. The present building, again damaged by tremors in 1940, is an 18th-century reconstruction of the early plans. Twin yellow towers sandwich an elaborate stone facade. Inside are several notable churrigueresque (Spanish baroque) altars and carved wooden choir stalls, but the cathedral is best known for the chapel where Francisco Pizarro lies and a small **Museo de Arte Religioso (Museum of Religious Art)** housed in the rear of the church.

Immediately to the right after you enter the church is a chapel decorated in magnificent Venetian mosaics and marble. In case you don't know whose earthly remains are inside the tomb, letters in mosaic tiles over the arch of the chapel spell out FRANCISCO PIZARRO. The founder of Lima and killer of the Incas' emperor was himself assassinated in the Plaza de Armas in 1541, but his remains weren't brought to the cathedral until 1985. (They were discovered in a crypt in 1977.) Look closely at the mosaic on the far wall, which depicts his coat of arms, Atahualpa reaching into his coffer to cough up a ransom in the hopes of attaining his release, and other symbols of Pizarro's life. The museum has a few fabulous painted-glass mirrors from Cusco, a collection of unsigned paintings, and a seated sculpture of Jesus, with his chin resting pensively on his hand; it's as bloody a figure of Christ as you're likely to see. Allow about an hour for a visit.

Plaza de Armas. ✆ **01/427-5980.** Admission to cathedral and museum S/10 adults, S/5 students. Guides available in English and Spanish (voluntary tip). Mon–Sat 10am–5pm.

Museo del Convento de San Francisco de Asis de Lima ★★ Probably the most spectacular of Lima's Colonial-era churches, the Convent of Saint Francis is a strikingly restored, yellow-and-white 17th-century complex that survived the massive earthquake in 1746. The facade is a favorite of thousands of pigeons, who rest on rows of ridges that rise up the towers—so much so that, from a distance, it looks like black spots add an unexpectedly funky flavor to the baroque church. Cloisters and interiors are lined with beautiful *azulejos* (glazed ceramic tiles) from Seville; carved *mudéjar* (Moorish-style) ceilings are overhead. The mandatory guided tour takes visitors past the cloisters to a fine museum of religious art, with beautifully carved saints and a series of portraits of the apostles by the studio of Francisco Zurbarán, the famed Spanish painter. For many, though, the most fascinating component of the visit is the descent into the catacombs, which were dug beginning in 1546 as a burial ground for priests and others. (As many as 75,000 bodies were interred here before the main cemetery was built.) File past loads of bones—it's unknown how many levels down they go—and see a round well lined with perfectly laid skulls and femurs. Also of great interest are the church, outfitted with an impressive neoclassical altar, and a fantastic 17th-century library with 20,000 books, many of which date to the first years after Lima's foundation. A breathtaking carved

Casa Aliaga **9**
Casa de Osambela Oquendo **1**
Casa Goyeneche **14**
Casa Riva-Agüero **10**
Convento de Santo Domingo **2**
Convento y Museo
 de San Francisco **6**
Iglesia de La Merced **13**
Iglesia de Las Nazarenas **12**
Iglesia de San Agustín **11**
Iglesia de San Pedro **16**
La Catedral **8**
Museo de la Inquisición **17**
Palacio del Gobierno **5**
Palacio Episcopal **7**
Palacio Torre Tagle **15**
Plaza de Ocho/Museo Taurino **4**
Puente de Piedra **3**

LIMA

6

WHAT TO SEE & DO

Moorish ceiling over a staircase is a reconstruction of the original from 1625. Allow 1½ hours to see it all, including waiting time for an English-language tour.

Ancash s/n (Plaza de San Francisco). ✆ **01/426-7377**. www.museocatacumbas.com. Admission S/5 adults, S/2.50 students. Guides available in English and Spanish. Daily 9am–6pm.

Museo de la Inquisición (Finds)   This magnificent mansion across the street from the House of Congress once belonged to the family considered the founders of Lima, but it became the tribunal for the notorious Spanish Inquisition. Today it is a museum that soberly addresses religious intolerance from the Middle Ages through colonial times. The handsomely restored house itself is worth a visit because it's a fine peek at the elegant rooms of a prominent 16th-century colonial home (including the intricately carved ceiling of the Tribunal room). But its unfortunate history is plainly evident in the catacombs, which served as prison cells; on view are several instruments of torture. At least 32 Peruvians died here during the Inquisition, which persisted until 1820. The guided tour lasts about an hour.

Plaza Bolívar (Junín 548). © 01/427-5980. Free admission. Guided tours in English, Spanish, French, and Portuguese. Daily 10am–6pm.

Colonial Church Roundup ★★

Lima Centro has a number of fine colonial-era churches worth visiting. Most are open Monday through Saturday for visits, and most have free admission.

Directly south of La Catedral on Azángaro at Ucayali, **San Pedro** ★ (© 01/428-3017), a Jesuit church that dates to 1638, is perhaps the best-preserved example of early colonial religious architecture in the city. The exterior is simple and rather austere, but the interior is rich with gilded altars and balconies. The bold main altar, with columns and balconies and sculpted figures, is particularly impressive. There are also some beautiful 17th- and 18th-century baroque *retablos* (altars) of carved wood and gold leaf. A small museum of colonial art is to the right of the entrance of the church, which is open Monday through Saturday from 7am to noon and 5 to 8pm; admission is free.

Iglesia de La Merced, Jirón de la Unión at Miró Quesada (© 01/427-8199), 2 blocks southwest of the Plaza de Armas, was erected on the site of Lima's first Mass in 1534. The 18th-century church has a striking carved baroque colonial facade. Inside, the sacristy, embellished with Moorish tiles, and the main altar are excellent examples of the period. The church also possesses a nice collection of colonial art. Yet it is perhaps most notable for the devoted followers of Padre Urraca, a 17th-century priest; they come daily in droves to pay their respects, praying and touching the large silver cross dedicated to him in the nave on the right, and leaving many mementos of their veneration. The church is open Monday through Saturday from 8am to noon and 4 to 8pm.

Practically destroyed during an 1895 revolution, **San Agustín,** at the corner of Jirón Ica and Jirón Camaná (© 01/427-7548), is distinguished by a spectacular churrigueresque facade, one of the best of its kind in Peru, dating to the early 18th century. San Agustín's official hours are daily from 8 to 11am and 4:30 to 7pm, but, in practice, it's frequently closed. The **Convento de Santo Domingo,** at the corner of Conde de Superunda and Camaná, toward the River Rímac (© 01/427-6793), draws many Peruvians to visit the tombs of Santa Rosa de Lima and San Martín de Porras. It is perhaps of less

---

Tips **Me Ama, No Me Ama, Me Ama . . .**

A curious park along the ocean at the edge of Miraflores, much beloved by Limeños looking to score, is the **Parque del Amor** (literally, "Love Park"), designed by the Peruvian artist Victor Delfín with a nod to Antoni Gaudí's Parque Güell in Barcelona, Spain. It features good views of the sea (when it's not shrouded in heavy fog), benches swathed in broken-tile mosaics, and, most amusingly, a giant, rather grotesque statue of a couple making out—which is pretty much what everyone does nearby. Benches are inscribed with sentimental murmurs of love, such as *vuelve mi palomita*. If it's Valentines Day, stand back.

interest to foreign visitors, although it does have a very nice main cloister. It's open Monday through Saturday from 9am to 12:30pm and 3 to 6pm; admission costs S/3.

Las Nazarenas, at the corner of Huancavelica and Avenida Tacna on the northwest edge of the colonial center (© **01/423-5718**), has a remarkable history. It was constructed in the 18th century around a locally famous painting of Christ by an Angolan slave. Known as "El Señor de los Milagros," the image, painted on the wall of a simple abode (many slaves lived in this area on the fringes of the city), survived the massive 1655 earthquake, even though everything around it crumbled. People began to flock to the painting, and soon the Catholic Church constructed a house of worship for it. Behind the altar, on the still-standing wall, is an oil replica, which is paraded through the streets on a 1-ton silver litter during the El Señor de los Milagros festival; this is one of Lima's largest festivals and is held on October 18, 19, and 28 and November 1. Everyone wears purple during the procession. Las Nazarenas is open Monday through Saturday from 6:30am to noon and 5 to 8:30pm.

Colonial Palace Roundup ★

The historic quarter of Lima, the old administrative capital of Spain's South American colonies, once boasted many of the finest mansions in the hemisphere. Repeated devastation by earthquakes and more recent public and private inability to maintain many of the superb surviving *casas coloniales,* however, has left Lima with only a handful of houses open to the public.

Casa Riva-Agüero, Camaná 459 (© **01/427-9275**), is an impressive 18th-century mansion with a beautiful green-and-red courtyard that now belongs to the Catholic University of Peru. It has a small folk-art museum in the restored and furnished interior. The house is open Tuesday through Saturday from 10am to 1pm and 2 to 7:30pm; admission costs S/25 museum only. **Casa Aliaga ★**, Jr. de la Unión 224 (© **01/427-6624**), is the oldest surviving house in Lima, dating from 1535. It is also one of Lima's finest mansions, with an extraordinary inner patio and elegant salons, and it continues to be owned and lived in by descendants of the original family. The house can be visited only as part of a city tour (S/75) conducted exclusively by **Lima Tours** (© **01/619-6900; www.limatours.com.pe**). A worthy alternative if you don't want to spring for a guided tour is **Casa de Osambela Oquendo,** Conde de Superunda 298 (© **01/428-7919**). The tallest house in colonial Lima, today it belongs to the Ministry of Education. Although it's still not officially open for visits, the caretaker, Lizardo Retes Bustamante, will show visitors around, including up four levels to the baby-blue cupola-mirador for views over the city. (The original owner built the house so he could see all the way to the port.) Next door is a 1770 house in a lamentable state; squatters inhabit it. The Osambela house has a spectacular patio, 40 bedrooms, and eight wooden balconies to the street, a sure sign of the owner's great wealth. It's open daily from 9am to 5pm; admission is free, but tips are accepted.

A couple blocks east of the Plaza de Armas at Ucayali 363 is **Palacio Torre Tagle ★**, the most famous palace in Lima and one of the most handsome in Peru. Today the early-18th-century palace, built by a marquis who was treasurer of the Royal Spanish fleet, belongs to the Peruvian Ministry of Foreign Affairs and, sadly, can no longer be visited by the public (though it may be worth inquiring at the Ministry, next door at Ucayali 318). Its exterior, with a gorgeous baroque stone doorway and carved dark-wood balconies, is very much worth a look (and you might get a peek inside the courtyard if a group of dark suits enters or leaves when you're passing by). Across the street from Torre Tagle,

Casa Goyeneche (also called **Casa de Rada**) is another impressive 18th-century mansion, with distinct French influences; it's also not open to the public (although you might be able to manage a peek at the patio). Those with a specific interest in colonial architecture might also want to have a look at the facades of **Casa Negreiros,** Jr. Azángaro 532; **Casa de las Trece Monedas,** Jr. Ancash 536; **Casa Barbieri,** Jirón Callao at Rufino Torrico; **Casa de Pilatos,** Jr. Ancash 390; and **Casa la Riva,** Jr. Ica 426.

THE TOP MUSEUMS

To locate the following museums, see the "Lima at a Glance" map on p. 107.

Museo Arqueológico Rafael Larco Herrera ★★★ Founded in 1926, this museum has the largest private collection of pre-Columbian art in the world. It concentrates on the Moche Dynasty, especially on its refined ceramics, with an estimated 45,000 pieces—including incredibly fine textiles, jewelry, and stonework from several other ancient cultures—all housed in an 18th-century colonial building. Rafael Larco Hoyle is considered the founder of Peruvian archaeology (he named the museum after his father); he wrote the seminal study *Los Mochicas* in 1938, although he succeeded in publishing only six chapters. (The rest has now been posthumously published.)

The Moche (A.D. 200–700), who lived along the northern coast in the large area near present-day Trujillo and Cajamarca, are credited with achieving one of the greatest artistic expressions of ancient Peru. The collection might be overwhelming to visitors who know little about the Moche, but one soon learns that the pottery gives clues to all elements of their society: diseases, curing practices, architecture, transportation, dance, agriculture, music, and religion. The Moche are also celebrated in the modern world for their erotic ceramics. The Sala Erótica here is removed from the general collection, like the porn section in a video store. It's outdoors, downstairs, and across the garden. The Moche depicted sex in realistic, humorous, moralistic, religious, and—above all—explicit terms; the most common and even a few deviant practices are represented. If you're traveling with kids, expect giggles or questions about the ancient Peruvians' mighty phalluses. Plan on spending 2 hours to see it all.

An attractive on-site restaurant, **Café del Museo** ★, a recent addition to the museum, is under the auspices of Peru's celebrity chef Gastón Acurio—so you may want to plan for lunch or an early dinner during your visit.

Av. Bolívar 1515, Pueblo Libre. ⓒ **01/461-1312.** www.museolarco.org. Admission S/30 adults, S/25 seniors, S/15 students. Private guides available in English and Spanish (tip basis, minimum S/10). Daily 9am–6pm. Take a taxi or the "Todo Brasil" colectivo to Avenida Brasil, and then another to Avenida Bolívar. If you're coming from the Museo Nacional de Arqueología, Antropología e Historia del Perú (p. 137), walk along the blue path.

Museo de la Nación ★★ (Kids) Peru's ancient history is exceedingly complicated—not to mention new territory for most visitors to the country. Indeed, Peru's pre-Columbian civilizations were among the most sophisticated of their times; when Egypt was building pyramids, people in Peru were constructing great cities. Lima's National Museum, the city's biggest and one of the most important in Peru, guides visitors through the highlights of overlapping and conquering cultures and their achievements, seen not only in architecture (including scale models of most major ruins in Peru), but also in highly advanced ceramics and textiles. The exhibits, spread over three rambling floors, are ordered chronologically—very helpful for getting a grip on these many cultures dispersed across Peru. They trace the art and history of the earliest inhabitants to the Inca Empire, the last before colonization by the Spaniards. In case you aren't able to

⊙Overrated All That Glitters Isn't Necessarily Gold

The privately held **Museo Oro del Perú (Gold Museum),** for decades the most visited museum in Peru, was part of a must-see museum triumvirate in Lima only a few years ago. But that was before the National Institute of Culture and the Tourism Protection Bureau declared just about everything in the museum—some 7,000 or more pieces—to be fake. The massive collection, mainly consisting of supposed pre-Columbian gold, was assembled by one man, Miguel Mujica Gallo—who, perhaps fortunately, died just days before the investigation into his collection was launched. Although the museum was expensive and poorly organized, all that glittering gold—augmented by hundreds (if not thousands) of ceremonial objects, tapestries, masks, ancient weapons, clothing, several mummies, and military weaponry from medieval Europe to ancient Japan—certainly caught many a visitor's eye over the years. Though the museum contends that everything on display is authentic, it's pretty difficult to recommend visiting a collection with such a fraudulent history. The museum is located at Av. Alonso de Molina 1100, Monterrico (ⓒ **01/345-1292;** www.museoroperu.com.pe; daily 11:30am–7pm; admission S/33 for adults, S/16 for students. A taxi is the most direct way here; coming by colectivo involves taking at least two buses along Arequipa to Avenida Angamos, changing to one marked UNIVERSIDAD DE LIMA, and asking the driver to let you off at the Museo de Oro.

make it to the archaeology-rich north of Peru, pay special attention to the facsimile of the Lord of Sipán discovery, one of the most important in the world in recent years. For the most part, explanations accompanying the exhibits are in both Spanish and English. Allow 2 to 3 hours for your visit.

Av. Javier Prado Este 2465, San Borja. ⓒ **01/476-9878.** Admission S/9 adults, S/3 seniors, S/1 students. Tues–Sun 9am–6pm. Guides in several languages can be contracted. You can get here by colectivo along Av. Prado from Av. Arequipa, but it is much simpler to take a taxi from Lima Centro or Miraflores/San Isidro.

Museo Nacional de Arqueología, Antropología e Historia del Perú ★ With
such a mouthful of an official name, you might expect the National Museum of Archaeology, Anthropology, and History to be the Peruvian equivalent of New York City's Metropolitan Museum of Art. It's not (especially because much of the museum's huge collection remains in storage), but it's a worthwhile and enjoyable museum that covers Peruvian civilization from prehistoric times to the colonial and republican periods. There are ceramics, carved stone figures and obelisks, metalwork and jewelry, and lovely textiles. On view are early ceramics from 2800 B.C. in the central Andes, the great granite Tello Obelisk from the Chavín period, burial tombs, and mummies in the fetal position wrapped in burial blankets. There's also a selection of erotic ceramics from the Moche culture, but it's not nearly as extensive as that of the Museo Arqueológico Rafael Larco Herrera (p. 136). Individual rooms are dedicated to the Nasca, Paracas, Moche, and Chimú cultures. Toward the end of the exhibit, which wanders around the central courtyard of the handsome 19th-century Quinta de los Libertadores mansion (once lived in

by South American independence heroes San Martín and Bolívar), is a large-scale model of Machu Picchu with buttons that allows visitors to identify key sectors of the complex. Basic descriptions throughout the museum are mostly in Spanish, although some are also in English. Allow about an hour for your visit. From the museum, you can follow a walking path along a painted blue line to the Rafael Larco Herrera Museum. It's about a mile away, or 20 minutes straight into traffic on Antonio de Sucre.

Plaza Bolívar s/n, Pueblo Libre. © **01/463-5070.** http://museonacional.perucultural.org.pe. Admission S/12 adults, S/3.50 seniors and students. Private guides available in English and Spanish (tip basis, minimum S/10). Tues–Sat 9am–5pm; Sun 10am–4pm. Take a taxi here, or take the "Todo Brasil" colectivo to Avenida Vivanco, and then take a 15-min. walk.

OTHER MUSEUMS

To locate Fundación Museo Amano and Museo de Arte Colonial Pedro de Osma, see the "Lima at a Glance" map, on p. 107.

Fundación Museo Amano (Finds) This nicely designed museum features a collection of artifacts belonging to a single collector, representing some of Peru's most important civilizations, including the Chimú and the Nasca. The textiles and ceramics are among the best displayed in Lima, and the collection really shows the strength of Chancay weaving (a culture from the northern coast), which you might not see a whole lot of elsewhere. You really have to want to see the collection, though (and qualify, as restrictive as that sounds); it's open for limited hours and only by previous appointment to small groups. Allow about an hour or more.

Calle Retiro 160, Miraflores. © **01/441-2909.** Free admission (donations accepted). Mon–Fri 3–5pm by appointment and guided tour in Spanish. Take a taxi to the 11th block of Av. Angamos Oeste/Av. Santa Cruz.

Museo Pedro de Osma ★ This private museum, located in a historic, ornate Barranco mansion (Palacio de Osma), focuses on colonial Peruvian art from areas that were among the most distinguished cultural centers of the day, including Cusco, Arequipa, and Ayacucho. The house is extraordinary, and the collection of religious art, including

---

Tips   Cool Breeze in Barranco ★★

Although it's a residential neighborhood and not immediately thought of as having many tourist sights, apart from the small Museo de Arte Colonial Pedro de Osma (p. 138), the charming seaside district of Barranco is still one of the highlights of Lima. Its serenity and laid-back artiness is a welcome contrast to the untidy and seedy character of rest of the city, and a stroll around the tranquil side streets of brightly colored bungalows is the best way to restore your sanity. It's little wonder that artists and writers have long been drawn to Barranco. Beneath the poetically named wooden footbridge Puente de los Suspiros (Bridge of Sighs) is a gentle passageway, La Bajada de Baños, which leads to a sea lookout and is lined with lovely, squat single-family houses, spindly trees, and stout cacti. During the daytime, the barrio is mellow and tropical-feeling, with sultry breezes coming in from the sea, but at night the area is transformed into Lima's hedonistic hot spot, with locals and visitors flocking to the discos and watering holes here—much to the dismay of local residents who don't own a bar or restaurant.

Archaeological Sites in Lima ★

Lima is hardly the epicenter of pre-Columbian Peru, and few visitors have more than the museums featuring ancient Peruvian cultures on their minds when they hit the capital. Surprisingly, there are a handful of *huacas*—adobe pyramids—that date to around A.D. 500 and earlier interspersed among the modern constructions of the city. The archaeological sites are junior examples of those found in northern Peru, near Chiclayo and Trujillo. If you're not headed north, Lima's huacas, which have small museums attached, are worth a visit.

In San Isidro is **Huaca Huallamarca** (also called Pan de Azúcar, or "Sugar Loaf"), at the corner of Avenida Nicolás de Rivera and Avenida El Rosario. The perhaps overzealously restored adobe temple of the Maranga Lima culture has several platforms and is frequently illuminated for special presentations. It's open Tuesday through Sunday from 9am to 5pm; admission is S/5 for adults and S/3 for students. Also in San Isidro is the **Huaca Juliana,** a pre-Inca mound dating to A.D. 400. It's at Calle Belén at Pezet and keeps the same hours as Huallamarca; admission is free. **Huaca Pucllana** ★★ is a sacred pyramid, built during the 4th century and still undergoing excavation, in Miraflores at the corner of calles General Borgoño (Block 8) and Tarapacá, near Avenida Arequipa (© **01/445-8695;** http://pucllana.perucultural.org.pe). It has a small park, a terrific restaurant (p. 126), and an *artesanía* gallery. From the pyramid's top, you can see the roofs of this busy residential and business district. It's open Wednesday through Monday from 9am to 4pm; admission is S/5 and S/3 for students.

Unfortunately, a few of these sites occasionally do not keep consistent hours, so you might find yourself staring through a chain-link fence if there's no one on hand to let you in.

polychrome sculptures, *retablos* (altarpieces), and paintings from the Cusco school, are exceptional for a small, private museum. Out back, across the gardens, is a separate building with a collection of 16th- to 19th-century silver. Plan on spending an hour here.

Pedro de Osma 421, Barranco. © **01/467-0141.** www.museopedrodeosma.org. Admission S/10 adults, S/5 students. Tues–Sun 10am–1:30pm and 2:30–6pm. By colectivo from Av. Tacna to Barranco.

6 ORGANIZED TOURS

Lima is a large, sprawling, and confusing city, so if you want to make quick work of a visit, an organized tour of the major sights might be the best option. Standard city tours are offered by innumerable agencies. Among the most dependable is **Lima Tours,** Belén 1040 (© **01/619-6900;** www.limatours.com.pe), which is the only organized tour with access to the Casa Aliaga, one of the most historic colonial mansions in Lima. A standard half-day tour of Lima Centro costs S/75. Lima Tours also offers visits to Pachacámac as part of its "Lima Arqueológica" tours, as well as highlights packages across Peru.

Peruvision, Jr. Chiclayo 444, Miraflores (✆ **01/447-7710;** www.peruvision.com), offers daylong sightseeing tours of Lima, including a choice of excursions for S/250, as well as 2-hour tours for S/70. **Contacto Lima** (✆ **01/224-3854;** contactolima@tsi.com. pe) offers half-day city tours of "colonial and modern Lima," full-day tours, museum tours, and trail riding on Peruvian pacing horses, as well as tours to Nasca and Paracas, south of Lima. **Fertur Perú ★,** Jr. Junín 211 (✆ **01/427-2626;** www.fertur-travel.com), with an office in the Hotel España (and a branch at Calle Schell 485 in Miraflores), is a highly professional outfit, run by a Peruvian-American couple, with reasonably priced city tours and 4-day packages to sights across Peru. **Class Adventure Travel (CAT) ★,** Grimaldo del Solar 463, Miraflores (✆ **01/444-2220;** www.cat-travel.com), is an excellent all-purpose agency run by a knowledgeable and friendly Dutch couple; it offers a 3-day city tour and travel arrangements around Peru.

Free short **walking tours** of Lima are frequently offered by the Municipalidad de Lima (Town Hall). For the latest schedule, call ✆ **01/427-4848** or 01/427-6080, ext. 222.

Mirabus (✆ **01/476-5213;** www.mirabusperu.com) is a double-decker bus that leaves from Parque Kennedy and offers several tours, from Centro Lima to a night tour and even a dinner buffet tour and visits outside of town to Pachacámac and Puerto del Callo. Tours range from S/8 for a downtown colonial tour to S/150 for the dinner bus. Finally, although it sounds a bit uncomfortably close to those stag or bachelorette bus parties where everyone drinks his or her way across town, dead set on making fools of the guest of honor, **El Bus Parrandero,** Av. Benavides 330, Of. 101, Miraflores (✆ **01/445-4755;** www.elbusparrandero.com), is a colorful party bus promoting gregarious evening tours of Lima, with unlimited drinks, snacks, and live music. Tours are given Monday through Saturday from 8 to 11pm, departing from Larcomar shopping mall; the ride costs S/70. It's perfect if you've got your heart set on reliving (or continuing) your college days while you're in Lima.

7 OUTDOOR ACTIVITIES & SPECTATOR SPORTS

BEACHES Although Lima is perched on the Pacific coast, Río de Janeiro it's not. Still, several beaches in Miraflores and Barranco are frequented by locals, especially surfers, in the summer months. The beaches are unfit for swimming, however: The waters are heavily polluted and plagued by very strong currents. Worse, they're stalking grounds for thieves. Although the beaches aren't that appealing in and of themselves, they might serve those with an interest in people-watching: The sands are very much frequented by Limeños in the summer (Dec–Mar). Much nicer and cleaner beaches are located immediately south of Lima (see "Side Trips from Lima," later).

BICYCLING & JOGGING Given Lima's chaotic traffic, jogging is best confined to parks. Probably the best area is the bicycling and jogging paths along the *malecón* in Miraflores, near the Marriott and Miraflores Park hotels. Contact the **Club de Bicicleta de Montaña (Mountain Bike Club),** Calle César Ortega s/n (✆ **01/872-4021**), which has information about routes near Lima and places to rent mountain bikes.

BULLFIGHTING Bullfighting, less of a national craze here than in Spain or Mexico, is held in July and in the main season from October to December at the 18th-century

Plaza de Acho, Jr. Hualgayoc 332, in Rímac (☎ **01/315-5000** or 01/481-1467), the third-oldest ring in the world. Events are held Sunday afternoon. The *fiestas taurinas* bring matadors from Spain and take place at the same time as the Señor de los Milagros in October. Tickets, which range from about S/60 to S/300 for a single event (depending on whether seats are in the shade), can be obtained at the box office at the bullring. They can also be purchased at **Farmacia Deza,** Av. Conquistadores 1140, San Isidro (☎ **01/440-3798**), or by phone from **Teleticket** (☎ **01/242-2823**). Inquire about advance tickets by sending an e-mail to plazadeacho@peru.com.

GOLF Golf courses in Lima aren't open to nonmembers. Your best bet for golf is to stay at one of the exclusive hotels with golf privileges at the Lima Golf Club in San Isidro: **Country Club Lima Hotel** (p. 120) and **Sonesta Hotel El Olivar Lima** (p. 122).

PERUVIAN PACING HORSES Peruvian Paso horses *(caballos de paso),* which have a unique four-beat lateral gait, are considered by many to be the world's smoothest riding horse and also one of the showiest of all horse breeds. If you're already a fan of the breed, or just a fan of horses in general, seeing them on their home turf could be exciting. There are *concursos* (show events) scheduled at different times of the year; there's a big one in April (free admission). Information about exhibitions is available from the **Asociación Nacional de Caballos Peruanos de Paso,** Bellavista 549, Miraflores (☎ **01/444-6920** or 01/447-6331).

SOCCER Important league and national *fútbol* (soccer) matches are held at the venerable 50-year-old **Estadio Nacional,** Paseo de la República, Blocks 7–9, located just 5 minutes from the city center. Popular teams include Alianza Lima, Alianza Atlético, Universitario (known as "La U"), and Sporting Cristal. Tickets (S/10–S/75) for most matches can be purchased the same day at the stadium or from **Teleticket** (☎ **01/242-2823**).

SURFING Although several beaches in Miraflores and Barranco are popular with surfers in summer and are fine for beginners, the best beaches in southern Peru—Punta Hermosa, Punta Rocas (highly recommended), Cerro Azul, and Pico Alto (which is supposed to have the biggest waves)—are beyond Lima. Surfing in southern Peru is best from April through December (and at its peak in May); surfers who hit the waves year-round usually do it in wet suits. Check out **www.wannasurf.com/spot/South_America/Peru/Lima** for specialist information, including a chart of southern beaches that specifies skill level and breaks. Information, equipment, boards (for sale only), and accessories are available at **O'Neills,** Av. Santa Cruz 851, Miraflores (☎ **01/242-4486**); and **Focus,** Leonardo DaVinci 208, San Borja (☎ **01/475-8459**).

8 SHOPPING

The capital has the greatest variety of shopping in Peru, from tony boutiques to artisan and antiques shops. Shopping at markets in *sierra* villages and buying direct from artisans on Lake Titicaca are better experiences, certainly, but don't discount the fact that, unless you ship the loot home, you'll most likely have to bring it back to Lima anyway. In Lima, you can find traditional handicrafts from across Peru; prices are not usually much higher, and the selection might be even better than in the regions where the items are made. One exception is alpaca goods, which are better purchased in the areas around Cusco, Puno, and Arequipa, in terms of both price and selection.

Miraflores is where most shoppers congregate, although there are also several outlets in Lima Centro and elsewhere in the city. Most shops are open daily from 9:30am to 12:30pm and 3 to 8pm.

ANTIQUES & JEWELRY

Look for silver jewelry and antiques along Avenida La Paz in Miraflores. In particular, there's a little pedestrian-only passageway at Av. La Paz 646 that's lined with well-stocked antiques shops, many with nice religious art, including **La Línea del Tiempo** (© 01/241-5461) and **SAS Antiquedades** (© 01/241-1092). *Platerías* and *joyerías* (silver and jewelry shops) worth a visit are **Ilaria ★★**, Av. Larco 1325 (© 01/444-2347); and **El Tupo,** La Paz 553 (© 01/444-1511). In downtown Lima, **Joyería Gold/Gems Perú,** Pasaje Santa Rosa 119 (© 01/426-7267), stocks Colombian emeralds and fashionable, inexpensive Italian steel jewelry. Miraflores antiques shops include **El Almacén de Arte,** Francia 339 (© 01/445-6264), and **Porta 735,** Porta 735 (© 01/447-6158). A shop I particularly like is **La Casa Azul ★**, Alfonso Ugarte 150 (© 01/446-6380), which specializes in colonial furniture, religious art, and other fantastic decorative pieces. The friendly owners can help arrange shipping and assist with getting export approval for especially valuable pieces.

HANDICRAFTS & TEXTILES

Miraflores houses the lion's share of Lima's well-stocked shops, which overflow with handicrafts from around Peru, including weavings, ceramics, and silver. A terrific shop with carefully chosen, unique items of artisanship is **Killari ★★**, Alcanfores 699 (© 01/447-8684). Several dozen large souvenir and handicrafts shops are clustered on and around Avenida Ricardo Palma (a good one is **Artesanías Miraflores,** no. 205) and Avenida Petit Thouars (try **Artesanía Expo Inti,** no. 5495).

Handicrafts shops elsewhere in Miraflores include **Agua y Tierra,** Diez Canseco 298 (© 01/445-6980), and **Silvania Prints,** Diez Canseco 378 (© 01/242-0667). Alpaca sweaters and other items can be had at **Alpaca 111,** Av. Larco 671 (Larcomar shopping center; © 01/447-1623); **Alpaca Peru,** Diez Canseco 315 (© 01/241-4175); **Mon Repos,** Centro Comercial Camino Real (© 01/221-5331); and **All Alpaca,** Av. Schell 375 (© 01/427-4704). One of the largest shops, which stocks a huge range of Peruvian handicrafts from all over the country, is **Peru Artcrafts ★**, in the Larcomar shopping mall, Malecón de la Reserva 610 (© 01/446-5429). Although it's considerably more expensive than other shops (all prices are in dollars), it's perhaps the best for last-minute and one-stop shopping.

Another great spot for handicrafts from around Peru in Lima Centro is the **Santo Domingo** *artesanía* **arcades** across the street from the Santo Domingo convent on Conde de Superunda and Camaná. In Miraflores, a giant *artesanía* market with dozens of stalls is **Mercado Indio ★**, 5245 Avenida Petit Thouars (at General Vidal). In fact, almost all of Avenida Petit Thouars, from Ricardo Palma to Vidal, is lined with well-stocked handicrafts shops.

In Barranco, the finest upscale purveyor of crafts and home furnishings is **Dédalo ★★**, Saenz Peña 295 (© 01/477-0562). If you arrive here around midday and hungry, you'll be happy to find a little cafe out back in the garden, serving salads, sandwiches, and tamales. A superb selection of folk art and handcrafts from across Peru can be found at **Las Pallas ★★★**, Cajamarca 212 (© **01/477-4629**); the owner, a British woman named Mari Solari has been collecting Peruvian folk art for three decades and displays it all in several rooms of her fine Barranco house. For fine *retablos* and artisanship typical of Ayacucho (which produces some of Peru's most notable pieces), visit the **Museo-Galería Popular de Ayacucho,** Av. Pedro de Osma 116, Barranco (© **01/247-0599**).

MARKETS & MALLS

Lima Centro's crowded **Mercado Central (Central Market)** is south of the Plaza Mayor, at the edge of Chinatown and it runs daily from 8am to 5pm; you'll find just about everything there, but you should take your wits and leave your valuables at home. The **Feria Artesanal** (Artisans' Market, also called the Mercado Indio, or Indian Market, but not to be confused with the Mercado Indio in Miraflores) has a wide variety of handicrafts of varying quality, but at lower prices than most tourist-oriented shops in Lima Centro or Miraflores (quality might also be a bit lower than at those shops). Haggling is a good idea. The market is located at Avenida de la Marina (blocks 6–10) in Pueblo Libre; it's open daily from noon to 8pm.

Small handicrafts markets, open late to catch bar and post-dinner crowds, are situated in the main squares in both Miraflores and Barranco. The **Jockey Plaza Shopping Center** (© 01/437-4100) is a modern American-style shopping mall—the newest, biggest, and best in Lima—with department stores, restaurants, movie theaters, a supermarket, and some 200 exclusive shops. It's next to the Jockey Club of Peru at Hipódromo de Monterrico, at the intersection of Javier Prado and Avenida Panamericana Sur in Surco. It's open daily from 11am to 9pm. **Centro Comercial Larcomar ★★** (© 01/445-7776) in Miraflores along the *malecón* and Parque Salazar (near the Marriott hotel), is one of the swankest malls in Lima, with a slew of restaurants, movie theaters, and upscale shops overlooking the ocean. It's open daily from 10am to 8pm and is a weekend destination for many Limeños.

A fascinating food-shopping experience is to visit the diverse **Mercado de Surquillo ★★** (Avenida Paseo de la Republica at Ricardo Palma, Miraflores/Surquillo), where Limeños and many of the top chefs in town go to get fresh produce, seafood, meats and a wide array of kitchen implements.

---

9 LIMA AFTER DARK

As the largest city in the country, with a population of immigrants from around the country and the most international flavor, Lima certainly has Peru's most varied nightlife scene. Whether you're into jazz, *criollo*, Latin, or rock music, you'll find it here. The best after-dark scenes are in Miraflores and particularly Barranco, which transforms from a sleepy artists' and writers' community during the day to party central at night. Although it has a number of high-octane clubs and discos, it also has some of the city's best peñas and bars, especially those with ocean views just past the Puente de los Suspiros, or "Bridge of Sighs."

Bars open at about 8pm, but discos and live-music clubs don't generally get started until 10pm or later. Many are open very late, until 3 or 4am or even later.

THE PERFORMING ARTS

Lima's stunning **Teatro Municipal,** the pride of the local performing-arts scene and the primary locale for theater, ballet, opera, and symphony performances, burned to the ground in 1998. Since then, the National Symphony Orchestra and the National Ballet

Company have performed at the **Museo de la Nación,** Avenida Javier Prado (© **01/476-9875**). The 1940s-era **Teatro Segura,** Huancavelica 265 (© **01/426-7206**) has picked up some of the slack for opera and music concerts. Frequent cultural events, including films and music recitals, are held every week at the **Centro Cultural Ricardo Palma,** Larco Herrera 770, Miraflores (© **01/446-3959**), and the **British Council,** Calle Alberto Lynch 110, San Isidro (© **01/221-7552**). The **Instituto Cultural Peruano Norteamericano,** at the corner of Angamos and Arequipa in Miraflores (© **01/446-0381**), hosts theater, jazz, classical, and folk music. See the daily newspaper *El Comercio* (www.elcomercioperu.com.pe) for updated lists of live performing-arts events in Lima (in Spanish only).

Lima has a good theater scene, although, as one might expect, nearly all plays are in Spanish. Two of Lima's best theaters are **Teatro Canout,** Av. Petit Thouars 4550, Miraflores (© **01/422-5373**), and **Teatro Auditorio Miraflores,** Av. Larco 1036, Miraflores (© **01/447-9378**). Tickets are available at the box offices.

BARS, LIVE MUSIC & CLUBS

Bars & Pubs

MIRAFLORES **Freiheit,** Lima 471, in front of Parque Kennedy (© **01/247-4630**), is a warmly decorated bar, in the style of a German tavern, but with a separate dance area. There's a drink minimum on weekends. **O'Murphy's Irish Pub,** Shell 627 (© **01/242-1212**), is a longtime favorite drinking hole with a small menu of pub grub. Expect a pool table, darts, Guinness on tap, and Brits and Irishmen hoisting it. They also host live music on Thursday. **Son de Cuba,** Bulevar San Ramón 277 (© **01/445-1444**), is on the pedestrian street called "Little Italy" by locals, but the club focuses on Caribbean rhythms and drinks Tuesday through Sunday. **Scena** ★, Francisca de Paula 226 (© **01/445-9688;** www.scena.com.pe) is a sleek modern restaurant with a good wine selection and lively bar scene; DJs spin tunes here in the evenings.

BARRANCO The area past the Puente de los Suspiros in Barranco has some of the coolest watering holes in Lima. My favorite is **Santos** ★★, Jr. Zepita 203 (© **01/247-4609**), a hip joint with an inventive decor, easygoing vibe and slender balcony with views out to the ocean; the place is packed on weekend nights. Right across the bridge is the slick, upscale bar and restaurant, **Picas** ★, Bajada de Baños 340 (© **01/252-8095;** www.picas.com.pe), serving great (but pricey) cocktails to a well-dressed crowd. Nearby, **La Posada del Mirador,** Pasaje La Ermita 104 (© **01/477-1120**) and **Nuevo Acantilado de Barranco,** Pasaje La Ermita 102 (© **01/247-2145**) both occupy old houses overlooking the ocean and have spectacular verdant settings with indoor and outdoor garden seating. For a real taste of old-school Peru, stop by the legendary **Bodega Juanito** ★★, Av. Grau 274 (© **01/994-96176**), a former apothecary that sports a plain, if charmingly retro (aka Soviet Union) look, with fluorescent lighting, industrial fans, and walls littered with theater and film posters. There's a peculiar rule that men not accompanied by women have to retreat to the back room to down their pitchers of beer. Juanito's is a longtime hangout for Barranco's artists and intellectuals, who smoke, drink and devour the fantastic, locally famous ham sandwiches.

New to the scene is an old train car parked just off the main park: **Expreso Virgen de Guadalupe Café Cultural,** Av. Prolongación San Martín 15 (© **01/252-8907**) is a charming 1920s *vagón* with gorgeous wood, stained-glass windows, and live piano music, specialty coffees, and cocktails. It's perfect if you're trying to escape some of the noisier joints in Barranco. One of the trendy bars drawing a younger crowd is **Amnesia,** Bulevar

Sánchez Carrión 153, just off the municipal square (✆ **01/477-9577**). It's open only **145**
Thursday through Saturday. **Posada del Angel**, Av. Pedro de Osma 164 (and 222;
✆ **01/247-0341**), is a baroque cafe-bar with two locations on the same street and occasional live jazz and folk music. **El Ekeko**, Av. Grau 266 (✆ **01/247-3148**), once an
atmospheric neighborhood bar with occasional live music, has become a rowdy sports bar
full of *fútbol*-watching and beer-swilling patrons. One of the hottest, and biggest, spots
of the moment is **Ayahuasca** ★★, Prolongación San Martín 130, Barranco (✆ **9810-
44745**), a stylish bar in a stately colonial mansion with swank furnishings, art exhibits
and great cocktails, including an impressive array of pisco sours.

LIMA CENTRO There are two excellent pubs downtown owned by the same folks.
One is **Rincón Cervecero**, a German-style bierhall, at Jr. de la Unión 1045 (✆ **01/428-
1422**). The other, **Estadio Fútbol Club**, Av. Nicolás de Piérola 926 (✆ **01/428-8866**),
is strictly for *fútbol* fans: It's a three-level bar (and disco on weekends) that amounts to a
museum of the sport, and with dozens of big-screen TVs, it can get pretty rowdy when
a big Peruvian or international game is on.

Live Music

BARRANCO My vote for best live-music club in Lima is **La Noche** ★★, Bolognesi
307 (✆ **01/477-1012**). Despite its prosaic name, this sprawling multilevel club feels like
a swank tree house, with a great stage and sound system and good bands every night that
run the gamut of styles (although it's frequently jazz), plus a hip mixed Limeño and
international crowd. Monday night jam sessions (no cover charge) are particularly good;
otherwise, cover charges range from S/5 to S/30. There's also a La Noche outpost in Central
Lima, at the corner of Jirón Camaná and Jirón Quilca. **La Estación de Barranco** ★,
Pedro de Osma 112 (✆ **01/247-0344**), is another nice place, housed in an old train
station, with live music Tuesday through Saturday and a slightly more mature crowd
(both locals and tourists); the music on tap is often *criolla*. The classic upstairs bar **La
Taberna de Barranco** ★, Av. Grau 268 (no phone), schedules both live rock and pop
for the youngsters (often early shows beginning at 9pm), and occasional peña and Afro-
Peruvian shows late on weekends for a more sophisticated crowd. **Bar Mochileros** ★,
Av. Pedro de Osma 135, Barranco (✆ **01/247-1225**), is a cool pub that hops with exotic
cocktails and young people spilling out into the courtyard; there's occasional live rock,
from punk to electronica, on weekends.

MIRAFLORES **Satchmo** ★, Av. La Paz 538 (✆ **01/444-4957**), is a sophisticated joint
with a variable roster of live bands, including jazz combos—as the name would indicate.
It's a good date spot. Cover charges range from S/20 to S/60. Another great spot for live
jazz (as well as bossa nova and Afro-Peruvian evenings) is **Jazz Zone** ★★, Av. La Paz 656,
Pasaje El Suche (✆ **01/241-8139**; www.jazzzoneperu.com). **Crocodilo Verde**, Francisca
de Paula 226 (✆ **01/445-7583**; www.cocodriloverde.com), has jazz on Wednesday and
a variable program of live music on weekends.

Peñas

You should check out at least one peña, a performance at a *criollo* music club that quite
often inspires rousing vocal and dance participation, during your stay in Lima.

MIRAFLORES **Caballero de Fina Estampa** ★, Av. del Ejército 800 (✆ **01/441-
0552**), named for one of the most famous Peruvian songs of all time, is one of the city's
chicest peñas, with a large colonial salon and balconies. The cover charge is S/50.
Sachún, Av. del Ejército 657 (✆ **01/441-4465**), is favored by tourists and middle-class

LIMA 6 LIMA AFTER DARK

Limeños who aren't shy about participating with their feet and vocal cords. The cover charge ranges from S/25 to S/45.

BARRANCO   De Rompe y Raja ★, Manuel Segura 127 (© **01/247-3271;** www.derompeyraja.net), is a favorite of locals that's open Thursday to Saturday nights. Look for the popular Matices Negros, an Afro-Peruvian dance trio. The cover is usually around S/35. **Peña del Carajo!** ★, Calle Catalino Miranda 158 (© **01/247-7023;** www.delcarajo.com.pe), is another cool peña with good live music, percussion, and dance shows Tuesday through Saturday starting at 10pm. Covers range from S/20 to S/45. **La Candelaria,** Bolognesi 292 (© **01/247-1314;** www.lacandelariaperu.com), is a comfortable club celebrating Peruvian folklore. It's open Friday and Saturday from 9pm onward; the cover is normally S/30. **Las Guitarras,** Manuel Segura 295 (© **01/479-1874**), is where locals go to play an active part in their peña. A cool spot, it's open Friday and Saturday only, with no cover charge and no credit cards accepted.

LIMA CENTRO   Brisas del Titicaca ★★, Jr. Walkulski 168, the first block of Avenida Brasil, near Plaza Bolognesi (© **01/332-1901;** www.brisasdeltiticaca.com), is a cultural institution featuring *noches folclóricas*—indigenous music-and-dance shows—that are some of the finest in Lima. Shows are Tuesday and Wednesday at 8pm, Thursday at 9:15pm, and Friday and Saturday at 10:15pm. You can even catch a dance show with lunch, Friday and Saturday from noon to 6pm. Covers range from S/30 to S/70.

Dance Clubs

Many of Lima's discos are predominantly young and wild affairs. Cover charges range from S/15 to S/50. The main drags in Barranco, Avenida Grau and Pasaje Sánchez Carrión (a pedestrian alley off the main square), are lined with raucous clubs that go late into the evening and annoy Barranco residents. Two very chic and popular discotheques, **Gotica** ★ (© **01/445-6343;** www.gotica.com.pe) and **Aura** ★ (© **01/242-5516;** www.aura.com.pe) face each other in the Larcomar shopping center, Malecón de la Reserva 610, Miraflores and feature interconnected open-air terraces, great sea views and dance music ranging from electronica to the Latin specialty, *pachanga*. Also check out **Deja-Vu,** Av. Grau 294 (© **01/247-6989**); the decor is based on TV commercials, and "waitress shows" tease horny patrons. It's a dancefest from Monday to Saturday; the music trips from techno to trance. **Café Bar Kitsch,** Bolognesi 743, Barranco (© **01/242-3325**), is one of Lima's hottest bars—literally, sometimes it turns into a sweatbox—with over-the-top decor and recorded tunes that range from 1970s and 1980s pop to Latin and techno. **Tequila Rock,** Diez Canseco 146, Miraflores (© **01/444-3661**), is one of Lima's long-standing popular discos, although it's a bit of a meat (or hooker's) market.

GAY & LESBIAN NIGHTLIFE

Although Peru as a whole remains fervently Catholic and many gay and lesbian Peruvians feel constricted in the expression of their lifestyle, Lima is the most progressive city in the country, with the most facilities and resources for gays and lesbians, including a significant number of nightclubs. Among the most popular are **Gitano 2050,** Berlín 231, Miraflores (no phone), probably the best-known gay disco in the city, with two cruising balconies overlooking the dance floor; **Downtown Vale Todo,** Pasaje los Pinos 160, Miraflores (© **01/444-6433**), currently the most popular club with go-go boys, with occasional shows and strippers; **Café Bar Kitsch,** Bolognesi 743, Barranco (no phone), a funky and highly original bar/disco that's also very popular with straights; and **Perseo Palace,** Av. Aviación 2514, San Borja (© **01/224-3731**), a lively disco with an eclectic soundtrack and large

dance floor. A gay-oriented combination sauna/gym/bar/video lounge is **Sauna Tivoli,** Av.
Petit Thouars s/n, San Isidro ((C) **01/222-1705**). All are open Wednesday through Saturday
(Gitano 2050 and Sauna Tivoli are open Sun as well); cover charges range from S/15 to
S/35. Visit **http://lima.queercity.info** for more information on gay Lima and gay Peru,
including all the latest bars, discos and saunas (bathhouses).

CINEMA

Most foreign movies in Lima are shown in their original language with subtitles. Art and
classic films are shown at the **Filmoteca de Lima** in the Lima Museo de Arte, Paseo
Colón 125, Lima Cercado ((C) **01/423-4732**), and **El Cinematógrafo,** Pérez Roca 196,
Barranco ((C) **01/477-1961**). Commercial movie houses worth checking out include
Multicines Starvisión El Pacífico, Av. José Pardo 121, near the roundabout at Parque
Central, Miraflores ((C) **01/445-6990**); **Cinemark Perú Jockey Plaza,** Av. Javier Prado
4200 ((C) **01/435-9262**); and **Multicines Larcomar,** Malecón de la Reserva 610, Mira-
flores ((C) **01/446-7336**). Most theaters in the suburbs cost more than the ones in Lima
Centro, but they're more modern and better equipped. Several have matinee prices and
discounts on Tuesday. For a list of films *subtituladas* (with subtitles), consult the Friday
edition of *El Comercio*. Note that the term *doblada* means "dubbed." Tickets run S/12 to
S/20.

CASINOS

Peruvians are big on casinos, and many of the larger upscale hotels in Lima have casinos
attached. Some of the better ones are the Stellaris Casino at the **JW Marriott Hotel**
(p. 118); **Grand Hotel Miraflores,** Av. 28 de Julio 151, Miraflores ((C) **01/447-9641**);
Country Club Lima Hotel (p. 120); and **Sheraton Hotel & Casino,** Paseo de la
República 170, Centro ((C) **01/433-3320**). Most casinos are open Monday through
Thursday from 5pm to 2am, and Friday through Saturday from 5pm to 5am.

---

10 SIDE TRIPS FROM LIMA

Most visitors to Lima, having seen the highlights of the colonial center and a few museums, head out on long-distance buses and planes to Cusco and Machu Picchu, Nasca,
Arequipa, and north to the jungle. However, if you have time for an excursion or two
closer to the Peruvian capital, consider the pre-Columbian ruins at Pachacámac or the
attractive beaches south of Lima.

THE SOUTHERN BEACHES

30–70km (19–43 miles) S of Lima

The best beaches easily accessible from Lima line the coast south of the city. Popular spots
along the shadeless, arid desert landscape are El Silencio, Punta Hermosa (a good place
for ceviche and fresh fish in any number of rustic seafood restaurants), Punta Negra,
Santa María, and Pucusana. Probably the best bet is Pucusana, a small fishing village,
although it's the farthest beach from Lima. The attractive beaches are very popular with
Limeños during the summer months; on weekends, the southern coast is a long line of
caravans of sun-seekers.

    Note: Even though you can swim in the ocean at this distance from the capital, the
currents are very strong, and great caution should be exercised. You should also be careful

with your possessions because thieves frequent these beaches. Finally, be forewarned that the beaches are only moderately attractive.

GETTING THERE   Unless you have wheels, the best way to tour the beaches south of Lima is to hop on a combi, like Limeños do. Those marked "San Bartolo" (another one of the beaches) leave from Angamos and Panamericana Sur in Lima; others at Jirón Montevideo and Jirón Ayacucho in Lima Centro will also get you to the beaches. You'll have to tell the driver where you want to get off (or hop off wherever a number of fellow bus travelers do), and then walk a mile or less down to the beach.

The ride costs S/5 and takes anywhere from 45 minutes to 2 hours. The beaches and their markers are as follows: El Silencio, Km 42; Punta Hermosa, Km 44; Punta Rocas, Km 45; Punta Negra, Km 46; San Bartolo, Km 52; Santa María, Km 55; and Pucusana, Km 65.

PACHACAMAC
31km (19 miles) S of Lima

The finest ruins within easy reach of Lima, **Pachacámac,** in the Lurín Valley, was inhabited by several pre-Columbian cultures before the Incas. The extensive site, a sacred city and holy place of pilgrimage, includes plazas, adobe-brick palaces, and pyramidal temples, some of which have been rebuilt by the Peruvian government. It makes for an interesting visit, especially if you're not planning on heading north to the archaeological sites near Chiclayo and Trujillo.

The earliest constructions here date to the 1st century, although the site reached its apex during the Huari (or Wari) culture (10th c.). Pilgrims came here to pay homage to the feared oracle and creator-god, Pachacámac, who was believed to be responsible for earthquakes and matters of state such as war. The Incas conquered the site in the 15th century, and it was one of the most important shrines in the Americas during their rule, although its ceremonial importance began to wane soon afterward. However, two of the most important structures on-site, the Temple of the Sun and the Acllahuasi (or Mamacuña) palace (where "chosen maidens" served the Inca), both date to the Inca occupation. Hernán Pizarro and his gold-hungry troops arrived in 1533 but were disappointed to find a paucity of riches. On the premises is a small museum of pre-Columbian artifacts, including textiles and the dual-personage carved wooden idol of Pachacámac, god of fire and son of the sun god.

The site (© 01/430-0168), which occupies a low hill, is large; allow at least a few hours to visit by foot (the visit from Lima can be completed in a half-day). English-speaking guides are usually available for hire at the entrance if you don't arrive with a guide-led group. The site's open daily from 9am to 4pm. Admission is S/6 for adults, S/3 for students, and S/1 for children.

GETTING THERE   Pachacámac is about 45 minutes from Lima by car or bus. Combis (with signs reading PACHACAMAC/LURIN) leave from Avenida Abancay and the corner of Ayacucho and Montevideo in Lima Centro. The most convenient way to visit—cheaper than hiring a taxi, unless there are several of you—is by a half-day organized tour, offered by Lima Vision, Lima Tours, and other companies; see "Organized Tours," earlier in this chapter. Most tours cost between S/75 and S/125 per person, including transportation and guide.

The Central Coast & Highlands

South of Lima along the coast, the hot and extraordinarily dry desert province of Ica—one of the most arid places on earth—contains one of Peru's most exotic, inscrutable sights: The Nasca Lines, huge pre-Columbian desert drawings, have raised many questions and given rise to wild theories about Peru's ancient past. The region forms part of the oldest geological strata in the country; fossils date back as far as the Tertiary or Quaternary eras. The Paracas and Nasca cultures that took root here (roughly 1300 B.C.–A.D. 700) were two of Peru's most advanced. Little was known about the two cultures until the 20th century, but they are acclaimed today for their exquisite textile weavings and ceramics, among the finest produced by pre-Columbian Peru.

This region, where the South American Plate collides with the Nazca Plate, is also one of the most seismically active regions of the world. The most recent tragedy struck in August 2007 when a massive earthquake, which registered 7.9 on the Richter scale, devastated much of Pisco and Ica, killing more than 500 people and leaving nearly 100,000 homeless. The hardest hit parts of the region will take years to rebuild, a factor that travelers should keep in mind if they intend to travel to the area in the very near future. For more info on the aftermath of the earthquake, see p. 158.

While Nasca, a small and unassuming town, escaped some of the heaviest 2007 earthquake damage, it was rocked just a few years ago by another major earthquake that nearly leveled it. It's fair to say that

Nasca might go entirely unnoticed by visitors to Peru were it not for the enigmatic Nasca Lines nearby. Besides that head-scratching site are others in and around Nasca intimately tied to the ancient cultures that once settled and irrigated these desert lands, including remarkable stone aqueducts—evidence of advanced engineering—and an evocative burial ground. Although the Nasca Lines reign as the undisputed highlight of the region, this stretch of arid coast and pampas south of Lima has other things to offer the visitor who's not in too much of a rush to roar on to Cusco, Arequipa, or Lake Titicaca.

Within easy reach of Nasca are the towns Ica and Pisco, and the nearby Reserva Nacional de Paracas (Paracas National Reserve), known for the Ballestas Islands, which locals liken to Ecuador's Galápagos Islands. That claim might be a slight (or even significant) exaggeration, but the maritime sanctuary, encompassing the Paracas Peninsula and a lovely bay with curious rock formations, swells with unusual flora and fauna, including thousands of sea lions, flamingos, and endangered Humboldt penguins. Pisco is a dusty, unremarkable town that will sound familiar to anyone who's had a drink in a Peruvian bar or restaurant: The country's famous cocktail, the pisco sour, is made with the white-grape brandy that shares its name with the town. The region's wineries (actually nearer to Ica) make Peru's best wines and, of course, pisco. Ica, the capital of the department, is a small, enjoyable town with stifling heat and a collection of attractive churches, notable colonial mansions, and one of the better small museums in the country. The nearby Huacachina Lagoon is a beautiful green-and-blue oasis in the midst of the monochrome desert.

Ayacucho, a lovely colonial town in the Central Highlands, is newly welcoming to outsiders after years spent in the grips of Peru's homegrown guerrilla movement, the Shining Path. Ayacucho has the country's finest collection of colonial-era churches, and it's also the epicenter of Peru's most celebrated artisans, whose folk art is shown across the country.

Paracas, Ica, and Nasca are all within striking distance of Lima, but for those with limited time, a visit to the region could complicate moving on to other places in Peru. The only flights available from Lima are 1-day Nasca Lines overflights. Otherwise, you'll need to travel overland along the desert coast to get to the department of Ica, and by land again if you're headed to any of the other major destinations in Peru—in all likelihood, adding a couple of days to your trip. (For many travelers, that will mean returning to the capital and catching a flight.) The vast Carretera Panamericana (Pan-American Hwy.), a two-lane strip of asphalt that extends the length of Peru from the Ecuadorian border all the way down to Chile, slices through this section of the desert lowlands, and bus travel is direct, if not always visually stimulating. Many visitors move on by bus from Nasca to Arequipa or Lake Titicaca. Although Ayacucho is a long and winding Andean bus ride from Lima or Ica, you can now fly there from the capital (but not yet from Cusco or other cities).

1 PISCO & THE RESERVA NACIONAL DE PARACAS ★

260km (162 miles) S of Lima; 75km (47 miles) NW of Ica; 205km (127 miles) NW of Nasca

The first town of any size to the south of Lima, Pisco is also the first settlement beyond the beaches outside the capital that draws the attention of travelers. Yet that interest has little to do with the (rather lacking) attributes of the town and almost everything to do with the natural attractions in abundance at the nearby Ballestas Islands and Paracas National Reserve, just 22km (14 miles) from the center of Pisco. A few kilometers west of the Pan-American Highway, Pisco is a small port and fishing village of very modest interest (beyond the Moorish-inspired Municipal Palace) that sometimes serves as a base for those wanting to visit Paracas Peninsula and Bay without paying the higher prices commanded by the resort.

Pisco was perhaps the hardest hit town by the 2007 earthquake that devastated the area. As much as 85% of central Pisco—where most homes were constructed of adobe—was destroyed, including nearly 20,000 homes and the city's San Clemente Church, where more than 130 people died while attending Mass. More modern buildings mostly survived, though the five-story Hotel Embassy in Pisco collapsed, killing 15 guests and employees.

ESSENTIALS
Getting There
There are frequent buses up and down the coast from Lima to Arequipa, with stops in between. From Lima, frequent buses normally take between 3 and 4 hours to reach Pisco. However, because the town is not directly on the Carretera Panamericana, not all coastal

buses stop there. Be sure to confirm that the bus won't merely leave you on the side of the road en route to Ica (which would result in the hassle of getting a *combi* to town).

Ormeño (01/472-5000; www.grupo-ormeno.com.pe) travels from Lima to Pisco and to Ica, Nasca, and Arequipa. In Lima, the office is located at Av. Carlos Zavala 177; the Pisco office (© **056/522-058**) is at San Francisco 259, 1 block from the Plaza de Armas. **Transportes Soyuz** (© **01/265-0501;** www.soyuz.com.pe) connects Pisco with Lima and Ica; you'll find an office in Lima at Av. México 331, La Victoria, and in Pisco (© **056/531-014**) at Av. Ernesto R. Diez Canseco 41. Bus terminals are located right in the center of town, on or just off the Plaza de Armas. Frequent *colectivos* travel to Ica from Pisco.

Visitor Information

The **Municipality of Pisco office** at the Plaza de Armas (© **056/532-525**) might be able to provide some rudimentary tourist information; a better bet is one of the travel agencies offering tours to Paracas and other places in the region. See "By Organized Tour" in "Getting Around," below.

FAST FACTS   **Banco de Crédito,** Pérez Figuerola 162 (© **056/532-954**), has a Visa-compatible ATM. You'll also find *cambistas,* or money exchangers, hovering around the Plaza de Armas. If you need medical attention, go to **Hospital Antonio Skrabonja Antoncich (ESSALUD),** San Francisco 322 (© **056/532-784**) or **San Juan de Dios,** Av. San Juan de Dios 350 (© **056/532-332**). In an emergency, you can reach the **police** at the Plaza de Armas, Calle San Francisco (© **056/532-165**). The **post office** is at Av. Federico Uranga 211, Independencia (© **056/220-208**). There's a **Telefónica del Perú** office at Bolognesi 298.

Getting Around

The best way to get around Pisco itself is on foot because anything of interest—hotels, restaurants, the cathedral—is only minutes from the Plaza de Armas. Taxis are readily available and cheap for any trip within the city (S/3–S/4). For transport to the Paracas National Reserve and other areas of interest, you can hire a taxi (about S/20) or travel by bus. The most efficient way to see the highlights of the area is with a tour company, especially because there is no public transportation on the peninsula or within the reserve.

BY BUS   Combis to the Ballestas Islands and Paracas National Reserve (marked EL CHACO–PARACAS) depart from the Pisco market on Fermín Tangus every half-hour at a rate of S/2.

BY BOAT   Boat tours of the Paracas Bay and Ballestas Islands are available right on the El Chaco waterfront (S/40 per person) or by arranging an organized tour.

BY ORGANIZED TOUR   The following companies all offer packages to the Ballestas Islands and Paracas National Reserve (as well as tours to Tambo Colorado and Nasca): **Zarcillo Connections,** Callao 137 (© **056/536-636;** www.zarcilloconnections.com); **Ballestas Travel Service,** San Francisco 249 (© **056/533-095**); and, near Ica, **Huacachina Tours,** Av. La Angostura 355, L-47, in front of the Hotel Las Dunas (© **056/256-582;** www.huacachinatours.com).

WHAT TO SEE & DO
Reserva Nacional de Paracas ★

The Paracas Bay and Peninsula, along with the small Ballestas Islands, compose the Paracas National Reserve, a place of gorgeous unpopulated beaches, strange desert vistas, and spectacular wildlife. Established in 1975, Paracas is the primary marine conservation center in Peru. The 14,504-sq.-km (5,600-sq.-mile) reserve, which can be visited year-round, is about two-thirds ocean, so don't come expecting to see a zoolike array of plants

Fun Facts   El Libertador

General José de San Martín—immersed in the continent-wide campaign for independence from Spain and already having liberated Chile and Argentina—made landfall with an army of 4,500 men at Paracas in 1819 and established his headquarters in Pisco. Here began his legendary battle for Peru's independence, which he declared in Huacho in 1821. San Martín was subsequently named the "Protector of Peru" and went about constructing its new republican government.

and animals at every turn—except on the Ballestas, where several thousand sea lions, in addition to many other species, lie about in plain view.

Exploring Paracas

What is not water in the Paracas National Reserve is hot and dry land, with no transportation to speak of except for independently hired taxis. For this reason, most tourists tend to visit the reserve as part of an organized tour. However, adventurous travelers with plenty of water, sunscreen, and stamina can get to know the peninsula and its rich marine birdlife on their own, camping far from other humans. Safety has become a concern in recent years, though, so camping alone is not a good idea.

Dirt roads crisscross the Paracas Peninsula, and a paved road goes around it, out toward Punta Pejerrey, near the Candelabro (see "Islas Ballestas," below). The dirt roads are the most interesting, reaching minuscule fishing villages such as attractive **Lagunillas** and a cliff-top lookout point, **Mirador de los Lobos,** with views of the ocean and lots of sea lions. Sadly, the August 2007 earthquake destroyed the famous **Cathedral** rock and cave formation, one of the National Reserve's great attractions.

Paracas Culture

Paracas might be best known for its great natural coastal beauty and wildlife, but the region is no less recognized (especially among archaeologists and historians) as the home of several advanced cultures that thrived in Peru before the Incas. The so-called *hombre de Santo Domingo* (Santo Domingo man), whose remains date to 7000 B.C., was found on the west shore of the Bay of Paracas.

Little was known about the Paracas culture, an ancient Amerindian civilization founded along the south-central coast more than 3,000 years ago, until 1925, when the Peruvian archaeologist Julio C. Tello discovered extraordinary burial sites, now referred to as the Paracas Necropolis, concealed by the desert sand dunes on the isthmus of the Península de Paracas. The arid climate and layers of sand had done wonders to protect extraordinary embroidered textiles—largely found within burial sites—that today are recognized as the finest representatives of pre-Columbian Peruvian woven art. The Paracas culture produced textiles of unrivaled color, technique, and design. The most exquisite examples of funereal textiles are found at Lima's Museo de la Nación (p. 136), but there are also fine pieces in Ica at the Museo Regional (p. 162) and at the Museo de Sitio Julio C. Tello within the Paracas National Reserve (p. 150).

Also found at the sites were skulls that reveal fascinating information about the Paracas social structure and notions of physical beauty. The Paracas employed methods to alter the shape of the skull, elongating it with weights and boards, to connote social status. Many of the skulls found in the Paracas Necropolis have stretched and sloped craniums. The Paracas people also practiced a crude form of brain surgery called trepanation. Like medieval physicians, who believed bloodletting aimed at the forehead was a cure-all, Paracas doctors surgically drilled holes in the skull to treat both physical trauma and, it seems, psychological disorders. The formation of scar tissue indicates that many of the patients actually survived the operations, although, of course, it's impossible to say how their physical or behavioral problems were affected.

The Paracas culture flourished from roughly 1300 B.C. to A.D. 200, but scholars are most knowledgeable about the late period of development, from 300 B.C. to A.D. 200. At the Paracas Necropolis, researchers discovered more than 400 funerary bundles, each consisting of a mummified priest or nobleman swathed in brilliantly woven and embroidered funeral tapestries. The large and exceptionally detailed, colorful weavings feature repetitive motifs of birds, fish, and other animals, revealing a keen sense of textile design and artistry.

Little is known about the disappearance of the Paracas culture around A.D. 200. Farther south along the coast, the Nasca culture reigned for about 5 centuries, itself eventually succeeded by the Huari and then Ica cultures, the last of which succumbed to the expanding Inca Empire by the 15th century.

Boat Tours

ATTRACTIONS ●
Candelabro **2**
Islas Ballestas **1**
Mirador de los Lobos **9**
Museo de Sitio
  Julio C. Tello **8**
Paracas Necropolis **7**

ACCOMMODATIONS ■
Doubletree Guest Suites **6**
Hotel El Mirador **4**
Hotel Paracas **5**

DINING ◆
El Chaco **3**

(i) Information
═══ Highway
- - - Road (unpaved)

THE CENTRAL COAST & HIGHLANDS

7

PISCO & THE RESERVA NACIONAL DE PARACAS

To hike around the peninsula, it's about 21km (13 miles) round-trip to the lookout point (5km/3 miles from the Tello Museum to Lagunillas). Begin at a turnoff left of the paved road beyond the museum. There are few facilities of any kind on the peninsula. You are allowed to camp on the beautiful beaches (where you might see no other humans, just pelicans and other birds), and there are a couple of seafood restaurants in Lagunillas—Tía Fela's is the best place around for fresh fish.

Museo de Sitio Julio C. Tello Named for the Peruvian archaeologist credited with uncovering many of the mysteries of the ancient Paracas culture, the Julio Tello Site Museum is located just past the entrance to the Paracas National Reserve, 5km (3 miles) from Paracas beach. The museum suffered considerable damage from the 2007 earthquake and while open, is still in the process of being renovated. It contains a small but instructive exhibit of ceramics and textiles that depict the evolution of the Paracas culture. The Paracas were experts at mummifying their dead; in the mummies, you can see the peculiar practices of cranial deformation and cranial trepanation, or brain surgery. The Paracas also admired trophy heads, and warriors often attached the heads of defeated foes to their armor to instill fear into their opponents.

> **Fun Facts   A Bird-Watcher's Boon**
>
> The Ballestas Islands are smack in the middle of the Humboldt Current, which flows 3,220km (2,000 miles) from Antarctica along the Pacific coastline. In the warm, shallow waters along the Peruvian coast, the current makes abundant growth of phytoplankton possible, which stimulates an ecological food chain that culminates in the largest concentration of birds on earth.

Near the museum is the **Paracas Necropolis** (100 B.C.–A.D. 300), comprising the archaeological sites of Cabezas Largas and Cerro Colorado. First explored in the 1920s, it is the oldest discovered site in the region. Tello uncovered Paracas burial sites containing superb funerary cloths, skulls, and other artifacts—all key elements in his groundbreaking studies of the Paracas culture. However, there is very little to see today at the sites. About 270m (886 ft.) toward the bay is a viewing tower, constructed to allow viewings of the dozens (or hundreds) of pink flamingos often gathered on the beach (usually July–Nov only).

Carretera Pisco, Km 27, Puerto San Martín, Paracas. © 056/620-436. Admission S/10 adults, S/5 students and seniors, S/3 children 9 and under. Daily 9am–5pm.

Islas Ballestas ★★

The primary focus of a visit to the reserve is a boat tour of the Ballestas (pronounced "Bah-yes-tahs") Islands. Although the islands can't possibly live up to locals' touting of them as the "Peruvian Galápagos," the Ballestas do afford tantalizing close-up views (without allowing visitors on the islands) of the habitat's rich roster of protected species, including huge colonies of barking sea lions, endangered turtles and Humboldt penguins, red boobies, pelicans, turkey vultures, and red-footed cormorants. During the summer months (Jan–Mar), baby sea lions are born, and the community becomes even more populous and noisy. The wall-like, cantilevered islands are literally covered with birds; 110 migratory and resident seabirds have been documented, and the bay is a stopover point in the Alaska-Patagonia migration route. Packs of dolphins are occasionally seen slicing through the water; less frequently, humpback whales and soaring Andean condors can also be glimpsed.

The islands are often referred to by locals as *las islas guaneras* because they are covered in bird droppings. (*Guano* is the Quechua word for excrement.) The nitrogen-rich *guano* is harvested every 10 years and made into fertilizer. (A factory can be seen on the first island.) No humans other than the *guano* collectors—no doubt a contender for worst job title in the world—are allowed on the islands, and all the species in the reserve are protected by law. In practice, however, there are no specially assigned police officers or boats available to enforce protection.

En route to the islands, boats pass the famous **Candelabro,** a giant candelabra-like drawing etched into a cliff overlooking the bay. The huge etching, 126m long and 72m wide (413×236 ft.), looks as though it could be a cousin to the Nasca Lines, and it is similarly shrouded in mystery. Some believe that it's a ritualistic symbol of the Paracas or Nasca cultures, while others contend that it dates only to the 18th or 19th century, when it served as a protective symbol and navigational guide for fishermen and sailors.

Most organized tours take visitors from the San Andrés port to the El Balneario resort, a beach playground for upscale residents of Lima, and then on to Playa El Chaco, where boats leave for 1-hour tours of the Ballestas. You can also independently contract an island boat tour here from one of the 13 operators on the main street. Tours run about S/40 per person, and each boat has an English- or French-speaking guide on board. Most start early in the morning, between 7 and 8am. Visitors are not allowed to set foot on the islands, although boats get close enough for good viewing. Sweaters and windbreakers, hats, and sunscreen are essential.

Tambo Colorado

An Inca fortress and probably the best-preserved ancient architectural complex on the central coast, this outpost is thought to have been an administration checkpoint for Andean coastal migration. It was probably also where the Inca chieftain and his minions stayed for periods as he traveled back and forth between the Inca capital, Cusco, and coastal settlements. Unlike other archaeological sites, where the characteristic vibrant colors have long faded, here at least some of the original red, white, and yellow walls are still preserved. (The name of the complex, *Colorado*, refers to the red color of the walls.) Also unique in the Inca canon, the structures here were constructed not of neatly cut stone, but of materials that could be used for long-term construction, given the lack of rain on the desert coast.

The complex contains a central plaza, storehouses, living quarters, and military installations. If you're headed to Cusco, you can be assured of seeing more impressive Inca sites, but Tambo Colorado is rewarding for archaeology fans and Inca completists.

The site is quite removed from Pisco—about 45km (28 miles) northeast of town. It lies about 5km (3 miles) outside the town of Humay, to which you can take a bus, but service is erratic. If you are intent on seeing Tambo Colorado, it's advisable to either go with an organized guided tour or hire a taxi, which will take you out to the site, wait for you, and return you to Pisco for about S/105. The site is open daily from 9am to 5pm; admission is S/5.

WHERE TO STAY

For years the Paracas National Reserve, despite its natural attractions, was decidedly lacking in upscale accommodations and resort activities. That niche has now been filled, with international chains arriving to transform the old Hotel Paracas and build a new Doubletree by Hilton hotel.

Tips Organized Tours

Most people visit the Paracas National Reserve and Ballestas Islands as part of organized tours. Guides, transportation, and entrance fees are all included in the price. Those who prefer to visit the reserve on their own must pay an entrance fee upon entering the reserve (S/5 for adults and students 14 and older; free for children 13 and under). You can enter the reserve without a guide, but it's highly recommended that you contract one in order to get the most out of a visit. Much that is unique about the area—its climate and conditions, and its migratory wildlife—is not always immediately obvious.

Earthquake Aftershocks

The massive 7.9 earthquake that rocked Pisco and Ica in late 2007 destroyed the famous Cathedral rock formation in the Paracas National Reserve, leveled major churches—Ica's Señor de Luren and Pisco's San Clemente—and severely damaged invaluable pre-Hispanic artifacts, including mummies and ceramics, in museums in Ica and Pisco. More than 37,000 homes were destroyed, half of them in Pisco. Officials estimated that 85% of central Pisco, where most homes in the region were constructed of adobe and incapable of withstanding the tremors, was destroyed.

While aid flooded in from around the world, and Peru sent in its military to keep the peace and try to get the most drastically affected communities back on their feet, it will take years for them to recover, and many who lost their homes may never be able to rebuild.

Expensive

Doubletree Guest Suites by Hilton ★★ (**Kids**) This contemporary new addition to the Paracas hotel scene is a welcome one. A large waterfront resort on Santo Domingo beach and next to the entrance to the Nature Reserve, with starkly modern furnishings, excellent views of Paracas Bay, a massive pool, and a bundle of outdoor activities, including a kid's club and nautical sports, this makes an ideal getaway for families. Accommodations are spacious, chic, and crisp, and overlook either the bay or the main pool (it goes without saying that the former are preferable). The resort is quite isolated, so understand that if you stay here, you'll likely eat all your meals here as well, either in the main restaurant or at the pool snack bar.

Urb. Santo Domingo, Paracas National Reserve, Pisco. ℂ **01/617-1000.** Fax 01/444-2171. http://double tree1.hilton.com. 120 units. $179–$259 double. AE, DC, MC, V. **Amenities:** Restaurant; bar; fitness center; outdoor pool; spa. In room: A/C, TV, fridge, Wi-Fi.

Hotel Paracas ★★ (**Kids**) Now wholly transformed as an upscale Starwood Luxury Collection property, this large Mediterranean-style hotel on the bay is perhaps the top place to stay in the region. Airy and beachy, with great views of the water and a new sophistication, it features an extraordinary infinity pool, lounge bar and deck, as well as a remodeled restaurant and a new spa. Rooms are spiffier, too, furnished with bamboo appointments, and they have either bay or garden views, and all have small terraces. With features including a children's playground, water-skiing, kayaks, and paddleboats, it's an especially good option for families. The hotel organizes its own Ballestas Islands visits, and it can arrange trips to the Nasca Lines as well. The hotel serves good lunch buffets, open to nonguests.

Av. Paracas s/n, Paracas National Reserve, Pisco. ℂ **056/581-333.** Fax 01/446-5079 in Lima. www.star woodhotels.com. 120 units. $225–$465 double; $625 suites. AE, DC, MC, V. **Amenities:** Restaurant; bar; fitness center; 3 outdoor pools; spa. In room: A/C, TV, fridge, Wi-Fi.

Moderate

Hotel El Mirador   Near the sand dunes at the entrance to the nature reserve, about 16km (10 miles) south of Pisco and quite removed from Paracas, El Mirador is an old-school, rather tired hotel. It has ample grounds and a nice terrace with sea views, as well as an appealing swimming pool. The well-furnished rooms are decent enough with carpeted floors and wood-beamed ceilings, but, for the price, I'd opt for one of the two better inexpensive hotels in town.

Carretera Paracas, Km 20, Paracas National Reserve, Pisco. ℂ/fax **564/545-086,** or ℂ/fax 01/423-8618 for reservations. www.elmiradorhotel.com. 35 units. $170 double. Rates include breakfast. AE, MC, V. **Amenities:** Restaurant; bar; outdoor pool.

Inexpensive

Hostal Posada Hispana ★ ⟨Value⟩   This small, charming, colonial-style hotel is managed by a Spaniard, a longtime resident of Peru, and his Peruvian wife. The popular and good-value inn is clean and quite nicely decorated for the price; it's also only 1½ blocks from the Plaza de Armas. The rooms have loft spaces and bathrooms, and the hotel has a backyard garden. The friendly *hostal* also operates a nice little restaurant that serves paella, pizzas, and Peruvian dishes.

Bolognesi 222, Pisco. ℂ/fax **056/536-363.** www.posadahispana.com. 24 units. $30 double. Rates include taxes. No credit cards. **Amenities:** Restaurant, bar. *In room:* TV, Wi-Fi.

Hostal Villa Manuelita ★ ⟨Value⟩   One of the most recent additions to the lackluster Pisco hotel scene is this charming, centrally located colonial house, which is colorfully and nicely restored. The 100-year-old house is just a half-block from the main square, and it offers spacious, handsomely decorated rooms that are a very good value. The house features a large living room and a Spanish-style central courtyard with a fountain— definitely a step up from most inexpensive accommodations.

San Francisco 227, Pisco. ℂ/fax **056/535-218.** www.villamanuelitahostal.com. 16 units. $30 double. Rates include taxes. No credit cards. **Amenities:** Restaurant/pizzeria; bar. *In room:* TV, fridge.

WHERE TO DINE

Most visitors to Paracas National Reserve dine at their hotels, and both the Doubletree and Hotel Paracas have good restaurants. Pisco offers nothing special in terms of restaurants, although the informal seafood eateries at the **El Chaco** waterfront in Paracas, where launches for the Islas Ballestas depart, are popular with travelers. The best bet there is **El Chorito,** El Chaco s/n (ℂ 056/545-054), which is part of a *hostal.* In Pisco, there are several inexpensive cafes and pizzerias on or near the Plaza de Armas, and a number of restaurants along the pedestrian boulevard (Comercio) with tourist *menus* (inexpensive set meals). **Hostal Posada Hispana** ★ (see "Where to Stay," above) has a good-value bistro-style restaurant serving pizzas, pastas, and paella, and is easily as good as anything you'll find in town. For inexpensive mussels and ceviche, try the *cevichería* **Los Choritos Mágicos,** 28 de Julio 116 (ℂ 056/534-158). **Restaurant El Catamarán,** Jr. Comercio 166 (ℂ **056/680-327**), serves the town's best pizzas and has a very cheap menu. The most upmarket of the restaurants along the walkway, **Don Manuel,** Jr. Comercio 179 (ℂ **056/532-035**), serves a variety of inexpensive meals, including *churrasco* (grilled meats) and good fresh fish.

2 ICA

300km (186 miles) S of Lima; 75km (47 miles) SE of Pisco; 130km (81 miles) NW of Nasca

Capital of the department and surrounded by sand dunes, Ica is a surprisingly large and bustling colonial town, given the scorching desert sun its inhabitants have to contend with. Like Pisco, most of the principal attractions are located beyond the city. Ica is known primarily for its bodegas, wineries that produce a range of wines and pisco, the white-grape brandy that is the essential ingredient in the national drink, the ubiquitous pisco sour (served as a welcome drink at bars, hotels, and restaurants throughout Peru). Also welcome to travelers in the unrelentingly dry, sandy pampas of the department is the Huacachina Lagoon, a pretty and unexpected oasis amid palm trees and dunes on the outskirts of Ica. In Ica proper is a small collection of interesting colonial mansions and churches, as well as the surprisingly excellent Museo Regional, with some splendid exhibits on the area's rich archaeological finds.

Ica was first settled as early as 10,000 years ago and then inhabited by a succession of advanced cultures, including the Paracas, Nasca, Wari, and Ica civilizations. The Inca Pachacútec incorporated the Ica, Nasca, and Chincha valley territories in the 15th century, but by the mid–16th century, the Spaniards had arrived, and Jerónimo Luis de Cabrera founded the Villa de Valverde del Valle de Ica, which grew in importance as a commercial center focusing on wine and cotton production.

Ica is still recovering from the great 2007 earthquake. The city's Señor de Luren church was leveled, and many residents lost their homes.

ESSENTIALS

Getting There

There are frequent buses from Lima to Ica (4 hr.), which drop passengers in the center of town. Frequent service also connects Ica to Nasca (2 hr.) and Pisco (45 min.). **Cruz del Sur,** Avenida Paseo de la República, Lima (© 01/311-5050; www.cruzdelsur.com. pe), and **Ormeño,** Av. Carlos Zavala 177, Lima (© 01/472-5000; www.grupo-ormeno. com.pe), both travel between Lima, Pisco, Nasca, and Arequipa. **Soyuz,** Av. México 331 (La Victoria), Lima (© 01/265-0501; www.soyuz.com.pe), connects Ica with Lima and Pisco, and is the fastest and best service (with the most frequent departures) from either city. Bus terminals in Ica are located in the center of town on or just off Jirón Lambayeque, a couple of blocks west of the Plaza de Armas.

Visitor Information

The **tourist information office** is located at Grau 150 (© 056/227-287), and the **tourism police** can be found on the Plaza de Armas (© 056/227-673).

FAST FACTS **Banco de Crédito,** Av. Grau 109, at the corner of Callao (© 056/233-711), has an ATM. You'll also find money exchangers on the Plaza de Armas.

For medical attention, go to **Hospital Félix Torrealva Gutiérrez,** Bolívar 1065 (© 056/234-798), or **Hospital de Apoyo,** Camino a Huacachina s/n (© 056/235-231, or 056/235-101 for emergencies). If you need the **police,** its headquarters are located at Lambayeque, block 1 (© 056/224-553). You'll find a **post office** at San Martín 156 (© 056/234-549) and a **Telefónica del Perú** office at Jr. Huanuco 289 (© 056/217-247).

ACCOMMODATIONS ■
El Huacachinero **12**
Hostería Suiza **13**
Hotel Las Dunas Sun Resort **2**
Hotel Mossone **12**

DINING ◆
El Otro Penoncito **7**
Nueva Castilla **4**
Restaurant Valasco **8**
La Villa de Ica **9**
Plaza 125 **10**

ATTRACTIONS ●
Bodega Catador **15**
Hacienda Tacama Bodega **1**
Iglesia de la Merced **5**
Iglesia de San Francisco **3**
Laguna de Huacachina **11**
Museo Cabrera **6**
Museo Regional de Ica **14**

Getting Around

Ica is quite spread out, and getting around town will most likely involve taking inexpensive taxis, which flood the streets. (Most trips in town cost less than S/7) Taxis are especially useful in visiting the wineries located outside of town. There are also *ciclotaxis,* or bicycle rickshaws, which are cheaper still but less secure. Some visitors enjoy taking them out to Huacachina.

You can arrange Nasca Lines overflights from Ica, although it's considerably more common (not to mention much, much cheaper) to organize them in Nasca. If you want to do it from Ica, contact **AeroCondor,** in the Hotel Las Dunas at Av. La Angostura 400

(© **056/256-820** or 01/442-5112). For other organized tours, contact **Huacachina Tours,** Av. La Angostura 355, L-47, in front of the Hotel Las Dunas (© **056/256-582;** www.huacachinatours.com); or **Pelican Travel & Service,** Jr. Independencia 156 and Jr. Lima 121 (© **056/225-211**). For additional flight information, call the Aeródromo de Ica, Carretera Panamericana Sur, Km 299 (© **056/256-230**).

WHAT TO SEE & DO
Museums

Museo Cabrera (Finds) An oddly idiosyncratic museum that specializes in purportedly ancient stones, this private unmarked collection is worth a visit if you prize the "art" of highly personal collecting. With more than 10,000 stones, including a series of fancifully engraved stones with depictions of primitive life (including dinosaurs), the collection makes an entertaining, if almost assuredly fraudulent, case for the nature of pre-Inca Peruvian civilizations. Dr. Javier Cabrera, a descendant of one of Ica's founders, claimed that his stones proved the validity of his unique theories that an unprecedented advanced Stone Age culture flourished in Peru long before the reign of the Inca Empire. Regardless of the truth, the stones were engraved by talented artisans, many of whom are still living today. A visit to this museum will be brief—in 20 minutes, you will have seen all you need to see.

Bolívar 170 (Plaza de Armas). © **056/231-933.** Admission by guided tour only, S/18. Mon–Sat 9am–1pm and 4–8pm (although hours are not always maintained).

Museo Regional de Ica ★ (Finds) Ica's Regional Museum, founded in 1946 and frequently hailed as one of the best small museums in the country, houses a very good collection of intricate Paracas textiles, Nasca ceramics, mummies, fossils, deformed skulls, and trophy heads, as well as colonial and republican art. The well-organized collection also includes important pieces from the Huari, Ica, Chincha, and Inca civilizations, giving visitors an excellent primer on the region's rich history and archaeology. You'll find *quipus,* knotted strings used by the Incas, who, in lieu of a writing system, made and maintained calculations, records, and historical notes with them; and a large-scale model (1/500) of the Nasca Lines behind the museum. Allow about 45 minutes for a visit.

Jirón Ayabaca, Block 8 s/n. © **056/234-383.** Admission S/6 adults, S/3 students. Mon–Sat 8am–7pm; Sun 9am–1pm. The museum is about a mile, or a 20-min. walk, from Ica's Plaza de Armas; you can also take bus 17 from the plaza to reach it.

Bodegas (Wineries)

Dispersed throughout the Ica countryside are some 85 traditional artisanal wineries that produce pisco and regular table wines. Several of the larger bodegas welcome visits; these can be interesting because pisco is such a unique Peruvian product, but they're unlikely to be the most fascinating winery tours you'll experience in your lifetime. They don't usually draw big crowds, so visits can be a little homespun and even haphazard. If you don't have your own transportation, the best way to visit the following bodegas is to either take a taxi or check with one of the travel agencies in town (see "Getting Around," above) about organized tours. Tours given on the premises of the wineries are frequently in Spanish only. For 3-day/2-night package tours from Lima to Ica, which include transportation, bodega visits, meals, city tours, and accommodations, call **Fly Peru/La Ruta del Pisco** at © **01/445-3900;** the cost is $69 to $99 per person, depending on the hotels.

Harvest time, from late February to April, is by far the best time to visit. At other times, the bodegas can be very quiet; it might be difficult finding someone to give a tour, but you might also have the chance to sit down for a drink with the owner.

(Tips) No Wine Until It's Time

Ica celebrates a wine-harvest festival *(Festival Internacional de la Vendimia)* during early March. The second Friday of the month is a major holiday throughout the Ica department. Many activities take place in the vineyards, although around town there are concerts, handicraft fairs, Peruvian *caballos de paso* (step horses) shows, beauty pageants, and cockfighting. (Don't these last two always go together?) It's a great time to get your fill of pisco. The lovely maiden chosen as the Queen of the Festival gets to doff her shoes and squish grapes in a huge wine vat, to the titillation of all.

Another date to remember: July 25 is the **Día Internacional del Pisco** across Peru, and everybody gets drunk on a national scale.

Bodega Catador   Located in the Subtanjalla district 7km (4⅓ miles) from Ica, this interesting and ancient bodega, resuscitated in 1970, offers free tours and tastings. It has a small wine museum, and a restaurant and tavern that often have live music. (The winery curiously calls this a "discothèque.") A small Centro Turístico displays photographs and videos of the production process.

Fondo Tres Esquinas 102 (Ctra. Panamericana Sur, Km 296), Subtanjalla, Ica. ℂ **056/403-295** or 056/403-427. Free admission. Daily 8am–6pm.

Bodegas Vista Alegre   Just 3km (1¾ miles) north of the center of Ica in the La Tinguiña district, this winery is one of the oldest and largest in Peru. It was a Jesuit hacienda until the late 18th century; in 1857, the winery was established by the Picasso brothers, and it's now well known for its pisco production. To get there on foot, walk on Avenida Grau from the Plaza de Armas, cross over the Ica River, and turn left; the gate entrance to the colonial hacienda is impossible to miss.

Camino a La Tinguiña Km 2, Ica. ℂ **056/232-919.** www.vistaalegre.com.pe. Free admission. Mon–Fri 9am–2pm.

Hacienda Tacama Bodega ★   About 10km (6¼ miles) northeast of Ica, housed in a 16th-century colonial hacienda, this winery, one of the largest producers in the region, is known internationally and exports its pisco and table wines—some of the finest in Peru—to a number of countries. The Olaechea family has owned the winery since 1889. Despite the farm building's age—it's one of the oldest in the valley—the bodega uses modern technology. The vineyard is still irrigated, incredibly, by the amazing Achirana irrigation canal built by the Incas. Note that for the time being, public tours of the winery have been suspended.

Camino a La Tinguiña s/n, Ica. ℂ **056/228-395.** Call for fees, if tours are operating. Daily 9am–3pm.

Ocucaje ★   About 35km (22 miles) south of Ica, on the grounds of a colonial hacienda, this remote traditional winery, which dates to the 16th century, is where the locally famous Vino Fond de Cave was born. The winery and its on-site resort suffered significant damages in the August 2007 earthquake.

Av. Principal s/n. ℂ **056/408-001** or 056/837-049. www.ocucaje.com. S/10 per person for tour. Mon–Fri 9am–noon and 2–5pm; Sat 9am–noon.

> ## (Fun Facts Pisco Sour
>
> The pisco sours that groups of tourists get served as welcome drinks at restaurants and hotels across the country are often light and frothy—pale imitations of more potent and tart pisco sours that are the real thing. However, there's been a real revival of interest in this classic Peruvian drink, and in addition to the traditional cocktail, mixologists have come up with delectable variations such as coca sours, maracuyá sours and lucumá sours, taking advantage of Peru's indigenous plants and fruits. Here's the recipe for an authentic pisco sour:
>
> 2 oz. pisco
> 1 oz. lime juice
> 1/4 oz. simple syrup
> 1/2 egg white
> 1 dash Angostura bitters
>
> Shake with ice and strain into glass; garnish with bitters on the creamy top.

Colonial Churches & Mansions

Ica has several colonial churches and mansions of note, even though many have been felled by earthquakes over the years. **Iglesia de La Merced** (also called **La Catedral**), on the southwest corner of the Plaza de Armas, is a late-19th-century colonial church with a handsomely carved altar. **Iglesia de San Jerónimo,** Cajamarca 262, is primarily of interest for its altar mural. **Iglesia de San Francisco,** though constructed in 1950, is notable for its stained glass; it's at Avenida Municipalidad, at Avenida San Martín. The most important church to worshipers, the neoclassical **Templo del Santuario de Luren,** Calle Ayacucho at Piura, was sadly destroyed by the 2007 earthquake that struck the region.

Among the most attractive of Ica's *casonas,* or colonial mansions, are the **Casona del Marqués de Torre** (today the Banco Continental), on the first block of Calle Libertad; **Casa Mendiola,** on Calle Bolívar; **Casona Alvarado,** a Greco-Roman imitation at Cajamarca 178; and **Casona Colonial El Portón,** Calle Loreto 223.

Outdoor Fun

LAGUNA DE HUACACHINA ★★ (Kids) If you stumble upon this gentle, beautiful oasis in the middle of the desert, surrounded by massive sand dunes and palm trees, you might think it's a mirage. Only 5km (3 miles) southwest of the center of Ica, Huacachina (pronounced "Wah-kah-*chee*-nah") Lagoon is a great place to relax and swim (although the water can be pretty murky) if you're suffering from the heat, and there's a small resort village with a few hotels and restaurants. A boardwalk rings the lagoon. Locals contend that the sulfur-rich waters of the lagoon have curative medicinal properties. Kids can go sand boarding on the dunes (one of the restaurants and the Hostal Rocha in town rent out boards) or paddleboat across the lagoon. Regular buses to Huacachina depart from the Plaza de Armas in Ica. Better yet, you can take an inexpensive and quick taxi; it's best to request one from your hotel and establish the price beforehand (rates run about $3–$4).

SAND BOARDING ★ (Kids) In the sand dune–laden desert landscapes in southern Peru, surfing the dunes on sand boards and rumbling across the sands in *areneros* (dune buggies) are popular sports. The largest sand dunes in South America, reaching a height of 2,000m (6,560 ft.), are just 8km (5 miles) from Nasca, and there are also really high dunes around the Huacachina Lagoon outside of Ica.

Sand boarding, a cross between downhill skiing and snowboarding on grainy stuff rather than white powder, is fairly easy to do (or that's what they tell me). You can really build up some speed, and accomplished boarders can maneuver almost like they would on the slopes. It can be very hot, though, and tough going, because there aren't any lifts to transport you back up the dune. After a few spills, you'll be covered in sand. Accidents can occur, so it's best to get some instruction from a local or the outfit renting the boards.

Adrenaline-fueled adventure trips in buggies are available through local tours (information is available at the **Hotel Paracas;** p. 158) or at the 210m (690-ft.) dunes around the Huacachina Lagoon outside of Ica, where a restaurant and the **Hostal Rocha** rent sand boards (about S/3 an hour; C 056/222-256).

WHERE TO STAY

Most of the best hotel options lie beyond the center of Ica; the majority of those in town are rather unappealing budget choices that have inconsistent hot water.

Moderate

Hotel Las Dunas Sun Resort ★ (Kids On the outskirts of Ica is this sprawling complex of white Mediterranean-style villas with pretty landscaped grounds, three swimming pools, and good sports opportunities, including horseback riding, golf, tennis, *frontón* (something like a cross between paddle tennis and jai alai), sand boarding, and volleyball. In terms of services and amenities, if not necessarily character, it's a step up from the other top hotel in the area, the Mossone (below). Rooms are surprisingly large and nicely furnished, and most have garden views. A terrific bonus is the planetarium that provides a good introduction to the Nasca Lines (admission S/20).

Av. La Angostura 400, Ica. C/fax **056/256-224** or 01/241-8000 for reservations. www.lasdunashotel. com. 106 units. Sun–Thurs S/366–S/458 double; Fri–Sat S/449–S/561 double; S/760–S/890 suite. Rates include taxes. AE, DC, MC, V. **Amenities:** Restaurant; cafeteria; bar; small gym; 2 outdoor pools; sauna. *In room:* A/C, TV, fridge.

Hotel Mossone (Kids A famous luxury resort hotel back in the 1920s, this century-old mansion at the Huacachina Lagoon is a fancy, colonial-style hotel that hasn't made much effort to keep up with the times. It slipped into neglect for a few decades and still feels a bit dilapidated, with the central patio—along with its lagoon location—its best feature. Rooms are dank and in need of updating, though the restaurant, featuring a relaxing deck overlooking the oasis, is an enjoyable place to relax. Most who choose the Mossone have their hearts set on staying at the lagoon and doing some sand boarding, but even to them it is likely to seem overpriced for what it is. El Huacachinero (below) is probably a better choice.

Balneario de Huacachina, Ica. C **056/236-136.** Fax 056/236-137. reservas@derramajae.org.pe. 43 units. $86 double. Rates include taxes. AE, DC, MC, V. **Amenities:** Restaurant; bar; outdoor pool. *In room:* TV.

Inexpensive

El Huacachinero ★ (Finds A convivial, cute little hostal, this is probably the best choice for staying right on the lagoon, and is understandably popular with backpackers. Rooms, well maintained and comfortable for the price, are built around an attractive outdoor pool with a sun terrace and bar. The hotel focuses on dune experiences, operating its own "green buggy" services and sand boarding trips, and the resident parrots are either entertaining or annoying, depending on your tolerance.

Avenida Perotti, Balneario de Huacachina, Ica. ℂ **056/217435.** Fax 056/256-814. www.elhuacachinero. com. 15 units. S/110 double. No credit cards. **Amenities:** Cafeteria; bar. *In room:* TV, minibar, Wi-Fi.

Hostería Suiza (**Kids**) Also at the edge of the Huacachina Lagoon, and operated by the family that once ran the elegant Hotel Mossone (above), this friendly, homey, and very comfortable hostal is a good value. Rooms, some of which overlook the lagoon, are very clean and attractive, if a bit spartan, and the bright tiled bathrooms are also quite nice. The outdoor pool and flower-filled gardens are a nice bonus at this price, at the high end of the budget range. The inn also operates desert sand buggy excursions, which are perfect for adventurous kids.

Balneario de Huacachina, Ica. ℂ **056/238-762.** Fax 056/219-516. hostesuiza@terra.com.pe. 22 units. $45 double. Rates include taxes. AE, DC, MC, V. **Amenities:** Restaurant; bar; outdoor pool. *In room:* No phone.

WHERE TO DINE

Despite its size, Ica doesn't offer much in the way of fine dining. Most locals and visitors tend to gravitate toward the Plaza de Armas and the handful of sandwich shops, rotisserie-chicken places, and informal restaurants there.

Grab some snacks, breakfast, or a tourist set lunch, along with some local wines, at **La Villa de Ica,** Lima 139 at the Plaza de Armas (ℂ **056/213-108**). **Plaza 125,** Lima 125 at the Plaza de Armas (ℂ **056/211-816**), serves grilled meats, rotisserie chicken, and barbecue, as well as regional specialties, to a mixed crowd of families and young people. **El Otro Peñoncito**★, Bolívar 422 (ℂ **056/233-920**), is the nicest restaurant in the city center, with a hugely varied menu of *criollo* (Creole) specialties and basic chicken, meat, and fish dishes, including some vegetarian plates. Sometimes there's live music in the evenings. **Nueva Castilla,** Libertad 252 (ℂ **056/213-140**), is a pretty nice restaurant serving Peruvian fare. After dinner on weekends, the music is pumped up and the restaurant becomes a disco of sorts. **Restaurant Velasco,** Libertad 137 (ℂ **056/218-182**), is a popular cafeteria-style restaurant and bakery serving both Peruvian and international dishes at very affordable prices, as well as a selection of baked goods and other desserts and coffee.

3 NASCA ★

443km (275 miles) S of Lima

Nasca (also spelled Nazca) would just be a dusty little desert town of little interest were it not for the strange presence of massive, mysterious drawings—the famous Nasca Lines—etched into the sands of the pampas more than a millennium ago. Ancient peoples created a vast tapestry of "geoglyphs"—trapezoids and triangles, 70-odd animal and plant figures, and more than 10,000 lines—that have baffled observers for decades. They are so large, with some figures reaching dimensions of 300m (1,000 ft.), that they can be appreciated only from the air. Over the years, theorists have posited that they were signs from the gods, agricultural and astronomical calendars, or even extraterrestrial airports. Some believe that the drawers of the lines must themselves have had the ability to fly, perhaps in hot-air balloons, over the designs below. The wildest theories, today discredited by all but fringe-dwelling true believers, prompted the old book and movie *The Chariots of the Gods.*

The town and the drawings are named for the Nasca culture (300 B.C.–A.D. 700), which succeeded the Paracas civilization along the southern desert coast. Little was

ACCOMMODATIONS ■	DINING ◆	ATTRACTIONS ●
Casa Andina Classic Nasca **9**	El Huarango **11**	Aqueductos de Cantalloc **2**
Hotel Alegría **5**	Las Líneas **10**	Casa-Museo María Reiche **1**
Hotel Cantayo Spa & Resort **4**	La Taberna **7**	Cementerios de Chauchilla **2**
Hotel Majoro **3**	Las Cañas **8**	Museo Antonini **12**
Hotel Nasca Lines **6**		

known about the Nasca until the beginning of the 20th century. Today the Nasca are renowned for their exquisitely stylized pottery, among the finest of pre-Columbian Peru. The small town of Nasca was devastated by a monstrous earthquake in 1996 and is just getting back on its feet. Most constructions in town were adobe, which crumbled and were replaced by hastily built concrete houses. The new construction adds to the dusty frontier feel of the town.

The surrounding desert is a strangely impressive place. Flying over the Nasca Lines, you see an unending expanse of craggy, dusty, origami-like folds in the sands, like deep wrinkles in a wizened face. Certainly, nothing in the region equals the impact of a flight over the lines, but the town does have a couple of good museums and two archaeological sites that evoke the Nasca culture that flourished in the area.

ESSENTIALS
Getting There
From Lima, **Cruz del Sur** buses (© **01/311-5050;** www.cruzdelsur.com.pe) pass through Nasca on the way to Arequipa; the trip to Nasca takes 6 to 7 hours. **Ormeño** (© **01/472-5000;** www.grupo-ormeno.com.pe) makes the trip from Lima as well as

> **Fun Facts   Say What?**
>
> The Nasca people were evidently deeply rooted in the hot and painfully arid southern desert landscape that they inhabited in spite of numerous earthquakes and that they fought valiantly to farm. The word "Nasca" comes from the Quechua *nanasca*, which means pain and suffering.

Cusco (24-plus hr.) and Arequipa (10 hr.), and, like Cruz del Sur, returns to Lima. **Expreso Wari** (© 01/423-6640; www.expresowari.com.pe) also makes the long journey between Cusco and Nasca (20–22 hr.).

Visitor Information

The **tourist information office** (© 056/522-418), Callao 783 (Plaza de Armas) in the Municipal building, offers maps, hotel and tourism packages and guide information. It's open Monday to Friday from 9am to 3pm. Tourist information can also be obtained from one of the travel agencies in town, such as **Alegría Tours,** although they are primarily interested in selling tour packages.

FAST FACTS   Banco de Crédito (© 056/522-445), at Avenidas Grau and Lima, has an ATM with the Visa logo, as does **Banco de la Nación** (no phone), Lima 431. For medical attention, go to **EsSalud,** María Reiche 308 (© 056/522-438), or **Hospital de Apoyo,** Callao s/n (at Morsesky; © 056/522-586). The **police** (© 056/522-442) are on Los Incas, next to the roundabout on Lima and Panamericana, near the Ormeño station.

The **post office** is at Fermín de Castillo 379, between Callao and Bolognesi. The **Telefónica del Perú** office (© 056/523-045) is at Lima 545.

WHAT TO SEE & DO

Visitors who want to see more than the Nasca Lines would probably benefit from arranging a group tour with one of the Nasca travel agencies because the major archaeological sites are scattered about the valley and complicated to get to. For flights over the lines, it's sometimes best to simply go to the airport and purchase tickets directly from one of the charter airlines there. The following agencies all offer city and regional packages and information on the area (as well as Nasca Lines packages): **Alegría Tours,** Jr. Lima 168 (© 056/523-431; www.alegriatoursperu.com); **Nanasca Tours,** Lima 160 (© 034/522-917); **Nasca Travel,** Lima 438 (© 056/522-085); and **Nasca Trails,** Jr. Bolognesi 299 (© 056/522-858; nascatrails@terra.com.pe). Going a bit beyond the standard Nasca Lines tours, offering helicopter flights over the Lines, dune buggy trips, and combo trips to the Cahuachi and Estaquería temples, is **Mystery Perú,** Ignacio Morsesky 126 (© 056/522-379; www.mysteryperu.com).

Nasca Lines ★★

The unique Nasca Lines remain one of the great enigmas of the South American continent. The San José desert, bisected by the great Pan-American Highway that runs the length of Peru, is spectacularly marked by 70 giant plant and animal figures, as well as a warren of mysterious geometric lines, carved into the barren surface. Throughout the Nasca Valley, an area of nearly 1,000 sq. km (390 sq. miles), there are at least 10,000 lines

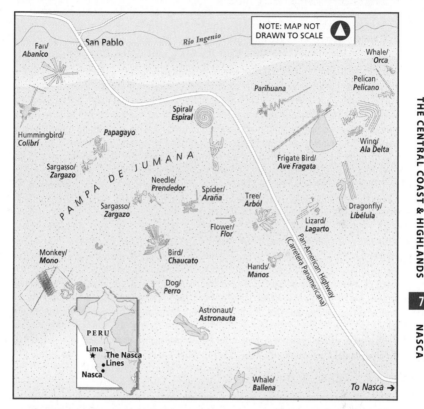

THE CENTRAL COAST & HIGHLANDS

7

NASCA

and 300 different figures. Most are found alongside a 48km (30-mile) stretch of the Pan-American Highway. Some of the biggest and best-known figures are about 21km (13 miles) north of Nasca. Most experts believe they were constructed by the Nasca (pre-Inca) culture between 300 B.C. and A.D. 700, although predecessor and successor cultures—the Paracas and Huari—might have also contributed to the desert canvas. The lines were discovered in the 1920s when commercial airlines began flights over the Peruvian desert. From the sky, they appeared to be some sort of primitive landing strips.

As enigmatic as they are, the Nasca Lines are not some sort of desert-sands Rorschach inkblot; the figures are real and easily identifiable from the air. With the naked eye from the window of an airplane, you'll spot the outlines of a parrot, hummingbird, spider, condor, dog, whale, monkey with a tail wound like a top, giant spirals, huge trapezoids, and, perhaps oddest of all, a cartoonish anthropomorphic figure with its hand raised to the sky that has come to be known as the "Astronaut." Some figures are as much as 300m (1,000 ft.) long, while some lines are 30m (100 ft.) wide and stretch more than 9.5km (6 miles).

Questions have long confounded observers. Who constructed these huge figures and lines? And, of course, why? Apparently, over many generations, the Nasca people removed hard stones turned dark by the sun to "draw" the lines in the fine, lighter-colored sand. The incredibly dry desert conditions—it rains only about 50 centimeters a year, on average—preserved the lines and figures for more than 1,000 years. Why the lines were constructed is more difficult to answer, especially considering that the authors were unable to see their work in its entirety without any sort of aerial perspective. The scientist who dedicated her life to study of the lines was a German mathematician, María Reiche. For 5 decades, she lived austerely in the Peruvian desert and walked alone among the lines, taking painstaking measurements and making drawings of the site. She concluded that the lines formed a giant astronomical calendar, crucial to calculating planting and harvest times. According to this theory, the Nasca were able to predict the arrival of rains, a valuable commodity in such a barren territory. Other theories abound, though. Nasca is a seismic zone, with 300 fault lines beneath the surface and hundreds of subterranean canals; an American scientist, David Johnson, proposed that the trapezoids held clues to subterranean water sources. Some suggest that the lines not only led to water sources, but that they also were pilgrimage routes, part of the Nasca's ritual worship of water. Notions of extraterrestrials and the Nasca's ability themselves to fly over the lines have been dismissed by most serious observers.

An observation tower *(mirador)* stands beside the Pan-American Highway (about 19km/12 miles north of Nasca), but it allows only a vague and partial view of three figures: the hands, lizard, and tree. The view from the tower (S/3 adults, S/2 students) is vastly inferior to the multiple bird's-eye views one gets on the overflight, but it's the best you'll be able to do if you can't take the stomach-turning dips and dives of the light-craft flights. (Only 10 min. into one recent flight, the four French travelers onboard with me were all tossing their *petits déjeuners* into the white plastic bags that had been thoughtfully provided.)

A half-dozen small charter airlines offer flights over the lines from the small airport in Nasca. Flights (35–45 minutes) cost $65 to $85—those originating in Ica run about $150 to $180. Pilots give very basic descriptions of the figures as they fly overhead. The small aircraft seat between three and five passengers.

If you're interested in seeing the lines only and you don't have time for the town of Nasca or the surrounding area, by far the most convenient—although certainly not the cheapest—way to see the lines is as part of a 1-day or overnight round-trip package from Lima with **AeroCondor's Nazca Conexxion,** Av. Aramburu 858, Surquillo (© **01/421-3105**); **AeroIca,** Diez Canseco 480B, Miraflores (© **01/445-0859;** www.aeroica.net/icahomeing.html); or **Aeroparacas,** Av. Santa Fe 274 (© **01/265-8073;** www.aeroparacas.com), with packages ranging from $599 to $699 per person. Unfortunately, there are no independent flights from Lima to Nasca (or from any other city to Nasca), so you'll have to get there by bus—an 8-hour ride; programs with bus transportation from AeroCondor range from $150 to $300 per person.

(Tips) **Take It from a Cartographer**

Frommer's cartographer Nick Trotter highly recommends picking up the Instituto Geográfico Nacional's extremely detailed topographical map of the Nasca Lines, available from IGN (www.ign.gob.pe) or from the South American Explorers (www.saexplorers.org). Nick says it's a must-have for any traveler who's serious about exploring the lines.

| **Tips** | **Cahuachi & El Estaquería** |

Cahuachi, an ancient adobe complex west of the Nasca Lines—said by some to be twice as large as Chan Chan, the massive city of the Chimú along the north coast—was the most important ceremonial and administrative center belonging to the Nasca culture. The ruins, in poor condition and, in large part, buried under sand, are still undergoing excavation. Because of ongoing work, only a handful of temples and pyramids may be visited, and only by guided tour. (The major agencies in Nasca usually offer the site as part of a group tour for around $25–$35 per person.) Also on the premises is **El Estaquería,** a construction of rows of *huarango* trees that probably marked important grave sites. The ruins are 30km (19 miles) from Nasca. The director of the Antonini Museum in Nasca has unearthed a spectacular collection of painted textiles, made with seven different dyes, at Cahuachi that he hopes to eventually exhibit in a new museum in Nasca. Many of the finest examples of Nasca ceramics in existence were also discovered at Cahuachi.

For the best visibility, try to go in the morning or late afternoon, but be prepared for conditions that frequently delay flights and occasionally make taking off impossible.

Companies operating Nasca Lines overflights from Nasca's Aeródromo de Nasca (© **056/523-665**), Carretera Panamericana Sur, Km 447 include: **AeroCondor, AeroIca,** and **Aeroparacas** (see above). Your best bet for arranging an overflight is with one of the Nasca agencies; Mystery Peru in particular has quite a number of overflight options, including a special in-depth 1-hour flight for $130. Alegría Tours and Mystery Peru both permit advance online reservations and purchases, in some cases with discounts.

Also worth a look for those with an interest in the Nasca Lines is the small **planetarium** at the Invertur Hotel Nazca Lines (p. 174).

Other Notable Sights Near Nasca

Acueductos de Cantalloc   About 4km (2½ miles) southwest of Nasca are very well-preserved stone aqueducts, part of a sophisticated subterranean system constructed by the Nasca to irrigate the fields in the pampas. There are 35 beautifully built Inca or pre-Inca aqueducts, or *puquios,* with surface air vents that form spirals descending to the water current. The canals, many S-shaped to slow the flow of water, still function and are used by local farmers. Nearby, Los Paredones, the ruins of an Inca trade center, is in poor shape, requiring a fertile imagination to conjure the activity that once reigned here.

Ctra. Puquio–Cusco. Admission $4. Daily 8am–5pm. To get here, you must come by taxi (about S/20 round-trip, incl. waiting time) or organized tour group ($15 per person).

Casa-Museo María Reiche   The German mathematician María Reiche was the foremost expert on the Nasca Lines, earning her the nickname "Dame of the Desert." She dedicated most of her adult life to studying them, debunking the loonier theories about their purposes, and doing more than even the Peruvian government to publicize the lines' existence. Reiche died in 1998 at the age of 95. Today the simple room where she worked and lived, which her tomb has been placed next to, has been converted into a small museum paying tribute to Reiche's life and the Lines, complete with maps, models, plans, and photos. The Casa-Museo (also variously referred to as Museo de Sitio María

> ## (Fun Facts) Nasca Culture
>
> The Nasca civilization is best known for its artistry on a grand scale: those mas-sive and monstrously baffling line drawings on the desert floor of the coastal pampas. But among scholars, the culture is acclaimed for producing the most sophisticated ceramists of pre-Columbian Peru and ingenious engineers who irri-gated their desert fields with hydraulic systems and aqueducts that carried underground water.
>
> The Nasca succeeded the Paracas in the desert region south of present-day Lima. Whereas the Paracas were extraordinary weavers and designers of textiles, the Nasca culture distinguished itself with highly artistic pottery. Its glazed ceramics featured vivid but earthy colors and symbolic motifs, and mineral-based pigments ensured lasting colors. Many of the stylized figures and lines on Nasca pottery closely echo the Nasca Lines, reinforcing theories about the latter's authorship.

Reiche Newman and Museo Regional María Reiche) is located in the district called San Pablo, between Ica and Nasca. Allow a half-hour to tour the museum.

Caserío la Pascana, Ctra. Panamericana Sur, Km 420 (27km/17 miles from Nasca), San Pablo. (℃) 056/234-383 or 056/522-428. Admission S/5. Mon–Fri 9am–7pm; Sat 8:30am–6:30pm; Sun 9am–1pm.

Cementerios de Chauchilla ★ (Finds) About 30km (19 miles) south of Nasca is an extensive valley of tombs from the Inca-Chincha period (A.D. 1000–1400). It is a necropolis rather than a mere cemetery: Thousands of graves have been uncovered in the area. Only 12 underground tombs are exposed for visitors, although they present a rich picture of the ancient culture of the desert valley. One tomb holds only children, and others are populated with the remains of adults with thick, Rasta-like dreadlocks. The cemetery has been open to the public since only 1997, and only in the past year were the tombs covered with thatch roofs, which is why many skulls appear whitewashed from the blazing desert sun. The desert's very dry conditions helped preserve the mummies over the centuries. Fragments of textiles, feathers, and even bone are scattered about the site, clues to the cemetery's discovery by *huaqueros* (grave robbers) and how underfunded this project remains. Allow about 3 to 4 hours for travel time and viewing the necropolis.

Chauchilla (30km/18 miles from Nasca). Admission S/5. Daily 8am–5pm. Getting to Chauchilla is compli-cated, as there is no public transportation to the site; taxi (about S/60 round-trip, incl. waiting time) and tour group ($15 per person) are the only options.

Museo Antonini ★ (Kids) This excellent private archaeology museum, a labor of love inaugurated by an Italian foundation in 1999, addresses local Nasca culture with excellent exhibits that detail the process as well as the results of archaeological excava-tions in the area. On view are fine ceramics, trophy heads worn by warriors after beheadings to inspire fear among enemies, musical instruments, and a few well-pre-served mummies. In the gardens out back are the Bisambra aqueduct, an ancient Nasca stone irrigation canal, reproductions of tombs, and scale models of the Nasca Lines. The director hopes one day soon to be able to open a new museum in Nasca to show off the world's greatest collection of painted textiles—made with seven different types of vegetable dyes—all uncovered from the huge adobe city of Cahuachi nearby. Plan to spend about an hour here.

WHERE TO STAY

There are plenty of low-end accommodations in Nasca and a handful of slightly more comfortable, if unspectacular, options in town and out by the airport.

Expensive

Hotel Cantayo Spa & Resort ★★ (Finds) Located next to the Cantalloc Aqueduct, this grand, mission-style hacienda has been converted into a sprawling spa hotel. Rustic and peaceful, it features sweeping panoramic mountain views, large rooms adorned with Balinese and Tibetan touches, a huge swimming pool, extensive gardens, and a jogging track. The Italian owners have positioned it as a relaxing refuge, which takes its cues from the region's more spiritual and mystical attractions, offering a menu of exoticism: tai chi, yoga, Japanese meditation, and not only massages and facials but also Watsu treatments. If you consider yourself more grounded than that, you can indulge in horseback riding and long walks around the property. The hotel's restaurant is the finest in Nasca and worth a visit even if you aren't staying here.

Carretera Puquio–Cusco, Nasca. ℂ **056/522-264** or 056/522-283 for reservations. Fax 056/522-283. www.hotelcantayo.com. 40 units. $190 double; $272 executive suite. Rates include breakfast. AE, DC, MC, V. **Amenities:** Restaurant; Jacuzzi; 2 outdoor pools; spa. *In room:* A/C, TV.

Moderate

Casa Andina Classic Nasca ★★ (Value) (Kids) Though there are no other chains in Nasca, Casa Andina, a still-growing group of Peruvian hotels, is making sure it's got all the top tourist spots in the country covered. This charming hotel, appreciated by families and more upscale travelers (for whom there are few good options in Nasca), follows the company's midsize, midrange, and always consistent formula. Located downtown, right on the pedestrian mall that's 1 block from the main square and about 5 minutes from the airfield where flights depart for the Nasca Lines, it is the largest hotel in Nasca. Rooms—built along a sunny, open-air interior corridor—are ample and nicely decorated, with colorful interiors and nice, clean bathrooms. The outdoor pool isn't large, but it features a large and cheery, bougainvillea-filled patio.

Jr. Bolognesi 367, Nasca. ℂ **056/523-563.** Fax 056/521-067. www.casa-andina.com. 60 units. $69–$99 double. Rates include breakfast buffet. AE, DC, MC, V. **Amenities:** Restaurant; small outdoor pool. *In room:* A/C, TV, hair dryer upon request.

Hotel Majoro ★ (Finds) (Kids) This rustic old hacienda features simple rooms around courtyards and tranquil, extensive gardens full of bougainvillea. Its new owners have pumped much-needed investment and life into the place, though it retains the feel of an elegant country house, with horse stables and open space. The common areas have been completely transformed and are now warm and inviting. Accommodations are spacious, clean, and charming where they were once dumpy. The two large, garden-like pools are terrific places to relax and let the kids run around. It's set in Majoro, a few kilometers along a dusty road beyond the airport. Check online for promotions, as the hotel advertises some good package deals that include Nasca Lines overflights and other excursions.

Ctra. Panamericana Sur, Km 452 (Majoro) Nasca. ℂ **056/522-481.** Fax 056/522-750. www.hotelmajoro. com. 39 units. $95–$140 double. Rates include breakfast. AE, DC, MC, V. **Amenities:** Restaurant; bar; 2 outdoor pools. *In room:* TV.

Hotel Nazca Lines For many years the most upscale hotel in town, the Hotel Nazca Lines has been surpassed by the new hotels and remodels, but is still pretty popular for its amenities: It has a pretty courtyard with a good-size clean pool and old tennis courts. The attractive-enough rooms, with tile and iron accents, have good air-conditioning but dated furnishings. The Lines' fabled caretaker, María Reiche, lived here for many years in room no. 130. On the premises are a restaurant and a planetarium named for Reiche, with Nasca Lines presentations.

Jr. Bolognesi s/n, Nasca. ℂ **056/522-293.** Fax 056/522-112. nazca@invertur.com.pe. 34 units. $85–$101 double. DC, MC, V. **Amenities:** Restaurant; outdoor pool; 2 tennis courts. *In room:* A/C, TV.

Inexpensive

Hotel Alegría ★ The down-to-earth and traveler-friendly Alegría, with a white-washed Andalusian look, is the most popular inexpensive hotel in town, and a good place to meet up with others exploring this region of Peru. Rooms are basic—clean but spartan—but the nice leafy patio garden and small pool are excellent bonuses for a hotel at this price point (although you could stay at the Casa Andina Classic for not much more). It operates a good travel agency and has loads of facilities and services, including free Internet access for guests, bus-station pickup, and luggage storage. Some of the new chalet-style rooms have air-conditioning.

Lima 168, Nasca. ℂ/fax **056/522-497.** www.hotelalegria.net. 43 units. $60 double. Rates include breakfast and prearranged pickup from bus stop. DC, MC, V. **Amenities:** Restaurant; bar; outdoor pool. *In room:* A/C in some units, TV.

WHERE TO DINE

Your dining choices are rather limited in Nasca, as they are throughout the region. Most people come just to view the Nasca Lines, they don't stay many nights, and they tend to eat at their hotels. Hotels with pretty good restaurants include **Casa Andina Classic Nasca** and **Hotel Alegría.** The restaurant at **Hotel Cantayo Spa & Resort ★★**, outside of town, is a cut above (see "Where to Stay," above).

Las Líneas, Jr. Arica 299-A (ℂ **056/522-066**), serves Peruvian fare such as ceviche and garlic chicken, even though it looks like a Chinese restaurant. **El Huarango,** Jr. Arica 602 (ℂ **056/521-287**), is one of the better restaurants in Nasca, offering good-value meals and a rooftop garden. **La Taberna ★**, Jr. Lima 321 (ℂ **056/806-783**), is a good restaurant—probably the best in town—with a varied international menu, live music on weekends, and the graffiti scrawlings of hundreds of international travelers who came before you. **Las Cañas,** Bolognesi 279 (ℂ **056/806-891**), serves a large menu of Peruvian and international dishes, including ceviche, pastas, salads, and hamburgers; it's quite a hangout on weekend nights.

4 A GEM IN THE CENTRAL HIGHLANDS: AYACUCHO ★★

585km (364 miles) SE of Lima; 337km (209 miles) NE of Pisco; 590km (367 miles) W of Cusco

Located high in the Central Andes—and hijacked in the 1980s by Shining Path terrorists who claimed the city as their base and cut it off from Peru and the rest of the world for much of the past 2 decades—dignified Ayacucho has at last escaped bloody conflict and is begging to be discovered. A colonial gem, with more of its Spanish architecture intact

ATTRACTIONS●

Basílica Menor (Catedral) **7**

Casona Cristóbal Castilla y Zamora **9**

Casona del Corregidor Nicolás Boza y Solis **10**

Casona del Marqués de Mozobamba
(Casona Olano) **13**

Casona Ruíz de Ochoa y Monreal
(Casona Jáuregui) **15**

Museo Cáceres (Casona Vivanco) **20**

Museo de Arte Popular Joaquín López Antay
(Casona Chacón) **6**

San Francisco de Asís **17**

Santa Clara de Asís **16**

Templo de la Compañía de Jesús **11**

Templo de San Cristóbal **22**

Templo de Santa María Magdalena **2**

Templo de Santa Teresa **21**

Templo de Santo Domingo **3**

Templo del Arco **1**

Templo y Convento de La Merced **18**

ACCOMMODATIONS■

Ayacucho Hotel Plaza **5**

Hostal La Florida **8**

Marquez de Valdelirios **23**

DINING◆

Café Bar New York **12**

El Monasterio **12**

La Casona **4**

Sandra **14**

Urpicha **19**

than almost any other city in Peru, the city claims the crown as the epicenter of Peruvian *artesanía* (popular art). The renowned *retablos* (see box on *retablos* below), ceramic churches, and whimsical red-clay figurines one sees all over Peru (and in Latin American shops from Austin to Amsterdam) are all produced locally.

Locals are fond of saying that the critical developments in Peruvian history are tied to Ayacucho. As the site of the earliest-known human presence in Peru, in nearby Pikim-achay, and the one-time capital of the powerful Huari culture (200–100 B.C.), Aya-cucho—originally called Huamanga, a name many locals insist on still using today—is best known as a place where crucial battles for the soul of Peru have taken place. The Chanca people bravely resisted the aggressively expanding Inca Empire, and the bloody Battle of Ayacucho against Spanish forces in 1824 launched the country's independence.

Given its history, it's not surprising that Ayacucho means "City of Blood" or "City of the Dead." Yet Ayacucho has much more to offer than its notoriety: Visitors will find it a welcoming and spectacularly serene city seemingly cleansed of its violent legacy. It's so easygoing and unassuming that it's almost inconceivable that it could have been held hostage for so long by terrorists intent on rending Peruvian society.

Still, this graceful colonial town can't escape its tumultuous past, and that's one of the best reasons to pay a visit before it becomes better known. As it continues to distance itself from the guerrilla violence of the 1980s and early 1990s, Ayacucho is keen to attract travelers on a large scale. Nestled into the Andes Mountains, the city boasts nearly 3 dozen colonial churches within blocks of the Plaza Mayor—and a spectacular Easter week festival and carnival celebrations for which it has become famous.

ESSENTIALS

Getting There

BY PLANE By far the best way to get to Ayacucho is to fly from Lima on **LC Busre** (© 01/619-1313; www.lcbusre.com.pe) or **Star Perú** (© 01/705-9000; www.starperu. com) which fly daily; the flight is 1 hour and costs about $99 one-way. The **Alfredo Mendivil Duarte** airport (© 066/812-418) is 4km (2½ miles) east of downtown on Av. del Ejército 950. Taxis, which charge S/8 to downtown, await arriving flights.

BY BUS Executive service buses from Lima via Pisco or Ica take about 9 hours on a very demanding road through the mountains; contact **Ormeño** (© 01/472-5000; www.grupo-ormeno.com.pe) or **Cruz del Sur** (© 01/311-5050; www.cruzdelsur.com.pe). Executive buses are infinitely preferable to regular service; note that they travel at night only on the direct return to Lima. There is no central bus terminal in Ayacucho; **Cruz del Sur** is located on Av. Mariscal Cáceres 1264 (© 066/812-813), and **Ormeño** is at Jr. Libertad 257 (© 066/812-495).

Visitor Information

A small **iPerú** tourist counter greets arriving planes at the airport every morning from 6:30 to 8:30am. The **iPerú** office at Portal Municipal 48 (Plaza Mayor; © 066/818-305) is extremely helpful and is open Monday through Saturday from 8:30am to 7:30pm, and Sunday from 8:30am to 2:30pm.

For guided tours and transportation in the area, contact **Wari Tours,** Portal Independencia 70 (© 066/311-415).

FAST FACTS **Banco de Crédito** (© 066/522-445) Portal Unión 27 (Plaza Mayor), has a Visa-compatible ATM. You'll also find money-changers hanging around the Plaza Mayor. Several pharmacies line Jirón 28 de Julio, including **Farmacia del Pino,** Jr. 28 de

Highest Railroad in the World

Lima is the starting point of the **Ferrocarril Central Andino** (☏ **01/226-6363;** www.ferrocarrilcentral.com.pe), the highest railway in the world, which runs from Lima to Huancayo in the Central Highlands (up to 4,781m/15,686 ft.). Unfortunately, the line has a problematic history (enough to discourage most reasonable travelers from planning their trips to Peru around it): The so-called "Tren Macho" was shut down for most of the 1980s and 1990s. It is again operating after long periods of inactivity, however. The incredibly scenic, 12-hour passenger train, which crosses 58 bridges and passes through 69 tunnels, runs once a month between July and November S/165 to S/300 round-trip). Trains leave Lima from the **Estación Central de Desamparados,** Jr. Ancash 201, just behind the Government Palace. Check for updates before you arrive in Peru.

Julio 123 (☏ 066/312-080). For emergencies, contact the **National Tourism Police** at Jr. 2 de Mayo 100 (at Jirón Arequipa; ☏ 066/312-055). The 24-hour **National Police** office is at Jr. 28 de Julio 325 (☏ 066/312-332). The main hospital is **Hospital Regional de Ayacucho,** Av. Independencia 355 (☏ 066/312-180). The **post office** is at Jr. Asamblea 295 (☏ 066/312-224).

Getting Around

The best way to get around Ayacucho itself is on foot because most places of interest—hotels, restaurants, the cathedral—are only minutes from the Plaza Mayor. Taxis and mototaxis are readily available and cheap for any trip within the city; taxis charge S/3 to S/4, and mototaxis charge S/2. A taxi to the Barrio de Santa Ana is a good idea, but if you want the driver to wait while you explore the *artesanía* galleries, negotiate a price beforehand.

For transport to Quinua and other outlying attractions, colectivos depart from the *paradero* at the corner of Jirón Salvador Cavero and Jirón Ciro Alegría in the eastern part of Ayacucho (Urbanización Santa Bertha).

WHAT TO SEE & DO
Museums & Colonial Houses

Ayacucho's pretty and placid **Plaza Mayor** ★★ (also called the **Plaza de Armas**), the epitome of a highland town square and the heart of the city, is lined by grand 16th- to 18th-century homes with stone arches and colonial red-tile roofs. It is one of the best surviving examples of colonial architecture in Peru. Eight walkways radiate out from the center in the form of a star, and you'll probably find yourself crisscrossing the square several times a day. The plaza's lovely gardens and soaring views of the cathedral and surrounding mountains make it a perfect place to occupy an iron bench and watch locals get their pictures made around the Monument to Antonio José de Sucre in the center.

On the south side of the plaza (Portal Municipal 49) is the Basílica Menor, or **La Catedral** ★, ordered built by King Philip in 1612 and completed in 1672. Beyond an ornate stone facade and two bell towers are three naves, an elaborately carved pulpit, silver and gold-leaf altars, and a collection of colonial-era religious paintings. The cathedral is open to visitors Monday through Saturday from 5 to 7pm, and Sunday from 9am to 5pm; admission is free.

Ayacucho's Renowned Retablos

Ayacucho has a long tradition of finely crafted *artesanía*, and the city and environs are said to produce 40 different specialized crafts. Perhaps most famous and emblematic of Ayacucho are the *retablos*, wooden boxes that open to show off two or three levels of busy scenes populated by dozens of laboriously hand-carved and -painted figures. A tradition brought by Spaniards and first produced in Peru during early colonial times in the 16th century, they were then known as Cajones de San Marcos or San Antonio, and they served as portable altars that devotees of St. Mark or St. Anthony carried with them on their travels through the Andes. The *retablos* were often used in efforts to convert indigenous peoples to Catholicism. Although the scenes depicted were once strictly religious, today they represent quotidian scenes of life in the *sierra*, from weddings to harvest scenes and popular festivals (although nativity scenes remain very popular).

The doors and exterior usually feature brightly painted flowers, and the *retablos* range from miniature versions with tiny figurines to others that are 1.8m (6 ft.) tall and hold 100 or more figures inside. *Retablos* are so identifiable with Ayacucho that enormous ones are displayed in the airport (more than 3m/10 ft. tall) at the luggage turnstile, and newspaper kiosks around the Plaza Mayor are decorated like oversize *retablos*.

Other handicrafts that are indigenous to the region are red-clay ceramics, including humorous depictions of groups of musicians and small bulls, and model churches; tightly woven and brightly colored *tejidos*, or textiles; carved alabaster, or *piedra de Huamanga*; figures of saints; crucifixes; chess sets; and art naïf *tablas de Sarhua*.

In a handsome colonial building on the east side of the Plaza Mayor, Portal Unión 28, is the **Museo de Arte Popular Joaquín López Antay** ★ (© **066/812-467**). The museum, which is the best place to get an overview of the highly prized artisanship and crafts that Ayacucho and surrounding villages are so renowned for, occupies several rooms around the central courtyard (the BCP bank inside the courtyard could be one of the best-looking banks you've seen). You'll find an excellent selection of colorful and tactile hand-woven rugs, filigreed silver, and ubiquitous ceramic churches and red-clay figures of musicians. On display are several works of Peru's most famous *retablista* (altar artist), for whom the museum is named. López Antay, who had a number of international exhibits and was awarded the National Culture Prize in 1975, considered himself a sculptor rather than an artisan. Don't miss the second floor, which has some of the finest examples of popular art, many of them valuable antiques. The museum is open Tuesday through Friday from 10:15am to 5:30pm, and Saturday from 9:45am to 12:15pm; admission is free.

The **Museo Cáceres** (also known as Casona Vivanco), Jr. 28 de Julio 508 (© **066/836-166**), is a good example of a historic colonial-era *casona*, or mansion. Inside is a collection of original Escuela Cusqueña art, carved baroque furniture, colonial ceramics, and leather Spanish trunks. The original inhabitant of the house, Mariscal Cáceres, was a hero of Peru's War of the Pacific with Chile. The museum is open daily from 9am to 1pm and from 2 to 6pm; admission is S/.4.

The Plaza Mayor is lined with other notable colonial houses, which belonged to the most powerful citizens of Ayacucho, including **Casona Cristóbal Castilla y Zamora,** Portal Municipal 50 (© 066/312-230; Mon–Fri 8:15am–3:45pm); and **Casona del Corregidor Nicolás Boza y Solís,** Portal Constitución 15 (© 066/312-229; Mon–Fri 8am–noon and 2–6pm). **Casona del Marqués de Mozobamba** (also known as **Casona Olano**), Jr. 28 de Julio 175, is one of the most distinguished examples of 16th-century colonial architecture in the city. **Casona Ruíz de Ochoa y Monreal** (better known as **Casona Jáuregui**), Jr. 2 de Mayo 210 (© 066/314-299; Mon–Fri 8am–5pm), facing Templo de La Merced, is a handsomely restored, bright yellow 18th-century house with stone arches and blue doors, balconies, and shutters.

Colonial Churches

Anyone with an interest in colonial churches will be in heaven in Ayacucho, which over-flows with 33 examples, dating back as far as 1540, in a relatively small downtown area. In fact, Ayacucho is one of the few Peruvian cities that retains a significant colonial architectural core. Most churches can be visited only during Mass hours on Sunday (except where noted below).

North of the Plaza Mayor, and perhaps the most visually striking of the collection, is the finely sculpted **Templo de Santo Domingo** (1548), Jirón 9 de Diciembre at Jirón Bellido, the city's second convent. Its unique facade is marked by rustic earth-colored bricks, two towers framing a row of spikes, and three Romanesque arches at the ground level.

The majority of churches are south and west of the Plaza Mayor. Little except for an exterior wall and an original squat bell tower remains of **Templo de San Cristóbal,** Jirón 28 de Julio at Jirón 2 de Mayo, the first church in Ayacucho, constructed in 1540 and one of the oldest churches in South America. Built of brick and adobe, it was quite evidently a simple and rustic design. **Templo de la Compañía de Jesús** (1605), Jirón 28 de Julio between Jirón Lima and Jirón San Martín, founded as a Jesuit school and church, is an imposing baroque brick structure a half-block west of the Plaza Mayor. Its massive towers were added in the 18th century. **Templo y Convento de La Merced** (1540), Jirón 2 de Mayo at Jirón San Martín, the second church and first convent in Ayacucho, is well worth a visit. It was begun the year of the Spanish founding of the city.

Templo de Santa Teresa (1703), Jr. 28 de Julio s/n, faces a pretty, serene plaza across from San Cristóbal. You must first enter the convent, to the right of the church, and ask permission to visit the church (it remains a convent of 20 cloistered Carmelite nuns), which is entered around the corner from the plaza. The main altar is a fabulously chunky example of gold-leaf carving. **Santa Clara de Asís** (1568), Jirón Grau at Nazareno, the first monastery in Ayacucho and the second in Peru, has the largest tower in the city. Inside are good examples of *mudéjar* (Moorish-style) woodcarving and an interesting sculpture of the Immaculate Conception on the main altar.

Other colonial churches of interest to completists are **San Francisco de Asís** (1552), Jirón 28 de Julio at Jirón Vivanco, the only church besides the cathedral to have three naves; the baroque **Templo de Santa María Magdalena** (1588), Jirón Sol at Avenida Mariscal Cáceres, founded by the Dominican order but a three-time victim of fire; and the small and sweet snow-white **Templo del Arco** (1822), Plazoleta María Parado de Bellido, near the Mercado Artesanal in the El Arco district (north of the Plaza Mayor).

In any direction you walk, however, there are lasting examples of religious architecture marking Ayacucho's colonial importance.

WHERE TO STAY

Given its years in the hinterlands of the tourism circuit, it's not surprising that Ayacucho isn't exactly overflowing with good hotel choices. Still, there's a large, if uninspiring, hotel that caters mostly to business travelers and a small selection of easygoing, family-run *hostales*.

Moderate

Ayacucho Hotel Plaza   Ayacucho's deceptively splendid facade hides a rather disappointingly plain hotel that is far more functional than luxurious. As the largest hotel in town, and one that offers a full complement of services and amenities—and a location only 2 blocks from the Plaza Mayor—the Ayacucho Hotel Plaza is the choice of business travelers to Ayacucho. Besides the exterior, about all that can be said for the hotel is that it's built around a central courtyard and that the rooms have high ceilings. Rooms are plain, if not dumpy, and not as good as a couple of *hostales* that charge one-third the price. And rooms facing the street can be very noisy. It's a shame because, with an upgrade that lent as much care to the rooms and service as to the attention-getting outside, it could be a nice place to stay. But I wouldn't hold my breath waiting for that development.

Jr. 9 de Diciembre 184 (at Jirón Lima), Ayacucho. © **066/812-202.** hplaza@derramajae.org.pe. 80 units. $60 double; $80 suite. AE, DISC, MC, V. **Amenities:** Restaurant; bar. *In room:* A/C, TV.

Inexpensive

Hostal La Florida (Value)   A relaxed and friendly, family-run small *hostal* just 3 blocks from the main square, this is one of the better spots in town. It's secure, quiet, and clean, and rooms on the top floor across the small, leafy courtyard have excellent views of the surrounding rooftops and mountains. En-suite bathrooms are small but very clean, and—a rarity at this price—rooms have cable TV. There's a cute little cafe next door, a good spot for breakfast and other informal meals.

Jr. Cusco 310, Ayacucho. © **066/812-565.** 12 units. $18 double. No credit cards. **Amenities:** Cafe. *In room:* TV.

Marquez de Valdelirios ★ (Finds)   My top choice in Ayacucho isn't luxurious, but this *hostal,* housed in a handsome colonial house, is a real find. On a very peaceful, well-manicured boulevard just a few blocks north of the busy downtown (a 10-min. walk from the Plaza Mayor), it feels like a retreat. On the outside, it looks almost high design, with artfully placed blue flowerpots against the stark white stucco walls and deep wood exterior. Rooms, which are all on the interior, are comfortably outfitted, if not overly large. They might not live up to the promise of the exterior, but for the bargain price, they're more than comfortable. Breakfast is served on the sunny terrace.

Alameda Bolognesi 720–724, Ayacucho. © **066/318-944** or 066/314-014. 14 units. $25 double. Rates include breakfast. No credit cards. **Amenities:** Bar. *In room:* TV.

WHERE TO DINE

Down-to-earth Ayacucho is a great place to sample traditional Quechua specialties. It's also known for its artisanal wheat bread. In addition to the restaurants below, a great spot for breakfast or a simple lunch is **Sandra,** Jr. 28 de Julio 183 (no phone), a cute little cafe

(Moments) Ayacucho's Celebrated Festivals

Ayacucho plays host to some of the most spectacular popular festivals in Peru. The weeklong Easter celebration, **Semana Santa** ★★★, features nightly candlelit processions and daily fairs. It culminates in a stunning and emotional procession on Easter Sunday that makes its way around the Plaza Mayor. The procession is marked by the annual appearance of a massive (15×8m/49×26-ft. high) throne made entirely of white wax and carried by 200 people. Note that all hotels and *hostales* in Ayacucho are booked months in advance for Easter week, although you might find additional lodging offered in private homes.

Carnaval Ayacuchano is an authentic Quechua carnival celebration, one of the most colorful in the country. For 3 days in February or March, dancing and festivities take over the streets of Ayacucho, including the official proclamation of the *Ño Carnavalon,* or giant papier-mâché figure of the Rey Momo. The celebration also includes the unveiling of political songs, elaborate masks, and the Festival del Puchero, a typical Carnaval Ayacuchano dish served on Tuesday of Holy Week. In rural areas, carnival celebrations are starkly traditional, marked by manifestations such as ancient fertility rites.

The **Bajada de los Reyes Magos (the arrival of the Three Kings)** on January 6 and **La Virgen de la Candelaria** on February 2 are two other notable festivals, though they're not nearly as popular as Carnaval and Semana Santa. For more information on festivals in Ayacucho, contact **iPerú** (✆ **066/318-305;** www.promperu.gob.pe).

and *juguería* (juice bar). It serves a huge *café con leche,* massive *jarras* of fresh juices, and tamales, salads, and sandwiches on herb-crusted pita bread. Within the courtyard of the Centro Cultural, Jr. 28 de Julio 178, there are a couple of good cafes for light meals, snacks, coffee, dessert, and breakfast; check out **Café Bar New York** (✆ **066/313-079**), which has seats outdoors overlooking the patio.

Inexpensive

El Monasterio (Value) PERUVIAN Occupying a corner of the Centro Cultural courtyard, with outdoor tables, this restaurant is essentially a *pollería*—a simple restaurant serving roasted chicken—in a slightly upscale location. There are other things on the menu, but I never once saw anyone order anything but the chicken. And with good reason: It's flavorful and plentiful, and it's a steal. For just a couple of bucks, you can get a quarter of a roasted chicken, french fries, and salad. The other items on the menu are mainly the usual Andean suspects, such as *lomo saltado* (strips of beef with fried potatoes, onions, and tomatoes over rice).

Jr. 28 de Julio 178 (in Centro Cultural). ✆ **066/313-905.** Reservations not accepted. Main courses S/8–S/18. No credit cards. Daily 11am–11pm.

La Casona ★ PERUVIAN Though brightly lit, this comfortable restaurant, as popular with locals as it is with visitors to Ayacucho, is a nice spot to sample a varied and good-value menu of Andean *criollo* cooking. Built around a pleasant, plant-filled courtyard, the restaurant features grilled meats, roast chicken, trout, and a host of *platos tradicionales,* or regional specialties, such as *chancho al horno con qapchi* (oven-baked pork). A nice appetizer is the huge avocado stuffed with chicken—a meal in itself. Most dishes come with either golden potatoes or salad.

Jr. Bellido 463. © **066/312-733.** Reservations recommended Fri–Sat. Main courses S/10–S/24. MC, V. Daily 7am–10pm.

Urpicha ★ (Finds) PERUVIAN   Tucked down a small alley off Jirón Londres, the winding street populated by dozens of hair salons, this laid-back restaurant inhabits the gorgeous interior of a colonial house decorated with Peruvian popular art and overlooking an abundant and sunny garden of cacti, ivy, and flowering plants. On a lazy afternoon, it's the perfect spot to linger on the lovely covered terrace and enjoy local *criollo sierra* specialties such as *adobo asado* (juicy roast pork), fried trout, and *ají de gallina*. More unusual dishes, such as *puca picante con chicharrón* (potatoes in red sauce with peanuts, rice, and pork), are available for the more adventurous diner. A good sampler plate mixes a half-dozen Andean specialties. The chilled pitchers of *chicha morada* (a blue corn beverage) are the perfect accompaniment to any meal here.

Jr. Londres 272. © **066/313-905.** Reservations recommended Fri–Sat. Main courses S/12–S/28. No credit cards. Daily 11am–4pm and 7–10pm.

SHOPPING

The best spot in town to shop for the famous *retablos,* ceramic churches, and other typical *artesanía* of the Ayacucho region is the **Mercado Artesanal Shosaku Nagase,** Plazoleta María Parado de Bellido (5 blocks north of the Plaza Mayor). At this sprawling facility, the government operates training programs for those wanting to work in the production of handicrafts, and there are two buildings full of stalls selling local works. Its selection is good, though perhaps similar to what you might find in Lima.

Barrio Santa Ana ★, some 10 blocks southwest of the Plaza Mayor, is the heart of Quechua culture and *artesanía.* Around the main square, Plazuela de Santa Ana, are several family-run galleries. At several, you can watch textiles and rugs being created. Some rugs are highly valued and have been exhibited internationally. Visit Alejandro Gallardo's **Galería Latina,** Plazuela de Santa Ana 105 (© 066/528-315); **Alfonso Sulca Chávez,** Plazuela de Santa Ana 83 (© 066/312-990); and **Galería Arte Popular de Fortunato Fernández,** Plazuela de Santa Ana 63–64 (© 066/313-192). **Galería Wari,** Mariscal Cáceres 302 (© 066/312-529), is the studio and home of Gregorio Sulca, a highly celebrated textile and plastic artist who has exhibited his sophisticated rugs, paintings, and other pieces based on deep research into the Quechua culture in Germany and the U.S. If he's around and you speak Spanish, it's worth engaging him in conversation for an explanation of some fundamental Quechua philosophy and the historical and theoretical underpinnings of his (very expensive) work.

The finest handicrafts shopping, however, is found at the source of most of the typical regional *artesanía.* The tiny pueblo **Quinua** is where most of the ceramic churches and *retablos* are made by local artisans, and it is a fascinating Quechua village. Prices are cheaper than in Ayacucho and much cheaper than in Lima or Cusco; the selection also is much better. See "A Trip to Quinua, Handicrafts Capital of Peru," below.

A TRIP TO QUINUA, HANDICRAFTS CAPITAL OF PERU ★★

Although Ayacucho is well known throughout the country as the popular arts capital of Peru, most of the famous *artesanía* originate from Quinua, a lovely and gentle *sierra* town located 37km (23 miles) northeast of Ayacucho. If you'd prefer to buy at the source, preferably from the artisan who crafted the work rather than from a mere salesperson,

Quinua is tops in Peru. The red-tile roof of nearly every house in town is topped with a ceramic church of the kind foreigners are more likely to buy and display on a table or bookshelf. The churches serve as roof-bound protectors against evil spirits.

A beautiful stone passageway leads up to the main cobblestone plaza, populated by whitewashed buildings and the village church. Even though local artisans export their ceramic churches and figures of musicians around the world, Quinua is still the kind of place where little girls whisper and point at visiting gringos.

Local Quechua artisans have become very adept at commercializing and marketing their artisanship. Traditionally, all the ceramic pieces were unpainted or in earth tones. Increasingly, artisans have introduced pastels and bright colors, and the two traditional church towers have gradually begun to bend outward fancifully. But classic pieces are still produced. A few of the best-known local ceramists, including Mamerto Sánchez, have now moved their studios to more profitable environs such as Lima, cutting out the middle man. There are touristy stalls near the main road and a couple of shops, but for the best shopping, you'll need to venture up the stairs to the heart of the village. The peaceful back streets behind the Plazuela de Armas, especially Jirón Sucre and Jirón San Martín, are where to find the best popular art galleries, and it's not unusual to find pottery firing and hand painting taking place.

Galería Familia Sánchez ★, Jr. San Martín 151 (© **066/810-212**), is the studio and gallery of Mamerto Sánchez's son. Walter follows in his father's footsteps, and his studio produces some of the best ceramic pieces and churches in Quinua. Across the street is **Galería Ayllu,** which also has a little outdoor bar. A number of galleries, including **Artesanía Anclla** and **Artesanía El Quinuino,** are clustered on Jirón San Martín. A medium-size church costs between S/40 and S/75. Antique *retablos* and churches are difficult to find; your best bet is with antiques dealers in Lima or Cusco.

A few restaurants and *hostales* can accommodate you if you want to linger or spend the night in peaceful Quinua. You won't have much to do besides visit *artesanía* galleries, but you'd be hard-pressed to find a simpler, prettier, and more authentic *sierra* town. The small **Hostal Las Américas,** Jr. San Martín s/n, above Artesanía Anclla (© **066/965-7721; S/30 double),** has comfortable rooms in the house of one of the best-known local artisans.

To get to Quinua, take a colectivo at the corner of Jirón Salvador Cavero and Jirón Ciro Alegría in the east part of Ayacucho (Urbanización Santa Bertha). The trip (S/3) takes about an hour, and vans return hourly.

On the way to Quinua, 22km (14 miles) north of Ayacucho, is the **Huari** (also spelled Wari) **archaeological complex ★**, one of the oldest urban walled centers in the Americas, dating to around A.D. 600. The Huari culture, perhaps the first centrally governed "nation" in the Andes, was one of the most important in early Peru; its empire stretched north to Cajamarca and south to Cusco. The massive (300-hectare/750-acre) ruins, though badly deteriorated, are of thick, 10m-high (33-ft.) stone walls, houses, tunnels, and flat ceremonial areas, and well worth a visit for anyone with an interest in pre-Inca archaeology. Archaeologists have theorized that Huari urban planning and their system of religious, political, and military organization served as a model for the Incas. The city, which contained three levels of underground burial chambers, once had as many as 50,000 inhabitants; it was abandoned around A.D. 800. On-site are a visitor center and small museum **(Museo de Sitio Wari)** exhibiting photographs, dioramas, and artifacts discovered at the complex. The ruins are open Tuesday through Sunday from 9am to 5pm; admission is S/3.

8

Cusco

The storied capital of the Inca

Empire and gateway to the imperial city of Machu Picchu, **Cusco** (also spelled Cuzco) ★★★ is one of the undisputed highlights of South America. Stately and historic, with stone streets and building foundations laid by the Incas more than 5 centuries ago, the town is much more than a mere history lesson; it is also surprisingly dynamic, enlivened by throngs of travelers who have transformed the historic center around the Plaza de Armas into a mecca of sorts for South American adventurers. Yet for all its popularity, Cusco is one of those rare places—perhaps like Bali, Katmandu, or Prague—that seems able to preserve its unique character and enduring appeal despite its growing prominence on the international tourism radar.

Cusco looks and feels like the very definition of an Andean capital. It's a fascinating blend of pre-Columbian and colonial history and contemporary *mestizo* culture. The Incas made *Q'osqo* (meaning "navel of the world" in Quechua) the political, military, and cultural center of their empire, which stretched up and down the Andes, from Ecuador through Bolivia and all the way to Chile. Cusco was the empire's holy city, and it was also the epicenter of the legendary Inca network of roads connecting all points in the empire.

The Spanish conquistadors understood that it was essential to topple the capital city to take control of the region, a feat they ultimately accomplished after an epic battle at Sacsayhuamán. The Spaniards razed most Inca buildings and monuments, but, in many cases, they found the structures so well engineered that they built upon the very foundations of Inca Cusco. Many perfectly constructed Inca stone walls, examples of unrivaled stonemasonry, still stand. After a devastating earthquake in 1650, Cusco became a largely baroque city.

The result is a city that showcases plainly evident layers of history. Cusco's highlights include both Inca ruins—such as Sacsayhuamán, a seemingly impregnable fortress on a hill overlooking the city, and Qoricancha, the Temple of the Sun—and colonial-era baroque and Renaissance churches and mansions. The heart of the historic center has suffered relatively few modern intrusions, and despite the staggering number of souvenir shops, travel agencies, hotels, and restaurants overflowing with visitors, it doesn't take an impossibly fertile imagination to conjure the magnificent capital of the 16th century.

Today Cusco thrives as one of the most vibrant expressions of Amerindian and *mestizo* culture anywhere in the Americas. Every June, the city is packed during Inti Raymi, the celebration of the winter solstice and the sun god, a deeply religious festival that is also a magical display of pre-Columbian music and dance. Thousands trek out to Paucartambo for the riveting Virgen del Carmen festival in mid-July. Other traditional arts also flourish. Cusco is the handicrafts center of Peru, and its streets and markets teem with merchants and their extraordinary textiles, many hand-woven using the exact techniques of their ancestors.

Spectacularly cradled by the bold southeastern Andes Mountains that were so fundamental to the Inca belief system, Cusco sits at a daunting altitude of 3,400m (11,000 ft.). The air is noticeably thinner here than in almost any city in South America, and the city, best explored on foot, demands arduous hiking up precipitous stone steps, leaving even the fittest of travelers gasping for breath and saddled with headaches and nausea. It usually takes a couple of days to get acclimatized before moving on from Cusco to explore the mountain villages of the Urubamba Valley (also known as the Sacred Valley), the Amazon basin, and, of course, Machu Picchu, but many visitors find Cusco so seductive that they either delay their plans to explore the surrounding region or add a few days to their trip to allow more time in the city. Increasingly, travelers are basing themselves in one of the lower-altitude villages of the Sacred Valley, but there is so much to see and do in Cusco that an overnight stay is pretty much required of anyone who hasn't previously spent time in the area.

Cusco's beautiful natural setting, colorful festivals, sheer number of sights—unparalleled in Peru—and facilities and services organized for travelers make it the top destination in Peru and one of the most exciting places in South America. It is loaded with good and, in many cases, inexpensive restaurants, *hostales* (inns), and lively bars that cater to enthusiastic crowds of young and old gringos outfitted with the latest in fleece wear, backpacks, and hiking boots. For the burgeoning crowd that comes to Peru to do justice to all that high-tech adventure gear, superb trekking, river-rafting, and mountain-biking opportunities abound throughout the Sacred Valley.

As well as Cusco seems to handle the burden of its popularity—which seems to increase steadily year by year—for some travelers, the incessant hawking of postcards, cigarettes, restaurants and travel agencies, and hordes of gringos who look just like they do can be a bit overwhelming. Those looking for a more peaceful introduction to the Andes might choose to spend more time in the Sacred Valley (see chapter 9). As much as I love Cusco, every time I visit, I find the city just a tiny bit more overwhelmed by its tourist industry. Although resilient Cusco is not yet Marrakech in terms of hassles and sensory overload, it might be headed there.

The positive side of the equation, of course, is the vital role that tourism plays in propping up the local economy. Cusco is one of the only provinces in Peru that is not mired in economic crisis. Cusqueños are understandably pleased to receive international visitors and are remarkably forgiving of their excesses, but many locals quietly voice concerns about being pushed out of the city while they watch every last colonial house give way to yet another hotel, cafe, or dance club.

1 ORIENTATION

ARRIVING
By Plane

Most visitors to Cusco arrive by plane from Lima (a 1-hr. trip). In high season, flights arrive by the dozens from Lima as well as Arequipa, Puerto Maldonado, and La Paz, Bolivia, at **Aeropuerto Internacional Velasco Astete** (© 084/222-611), located 5km (3 miles) southeast of the historic center of Cusco. All major Peruvian airlines fly into Cusco, including **LAN** (© 01/213-8200; www.lan.com) **Taca** (© 01/511-8222; www.taca.com); and a new airline, **Peruvian Airlines** (© 01/716-6000; www.peruvian airlines.pe), which recently began offering flights from Lima to Cusco. A number of tour operators have sales booths in the arrivals terminal, and there are also a tourist information booth, an ATM, and currency exchange.

(Tips) Making the Connection to Cusco

Flights to Cusco are massively popular, so make your reservations as far in advance as possible if you are arriving from another Peruvian city. Flights are occasionally delayed by poor weather, and sometimes from Lima it is necessary to go through Arequipa if direct flights to Cusco are sold out. Although it is possible to arrive from North America on an overnight flight that theoretically will put you into Lima in time for an early morning flight to Cusco, the window is often quite tight, and a fair number of travelers miss their connecting flights. Also, be sure that your travel agent or airline hasn't inadvertently booked you on a charter, rather than regular, flight to Cusco.

Transportation from the airport to downtown Cusco, about 20 minutes away, is by taxi or private hotel car. (A less convenient *combi,* or small bus, passes outside the airport car park and goes to Plaza San Francisco; unless you have almost no baggage and your hotel is right on that square, it's not worth the few *soles* you'll save to take a combi.) Most hotels, even less expensive *hostales,* are happy to arrange airport pickup. If you take a taxi, note that the fare is likely to drop precipitously if you merely refuse the first offer you get (likely to be S/15–S/20). Taxi fare to Cusco is officially S/10 from the airport to the center, although if you really want to negotiate you can occasionally get one for as little as S/6.

When you exit with your luggage, you will be besieged with offers from taxi and tour-company representatives, many of whom will pretend to have your name on their "arrivals list," just to take you into town and try to score a commission from one of hundreds of tour operators. If you have arranged for your hotel to pick you up, be certain that you are dealing with someone authorized by the hotel and who possesses your exact arrival information.

The airport departure tax is S/18 for domestic flights and S/36 for international flights.

By Bus

Buses to Cusco arrive from Lima, Arequipa, Puno/Juliaca, and Puerto Maldonado in the Amazon basin. The journey from Lima to Cusco takes 26 hours by land; from Puno, 9 to 10 hours; and from Arequipa, 12 hours. There is no single, central bus terminal in Cusco. Most buses arrive at the **Terminal Terrestre,** Av. Vellejos Santoni, Cdra. 2, Santiago (© **084/224-471**), several kilometers from the city center on the way to the airport. Buses to and from the Sacred Valley (Urubamba buses, which go through either Pisac or Chinchero) use small, makeshift terminals on Calle Puputi s/n, Cdra. 2, and Av. Grau s/n, Cdra. 1. For service from Lima, contact the major companies, including **Ormeño** (© **01/472-5000**; www.grupo-ormeno.com.pe), **Cruz del Sur** (© **01/311-5050**; www.cruzdelsur.com.pe), **Oltursa** (© **01/708-5000**; www.oltursa.com.pe), and **Transportes Civa** (© **01/418-1111**; www.civa.com.pe). From Puno, the following offer daily service to Cusco: **Cruz del Sur** (see above), **Inka Express** (© **084/247-887**; www.inkaexpress.com), and **Imexso Tours** (© **084/240-801**; www.perucuzco.com/imexsotours). From Arequipa, your best bests are **Civa** and **Cruz del Sur.**

By Train

Cusco has two main PeruRail train stations. Trains from Puno arrive at **Estación de Huanchaq** (also spelled Wanchaq), Av. Pachacútec s/n (℃ **084/581-414;** www.perurail. com), at the southeast end of Avenida El Sol. Trains from Ollantaytambo and Machu Picchu arrive at **Estación Poroy** (℃ **084/581-414**), on the outskirts of Cusco. Visitors should be particularly cautious at train stations, where thieves have been known to prey on distracted passengers.

VISITOR INFORMATION

As the top tourist destination in Peru, Cusco is well equipped with information outlets. There's a small, occasionally unoccupied branch of the **Oficina de Información Turística** (℃ **084/237-364**) at the Velasco Astete Airport in the arrivals terminal; it's open daily from 6:30am to 12:30pm. The principal **Oficina de Información Turística** is located on Mantas 117-A, a block from the Plaza de Armas (℃ **084/222-032**). It's open Monday through Saturday from 7am to 7pm and Sunday from 7am to noon. It sells the essential *boleto turístico* (tourist ticket; see "Cusco's *Boleto Turístico*" on p. 216). However, the **iPerú office,** Av. El Sol 103, Of. 102 (℃ **084/252-974**), has been better stocked with information and much more helpful on recent visits; it's open daily from 8:30am to 7:30pm. Another information office is in the **Terminal Terrestre de Huanchaq** train station, Av. Pachacútec s/n (℃ **084/238-722**); it's open Monday through Saturday from 8am to 6:30pm.

South American Explorers has an office and club in Cusco at Choquechaca 188, no. 4 (℃ **084/245-484;** www.saexplorers.org). The office stores luggage, maintains lists of trail reports for members, and has a library of useful information for trekking and mountaineering. If you're traveling extensively, and independently, through Peru, it's worth becoming a member of this helpful group.

For up-to-date information on cultural happenings, bars and restaurants, check out **www.agendacusco.com.**

(Tips) Altitude Acclimatization

You'll need to take it easy for the first few hours or even couple of days in Cusco—which sits at an altitude of just over 11,000 feet—to adjust to the elevation. Pounding headaches and shortness of breath are the most common ailments, though some travelers are afflicted with severe nausea (others may little feel effects of the altitude except when walking up Cusco's steep hills). Drink lots of water, avoid heavy meals, and do as the locals do: Drink *mate de coca,* or coca-leaf tea. (Don't worry, you won't get high or arrested, but you will adjust a little more smoothly to the thin air.) If that doesn't cure you, ask whether your hotel has an oxygen tank you can use for a few moments of assisted breathing. If you're really suffering, look for an over-the-counter medication in the pharmacy called "Soroche Pills." And if that doesn't do the trick, it may be time to seek medical assistance; see "Fast Facts: Cusco," below. Those who think they may have an especially hard time with the altitude might consider staying the first couple of nights in the slightly lower Sacred Valley (near Urubamba, Yanahuara, or Ollantaytambo); see chapter 9.

Tips   **Cusco = Cuzco = Q'osqo**

Spanish and English spellings derived from the Quechua language are a little haphazard in Cusco, especially because there has been a linguistic movement to try to recuperate and value indigenous culture. Thus, you might see Inca written as Inka; Cusco as Cuzco, Qosqo, or Q'osqo; Qoricancha as Coricancha or Koricancha; Huanchaq as Huanchac or Wanchac; Sacsayhuamán as Sacsaywaman; and Q'enko as Qenko, Kenko, or Qenqo. You're likely to stumble across others, with similar alphabetical prestidigitation, all used interchangeably.

CITY LAYOUT

The Incas designed their capital in the shape of a puma, with the head at the north end, at Sacsayhuamán (whose zigzagged walls are said to have represented the animal's teeth). This is pretty difficult to appreciate today; even though much of the original layout of the city remains, it has been engulfed by growth. Still, most of Cusco can be seen easily on foot, and walking is certainly the best way to take in this historic mountain city that is equal parts Inca capital, post-Conquest colonial city, and modern tourist magnet. For outlying attractions, such as the handful of Inca ruins that lie just beyond the center of town, taxis are the best option.

The old center of the city is organized around the stunning and busy Plaza de Armas, the focal point of life in Cusco. The streets that radiate out from the square—Plateros, Mantas, Loreto, Triunfo, Procuradores, and others—are loaded with travel agencies, shops, restaurants, bars, and hotels. The major avenue leading from the plaza southeast to the modern section of the city is Avenida El Sol, where most banks are located. The district of San Blas is perhaps Cusco's most picturesque barrio; the labyrinthine neighborhood spills on cobblestone streets off Cuesta San Blas, which leads to crooked alleys and streets and viewing points high above the city.

Much of what interests most visitors is within easy walking distance of the Plaza de Armas. The major Inca ruins are within walking distance for energetic sorts who enjoy a good uphill hike.

2 GETTING AROUND

Getting around Cusco is straightforward and relatively simple, especially because so many of the city sights are within walking distance of the Plaza de Armas in the historic center. You will mostly depend on leg power and omnipresent, inexpensive taxis to make your way around town.

BY FOOT

Most of Cusco is best navigated by foot, although because of the city's 11,000-foot elevation and steep climbs, walking is demanding. Allow extra time to get around, and carry a bottle of water. You can walk to the major ruins just beyond the city—Sacsayhuamán and Q'enko—but you should be rather fit to do so. It's also best to undertake those walks in a small group and not alone.

BY TAXI

Cusco is crawling with taxis. Unlike in Lima, taxis are regulated and charge standard rates (although they do not have meters). Taxis are inexpensive (S/3 for any trip within the historic core during the day, S/4–S/5 at night) and are a good way to get around, especially at night. Hailing a cab in Cusco is considerably less daunting than in Lima, but you still should call a registered taxi when traveling from your hotel to train or bus stations or the airport, and when returning to your hotel late at night (there have been reports of muggings and even rapes tied to rogue taxis). Licensed taxi companies include **Okarina** (© 084/247-080) and **Aló Cusco** (© 084/222-222). Taxis can be hired for return trips to nearby ruins or for half- or full days. To the airport, taxis charge S/10 from the city center; to the distant Terminal Terrestre (bus station), they charge S/8.

BY TRANVIA

A *tranvía* is a vehicle designed to look like the old mule-pulled streetcars that once traversed Cusco; they cart visitors around the city on sightseeing tours for a modest sum (though the city, despite its hills, is much better appreciated on foot). Catch the **Tranvía de Cusco** on the Plaza de Armas, departing at 10 and 11:30am and 2, 3:30, and 5pm. Tours last 85 minutes and cost S/15 for adults and S/8 for students. For more information, call © **084/223-840** or visit www.tranviacusco.com.

BY BUS

Most buses—called variously *colectivos, micros,* and *combis*—cost S/1.50, slightly more after midnight, on Sunday, and on holidays. You aren't likely to need buses often, or ever, within the city, though the colectivos that run up and down Avenida El Sol are also a

---

> **(Tips) A Safety Note**
>
> Over the years, Cusco, which on the surface seems to be an easygoing, if increasingly congested, Andean city, has earned a reputation for being somewhat unsafe for foreign visitors, especially at night, when violent muggings (some using the "chokehold" method) have been known to occur on empty streets. There have also been reports of rapes, attempted rapes, and other sexual assaults in the past couple of years. While I have never had a problem in the city in more than 20 years, it's advisable to take some precautions and remain vigilant at all times. Incidents of drink-spiking have been reported; be aware of your drinking companions in bars and don't allow strangers to buy you drinks. Do not walk alone late at night (young women should travel in groups larger than two); have restaurants and bars call registered taxis to transfer you to your hotel. Be wary of unlicensed, rogue taxis in the city and surrounding environs. Young people staying in inexpensive hostels should be particularly cautious of hotel visitors and belongings. It's a good idea to be at your most vigilant, especially in the neighborhoods of San Blas, in the side streets leading off the Plaza de Armas, near the Central Market, and at bus and train hubs; still, robberies and attacks have occurred at the ruins at Sacsayhuamán on the outskirts of the city and even along the Inca Trail.

CUSCO

8

GETTING AROUND

useful option for some hotels, travel agencies, and shopping markets (taxis are much easier and not much more expensive). A bus departs from Plaza San Francisco to the airport, but it isn't very convenient. Buses and combis are most frequently used to travel from Cusco to towns in the Sacred Valley, such as Pisac, Calca, and Urubamba. Those buses depart from small terminals on Calle Puputi s/n, Cdra. 2 (via Pisac) and Av. Grau s/n, Cdra. 1 (via Chinchero).

BY TRAIN

The most popular means to visit Machu Picchu and the Sacred Valley sights is by train. PeruRail trains from Cusco to Ollantaytambo and Machu Picchu Pueblo (also called Aguas Calientes) leave from **Estación Poroy,** a 15-minute cab ride from downtown. Reservations for these trains, especially in high season (May–Sept), should be made several days or weeks in advance. Make reservations online at www.perurail.com; also see p. 263 in chapter 9 for more information, including trains that travel between Machu Picchu and the Sacred Valley only.

BY CAR

Renting a car in the Cusco region—more than likely to visit the beautiful Sacred Valley mountain villages—is a more practical idea than in most parts of Peru. Rental agencies include **Avis,** Av. El Sol 808 (✆ **084/248-800**) and **Localiza,** Av. Industrial J-3, Urbanización Huancaro (✆ **084/233-131**). Rates range from $50 per day for a standard four-door to $75 or more per day for a Jeep Cherokee four-wheel-drive. Check also with **4x4 Cusco,** Urb. San Borja, Huanchaq (✆ **084/227-730**) which has pickups and even Toyota Land Cruisers.

For information on driving around the Cusco department, and in case of emergencies, contact the **Touring Automóvil Club del Perú,** Av. El Sol 349, 2nd Floor (✆ **084/224-561**). The office is open Monday through Friday from 9am to 1pm and 3:30 to 7:30pm, and Saturday from 9am to 1pm.

(*Fast Facts* Cusco

Airport See "Arriving" in "Orientation," earlier in this chapter.

Banks & Currency Exchange Most Peruvian and international banks with currency-exchange bureaus and ATMs are located along Avenida El Sol. Moneychangers, usually wearing colored smocks, patrol the main streets off the Plaza de Armas and Avenida El Sol. Banks include **Banco Santander Central Hispano,** Av. El Sol 459; **Banco de Crédito,** Av. El Sol 189; and **Banco Continental,** Av. El Sol 366. The external ATMs nearest the Plaza de Armas are at **Banco de Crédito,** Av. El Sol 189; **Banco del Sur,** Av. El Sol 457; and **Banco Latino,** Av. El Sol 395. A couple are also located at the entrances to stores and restaurants on the Plaza de Armas and at the Huanchaq train station. Several small *casas de cambio,* with similar rates to banks, operate out of travel agencies and shops on Plaza de Armas and Avenida El Sol.

Car Rentals See "Getting Around," above.

Consulates The U.S. consulate is located at Av. Pardo 845 (✆ **084/231-474,** or CoresES@state.gov.). The honorary U.K. consulate is at Manu Expeditions,

Urbanización Magisterial, G-5 Segunda Etap ((©) **084/239-974;** bwalker@terra.com.pe). Both are open daily from 9am to noon and 3 to 5pm.

Dentists & Doctors In an emergency, contact the **Tourist Medical Assistance (TMA),** Heladeros 157 ((©) **084/260-101**). It offers 24-hour emergency medical services, health information, and legal assistance.

Drugstores For locations, consult a phone book Yellow Pages under "Farmacias" and "Boticas."

Emergency For general emergencies and the **police,** call (©) 105. For the **tourist police,** call (©) 084/249-654. To report a **fire,** call (©) 103. In a medical emergency, go to **Hospital EsSalud,** Av. Anselmo Álvarez s/n ((©) 084/223-030), or contact **Tourist Medical Assistance** ((©) 084/260-101).

Hospitals English-speaking medical personnel are available at the following hospitals and clinics: **Hospital EsSalud,** Av. Anselmo Álvarez s/n ((©) 084/237-341); **Clínica Pardo,** Av. de la Cultura 710 ((©) 084/624-186); **Hospital Antonio Loren,** Plazoleta Belén 1358 ((©) 084/226-511); **Hospital Regional,** Av. de la Cultura s/n ((©) 084/223-691); and **Clínica Paredes,** Lechugal 405 ((©) 084/225-265).

For **yellow-fever** vaccinations, try Hospital Antonio Loren on Tuesday or Hospital Regional on Saturday from 9am to 1pm.

Internet Access Internet *cabinas* are everywhere in the old section of Cusco, and many permit cheap oversees Internet-based (Web2Phone) calls for as little as S/1 per minute. Rates are generally S/1.50 per hour. Most keep very late hours, opening at 9am and staying open until 11pm or midnight. A few of the many cabinas around town include **Explora,** Arequipa 251; **Speed X,** Procuradores 50 and Tecsecocha 400; **@Internet,** Portal de Panes 123; and **Cyber-Planet,** Almagro 200. Several cafes and nightspots, including **Trotamundos, Ukuku's,** and **Mama Africa** (see "Cusco After Dark," later in this chapter), also have computers and Internet access, which is convenient if you got an e-mail address rather than a phone number from a guy or girl at the bar.

Language Schools For intensive Spanish courses, try **AMAUTA Spanish School,** Suecia 480 ((©) **084/262-345;** www.amautaspanish.com), **Academia Latinoamericana de Español,** Av. El Sol 580 ((©) **084/243-364;** www.latinoschools.com), or **San Blas Spanish School,** Tandapata 688 ((©) **084/247-898**). All are very popular with short- and long-term visitors to Cusco.

Laundry Laundromats offering good, rapid service include: **Lavandería Louis,** Choquechaca 264 ((©) **084/243-485**); **Easy Wash,** Ruinas 457 ((©) **084/238-124**); **Lavandería Inka,** Ruinas 493 ((©) **084/223-421**) and **Totem Wash,** Saphy 726 ((©) **084/145-367**).

Maps The main tourist information office gives out free maps, and, for most visitors, these should be sufficient. (Cusco is easy to manage and a joy to wander around and even get lost in.) More detailed maps, and maps of the Inca Trail and other hiking trails in the Cusco region, are available at bookstores.

Massage On virtually every street in the old town are young women advertising "massage, massage," often for as little as $7. They're generally of questionable quality or intent. Several legitimate spots are in town, some more professional than others, but the best massage I've had in Peru was from Olga at **Ying Yang**

Massage, Av. El Sol 106 (Galerías La Merced; © **084/243-592;** yinyang_masajes@ hotmail.com), where the rooms are nice and a 1-hour full-body massage will set you back S/75; hotel visits are also possible for a small supplement. The swankest massage center in town is **Inca Spa,** within the Hotel Eco Inn, Av. El Sol 1010 (© **084/581-280;** www.incaspa.com.pe); it's excellent but prices are about double its competitors.

Police The **Policía Nacional de Turismo (National Tourism Police)** has an English-speaking staff that is specifically trained to handle the needs of foreign visitors. The office is at Saphy 510 (© **084/249-654**). You can also contact **iPerú/ INDECOPI** (Servicio de Protección al Turista, or Tourist Protection Bureau), Portal Carrizos 250, Plaza de Armas (© **084/252-974**); the staff is available daily from 8am to 8pm.

Post Office & Mail Cusco's main post office, Serpost, is at Av. El Sol 800 (© **084/224-212**). A **DHL/Western Union** office is at Av. El Sol 627-A (© **084/244- 167**).

Safety See "A Safety Note" above for info.

Taxis See "Getting Around," above.

Telephone Cusco's area code is 084. The principal **Telefónica del Perú** office, for long-distance and international calls, is at Av. El Sol 382-6 (© **084/241-114**). It's open Monday through Saturday from 8am to 10pm.

Tour Operators & Travel Agencies Cusco is swimming in travel agencies—several hundred of all sizes, and many that offer almost the exact same packages compete for your attention. Only a few dozen have solid reputations, however, and many should be flat-out avoided. Do not contract any would-be travel agent on the street, and do not hand over money for a trip or package without visiting the outfit in its office. If you have any questions about an agency, particularly one not listed by name and recommended in this chapter, do not hesitate to inquire about its reputation in the Tourist Information Office.

For travel arrangements around Peru, as well as city tours and Sacred Valley, Machu Picchu, Inca Trail, and Amazon jungle trips, see the relevant sections below and in chapters 9 and 11.

3 WHERE TO STAY

As the top tourist destination in Peru, where virtually every visitor seems to pass and stay a few days, Cusco has developed a remarkable cornucopia of lodgings, with hundreds of hotels, inns, and *hostales* of all stripes and prices. More continue to sprout, and few seem to close. Although the sheer number of offerings, particularly at the midrange and budget levels, means that you can pretty confidently land in Cusco without a reservation (outside of popular festivals like Inti Raymi and Fiestas Patrias at the end of June and July) and find a decent place to stay, many of the better and more popular hotels at all levels fill up throughout high season and even in shoulder months. In my opinion, it's better to firm up a reservation as soon as you know your dates of stay in Cusco.

> **ⓘ Tips   No Sleeping In**
>
> Most Cusco hotels have annoyingly early checkout times—often 9 or 9:30am—due to the deluge of early morning flight arrivals to the city. At least in high season, hotels are very serious about your need to rise and shine (and many travelers are up and out very early anyway, on their way to Machu Picchu or trekking excursions), but you can always store your bags until later.

Most of the city's most desirable accommodations are very central, within walking distance of the Plaza de Armas. The artsy San Blas neighborhood is also within walking distance, although many hotels and *hostales* in that district involve some steep climbs up the hillside. (The upside is that guests are rewarded with some of the finest views in the city.) Some visitors may want to avoid hotels and inns too close to the Plaza de Armas; that zone's crowded bars and discos, many of which are open until sunrise, tend to produce throngs of rambunctious and usually inebriated young people who stumble downstairs and howl at the moon or bellow at the people who just rejected them inside.

Hot water is an issue at many hotels, even those that swear they offer 24-hour hot showers. Many hotels and inns will arrange free airport transfers if you communicate your arrival information to them in advance.

Cusco possesses only a couple of truly excellent high-end hotels (though there are several new ones on the way), and few good hotels at the next tier. In Cusco, an eternal backpackers' delight, there remains a glut of accommodations at the moderate and budget levels. However, several *hostales* have more atmosphere and are likely to provide a better overall experience than more expensive—and more institutional—hotels. Prices listed below are rack rates for travel in high season; unless otherwise noted, rates do not include taxes or service charges. During the low season (Nov–Apr), prices often drop precipitously, even at midrange inns and backpacker hostels—sometimes as much as 50%—as the glut of hotels fights for a much-reduced number of visitors.

Several of the *hostales* reviewed below are cozy, family-run places, but travelers looking for even greater contact with a Peruvian family might want to check out the very inexpensive inns belonging to the **La Asociación de Casas Hospedaje (The Association of Hospitality Houses),** which operates a website (www.cusco.net/familyhouse) with listings of guesthouses with one or more rooms available for short- or long-term stays.

NEAR THE PLAZA DE ARMAS
Very Expensive
Fallen Angel: The Guest House ★★★ Ⓕ**Finds**   It's nearly impossible to do this wildly unique, idiosyncratic, sumptuous and fantasylike guest house justice. The brainchild of Andrés Zuniga, who created the surreal restaurant Fallen Angel, it takes that concept one step further—literally upstairs. With just four rooms (with names like Passion, Liberty and Tranquility), each decorated to the hilt as if part of some avant-garde art installation, this is a solar system removed from your expected Andean lodgings. A place for sybarites, rooms, filled with incredible original art and furnishings, are impossibly large and grand, adhering to an eclectic vision that's part Pedro Almodóvar, part Damien Hirst and part Peter Greenaway. Staying here is something akin to sleeping on

CUSCO

8

WHERE TO STAY

a trippy film set, so you need to have an open mind and sense of humor. If you do, Fallen Angel is a place you're unlikely to ever forget.

Plazoleta Nazarenas 221, Cusco. ℂ **084/258-184.** www.fallenangelincusco.com. 4 units. $280–$330 suite. Rates include breakfast, airport transfer and massage. MC, V. **Amenities:** Restaurant; bar. *In room:* A/C, TV/DVD, fridge, hair dryer, Wi-Fi.

Hotel Monasterio ★★★   Still Cusco's most extraordinary place to stay, though competition is on the rise, this beautiful hotel occupies the San Antonio Abad monastery, constructed in 1592 on the foundations of an Inca palace. An Orient-Express property, the Hotel Monasterio exudes grace and luxury. As much a museum as a hotel, it has its own opulent gilded chapel and 18th-century Escuela Cusqueña art collection. Located on quiet Las Nazarenas square between the bohemian San Blas district and the main square, the hotel makes fine use of several courtyards with stone arches; one is set up for lunch outdoors, about as beautiful a setting as is to be found in Cusco. Rooms are impeccably decorated in both colonial and modern styles, with large Cusqueña School paintings; the accommodations off the first courtyard are more traditionally designed and feel more authentic. For a special treat, consider one of the two-story junior suites. One restaurant, Tupay, is housed in the original vaulted refectory of the monastery; early risers, many on their way to Machu Picchu, can enjoy a terrific breakfast buffet as they're serenaded by Gregorian chants. As a special bonus, the hotel was the first in the world to offer oxygen piped directly into rooms through the ventilation ($40 per day). It sounded gimmicky to me, but my wife, who was suffering from a bout of *soroche* (altitude sickness), says she slept wonderfully and woke up without a pounding headache.

Palacios 136 (Plazoleta Nazarenas), Cusco. ℂ **084/241-777.** Fax 084/246-983. http://monasterio.orient-express.com. 122 units. $399–$499 deluxe double; $580–$1,089 suite. Rates include breakfast buffet. AE, DC, MC, V. **Amenities:** 2 restaurants; cafe; bar; concierge. *In room:* A/C, TV/VCR, fridge, hair dryer, oxygen on demand.

La Casona ★★★   A new (2009) entry into the ultraluxe category is this small and eminently polished boutique hotel, inhabiting a magnificently16th-century colonial manor house just across Plazoleta Las Nazarenas from Hotel Monasterio, the only other hotel in Cusco with a similar historic sophistication. The difference here is that La Casona, a Relaís & Chateaux property, is meant not to feel like a hotel at all, but an elegant palace-home where guests are lucky (and affluent) enough to spend the night. There's no bell (or even sign) out front, no traditional lobby or check-in desk, and rooms have neither numbers nor names. Owned by Inkaterra, which operates a great hotel at Machu Picchu (p. 284), the inn is all about full-on luxury and attentive service (personal concierges take care of guests' every whim). Accommodations (all suites) built around the elegant central courtyard are enormous, and the marble-and-stone bathrooms all the more so; they're the size of most NYC apartments. Rooms are outfitted with exquisite antiques, authentic Cusqueña School paintings, and they feature radiant heat in the flooring. The elegant small dining room and sitting room are suitable for visiting dignitaries, which guests may well consider themselves.

Plazoleta Nazarenas 167, Cusco. ℂ **800/442-5042** in U.S. and Canada, or 01/610-0400 for reservations. Fax 084/244-669. www.inkaterra.com/en/cusco. 11 units. $720–$1,128 suite. Rates include breakfast buffet. AE, DC, MC, V. **Amenities:** Restaurant; concierge. *In room:* A/C, TV/DVD, fridge, hair dryer, Wi-Fi.

Libertador Palacio del Inka ★★   One of Cusco's top hotels, now competing with more than just the Monasterio at the top end, the Libertador could just as easily be called the Conquistador. Directly across from the Inca Temple of the Sun and built on the

Albergue Municipal **15**
Casa Andina Classic—
  Cusco Catedral **21**
Casa Andina Classic—Cusco Plaza **9**
Casa Andina Classic—
  Cusco Koricancha **24**
Casa Andina Private Collection **26**
El Andariego Hostal **11**
El Balcón **1**
Fallen Angel The Guest House **20**
Hostal Corihuasi **16**
Hostal Loreto **22**
Hostal Los Aticos Quera **12**
Hostal Oblitas **7**
Hostal Resbalosa **14**
Hostal Rikch'airy **2**
Hostal Rumi Punku **18**
Hostal Suecia I **13**
Hostal Virrey **8**
Hotel El Arqueólogo **17**
Hotel Monasterio **19**
Hotel Royal Qosqo **6**
La Casona **20**
Liberator Palacio del Inka **24**
Niños Hotel **3**
Niños Hotel II **4**
Novatel Cusco **23**
Pariwana Hostel Cusco **10**
Torre Dorada **27**

foundations of the "Aclla Huyasi," where the Inca chieftain kept maidens, this elegant traditional hotel occupies a historic house once inhabited by none other than Francisco Pizarro. The handsome art- and antiques-filled hotel, just 4 blocks from the Plaza de Armas, is built around a dramatic colonial courtyard marked by perfect arches, terra-cotta tiles, and a Spanish-style fountain. The swank lobby has a massive pyramidal sky-light and exposed Inca walls. Guest rooms are spacious and refined; furnishings have rustic colonial touches, and the marble bathrooms are large and well equipped. Many rooms have small terraces. But the Libertador perhaps most distinguishes itself with extremely attentive and professional service. The fine but pricey restaurant, Inti Raymi, is built around the edges of the courtyard and features a nightly dance and music show.

San Agustín 400 (Plazoleta Santo Domingo 259), Cusco. ℂ **084/231-961.** Fax 01/233-152. www.summithotels.com. 254 units. $305 deluxe double; $345 suite AE, DC, MC, V. **Amenities:** Restaurant; coffee shop; concierge; fitness center; sauna. *In room:* A/C, TV/VCR, fridge, hair dryer.

Expensive

Casa Andina Private Collection ★★ Ⓥalue
Inhabiting one of the city's loveliest colonial structures, an 18th-century mansion on a small square in the heart of the old city, this sensitively restored hotel built around four interior patios is like a budget version of the very elegant, and very expensive, Hotel Monasterio. For travelers looking for a bit of that hotel's ambience but not its elevated price tag, Casa Andina is one of the best-value luxury options in town. Rooms are spacious and cleanly outfitted, with a minimalist take on Andean decor. While my favorites are the suites in the old section of the hotel, the newer rooms thankfully are not distractingly modern, and, tucked away as they are from the street, they're nice and quiet. The gorgeous, deep-red sitting room, with its massive, roaring fire-place, is the perfect place to sip a pisco sour or coca tea and warm up on a chilly Cusco night. And the gourmet restaurant, named for the plaza it sits on, features stone arches, strong colors, and Cusco-school paintings, as well as a very fine haute Andean menu, making it one of those all too rare hotel restaurants that merits staying in for the night.

Plazoleta de Limacpampa Chico 473, Cusco. ℂ **084/232-610.** For reservations in the U.S. ℂ **866/220-4434,** Lima ℂ 01/213-9739. Fax 084/232-629. www.casa-andina.com. 100 units. $124–$207 double; $279 suite. Rates include breakfast buffet. AE, DC, MC, V. **Amenities:** Restaurant; bar; babysitting; concierge. *In room:* TV, fridge, hair dryer, Wi-Fi.

Novotel Cusco ★ Ⓥalue
This member of the French Novotel chain is built around the guts of a 16th-century colonial building with a lovely central courtyard. Most of the rooms, however, are in newly built additions. The hotel is modern and dependable, with good services and amenities, although, in most regards, it's a notch below the city's two top-flight luxury hotels. The modern rooms are well equipped and brightly colored, but are otherwise standard accommodations. At this level, it's worth spending the extra money to get one of the superior rooms in the converted colonial section of the hotel; they are larger and much more atmospheric. The hotel, a short distance from the Plaza de Armas, features a nice garden-side restaurant serving French fare, and a warm bar with a fireplace. Deals are often available online.

San Agustín 239 (corner of Pasaje Santa Mónica), Cusco. ℂ **084/881-030.** Fax 084/228-855. www.novotel.com. 99 units. $109–$170 double. Rates include breakfast. AE, DC, MC, V. **Amenities:** Restaurant; bar; babysitting; concierge; sauna. *In room:* A/C, TV, fridge, hair dryer.

Picoaga Hotel ★
A nice, more reasonably priced alternative to Cusco's top two luxury hotels, Picoaga also occupies a historic building—in this case a 17th-century man-sion that once belonged to a Spanish nobleman, the marquis of Picoaga. Just minutes

---

(Kids) Family-Friendly Hotels

Hostal Marani (p. 204)   This relaxed and inviting, inexpensive boutique hotel has a mission similar to Niños Hotel. Families can learn about the programs of the HoPe Foundation, which funds schools and hospitals in the region.

Hotel Rumi Punku (p. 198)   This family-owned *hostal* has a pretty, flower-filled colonial courtyard, gardens, and a historic Inca wall. There's plenty of room for the kids to run about behind the massive Inca portal.

Niños Hotel (p. 199)   The very definition of a family-friendly hotel, this one was built to allow Cusco street kids to become part of a family. Profits go to care for another 500 needy children. The restored colonial house is one of the most charming and best-maintained small inns around. Reserve well in advance. Families should inquire about a second location and the excellent-value apartments for longer stays.

---

from the Plaza de Armas, the hotel is set around a lovely arcaded courtyard—or, at least, one portion of it is. A newer wing is in a dated and much less appealing modern section at the rear of the hotel. Ask for a room in the front section overlooking the patio. Rooms there, about a third of the total, are larger, have high ceilings, and are decorated with colonial-style furniture and floral prints. Rooms are nice but certainly not over-the-top elegant. (*Another tip:* Request a room on the back side of the courtyard rather than one facing the street because traffic and street noise on Santa Teresa fires up right about 5:39am.) Picoaga has more colonial character than the Novotel Cusco, although the latter offers better service.

Santa Teresa 344, Cusco. (℃) **084/252-330.** Fax 084/221-246. www.picoagahotel.com. 70 units. $160–$180 double; $220–$250 suite. Rates include breakfast buffet. AE, DC, MC, V. **Amenities:** 2 restaurants; fireplace cocktail bar; concierge. *In room:* A/C, TV, fridge, hair dryer, Wi-Fi.

Moderate

Casa Andina Classic—Cusco Koricancha ★ (Value)   This very professionally run, midprice hotel is one of five in Cusco belonging to this upstart Peruvian hotel chain. Visitors to Casa Andina know what to expect: excellent service and clean, ample, colorfully decorated rooms. The Koricancha hotel on San Agustín, 3 blocks from the main square, is built around a restful colonial courtyard and is in a somewhat quieter neighborhood, while the other two, smaller locations, are virtually on top of the Plaza de Armas. All have similar prices and features (though the Cusco Catedral hotel has an Inca wall within the hotel and the smaller Cusco Plaza has views of the Plaza de Armas from its breakfast room). All are just within blocks of the main square, but those looking to be in Cusco's coolest and hilliest neighborhood, with great views of the city, should gravitate toward the Casa Andina Classic in San Blas, on Calle Chihuampata 278. Those in the market for a bit more luxury should check out the Casa Andina Private Collection (see above).

San Agustín 371, Cusco. (℃) **084/252-633.** For reservations in the U.S. (℃) **866/220-4434,** Lima (℃) 01/213-9739. Fax 084/222-908. www.casa-andina.com. 57 units. $99–$130 double. Rates include breakfast buffet. AE, DC, MC, V. **Amenities:** Concierge. *In room:* TV, fridge, hair dryer on request.

El Andariego Hostal (Finds) This family-owned, cozy, and centrally located, though well hidden, *hostal* is a quiet, genial place that retains a great deal of the flavor of a 19th-century Cusco colonial house. Set back from a busy street across an interior patio, it has just eight rooms, a few of which are great values. Room nos. 101 (which fronts a small garden) and 103, both of which have functioning wood-burning fireplaces and exposed stone walls, are my favorites. They're large and comfortable, with hardwood floors and a smattering of antiques as well as clean tile bathrooms. Other rooms are also nice, if not quite as unique. The owners will prepare dinners on request.

San Andrés 270, Cusco. ©/fax **084/225-593.** www.andariegocusco.com. 14 units. $52–$55 double; $50 suite. Rates include continental breakfast. MC, V. **Amenities:** Restaurant; bar. *In room:* TV, Wi-Fi.

Hotel Arqueologo ★ It takes a little bit of effort to uncover this small hotel, named for the profession responsible for discovering so much of Peru's pre-Columbian past and owned by a Frenchman who's a longtime Cusco resident. Down a stone alleyway and tucked behind the unprepossessing facade of a late-19th-century house, it certainly doesn't jump out at you, but once inside, you'll find a lovely interior courtyard and sunny garden—with ample space for kids to play—and rooms that run along a corridor over-looking the patio. Rooms are cozy, warm and even romantic, with nice hardwood floors and quality bedding and linens; some feature peaked ceilings.

Pumacurco 408, Cusco. © **084/232-522.** Fax 084/235-126. www.hotelarqueologo.com. 20 units. $99–$120 double; $180 suite. Rates include breakfast buffet. MC, V. **Amenities:** Restaurant. *In room:* TV, hair dryer, Wi-Fi, no phone.

Hotel Rumi Punku ★ (Finds)(Kids) A glance at the name or address of this idiosyncratic family-owned hostel will give you an indication of its strong connection to Cusco's Inca roots. The massive portal to the street is a fascinating original Inca construction of perfectly cut stones, once part of a sacred Inca temple. (The door is one of only three belonging to private houses in Cusco, and elderly residents of the city used to do the sign of the cross upon passing it.) There's more to the *hostal* than might appear from the street. Inside is a charming, flower-filled colonial courtyard with a cute little chapel and gardens along a large Inca wall. The clean bedrooms are ample, with hardwood floors and Norwegian thermal blankets. The top-floor dining room, where breakfast is served, has excellent panoramic views of Cusco's rooftops. The hostel is on the way up to Sacsayhuamán, but only a short walk from the Plaza de Armas. Rumi Punku, by the way, means "door of stone" in Quechua. New features include a "Finnish" sauna and Jacuzzi tub, perfect to take the edge off the altitude and area hikes.

Choquechaca 339, Cusco. © **084/221-102.** Fax 084/242-741. www.rumipunku.com. 30 units. $90 per person. Rates include continental breakfast buffet. MC, V. **Amenities:** Restaurant.

Inexpensive

Hostal Resbalosa (Finds) A longtime favorite of backpackers, this inn is named for the steep cobblestoned street it's on (which makes access a little tricky) rather than any innate shady quality. (*Resbalosa* means "slippery.") The good-size rooms have hardwood floors, large windows, and immaculate bathrooms with pretty dependable hot-water showers. Try to get a room with a view. There's a large rooftop terrace, perfect for sunning and just hanging out, enjoying the 180-degree views. The steep, pedestrian-only cobblestone street means you'll have to haul your pack up, but it's good training for the Inca Trail.

Resbalosa 494, Cusco. © **084/224-839.** www.hostalresbalosa.com. 20 units. $15 double with shared bathroom; $22 double with private bathroom. No credit cards. *In room:* No phone.

Niños Hotel ★★★ (Value) (Kids) The Dutch owner of the charming "Children's
Hotel" says she has a story to tell, and it's certainly an inspirational one. Jolanda van den
Berg, in just over a decade in Peru, has mounted a rapidly expanding empire of goodwill
through the Foundation Niños Unidos Peruanos: Soon after arriving in Peru, she adopted
12 Peruvian street children, and constructed an extremely warm, stylish, and inviting (not
to mention great-value) hotel in the old section of Cusco that puts all its profits toward care
for needy children. The project quickly grew to encompass a learning center, two restaurants feeding 500 kids a day, and athletic and day-care facilities with medical attention for
other disadvantaged youths of Cusco. The ambitious Niños foundation has now added a
second hotel, also in a historic building, and, incredibly, has taken in two more adoptive
families (totaling 20 girls and another two boys). On the same street as the second hotel are
four terrific apartments for longer stays, ideal for small families.

The good news for travelers is that, if you are lucky enough to get a room (reservations
generally must be made about 6 months in advance for high season, though especially in
off-season it's sometimes possible to score a reservation only days in advance, and occasionally even the day of your arrival), you won't have to suffer for your financial contribution to such an important cause. The main hotel, in a restored colonial house just 10
minutes from the Plaza de Armas, is one of the finest, cleanest, and most comfortable
inexpensive inns in Peru. The large rooms—named for the owner's adopted children—
are minimalist chic, with white-painted hardwood floors and quality beds, and they ring
a lovely sunny courtyard, where breakfast is served. The sister hotel, just 2 blocks away,
is very similar in style and amenities. An excellent new option, for those also interested
in visiting the countryside outside Cusco, is the **Niños Hotel Hacienda,** a beautiful,
rustic inn in the town of Huasao, just 30 minutes from Cusco (rates start at $90, includ-
ing transportation, lunch and dinner, and a tour of the local ruins).

Meloq 442, Cusco. ℂ **084/231-424.** www.ninoshotel.com. 20 units. $44 double with private bathroom;
$40 double with shared bathroom; apartments $32 per person per day or $350 per month (2nd person
an additional $130 per month). No credit cards. **Amenities:** Restaurant; cafe. *In room:* No phone.

Pariwana Hostel Cusco ★ (Value) This new hostel is certain to become the choice
for students and young backpackers. Unusual for such a low-priced option, it occupies
stately digs—an elegant 16th-century colonial manor house built around a beautiful courtyard just 2 blocks from the Plaza de Armas. Rooms are clean, safe and very well thought
out, with lockers and loads of options, from double rooms with bathrooms to standard
dorm rooms of several sizes (overall capacity is for 220 people), including dorm rooms for
women only. The hub of activity is the very cool bar/lounge (with video, Play Station, and
ping-pong and pool tables), and all sorts of nightly group activities and excursions are
offered. If you've come to Cusco to hang out, meet fellow travelers and make new travel
plans, this is the place. Knowing its audience well, breakfast is served until 1pm!

Mesón de la Estrella 136, Cusco. ℂ **084/233-751.** www.pariwana-hostel.com. 60 units. S/90 double;
S/23–S/33 per person in dorm room with shared bathroom. Rates include breakfast. No credit cards.
Amenities: Restaurant; bar; lockers. *In room:* Wi-Fi, no phone.

SAN BLAS
Moderate
Casa de Campo Hostal (Finds) Lodged in the hills of the traditional neighborhood
San Blas, Casa de Campo means "country house," and the air up here, high above Cusco,
has the freshness of country air. An organic complex, its chalet-style rooms appear to have
sprouted one from the other. A friendly and comfortable place, it's nonetheless not for

everyone, especially not those who are tired of climbing the steps of Inca ruins. The climb up to the hotel is taxing enough, but once inside the gate, guests must use their remaining reserves to amble up several more flights of stone steps.

Once there, though, you're rewarded with nice gardens and several terraces with unparalleled sweeping views of the city and surrounding mountains, as well as a cozy lounge with a large fireplace. Rooms are rather small, but they have good, firm beds and are rustically decorated, with exposed wood beams and thick wool blankets. (It's generally considerably cooler up here than just 15 min. down in Cusco.) One special room has a fireplace (for the same price as a regular room); another is like a cottage towering above the city. The staff will build a fire in the bar on request and arrange a free city tour in Cusco. The owners also operate the Amauta Spanish-language school and Tertulia travel agency, as well as a rustic hotel (www.hotelcasadecampourubamba.com; $55 double) in Urubamba in the Sacred Valley.

Tandapata 296, San Blas, Cusco. ℭ **084/244-404.** Fax 084/243-069. www.hotelcasadecampo.com. 25 units. $55 double; $75 suite. Rates include continental breakfast and airport pickup. AE, MC, V. **Amenities:** Restaurant. *In room:* Phone in some units.

Casa San Blas Boutique Hotel

A modern boutique hotel tucked down a small, dead-end alleyway off pedestrian-only Cuesta San Blas, and approaching the artsy neighborhood of the same name, this place has a lot going for it. Excellent location and good services are principal among its advantages. I would opt for one of the two-level junior suites with kitchenettes and spectacular views of Cusco from upstairs; though the prices are up a bit from previous years, they're comparatively better value than the regular rooms, which are comfortable but plain and not nearly as inviting (all doubles are interior with no views). The hotel's panoramic-view terrace, though, is an excellent spot to relax and check out the city creeping up into the hills.

Tocuyeros 566, San Blas, Cusco. ℭ **888/569-1769** in the U.S. and Canada or 084/237-590063. Fax 084/237-900. www.casasanblas.com. 18 units. $110 double; $156–$192 suite. Rates include airport transfer and breakfast. AE, DC, MC, V. **Amenities:** Restaurant; piano bar; free Internet (in lobby); massage room; room service. *In room:* TV, Wi-Fi.

Casona Les Pleiades ★ (Value)

A small, French-owned boutique hotel tucked away on a pedestrian-only, hilly street in the San Blas neighborhood, this agreeable place is a relaxed refuge. A three-story house renovated in 2005, it has a treasured sunny terrace, which is a great place to read and relax (and dry laundry), and to soak in great views of Cusco below. Rooms, accessed from an interior patio, are ample and colorfully decorated with bright down comforters. The friendly owners, Philippe and Melanie, are on hand to offer personal advice about activities in Cusco and the region, though Melanie spends a good part of each year working in California.

Tandapata 116, San Blas, Cusco. ℭ **084/506-430.** www.casona-pleiades.com. 7 units. $50 double. Rates include continental breakfast. AE, MC, V. **Amenities:** Video lounge. *In room:* Cable TV, no phone, Wi-Fi.

Los Apus Hotel & Mirador ★

Swiss-managed, with a bit of a chalet feel, this small hotel on a quiet, hilly street in San Blas is a nice, homey find. It has a handsome, airy lobby atrium, tranquil reading areas, and an attractive rooftop terrace with excellent views of Cusco. Accommodations pale a bit in comparison with the hotel's public amenities, but on the whole they are a pretty good value. The first-floor rooms have higher ceilings, but those on the third and fourth floors—many of which have private balconies—have the best views.

ACCOMMODATIONS ■
Amaru Hostal **11**
Casa Andina Classic—San Blas **18**
Casa de Campo Hostal **1**
Casa Hospedaje Kuntur Wasi **2**
Casa de la Gringa **9**
Casa San Blas Boutique Hotel **15**
Casona Les Pleiades **8**
Hospedaje Turístico San Blas **14**
Hostal Marani **7**
Los Apus Hotel & Mirador **4**
Orquidea Real Hostal **17**
Second Home Cusco **3**
Tik'a Wasi Hostal **6**

DINING ◆
Granja Heidi **12**
Jack's Café Bar **13**
Macondo **10**
PachaPapa **16**
Quinta Eulalia **5**
Quinta Zarate **19**

CUSCO

8

WHERE TO STAY

Atocsaycuchi 515 (corner of Choquechaca), San Blas, Cusco. ✆ **084/264-243.** Fax 084/264-211. www. losapushotel.com. 20 units. $109 double. Rates include breakfast. AE, DC, MC, V. **Amenities:** Restaurant. *In room:* TV.

Orquidea Real Hostal (Finds) Hidden away along a narrow street wedged into the hill to San Blas, this tiny, unassuming inn has several surprises inside, beginning with some of the greatest views in Cusco and continuing to the rarity of a working fireplace in each room (a true benefit at this chilly elevation). The colonial building has original Inca walls and exposed wood beams, and the rustic accommodations are simply decorated in a cozy mountain lodge aesthetic (even though the old-school comforters really need to go; they make the place feel dowdier than it is). All rooms are oriented toward Cusco below, offering panoramic views; no. 20 is a suite with a little sitting room, available for the same price. There's hot water 24 hours a day. The company that owns the inn also offers a wide variety of all-inclusive package deals and tours in Cusco and across Peru (see its website).

Alabado 520, San Blas, Cusco. ✆ **084/221-662.** For reservations in the U.S. ✆ **877/260-2423.** Fax 01/242-1273. www.cusco-hotel.net. 11 units. $44 double; $55 suite. Rates include continental breakfast and airport pickup. AE, MC, V. **Amenities:** Cafeteria. *In room:* TV.

More Hotels & Hostales in Cusco

Despite the amazing number of accommodations strewn across the city, Cusco can get very crowded in high season; particularly if you're in town during the Inti Raymi festival (late June), July, and August, finding a place to rest your head can be headache inducing. Here are a few more recommended places to try (although a couple of them are often full).

Casa de la Gringa ★ (Finds) This tranquil and friendly South African–owned house is a real find and a favorite of those who come to Cusco on spiritual and mystical journeys. Its rooms are nicely decorated, with a touch of bohemian flair and lively, colorful art. It features a lounge and an annexed cottage, with a patio with glass-enclosed roof for star-gazing. Pasnapacana 148 (corner Tandapata), San Blas, Cusco. (②)/fax **084/241-168.** www.casadelagringa.com. $15 per person double.

Casa Hospedaje Kuntur Wasi This tiny, family-run inn is popular with Europeans, tucked up in the San Blas district. The small terrace has amazing views of Cusco. Rooms are plain, but they have pretty good beds, and there's laundry service. Tandapata 352, San Blas, Cusco. (②)/fax **084/227-570.** $20 double with shared bathroom; $25 double with private bathroom.

El Balcón ★ (Finds) This handsome and sprawling early-17th-century colonial building has beautiful long balconies and excellent views of the city. The rooms are comfortable, and there's an inviting atmosphere throughout. Tambo de Montero 222, Cusco. (②) **084/236-738.** Fax 084/225-352. www.balconcusco. com. $60–$70 double (breakfast included).

Hostal Corihuasi (Finds) On a street leading up above Cusco, this small, cozy and rustic *hostal* has a great living room/breakfast area with a fireplace and superlative panoramic views; those same views come with a handful of rooms (nos. 1, 6, 8, 10, and 20). Suecia 561, Cusco. (②)/fax **084/232-233.** www. corihuasi.com. $49–$55 double (continental breakfast and airport pickup included).

Hostal Loreto This newly remodeled *hostal* is popular with many travelers for the original Inca stone walls featured in some rooms. The rooms can be very chilly, despite electric heaters. Still, it's just a few paces from Qoricancha and the Plaza de Armas—which is what you're paying for—and all rooms have private bathrooms with hot water. Loreto 115, Cusco. (②) **084/226-352.** $45 double.

Hostal Oblitas Just up the street from the Plaza de Armas, this small family-run hotel is homey and an excellent value. Breakfast is served in a dining room that will make you feel like you're staying at a Peruvian friend's house. Plateros 358A, Cusco. (②)/fax **084/223-871.** $40 double.

Hostal Rikch'ariy   Popular with backpackers, this small place has nice basic rooms, laundry service, and a pretty garden with good views, as well as helpful English-speaking owners. Tambo de Montero 219, Cusco. ℰ **084/236-606.** $15 per person.

Hostal San Isidro Labrador   The Labrador is a pleasant and safe but slightly overpriced choice, with 14 rooms set back from busy Calle Saphy in colonial digs set around a long courtyard. Rooms are rather small and dark but clean; several second-floor rooms have high ceilings, wood beams, and skylights. Saphy 440, Cusco. ℰ **084/226-241.** labrador@qnet.com.pe. $45 double.

Hostel Suecia Bed & Breakfast (Value)   This friendly and consistently popular backpackers' inn, housed in a 16th-century house 2 blocks from the main square, is a notch above most of Cusco's most economical *hostales*. It has comfortable rooms, an enclosed and covered courtyard, hot water, and nice beds. It's usually a great place to form Inca Trail groups. Suecia 332, Cusco. ℰ **084/233-282.** www.hostalsuecia1.com. $15 double with shared bathroom; $20 double with private bathroom.

Hotel Royal Qosqo   This popular little inn has a good vibe and a good location near the top of Procuradores. If you want to hang where the action is, this is one of your better bets, though rooms vary greatly. Tecsecocha 2, Cusco. ℰ/fax **084/226-221.** $60 double with shared bathroom.

Hostal Virrey   If you're dying to be right on the Plaza de Armas, you can't do much better than this small inn. Two rooms have stunning views of classic Cusco. Portal Comercio 165, Cusco. ℰ **084/221-771.** Fax 084/235-349. $50 double.

Los Aticos de Quera (Kids)   A great option for families, these cozy, clean rooms and apartments have a separate bedroom with a double bed, a living room with a sofa bed, a kitchenette, and a desk. It's excellent for long stays. Quera 253, Cusco. ℰ **084/231-710.** Fax 084/231-388. www.losaticos.com. $50 apartment (up to 4 people); $40 double.

Pensión Alemana   This small, German-run San Blas hotel is like a large B&B. It is very clean, if a little spartan and functional-feeling, with a nice garden area and terrace with views of Cusco below. Room no. 1, which is large and light, has great views and is your best bet. Tandapata 260, San Blas, Cusco. ℰ **084/226-861.** www.cuzco.com.pe. $50–$55 double.

Tik'a Wasi Hostal   An *hostal* with vehicular access—a rarity in this neighborhood—this clean and attractive inn has a cafeteria, comfortable carpeted rooms, a TV lounge, room service (another rarity among small *hostales*), and laundry service. Tandapata 491, San Blas, Cusco. ℰ/fax **084/231-609.** www.tikawasi.net. $50 double.

Second Home Cusco ★★ (**Finds**) Literally part of the family, a sister property of my favorite place to stay in Lima (p. 123)—the owner, Carlos, is the brother of Lillian who runs Second Home Peru, and both are the children of the famous Peruvian artist Victor Delfín—this tiny guest house has just three rooms, but it's a lovely and personable place to stay, and a very good value to boot. In fact, it has the comfort and exclusiveness of much more expensive and larger expensive hotels. In a meticulously reformed, colonial San Blas home with high ceilings, the inn is true to its name; it's like coming to stay at a friend's home. Rooms have a modern sensibility, along with top-quality bedding and linens, and nicely appointed bathrooms. The house has several of Delfín's unique art pieces, including a stunning chimney, shaped like the massive head of a puma, in the entryway. Breakfast is a communal (but made-to-order) affair, and Carlos, the genial host, is generally around to share impressions of his new home, Cusco (he previously lived many years in New York City, where he operated a Manhattan guest house).

Atocsaycuchi 616, San Blas, Cusco. © 084/235-873. www.secondhomecusco.com. 3 units. $95 double; $120 suite. Rates include breakfast. MC, V. *In room:* TV, Wi-Fi.

Inexpensive

Amaru Hostal ★ (**Value**) Popular with legions of backpackers, this hostel, in a pretty colonial-republican house in the midst of the San Blas artist studios and shops, has a lovely balconied patio, with a very nice garden area that tends to attract sunbathers and with good views of Cusco. Rooms are very comfortable, attractively decorated, and a good value (although some are quite small). Several have colonial-style furnishings and lots of natural light. (Ask to see several rooms, if you can.) It's a very friendly and relaxed place, as is its nearby sister property, Amaru Hostal II, on Chihmpata 642 (© 084/223-521; www.amaruhostal.com).

Cuesta San Blas 541, San Blas, Cusco. ©/fax 084/225-933. www.cusco.net/amaru. 16 units. $40–$48 double with bathroom; $23 double with shared bathroom. Rates include continental breakfast. No credit cards. **Amenities:** Coffee shop. *In room:* No phone.

Hostal Marani ★ (**Kids**) (**Value**) Similar in commitment and heritage to the better-known and slightly more stylish Niños Hotel—both are Dutch-owned and very active in social programs to benefit disadvantaged Peruvian children—this handsome *hostal* is very well designed and maintained. It occupies an attractive colonial-era house in San Blas and features spacious, light, and impeccable rooms with spotless tiled bathrooms. The rooms are located around a traditional Spanish-style courtyard, where guests often take their breakfasts and read in the afternoon. Ask about off-season discounts. The *hostal* has a close affiliation with the HoPe Foundation, a Dutch nonprofit that has funded dozens of schools, hospitals, and other development programs in Cusco and rural Andean villages.

Carmen Alto 194, San Blas, Cusco. ©/fax 084/249-462. www.hostalmarani.com. 17 units. $51 double. Rates include buffet breakfast and airport/bus station pickup. No credit cards. **Amenities:** Cafe. *In room:* No phone.

San Blas Hospedaje Turístico About halfway up the principal artery that wends its way up (and up) the artsy San Blas district is one of its most attractive inexpensive inns. Rooms are pretty spacious and warmly decorated. The airy colonial house has a glassed-in courtyard and a sun terrace with good views (and 24-hr. hot water). This inn is a nice step up from run-of-the-mill budget options in Cusco, and it's a good place to meet up with fellow travelers.

Cuesta San Blas 526, San Blas, Cusco. © 084/244-481. Fax 084/225-781. www.sanblashostal.com. 20 units. S/110 double. Rates include continental breakfast and airport pickup. No credit cards. **Amenities:** Coffee shop. *In room:* No phone.

Torre Dorada ★ (Value In general, I don't recommend many hotels outside city centers, because convenience is of the utmost importance to me and most travelers. However, this personalized boutique hotel in a quiet residential neighborhood (just 5 min. from downtown, and the hotel generously ferries its guests back and forth for free) is so exceptional that I can't overlook it. While not luxurious, the four-story, modern construction offers services and attention to detail that are nearly the equal of five-star hotels (but it's much friendlier doing it). It's a particularly good place to stay if you are concerned about safety, undisturbed about not being able to walk to and from the city, and perhaps uncertain about a trip to Cusco or lacking in Spanish skills. The staff goes out of its way to look out for guests and make their trips enjoyable and easygoing; I've never encountered anyone like Peggy and her hotel family. Rooms are very well outfitted and impeccable. The breakfast buffet, served in a top-floor dining room with great views, outclasses most luxury hotels.

Calle los Cipreses, Residencial Huancaro, Cusco. ⓒ **084/241-698.** Fax 084/224-255. www.torredorada. com.pe. 21 units. $85 double. Rates Include airport pickup and buffet breakfast. AE, DC, MC, V. **Amenities:** TV lounge; free taxi service to downtown; Wi-Fi.

4 WHERE TO DINE

Visitors to Cusco have a huge array of restaurants and cafes at their disposal; eateries have sprouted up even faster than *hostales* and bars, and most are clustered around the main drags leading from Plaza de Armas. Many of the city's most popular restaurants are large tourist joints with Andean music shows, while many more are economical, informal places favored by backpackers and adventure travelers—some offer midday three-course meals *(menus del día)* for as little as S/10. However, Cusco is also blessed with a growing number of upscale dining options, and the dining scene has improved every year as it expands to accommodate new, and more sophisticated, visitors to the city. Prices, too, have crept steadily upward at the top end of the scale. Though you can still eat very inexpensively, Cusco is now also a place to reward yourself with a good meal if you've been in the jungle or been trekking in the mountains.

Cheap eateries line the narrow length of Calle Procuradores, which leads off the Plaza de Armas across from the Compañía de Jesús church and is sometimes referred to as "Gringo Alley." Many are pizzerias, as Cusco has become known for its wood-fired, crispy-crust pizzas. Lurking on Procuradores and Plaza de Armas are hawkers armed with menus, hoping to lure you inside restaurants. Most represent decent, upstanding restaurants (though some occasionally offer drugs and other services), but if you know where you want to dine, a polite "no, gracias" is usually all it takes to get them off your trail. Horror of horrors, McDonald's recently took over a coveted storefront right on the stately, ancient Plaza de Armas; fortunately, it's fairly discreet, with no giant glowing "M" to disrupt the harmonious appearance.

Several cool bars, such as Los Perros and The Muse, also double as (often quite good) restaurants, primarily for their young and hip clients who'd prefer to get their food the same place as their cocktails. Baco, owned by the folks that operate one of the best restaurants in Cusco, Cicciolina, is as much chic restaurant as wine bar, and serves great gourmet pizzas (closed on Sundays); see p. 231.

Not all restaurants in Cusco accept credit cards; many of those that do, especially the cheaper places, will levy a 10% surcharge to use plastic, so you're better off carrying cash (either soles or dollars). Top-flight restaurants often charge both a 10% service charge and 18% sales tax, neither of which is included in the prices listed below.

For restaurants in San Blas, see the "Where to Stay & Dine in San Blas" map, on p. 201.

VERY EXPENSIVE

MAP Café ★★ INTERNATIONAL/NOVO ANDINO Though the name might seem a bit misleading, causing one to conjure a globe-trotter's bohemian hangout, this is in fact one of Cusco's most stylish and elegant restaurants. Housed in a modern, minimalist glass-and-steel box with few adornments other than views of the handsome colonial patio it sits in the middle of—Casa Cabera, now the beautifully designed Museo de Arte Precolombino—it places its focus squarely on the elegantly prepared and artistically presented food. At dinner, the chef presents a prix-fixe menu (including a pisco sour), which is a bit pricey for Cusco. Standouts include the fresh trout tartare and sampling of Lima-style *causas* (cold mashed-potato-and-vegetable casseroles). For diners in the mood for a taste of creative Andean cuisine, the guinea pig confit is a daring dish. As a bonus, the museum is open until 10pm, making it possible to make a dinner and pre-Columbian date of the evening.

Casa Cabrera (in Museo de Arte Precolombino), Plaza Nazarenas 231. © **084/242-476.** Reservations required. Main courses S/24–S/50; Pre-fixe dinner menu $50. AE, DC, MC, V. Daily noon–3pm and 6pm–midnight.

EXPENSIVE

Chi cha ★★★ (Finds NOVO ANDINO/PERUVIAN Gastón Acurio, Peru's leading celebrity chef who seemingly turns every kitchen he walks into to gold, has expanded beyond Lima and outposts in South and North America and put his spin on regional Peruvian cooking. His new restaurant Chi cha is his interpretation of Cuzqueña highland cuisine. In a warm and chic, nearly hidden second-story rectangular space with a high peaked ceiling painted white and dark stained wood floors, bookended by the open kitchen and the bar, Acurio works his magic again. Some have called this his least successful venture, but I disagree. Using local ingredients like quinoa for his tabbouleh and daring to offer an upscale version of *pachamanca* (a traditional countryside barbecue of meat and potatoes cooked underground), nearly everything works. I particularly loved the *codillo croquante,* slow-cooked pork shoulder wrapped in a thick slab of crunchy bacon. You can also get the ceviche and *causas* he made famous in Lima, and cocktails and desserts (including a tasting of three desserts using choclo, or large-kernel corn) are exquisite. Note that there's no sign on the street; the entrance is to the right of the touristy restaurant El Truco and up the stairs.

Plaza Regocijo 261, 2nd floor. © **084/240-520.** Reservations recommended. Main courses S/26–S/49. AE, DC, MC, V. Mon–Sat noon–11pm; Sun noon–5pm.

Cicciolina ★★★ (Finds MEDITERRANEAN/NOVO ANDINO Upstairs in the same courtyard as the restaurant A Mi Manera (below) is this delightfully chic restaurant, one of the hottest and most stylish in Cusco. The restaurant looks ripped from the Tuscan countryside. The long and often boisterous country-elegant bar is decorated with bunches of garlic, peppers, and fresh-cut flowers and is a great spot for one of the excellent cocktails (such as a maracuyá sour), or dinner itself, especially if you're in the mood

Al Grano **15**
A Mi Manera **11**
Brava **2**
Chez Maggy **4**
Cicciolina **13**
Chi Cha **1**
El Cuate **6**
Fallen Angel **12**
Greens **14**
Inka Grill **9**
Kusikuy **7**
La Tertulia **5**
Limo **10**
Moni Cafe
    Restaurante **16**
Pucara **3**
Two Nations **8**

for creative tapas (which are served only in the bar). The high-ceilinged dining room at the back, one of the few places in Cusco for true fine dining, features high-backed chairs, deep-red walls, contemporary art, and large antique mirrors. The menu focuses on unusual spices and accents, with a number of adventurous dishes. You might start with porcini mushroom soup (topped with a pisco froth) or spicy barbecued calamari, prawns, and scallops, which is served with a minty rice noodle salad. Main courses include large, superb salads (including a yummy mix of rare roast beef and vegetables), excellent home-made pastas, and alpaca filet. At lunchtime, there's usually a great pasta special, just S/20 with a lemonade or S/28 with a glass of wine, and breakfast from the bakery downstairs is served daily.

Triunfo 393, 2nd floor. (C) **084/239-510.** Reservations recommended. Main courses S/23–S/48. AE, DC, MC, V. Daily 8am–midnight.

Fallen Angel ★★ (Finds NOVO ANDINO/STEAK   It may be hard to conceive of this wildly eccentric, artistically designed funhouse as a restaurant rather than a night-club, but it is, and quite a good one at that. Though it takes a while to focus on the menu given the maximalist surroundings of flying pigs and floating cherubs, once you do, carnivores will be in heaven: it is dominated by beef tenderloin, with a choice of 15 different salsas, some with Asian and exotic combinations. Other than meat, the emphasis is on local produce and ingredients from the Sacred Valley (where the creative owner spent much of his youth on a farm) for sides and salads. Non–meat eaters can also opt for pastas, such as sweet-potato tortellini, and ceviche, but the best bet by far are the steaks. From the baroque décor to the menu, though, the adventurous Fallen Angel is definitely a love-it-or-hate it kind of place.

Plazoleta Nazarenas 221. (C) **084/258-184.** Reservations recommended. Main courses S/45. MC, V. Mon–Fri 11am–11pm; Sat–Sun 2–11pm.

Greens ★★ HEALTH FOOD/NOVO ANDINO   Once *the* destination restaurant in the bohemian heart of San Blas, Greens, now on the second floor in an old building just off the Plaza de Armas, remains one of Cusco's most stylish and intimate restaurants. More sedate and less funky than its previous incarnation, it appeals to a wider audience, even as its organic menu caters to a healthy-eating crowd (though that shouldn't scare off those who'd normally steer clear of such places). The romantic space, with overhead beams and warm woods, has just a handful of candelit tables and a soundtrack of laid-back dance beats. The creative and consistently good menu features a large number of vegetarian options, including delicious salads, as well as steaks, rack of lamb, and tropical chicken curry.

Santa Catalina Angosta 135, 2nd floor. (C) **084/243-579.** Reservations recommended. Main courses S/28–S/42. No credit cards. Daily 11am–11pm.

Inka Grill ★ PERUVIAN/NOVO ANDINO   A large and attractive modern two-level place right on the Plaza de Armas, popular with both young and old, the distinguished but somewhat pricey Inka Grill serves *novo andino* (modern Andean) fare and is consistently one of Cusco's most dependable dining experiences. Start with a bowl of yummy *camote* (sweet potato) chips and green salsa. The best dishes are Peruvian standards such as sautéed alpaca tenderloin served over *quinoa* (a grain) and *ají de gallina* (shredded chicken with nuts, cheese, and chili peppers), and desserts such as a coca-leaf crème brûlée. The extensive menu also includes a wide range of international dishes such as pizza, pasta, and risotto. If you like Inka Grill, check out its similarly relaxed but larger cousin, **Incanto** (across Plaza de Armas, at Santa Catalina Angosta 135; (C) **084/254-753**); it focuses more on homemade pastas and pizzas from a wood-burning oven.

Portal de Panes 115. (C) **084/262-992.** www.cuscorestaurants.com. Reservations recommended. S/23–S/55. AE, DC, MC, V. Mon–Sat 8am–midnight.

Limo ★★★ (Value) PERUVIAN/SUSHI   This chic and contemporary new restaurant, along with Chi cha the most stylish in Cusco, has so much going for it that it's a place I—and I suspect many visitors—will return to multiple times, even on a short trip. The stupendous views of the Plaza de Armas and surrounding mountains from the enclosed terrace would alone be enough to recommend it. The sleek design, a tasteful transformation of a colonial structure that preserved the high ceilings and beams (now painted a thick white) is complimented by modern white chairs and bold, large-format photographs. Start with a superb (and innovative) cocktail, perfect to accompany the complimentary starter of French-fried potatoes and three salsas served in a lime-green pot. Then graduate to *causita* balls, ceviche and one of the imaginative sushi rolls (which have a Peruvian bent) or *tiraditos* (Peruvian-style sashimi). Though seafood is truly the great attraction of Limo, meat-eaters can opt for more traditional highland entrees, such as pork shoulder and *adobo de cerdo*. Everything is gorgeously presented and carefully exe- cuted, and though it's not inexpensive for Cusco, for most international travelers it's a steal. Because Limo belongs to a group of very successful and dependable Cusco restaurants (others include Greens, MAP Café, and Incanto), I knew it would be good. But it's even better than I expected.

Portal de Carnes 236, 2nd floor. ℂ **084/240-668.** www.cuscorestaurants.com. Reservations recommended. Main courses S/16–S/40. AE, DC, MC, V. Daily noon–midnight.

MODERATE

A Mi Manera ★ (Finds ANDEAN A handsome and friendly little upstairs restaurant—entered through the colonial courtyard—on an overlooked little square 1 block from Plaza Nazarenas, this is one of the most relaxed spots in town. It serves excellent, creative Andean dishes with plenty of vegetarian options. Traditionalists should check out the *rocoto relleno* (stuffed peppers with meat, peanuts, and raisins), *adobo* (chicken made with chichi and *yuca*), or the *orgía de papas* (an "orgy" of spicy and cheesy potatoes). The house specialty is the traditional oven-baked *cuy* (guinea pig) with stuffed pepper and potatoes (which requires a reservation 3 hr. in advance). There are also homemade pastas, including several with twists, such as the Andean quinoa gnocchi. The wine list is pretty good, but for Andean dishes, the best accompaniment is *chicha morada,* the chilled nonalcoholic beverage brewed from purple corn. Breakfast is also served daily.

Triunfo 393, 2nd floor. ℂ **084/243-629.** Reservations recommended. Main courses S/20–S/50. AE, DC, MC, V. Daily 8am–11pm.

Brava (Value PERUVIAN In the space where Don Esteban & Don Pancho used to be, this sleek-looking, modern little restaurant—a nice change from the typical Andean rustic spots around town—has adopted a less daring menu of standard, but well-prepared pastas and pizzas. It still has the cool river-rock and stone floors, brown-and-white booths, and stylish straw chairs, making it one of the more attractive restaurants in Cusco, at least to those with a modern sensibility. You'll also find a few classic Peruvian dishes on the menu, and there's a daily special *menu* for S/20.

Portal Espinar 144. ℂ **084/243-629.** Reservations recommended. Main courses S/15–S/25. AE, DC, MC, V. Daily 11:30am–10:30pm.

Kusikuy ANDEAN/INTERNATIONAL If you've resisted trying the Andean specialty that makes most foreigners recoil or at least raise an eyebrow, this could be the place to get adventurous. The restaurant's name in Quechua means "happy little guinea pig," so *cuy al horno* is, of course, the house dish. The rest of the menu focuses on other typical Peruvian dishes and adds stuff for gringos, such as pastas and basic chicken and meat dishes. It also serves a good-value lunch *menu* (which one day featured soup, chicken in red wine with rice, and pudding, plus juice). The cozy and good-looking loft-like space, on a hilly street above the Plaza de Armas, is warmly decorated with hardwood tables and couches and a mix of antiques and musical instruments from the Amazon. It's a cool, relaxed spot for a drink.

Suecia 339. ℂ **084/262-870.** Reservations not accepted. Main courses S/14–S/38. MC, V. Mon–Sat 8am–midnight.

Macondo ★ INTERNATIONAL/LATIN AMERICAN This hip cafe/bar puts its claim to insider coolness on the door—the name is a reference to the town that is the setting for García Márquez's *One Hundred Years of Solitude*. Macondo looks more like an

Cusco's Quintas

When the day warms up under a huge blue sky in Cusco, you'll want to be outside. Cusco doesn't have many sidewalk cafes, but it does have a trio of *quintas,* traditional open-air restaurants that are most popular with locals on weekends. These are places to get large portions of good-quality Peruvian cooking at pretty reasonable prices. Among the dishes they all offer are tamales, *cuy chactado* (fried guinea pig with potatoes), *chicharrón* (deep-fried pork, usually served with mint, onions, and corn), alpaca steak, *lechón* (suckling pig), and *costillas* (ribs). You can also get classics such as *rocoto relleno* (stuffed hot peppers) and *papa rellena* (potatoes stuffed with meat or vegetables). Vegetarian options include *sopa de quinoa* (grain soup), fried *yuca,* and *torta de papa* (potato omelets). *Quintas* are open only for lunch (noon–5 or 6pm), and most people make a visit their main meal of the day. Main courses cost between S/15 and S/45.

Pachapapa ★ Across from the small church in San Blas, this popular *quinta* serves a full menu of authentic Andean dishes. Its delightful setting, in a relaxing and attractive courtyard with potted plants and whitewashed walls, also makes it an excellent place to take a breather while traipsing around hilly San Blas, to enjoy light items like soups and salads, as well as a full bar menu. From the wood-fired oven comes one of the house specialties, *cuy* (guinea pig served with Huacatay mint), as do the trout and even a spicy ham and cheese calzone. Plazoleta San Blas 120. ℘ **084/241-318.**

Quinta Eulalia ★ **(Kids)** Eulalia has been around since 1941, making it Cusco's oldest *quinta.* From a lovely colonial courtyard (only a 5-min. walk from the Plaza de Armas), there are views of the San Cristóbal district to the surrounding hills from the upper eating area. It's a great place to dine on a sunny day, and the Andean specialties are reasonably priced. Choquechaca 384. ℘ **084/224-951.**

Quinta Zarate **(Finds)** Located at the eastern end of town, this relaxed place has a lovely, spacious garden area with great views of the Cusco valley. Portions are very large, and the trout is a standout; try the *ceviche de trucha* (trout marinated in lime and spices). This *quinta* isn't difficult to find, though it's a decent hike from the square in San Blas. Totora Paccha 763, at the end of Calle Tandapata. ℘ **084/245-114.**

artsy coffeehouse than a restaurant, and the soundtrack is generally trendy tropical rhythms. The cooking is nearly as funky and imaginative as the decor. Dishes, such as the alpaca mignon with bacon in mushroom and white-wine sauce, are very well presented and served in generous portions. Much of the menu echoes the laid-back tropical theme. *Juanes* are chicken, rice, and salsa wrapped in a Bijao leaf, and chicken kabobs are accompanied by peanut sauce, like a satay. Well suited for the bohemian neighborhood of San Blas, this friendly cafe serves a variety of splashy cocktails (with two daily happy

hours) and is gay-friendly. Its owners also operate the bar-restaurant Fallen Angel **211**
(p. 207) on Plaza Nazarenas.

Cuesta San Blas 571, San Blas. © **084/229-415.** Reservations not accepted. Main courses S/19–S/30. MC, V. Mon–Sat 8:30am–10pm; Sun 3–10pm.

Pucara INTERNATIONAL/PERUVIAN   Just off the Plaza de Armas, this intimate, dimly lit restaurant has small wood tables, exposed wood beams, and cloth lamps hanging low over the tables. As one of the first restaurants tourists stumble onto right off the main square, and as one of the better values in the historic center, it's generally packed. It has a few odd touches: On the walls are framed picture cutouts of the dishes, and the waitstaff is a group of local women in yellow jackets and hairnet caps. But don't let that turn you off; it has a nice selection of traditional Peruvian and international dishes, including a tasty *lomo saltado* (strips of beef with fried potatoes, onions, and tomatoes), several different soups, and a variety of whitefish preparations.

Plateros 309. © **084/222-027.** Reservations not accepted. Main courses S/14–S/32. No credit cards. Mon–Sat 12:30–10pm.

Two Nations ★ (**Value**) ANDEAN   Owned and helmed by an Australian chef, this agreeable, laid-back joint—scruffy enough to have the graffiti of global travelers covering the walls and to offer beer by the minikeg—is best known for its Aussie burger (with fried egg and beetroot), but it also offers a long list of Andean specialties, such as *palta la reyna* (stuffed avocado) and *rocoto relleno* (stuffed spicy pepper). At night it's popular with a young, international crowd, who take advantage of the all-day happy hour (oxymoron alert!) and familiar fare like a BLT (or exotic twists on standards, such as alpaca tenderloin and carmelized onions on the Two Nations burger). There's a killer lunch deal, too: just S/10 for three courses and homemade lemonade. English-language books are available for sale or exchange.

Huaynapata 410. © **084/**240-198. Reservations recommended. Main courses S/12–S/30. AE, DC, MC, V. Mon–Sat 8am–11pm.

INEXPENSIVE

Al Grano ASIAN   A quiet corner cafe, with lots of natural light and decorated with Andean textiles and featuring exposed Inca stonework, this little place doesn't specialize in standard *criollo* (Creole) fare, as you might expect. On the menu are items from Indonesia, India, Pakistan, and Sri Lanka, including chutneys, vegetarian curries, and lamb in spices and yogurt. Most dishes are pretty mild. There's a very cheap daily menu, served until 3pm, as well as daily specials. Al Grano also has a range of great baked goods for dessert (try the brownie or spice cake) and good coffee and tea.

Santa Catalina Ancha 398 (at San Agustín). © **084/228-032.** Reservations not accepted. Main courses S/7–S/24. No credit cards. Mon–Sat 10am–9pm.

Chez Maggy (**Value**) (**Kids**) PERUVIAN/PIZZERIA   This bustling little joint, which has been around for almost 30 years and spawned several branches in Cusco and other parts of Peru, has a bit of everything, from trout and alpaca to homemade pastas to Mexican food, but most people jam their way in for the freshly baked pizzas made in a traditional wood-burning brick oven. They're some of the best in Cusco (even though every other restaurant in Cusco seems to be a pizzeria). Chez Maggy is usually packed in the evenings, and there's often live Andina music when roaming street musicians pop in to entertain diners. The restaurant is a long corridor with shared bench tables full of

CUSCO

8

WHERE TO DINE

gringos—you might just meet other travelers as you jockey for elbow space. Incredibly, three other locations are along Procuradores, better known as Gringo Alley. If you want a pizza on the terrace of your *hostal,* Chez Maggy will deliver for free.

Plateros 348. © **084/234-861.** Reservations not accepted. Main courses S/12–S/30. MC, V. Daily 6–11pm.

El Cuate (Kids) MEXICAN I'm usually wary about trying out Mexican restaurants while traveling in countries other than Mexico because they almost always serve a crummy imitation of Tex-Mex under a cheesy sombrero on the wall. But this animated hole in the wall on "Gringo Alley" dishes out good-value, pretty authentic Mexican food for scores of backpacker types. El Cuate was Cusco's first Mexican restaurant, and its success has spawned several imitators who've felt compelled to add Mexican dishes to their Peruvian and Italian menus. But if you're sure you want Mexican, this is still the place to come. It has a number of bargain menus at lunch and dinner; and dishes such as *enchiladas suizas* (cheese enchiladas), Mexican soup, tacos, and burritos. With long bench tables, often shared, it's a jovial place.

Procuradores 386. © **084/227-003.** Reservations not accepted. Main courses S/12–S/28. MC. Daily 11am–midnight.

Granja Heidi ★ (Finds) HEALTH FOOD/VEGETARIAN Although easily over-looked, given its second-floor interior location in San Blas, this easygoing eatery with an emphasis on healthy, good-value meals (especially outstanding breakfasts) is worth track-ing down. With a high ceiling and the airy, sun-filled look of an art studio, it's perfect for the neighborhood. Run by a German woman who has a farm of the same name outside Cusco, the restaurant features fresh ingredients and products, such as yogurt, cheese, and quiches, that taste like they came straight from the farm. You might expect only stuff that's strictly good for you, but the menu also offers surprising meat dishes, including ostrich steak, and typical Peruvian dishes. The daily menu (served until 9:30pm) offers vegetarian and nonvegetarian choices and might start with pumpkin soup, followed by lamb or a veggie stir-fry, fruit salad, and tea. Don't pass on dessert, or you'll miss excellent home-baked cakes, such as the cheesecake.

Cuesta San Blas 525, San Blas. © **084/238-383.** Reservations not accepted. Main courses S/9–S/25. No credit cards. Daily 8am–9:30pm.

Jack's Café Bar ★★ (Value) CAFE/INTERNATIONAL One of the most popular gringo hangouts in Cusco, owned by the guy who runs a thriving Irish pub in town, Jack's isn't just a spot to have a drink and check out some American and British maga-zines; it serves very fresh, very good, and frequently very large meals throughout the day, and features enough variety that you wouldn't be the first to eat here several times during your stay. For breakfast, try the big, fluffy pancakes. At lunch, order one of the towering salads or creative gourmet sandwiches (such as caramelized onions and salami). Finish with a dinner of "really hot green chicken curry" or a red wine, beef, and mushroom casserole. There are plenty of items for vegetarians, smoothies, wine and beer, as well as great coffee drinks and hot chocolate (for those cool Andean nights). And it's a friendly place to linger and meet fellow travelers, to boot.

Choquechaca 509 (corner of Cuesta San Blas). © **084/806-960.** Reservations not accepted. Main courses S/12–S/22. No credit cards. Daily 7am–10pm.

La Tertulia (Value) (Kids) BREAKFAST/CAFE FARE A classic Cusco spot for breakfast or other light meals, this little restaurant, up a tight spiral staircase from a travel agency, is a gringo hangout par excellence. The name means "discussion," which is fitting because people gather here to read newspapers and foreign magazines, and to exchange books and advice on hiking the Inca Trail and other far-flung adventures across South America. Many come to fuel up as early as 6:30am before setting out on one of those trips, and the superb breakfast buffet does the trick. You'll get all-you-can-eat eggs, fruit salads, yogurt, granola, amazing homemade whole-meal bread, French toast, tamales, fresh juices, and coffee—truly the breakfast of champions and an excellent value. The breakfast menu also features 16 types of crepes. There's a set-lunch deal and a nice salad bar, as well as pizzas, sandwiches, and fondues. If you feel bad about stuffing yourself at breakfast, you can feel good about the fact that La Tertulia donates S/1 of each buffet to a Peruvian orphanage. You can also take salsa dance classes here, but I wouldn't recommend trying it right after breakfast.

Procuradores 44, 2nd floor. © **084/241-422.** Reservations not accepted. Main courses S/8–S/24. MC, V. Daily 7am–3pm and 5–11pm.

Moni Café Restaurant ⟨Finds⟩ HEALTH FOOD/VEGETARIAN This tiny cafe, a couple of blocks off the Plaza de Armas, is an unpretentious gringo hangout and a good spot for freshly prepared vegetarian fare. It offers appetizers like Nepalese tomato soup and main courses like eggplant curry and spinach and ricotta lasagna, accompanied by juices, beers, and smoothies. Everything is made to order.

San Agustín 311. © **084/231-029.** Reservations not accepted. Main courses S/18–S/29. No credit cards. Mon–Sat 9am 3pm and 6–9pm.

5 WHAT TO SEE & DO

The stately and lively **Plaza de Armas** ★★, lined by arcades and carved wooden balconies, and framed by the Andes, is the focal point of Cusco. After Machu Picchu, it is one of the most familiar sights in Peru. You will cross it, relax on the benches in its center, and pass under the porticoes that line the square with shops, restaurants, travel agencies, and bars innumerable times during your stay in Cusco. The plaza—which was twice its present size in Inca days—has two of Cusco's foremost churches and the remains of original Inca walls on the northwest side of the square, thought to be the foundation of the Inca Pachacútec's palace.

Many principal sights within the historic quarter of Cusco and beyond the city are included in the *boleto turístico* (below), but a few very worthwhile places of interest, such as the Templo del Qoricancha (Temple of the Sun) and Museo de Arte Precolombino (MAP), are not included.

AROUND THE PLAZA DE ARMAS

Convento y Museo de Santa Catalina ★★ A small convent a couple of blocks west of the Plaza de Armas, Santa Catalina was built between 1601 and 1610 on top of the Acllawasi, where the Inca emperor sequestered his chosen Virgins of the Sun. The convent contains a museum of colonial and religious art. The collection includes an excellent selection of Escuela Cusqueña paintings, featuring some of the greatest works of Amerindian art—a combination of indigenous and typically Spanish styles—in Cusco. The collection also includes four paintings of the Lord of the Earthquakes (El Señor de los Temblores) painted by Amerindians. The interior of the monastery is quite beautiful, with painted arches and an interesting chapel with baroque frescoes of Inca vegetation. Other items of interest include very macabre statues of Jesus and an extraordinary trunk that, when opened, displays the life of Christ in 3-D figurines. (It was employed by the Catholic Church's "traveling salesmen," who were used to convert the natives in far-flung regions of Peru.)

Santa Catalina Angosta s/n. ℭ **084/226-032.** Admission not included in *boleto turístico;* S/8 adults, S/5 students. Daily 8am–5:30pm.

La Catedral ★★★   Built on the site of the palace of the Inca Viracocha, Cusco's cathedral, which dominates the Plaza de Armas, is a beautiful religious and artistic monument. Completed in 1669 in the Renaissance style and now handsomely restored, the cathedral possesses some 400 canvasses of the distinguished Escuela Cusqueña that were painted from the 16th to 18th centuries. There are also amazing woodcarvings, including the spectacular cedar choir stalls. The main altar—which weighs more than 401 kilograms (884 lb.) and is fashioned from silver mined in Potosí, Bolivia—features the patron saint of Cusco. To the right of the altar is a particularly Peruvian painting of the Last Supper, with the apostles drinking *chicha* (fermented maize beer) and eating *cuy* (guinea pig). The **Capilla del Triunfo** (the first Christian church in Cusco) is next door, to the right of the main church. It holds a painting by Alonso Cortés de Monroy of the devastating earthquake of 1650. To the right of the entrance to the Capilla (the right nave, next to the choir stalls) is an altar adorned by the locally famous "El Negrito" (also known as "El Señor de los Temblores," or Lord of the Earthquakes), a brown-skinned figure of Christ on the cross known as the protector of Cusco. The figure was paraded around the city by frightened residents during the 1650 earthquake (which, miracle or not, ceased shortly thereafter). So strong is continued faith in El Negrito that locals deliver dozens of fresh flowers in his honor on a daily basis. The figure's crown was stolen a couple of years ago and not recovered; the one now adorning his head is gold, a gift of a parishioner.

The entrance to the cathedral and ticket office, where you can purchase the *boleto turístico,* is actually at the entrance to the **Capilla de la Sagrada Familia,** to the left of the main door and steps.

Plaza de Armas (north side). No phone. Admission not included in *boleto turístico;* S/25 adults, S/12.50 students. Mon–Sat 10am–6pm, Sun 2–6pm.

Museo Inka ★   Housed in the impressive Admirals Palace, this museum contains artifacts designed to trace Peruvian history from pre-Inca civilizations and Inca culture, including the impact of the Conquest and colonial times on the native cultures. On view are ceramics, textiles, jewelry, mummies, architectural models, and an interesting collection—reputed to be the world's largest—of Inca drinking vessels *(qeros)* carved out of wood, many meticulously painted. The museum is a good introduction to Inca culture, and there are explanations in English. The palace itself is one of Cusco's finest colonial mansions, with a superbly ornate portal indicating the importance of its owner; the house was built on top of yet another Inca palace at the beginning of the 17th century. In the courtyard is a studio of women weaving traditional textiles. Allow 1½ to 2 hours to see the entire collection.

Cuesta del Almirante 103 (corner of Ataúd and Tucumán). ℭ **084/237-380.** Admission not included in *boleto turístico;* S/10 adults, S/5 students. Mon–Sat 9am–6pm.

Templo de la Compañía de Jesús ★   Cater-cornered to the cathedral is this Jesuit church, which rivals the former in grandeur and prominence on the square (an intentional move by the Jesuits, and one that had Church diplomats running back and forth

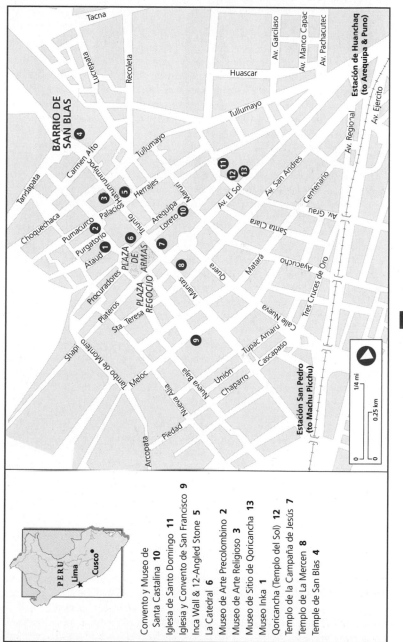

Convento y Museo de
Santa Catalina **10**

Iglesia de Santo Domingo **11**

Iglesia y Convento de San Francisco **9**

Inca Wall & 12-Angled Stone **5**

La Catedral **6**

Museo de Arte Precolombino **2**

Museo de Arte Religioso **3**

Museo de Sitio de Qoricancha **13**

Museo Inka **1**

Qoricancha (Templo del Sol) **12**

Templo de la Campaña de Jesús **7**

Templo de La Mercen **8**

Temple de San Blas **4**

(Value) Cusco's Boleto Turístico

Cusco's municipal tourism (Calle Mantas 117-A) office sells a tourist ticket, or **boleto turístico,** that is virtually essential for visiting the city and surrounding areas. It is your admission to 16 of the most important places of interest in and around Cusco, including some of the major draws in the Sacred Valley. Though it has more than doubled in price in the last few years and is no longer much of a bargain, the *boleto* is the only way you can get into a number of churches, museums and ruins sites. The full ticket costs S/130 for adults and S/70 students with ID and children, is valid for 10 days, and is available at the tourism office at Mantas 117-A (📞 **084/263-176**), open Monday through Friday from 8am to 6:30pm and Saturday from 8am to 2pm.

In addition to the main Tourist Office, the *boleto* can be purchased at OFEC, Av. El Sol 103, office 101 (Galerías Turísticas; 📞 **084/227-037**), from 8am to 6pm Monday through Saturday, and Casa Garcilaso, at the corner of Garcilaso y Heladeros s/n (📞 **084/226-919**), from 8am to 5pm Monday through Friday, and 8am to 4pm Saturday.

The full *boleto* allows admission to the following sights: in Cusco, Museo Municipal de Arte Contemporáneo, Museo Histórico Regional, Museo de Sitio Qoricancha, Museo de Arte Popular, Centro Qosqo de Arte Nativo, Monumento al Inka Pachacuteq; the nearby Inca ruins of Sacsayhuamán, Q'enko, Pukapukara, Tambomachay, Pikillacta, and Tipón; and the Valle Sagrado attractions of Pisac, Ollantaytambo, and Chinchero.

La Catedral, the imposing cathedral on the Plaza de Armas, formerly included in the *boleto,* now charges a separate admission fee (although there is a combination ticket that covers the cathedral and other principal Cusco attractions not covered by the *boleto,* including Templo de San Blas, Iglesia de la Compañía de Jesús, and Palacio Arzobispal, for S/50 adults, S/25 students).

Not all of these attractions are indispensable, and you probably won't end up checking off absolutely everything on your color photo-coded *boleto,* but it remains the best admission ticket in Cusco. You can also buy a partial ticket for S/70 that only covers either attractions in the city, or ruins outside of Cusco. Make sure you carry the ticket with you when you're planning to make visits (especially on day trips outside the city), as guards will demand to see it so that they can punch a hole alongside the corresponding picture. Students must also carry their International Student Identification Card (ISIC), as guards often demand to see that ID to prove that they didn't fraudulently obtain a student *boleto.* For additional information, visit www.boletoturisticocusco.com.

to the Vatican). Begun in the late 16th century, it was almost entirely demolished by the quake of 1650, rebuilt, and finally finished 18 years later. Like the cathedral, it was also built on the site of an important palace, that of the Inca Huayna Cápac (said to be the most beautiful of all the Inca rulers' palaces). Inside, it's rather gloomy, but the gilded altar is stunning, especially when illuminated. The church possesses several important works of art, including a picture of Saint Ignatius de Loyola, by the local painter Marcos

Zapata, and the Cristo de Burgos crucifixion by the main altar. Also of note are the paint- ings to either side of the entrance, which depict the marriages of Saint Ignatius's nephews; one is the very symbol of Peru's *mestizo* character, as the granddaughter of Manco Inca weds the man who captured the last Inca, Tupac Amaru, the leader of an Indian uprising.

Plaza de Armas (southeast side). Admission not included in *boleto turístico;* S/10 adults, S/5 students. Mon–Sat 11am–noon and 3–4pm.

SOUTH & EAST OF THE PLAZA DE ARMAS

Barrio de San Blas ★★   Cusco's most atmospheric and picturesque neighborhood, San Blas, a short but increasingly steep walk from the Plaza de Armas, is lined with artists' studios and artisans' workshops, and stuffed with tourist haunts—many of the best bars and restaurants and a surfeit of hostels. It's a great area to wander around—many streets are pedestrian-only—though you should exercise caution with your belongings, especially at night. The neighborhood also affords some of the most spectacular panoramic vistas in the city. In the small plaza at the top and to the right of Cuesta San Blas is the little white **Templo de San Blas ★**, said to be the oldest parish church in Cusco (no phone; admission apart from *boleto turístico;* S/15 adults, S/7.50 students; Mon–Sat 2–5:30pm). Although it's a simple adobe structure, it contains a marvelously carved churrigueresque cedar pulpit. Some have gone as far as proclaiming it the finest example of woodcarving in the world; carved from a single tree trunk, it is certainly impressive. The pulpit comes with an odd story, and it's difficult to determine whether it's fact or folklore: It is said that the carpenter who created it was rewarded by having his skull placed within his masterwork (at the top, beneath the feet of St. Paul) upon his death. Also worth a look is the baroque gold-leaf main altar.

Begins roughly at Calle Choquechaca, as the neighborhood climbs into the hills.

Museo de Arte Precolombino (MAP) ★★ (Finds   This sophisticated and sumptu- ously designed archaeological museum features part of the vast collection of pre-Colum- bian works belonging to the Museo Larco in Lima. Housed in an erstwhile Inca ceremonial court, Santa Clara convent, and later colonial mansion (Casa Cabrera) of the Conquistador Alonso Díaz are 450 pieces—about 1% of the pieces in storage at the museum in Lima—dating from 1250 B.C. to A.D. 1532. Beautifully illuminated halls carefully exhibit gold and silver handicrafts, jewelry, ceramics, and other artifacts depict- ing the rich traditions from the Nasca, Moche, Huari, Chimú, Chancay, and Inca cul- tures. Although the number of pieces isn't overwhelming, they are all beautifully lighted and displayed. Scattered about are comments about "primitive" art by major Western artists such as Paul Klee, and deviating from the museum's main thrust is a room of Cusqueña School religious painting. The museum is especially worthwhile for anyone unable to visit the major museums in Lima or any of the premier sites in northern Peru. Allow 1 or 2 hours for your visit. Within the courtyard, housed in a minimalist glass box, is MAP Café (p. 206), one of Cusco's most exclusive restaurants.

Casa Cabrera, Plaza de las Nazarenas s/n. © **084/237-380.** S/22 adults, S/11 students and children. Daily 10am–10pm.

Museo de Arte Religioso (Palacio Arzobispal)   On the corner of one of Cusco's most extraordinary streets, Hatunrumiyoc, a pedestrian alleyway lined with magnificent Inca stonemasonry (see "The Magic of Inca Stones: A Walking Tour" on p. 220), the Museum of Religious Art is housed in a handsome colonial palace that previously belonged to the Archbishop of Cusco (before that, it was the site of the palace of Inca

The Cusco School of Art

The colonial-era **Escuela Cusqueña,** or Cusco School of Art, that originated in the ancient Inca capital was a synthesis of traditional Spanish painting with local, *mestizo* elements—not surprising, perhaps, because its practitioners were themselves of mixed blood. Popular in the 17th and 18th centuries, the style spread from Cusco as far as Ecuador and Argentina. The most famous members of the school were Diego Quispe Tito, Juan Espinosa de los Monteros, and Antonio Sinchi Roca, even though the authors of a large majority of works associated with the school are anonymous. Most paintings were devotional in nature, with richly decorative surfaces. Artists incorporated recognizable Andean elements into their oil paintings, such as local flora and fauna, customs, and traditions—one depiction of the Last Supper has the apostles feasting on guinea pig and drinking maize beer—and representations of Jesus looking downward, like the Indians who were forbidden to look Spaniards in the eye. Original Escuela Cusqueña works are found in La Catedral, the Convent of Santa Catalina, the Museum of Religious Art, and a handful of other churches in Cusco. Reproductions of original paintings, ranging from excellent in quality to laughable, are available across Cusco, particularly in the galleries and shops of San Blas.

Roca and then the home of a Spanish marquis). Inside is a nice collection of colonial religious paintings, notable for the historical detail they convey, but the extravagant old house—with its impressive portal and Moorish-style doors, balcony, carved-cedar ceilings, stunning stained-glass windows, and small chapel—is pretty nearly the main draw. Plan to spend about 1 to 2 hours here.

Corner of Hatunrumiyoc and Palacio. © **084/225-211.** Admission not included in *boleto turístico;* S/10 adults, S/5 students. Mon–Fri 8am–12:30pm and 3–6pm.

Museo de Sitio de Qoricancha   In three small rooms, this underground museum, located across the garden from the vastly more interesting Temple of the Sun and Church of Santo Domingo, presents a decent collection of ceramics, metalwork, and textile weavings of Inca and pre-Inca civilizations, as well as a host of other archaeological finds. The museum pales in comparison to the Museo de Arte Precolombino and Museo Inka, however. Allow about a half-hour for your visit, tops.

Av. El Sol s/n (across the esplanade from Qoricancha). Admission by *boleto turístico.* Mon–Sat 9:30am–5:30pm.

Qoricancha (Templo del Sol) & Santo Domingo ★★★   Qoricancha and Santo Domingo together form perhaps the most vivid illustration in Cusco of Andean culture's collision with western Europe. Like the Great Mosque in Córdoba, Spain—where Christians dared to build a massive church within the perfect Muslim shrine—the temple of one culture sits atop and encloses the other. The extraordinarily crafted Temple of the Sun was the most sumptuous temple in the Inca Empire and the apogee of the Incas' naturalistic belief system. Some 4,000 of the highest-ranking priests and their attendants were housed here. Dedicated to worship of the sun, it was apparently a glittering palace straight out of El Dorado legend: *Qoricancha* means "golden courtyard" in Quechua, and in addition to hundreds of gold panels lining its walls, there were life-size gold figures, solid-gold altars, and a huge golden sun disc. The sun disc reflected the sun and bathed the temple in light. During the summer solstice, the sun still shines directly into a niche where only the Inca chieftain was permitted to sit. Other temples and shrines existed for the worship of lesser natural gods: the moon, Venus, thunder, lightning, and rainbows. Qoricancha was the main astronomical observatory for the Incas.

After the Spaniards ransacked the temple and emptied it of gold (which they melted down, of course), the exquisite polished stone walls were employed as the foundations of the Convent of Santo Domingo, constructed in the 17th century. The baroque church pales next to the fine stonemasonry of the Incas—and that's to say nothing about the original glory of the Sun Temple. Today all that remains is Inca stonework. Thankfully, a large section of the cloister has been removed, revealing four original chambers of the temple, all smoothly tapered examples of Inca trapezoidal architecture. Stand on the small platform in the first chamber and see the perfect symmetry of openings in the stone chambers. A series of Inca stones displayed reveals the fascinating concept of male and female blocks, and how they fit together. The 6m (20-ft.) curved wall beneath the west end of the church, visible from the street, remains undamaged by repeated earthquakes and is perhaps the greatest extant example of Inca stonework. The curvature and fit of the massive dark stones is astounding.

Once the Spaniards took Cusco, Francisco Pizarro's brother Juan was given the eviscerated Temple of the Sun. He died soon afterward, though, at the battle at Sacsayhuamán, and he left the temple to the Dominicans, in whose hands it remains.

Plazoleta Santo Domingo. © **084/222-071.** Admission not included in *boleto turístico*; S/10 adults, S/5 students and children. Mon–Sat 8:30am–6:30pm; Sun 2–5pm.

CUSCO

8

WHAT TO SEE & DO

(Fun Facts) Hang a Right at Donkey Lips

Cusco is littered with difficult-to-pronounce, wildly spelled street names that date to Inca times. In the bohemian neighborhood of San Blas, though, they're particularly colorful. Here's a primer of atmospheric street names and their literal meanings:

Atoqsayk'uchi Where the fox got tired
Tandapata Place of taking turns
Asnoqchutun Donkey lips
Siete Diablitos Seven Little Devils
Siete Angelitos Seven Little Angels
Usphacalle Place of sterility/place of ashes
Saqracalle Where the demons dwell
Pumaphaqcha Puma's tail
Cajonpata Place shaped like a box
Rayanpata Place of myrtle flowers
One to seek out: **P'asñapakana** Where the young women are hidden
And, finally, one to avoid: **P'aqlachapata** Place of bald men

The Magic of Inca Stones: A Walking Tour ★★

Dominating the ancient streets of Cusco are dramatic **Inca walls,** constructed of mammoth granite blocks so exquisitely carved that they fit together without mortar, like jigsaw-puzzle pieces. The Spaniards razed many Inca constructions but built others right on top of the original foundations. (Even hell-bent on destruction, they recognized the value of good engineering.) In many cases, colonial architecture has not stood up nearly as well as the Incas' bold structures, which were designed to withstand the immensity of seismic shifts common in this part of Peru.

Apart from the main attractions detailed in this section, a brief walking tour will take you past some of the finest Inca constructions that remain in the city. East of the Plaza de Armas, **Calle Loreto** is one of the best-known Inca thoroughfares. The massive wall on the left side, composed of meticulously cut rectangular stones, was once part of the Acllahuasi, or the "House of the Chosen Maidens," the Inca emperor's Virgins of the Sun. This is the oldest surviving Inca wall in Cusco and one of the most distinguished. Northeast of the Plaza de Armas, off Calle Palacio, is **Hatunrumiyoc,** a cobblestone street lined with impressive walls of polygonal stones. Past the Archbishop's Palace on the right side is the famed **12-angled stone** (now appropriated as the symbol of Cuzqueña beer), which is magnificently fitted into the wall. Originally, this wall belonged to the palace of the Inca Roca. This large stone is impressively cut; the Incas almost routinely fitted many-cornered stones (with as many as 32, as seen at Machu Picchu, or even 44 angles) into structures. From Hatunrumiyoc, make your first right down another pedestrian alleyway, Inca Roca; about halfway down on the right side is a series of stones said to form the shape of a **puma,** including the head, large paws, and tail. It's not all that obvious, so if you see someone else studying the wall, ask him to point out the figure. **Siete Culebras (Seven Snakes),** the alleyway connecting Plaza Nazarenas to Choquechaca, contains Inca stones that form the foundation of the chapel within the Hotel Monasterio. Other streets with notable Inca foundations are **Herrajes, Pasaje Arequipa,** and **Santa Catalina Angosta.** Only a couple genuine Inca **portals** remain. One is at Choquechaca 339 (the doorway to a recommended *hostal,* Rumi Punku), and another is at Romeritos 402, near Qoricancha.

Not every impressive stone wall in Cusco is Incan in origin, however. Many are transitional period (post-Conquest) constructions, built by local masons in the service of Spanish bosses. Peter Frost's *Exploring Cusco* (available in local bookstores) has a good explanation of what to look for to distinguish an original from what amounts to a copy.

SOUTHWEST OF THE PLAZA DE ARMAS

Iglesia y Convento de San Francisco   This large and austere 17th-century convent church, thoughtfully restored, extends the length of the square of the same name. It is best known for its collection of colonial artworks, including paintings by Marcos

Zapata and Diego Quispe Tito, both of considerable local renown. A monumental can- **221**
vas (12×9m/39×30 ft.) that details the genealogy of the Franciscan family (almost 700
individuals) is by Juan Espinoza de los Monteros. The Franciscans also decorated the
convent with ceiling frescoes and a number of morbid displays of skulls and bones. The
church is worth a visit mainly for those with extra time in Cusco.

Plaza de San Francisco s/n. ☎ **084/221-361.** Admission S/5 adults, S/3 students. Mon–Sat 9am–4pm.

Templo de La Merced ★ Erected in 1536 and rebuilt after the great earthquake in
the 17th century, La Merced ranks just below the cathedral and the La Compañía church
in importance. It has a beautiful facade and lovely cloisters with a mural depicting the
life of the Merced Order's founder. The sacristy contains a small museum of religious art,
including a fantastic solid-gold monstrance swathed in precious stones. In the vaults of
the church are the remains of two famous conquistadors, Diego de Almagro and Gonzalo
Pizarro.

Calle Mantas s/n. ☎ **084/231-831.** Admission S/5 adults. Mon–Sat 8:30am–noon and 2–5pm.

INCA RUINS NEAR CUSCO ★★★

The easiest way to see the following set of Inca ruins just outside Cusco is as part of a
half-day tour. The hardy might want to approach it as an athletic archaeological expedition: If you've got 15km (9⅓ miles) of walking and climbing at high altitude in you, it's
a beautiful trek. Otherwise, you can walk to Sacsayhuamán and nearby Q'enko (the
climb from the Plaza de Armas is strenuous and takes 30–45 min.), and take a colectivo
or taxi to the other sites. Alternatively, you can take a Pisac/Urubamba minibus (leaving
from the bus station at Calle Intiqhawarina, off Avenida Tullumayo, or Huáscar 128) and
tell the driver you want to get off at Tambomachay, the ruins farthest from Cusco, and
work your way back on foot. Some even make the rounds by horseback. You can easily
and cheaply contract a horse at Sacsayhuamán, but don't expect a chance to ride freely in
the countryside—you'll walk rather slowly to all the sites alongside a guide.

Visitors with less time in Cusco or less interest in taxing themselves might want to join
a guided tour, probably the most popular and easiest way to see the sites. Virtually any
of the scads of travel agencies and tour operators in the old center of Cusco offer them.
Some well-rated traditional agencies with a variety of programs include **Milla Turismo,**
Av. Pardo 689 (☎ **084/231-710;** www.millaturismo.com), and **SAS Travel,** Garcilaso
270, Plaza San Francisco (☎ **084/249-194;** www.sastravelperu.com).

Admission to the following sites is by *boleto turístico,* and they are all open daily from
7am to 6pm. Guides, official and unofficial, hover around the ruins; negotiate a price or
decide upon a proper tip. There are a handful of other Inca ruins on the outskirts of
Cusco, but the ones discussed below are the most interesting.

(Fun Facts) Those Fabulously "Sexy" Ruins

The pronunciation of Sacsayhuamán, like many Quechua words, proves difficult
for most foreigners to wrap their tongues around, so locals and tour guides have
several jokes that point to its similarity to the words "sexy woman" in English. You
haven't really experienced Cusco until you've heard the joke with that punch line
a dozen times—from old men, guides, and even little kids.

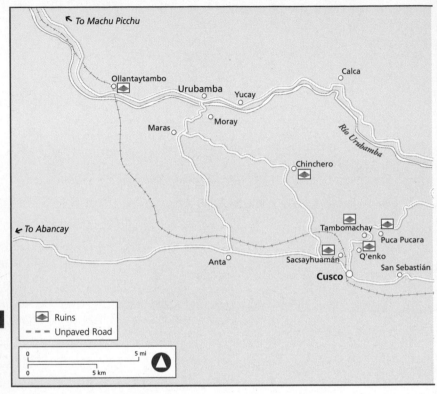

These sites are generally safe, but at certain times of day—usually dawn and dusk before and after tour groups' visits—several ruins are said to be favored by thieves. It's best to be alert and, if possible, go accompanied.

Note that new finds are continually being uncovered here, even as close to Cusco as the vicinity around Sacsayhuamán. Archaeologists recently announced the discovery of an ancient, pre-Inca temple, irrigation canals, and a series of rooms that held mummies and idols. The temple is believed to have been built by the Killke culture, which occupied the region around present-day Cusco from A.D. 900 to 1200.

Sacsayhuamán ★★★

The greatest and nearest to Cusco of the Inca ruins, Sacsayhuamán reveals some of the Incas' most extraordinary architecture and monumental stonework. Usually referred to as a garrison or fortress—because it was constructed with forbidding, castlelike walls—it was more likely a religious temple, although most experts believe it also had military significance. The Inca emperor Pachacútec began the site's construction in the mid–15th century, although it took nearly 100 years and many thousands of men to complete it. Massive blocks of limestone and other types of stone were brought from as far as 32km (20 miles) away.

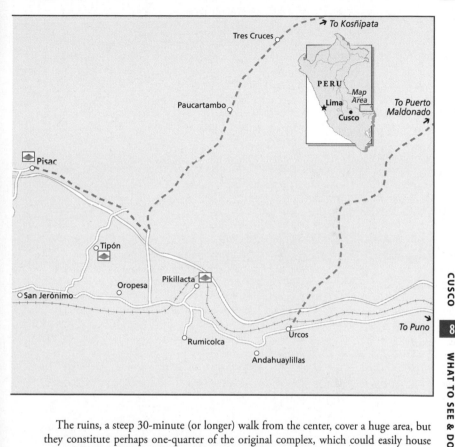

The ruins, a steep 30-minute (or longer) walk from the center, cover a huge area, but they constitute perhaps one-quarter of the original complex, which could easily house more than 10,000 men. Today, what survive are the astounding outer walls, constructed in a zigzag formation of three tiers. (In the puma-shaped layout of the Inca capital, Sacsayhuamán was said to form the animal's head, and the zigzag of the defense walls forms the teeth.) Many of the base stones employed are almost unimaginably massive; some are 3.5m (11 ft.) tall, and one is said to weigh 300 tons. Like all Inca constructions, the stones fit together perfectly without aid of mortar. It's easy to see how hard it would have been to attack these ramparts with 22 distinct zigzags; the design would automatically expose the flanks of an opponent.

Above the walls are the circular foundations of three towers that once stood here; they were used for storage of provisions and water. The complex suffered such extensive destruction that the primary function of Sacsayhuamán continues to be debated. What is known is that it was the site of one of the bloodiest battles between the Spaniards and native Cusqueños. More than 2 years after the Spaniards had initially marched on Cusco and installed a puppet government, the anointed Inca (Manco Inca) led a seditious campaign that took back Sacsayhuamán and nearly defeated the Spaniards in a siege of the Inca capital. Juan Pizarro and his vastly outnumbered but superior armed forces stormed

Cusco's Spectacular Celebrations

Cusco explodes with joyous celebration of both its Amerindian roots and Christian influences during festivals, which are crowded but splendid times to be in the city if you can find accommodations. It's worth planning your trip around one of the following fiestas, if possible.

Inti Raymi ★★★, the fiesta of the winter solstice (June 24, but lasting for days before and afterward), is certainly the star attraction. It's an eruption of Inca folk dances, exuberant costumes, and grand pageants and parades, including a massive one that takes place at the stately Sacsayhuamán ruins overlooking the city. Inti Raymi is one of the finest expressions of local popular culture on the continent, a faithful reenactment of the traditional Inca Festival of the Sun. It culminates in high priests sacrificing two llamas, one black and one white, to predict the fortunes of the coming year. Cusco's **Carnaval week,** with lots of music, dance, and processions of its own, is part of the buildup for Inti Raymi.

Semana Santa, or Easter week (late Mar or Apr), is an exciting traditional expression of religious faith, with stately processions through the streets of Cusco, including a great procession led by El Señor de los Temblores (Lord of the Earthquakes) on Easter Monday. On Good Friday, booths selling traditional Easter dishes are set up on the streets.

In early May, the **Fiesta de las Cruces (Festival of the Crosses),** a celebration popular throughout the highlands, is marked by communities decorating large crosses that are then delivered to churches. Crucifix vigils are held on all hilltops that are crowned by crosses. Festivities, as always accompanied by lively dancing, give thanks for bountiful harvests. Early June's **Corpus Christi** festival is another momentous occasion, with colorful religious parades featuring 15 effigies of saints through the city and events at the Plaza de Armas and the cathedral (where the effigies are displayed for a week).

On December 24, Cusco celebrates the **Santuranticuy Festival,** one of the largest arts-and-crafts fairs in Peru. Hundreds of artisans lay out blankets in the Plaza de Armas and sell carved Nativity figures and saints' images, in addition to ceramics and *retablos* (altars). The tradition was begun by the Bethlehemite Order and Franciscan Friars.

A hugely popular Andean festival that attracts droves from Cusco and the entire region is the **Virgen del Carmen,** celebrated principally in Paucartambo (see "Side Trips from Cusco," later in this chapter) and with only a slightly lesser degree of exuberance in Pisac and smaller highland villages.

Sacsayhuamán in a horrific battle in 1536 that left thousands dead. Legend speaks of their remains as carrion for giant condors in the open fields here. After the defeat of the Inca troops and the definitive Spanish occupation of Cusco, the Spaniards made off with the more manageably sized stone blocks from Sacsayhuamán to build houses and other structures in the city below.

The Inti Raymi festival is celebrated here annually, and it is truly a great spectacle— one of the finest in Peru (see "Cusco's Spectacular Celebrations" on p. 224). A flat, grassy esplanade (where the main ceremony of the festival is celebrated) separates the defense walls from a small hill where you'll find the "Inca's Throne" and large rocks with well-worn grooves, used by children and often adults as slides. Nearby is a series of claustrophobia-inducing tunnels—pass through them if you dare.

Night visits to the ruins are permitted from 8 to 10pm. Under a full moon in the huge starlit Andean sky, Sacsayhuamán is so breathtaking that you'll instantly grasp the Incas' worship of the natural world, in which both the sun and the moon were considered deities. If you go at night, take a flashlight and a few friends; security is a little lax, and assaults on foreigners have occurred.

Walking directions: A couple of paths lead to the ruins from downtown Cusco. You can take Almirante, Suecia, or Plateros. Head northwest from the Plaza de Armas. Take Palacio (behind the cathedral) until you reach stairs and signs to the ruins; or at the end of Suecia, climb either Huaynapata or Resbalosa (the name means "slippery") until you come to a curve and the old Inca road. Past the San Cristóbal church at the top, beyond a plaza with fruit-juice stands, is the main entrance to the ruins. Plan to spend about an hour here for a brief run-through, and up to 3 hours if you're a photography buff or if you have kids who want to play on the slides and in the tunnels.

Q'enko ★

The road from Sacsayhuamán leads past fields where, on weekends, Cusqueños play soccer and have cookouts, to the temple and amphitheater of Q'enko (*Kehn*-koh), a distance of about a kilometer (½ mile). The ruins are due east of the giant white statue of Christ crowning the hill next to Sacsayhuamán; follow the main road, and you'll see signs for Q'enko, which appears on the right. A great limestone outcrop was hollowed out by the Incas, and, in the void, they constructed a cavelike altar. (Some have claimed that the smooth stone table inside was used for animal sacrifices.) Visitors can duck into the caves and tunnels beneath the rock. You can also climb on the rock and see the many channels cut into the rock, where it is thought that either *chicha* or, more salaciously, sacrificial blood coursed during ceremonies. (Q'enko might have been a site of ritual ceremonies performed in fertility rites and solstice and equinox celebrations.) Allow a half-hour to tour the site, not including travel time.

Puca Pucara

A small fortress (the name means "red fort") just off the main Cusco-Pisac road, this might have been some sort of storage facility or lodge, or perhaps a guard post on the road from Cusco to the villages of the Sacred Valley. It is probably the least impressive of

---

(Fun Facts) Can't Leave Well Enough Alone

The Peruvian authorities are notorious for messing with ancient Inca ruins, trying to rebuild them rather than let them be what they are: ruins. You'll notice at Sacsayhuamán and other Inca sites that unnecessary and misleading restoration has been undertaken. The grotesque result is that small gaps where original stones are missing have been filled in with obviously new and misplaced garden rocks—a disgrace to the perfection pursued and achieved by Inca stonemasons.

the area sites, although it has nice views of the surrounding countryside. From Q'enko, Puca Pucara is a 90-minute to 2-hour walk along the main road; allow a half-hour for your visit.

Tambomachay

On the road to Pisac (and a short, signposted walk off the main road), this site is also known as Los Baños del Inca (Inca Baths). Located near a spring just a short walk beyond Puca Pucara, the ruins consist of three tiers of stone platforms. Water still flows across a sophisticated system of aqueducts and canals in the small complex of terraces and a pool, but these were not baths as we know them. Most likely this was instead a place of water ceremonies and worship. The exquisite stonework indicates that the baños were used by high priests and nobility only. Plan on spending an hour here.

---

6 ESPECIALLY FOR KIDS

Cusco is a blast to walk around, so entertaining the kids and finding suitable restaurants and things to do shouldn't be a problem for most families. Kids old enough to appreciate a bit of history might enjoy the exceptionally laid-out **Museo de Arte Precolombino (MAP),** as well as the **Museo Inka,** both of which will give them a good grounding in pre-Columbian civilizations and Inca culture. Beside ceramics and textiles, the Museo Inka displays cool mummies and tiny hand-painted Inca drinking vessels. You'll find Andean women weaving traditional textiles in the courtyard.

Cusco resonates with remnants of the ancient capital; a walking tour with the kids will take you past **Inca walls** with giant granite blocks that look like the pieces of a giant jigsaw puzzle. Have the kids count the hand-cut angles in the 12-angled stone and find the outlines of the puma stone (see "The Magic of Inca Stones: A Walking Tour" on p. 220). Observing the walls will give you a chance to impress your family with your knowledge of Andean history. Explain that the Incas built these massive walls without mortar or cement of any kind and with no knowledge of the wheel or horses, and that they constructed one of the world's greatest empires, reaching from one end of South America to another, without a written language and with runners who relayed messages to rulers.

Another good activity for artistically inclined children is to pop into **artists' studios** in the funky neighborhood of San Blas. Then walk—if you have the energy—up to the ruins of **Sacsayhuamán.** There you'll find more massive stones and gorgeous views of the city and surrounding mountains, but kids will really dig the huge rocks with slick grooves that make fantastic slides. There are also some cool tunnels cut into stones nearby, which kids might enjoy much more than their parents.

And, of course, the biggest family attraction of all lies beyond Cusco: Few are the kids who aren't fascinated by the ruins of **Machu Picchu.** The easygoing towns of the **Sacred Valley** are also great spots for families; see chapter 9 for info.

---

7 SHOPPING

Cusco is Peru's acknowledged center of handicraft production, especially hand-woven textiles, and along with Lima the country's premier shopping destination. Many Cusqueño artisans still employ ancient weaving techniques, and they produce some of the finest textiles in South America. Peru's top tourist draw overflows with shops stuffed with colorful, enticing wares. From tiny one-person shops to large markets with dozens of stalls, there are few better places to shop than Cusco for excellent-value Andean handicrafts.

Items to look for (though you certainly won't have to look too hard because shopping opportunities are pretty much everywhere you turn) include alpaca-wool sweaters, shawls, gloves, hats, scarves, blankets, ponchos (in fact, there are so many cool and cheap cold-weather items here that many people end up replacing the things they've brought for the chilly nights); silver jewelry; antique blankets and textiles, beautiful but pricey; woodcarvings, especially nicely carved picture frames; fine ceramics; and Escuela Cusqueña reproduction paintings.

The barrio of **San Blas,** the streets right around the **Plaza de Armas** (particularly calles Plateros and Triunfo), and **Plaza Regocijo** are the best and most convenient haunts for shopping outings. Many merchants sell similar merchandise, so some price comparison is always helpful. If sellers think you've just arrived in Peru and don't know the real value of items, your price is guaranteed to be higher. Although bargaining is acceptable and almost expected, merchants in the center of Cusco are confident of a steady stream of buyers, and, as a result, they are often less willing to negotiate than their counterparts in markets and more out-of-the-way places in Peru. Most visitors will find prices delightfully affordable, though, and haggling beyond what you know is a fair price, when the disparity of wealth is so great, is generally viewed as bad form.

ALPACA & ANDEAN FASHIONS

It's difficult to walk 10 feet in Cusco without running into an alpaca goods shop. Almost everyone in Cusco will try to sell you what they claim to be 100% alpaca scarves and sweaters, but many sold on the street and in tourist stalls are inferior quality (and might even be mixed with man-made materials such as fiberglass). What is described as "baby alpaca" might be anything but. (A trekking guide once joked that if you listen carefully, sellers claiming their wares are "baby alpaca" are in fact saying "may be alpaca.") To get better quality, not to mention more stylish and original, examples, you need to visit a store that specializes in upscale alpaca fashions; they are more expensive but, compared to international alpaca prices, still a true bargain. The following stores are some of the best, and they all feature great-looking shawls, jackets, sweaters, scarves and more: **Alpaca 3,** Ruinas 472 (© 084/226-101); **Alpaca's Best** ★★, Plaza Nazarenas 197–199 (© 084/245-331); **Kuna** ★★, Plaza Recocijo 202 (© 084/243-233) and Portal de Panes 127/Plaza de Armas; **Alpaca Treasures,** Heladeros 172 (© 084/438-557); and **World Alpaca,** Portal de Carnes 232/Plaza de Armas (© 084/244-098).

Many shops in Cusco feature sheep's wool or alpaca *chompas,* or jackets, with Andean designs (often lifted directly from old blankets and weavings). A different take on Peruvian fashions, sure to appeal to plenty of stylish backpackers, is available at **Mundo Hemp,** Qanchipata 596, San Blas (© 084/258-411), where you'll find 100% natural hemp clothes and housewares, as well as a funky little cafe. For t-shirts with hip Andean motifs, check out **Mullu Arte Contemporáneo,** Triunfo 120 (© 084/229-831).

ANTIQUES

Most of the best antiques dealers are found in the San Blas district. **Antigüedades y Artesanías Sayre,** at Triunfo 352-B (© 084/236-981), and **Galería de Arte Cusqueño Antigüedades,** at Plazoleta San Blas 114 (© 084/237-857), have lots of different antiques, ranging from textiles to art and furniture. Another shop worth a peek is **El Armario,** Carmen Alto 118 (© 084/229-809).

Especially noteworthy is the **Centro de Textiles Tradicionales del Cusco ★★**, Av. El Sol 603 (© **084/228-117;** www.textilescusco.org), an organization dedicated to "fair trade" practices. It ensures that 70% of the sale price of the very fine textiles on display goes directly to the six communities and individual artisans it works with. On-site is an ongoing demonstration of weaving and a very good, informative textiles museum. Prices are a bit higher than what you may find in generic shops around town, though the textiles are also higher quality, and much more of your money will go to the women who work for days on individual pieces. (There's also a small outlet of the Centro in the courtyard at the Museo de Arte Precolombino, Plaza Nazarenas 231.) **Casa Ecológica Cusco,** Portal de Carnes 236 (interior; © **084/255-427**) has a good selection of high-quality, handmade textiles from highland communities (in addition to natural medicines and organic food products). For a massive selection of antique Andean textiles, visit the small shop that appears to have no name, but which the proud owner calls **Tienda-Museo de Josefina Olivera ★**, Portal Comercio 173, Plaza de Armas (© **084/233-484**). They stock some fantastic vintage alpaca ponchos and blankets, though some age claims may be slightly exaggerated. For antique textiles, there's also a very good little stall ★ at the end of the corridor (on the right side as you enter) within the **Feria Artesanal** at Plateros 334 (below). The stalls aren't numbered, and you might have to ask the owner to pull his older, more valuable pieces from a trunk he keeps them in, but he has some of the finest quality ceremonial textiles in Cusco.

For a general selection of *artesanía,* **Galería Latina,** Zetas 309 (© **084/236-703**), has a wide range of top-end antique blankets, rugs, alpaca-wool clothing, ceramics, jewelry, and handicrafts from the Amazon jungle in a large, cozy shop. **Centro Artesanal Cusco,** at the end of Avenida El Sol, across from the large painted waterfall fountain and the Hotel Savoy, is the largest indoor market of handicrafts stalls in Cusco, and many goods are slightly cheaper here than they are closer to the plaza. Other centers with stalls and similar goods are **Feria Artesanal Tesoros del Inca,** Plateros 334 (© **084/233-484**); **Centro Artesanal "Conde de Gabucha,"** Zetas 109 (© **084/248-250**); **Centro Artesanal El Inca,** San Andrés 218; **Centro Artesanal Sambleño,** Cuesta de San Blas 548; and **Feria Artesanal Yachay Wasi,** Triunfo 374. **Puquna,** Choquechaca 408 (© **084/255-257**) is a stylish little shop with original design and popular art objects, including photography, textiles and jewelry; **Indigo Arte y Artesanía ★**, San Agustín 403-407 (© **084/240-145**) is similar, though more traditional and loaded with good gift ideas from across Peru.

San Blas is swimming with art galleries, artisan workshops, and ceramics shops. You'll stumble upon many small shops dealing in reproduction Escuela Cusqueña religious paintings and many workshops where you can watch artisans in action. Several of the best ceramics outlets are also here, and a small handicrafts market usually takes over the plaza on Saturday afternoon. Check out **Artesanías Mendivil ★★**, known internationally for its singular saint figures with elongated necks, but also featuring a nice selection of mirrors, carved wood frames, Cusco School reproductions, and other ceramics; it has locations at Plazoleta San Blas 619 (© 084/233-247), Hatunrumíyoc 486 (© 084/233-234), and Plazoleta San Blas 634 (© 084/240-527). **Artesanías Olave ★★**, the outlets of a high-quality crafts shop that does big business with tourists, are located at Triunfo 342 (© 084/252-935), Plazoleta San Blas 100 (© 084/246-300), and Plazoleta San Blas 651 (© 084/231-835). **Juan Garboza** *taller* (workshop), Tandapata 676, Plazoleta San Blas (© 084/248-039), specializes in pre-Inca-style ceramics. **Aqlla ★**, at Cuesta de San

Blas 565 and marked by a sign that says ETHNIC PERUVIAN ART (© 084/249-018), has great silver jewelry, folk and religious art, and fine alpaca items. **Galería Sur,** Hatunrumiyoc 487-B (© 084/238-371) sells fine, distinctive tapestries from Ayacucho.

Several artists in the San Blas area open their studios as commercial ventures, although the opportunity to watch a painter work can be fairly expensive. Look for flyers in cafes and restaurants in San Blas advertising such workshops.

DESIGNER APPAREL

For women only, **Montse Aucells** ★★★, a Catalan designer resident in Cusco, has a small shop at Palacio 116 (© **084/226-330**) that features some of the most fashionable and original—but still largely traditional—alpaca designs and knitwear for women in town. **Werner & Ana** ★, a Dutch-Peruvian design couple, sell stylish clothing in fine natural fabrics, including alpaca; they have a shop on Plaza San Francisco 295-A (at Garcilaso; © **084/231-076**). But the most unique designer that I've found in Cusco, or pretty much anywhere in Peru, for that matter, is a northern Irish woman, Eibhlin Cassidy, who sells her original clothing designs for women at her shop, **Hilo** ★★★, Carmen Alto 260, San Blas (© **084/254-536**). Eibhlin has a keen eye for patterns and sometimes startling combinations of fabrics and color and adornments like buttons; her whimsical but beautiful tops and jackets may not be for everyone, but to me it's wearable art. Young, trendy sorts should check out the small shop **Pulga,** Carmen Alto 237, San Blas (© **084/9844-93537;** www.pulgalatienda.com), which focuses exclusively on the funky clothing, bags and accessories (for both men and women) of young Peruvian designers from Lima and around the country. Also contemporary with an emphasis on wildly colorful is the shop **Peru Moderno** ★, Choquechaca 162 (© **084/244-135;** www.perumoderno.com), with hip (and often neon) clothing, bag and accessory designs.

FOODSTUFFS & MERCADO CENTRAL

Cusco's famous, frenzied **Mercado Central (Central Market)** ★ near the San Pedro rail station is shopping of a much different kind—almost more of a top visitor's attraction than a shopping destination. Its array of products for sale—mostly produce, food, and household items—is dazzling. Even if you don't come to shop, this rich tapestry of modern and yet highly traditional Cusco still shouldn't be missed. If you're an adventurous type who doesn't mind eating at street stalls (which are generally pretty clean), you can get a ridiculously cheap lunch for about $1. Don't take valuables (or even your camera), though, and be on guard because the market is frequented by pickpockets targeting tourists. The market is open daily from 8am to 4pm or so.

A great selection of homemade chocolates can be had at a small shop in San Blas, called, appropriately enough, **Chocolate,** Choquechaca 162 (© 084/229-001). **Mundo Hemp,** Qanchispata 596, San Blas (© **084/258-411;** www.mundohemp.com), has hemp-based sweets and soups in its cafe, in addition to the more expected hemp t-shirts and clothing and home-design accessories. **The Coca Shop,** Carmen Alto 115, San Blas (© **084/260-774;** www.thecocashop.com), features all things derived from coca leaves (save the obvious), including coca- and lúcuma-infused chocolates and teas.

JEWELRY & SILVER

Ilaria ★★★, one of the finest jewelry stores in Peru, deals in fine silver and unique Andean-style pieces, and has several branches in Cusco: at Hotel Monasterio, Palacios 136 (© **084/221-192**); at the Casa Andina Private Collection, Plazoleta de Limacpampa

Chico 473 (p. 196); at Hotel Libertador, Plazoleta Santo Domingo 259 (© **084/223-192**); and another at Portal Carrizos 258 on the Plaza de Armas (© **084/246-253**). Many items, although not inexpensive, are an excellent value for handmade silver.

The contemporary jewelry designer **Carlos Chaquiras,** Triunfo 375 (© **084/227-470**), is an excellent craftsman; many of his pieces feature pre-Columbian designs. **Claudia Lira ★★**, a Lima designer, has her elegant and unique gold and silver pieces within the funky shop Peru Moderno, Choquechaca 162 (© **084/244-135;** www.claudia lira.com). Another nice shop with silver items is **Platería El Tupo,** Portal de Harinas 181, Plaza de Armas (© **084/229-809**). **Chimú Art & Gifts,** Carmen Alto 187-B, San Blas (© **084/801-968**), is a funky shop featuring cool contemporary designs in silver, many based on interpretations of Chimú culture art. Rocío Pérez shows her original designs (packaged in handmade bags) at her little shop, **Jewelry Esma,** in the entryway to the Quinta Paccha Papa restaurant, at Plaza San Blas 120.

OUTDOOR GEAR

As the gateway to outdoor highlands and Sacred Valley activities, including mountain climbing, trekking and cycling, Cusco is well stocked with outdoor gear shops for those who aren't adequately equipped for their adventures. In the last few years, the selection of international, high-end name brands has increased while prices have come down to pretty standard international levels. **Tatoo Adventure Gear ★★**, Calle del Medio 130 leading just off Plaza de Armas (© **084/224-797**) has probably the best selection of camping, trekking and mountain climbing shoes, backpacks and equipment. Another good nearby shop with similar goods is **Cordillera ★**, Garcilaso 210 (© **084/244-133**).

WOODWORK

Lots of shops have hand-carved woodwork and frames. However, the best spots for handmade baroque frames (perfect for your Cusco School reproduction or religious shrine) are **La Casa del Altar,** Mesa Redonda Lote A, near the Plaza de Armas (© **084/244-712**), which makes *retablos* (altarpieces) and altars in addition to frames; and the small *taller* (studio) where Miguel Angel León Sierra and children and grandchildren make splendid handmade cedar frames to order (the kind one sees on most art from the Escuela Cusqueña originals and imitations). The *taller* is just off Plaza de Nazarenas, at Córdoba del Tucumán 372 (© **084/236-271**).

8 CUSCO AFTER DARK

Most first-time visitors to Cusco are surprised to find that this Andean city with such a pervasive, gentle Amerindian influence and colonial atmosphere also has such a rollicking nightlife. It's not as diverse (or sophisticated) as Lima's, but the scene, tightly contained around the Plaza de Armas, is predominantly young and rowdy, a perfect diversion from the rigors of trekking and immersion in Inca and colonial history. Some older visitors might find the late-night, spring break party atmosphere a little jarring in such a historic, stately place. But even for those with a lower-key night in mind, Cusco is especially entrancing in the early evening, as lights twinkle in the hills and the street lamps in the Plaza de Armas give a golden glow to the square.

Even though the city is inundated with foreigners during many months of the year, bars and discos happily aren't just gringolandia outposts. Locals (as well as Peruvians from other cities, principally Lima, and other South Americans) usually make up a pretty healthy percentage of the clientele. Clubs are in such close range of each other—in the **231** streets just off the Plaza de Armas and in San Blas (where the city's artsy bars and cafes proliferate)—that virtually everyone seems to adopt a pub-crawl attitude, bopping from one bar or disco to the next, often reconvening with friends in the plaza before picking up a free drink ticket and free admission card from one of the many girls on the square handing them out.

For those who are saving their energy for the Inca Trail and other treks, there are less rowdy options, such as Andean music shows in restaurants, more sedate bars, and English-language movies virtually every night of the week.

BARS & PUBS

In high season, bars are often filled to the rafters with gringos hoisting cheap drinks and trading information on the Inca Trail or their latest jungle or rafting adventure (or just trying to pick up Peruvians or each other). Most bars are open from 11am or noon until 1 or 2am. Many have elastic happy hours offering half-price drinks, making it absurdly cheap to tie one on. (Travelers still adjusting to Cusco's altitude, though, should take it easy on alcohol in their first days in the city.)

A cocktail bar specializing in Peruvian piscos (and a dizzying array of pisco sours) is **El Pisquerito** ★★, Santa Teresa 172 (✆ **084/235-223**), popular with locals and visitors and 1 block from Plaza Regocijo. **Los Perros** ★★, Tecsecocha 436 (✆ **084/241-447**), is a laidback lounge bar owned by an Australian-Peruvian couple. "The Dogs" has comfy sofas, good food and cocktails (including hot wine), and a hip soundtrack, including live jazz on Sunday and Monday nights. The bar attracts an international crowd that takes advantage of the book exchange and magazines, and plenty of folks quickly become regulars, making it their spot for dining as well as just hanging out and drinking. **The Muse** ★, now moved from San Blas to Plateros 316 (same entrance as Ukuku's; ✆ **084/231-717**), has a similar vibe, though it's a bit scruffier. **Baco** ★, Calle Ruinas 465 (✆ **084/242-808**), a sleek wine bar that's as much a restaurant as it is an oenophile hangout—offering gourmet pizzas and sophisticated *novo andino* and international fare—is owned by the same people behind the excellent restaurant Cicciolina. **Cicciolina** ★★ itself (p. 206) has a very appealing wine and cocktail bar, with tons of ambience; it's a good place to begin or end the evening. Next door, the sedate and good-looking cocktail lounge **Marcelo Batata,** Palacios 121 (✆ **084/224-424**) has a coveted rooftop terrace. Way too unique and inspired to be merely another restaurant, **Fallen Angel** ★★★ (p. 207), Plaza de Nazarenas 221 (✆ **084/258-184**), has such a wild, over-the-top

---

ⓘ Tips Raw Fish: A Cure for What Ails You

If you hang out so much and so late in Cusco that you wind up with a wicked hangover—which is even more of a problem at an altitude of 3,300m (11,000 ft.)— adopt the tried-and-true Andean method of reviving yourself. For once, the solution is not coca-leaf tea—it's ceviche that seems to do the trick. Something about raw fish marinated in lime and chili makes for a nice slap in the face. When I lived in Ecuador (a country that fights with Peru not only over boundaries, but also over credit for having invented ceviche), late Sunday mornings at the *cevichería* were part of the weekly routine for pale-faced folks hiding behind sunglasses.

CUSCO

8

CUSCO AFTER DARK

look—complete with glass tables topping porcelain bathtubs filled with brightly colored (live) fish—that it also makes a scene-stealing spot for a drink (note that it closes promptly at 11pm, however).

One of the oldest pubs in town is the **Cross Keys** ★, Triunfo 350 (✆ **084/229-227**), owned by the English honorary consul and especially popular with Brits who come to play darts or catch up on European soccer on satellite, and knock back pints of ale; it's stuffed to the gills late at night. Pub grub is available, if you can manage to get an order in. American-owned **Norton Rat's Tavern,** Santa Catalina Angosta 116 (✆ **084/246-204**), next door to the La Compañía church, is a rough-and-tumble bar, the type of biker-friendly place that you might find in any American Midwestern city. Nice balconies overlook the action below on the plaza. **Paddy Flaherty's,** Triunfo 124, Plaza de Armas (✆ **084/247-719**), is an Irish pub serving Guinness on draft. It's cozy, relaxed, and often crowded, with expats catching up on *fútbol* (soccer, of course) and rugby. **Rosie O'Grady's,** Santa Catalina Ancha 360 (✆ **084/247-935**), is the other Irish tavern of note, with considerably fancier digs in which to down your (canned) Guinness. There's live music Thursday through Saturday, and several happy hours throughout the day. If you really want to get your drink on, **La Chupitería,** Tecsecocha 400 (✆ **084/984-725-241**) calls itself a "revolutionary shot bar," and in addition to any number of shots, it's got a whole lineup of spring break-like drink combos with suggestive or plain vulgar names. (You've been warned.) Rowdy late into the night in San Blas is **7 Angelitos,** Calle Siete Angelitos 638 (✆ **084/806-070**), with live music most nights; it's the place to go when all other bars have closed—its owners will still be buying folks drinks and encouraging hang-overs. For a real local taste, check out the rustic and hugely popular bar (with live music on weekends) **Pepe Zeta** ★, Tecsecocha 415 (✆ **084/223-082**). You may need at least some rudimentary Spanish, but it's a great place to meet Peruvian young people.

LIVE MUSIC

Live music is a nearly constant feature of the Cusco nightlife scene, and it's not all itinerant bands of *altiplano* musicians in colorful vests and sandals playing woodwind instruments—not by a long shot. Live music tends to begin around 11pm in most clubs, and happy hours are generally from 8 to 9 or 10pm.

Teatro Municipal, Mesón de la Estrella 149 (✆ **084/221-847**), and particularly the long-running **Centro Q'osqo de Arte Nativo** ★, Av. El Sol 684 (✆ **084/227-901**), schedule music and folkloric dance performances. Check with the tourist information office for a schedule of events.

You can catch traditional Peruvian bands with a beat at Ukuku's (below) and Rosie O'Grady's (above), but for a traditional folklore music-and-dance show with panpipes and costumes—well, ponchos, alpaca hats, and sandals, at a minimum—you'll need to check out one of the tourist-oriented restaurants featuring nightly entertainment. In addition to the long-time show restaurants **El Truco** (Plaza Regocijo 261; ✆ **084/232-441**) and **La Retama** (Portal de Panes 123, 2nd Floor; ✆ **084/226-372**), **Tunupa,** Portal Confiturías 233, 2nd Floor (✆ **084/252-936**), offers a good traditional music-and-dance show, as well as a panoramic view of the Plaza de Armas.

One of the coolest places in Cusco for nightly live music is **Ukuku's** ★★, Plateros 316, second floor (✆ **084/227-867**). The range of acts extends from bar rock to Afro-Peruvian, and the crowd comes to get a groove on, jamming the dance floor. Often the mix is half gringo, half Peruvian. If you're looking to pick up a Peruvian *chico* or *chica,* or at least practice your Spanish, it's one of the best spots in town. Ukuku's is open until the wee hours, and there's a room with computer terminals, 24-hour Internet access, and

Cafe Society

If you really just want to chill out and have a coffee, a beer, or some dessert, drop into one of the city's comfortable cafes. The following are all good places for a light meal during the day, but at night they tend to take on some of that smoky Euro-cafe sheen, and travelers get all metaphysical about their treks through the Andes.

Café Ayllu ★, Almagro 133 (② 084/232-357), is a busy little place, a traditional Cusco café drawing as many locals as gringos. It's known for its *ponche de leche* (a milky beverage, often served with a shot of pisco) and *lenguas* (a flaky pastry with manjar blanco crème in the middle). It also offers good breakfasts, sandwiches, and the mainstay, coffee. Trotamundos ★, Portal de Comercio 177, second floor (② 084/239-590), has an excellent balcony on the main square, facing the cathedral. It also has an open fireplace, which is perfect for cold evenings, and a convenient Internet cafe. It's a good spot for coffee and cakes, and a lively nighttime bar atmosphere. La Tertulia, Procuradores 44 (② 084/241-422), is more of a breakfast and lunch hangout, while Café Varayoc, Espaderos 142 (② 084/232-404), is a sophisticated place to read and chill over coffee and excellent pastries and desserts, especially cheesecake.

Removed from the center, but well located if you're making the rounds of Manu travel operators, **Manu Café** is a chic rainforest-style cafe, very swish for Cusco; it's attached to Manu Nature Tours at Av. Pardo 1046 (② 084/252-721). It serves excellent coffee (including imported roasts from around the world) and light meals, and there are racks of foreign newspapers for your perusal.

CUSCO

8

CUSCO AFTER DARK

a pizza bar, as well as daily movies in the afternoon. Get your hands on a pass for free entrance so you don't get stuck paying a cover (although often it's not even necessary to have a pass; gringos often sail right in).

Kamikase ★, Plaza Regocijo 274, 2nd Floor (② 084/233-865), is the senior citizen of Cusqueño nightclubs, inaugurated long before the tourist explosion, back in 1985. It's a comfortable, well-worn place, a two-level bar and a live music area with tables and funky decor. The music ranges from rock en Español to reggae, and there are lots of locals—occasionally, Peruvians even outnumber gringos. (Imagine that!) There are nightly drink specials on things such as caipirinhas. If you've imbibed one too many of those, you might want to take a breather before tackling the stairs to the street. I once had to carry a friend out (don't ask), and it was a real challenge. **Pepe Zeta** ★ (see above) is a fun, local hangout with live Peruvian music on weekends. **Garabato Video Pub,** Espaderos 135, 3rd Floor (② 084/620-336), is a bar/restaurant that features nightly movies on a large screen, a variety of live shows, and a dance floor and lounge. It's one of Cusco's one-stop-shopping outlets for nightlife.

DANCE CLUBS

Several late-night dance clubs have come and gone in the last few years, but a few of the old warhorses remain popular. A pretty young crowd, both backpackers and young Peruvians, is lured to the discos by all the free drink cards handed out on the Plaza de Armas.

Mama Africa, Portal de Panes 108, 2nd Floor (© **084/246-544**), boasts sweaty charm and features occasional live music and DJs who spin an international dance mix of Latin, reggae, rock, and techno music for a mix of locals and gringos. The original club is now called **Mama Amerika,** Portal Belén 115, 2nd Floor (© **084/245-550**). It's just as crowded as ever, and besides serving free and cheap drinks, it also has good munchies and a large screen showing videos.

    Eko Club ★, Plateros 334, 2nd Floor (no phone), is one of Cusco's hottest dance clubs. The large dance floor throbs until dawn with a variety of rock, trance, and Euro-techno; for those who need a break, there's a laid-back lounge out back, good for a chair, a smoke, and a drink. **Up Town,** Suecia 302 (© **084/227-241**), is Cusco's island resort disco on spring break. It offers free salsa, samba, and merengue dance classes (in English), and it's popular with locals. With two bars and a fleet of young girls enticing visitors with free drink cards, **Extrem,** Portal de Carnes 298 (© **084/240-901**), swarms with one of Cusco's youngest and most frenetic crowds who come for happy hour and free drinks. Those who need to rest their hips can hang by the fireplace, catch a movie, or fortify themselves at the pizzeria.

CINEMA

There aren't many traditional cinemas in central Cusco, but there are a number of places showing movies, mostly to entertain international visitors in need of a break from trekking and sightseeing. Probably the best selection of international films, ranging from classic to art house to children's flicks, but mostly American, is found at **The Film Lounge & Danish Café,** Procuradores 389, second floor (© **084/123-236**); it's got a cute little bar, serves food and drinks, and has three screenings daily (S/4). Other screens showing movies on a daily basis are **Garabato Video Pub,** Espaderos 135, third floor (© **084/620-336**); and **Ukuku's,** Plateros 316 (© **084/227-867**).

THEATER

An excellent counterpoint to the town's ubiquitous bars, discos, and half-hearted tourist musical programs, **Kusikay** ★★★ at the Garcilaso Theater, 117 Calle Unión, presents a superb music and theater program that's equal parts Broadway theater, Cirque du Soleil, and modern dance. The engaging production (the second-season program is called "Paukartanpu"), set in a beautifully renovated historic theater with superb sound and brilliant costumes and choreography, tells an Andean fable through song and dance, and the Spanish and Quechua dialogue is translated into English on an overhead screen, like in some opera houses. It's an excellent outing for families, though some very small children may be frightened by the costumes. For more information, visit www.kusikay.com, call © **084/255-414,** or look for one of the brochures in hotels and around town. Tickets are $35; shows are Monday through Saturday at 7:30pm.

9 SIDE TRIPS FROM CUSCO

Many visitors "do" Machu Picchu in a single day, taking a morning train out and a late-afternoon train back to Cusco. In my book, Machu Picchu is much too important and impressive a sight to relegate it to a day trip, but that's all many people have time for. The Sacred Valley villages and famed markets (especially Pisac and Chinchero) also constitute day trips for loads of travelers. Again, though, the area is so rich and offers so much for

(Tips) Jungle Adventure

Cusco is the gateway to the southern Amazon region. If you're interested in a jungle expedition to the Manu Biosphere Reserve or the Tambopata National Reserve, don't miss chapter 11.

travelers with time to do more than whiz through it that the area—including Pisac, Urubamba, Ollantaytambo, Calca, Chinchero, and Moray—is treated separately in chapter 9, along with the great Inca ruins of Machu Picchu.

A Cusco-area **ruins hike,** either on foot or on horseback, of the Inca sites within walking distance of the capital—Sacsayhuamán, Q'enko, Puca Pucara, and Tambomachay—makes for a splendid daylong (or half-day, if you make at least some use of public transportation or a taxi) excursion. For more information on the individual sites, see the earlier "Inca Ruins Near Cusco" section and the map in "What to See & Do in Cusco," earlier in this chapter.

Adventure travelers might want to concentrate on other **outdoor sports,** including treks, biking excursions, and white-water rafting that can be done around Cusco. See "Extreme Sacred Valley: Outdoor Adventure Sports" in chapter 9.

PAUCARTAMBO ★★

110km (68 miles) NE of Cusco

Most visitors who venture to very remote Paucartambo (and there aren't many of them) do so for the annual mid-July **Fiesta de la Virgen del Carmen** ★★★, one of Peru's most outrageously celebrated festivals (it lasts several days, and most attendees, be they villagers or foreigners, camp out because there is nowhere else to stay); see the "Cusco's Spectacular Celebrations" box on p. 224 for more details. Yet the beautiful, small, and otherwise quiet mountain village might certainly be visited during the dry season (May–Oct), if you've got the patience to venture way off the beaten track. A few travelers stop en route to Puerto Maldonado and the Manu Biosphere Reserve.

The peaceful colonial town, once a mining colony, has cobblestone streets and a lovely Plaza de Armas with white structures and blue balconies, but not a whole lot else—that is, until it is inundated by revelers donning wildly elaborate and frequently frightening masks, and drinking as if Paucartambo were the last surviving town on the planet. The colorful processions and traditional dances are spectacular, and a general sense of abandonment of inhibitions (senses?) reigns. Mamacha Carmen, as she's known locally, is the patron saint of the *mestizo* population. During the festival, there's a small office of tourist information on the south side of the plaza. More information on the celebrations is available from the main tourist office in Cusco (p. 187).

Depending on when you visit, you might be able to get a simple bed at one of two small and very basic inexpensive inns in town: the **Hostal Quinta Rosa Marina** and the **Albergue Municipal** (neither has a phone).

Another 45km (28 miles) beyond Paucartambo is **Tres Cruces (Three Crosses)** ★, sacred to the nature-worshiping Incas and still legendary for its mystical sunrises in the winter months (May–July are the best). Tres Cruces occupies a mountain ridge at the edge of the Andes, before the drop-off to the jungle. From a rocky outcropping at nearly 4,000m (13,100 ft.) above sea level, hardy travelers congratulate themselves (for having gotten there,

And Then There Were 12: The Inca Emperors

The Inca Empire, one of the greatest the Americas has ever known, had 12 rulers over its lifetime from the late 12th century to the mid–16th century. The emperors, or chieftains, were called Incas; the legendary founder of the dynasty was Manco Cápac. The foundations of the palaces of the sixth and eighth leaders, Inca Roca and Viracocha Roca, respectively, are still visible in Cusco. Pachacútec was a huge military figure, the Inca responsible for creating a great, expansive empire. He was also an unparalleled urban planner. He made Cusco the capital of his kingdom, and, under his reign, the Incas built Qoricancha, the fortresses at Pisac and Ollantaytambo in the Sacred Valley, and mighty Machu Picchu. Huayna Cápac, who ruled in the early 16th century, was the last Inca to oversee a united empire. He divided the Inca territory, which by that time stretched north to Ecuador and south to Bolivia and Chile, between his sons, Huáscar and Atahualpa, which resulted in a disastrous civil war. Atahualpa eventually defeated his brother but was captured by Francisco Pizarro in Cajamarca and killed by the Spaniards in 1533, which led to the ultimate downfall of the Incas. The 12 Incas, in order, are as follows:

1. Manco Cápac
2. Sinchi Roca
3. Lloque Yupanqui
4. Mayta Cápac
5. Cápac Yupanqui
6. Inca Roca
7. Yahuar Huácac
8. Viracocha Inca
9. Pachacútec
10. Tupac Inca
11. Huayna Cápac
12. Atahualpa

as much as for the sight they've come to witness) as they gaze into the distance out over the dense, green Amazon cloud forest. The sunrise is full of intense colors and trippy optical effects (including multiple suns). Even for those lucky enough to have experienced the sunrise at another sacred Inca spot, Machu Picchu, it is truly a hypnotic sight.

GETTING THERE Gallinas de Rocas minibuses leave daily for Paucartambo from Cusco's Avenida Huáscar, near Garcilaso (departure times vary; the journey takes 4–6 hr.). For the Virgen del Carmen festival (July 15–17), some small agencies organize 2- and 3-day visits, with transportation, food, and camping gear (or arrangements for use of a villager's bed or floor) included. Look for posters in the days preceding the festival. To get to Tres Cruces, see whether any Cusco travel agencies are arranging trips; otherwise, you'll either have to hire a taxi from Cusco or hitchhike from Paucartambo. (Ask around; some villagers will be able to hook you up with a ride.) Make sure you leave in the middle of the night to arrive in time for the sunrise.

TIPON ★

23km (14 miles) SE of Cusco

Rarely visited by tourists, who are in more of a hurry to see the villages and Inca ruins of the Sacred Valley north of Cusco, the extensive complex of Tipón is nearly the equal of the more celebrated ruins found in Pisac, Ollantaytambo, and Chinchero. For fans of Inca stonemasonry and building technique, Tipón's well-preserved agricultural terracing is among the best created by the Incas and makes for a rewarding, if not easily accessible, visit. Peter Frost writes in *Exploring Cusco* (Nuevas Imágenes, 1999) that the terracing is so elaborately constructed that it might have been instrumental in testing complex crops rather than used for routine farming. There are also baths, a temple complex, and irrigation canals and aqueducts that further reveal the engineering prowess of the Incas. The ruins are a healthy hour's climb (or more, depending on your physical condition) up a steep, beautiful path, or by car up a dirt road. The uncluttered distant views are tremendous. The truly adventurous and fit can continue above the first set of ruins to others perched even higher (probably another 2 hr. of climbing). During the rainy season (Nov–Mar), it's virtually impossible to visit Tipón.

GETTING THERE Combis for "Urcos" leave from Avenida Huáscar in Cusco; request that the driver drop you off near Tipón, which is between the villages of Saylla and Oropesa. The site is 4km (2½ miles) from the highway; it's open daily from 7am to 5:30pm. Admission is by Cusco's *boleto turístico*.

PIKILLACTA & RUMICOLCA

38km (24 miles) SE of Cusco

These pre-Inca and Inca ruins might go unnoticed by most, were it not for their inclusion on the Cusco tourist ticket. Although the Cusco region is synonymous with the Incas, the Huari and other cultures preceded them. **Pikillacta** is the only pre-Inca site of importance near Cusco. The Huari culture built the complex, a huge ceremonial center, between A.D. 700 and 900. The two-story adobe buildings, of rather rudimentary masonry, aren't particularly good shape, although they are surrounded by a defensive wall. Many small turquoise idols, today exhibited in the Museo Inka in Cusco, were discovered at Pikillacta.

Less than a kilometer from Pikillacta, across the main road, is **Rumicolca,** an Inca portal—a gateway to the Valle Sagrado—constructed atop the foundations of an ancient aqueduct that dates to the Huari. The difference in construction techniques is readily apparent. The site was a travel checkpoint controlling entry to the Cusco Valley under the Incas.

GETTING THERE Combis for "Urcos" leave from Avenida Huáscar in Cusco and drop passengers for Pikillacta near the entrance. Both sites are open daily from 7am to 5:30pm. Admission is by Cusco's *boleto turístico.*

Machu Picchu & the Sacred Valley of the Incas

The **Urubamba Valley**, better known as **El Valle Sagrado de los Incas (the Sacred Valley of the Incas)** ★★★, is a relaxed and incomparably beautiful stretch of small villages and ancient ruins spread across broad plain and rugged mountain slopes northwest of Cusco. The magnificent Inca ruins found from Pisac to Ollantaytambo and beyond—some of the finest not only in Peru, but also in all of the Americas—are testaments to the region's immense ceremonial importance. The Incas built several of the empire's greatest estates, temples, and royal palaces between the sacred centers of Cusco and Machu Picchu, positioned like great bookends at the south and north ends of the valley.

Through the valley rolls the revered Río Urubamba (called the Willcamayu by the Incas; today it is also called the Vilcanota in one section), a pivotal religious element of the Incas' cosmology. The Incas believed not only that the flow of the Urubamba was inexorably tied to the constellations and the mountain peaks, but also that the river was the earthbound counterpart of the Milky Way. With the river as its source, the fertile valley was a major center of agricultural production for the Incas, who grew native Andean crops such as white corn, coca, potatoes, and other fruits and vegetables in expansive fields and along spectacularly terraced mountain slopes. The valley continues to serve as a breadbasket for Cusco, providing grains, peaches, avocadoes, and much more.

Even though the villages of the Sacred Valley, stretching about 100km (62 miles) from Pisac to Ollantaytambo, are highlights of many tourist itineraries and are coveted by hotel developers, they remain starkly traditional. Quechua-speaking residents work the fields with primitive tools and harvest salt with methods unchanged since the days of the Incas, and market days—although now conducted to attract the tourist trade as well as intervillage commerce—remain important rituals.

Along with Cusco and Machu Picchu, the Valle Sagrado is one of the highlights of Peru and is really beginning to take off as a destination on its own, rather than just an add-on to Cusco or Machu Picchu. If like most you're visiting either of the two biggest attractions in Peru, it would be a shame not to spend at least an extra day or two in the Valley. Many visitors without a lot of time on their hands whip through the valley's highlights and markets on a daylong guided bus tour, sandwiching it between Cusco and Machu Picchu on the Inca itinerary. Seeing it blitzkrieg-style is certainly doable, but it can't compare to a leisurely pace that allows you an overnight stay or two in the valley and the chance to soak up the area's immense history, relaxed character, huge sky, stunning scenery, and, in the dry season, equally gorgeous springlike weather. The valley is also about 300m (1,000 ft.) lower than

Aranwa Sacred Valley **7**
Casa Andina Private Collection **2**
The Green House **8**
Hotel Pisaq/Hostal Paz y Luz **9**
Las Chullapas **4**
Liberator Valle Sagrado Lodge **1**
Sol y Luna Lodge/Spa & K'uychi Rumi **3**
Sonesta Posadas del Inca Sacred Valley **6**
Ticllabamba Maison d'Hôtes **5**

Cusco, making it much more agreeable for those potentially afflicted with altitude-related health problems. As a way to ease into Peru, it may make more sense to begin in the Sacred Valley and see Machu Picchu before visiting Cusco.

More visitors are doing exactly that, spending several days in the valley, even choosing to base themselves at least initially in Pisac, Urubamba, or Ollantaytambo rather than the regional capital, Cusco. With the increased number of services (and more on the way) geared toward visitors in and around centrally located Urubamba and Ollantaytambo, this is more attractive than ever. The Sacred Valley now has some of the finest country-style hotels in Peru, especially geared toward visitors who are looking for an easy pace or all the outdoor activities they can take advantage of (see "Extreme Sacred Valley: Outdoor Adventure Sports" on p. 244). Several highlights of the Sacred Valley, such as the ruins of Pisac and Ollantaytambo, and the market town Chinchero, are visited as part of the Cusco *boleto turístico* (see "Cusco's *Boleto Turístico*" on p. 216 in chapter 8 for complete details).

(Tips) Getting Around the Sacred Valley

Local buses (usually small *combis* or *colectivos*) are the easiest and cheapest way to get to and around the Sacred Valley. They are often full of local color, if not much comfort. (Tall people forced to stand will not find them much fun.) Buses to towns and villages in the Sacred Valley—primarily to Pisac, Urubamba, and Chinchero—use small, makeshift terminals on Calle Puputi s/n, Cdra. 2 and Av. Grau s/n, Cdra. 1, in Cusco. They leave regularly throughout the day, departing when full; no advance reservations are required. Fares are S/3.

Nearly every Cusco travel agency offers a good-value, 1-day Sacred Valley tour (as little as $25, per person for a full-day guided tour), and most provide English-speaking guides. The tours tend to coincide with market days (Tues, Thurs, and Sun) and generally include Pisac, Ollantaytambo, and Chinchero. It's not enough time to explore the ruins, though a quickie tour gives at least a taste of the Valley's charms. An even better way to explore the Urubamba Valley, if you have the time, is to advance town by town toward Machu Picchu or vice versa, starting out from the great citadel and returning piecemeal toward Cusco. The first Sacred Valley visit on most itineraries is Pisac. *A caveat:* Although you will travel comfortably by chartered, air-conditioned bus and will not have to worry about connections, you won't be able to manage your time at each place (indeed, you'll have precious little time in each place—only enough for a quick look around and a visit to ruins or the local market).

You can also hire a taxi from Cusco to get to any of the valley towns or for a daylong tour of the Sacred Valley—expect to pay about S/90. Shared private cars *(autos)* to Urubamba leave from Calle Pavitos 567, with four passengers per car (they're generally station wagons with room for luggage in back and take just 50 min.) for just S/10 per person.

Beckoning at the end of the line, of course, is Machu Picchu. The most celebrated ruins in South America and a place that retains its mystery, allure, and spectacular beauty despite its enduring (and still growing!) popularity, Machu Picchu is one of the most dramatic places on earth, one that holds a mystical appeal for many Peruvians and visitors. The classic route to Machu Picchu is via the Camino Inca (Inca Trail), a marvel of sensitive development and religious appreciation for nature. Hiking the trail requires 4 days (or 2 days along the shorter, less traditional path) of pretty tough trekking across mountain passes, but the experience is unforgettable. Because of the overwhelming popularity of the Camino Inca, a number of alternative ruins treks, such as Choquequirao and Salcantay, have begun to attract attention for adventurers seeking solitude and authenticity. But if you don't have time or interest in walking and camping, the train to Machu Picchu nearly rivals the trail for scenic beauty, even if it doesn't provide the payoff of arriving shortly after sun-up as the mist begins to clear and rays of sunshine bathe the ruins.

32km (20 miles) NE of Cusco

The pretty Andean village of Pisac lies at the eastern end of the valley. Although the town is prized principally for its hugely popular Sunday artisan market, an obligatory stop on most Sacred Valley tours, Pisac deserves to be more widely recognized for its splendid Inca ruins, which rival those of Ollantaytambo and even Machu Picchu. Perched high on a cliff is the largest fortress complex built by the Incas. The commanding, distant views from atop the mountain, over a luxuriously long valley of green patchwork fields, are breathtaking.

ESSENTIALS
Getting There
The bus (*combi;* S/5) from Cusco (Calle Puputi s/n, Cdra. 2; no phone) to Pisac takes 45 minutes to an hour. Colectivos drop passengers just across the river at the edge of town, a 3-block walk uphill from the main square (and market). From Pisac, buses return to Cusco and depart for other parts of the valley—Yucay, Urubamba (both a half-hour journey), and Ollantaytambo (1 hr.)—from the same spot.

Although a taxi to Pisac on your own costs about S/35, it is often possible to go by private car for as little as S/10 per person. Private cars congregate near the bus terminal and leave when they have three or four passengers; just get in and ask the price (everyone pays the same fare).

Visitor Information
You're best off getting information on Pisac and the entire Sacred Valley before leaving Cusco at the **Tourist Information Office,** Mantas 117-A, a block from the Plaza de Armas (*©* **084/263-176**) or the **iPéru office,** Av. El Sol 103, Of. 102 (*©* **084/252-974**). Cusco's **South American Explorers Club** (*©* **084/245-484**) is also an excellent source of information, particularly on the Inca Trail and alternative treks, mountaineering, and white-water rafting in the valley. Inquire there about current conditions and updated transportation alternatives. Beyond that, the best sources of information are hotels.

Though you'll find an ATM on the main square, it's probably wise to exchange much of the money you'll need before leaving Cusco (especially if coming on Sun to the crowded market). There's a post office on the corner of Comercio and Intihuatana.

ⓘ Tips   Boleto Turístico in the Valle Sagrado

The Cusco *boleto turístico* (tourist pass) is pretty much essential for visiting the Sacred Valley, in particular for the ruins of Pisac and Ollantaytambo, as well as the market and town of Chinchero. You can purchase it at any of those places if you haven't already bought it in Cusco before traveling to the Valley. You can purchase the partial ticket that just covers the Sacred Valley sites if you aren't planning to make use of the full ticket in Cusco. See p. 216 in chapter 8 for more information.

The Market

Pisac's famed **artisans' and antiques market** ★ draws many hundreds of shoppers on Sunday morning in high season, when it is without a doubt one of the liveliest in Peru. (There are slightly less popular markets on Tues and Thurs as well.) Hundreds of stalls crowd the central square—marked by a small church, San Pedro el Apóstolo, and massive *pisonay* trees—and spill down side streets. Sellers come from many different villages, many of them remote populations high in the Andes, and wear the dress typical of their village. Dignitaries from the local villages usually lead processions after Mass (said in Quechua), dressed in their versions of Sunday finery. The market is much like Cusco: rather touristy, though endearing and an essential experience in Peru. Even if you're not a committed shopper, it's an event. If you're never been to a Peruvian market, this is the place to start, though the market at Chinchero (p. 254) strikes me as considerably more authentic.

The goods for sale at the market—largely sweaters and ponchos, tapestries and rugs, musical instruments, and carved gourds—are familiar to anyone who's spent a day in Cusco, but prices are occasionally lower on selected goods such as ceramics. While tourists shop for colorful weavings and other souvenirs, locals are busy buying and selling produce on small streets leading off the plaza. The market begins at around 9am and lasts until midafternoon. It is so well-worn on the Cusco tourist circuit that choruses of, *"¿Foto? Propinita,"* (photograph for a tip) ring out among the mothers and would-be mothers who come here to show off their children, dressed up in adorable local outfits. On nonmarket days, bustling Pisac becomes a very quiet, little-visited village with few activities to engage travelers.

The Pisac Ruins ★★

The Pisac ruins are some of the finest and largest in the entire valley. Despite the excellent condition of many of the structures, little is conclusively known about the site's actual purpose. It appears to have been part city, part ceremonial center, and part military complex. It might have been a royal estate of the Inca emperor (Pachacútec). It was certainly a religious temple, and although it was reinforced with the ramparts of a massive citadel, the Incas never retreated here to defend their empire against the Spaniards (and Pisac was, unlike Machu Picchu, known to Spanish forces).

The best but most time-consuming way to see the ruins is to climb the hillside, following an extraordinary path that is itself a slice of local life. Trudging along steep mountain paths is still the way most Quechua descendants from remote villages get around these parts; many people you see at the Pisac market will have walked a couple of hours or more through the mountains to get there. To get to the ruins on foot (about 5km/3 miles, or 60 min.), you'll need to be pretty fit and/or willing to take it very slowly. Begin the ascent at the back of Pisac's main square, to the left of the church. (If you

---

Moments   The Virgen del Carmen Festival

Pisac celebrates the Virgen del Carmen festival (July 16–18) with nearly as much enthusiasm as the more remote and more famous festival in Paucartambo (p. 235). It's well worth visiting Pisac during the festival if you are in the area.

haven't already purchased a *boleto turístico,* required for entrance, you can do so at the small guard's office at the beginning of the path as you climb out of town.) The path bends to the right through agricultural terraces. There appear to be several competing paths; all of them lead up the mountain to the ruins. When you come to a section that rises straight up, choose the extremely steep stairs to the right. (The path to the left is overgrown and poorly defined.) If an arduous trek is more than you've bargained for, you can hire a taxi in Pisac (easier done on market days) to take you around the back way. (The paved road is some 9.5km/6 miles long.) If you arrive by car or colectivo rather than by your own power, the ruins will be laid out the opposite of the way they are described below.

From a semicircular terrace and fortified section at the top, called the **Qori-huayrachina,** the views south and west of the gorge and valley below and agricultural terraces creeping up the mountain slopes are stunning. Deeper into the nucleus, the delicately cut stones are some of the best found at any Inca site. The most important component of the complex, on a plateau on the upper section of the ruins, is the **Templo del Sol (Temple of the Sun),** one of the Incas' most impressive examples of masonry. The temple was an astronomical observatory. The **Intihuatana,** the so-called "hitching post of the sun," resembles a sundial but actually was an instrument that helped the Incas to determine the arrival of important growing seasons rather than to tell the time of day. Sadly, this section is now closed to the public, due to vandals who destroyed part of it a few years ago. Nearby (just paces to the west) is another temple, thought to be the **Templo de la Luna (Temple of the Moon),** and beyond that is a ritual bathing complex, fed by water canals. Continuing north from this section, you can either ascend a staircase path uphill, which forks, or pass along the eastern (right) edge of the cliff. If you do the latter, you'll arrive at a tunnel that leads to a summit lookout at 3,400m (11,200 ft.). A series of paths leads from here to defensive ramparts **(K'alla Q'asa),** a ruins sector called **Qanchisracay,** and the area where taxis wait to take passengers back to Pisac.

In the hillside across the Quitamayo gorge, at the back side (north end) of the ruins, are hundreds of dug-out holes where *huaqueros* (grave robbers) have ransacked a cemetery that was among the largest known Inca burial sites.

The ruins are open daily from 7am to 5:30pm; admission is by Cusco's *boleto turístico* (p. 216). Note that to explore the ruins thoroughly by foot, including the climb from Pisac, you'll need 3 to 4 hours. Most people visit Pisac as part of a whirlwind day tour through the valley, which doesn't allow enough time either at the market or to visit the ruins. Taxis leave from the road near the bridge and charge around S/15 to take you up to the ruins.

WHERE TO STAY

If either of the two places below is full or beyond your budget, check out these inexpensive basic inns in town: **Hospedaje Buho,** Intihuatana 642, Camino Ruinas (© 084/203-001), on a side street near the main square, with rooms (even a few with private bathrooms) around a central patio and an *artesanía* shop; or **Kinsa Cocha Hospedaje,** Arequipa 307 (© 084/203-101), a family-run place with clean dorm rooms near the main plaza.

Hotel Pisaq ★ (Value) Owned by a friendly Peruvian-American couple, this small, pleasant, and central inn is a superb option in town. Located right on the main square in Pisac (the sign outdoors says "Pisac Inn"), it features nicely decorated rooms full of Andean textiles, murals hand-painted by the owners, a sauna, and an attractive courtyard

Extreme Sacred Valley: Outdoor Adventure Sports

Peru has become a star on South America's burgeoning adventure and extreme sports travel circuit, a far cry from the days when just traveling to Peru was adventure enough. These days, many gringos in Peru have Gore-Tex boots on their feet and adrenaline rushes on their minds.

The Cusco–Sacred Valley region is one of the best in Peru—and the whole of South America—for white-water rafting, mountain biking, trekking, hang gliding, and paragliding.

Many tour operators in Cusco organize adventure trips, some lasting a single day and some lasting multiple days, with a focus on one or more extreme sports. Participants range from novices to hard-core veteran adventure junkies; no experience is required for many trips, but make sure you sign up for a program appropriate for your level of interest and ability. Extreme sports being what they are, I suggest that you thoroughly check out potential agencies and speak directly to the guides, if possible. Booking a tour in Cusco rather than your home country may lead to a large discount. Trips booked in advance may be changed if there are not enough participants or farmed out to another, subcontracting, agency.

Bungee Jumping   New to the Sacred Valley (and as far as I know, Peru) is this favorite activity of thrill-seekers the world over. **Action Valley Cusco Adventure Park,** Calle Santa Teresa 325 (Plazoleta Regocijo), Cusco (✆ **084/240-835;** www.actionvalley.com) is an adventure park 11km (7mi) from Cusco, with not just bungee jumping but paintball and other suspended line activities, such as "swing" and "slingshot."

Horseback Riding   **Perol Chico,** Carretera Urubamba-Ollantaytambo Km 77, Urubamba (✆ **01/994-147-267** or 084/984-624-475; www.perolchico.com), is a ranch in the Sacred Valley and one of the top horseback-riding agencies in Peru. It offers full riding vacations, with Peruvian Paso horses and stays at the ranch (in rustic cottages), as well as 1- and 2-day rides.

Hot-Air Ballooning & Paragliding   Now that you can no longer hop a helicopter to Machu Picchu, there are other, less intrusive ways to get aerial views of the Sacred Valley. **Aero Sports Club of the Sacred Valley,** Av. de la Cultura 220, Ste. 36 (✆ **084/232-352;** www.globosperu.com), run by an American, Jeff Hall is the only outfit organizing such trips. If you've got the money (ballooning isn't cheap, no matter where you do it) and you want aerial panoramas of the Sacred Valley, Inca ruins, and the majestic Andes, contact Aero Sports Club to verify current flight programs. You might also check around Cusco for posters advertising tandem paraglide flights over the Sacred Valley.

Mountain Biking   Mountain biking has started to catch on in Peru, and tour operators are rapidly expanding their services and equipment. Cusco's nearby ruins and the towns, villages, and gorgeous scenery of the Sacred Valley (and the Manu jungle, for more adventurous excursions) are the best areas. **Peru Discovery,** Santa Maria F-3, San Sebastian, Cusco (✆ **054/274-541;** www. perudiscovery.com) is one of the top specialists, with a half-dozen bike trips that include hard-core excursions. **Amazonas Explorer, Apumayo Expedicio-nes, Eric Adventures, Instinct Travel** (for contact information, see "White-Water Rafting," below), and **Manu Adventures,** Plateros 356, Cusco (✆ **084/ 261-640;** or 213/283-6987 in the U.S. or Canada; www.manuadventures.com), all offer 1- to 5-day organized mountain-biking excursions ranging from easy to rigorous. For a great locally based group, including mountain bike rentals and extended as well as shorter cyclotourism rides around Urubamba, with top equipment, contact Omar Zarzar at **Eco Montana** (www.ecomontana.com). If you're anything close to hard-core, Omar's your guy in the Sacred Valley.

Trekking   Too many highland-trekking adventures are offered to fully describe here. In addition to the groups listed in "Inca Trail Tour Agencies" (p. 278) and "The Road Less (or More Comfortably) Traveled: Alternatives to the Inca Trail," on p. 280, which organize Inca Trail and other regional treks, the following companies handle a wide variety of trekking excursions: **Apuandino Expedi-ciones,** Calle Tupac Katari, San Sebastian, Cusco (✆ **084/274-789;** www. apuandino-expeditions.com); **Aventours,** Saphi 456, Cusco (✆ **084/224-050;** www.ecoinka.com); **Enigma,** Jirón Clorinda Matto de Turner, 100 Urbanización Magisterial 1 Etapa, Cusco (✆ **084/221-155;** www.enigmaperu.com); **Manu Expeditions,** Clorinda Matto de Turner 330, Urbanizacion Magisterial Primero Etapa, Cusco (✆ **084/225-990;** www.manuexpeditions.com); and U.S.-based **Andean Treks** ★★ (✆ 800/683-8148 or 617/924-1974; www.andeantreks. com); and **Peru for Less** ★★(✆ 877/2609-0309; www.peruforless.com). **Peru Discovery** (see "Mountain Biking," above) also organizes excellent trekking expeditions, and Chalo, the Chilean-born owner of the cool ecostyled lodge **Las Chullpas** in Urubamba (p. 250), leads small-group treks into nearby ranges.

White-Water Rafting   There are some terrific Andean river runs near Cusco, ranging from mild Class II to moderate and world-Class IV and V, including 1-day Urubamba River trips (Huambutío-Pisac and Ollantaytambo-Chillca), multiday trips to the more difficult Apurímac River, and, for hard-core rafters, the Tambopata (10 days or more) in the Amazon jungle. Recommended agen-cies include **Amazonas Explorer** ★★Av. Collasuyo 910, Urb. Miravalle, Cusco (✆ 084/252-846; www.amazonas-explorer.com); **Apumayo Expediciones,** Jr. Ricardo Palma N-5, Santa Mónica, Wanchaq, Cusco (✆ 084/246-018; www. apumayo.com); **Eric Adventures,** Urb. Velasco Astete B-8-B, Cusco (✆ 084/234-764; www.ericadventures.com); **Instinct Tour Operator,** Av. de la Cultura 1318, Cusco (✆ 084/233-451; www.instinct-travel.com); **Loreto Tours,** Calle del Medio 111, Cusco (✆ 084/228-264; www.loretotours.com); **Mayuc,** Portal Con-fiturías 211, Plaza de Armas, Cusco (✆ 084/242-824; www.mayuc.com); and **Swissraft Peru** ★ Heraderos 129 (✆ 084/264-124; www.swissraft-peru.com).

Ziplining   Claiming to be the highest zipline in South America, Cola de Mono Canopy (✆ **084/792-413;** www.canopyperu.com), offers exciting high-wire zipping of up to 60 kmph through the lush treetops in Santa Teresa, 15 km (9mi) from Machu Picchu.

with flowers. The hotel also operates a small bar/restaurant with good pizza from a wood-burning oven and home-cooked meals.

Plaza Constitución 333, Pisac. (℃)/fax **084/203-062.** www.hotelpisaq.com. 11 units. $50–$65 double with private bathroom; $40–$45 with shared bathroom. No credit cards. **Amenities:** Restaurant; bar; sauna. *In room:* No phone.

Paz y Luz ★ (Finds)   About a 20-minute walk from the village along a road up to the Inca ruins is this convivial B&B and healing center run by a woman from New York, Diane Dunn, author of the book Cusco: Gateway to Inner Wisdom. It spells out its mission in the name: Peace and Light (also the names of the two dogs that make their home at the inn). Andean healing workshops, meditation, and sacred-plant ceremonies (administered by Javier, a Swiss national of Spanish descent) are a good part of the attraction for guests interested in the Sacred Valley's spiritual offerings and self-exploration, though plenty of guests come simply for the restful spirit and perhaps a massage—treating it as a relaxed country inn. Rooms are in comfortable and colorful adobe bungalows with thick blankets, high ceilings, and splendid views of the Pisac ruins and surrounding valley.

Carretera Pisac Ruinas s/n (℃) **084/203-204.** www.pazyluzperu.com. 86 units. S/160 double; S/220 suite (weekly and monthly rates also available). Rates include taxes and continental breakfast. AE, DC, MC, V. **Amenities:** Massage; healing workshops and sacred plant ceremonies. *In room:* No phone.

WHERE TO DINE

For eats in Pisac, check out **Ulrike's Café**★, Plaza de Armas 828 ((℃) **084/203-195**), a relaxed spot on the main square. Run by a German expat, Ulrike's is a genial and inexpensive place for any meal, from breakfast to hearty lunches and vegetarian options, such as homemade lasagna, omelets, salads, and great desserts (like Ulrike's famous strudel or any number of cheesecakes). It serves a great-value lunch menu (S/18, for a three-course meal). For a snack or lunch on the run, check out the excellent *hornos coloniales* (colonial bakeries), which use traditional, wood-fired ovens; one, called Santa Lucía, is on the corner of the main square next to Hotel Pisaq, while the other (unnamed) on Mariscal Castilla 372, a short walk from the plaza. Both serve excellent empanadas and breads, and are especially popular on market days (often selling out of empanadas by 2pm). Another good lunch or dinner option is **Ayahuasca,** Bolognesi s/n ((℃) **084/797-625**), a cute little cafe a couple blocks from the Plaza, on the way to the bus stops. You can get a simply prepared but very good-value menu (lomo saltado and other classic Peruvian highlander dishes) for just S/10.

SHOPPING

Of course the thrice-weekly market in Pisca gets all the attention, but one personal favorite shop is **La Casa del Té y Arte,** next to Ulrike's Café right on the Plaza de Armas ((℃) **084/984-730-862**), which features the uniquely designed felt slippers and funky hats made by hand by an Austrian woman and her Peruvian husband. Both items make great gifts.

2 URUBAMBA & ENVIRONS ★★

78km (48 miles) NW of Cusco

Centrally located Urubamba, a transportation hub, is the busiest of the Sacred Valley towns and the best equipped to handle visitors. The town itself doesn't have a whole lot more than a handsome main plaza and a few restaurants to offer, but the surrounding region is lovely, and several of the best hotels in the region are located within a radius of **247** a few miles, either just south near Yucay, an attractive colonial village, or north on the road toward Ollantaytambo. The area as a whole makes a fine base from which to explore the Sacred Valley.

ESSENTIALS
Getting There
BY BUS   To Urubamba (1½–2 hr. from Cusco), you can go either via Pisac or via Chinchero (a slightly more direct route). Buses, or combis (S/5), depart from Av. Grau s/n, Cdra. 1, in Cusco and arrive at **Terminal Terrestre** (no phone), the main bus terminal, about a kilometer (½ mile) from town on the main road to Ollantaytambo. Buses from the Urubamba terminal depart for Cusco and Chinchero (1 hr.), as well as Ollantaytambo (30 min.). Combis for other points in the Sacred Valley depart from the intersection of the main road at Avenida Castilla. To continue on to Yucay, just a couple of kilometers down the road, catch a mototaxi or a regular taxi in Urubamba or a colectivo along the highway (headed east, the opposite direction of the bus terminal from town).

BY TAXI   From Cusco, you can catch a cab to Urubamba for about S/70. Shared cars in Cusco leave from Calle Pavitos 567 for Urubamba; they charge just S/10 per person and take about an hour. If you're headed directly to the Valley upon arrival in Cusco, have your hotel arrange for pickup at the airport. If it's a market day, you can easily arrange for the driver to take you to Pisac or Chinchero for a brief stopover along the way. For taxi or minivan trips around the Valley, try **Roberto Angles Ochoa** (© 084/984-752-565).

Visitor Information
You should pick up information on the Sacred Valley before leaving Cusco, at the main **Tourist Information Office,** Mantas 117-A, a block from the Plaza de Armas (© 084/263-176); iPerú Av. El Sol 103, Of. 102 (© 084/252-974), or from Cusco's **South American Explorers Club** (© 084/245-484). In Urubamba, you might be able to scare up some limited assistance at Av. Cabo Conchatupa s/n; in Yucay, try the office of **Turismo Participativo,** Plaza Manco II 103 (© 084/201-099).

FAST FACTS   If you need cash, you'll find ATMs on either side of the main road to Yucay from Urubamba. For medical assistance, go to **Centro de Salud,** Av. Cabo Conchatupa s/n (© 084/201-334), or **Hospital del Instituto Peruano de Seguridad Social,** Av. 9 de Noviembre s/n (© 084/201-032).

Urubamba is the best spot for Internet *cabinas* in the Sacred Valley region, with a good supply of machines and fast connections all around town. **Academia Internet Urubamba** (no phone), established with the help of an American exchange student, is 2 blocks northeast of the Plaza de Armas, on the corner of Jirón Belén and Jirón Grau. There are also a couple of Internet cabinas on the main square. If you need a post office in Urubamba, you'll also find one on the Plaza de Armas.

WHAT TO SEE & DO
The main square of Urubamba, the **Plaza de Armas,** is attractively framed by a twin-towered colonial church and pisonay trees. Dozens of *mototaxis*, a funky form of local transportation not seen in other places in the valley (and widely seen in only a few other places in Peru), buzz around the plaza in search of passengers. Worth visiting in town is the beautiful home workshop of **Pablo Seminario** ★ , a ceramicist whose whimsical

work features pre-Columbian motifs and is sold throughout Peru. Visitors either love or hate the style, which was once sold by Pier 1 Imports in the U.S. The grounds of the house, located at Berriozábal 111 (© **084/201-002;** www.ceramicaseminario.com), feature a minizoo, with llamas, parrots, nocturnal monkeys, falcons, rabbits, and more. The workshop is open Monday through Saturday from 10am to 6pm. Seminario now has shops in the Sonesta Posadas del Inca hotel in Yucay as well as Cusco. **Lanandina** ★ (© **084/201-390;** call for directions), operated by an Austrian resident of Urubamba, makes fantastic handmade wool house shoes, bags, and hats using a centuries-old Mongolian formula (there's also a shop in Pisaq on the main square, **Casa del Arte y Te,** where you can find the slippers and hats).

Yucay, just south of Urubamba, is a pleasant and quiet little village with extraordinary views of the surrounding countryside. The Spaniards "bequeathed" the land to their puppet Inca chieftain, Sayri Tupac, who built a palace here. Inca foundations are found around the attractive **main plaza,** and some of the best agricultural terracing in the valley occupies the slopes of mountains around the village. Worthwhile side trips from Urubamba and Yucay are the ancient Inca salt pans of Maras or the Inca site at Moray; see "Beyond Urubamba," below, for additional information.

WHERE TO STAY

This section of the Sacred Valley continues to attract hoteliers and developers, who all seem intent on adding new country luxury resort hotels—a sure sign of the region's growing importance and affluence, at least in terms of foreign travelers. A simpler, in-town alternative to the more upscale hotels reviewed below is the pleasant and good-value **Posada Las Tres Marías,** Jr. Zavala 307, Urubamba (© **084/201-006** or 984-650-225; www.posadatresmarias.com), a modern house in the center of town with gardens and seven large rooms (doubles $50).

Very Expensive

Aranwa Sacred Valley ★★★ (Kids) Sacred Valley hotels have been trending upscale for the last few years, but this extraordinary new (2009) property, part of a small Peruvian hotel group begun by a Lima doctor, takes it to an entirely new level–and has instantly vaulted to the top of the heap among country hotels in Peru. Well conceived and picturesquely located, it has so much to offer that it may preclude some guests from exploring the Valley! The sprawling complex, part of which was originally a 17th-century hacienda, contains a lake, riverside trails, a movie theater, colonial chapel, art gallery, beautifully landscaped grounds, and massive luxe spa. The spacious, elegant accommodations feature lovely antique pieces and are divided by small "villages": colonial manor house rooms and modern rooms and suites on the bank of the river and lake (suites have kitchenettes and Jacuzzis). And while it may seem a bit over the top for some, in the rustic, peaceful Sacred Valley, it is leagues removed from your typical, faceless all-inclusive resort; in fact, it blends nicely with its rustic surroundings. It's a luxury country estate hotel, with a ton of services and attractions. For all it offers, at least for now, it is a good value at the high end, and deals can be found through the hotel Website.

Antigua Hacienda Yaravilca, Huayllabamba. © **01/434-1452** for reservations, or 084/205-080. Fax 01/434-6199. www.aranwahotels.com. 115 units. $225–$250 double; $400 and up suite. Rates include breakfast buffet. AE, DC, MC, V. **Amenities:** 3 restaurants; bar; concierge; exercise room; outdoor pool; spa; theater. *In room:* TV, fridge, Wi-Fi.

Ticllabamba Maison d'Hôtes ★★ (Finds) A tiny, hidden gem in the mountains above Yucay, surrounded by terraces built by the Inca Huayna Capac, this restored colonial

farm has been converted into a tiny and intimate luxury country "homestay" by a Peruvian former top model, Suzy Dyson. The property, built on a 16th-century Royal Inca estate, is an exclusive and out-of-the-way retreat (perfect for adventurous and discerning travelers looking for something different in the Sacred Valley). Ms. Dyson describes it as a *maison de charme* rather than a hotel; decorated with breezy, personal style, it has just two elegant rooms, with furniture designed by Suzy herself and linens and carpets handmade by local artisans. Nestled among the ancient Inca terraces are a cold plunge pool and Jacuzzi, as well as an Andean steam sauna.

Camino a Vinopata, Yucay. © **01/999-352-664.** www.aracari.com/hotels/ticllabamba-maison-dhotes-cuzco-cuzco-area.html. 4 units. $280 double. Rates include breakfast and light dinner. AE, MC, V. **Amenities:** Jacuzzi; plunge pool; sauna.

Expensive

Casa Andina Private Collection ★★ (Kids) One of the upstart Casa Andina group's select upscale offerings, this large, mountain-chalet type hotel is very professionally run and has a beautiful setting, with abundant gardens and excellent views of the countryside. Rooms are large and handsomely decorated, with high ceilings and spacious bathrooms; the two-story suites with balconies are especially enticing. The hotel features a very good, though occasionally boisterous restaurant, a spectacular full-service Andean-styled spa—one of the finest I've seen in Peru—and even a planetarium and observatory for stargazing in the huge, clear sky, making this an excellent retreat for sybarites, families, and groups of diverse size. A full range of activities, such as river rafting, trekking, mountain biking, and horseback riding, is offered.

Quinto paradero, Yanahuara. © **084/984-765-501.** Fax 01/445-4775. www.casa-andina.com. 85 units. $125–$185 double; $295 suite. Rates include breakfast buffet. AE, DC, MC, V. **Amenities:** Restaurant; concierge; exercise room; room service; spa. *In room:* TV, fridge, Wi-Fi.

Libertador Valle Sagrado Lodge ★ (Finds) This intimate and charming—if rather isolated—lodge feels more like an inn than hotel. It's constructed like a small colonial village with individual buildings of stucco and red-tile rooms, and gardens with fountains and trickling canals strewn throughout the property. Its elevated and secluded location provides fantastic mountain and valley views and makes it an excellent place to get away from it all (though you'll still be very close to Ollantaytambo and Machu Picchu). It's not ideal if you're planning on dashing about the Sacred Valley too much, since getting in and out requires a taxi for all but the hardiest walkers. However, if it's peace and quiet you seek, it's hard to do better at this level. Double rooms (with either mountain or garden views) are spacious, warmly decorated, and nicely distributed among the grounds. Given its small size, it hosts individuals and very small groups only.

Quinto paradero, Yanahuara (sector Pucará). © **084/201-408.** Fax 084/812-895. www.vallesagrado lodge.com. 16 units. $130 double. Rates include breakfast buffet. AE, DC, MC, V. **Amenities:** Restaurant; lounge; room service. *In room:* TV, hair dryer, minibar, safe.

Sol y Luna Lodge & Spa ★ (Kids) The continually expanding Sol y Luna is one of the more attractive properties in the valley. Though the hotel has many fans, travelers may find that they can do as well or better at one of its newer competitors. Set back from the main road on the way to Ollantaytambo, amid spectacularly landscaped gardens, the French- and Swiss-owned cluster of invitingly decorated, circular bungalow-style rooms (including four family bungalows) comes with rustic decor, private terraces, and gorgeous mountain views. The hotel has a nice but rather small outdoor pool, a super-sleek restaurant and pub, appealing spa, and horse stables. New for 2010 are five superluxe suites.

Ctra. Urubamba-Ollantaytambo s/n, Huicho (2km/1¼ miles west of Urubamba). ✆ **084/201-620.** Fax 084/201-084. www.hotelsolyluna.com. 33 units. $235 double; $245 family bungalow. Rates include breakfast buffet. AE, DC, MC, V. **Amenities:** Restaurant; pub; small pool; room service; tennis court. *In room:* TV.

Moderate

K'uychi Rumi ★ (**Kids**) (**Finds**) One of the more interesting and relaxing, if least pronounceable, lodging options in the Sacred Valley, this property isn't a hotel, per se. It's a complex of a half-dozen condos: rustic two-story, two-bedroom adobe houses, individually owned and rented when the owners aren't around (which is most of the time). The houses are connected by walkways and gardens, and all have excellent mountain views. For a couple who wants a bit of space, privacy, a kitchen, and a great fireplace, it's perfect. It's also a bargain for families or two couples who occupy the whole house. The architect who built the houses lives on-site with his wife and administers the property; their quartet of dogs is liable to be on your front porch in the morning, waiting for you to emerge. A buffet breakfast is extra (S/25), and there's no restaurant on the premises (although there are several restaurants nearby, and Urubamba is just up the road). Still, if you're looking for a serene retreat, this might be it.

Carretera Urubamba-Ollantaytambo s/n, Urubamba. ✆/fax **084/201-169.** www.urubamba.com. 6 units. S/430 double; S/720 family bungalow (4 people). AE, DC, MC, V. *In room:* Kitchen, fridge.

✓Sonesta Posadas del Inca Sacred Valley ★★ (**Kids**) This handsome ranch-style hotel, recently updated, remains one of the best in the valley, even as its high-end competition has grown. Originally a monastery in the late 1600s and then a hacienda, it was converted into an atmospheric colonial-village-like complex with mountain views and relaxed comfort in 1982. The grounds feature a chapel brought in whole from a provincial town, nice gardens, a good restaurant, and a cool little museum with ancient ceramics and textiles. Room no. 115 in the old section is a nice loft space, and room no. 312 has fantastic windows and superior views. It recently added a nice spa with massages, yoga, sauna, outdoor Jacuzzi, and other treatments. There are mountain bikes for guests' use; and lots of excursion and soft-adventure programs, including rafting, mountain biking, horseback riding, and trips to the salt pans of Maras or the Inca site at Moray, are offered.

Plaza Manco II de Yucay 123, Yucay. ✆ **084/201-107,** or 01/222-4777 for reservations (800/SONESTA [766-3782] in the U.S. and Canada). Fax 084/201-345. www.sonesta.com. 84 units. $109–$180 double; $150–$250 suite. Rates includes breakfast buffet. AE, DC, MC, V. **Amenities:** Restaurant; bar; lounge; spa. *In room:* TV, fridge.

Inexpensive

Las Chullpas Ecolodge ★ (**Finds**) This self-described "ecological guesthouse" is the sort of place you'd expect to find in the Amazon cloud forest rather than the Sacred Valley. It's a funky, and fun, place to stay, with a bohemian feel but enough creature comforts (including, importantly, great hot showers) for all but the most demanding guests. That being said, it's mostly a place for young and young-at-heart people. Run by a young Chilean and his German ex-wife (a midwife who works with *campesina* women from the countryside), the nine rooms are connected huts that have the feel of tree forts, but with an abundance of artisanal style, including comfortable beds, stovepipe heaters, and hand-painted, glazed tiles in the bathrooms. Profits from the huge suite go toward Leonie's midwifery practice—making it the perfect, feel-good splurge. The inn is secluded, up a long dirt road 3km (2 miles) from Urubamba. Chalo prepares excellent organic and vegetarian meals in the cozy, fireplace-warmed dining room. He's sensitive to the ecological impact of tourism and questions of sustainable development in the region, and **251** he's also a great mountain guide, who runs multiday treks into the Urubamba mountain range (visit www.peru.uhupi.com for info).

Gonzalo Múnoz s/n. (© **084/201-568.** www.chullpas.uhupi.com. 9 units. $50 double; $70 suite. Rates include breakfast buffet. No credit cards. **Amenities:** Restaurant. *In room:* No phone, Wi-Fi.

The Green House Hotel ★★ (Finds) A unique, secluded B&B at the edge of the Sacred Valley, this terrifically relaxing inn, run by an Englishman and his Argentine partner (who live on the grounds), features extensive gardens with great mountain views; a soaring, wall-of-glass living space with a fireplace—ideal for reading, relaxing and meeting other travelers—and simple, cozy rooms with attractive tiled bathrooms. In the less-traveled section of the Valley, Huarán (11km/7 miles from Urubamba), it's the kind of place I could easily see hanging out at for many more days than I'd originally planned to stay in the region. Gabriel, the Argentine, prepares delicious home-cooked meals in the evenings, the three dogs keep visitors company in the gardens and on walking trails leading from the property, and hiking, rafting, horseback riding, and biking tours can be arranged.

Carretera, Km 60, Pisac-Ollantaytambo, Calca. (© **084/984-770-130.** www.thegreenhouseperu.com. 4 units. S/150 double. Rates include breakfast. No credit cards. **Amenities:** Restaurant, video lounge. *In room:* No phone, Wi-Fi.

WHERE TO DINE

Because so many hotels are scattered about the Urubamba region, and somewhat isolated, many guests, especially at the upscale accommodations in the region, dine at their hotels; the major ones listed above (Casa Andina, Libertador, and Sonesta) all have very good restaurants. Perhaps best for drop-ins is the fine—but pricey for the area—restaurant of Sol y Luna Lodge & Spa (p. 249). Its restaurant **Wayra** is a two-story space with an open fireplace and pub on the second floor, and it serves very nicely prepared *criollo* and Nouveau Andean specialties, including *ají de gallina* (spicy, creamy chicken) and stuffed river trout, as well as fresh pastas. The restaurant's new incarnation has gone very upscale and gourmet, with wine-pairing dinners and the like. Call for reservations because the restaurant is often full with hotel guests.

However, easily the best and coolest restaurant in the Urubamba area is right in town: **El Huacatay** ★★★, Jr. Arica 620 (© **084/201-790;** www.elhuacatay.com), popular with both wealthier Peruvians and visiting gringos. A few blocks from the main square, this surprising gourmet restaurant, in an old home built around a garden set back from a nondescript Urubamba street, is the perfect place for a long, relaxing lunch on the patio under bamboo shade or a more elegant dinner in the warm, intimate dining room (which has only five tables) or brightly colored lounge area. Run by a Peruvian chef, Pío, and his German wife Iris, the restaurant's chef-driven menu is a bit of a rarity in these parts, and it focuses on Andean specialties, such as quinoa soup, alpaca lasagna, and coca-infused (but street-legal!) gnocchi. Portions are large and attractively presented, and although fairly priced for the setting, service, and quality, the restaurant is more upscale than most in the area. Open Monday to Saturday from 2 to 10pm, the restaurant accepts only cash and Visa cards; reservations on weekends and evenings are recommended.

Another unique Valle restaurant for fine dining is **Huayoccari Hacienda Restaurant** ★★, Carretera Cusco-Urubamba, Km 64 (© **084/962-2224** or 084/226-241 in Cusco), several miles southeast of Urubamba. The restaurant, in an exceedingly elegant farmhouse high in the hills above the Sacred Valley, is tough to make reservations at and hard to find. (It works almost exclusively with tour agencies such as **Lima Tours,** *C* **01/424-5110,** to arrange lunches and dinners; if you're not with a group, it's worth having your hotel call to see if it's possible to get in and get directions.) The $35 (cash only) prix-fixe menu starts with a pisco sour in the antique-filled common room or out among the gardens. Then diners, who feel as though they belong to an exclusive club, are admitted to the wood-paneled dining room—which has large picture windows framing views of the Andes—for a simple but well-prepared meal of local vegetables, soups (such as *crema de maiz*), and fresh river trout. The place is rather emphatically designed to feel like one is a guest in the home of a local agricultural patron (and in fact, the home and restaurant belong to the Orihuela family, one of the valley's most distinguished, and oldest, families).

Several restaurants are scattered about the main valley highway and cater to groups that storm through the Sacred Valley three times a week on market day. **Tunupa,** Km 77, Carretera Pisaq-Ollantaytambo (on the left side of the road on the way to Ollanta; *C* **084/963-0206**), owned by the same folks who own the restaurant of the same name in Cusco, is one of the most popular. In a massive, purpose-built hacienda with long corridors that form dining halls overlooking the Urubamba River, it's something akin to a Peruvian bier hall. It must seat at least 300 diners, and it's all buffet, all the time. Even though it can get crowded on market days at lunchtime, it's a fair value for an all-you-can-eat buffet for $15, including a pisco sour. Even better is **Alhambra ★**, Ctra. Urubamba-Ollantaytambo s/n (near Hotel Sol y Luna; *C* **084/201-200**), also a hacienda-style restaurant targeting bus tours, but in a more relaxed and intimate manner. The dining rooms are smaller, and there are tables outdoors under a thatched roof, with lovely garden and mountain views. Its buffets are only on market days (Tues, Thurs, and Sat). At other times, the three-course *menu turístico* ($15) is excellent; choose main courses such as stuffed lake trout with quinoa in a nut sauce.

On the main road going toward Yucay, **Quinta Los Geranios,** Av. Cabo Conchatupa s/n (*C* **084/201-093**), is a pretty good open-air restaurant set around a garden. It gets hit midday with tour buses but still manages to concoct fine versions of Peruvian standards such as *rocoto relleno* (stuffed hot peppers) and a number of indigenous soups. The three-course lunch *menu* is a good value. A similar tourist-group restaurant across the street is **El Maizal,** Av. Cabo Conchatupa s/n (*C* **084/201-054**); it offers a buffet lunch and has both indoor and outdoor seating.

In Urubamba itself, **The Muse Too,** Plaza de Armas (at the corner of Comercio and Grau; *C* **084/201-280**), a sister establishment of the San Blas bar The Muse, in Cusco, is a low-key two-story pub/restaurant with a single corner balcony upstairs. It features good soups, sandwiches, and lasagna, as well as breakfast all day. At night, it operates more as a bar than restaurant, focusing on its long list of martinis and specialty drinks. For good pizzas from a wood-fired oven and pastas, or cocktails downstairs, try **The Green House** (not related to the inn, above), Jirón Arica at Comercio (no phone; www.greenhouseurubamba.com).

URUBAMBA AFTER DARK

The Muse Too ★ (see "Where to Dine" above) is a nice spot for laid-back cocktails and the camaraderie of international travelers. A groovy bar also in Urubamba is **Inti Killa,** Av. Grau 708 (no phone), which sounds as though it could be named for a Peruvian rap star (though the word "Killa" is Quechua for house). About a block from the main square, the bar/club has hip dance beats, a large dance floor separate from the bar and a lounge area, and good pitchers of pisco sours.

Salineras De Maras ★★
10km (6 miles) NW of Urubamba

Near Urubamba (about 6km/3½ miles down the main road toward Ollantaytambo but from there only accessible by foot) is the amazing sight of the **Salineras de Maras** (also called Salinas), thousands of individual ancient salt mines that form unique terraces in a hillside. The mines, small pools thickly coated with crystallized salt like dirty snow, have existed in the same spot since Inca days and are still operable. Families pass them down like deeds and continue the backbreaking and poorly remunerated tradition of salt extraction (crystallizing salt from subterranean spring water). Although the site as a whole is extraordinary and photogenic—from afar it looks like a patchwork quilt spread over a ravine, or some sort of sprawling, multilevel cake with white and caramel-colored icing—and I found it almost surreal to watch workers standing ankle-deep and mining salt from one of nearly 6,000 pools cascading down the hillside, I supposed there are some travelers who might be somewhat less captivated by the sight of salt pans. If you have a good sense of balance, you can walk among salt-encrusted paths to get good close-up photographs. A small fee (S/5) is collected at the entrance; opening hours are from dawn to dusk.

GETTING THERE   To get to Salineras, take a taxi (S/10) from Urubamba to a point near the village of Tarabamba (next to the restaurant Tunupa); you can either have the taxi wait for you or hail a combi on the main road for your return. From there, it's a lovely 4km (2½-mile), or 1-hour, walk under a huge sky and along a footpath next to the river. There are no signs; cross the footbridge and bend right along the far side of the river and up through the mountains toward the salt pans. As you begin the gentle climb up the mountain, stick to the right path to avoid the cliff-hugging and only inches-wide trail that forks to the left. Even better is the walk (5km/3 miles) along a path (a little over an hour) from the village of Maras, a route taken by some of the salt-mine workers do (as if their work weren't grueling enough). Still more extreme and rewarding is the trek to the salt mines from the Inca ruins at Moray. It is one of the most stunningly beautiful walks in the region, a feast of blue-green cacti, deep red-brown earth, snowcapped mountains, plantings of corn and purple flowering potatoes, and small children tending to sheep. It's only for those who are in good shape, however; allow about 3 hours to cover the entire 14km (7½ miles).

Moray ★★
9km (5¹/₂ miles) NW of Maras

Among the wilder and more enigmatic Inca sites in Peru are the concentric ring terraces found in Moray. Unique in the Inca oeuvre, the site is not the ruins of a palace or fortress or typical temple, but what almost appears to be a large-scale environmental art installation. Three main sets of rings, like bowls, are set deep into the earth, forming strange sculpted terraces. The largest of the three has 15 levels. From above, they're intriguing, but it's even cooler to go down into them and contemplate their ancient functions. Many spiritually inclined travelers who come to the Sacred Valley for its special energy find that Moray possesses a very strong, and unique, vibe. The site may have had ritualistic purposes, but most likely, it was an agricultural development station where masterful and relentlessly curious farmers among the Incas tested experimental crops and conditions. The depressions in the earth (caused by erosion) produced intense microclimates, with

9

> **Tips   Chicha Here, Get Your Warm Chicha**
>
> Throughout the valley, you'll see modest homes marked by long poles topped by red flags (or red balloons). These *chicha* flags indicate that home-brewed fermented maize beer, or *chicha,* is for sale inside. What you'll usually find is a small, barren room with a handful of locals quietly drinking huge tumblers of pale yellow liquid. Tepid *chicha,* which costs next to nothing, is definitely an acquired taste.

remarkable differences in temperature from top to bottom, that the Incas were evidently studying. Moray is at its most spectacular after the end of the rainy season, when the terraces are a magnificent green.

GETTING THERE   Unfortunately, Moray is not easy to get to because it's removed from the main road that travels from Urubamba to Chinchero, with no public transportation of any kind, so it tends to draw only independent travelers and Inca completists, although increasingly Sacred Valley tours are beginning to include the site on their itineraries. The most convenient option is to take a taxi from either Urubamba or Chinchero; the driver will have to wait for you because there's nothing nearby, so the trip is sure to set you back at least S/130. Another option is to take a colectivo or bus that climbs up to Chinchero from Urubamba (or vice versa), getting off on the road to the village of Maras. (Make sure you ask the driver for the *desvío a Maras.*) From that point, there are usually taxis waiting to take visitors to Moray (negotiate a round-trip price). If you do go to Moray, it's possible to add on to your hike by walking another 9km (5½ miles) along a trail down to the Salineras de Maras. (See the trek described above, under "Salineras de Maras.") Along the path you'll likely encounter workers from the salt mines, who walk the distance back and forth to work.

Chinchero ★

28km (17 miles) NW of Cusco

Popular among tour groups for its bustling Sunday market that begins promptly at 8am, Chinchero is spectacularly sited and much higher than the rest of the valley and even Cusco; at 3,800m (12,500 ft.) and far removed from the river, technically Chinchero doesn't belong to the Urubamba Valley. The sleepy village has gorgeous views of the snowy peak of Salcantay and the Vilcabamba and Urubamba mountain ranges in the distance. Sunset turns the fields next to the church—where child shepherds herd their flocks and grown men play soccer without goal posts—gold against the deepening blue sky.

It might once have been a great Inca city, but except on the main market day, Chinchero remains a graceful, traditional Andean Indian village. Its 15,000 inhabitants represent as many as 12 different indigenous communities. The town's main points of interest, in addition to the fine market, are the expansive main square, with a handsome colonial church made of adobe and built on Inca foundations, and some Inca ruins, mostly terraces that aren't quite as awe-inspiring today as their counterparts in Ollantaytambo and Pisac.

In the main plaza is a formidable and famous Inca wall composed of huge stones and 10 trapezoidal niches. The foundations once formed the palace of the late-15th-century Inca Tupac Yupanqui. The early-17th-century *iglesia* (church) ★ has some very interesting, if faded, frescoes outside under the porticoes and mural paintings that cover the

entire ceiling. The church is open Monday through Saturday from 9am to 5pm and **255**
Sunday from 9am to 6pm. Across the plaza is a **Museo de Sitio** (no phone), the rather
spare municipal museum that holds a few Inca ceramics and instruments; it's open Tuesday through Sunday from 8am to 5pm, and admission is free.

The market comprises two marketplaces: one focusing on handicrafts and the other
consisting mainly of produce. The **Chinchero market ★★** is one of the best places in
the entire valley for Andean textiles and common goods such as hats, gloves, and shawls.
Even on Sunday, it is more authentic than the one at Pisac (although some visitors might
find Pisac more lively and fun). Chinchero's sellers of *artesanía*—who are more often
than not also the craftspeople, unlike the mere agents you'll find in Pisac and other
places—dress in traditional garb, and even the kids seem less manipulative in pleading
for your attention and soles. Midweek (especially Tues and Thurs), there are usually fewer
sellers who set their wares on blankets around the main square, and you'll have a better
chance of bargaining then.

Through the terraces to the left of the church is a path leading toward a stream and to
some finely sculpted Inca masonry, including stone steps, water canals, and huge stones
with animal figures.

GETTING THERE   Colectivos leave every half-hour or so from Tullumayo in Cusco for
Chinchero (a 90-min. journey). Buses also leave every 20 minutes or so from the Terminal Terrestre in Urubamba (a 50-min. trip). Entrance to Chinchero—officially to just the
market and church, but, in practice, to the whole town, it seems—is by *boleto turístico*
(see p. 216). If you try to visit the church and main square without a *boleto,* you will be
asked to purchase one (you can purchase the partial version that covers only Sacred Valley sites if you wish, rather than the entire Cusco ticket). Nearly everyone visits Chinchero on a half-day visit from either Cusco or Urubamba; there's not much else in the
way of infrastructure to detain you, although there are a handful of inexpensive restaurants on the main road where the bus drops you off for lunch. One serving pretty good
Andean specialties is **Abarrotes Bar Restaurant,** Av. Mateo Pumacahua 143 (© **084/306-
052**). There are a just a couple of spots in town to spend the night (the better of the two
is the small and inexpensive Hostal Los Incas), unless you want to camp in the fields just
beyond the plaza where the market is held. You're much better off visiting during the day
and staying elsewhere in the Sacred Valley, where there are considerably more services.

3 OLLANTAYTAMBO ★★★

97km (60 miles) NW of Cusco; 21km (13 miles) W of Urubamba

A tongue twister of a town—the last settlement before Aguas Calientes and Machu Picchu—this historic and lovely little place at the northwestern end of the Sacred Valley is
affectionately called Ollanta (Oh-*yahn*-tah) by locals. Plenty of outsiders who can't pro-
nounce it fall in love with the town, too, and the town, which was oh-so-quiet just a few
years ago, is now firmly on the tourist trail, fast on its way to becoming a mini Cusco.
New cafes, restaurants and *hostales* now ring the main square and line the street that connects the old town to the ruins, but Ollanta is trying to negotiate its newfound popularity and doing its best to avoid being overrun with shoddy tourist establishments like
Aguas Calientes. Despite its quick transformation, though, Ollantaytambo remains one
of the most enjoyable places in the Sacred Valley, the one place (other than Machu Picchu, of course) not to be missed. The scenery surrounding Ollantaytambo is stunning:

The snowcapped mountains that embrace the town frame a much narrower valley here than at Urubamba or Pisac, and both sides of the gorge are lined with Inca stone *andenes,* or agricultural terraces. Most extraordinary are the precipitous terraced ruins of a massive temple-fortress built by the Inca Pachacútec. Below the ruins, Ollantaytambo's old town is a splendid grid of streets dating to Inca times and lined with adobe brick walls, blooming bougainvillea, and perfect canals, still carrying rushing water down from the mountains. Though during much of the day tour buses deposit large groups at the foot of the fortress (where a handicrafts market habitually breaks out to welcome them) and tourists overrun the main square, the old town remains pretty quiet, a traditional and thoroughly charming Valle Sagrado village.

Ollantaytambo is one of the best spots to spend the night in the Sacred Valley—although accommodations are limited to small inns and simple hotels—especially if you want to be able to wander around the ruins alone in the early morning or late afternoon, before or after the groups overtake them. With the town's expanding roster of traveler services, it's now a good place to hang out for several days, not just an overnight on the way to or back from Machu Picchu.

ESSENTIALS
Getting There

BY TRAIN Ollantaytambo lies midway on the Cusco–Machu Picchu train route. Trains traveling to Aguas Calientes (Machu Picchu) from Cusco stop first at Ollantaytambo; two new competitors of PeruRail originate in Ollanta for travel to Machu Picchu. Peru Rail trains depart Cusco from **Estación Poroy** (© 084/221-352) a 15-minute taxi ride from Cusco and arrive in Ollantaytambo 90 minutes later. The train station in Ollantaytambo is a long 15-minute walk from the main square. Peru Rail's **Backpacker shuttle** ($31–$43 adults one-way) departs Ollantaytambo starting at 5:45am, with the last train leaving for Machu Picchu at 5:55pm. Coming back, the first train leaves at 5:45am and the last at 8:40pm. The slightly more upscale **Vistadome Valle** train ($43–$60 adults one-way) departs Ollantaytambo beginning at 6:40am, with the last train leaving at 4:05pm. The first Backpacker leaves Machu Picchu for Ollantaytambo at 8:30am and the last at 6:55pm. For additional details, including Peru Rail's two new competitor trains that travel back and forth from Machu Picchu to Ollantaytambo, see "Getting There" in "Machu Picchu & the Inca Trail," later in this chapter.

BY BUS The cheapest way to Ollantaytambo is to catch a combi or colectivo from Cusco to Urubamba (S/5) and transfer at the terminal there to a frequent combi (S/3) for Ollanta (30 min.). Buses drop passengers at the Plaza de Armas in the old town, about a kilometer (½-mile) from the ruins.

BY TAXI Taxis between Ollantaytambo and Cusco generally charge about S/100 each way. Shared taxis (for about S/10 per person) to Urubamba are frequently available; a private taxi from the bus station in Urubamba to Ollanta will run another S/10 to S/15.

Visitor Information

You're better off getting information on the Sacred Valley before leaving Cusco, either at the main **Tourist Information Office** (© 084/263-176), Av. El Sol 103, or at Cusco's branch of the **South American Explorers Club** (© 084/245-484). Your best bet for exchanging cash in Ollantaytambo is in small shops. If you need medical assistance, go to **Centro de Salud,** Calle Principal (© 084/204-090). The **post office** is on the Plaza de Armas.

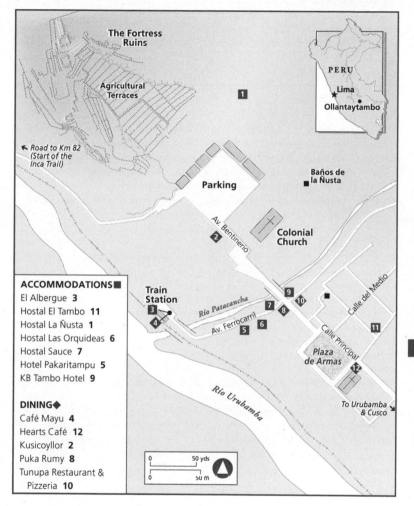

ACCOMMODATIONS
El Albergue **3**
Hostal El Tambo **11**
Hostal La Ñusta **1**
Hostal Las Orquideas **6**
Hostal Sauce **7**
Hotel Pakaritampu **5**
KB Tambo Hotel **9**

DINING
Café Mayu **4**
Hearts Café **12**
Kusicoyllor **2**
Puka Rumy **8**
Tunupa Restaurant & Pizzeria **10**

WHAT TO SEE & DO

Fortress Ruins ★★★

The Inca elite adopted Ollantaytambo, building irrigation systems and a crowning temple designed for worship and astronomical observation. Rising above the valley and an ancient square (Plaza Mañaraki) are dozens of rows of stunningly steep stone terraces carved into the hillside. The temple ruins, which appear both forbidding and admirably perfect, represent one of the Inca Empire's most formidable feats of architecture. The Incas were able to successfully defend the site against the Spanish in 1537, protecting the

(Tips   When Not to Go

The Inca ruins at Ollantaytambo are often overrun with tourists doing the bus tour of the Sacred Valley on Sunday afternoons, typical market day. The ruins are so special and so enjoyably serene on other days that if you can't get there early in the morning on Sunday, it's worthwhile visiting another day, if you can.

rebel Manco Inca after his retreat here from defeat at Sacsayhuamán. In all probability, the complex was more a temple than a citadel to the Incas.

The upper section—reached after you've climbed 200 steps—contains typically masterful masonry of the kind that adorned great Inca temples. A massive and supremely elegant doorjamb—site of many a photo—indicates the principal entry to the temple; next to it is the **Temple of Ten Niches.** On the next level are six huge pink granite blocks, amazingly cut, polished, and fitted together; they appear to be part of rooms never completed. This **Temple of the Sun** is one of the great stonemasonry achievements of the Incas. On the stones, you can still make out faint, ancient symbolic markings in relief. Across the valley is the quarry that provided the stones for the structure; a great ramp descending from the hilltop ruins was the means by which the Incas transported the massive stones—thousands of workers essentially dragged them around the river—from several kilometers away.

A footpath wends up the hill behind an outer wall of the ruins to a clearing and a wall with niches that have led some to believe prisoners were tied up here—a theory that is unfounded. Regardless of the purpose, the views south over the Urubamba Valley and of the snowcapped peak of Verónica are outstanding.

The ruins are open daily from 7am to 5:30pm; admission is by *boleto turístico* only (see p. 216). To experience the ruins in peace before the tour buses arrive, plan on getting to them before 11am. Early morning is best of all, when the sun rises over mountains to the east and then quickly bathes the entire valley in light.

At the bottom of the terraces, next to the Patacancha River, are the **Baños de la Ñusta (Princess Baths),** a place of ceremonial bathing. Wedged into the mountains facing the baths are granaries built by the Incas (not prisons, as some have supposed). Locals like to point out the face of the Inca carved into the cliff high above the valley. (If you can't make it out, ask the guard at the entrance to the ruins for a little help.)

Old Town ★★

Below (or south of) the ruins and across the Río Patacancha is the finest extant example of the Incas' masterful urban planning. Many original residential *canchas,* or blocks, each inhabited by several families during the 15th century, are still present; each *cancha* had a single entrance opening onto a main courtyard. The finest streets of this stone village are directly behind the main square. On my last visit to Ollanta, stonemasons were busy redoing every last old cobblestone street, so the Old Town should be in pristine shape again. Get a good glimpse of community life within a *cancha* by peeking in at **Calle del Medio** (Chautik'ikllu St.), where a couple of neighboring houses have a small shop in the courtyard and their ancestors' skulls are displayed as shrines on the walls of their living quarters. The entire village retains a solid Amerindian air to it, unperturbed by the crowds of gringos who wander through it, snapping photos of children and old women. It's a starkly traditional place, largely populated by locals in colorful native dress and women who pace up and down the streets or through fields absent-mindedly spinning the ancient spools used in making hand-woven textiles.

Ollantaytambo is an excellent spot in the valley for gentle or more energetic walks around the valley and into the mountains. One of the more accessible walks is the climb up into the hills overlooking the old town; take the stairs off Calle Lares K'ikllu, northeast of the Plaza de Armas and with the widest rushing canals in town. A simple sign reads "To Pinkuylluna." Though the climb is initially very steep, you can clamber over the entire hilltop and explore old Inca granaries. The views of Ollantaytambo, across town to the ruins and of the surrounding the valley are stupendous.

SHOPPING

While most shoppers beeline for the market directly in front of the entrance to the ruins, those in search of higher-quality, hand-woven textiles (with all-natural dyes and fibers), produced by artisans from Quechua mountain communities, should visit **Awamaki** ★, Calle Chaupi (© 084/792-529), the retail outlet of an NGO that runs a weaving project and ensures that profits make it back to the women of the Patacancha Valley. The organization also organizes trips to the Patacancha communities for weaving demonstrations and visits with local families and artisans.

WHERE TO STAY

In addition to the hotels below, budget travelers gravitate toward the first inexpensive options (which for the most part don't offer hot water) they come across: **KB Tambo Hotel** (no phone; www.kbtambo.com), owned by a mountain-biking American and with nice new rooms constructed a couple of years ago ($15–$28 per person); **Hostal Las Orquídeas,** Av. Ferrocarril s/n (© 084/204-032), which has clean and simple rooms with a shared bathroom around a courtyard for $20; and **Hostal La Ñusta,** Carretera Ocobamba (© 084/204-035), a clean and friendly place with good views from the balcony but small and plain rooms, $20 for a double. Tucked into the old town on a quiet street, simple and comfortable **Hostal El Tambo,** Calle Horno s/n (© 084/204-003), is built around an attractive, verdant patio. Rates are $15 for a double.

Tips **Sacred Valley Festivals**

The traditional Andean villages of the Sacred Valley are some of the finest spots in Peru to witness vibrant local festivals celebrated with music, dance, and processions. Among the highlights are Christmas, **Día de los Reyes Magos (Three Kings Day,** Jan 6), **Ollanta-Raymi** (celebrated in Ollantaytambo the week after its big brother, Cusco's Inti Raymi, during the last week of June), and Chinchero's **Virgen Natividad** (Sept 8), the most important annual fiesta in that village. The **Fiesta de las Cruces (Festival of the Crosses,** May 2–3) is celebrated across the highlands with enthusiastic dancing and the decoration of large crosses. Pisac celebrates a particularly lively version of the **Virgen del Carmen** festival held in Paucartambo (July 16).

Expensive

Hotel Pakaritampu ★   On the road from the train station to town, this hotel is surprisingly upscale for unassuming Ollantaytambo. With beautiful gardens, great views, and cozy touches such as a fireplace lounge and a library, it has a reasonably authentic, lived-in country feel. Rooms are tasteful, with sturdy, comfortable furnishings, and there's a nice restaurant/bar. It's owned by one of Peru's best-known athletes, a former Olympic volleyballer.

Av. Ferrocarril s/n, Ollantaytambo. ℂ **084/204-020.** Fax 084/205-105. www.pakaritampu.com. 39 units. S/396 double. Rates include breakfast. AE, DC, MC, V. **Amenities:** Restaurant; bar.

Moderate

El Albergue ★★ (Value   This rustic and homey *hostal*, owned by a longtime American resident of Ollantaytambo, may not be the most luxurious spot in town but it's still my favorite place to stay. It has large, comfortable, and nicely furnished rooms—the governing aesthetic is a kind of clean, modern rusticity—with excellent beds, luxuriant gardens, a wood-fired sauna, Labrador retrievers roaming the grounds, and a spot right next to the train to Machu Picchu. It's frequently full—Inca Trail groups come through regularly—even though it's more expensive than other budget accommodations in town (and prices have climbed steadily over the years). You can't miss the *hostal;* it's right next to the train terminal, and painted on the wall is the name of the proprietor in capital letters: Wendy Weeks. The inn now sports an excellent cafe/restaurant, **Café Mayu,** with its entrance through the hotel or from the train tracks; it's my favorite spot in town for a meal or even just dessert and coffee.

Av. Estación s/n (next to the railway station platform), Ollantaytambo. ℂ/fax **084/204-014.** www.elalbergue.com. 6 units. $58–$74 double with shared bathroom. Rates include continental breakfast. No credit cards. **Amenities:** Restaurant; cafe; sauna. *In room:* No phone.

Hostal Sauce   Sandwiched between the main square of the village and the road to the ruins, this modern and comfortable free-standing building has a smattering of very clean, nicely equipped rooms and a small restaurant. Some rooms have superb views of the ruins. The inn's name, which might strike some English speakers as a little odd, refers to the *sauce* tree out front.

Ventiderio 248, Ollantaytambo. ℂ **084/204-044.** Fax 084/204-048. www.hostalsauce.com.pe. 8 units. S/274 double ($10 discount if paying cash). Rates include breakfast. V. **Amenities:** Restaurant; bar.

WHERE TO DINE

Every year more and more small, tourist-oriented cafes and restaurants pop up in Ollantaytambo to cater to the crowds that hang out in the day and increasingly spend the night here. If you're staying in Ollanta and don't mind a drive, you might also consider catching a taxi to one of the fine restaurants along the main road from Urubamba to Ollantaytambo; see "Where to Dine" in "Urubamba & Environs," earlier in this chapter.

My favorite spot in Ollantaytambo is the new **Cafe Mayu ★★**, Estación de Tren Ollantaytambo (ℂ **084/204-014;** www.elalbergue.com), part of El Albergue *hostal* (see above) and right on the train tracks. The attractive cafe, which looks like it's been around much longer than it has, features homemade pastas (such as fettuccine with three Andean cheeses), quinoa and other salads, and tasty sandwiches. It also serves excellent breakfasts and great coffee and a locally famous brownie with vanilla ice cream. If you're headed out on a hike or to Machu Picchu, you can also pick up a boxed lunch for S/30. The next best choice, although simple and unadorned, may be **Hearts Café,** Plaza de Armas

Hiking Trails in the Sacred Valley

Energetic travelers with a fierce desire to get outdoors and exercise their legs in the Sacred Valley can do much more than the standard ruins treks and even the Inca Trail, although the latter is certainly the best known trek in Peru. Other trails are considerably less populated, so if you're looking for isolation in the Andes, give some of the following treks a try.

The entire valley is virtually tailor-made for treks, but Ollantaytambo and Yucay are particularly excellent bases for treks into the lovely, gentle hillsides framing the Urubamba Valley. The Cusco office of **South American Explorers** (© 084/245-484) is very helpful with trip and trail reports for members.

- **Km 82 of the Inca Trail:** Whether or not you're planning to do the Inca Trail, hiking the section from Km 82 to Km 88 is a nice addition to the classic or mini route. By staying to the north (or railroad) side of the Río Urubamba, you'll pass several good ruins sites, including Salapunku and Pinchanuyoq, finally reaching the Inca bridge at Km 88.
- **Pumamarca ruins:** You can reach the small but well-preserved Inca ruins of Pumamarca by a pretty trek along the banks of the Río Patacancha, which takes you through tiny villages. The walk from Ollantaytambo takes about 5 hours round-trip. To get there, take the road that leads north out of Ollanta along the Patacancha. After it crosses the river, it turns into a footpath and passes the village of Munaypata. Veer left toward the valley and terracing, and then turn sharply to the right (northeast), toward the agricultural terraces straight ahead.
- **Pinkulluna:** The mountain looming above Ollantaytambo makes for an enjoyable (though initially very steep) couple-hour trek up, past Inca terracing and old granaries. However, the trail isn't very clearly marked in sections, so it might be worthwhile to ask around town for a guide.
- **Huayoccari:** Adventurous trekkers in search of solitude should enjoy the 2-day hike (one-way) from Yucay to the small village of Huayoccari, which passes some of the valley's loveliest scenery, from the Inca terraces along the San Juan River ravine to Sakrachayoc and ancient rock paintings overlooking caves. After camping overnight, trekkers continue to the Tuqsana pass (4,000m/13,100 ft.) and descend to Yanacocha Lake before arriving at Huayoccari.

(© 084/204-078) begun by a British woman, Sonia Newhouse, who operates an NGO (www.livingheartperu.org) that works with highland community women and children—to which all profits of this restaurant are donated. Besides feeling good about spending your *soles* here, it's a cozy little spot for breakfast (served all day), sandwiches, empanadas, fruit juices and full, good-value dinners.

Puka Rumi, Av. Beniterio s/n (© 084/204-091), is a little bar/cafe that serves everything from eggs to *churrasco* (barbecue) and chicken; it's especially good for a cold beer on the tiny terrace. Across the street, **Tunupa Restaurant & Pizzeria** ★, Av. Beniterio s/n (℗ **084/204-077**), the main drag between the ruins and Old Town, is an inexpensive family-run terrace joint with a very agreeable open-air atmosphere. It serves breakfast, lunch, and dinner, from pancakes to pizza and chifa (Peruvian-Chinese dishes). Other cheap restaurants in Old Town, mostly serving cheap, serviceable pizzas, such as **Bar Ollantay** and **La Fortaleza,** ring the main square.

Right next to the entrance to the ruins, **Kusicoyllor,** Plaza Araccama s/n (℗ **084/204-114**), is a cozy cafe/bar that is expectedly a tad touristy and overpriced. It serves standard Peruvian and predominantly Italian dishes and offers a fixed-price *menu.* Breakfast is especially good, making it a fine stop after an early morning tour of the ruins.

4 MACHU PICCHU ★★★ & THE INCA TRAIL ★★★

120km (75 miles) NW of Cusco

The stunning and immaculately sited Machu Picchu, the fabled "lost city of the Incas," is South America's greatest attraction, one that draws ever-increasing numbers of visitors from across the globe. The Incas hid Machu Picchu so high in the clouds that it escaped destruction by the empire-raiding Spaniards, who never found it. It is no longer lost, of course—you can zip there by high-speed train or trek there along a 2- or 4-day trail—but Machu Picchu retains its perhaps unequaled aura of mystery and magic. No longer overgrown with brush, as it was when it was rediscovered in 1911 by the Yale archaeologist and historian Hiram Bingham with the aid of a local farmer who knew of its existence, from below it is still totally hidden from view. The majestic setting the Incas chose for it also remains unchanged: The ruins are nestled in almost brooding Andes Mountains and are frequently swathed in mist. When the early morning sun rises over the peaks and methodically illuminates the ruins' row by row of granite stones, Machu Picchu leaves visitors as awe-struck as ever.

Machu Picchu's popularity continues to grow by leaps and bounds, straining both its infrastructure and the fragile surrounding ecosystem, forcing state officials to limit the number of visitors in high season. The great majority of visitors to Machu Picchu still visit it as a day trip from Cusco, but many people feel that a few hurried hours at the ruins during peak hours, amid throngs of people following guided tours, simply do not suffice. That certainly is my opinion. By staying at least 1 night, either at the one upscale hotel just outside the grounds of Machu Picchu or down below in the town of Aguas Calientes (also officially called Machu Picchu Pueblo, although most Peruvians still call it by the original name), you can remain at the ruins later in the afternoon after most of the tour groups have gone home, or get there for sunrise—a dramatic, unforgettable sight. Many visitors find that even a full single day at the ruins does not do it justice.

The base for most visitors, Aguas Calientes is a small and humid, ramshackle tourist trade village with the feel of a frontier town, dominated by sellers of cheap *artesanía* and souvenirs, and weary backpackers resting up and celebrating their treks along the Inca Trail over cheap eats and cheaper beers. The Peruvian government, along with the help of PeruRail, is doing its level best to spruce up the town, lest its ramshackle look turn off visitors to Peru's greatest spectacle. It has fixed up the Plaza de Armas, built a nicely paved *malecón* riverfront area, and added new bridges over and new streets along the river, and the town does look better than at any time I can remember. It's still probably not a place you want to hang out for long, though. There are some additional good hikes in the area, but most people head back to Cusco after a day or so in town.

ESSENTIALS
Getting There

If you were hoping to soar over the Andes to Machu Picchu in a helicopter, you're out of luck: All flights have been suspended indefinitely, due to very real environmental concerns.

BY TRAIN Most people travel to Machu Picchu by train; one can go to Aguas Calientes, at the base of the ruins, from either Cusco or Ollantaytambo in the Sacred Valley. The 112km (70-mile) train from Cusco is a truly spectacular journey. It zigzags up Huayna Picchu and then through lush valleys hugging the Río Urubamba, with views of snowcapped Andes peaks in the distance. From Cusco, **Perurail** (© **01/612-6700** in Lima, 084/581-414 in Cusco; www.perurail.com) operates three tourist trains from Cusco, all arriving in under 4 hours: the **Backpacker,** the slowest and least expensive ($48 one-way); the **Vistadome,** the faster first-class service ($71); and the top-of-the-line and very pricey luxury line **Hiram Bingham★★**, named after the discoverer of Machu Picchu ($307 to $334 one-way, including two meals, cocktails, and a guided tour at the ruins). The *Backpacker* departs Cusco daily at 7:42am and arrives in Aguas Calientes at 10:51am (returning at 4:43pm and arriving in Cusco at 8:13pm); the *Vistadome* leaves at 6:53am and arrives at 9:52am (returning at 3:20pm and arriving at 6:50pm); and the Hiram Bingham leaves Cusco at 9:05am and arrives in Aguas Calientes at 12:24pm (returning at 5:50pm and arriving in Cusco at 9:16pm). Perurail's tourist trains depart from Cusco's **Estación Poroy,** a 15-minute taxi from Cusco, 6 days a week in high season (May–Oct) and 4 days a week in low season (Nov–Mar). Make your train reservations as early as possible; tickets can be purchased online or at **Estación Huanchaq** on Avenida Pachacútec (in cash, dollars or *soles*) for tickets reserved in advance. It's open Monday through Friday from 8:30am to 5:30pm, Saturday and Sunday from 8:30am to 12:30pm. See below for phone numbers for specific train stations.

Travelers based in the Urubamba Valley have additional options to travel by train to Machu Picchu, with two new rail lines challenging the decade-long monopoly held by

---

Tips Train Schedules to Machu Picchu

Train schedules have changed with alarming frequency in the past few years, according to season and, it seems, the whims of some scheduler—and that's likely to be especially true now that there are three companies handling service (rather than just one), all employing the same tracks. It's wise to make your reservation at least several days (or more) in advance, especially in high season. For Perurail's luxury Hiram Bingham service, reservations several weeks or more in advance are recommended. It's also smart to verify hours and fares at your hotel (if you're staying in one of the better ones with good service and informed personnel), the Tourist Information Office in Cusco (p. 187), or via Perurail (© **084/ 238-722;** www.perurail.com); Inca Rail (© **084/233-030;** www.incarail.com); or Machu Picchu Train (© **084/221-199;** www.machupicchutrain.com).

Endangered Machu Picchu

Machu Picchu survived the Spanish onslaught against the Inca Empire, but in the last few decades it has suffered more threats to its architectural integrity and pristine Andean environment than it did in nearly 500 previous years of existence. In the past, UNESCO has threatened to add Machu Picchu to its roster of endangered World Heritage Sites and not to withdraw that status unless stringent measures were taken by the Peruvian government to protect the landmark ruins.

Clearly, the preservation of Machu Picchu continues to face significant challenges. The ruins in the past few years have again been named to another notorious list, the 2010 World Monuments Watch, which details the 100 Most Endangered Sites in the World. (In 2002, in recognition of the Peruvian government's adoption of tougher regulations on the Inca Trail and the suspension of a proposed cable-car plan, Machu Picchu was removed from the list.) Today, World Monuments Fund maintains that "little has been done to address the impacts of tourism on the site or the resulting environmental degradation of the area." Planned projects, which include building a bridge across the Vilcanota River, are representative of "uncontrolled development and environmental mismanagement in Aguas Calientes." Add to that the reality that tourism at Machu Picchu has increased from 9,000 visitors in all of 1992 to close to 5,000 on a single busy day (the site receives nearly 1 million visitors annually), and Peru has significant environmental and conservation issues to face.

In 2001, a film company shooting a TV ad for a Peruvian beer sneaked equipment into the site and irreparably damaged the stone Intihuatana atop the ruins (the camera crane operator was sentenced to 6 years in prison in 2005). Developers' plans for a tram to the site have not been entirely dropped, as once reported, though they have been altered to minimize its impact should it ever be built. The Peruvian government has only slowly responded to pressure from UNESCO, foreign governments, and watchdog groups, introducing measures to clean up and restrict access to the historic Inca Trail. One unique measure adopted was a debt-swap initiative, in which the government of Finland traded 25% of Peru's outstanding debt (more than $6 million) for conservation programs targeting Machu Picchu. Yet clearly much more needs to be done to protect these singular ruins, Peru's most acclaimed treasure.

Peru Rail. From Ollantaytambo, the journey takes about 90 minutes. On the new **Inca Rail,** Av. El Sol 611, in Cusco (© **084/233-030;** www.incarail.com), first-class travel from Ollantaytambo to Machu Picchu is $75; executive class is $50. Trains (3 per day) run beginning at 6:40am, with the last return at 7pm. On the similarly just-launched **Machu Picchu Train,** Av. El Sol 576, in Cusco (© **084/221-199;** www.machu picchutrain.com), full fare from Ollantaytambo to Machu Picchu is $59. Perurail's Backpacker Cerrojo and Vistadome services also originate in Ollantaytambo, leaving several

class, \$43 to \$60 in Vistadome. *Tip:* For the best views on the way to Machu Picchu, sit
on the left side of the train.

Estación **Machu Picchu Pueblo,** the train station in Aguas Calientes, is along the
river side of the tracks, just beyond the market stalls of Avenida Imperio de los Incas.
Porters from several hotels greet the trains upon arrival each morning.

BY BUS   You can't travel from Cusco to Machu Picchu by bus until the final leg of the
journey, when buses wend their way up the mountain, performing exaggerated switchbacks for 15 minutes before suddenly depositing passengers at the entrance to the ruins.
The cost is \$14 round-trip. There's no need to reserve in advance; just purchase your
ticket at the little booth in front of the lineup of buses, at the bottom of the market stalls.
Buses begin running at 6:30am and come down all day, with the last one descending at
dusk. Some people choose to purchase a one-way ticket (\$7) up and walk down (30–45
min.) to Aguas Calientes.

BY FOOT   The celebrated **Inca Trail (Camino del Inca,** or Camino Real) is almost as
famous as the ruins themselves, and the trek is rightly viewed as an attraction in itself
rather than merely a means of getting to Machu Picchu under your own power. There
are two principal treks: one that takes 4 days (43km/27 miles) and another shorter and
less demanding route that lasts just 2 days. The trails begin outside Ollantaytambo (at
Km 82 of the Cusco–Machu Picchu railroad track); you can return to Cusco or Ollantaytambo by train. See "Hiking the Inca Trail," later in this section, for more details;
many new regulations have been introduced in the past few years.

For those who take the train to Aguas Calientes but still want a small dose of what it's
like to walk to Machu Picchu, it's straightforward (if a little difficult) to walk up to the
ruins from town up a steep path that cuts across the switchback road. It takes a little over
an hour to make it up and about 45 minutes to descend. Because you'll probably want
to save your energy for exploring Machu Picchu, if you are fit and want to walk at least
one-way, I recommend walking down from the ruins (which is still pretty strenuous on
one's knees).

Visitor Information

Aguas Calientes has an **iPerú** office, Av. Pachacútec, Cdra. 1 s/n (✆ **084/211-104**),
about one-third of the way up the main drag in town. It has photocopies of town maps
and some basic hotel and Machu Picchu information.

FAST FACTS   There are no banks in Aguas Calientes. To exchange money (cash or
traveler's checks), try **Gringo Bill's Hostal** at Colla Raymi 104, just off the main square.
Shops and restaurants along the two main streets, Avenida Imperio de los Incas and
Avenida Pachacútec, buy dollars from gringos in need at standard exchange rates.

You'll find the **police** on Avenida Imperio de los Incas, down from the railway station
(✆ **084/211-178**).

There are Internet cabinas at the **Café Internet** (no phone) on Avenida Imperio de los
Incas, a block away from the main square on the railroad tracks, and at a couple of places
on the Plaza de Armas. **Gringo Bill's Hostal** (✆ **084/211-046**), on Colla Raymi 104,
also has Internet access. There's a **post office** on the corner of Manco Cápac at Avenida
Imperio de los Incas. The **Telefónica del Perú** office (no phone) is at Av. Imperio de los
Incas 132.

SOUTH AMERICA'S TOP ATTRACTION:
MACHU PICCHU ★★★

Since its rediscovery in 1911 and initial exploration by an American team of archaeologists from Yale during the next 4 years, the ruins of Machu Picchu have resonated far beyond the status of mere archaeological site. Reputed to be the legendary "lost city of the Incas," it is steeped in mystery and folklore. The unearthed complex, the only significant Inca site to escape the ravenous appetites of the Spanish conquistadors in the 16th century, ranks as the top attraction in Peru, arguably the greatest in South America and, for my money, one of the world's most stunning sights. Countless glossy photographs of the stone ruins, bridging the gap between two massive Andean peaks and swathed in cottony clouds, just can't do it justice. I distinctly remember seeing pictures of Machu Picchu in- a textbook when I was 5 years old and dreaming that someday I would go there. When I did, for the first time in 1983, the glorious city of the Incas more than lived up to all those years of expectation. It is dreamlike-and remains so, even though it's a mandatory visit for virtually everyone who travels to Peru.

Invisible from the Urubamba Valley below, Machu Picchu lay dormant for more than 4 centuries, nestled nearly 2,400m (8,000 ft.) above sea level under thick jungle and known only to a handful of Amerindian peasants. Never mentioned in the Spanish chronicles, it was seemingly lost in the collective memory of the Incas and their descendants. The ruins' unearthing, though, raised more questions than it answered, and experts still argue about the place Machu Picchu occupied in the Inca Empire. Was it a citadel? An agricultural site? An astronomical observatory? A ceremonial city or sacred retreat for the Inca emperor? Or some combination of all of these? Adding to the mystery, this complex city of exceedingly fine architecture and masonry was constructed, inhabited, and deliberately abandoned all in less than a century—a mere flash in the 4,000-year-history of Andean Peru. Machu Picchu was very probably abandoned even before the arrival of the Spanish, perhaps as a result of the Incas' civil war. Or perhaps it was drought that drove the Incas elsewhere.

Bingham mistook Machu Picchu for the lost city of Vilcabamba, the last refuge of the rebellious Inca Manco Cápac (see "Bingham, the 'Discoverer' of Machu Picchu" on p. 272). Machu Picchu, though, is not that lost city (which was discovered deeper in the jungle at Espíritu Pampa). Most historians believe that the 9th Inca emperor, Pachacútec (also called Pachacuti Inca Yupanqui)—who founded the Inca Empire, established many of the hallmarks of its society, and built most of the greatest and most recognizable of Inca monuments—had the complex constructed sometime in the mid-1400s, probably after the defeat of the Chancas, a rival group, in 1438. Machu Picchu appears to have been both a ceremonial and agricultural center. Half its buildings were sacred in nature, but the latest research findings indicate that it was a royal retreat for Inca leaders rather than a sacred city, per se. Never looted by the Spaniards, many of its architectural features remain in excellent condition—even if they ultimately do little to advance our understanding of the exact nature of Machu Picchu.

One thing is certain: Machu Picchu is one of the world's great examples of landscape art. The Incas revered nature, worshiping celestial bodies and more earthly streams and stones. The spectacular setting of Machu Picchu reveals just how much they reveled in their environment. Steep terraces, gardens, and granite and limestone temples, staircases, and aqueducts seem to be carved directly out of the hillside. Forms echo the very shape of the surrounding mountains, and windows and instruments appear to have been constructed to track the sun during the June and December solstices. Machu Picchu lies

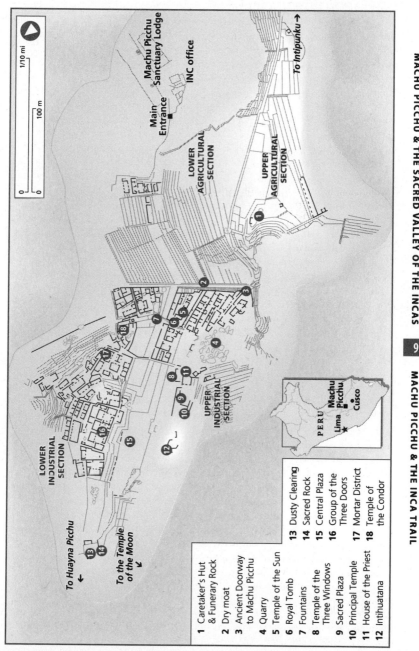

1   Caretaker's Hut
    & Funerary Rock
2   Dry moat
3   Ancient Doorway
    to Machu Picchu
4   Quarry
5   Temple of the Sun
6   Royal Tomb
7   Fountains
8   Temple of the
    Three Windows
9   Sacred Plaza
10 Principal Temple
11 House of the Priest
12 Intihuatana
13 Dusty Clearing
14 Sacred Rock
15 Central Plaza
16 Group of the
    Three Doors
17 Mortar District
18 Temple of
    the Condor

We Call It Choclo: Foods of the Incas

Wondering what the Incas cultivated on all those amazing, steeply terraced fields that so elegantly grace the hillsides? Sure, they grew *papas* (potatoes) and *coca* (coca leaves), but corn was perhaps the Incas' most revered crop. Although corn was important throughout the Americas in pre-Columbian times, the Inca Empire raised it to the level of a sacred state crop. Corn was a symbol of power, and the Incas saved their very best lands for its cultivation. The *choclo* of Cusco and the Sacred Valley was considered the finest of the empire. It is still an uncommon delight: Huge, puffy, white kernels with a milky, sweet taste, it's best enjoyed in classic corn-on-the-cob style, boiled and served with a hunk of mountain cheese.

Pachamanca is a classic *sierra* dish, an indigenous barbecue of sorts, perfected by the Incas. The word is derived from *Pachamama,* or "Mother Earth," in Quechua. A *pachamanca* is distinguished by its underground preparation. Several types of meat, along with potatoes, chopped *ají* (hot pepper), herbs, and cheese, are baked in a hole in the earth over hot stones. Banana leaves are placed between the layers of food. The act of cooking underground was symbolic for the Incas; they worshiped the earth, and to eat directly from it was a way of honoring Pachamama and giving thanks for her fertility. Peruvians still love to cook *pachamancas* in the countryside.

Quinoa, which comes from the word that means "moon" in Quechua (another central element in the Inca cosmology), was the favored grain of the Incas. The grain, which expands to four times its original volume when cooked and contains a greater quantity of protein than any other grain, remains central to the Andean diet. Most often seen in *sopa a la criolla,* it is often substituted for rice and incorporated into soups, salads, and puddings.

300m (1,000 ft.) lower than Cusco, but you'd imagine the exact opposite, so nestled are the ruins among mountaintops and clouds. The ruins are cradled at the center of a radius of Andean peaks, like the pistil at the center of a flower.

Appreciating Machu Picchu for its aesthetic qualities is no slight to its significance. The Incas obviously chose the site for the immense power of its natural beauty. They, like we, must have been in awe of the snowcapped peaks to the east; the rugged panorama of towering, forested mountains and the sacred cliff of Putukusi to the west; and the city sitting gracefully like a proud saddle between two huge *cerros,* or peaks. It remains one of the most thrilling sights in the world. At daybreak, when the sun's rays creep silently over the jagged silhouette, sometimes turning the distant snowy peaks fiery orange, and then slowly, with great drama, cast brilliant light on the ruins building by building and row by row, it's enough to move some observers to tears and others to squeals of delight.

Visiting the Ruins

Named a UNESCO World Heritage Site in 1983 and declared one of the "New Seven Wonders of the World," Machu Picchu's image around the world continues to grow, as does the number of people who want to visit the ruins. As many as 5,000 visitors a day visit Machu Picchu during high season, from May to October, and close to 1 million people visit Machu Picchu annually. You've got to arrive very early or stay pretty late for a bit of splendid Inca isolation, but Machu Picchu's huge numbers of visitors are rarely overwhelming. The place is large enough to escape most tour-group bottlenecks, although people fearful of the crush should plan to arrive as early as possible in the morning, especially to see the sun rise, and/or stay past 3pm. Perhaps the worst times to visit are from July 28 to August 10, when Peruvian national holidays land untold groups of schoolchildren and families at Machu Picchu, or solstice days (June 21 and Dec 21), when everyone descends on the ruins for a glimpse of the dazzling effects of the sun's rays. During the rainy season (Nov–Mar), you are very likely to get rain for (often) brief periods during the day, and Machu Picchu is usually obscured by clouds in the morning.

For information on the shuttle buses to the ruins, see "Getting There," earlier.

The ruins are open daily from dawn to dusk: The first visitors, usually those staying at the hotel or arriving from the Inca Trail, enter at 6am. Everyone is ushered out by 6pm. Tickets no longer can be purchased at the entrance; they must be purchased (take your passport) at the **Machu Picchu Cultural Center** in Aguas Calientes, Av. Pachacútec s/n (© **084/211-196**), near the main plaza. They may also be purchased at the **Instituto Nacional de Cultural (INC)** offices in Cusco, on Calle San Bernardo s/n (© **084/246-074**) several blocks from the Plaza de Armas. The entrance fee has doubled in the last few years to S/124 (half-price with an ISIC card; S/62 ages 8–21; free for children under 8). Some speculate that the fee may increase again in the near future, perhaps as by as much as 100%. Tickets are valid for 3 days from date of purchase, but are good for a single day's entrance only.

Along with your ticket, you will be given an official Institute of National Culture map of the ruins, which give the names of the individual sections, but no detailed explanations. The numbers indicated in brackets below follow our own map, "Machu Picchu," on p. 267. English-speaking guides can be independently arranged on-site; most charge around $30 for a private 2-hour tour. Individuals can sometimes hook up with an established group for little more than $5 per person.

Inside the Ruins

After passing through the entrance, you can either head left and straight up the hill, or go down to the right. The path up to the left takes you to the spot above the ruins, near the **Caretaker's Hut** and **Funerary Rock ❶** that affords the classic postcard overview of Machu Picchu. If you are here early enough for sunrise (6:30–7:30am), by all means do this first. The hut overlooks rows and rows of steep agricultural terraces (generally with a few llamas grazing nearby). In the morning, you might see exhausted groups of trekkers

---

ⓕun Facts Not a Woman's World

For years, the world thought Machu Picchu had been almost entirely populated by the Inca's chosen "Virgins of the Sun." Bingham and his associates originally reported that more than three-quarters of the human remains found at the site were female. Those findings have been disproved, however; the sexual makeup of the inhabitants of Machu Picchu was no different than anywhere else in society: pretty much 50/50.

arriving from several days and nights on the Inca Trail. (Most arrive at the crack of dawn for their reward, a celebratory sunrise.)

From this vantage point, you can see clearly the full layout of Machu Picchu, which had defined agricultural and urban zones; a long **dry moat ❷** separates the two sectors. Perhaps a population of 1,000 lived here at the high point of Machu Picchu.

Head down into the main section of the ruins, past a series of burial grounds and dwellings and the **main entrance to the city ❸** . A section of stones, likely a **quarry ❹** , sits atop a clearing with occasionally great views of the snowcapped peaks (Cordillera Vilcabamba) in the distance (looking southwest).

Down a steep series of stairs is one of the most famous Inca constructions, the **Temple of the Sun ★★★ ❺** (also called the Torreón). The rounded, tapering tower has extraordinary stonework, the finest in Machu Picchu: Its large stones fit together seamlessly. From the ledge above the temple, you can appreciate the window perfectly aligned for the June winter solstice, when the sun's rays come streaming through at dawn and illuminate the stone at the center of the temple. The temple is cordoned off, and entry is not permitted. Below the temple, in a cave carved from the rock, is a section traditionally called the **Royal Tomb ❻** , even though no human remains have been found there. Inside is a meticulously carved altar and series of niches that produce intricate morning shadows. To the north, just down the stairs that divide this section from a series of dwellings called the **Royal Sector,** is a still-functioning water canal and series of interconnected **fountains ❼** . The main fountain is distinguished by both its size and excellent stonework.

Back up the stairs to the high section of the ruins (north of the quarry) is the main ceremonial area. The **Temple of the Three Windows ★★ ❽** , each trapezoid extraordinarily cut with views of the bold Andes in the distance across the Urubamba gorge, is likely to be one of your lasting images of Machu Picchu. It fronts one side of the **Sacred Plaza ❾** . To the left, if you're facing the Temple of the Three Windows, is the **Principal Temple ❿** , which has masterful stonework in its three high walls. Directly opposite is the **House of the Priest ⓫** . Just behind the Principal Temple is a small cell, termed the **Sacristy,** renowned for its exquisite masonry. It's a good place to examine how amazingly these many-angled stones (one to the left of the doorjamb has 32 distinct angles) were fitted together by Inca stonemasons.

ⓘ Tips Package Visits to Machu Picchu

Machu Picchu packages that include round-trip train fare between Cusco and Aguas Calientes, shuttle bus and admission to the ruins, a guided visit, and sometimes lunch at Machu Picchu Sanctuary Lodge for same-day visits can be purchased from travel agencies in Cusco. Package deals generally start at around $150; it's worth shopping around for the best deal. Try **Milla Turismo,** Av.Pardo 689 (☏ **084/231-710;** www.millaturismo.com); **SAS Travel,** Calle Garcilaso 270, Plaza San Francisco (☏ **084/249-194;** www.sastravelperu.com); **Chaska Tours,** Garcilaso 265, 2nd Floor (☏ **084/240-424;** www.chaskatours.com); or any of the tour agencies listed later in this section that organize Inca Trail treks. Packages that include overnight accommodations at the ruins or in Aguas Calientes can also be arranged.

of the sun." It looks to be a ritualistic carved rock or a sort of sundial, and its shape echoes that of the sacred peak Huayna Picchu beyond the ruins. The stone almost certainly functioned as an astronomical and agricultural calendar (useful in judging the alignment of constellations and solar events and, thus, the seasons). It does appear to be powerfully connected to mountains in all directions. The Incas built similar monuments elsewhere across the empire, but most were destroyed by the Spaniards (who surely thought them to be instruments of pagan worship). The one at Machu Picchu survived in perfect form for nearly 5 centuries until 2001, when a camera crew sneaked in a 1,000-pound crane, which fell over and chipped off the top section of the Intihuatana.

Follow a trail down through terraces and past a small plaza to a **dusty clearing** ⓭ with covered stone benches on either side. Fronting the square is a massive, sculpted **Sacred Rock** ⓮ , whose shape mimics that of Putukusi, the sacred peak that looms due east across the valley. This area likely served as a communal area for meetings and perhaps performances. Many locals (as well as visitors) believe that the Sacred Rock transmits a palpable force of energy; place your palms on it to see if you can tap into it.

To the left of the Sacred Rock, down a path, is the gateway to **Huayna Picchu**★★ , the huge outcrop that serves as a dramatic backdrop to Machu Picchu. Although it looks forbidding and is very steep, anyone in reasonable shape can climb it. The steep path up takes most visitors about an hour or more, although some athletic sorts ascend the peak in less than 25 minutes. Guards at a small booth require visitors to sign in and out. Note, however, that only 400 people per day are permitted to make the climb; if you are keen on ascending Huyana Picchu for the views and exercise, arrive early. (The path is open 7am–1pm, and the first group of 200 must exit by 10am.) At the top, you'll reach a platform of sorts, which is as far as many get, directly overlooking the ruins. Others who've come this far and are committed to reaching the apex continue on for a few more minutes, up through a tight tunnel carved out of the stone, to a rocky perch with 360-degree views. There's room for only a handful of hikers up there, and the views are so astounding that many are tempted to hang out for hours—so new arrivals might need to be patient to win their place on the rock. The views of Machu Picchu below and the panorama of forested mountains are quite literally breathtaking.

Ascending Huayna Picchu is highly recommended for energetic sorts of any age (I've seen octogenarians climb the path at an enviable clip), but young children are not allowed. In wet weather, you might want to reconsider, though, because the stone steps can get slippery and become very dangerous.

Returning back down the same path (frighteningly steep at a couple points) is a turn-off to the **Temple of the Moon,** usually visited only by Machu Picchu completists. The trail dips down into the cloud forest and then climbs again, and is usually deserted. Cleaved into the rock at a point midway down the peak and perched above the Río Urubamba, it almost surely was not a lunar observatory, however. It is a strangely forlorn and mysterious place of caverns, niches, and enigmatic portals, with some terrific stone-work, including carved thrones and an altar. Despite its modern name, the temple was likely used for worship of the Huayna Picchu mountain spirit. The path takes about 1 to 1½ hours round-trip from the detour.

Passing the guard post (where you'll need to sign out), continue back into the main Machu Picchu complex and enter the lower section of the ruins, separated from the spiritually oriented upper section by a **Central Plaza** ⓯ . The lower section was more prosaic in function, mostly residential and industrial. Eventually, you'll come to a series

Bingham, the "Discoverer" of Machu Picchu

Hiram Bingham is credited with the "scientific discovery" of Machu Picchu, but, in fact, when he stumbled upon the ruins with the aid of a local campesino, he didn't know what he'd found. Bingham, an archaeologist and historian at Yale University (and later governor of Connecticut), had come to Peru to satisfy his curiosity about a fabled lost Inca city. He led an archaeological expedition to Peru in 1911, sponsored by Yale University and the National Geographical Society. Bingham was in search of Vilcabamba the Old, the final refuge of seditious Inca Manco Cápac and his sons, who retreated there after the siege of Cusco in 1537.

From Cusco, Bingham and his team set out for the jungle through the Urubamba Valley. The group came upon a major Inca site, which they named Patallacta (Llaqtapata), ruins near the start of the Inca Trail. A week into the expedition, at Mandorpampa, near today's Aguas Calientes, Bingham met Melchor Arteaga, a local farmer, who told Bingham of mysterious ruins high in the mountains on the other side of the river and offered to guide the expedition to them. In the rain, the two climbed the steep mountain. Despite his grandiose claims, the ruins were not totally overgrown; a small number of campesinos were farming among them.

In *The Lost City of the Incas,* Bingham writes: "I soon found myself before the ruined walls of buildings built with some of the finest stonework of the Incas. It was difficult to see them as they were partially covered over by trees and moss, the growth of centuries; but in the dense shadow, hiding in bamboo thickets and toggled vines, could be seen here and there walls of white granite ashlars most carefully cut and exquisitely fitted together . . . I was left truly breathless."

Bingham was convinced that he'd uncovered the rebel Inca's stronghold, Vilcabamba. Yet Vilcabamba was known to have been hastily built—and Machu Picchu clearly was anything but—and most accounts had it lying much deeper in the jungle. Moreover, the Spaniards were known to have ransacked Vilcabamba, and there is no evidence whatsoever of Machu Picchu having suffered an attack. Despite these contradictions, Bingham's pronouncement was accepted for more than 50 years. The very name should have been a dead

of cells and quarters, called the **Group of the Three Doors** 🔟 and the **Mortar District** or Industrial Sector 🔟. By far, the most interesting part of this lower section is the **Temple of the Condor** 🔟. Said to be a carving of a giant condor, the dark rock above symbolizes the great bird's wings and the pale rock below quite clearly represents its head. You can actually crawl through the cave at the base of the rock and emerge on the other side.

Apart from the main complex, west of Machu Picchu, is **the Inca Bridge,** built upon stacked stones and overlooking a sheer, nearly 2,000 ft drop. Critical to the citadel's defense, the bridge can be reached in an easy half hour from a clearly marked narrow trail.

giveaway: Vilcabamba means "Sacred Plain" in Quechua, hardly a description one would attach to Machu Picchu, nestled high in the mountains.

In 1964, the U.S. explorer Gene Savoy discovered what are now accepted as the true ruins of Vilcabamba, at Espíritu Pampa, a several-day trek into the jungle. Strangely enough, it seems certain that Hiram Bingham had once come across a small section of Vilcabamba, but he dismissed the ruins as minor.

The Machu Picchu ruins were excavated by a Bingham team in 1915. A railway from Cusco to Aguas Calientes, begun 2 years earlier, was finally completed in 1928. The road up the hillside to the ruins, inaugurated by Bingham himself, was completed in 1948. Bingham died still believing Machu Picchu was Vilcabamba, even though he'd actually uncovered something much greater—and more mysterious.

Bingham took some 11,000 pictures of Machu Picchu on his second visit in 1912 and eventually removed more than 45,000 artifacts for study in the U.S. (with the permission of the Peruvian government under the agreement that they would be returned to Peru when there was a suitable place for their storage and continued study). Peru claims the agreement was for 18 months, but the objects until now have remained at Yale University's Peabody Museum in New Haven, Connecticut for nearly a century. A U.S. traveling exhibition was organized in 2003, and after years of negotiations and threats of lawsuits, Yale and the Peruvian government have finally come to an agreement that recognizes that Peru holds title to the artifacts (though the former first lady of Peru, Eliane Karp-Toledo, has argued that Yale still has not relinquished its claim to all of the items taken from Machu Picchu; Yale disputes this and contends that the agreement does recognize Peru's sole title to all materials). Some 400 museum-quality Bingham artifacts will now be returned to Peru, and some items will remain at Yale for continued research. Under the agreement, Yale will assist Peru in organizing an international touring exhibit of 350 artifacts and serve as an advisor for a new $5-million museum to be built in Cusco for the collection. Further research, both sides say, will be based on collaboration rather than contention.

For those who haven't yet had their fill of Machu Picchu, the climb up to **Intipunku (Sun Gate)** is well worth it. The path just below the **Caretaker's Hut** leads to the final pass of the route Inca Trail hikers use to enter the ruins. The views from the gateway, with Huayna Picchu looming in the background, are spectacular. Two stone gates here correspond to the all-important winter and summer solstices; on those dates, the sun's rays illuminate the gates like a laser.

For a more detailed guide of the ruins and Machu Picchu's history, Peter Frost's *Exploring Cusco* (Nuevas Imágenes, 1999), available in Cusco bookstores, is quite excellent.

At its most basic, the Inca Trail (Camino del Inca) was a footpath through the Andes leading directly to the gates of Machu Picchu. Contrary to its image as a lone, lost, remote city, Machu Picchu was not isolated in the clouds. It was the crown of an entire Inca province, as ruins all along the Inca Trail attest. Machu Picchu was an administrative center in addition to its other putative purposes. That larger purpose is comprehensible only to those who hike the ancient royal route and visit the other ruins scattered along the way to the sacred city.

More than that, though, the Incas conceived of Machu Picchu and the great trail leading to it in grand artistic and spiritual terms. Hiking the Inca Trail—the ancient royal highway—is, hands down, the most authentic and scenic way to visit Machu Picchu and get a clear grasp of the Incas' overarching architectural concept and supreme regard for nature. As impressive as Machu Picchu itself, the trail traverses a 325-sq.-km (125-sq.-mile) national park designated as the Machu Picchu Historical Sanctuary. The entire zone is replete with extraordinary natural and man-made sights: Inca ruins, exotic vegetation and animals, and dazzling mountain and cloud-forest vistas.

Today the Inca Trail—which, as part of the Machu Picchu Historical Sanctuary, has been designated a World Heritage natural and cultural site—is the most important and most popular hiking trail in South America, followed by many thousands of ecotourists and modern-day pilgrims in the past 3 decades. Its extreme popularity in recent years—more than 75,000 people a year hike the famous trail—has led to concerns among environmentalists and historians that the trail is suffering potentially irreparable degradation. The National Institute of Culture (INC) and the Ministry of Industry, Tourism, Integration, and International Trade (MITINCI), reacting to pressure from groups such as UNESCO (which threatened to rescind Machu Picchu's World Heritage Site status), instituted far-reaching changes in practices designed to limit the number of visitors and damage to Machu Picchu and the Inca Trail, though these alone may not be enough to forestall the trail's damage; see the "Inca Trail Regulations" box on p. 279.

There are two principal ways to walk to Machu Picchu: either along the traditional, fairly arduous 4-day/3-night path with three serious mountain passes, or as part of a more accessible 2-day/1-night trail (there's also an even shorter 1-day trek that covers just the last part of the trail, which is suitable for inexperienced walkers). You can hire porters to haul your packs or suck it up and do it the hard way. Independent trekking on the Inca Trail without an official guide has been prohibited since 2001. **You must go as part of an organized group arranged by an officially sanctioned tour agency** (at last count, 140 agencies, both in Cusco and beyond, were allowed to sell Inca Trail packages). A couple or a small number of people can organize their own group if they are willing to pay higher prices for the luxury of not having to join an ad-hoc group.

Sadly, even with the new regulations, hiking the Inca Trail, beautiful and mystical as it remains for most, is not a silent, solitary walk in the clouds. At least in high season, you will contend with groups walking the trail both in front of and behind you, and some will invariably be noisy student groups.

Preparing for Your Trek

The classic **4-day route** is along hand-hewn stone stairs and trails through sumptuous mountain scenery and amazing cloud forest, past rushing rivers and dozens of Inca ruins. The zone is inhabited by rare orchids, 419 species of birds, and even the indigenous spectacled bear. The trek begins at Qorihuayrachina near Ollantaytambo—more easily described as Km 88 of the railway from Cusco to Aguas Calientes. The 43km (26-mile) route passes three formidable mountain passes, including the punishing "Dead Woman's Pass," to a maximum altitude of 4,200m (13,800 ft.). Most groups enter the ruins of Machu Picchu at sunrise on the fourth day, although others, whose members are less keen on rising at 3:30am to do it, trickle in throughout the morning.

The **2-day version** of the trail is being promoted by authorities as the Camino Sagrado del Inca, or "Sacred Trail," although it might also be called the Camino "Lite." It is a reasonable alternative to the classic trail if time or fitness is lacking. The path rises only to an elevation of about 2,750m (9,020 ft.) and is a relatively easy climb to Huiñay Huayna and then down to Machu Picchu. The minitrail begins only 14km (8¾ miles) away from Machu Picchu, at Km 104, and it circumvents much of the finest mountain scenery and ruins. Groups spend the night near the ruins of Huiñay Huayna before arriving at Machu Picchu for sunrise on the second day. More and more people of all ages and athletic abilities are tackling the Inca Trail; the Peruvian government, in addition to adopting more stringent regulations governing its use, also placed flush toilets in campsites several years ago in an attempt to make the trail cleaner and more user-friendly.

Either way you go, it is advisable to give yourself a couple of days in Cusco or a spot in the Sacred Valley to acclimatize to the high elevation. Cold- and wet-weather technical

On the Trail of "New" Inca Cities: The Discovery Continues

Ever since the demise of the Inca Empire, rumors, clues, and fabulous tales of a fabled lost Inca city stuffed with gold and silver have rippled across Peru. The tales prompted searches, discoveries, and, often, reevaluations. Machu Picchu wasn't the lost and last city Hiram Bingham thought it was—Vilcabamba the Old was the last refuge of the Incas. The search continues, though, and incredibly, new discoveries continue to occur in the Andes. First, it was Choquequirao in the early 1990s. More recently, other teams have announced the discoveries of other lost Inca cities.

The discovery of **Qorihuayrachina** (also called **Cerro Victoria,** the name of the peak it rests on), 35km (22 miles) southwest of Machu Picchu in the Andes, was announced by the National Geographic Society in March 2002. Led by Peter Frost, a group of explorers uncovered the ruins of a large settlement that might have been occupied by the Incas long before they'd built a continent-spanning empire. Among the ruins are tombs and platforms, suggestive of an important burial site and sacred rites, although there are also indications that the site was an entire city. The ruins cover 6 sq. km (2^1/$_3$ sq. miles) and occupy a spectacular mountaintop location with panoramic views of the Vilcabamba range's snowcapped peaks, which were considered sacred by the Incas. Archaeologists, claiming that Qorihuayrachina is one of the most important sites found in the Vilcabamba region since it was abandoned by the Incas nearly 500 years ago, have high hopes that the ruins will help them piece together the Inca Empire from beginning to end.

Frost claimed the site was the largest of its kind found since 1964. Comprising 100 structures, including circular homes, storehouses, cemeteries, funeral towers, roadways, waterworks, farming terraces, a dam, and a pyramid, the city might have been occupied by the Incas who fled Cusco after the Spanish conquest. The ruins are secluded in cloud forest in the remote Vilcabamba region.

Just months after the discovery of Qorihuayrachina in 2002, the British Royal Geographic Society, led by Hugh Thompson and Gary Ziegler, announced the finding of a major new Inca site, **Cota Coca,** only a few kilometers away but across a deep canyon from Choquequirao (a road might have connected the two). Wholly unknown to the outside world until its discovery, Cota Coca—97km (60 miles) west of Cusco—appears to have been an administrative and storage center.

Llaqtapata, rediscovered by a U.S. and British team using remote (aerial) infrared technology and reported in November 2003, is the most recent Inca city to (re)surface. Just 3km (1^3/$_4$ miles) from Machu Picchu, it, too, had been visited by Bingham and several explorers in the 1980s, so it's open to interpretation how new its "discovery" in fact is.

How long these discoveries might go on is anyone's guess. According to Hugh Thomson, "The physical geography of southeast Peru is so wild, with its deep canyons and dense vegetation, that it is possible that there are even more ruins waiting to be discovered. The fact that we have found two in 2 years means there could be many more out there."

gear, a solid backpack, and comfortable, sturdy, broken-in (and waterproof) hiking boots **277** are musts (also needed: sleeping bag, flashlight/headlamp, and sun block). Above all, respect the ancient trail and its environment. Whatever you pack in, you must also pack out. You should also choose your dates carefully. The dry season (June–Oct) is the most crowded time on the trail, but it's excellent in terms of weather. Shoulder seasons can be best of all, even with the threat of a bit of rain; May is perhaps best, with good weather and low numbers of trekkers. Other months—especially December through March—are simply too wet for all but the hardest-core trail vets. The entire trail is now closed for maintenance and conservation during the month of February—which was one of the rainiest and least appealing months for trekking to Machu Picchu anyway. For the most popular months (May–Sept), early booking (at least 3 months in advance) is essential.

The Peruvian government has sought to limit the number of trekkers on the Inca Trail (now capped at 200 trekkers or 500 total, including trek staff, per day), but also to maximize revenue from one of its foremost attractions. Thus, the cost of hiking the trail has steadily climbed—it now costs at least three times what it did just a few years ago. Standard-class 4-day treks, the most common and economical service, start at about $450 per person, including entrance fees ($88 adults, $44 students) and return by tourist trail. Independent trekkers generally join a mixed group of travelers; groups tend to be between 12 and 16 people, with guaranteed daily departures. The cost includes a bus to Km 88 to begin the trek, an English-speaking guide, tents, mattresses, three daily meals, and porters who carry all common equipment. Tips for porters or guides are extra. Personal porters, to carry your personal items, can be hired for about $130 for the 4 days. Premium-class services generally operate smaller group sizes (a maximum of 10 trekkers), and you generally get an upgrade on the return train. Prices for premium group treks, organized for private groups, range from $750 to as high as $1,000 per person.

Prices vary for trail packages based on services and the quality and experience of the agency. In general, you get what you pay for. Rock-bottom prices will probably get you an inexperienced guide who speaks little English, food that is barely edible, camping equipment on its last legs, and a large, rowdy group (usually 16 young trekkers). Especially important is the ability of an agency to guarantee departure even if its desired target number of travelers is not filled.

Never purchase Inca Trail (or, for that matter, any tour) packages from anyone other than officially licensed agencies, and be careful to make payments (and get official receipts) at the physical offices of the agencies. If you have questions about whether an agency is legitimate or is authorized to sell Inca Trail packages, ask for assistance at the main tourism information office in Cusco.

To guarantee a spot with an agency (which must request a trek permit for each trekker) it is imperative that you make a reservation and pay for your entrance fee a minimum of

Tips   Howling at the Moon

For a truly spectacular experience on the Inca Trail, plan your trip to coincide with a full moon (ideally, departing 2 or 3 days beforehand). Locals say the weather's best then, and having your nights illuminated by a full or near-full moon, especially for the early rise and push into Machu Picchu on the last day, is unforgettable.

15 days in advance (though in practice you'd be wise to do this at least 4–6 months or more in advance if you plan to go during peak months of May–Oct). Reservations can be made as much as a year in advance. Gone are the days when trekkers could simply show up in Cusco and organize a trek on the fly. Changing dates once you have a reservation is difficult, if not impossible. If spots remain on agency rosters, they are offered on a first-come, first-served basis.

The entrance ticket for the 2-day Camino Sagrado, purchased in Cusco, is $47 for adults and $27 for students. Basic pooled service (maximum 16 trekkers) costs about $150 per person (including the entrance fee). There are no premium-class services for the 2-day trek.

Inca Trail Tour Agencies

Only officially sanctioned travel agencies are permitted to organize group treks along the Inca Trail; at least 160 tour operators (!)—both Peruvian and international—have been granted government licenses to sell and operate Inca Trail treks. With the higher-end agencies, it is usually possible to assemble your own private group, with as few as two hikers. Budget trekkers will join an established group. In addition to cost, hikers should ask about group size (12 or fewer is best; 16 is the most allowed), the quality of the guides and their English-speaking abilities, the quality of food preparation, and porters and equipment. You should also make certain that the agency guarantees daily departures so that you're not stuck waiting in Cusco for a group to be assembled.

Recommended agencies that score high on those criteria follow. (Note that the addresses and phone numbers below change frequently; the websites are more reliable sources of info.)

- **Andean Life,** Plateros 372 (© 084/221-491; www.andeanlifeperu.com): A reputable midrange company offering both pooled basic and premium private treks with good guides.
- **Andean Treks ★★**, Av. Pardo 705 (© 800/683-8148 in the U.S. and Canada, 084/225-701 in Cusco; www.andeantreks.com): A longtime (since 1980), well-thought-of outdoors operator based in Watertown, Massachusetts, running 5-day treks along the Inca Trail as well as numerous other programs in Latin America.
- **Andina Travel,** Plazoleta Santa Catalina 219 (© 084/251-892; www.andinatravel.com): An upstart, progressive company interested in sustainable development, owned by a Cusco native and his North American business partner.
- **Big Foot Tour Operator,** Triunfo 392, 2nd Floor (© 084/991-3851; fax 084/222-123; www.bigfootcusco.com): A popular budget agency.
- **Chaska Tours,** Garcilaso 265, 2nd Floor (© 084/240-424; www.chaskatours.com): A very capable midrange company, run by a Dutch and Peruvian team, praised for its private and group treks to Machu Picchu as well as Choquequirao.
- **Enigma ★**, Jirón Clorinda Matto de Turner, 100 Urbanización Magisterial 1 Etapa (© 084/221-155; fax 084/221-153; www.enigmaperu.com): A relatively new adventure travel operator with a good reputation and specialized and alternative hiking and trekking options, good for small-group and private treks.
- **Explorandes ★★**, Av. Garcilaso 316-A (© 084/238-380; fax 084/233-784; www.explorandes.com): One of the top high-end agencies and the most experienced in treks and mountaineering across Peru. Especially good for forming very small private groups.
- **Inca Explorers ★★**, Ruinas 427 (© 084/241-070; fax 084/239-669; www.incaexplorers.com): One of the best agencies, offering midrange, comfortable Inca Trail treks. Porters carry hikers' packs, and groups are small (including private group treks).

Inca Trail Regulations

For decades, individuals trekked the Inca Trail on their own, but hundreds of thousands of visitors—more than 75,000 a year—have left behind so much detritus that not only was the experience compromised for most future trekkers, but the very environment was also placed at risk. The entire zone has suffered grave deforestation and erosion. The Peruvian government, under pressure from international organizations, has finally instituted changes and restrictions designed to lessen the human impact on the trail and on Machu Picchu itself: In the first couple of years, regulations were poorly enforced, but in 2003, the government announced its intentions to fully and strictly enforce them.

All trekkers are now required to go accompanied by a guide and a group. In addition, the overall number of trekkers permitted on the trail was significantly reduced, to 200 per day; the maximum number of trekkers per group outing is capped at 16; only professionally qualified and licensed guides are allowed to lead groups on the Inca Trail; the maximum loads porters can carry has been limited to 20 kilograms (44 lb.); tourists are no longer permitted to travel on the local train from Aguas Calientes to Machu Picchu (or vice versa); and all companies must pay porters the minimum wage (about $15 per day).

These changes have cut the number of trekkers on the trail in half and have made reservations essential in high season. Guarantee your space on the trail by making a reservation at least 15 days in advance of your trip (but 4–6 months or more in advance for high season May–Oct; reservations can be made as much as a year in advance). Travelers willing to wing it stand an outside chance of still finding available spots a week or few days before embarking on the trail, perhaps even at discounted rates, but waiting until you arrive in Cusco is a ridiculous risk if you're really counting on doing the Inca Trail.

The key changes for travelers are that it is no longer possible to go on the trail independently and no longer dirt-cheap to walk 4 days to Machu Picchu. The good news is that the trail is more organized and that hope for its preservation is greater.

- **Mayuc** ★, Portal de Confiturías 211, Plaza de Armas (© **866/777-9213** in the U.S. and Canada or 084/242-824 in Cusco; www.mayuc.com): Especially good for pampered Inca Trail expeditions (porters carry all packs). It aims to be low impact, and hosts smaller groups.
- **Q'Ente** ★, Garcilaso 210 (© **084/222-535;** fax 084/222-535; www.qente.com). Receives very high marks from budget travelers. It's very competitively priced, with responsible, good guides, and also offers a premium trek with a maximum of eight trekkers.
- **SAS Travel,** Garcilaso 270, Plaza San Francisco (© **084/249-194;** fax 084/225-757; www.sastravelperu.com): Large, long-established agency serving budget-oriented trekkers. Very popular, responsible, and well organized.
- **United Mice** ★, Plateros 351 (© **084/221-139;** www.unitedmice.com): Started by one of the trail's most respected guides, this is another of the top agencies organizing affordable midrange treks.

(Tips) The Road Less (or More Comfortably) Traveled: Alternatives to the Inca Trail ★★★

The legendary Inca Trail was once very much off the beaten path and at the cutting edge of adventure travel—for hard-core trekkers only. Although the Peruvian government adopted new measures to restrict the numbers of trekkers along the trail, it has become so popular and well-worn that in high season it's tough to find the solitude and quiet contemplation such a sacred path deserves. Trekkers and travelers looking for more privacy, greater authenticity, or bragging rights are seeking out alternatives, and many adventure-travel companies are catering to them by offering less accessible trails to keep one step ahead of the masses. Several international operators now offer custom-designed alternatives to the traditional Inca Trail, and many Peru cognoscenti believe this is the future of trekking in Cusco and the Sacred Valley. Some of the challenging treks terminate in visits to Machu Picchu, while others explore stunning but much less-visited Inca ruins like Choquequirao. **Adventure Life** ★ (© 800/344-6118; www.adventurelife.com) promotes a 10-day Cachiccata trek and 11-day Ausangate trip Alternative; **Andean Treks** ★★ (© 800/683-8148; www.andeantreks.com) offers a 4-day "Moonstone to Sun Temple" trek, as well as others to Choquequirao and Ausangate; **Mountain Travel Sobek** ★★ (© 888/831-7526; www.mtsobek.com) offers a 12-day (7 days hiking) "Other Inca Trail"; **Peru for Less** ★★ (© 877/2609-0309; www.peruforless.com), originally based in the U.S., recently launched a series of small-group, alternative treks in the Vilcabamba region, with trips to Choquequirao, Ausangate, and Espíritu Pampa; and **Wilderness Travel** ★★ (© 800/368-2794; www.wildernesstravel.com) has a 17-day (13 days hiking) "Choquequirao to Machu Picchu Hidden Inca Trail" tour. Most treks range from about $600 to $4,000 per person.

The trend toward luxury, or soft, adventure is also gaining traction in the Peruvian Andes, and companies offering treks to Machu Picchu and other highland destinations are targeting more affluent and creature comfort–oriented travelers who want the adventure experience without roughing it too much. **Mountain Lodges of Peru** ★★★ (© 01/421-7777 or 510/525-8846 in the U.S. and Canada; www.mountainlodgesofperu.com), a Peruvian adventure

Day-by-Day: The Classic 4-Day Inca Trail Trek

The following is typical of the group-organized 4-day/3-night schedule along the Inca Trail.

DAY 1 Trekkers arrive from Cusco, either by train, getting off at the midway stop, Ollantaytambo, or Km 88; or by bus, at Km 82, the preferred method of transport for many groups. (Starting at Km 82 doesn't add an appreciable distance to the trail.) After crossing the Río Urubamba (Vilcanota), the first gentle ascent of the trail looms to Inca ruins at **Llaqtapata** (also called **Patallacta,** where Bingham and his team first camped on the way to Machu Picchu). The path then crosses the Río Cusicacha, tracing the line of the river until it begins to climb and reaches the small village (the only one still inhabited travel company, has constructed four lodges on private lands in the Vilcabamba mountain range west of the Sacred Valley. The inns are stunning, not only for their high-altitude locations but also their sophisticated architecture and amenities—which include whirlpools, hot showers, fireplaces, and sleek dining rooms. Mountain Lodges offers its own 7-day treks ($2,650 per person), culminating in a visit to Machu Picchu, but the company has also contracted with international trekking and adventure companies, including **Backroads** (℃ **800/462-2848;** www.backroads.com), **Wilderness Travel,** and **Mountain Travel Sobek** (above), which have booked the lodges for their own 9-day (5 days trekking) "Machu Picchu Lodge to Lodge" or "Inn to Inn" packages. Prices for full trips, including stays in Cusco, run to $4,995 per person. **Andean Lodges ★** (℃ **084/224-613;** www.andeanlodges.com), a rare joint initiative between the tour group Auqui Mountain Spirit and local Quechua shepherding communities, operates four simple and ecofriendly mountain lodges, which it claims are the highest altitude lodges in the world (at 13,000–15,000 ft.), along the Camino del Apu Ausangate (in the Vilcanota range). Trek prices start at $845 per person.

If the notion of luxury adventure travel doesn't excite your inner hard-core adventurer, consider one of the spectacularly scenic (and arduous 4- to 11-day) treks that have gained wider traction in the last few years: **Salcantay, Vilcabamba, Espíritu Pampa,** and **Choquequirao,** the last two "lost" Inca cities only truly unearthed in the past decade. All are increasingly offered by local trek tour agencies in Cusco and some of the most established international trekking and Peruvian travel companies (see above). Much as I hate to disparage the legendary Camino Inca, it has become too popular and laden with restrictions and hassles for many adventure travelers to enjoy it the way it was intended. By going off the standard trekking grid, not only can you be sure that when you get back to Cusco not everyone in the coffeehouse will have the same bragging rights, you are likely to have a more authentic, peaceful and exhilarating outdoors and cultural experience.

along the trail) of **Huayllabamba**—a 2- to 3-hour climb. Most groups spend their first night at campsites here. Total distance: 10 to 11km (6¼–6¾ miles).

DAY 2 Day 2 is the hardest of the trek. The next ruins are at **Llullucharoc** (3,800m/12,460 ft.), about an hour's steep climb from Huayllabamba. **Llulluchapampa,** an isolated village that lies in a flat meadow, is a strenuous 90-minute to 2-hour climb through cloud forest. There are extraordinary valley views from here. Next up is the dreaded Abra de Huarmihuañusqa, or **Dead Woman's Pass,** the highest point on the trail and infamous among veterans of the Inca Trail. (The origin of the name—or who the poor victim was—is anybody's guess.) The air is thin, and the 4,200m (13,780-ft.) pass is a killer for most: a punishing 2½-hour climb in the hot sun, which is replaced by cold winds at the top. It's not uncommon for freezing rain or even snow to meet trekkers atop the pass. After a deserved rest at the summit, the path descends sharply on complicated stone steps to **Pacamayo** (3,600m/11,810 ft.), where groups camp for the night. Total distance: 11km (6¾ miles).

DAY 3   By the third day, most of the remaining footpath is the original work of the Incas. (In previous sections, the government "restored" the stonework with a heavy hand.) En route to the next mountain pass (1 hr.), trekkers encounter the ruins of **Runcuracay.** The circular structure (the name means "basket shaped") is unique among those found along the trail. From here, a steep 45-minute to 1-hour climb leads to the second pass, **Abra de Runcuracay** (3,900m/12,790 ft.), and the location of an official campsite just over the summit. There are great views of the Vilcabamba mountain range. After passing through a naturally formed tunnel, the path leads past a lake and a stunning staircase to **Sayacmarca** (3,500m/11,480 ft.), named for its nearly inaccessible setting surrounded by dizzying cliffs. Among the ruins are ritual baths and a terrace view point overlooking the Aobamba Valley, suggesting that the site was not inhabited but instead served as a resting point for travelers and as a control station.

The trail backtracks a bit on the way to **Conchamarca,** another rest stop. Here, the well-preserved Inca footpath drops into jungle thick with exotic vegetation, such as lichens, hanging moss, bromeliads, and orchids, and some of the zone's unique bird species. After passing through another Inca tunnel, the path climbs gently for 2 hours along a stone road, toward the trail's third major pass, **Phuyupatamarca** (3,800m/12,460 ft.); the final climb is considerably easier than the two that came before it. This is a spectacular section of the trail, with great views of the Urubamba Valley. Some of the region's highest snowcapped peaks (all over 5,500m/18,040 ft.), including Salcantay, are clearly visible, and the end of the trail is in sight. The tourist town of Aguas Calientes lies below, and trekkers can see the backside of Machu Picchu (the peak, not the ruins).

From the peak, trekkers reach the beautiful, restored Inca **ruins of Phuyupatamarca.** The ancient village is another one aptly named: It translates as "Town above the Clouds." The remains of six ceremonial baths are clearly visible, as are retaining-wall terraces. A stone staircase of 2,250 steps plummets into the cloud forest, taking about 90 minutes to descend. The path forks, with the footpath on the left leading to the fan-shaped **Intipata terraces.** On the right, the trail pushes on to the extraordinary ruins of **Huiñay Huayna** ★★, which are actually about a 10-minute walk from the trail. Back at the main footpath, there's a campsite and ramshackle trekker's hostel offering hot showers, food, and drink. The grounds are a major gathering place for trekkers before the final push to Machu Picchu, and for some, they're a bit too boisterous and unkempt, an unpleasant intrusion after all the pristine beauty up to this point on the trail. Although it's closest to Machu Picchu, the Huiñay Huayna ruins, nearly the equal of Machu

---

ⓘ Tips   About Tipping

At the end of the Inca Trail, guides, cooks, and especially porters expect—and fully deserve—to be tipped for their services. They get comparatively little of the sum hikers pay to form part of the group, and they depend on tips for most of their salary, much like waitstaff in American restaurants. Tip to the extent that you are able.

Picchu, were only discovered in 1941. Its name, which means "Forever Young," refers not to its relatively recent discovery, but to the perpetually flowering orchid of the same name that is found in abundance nearby. The stop was evidently an important one along the trail; on the slopes around the site are dozens of stone agricultural terraces, and 10 ritual baths, which still have running water, awaited travelers. Total distance: 15km (9⅓ miles).

DAY 4   From Huiñay Huayna, trekkers have but one goal remaining: reaching Intipunku (the Sun Gate) and descending to Machu Picchu, preferably in time to witness the dramatic sunrise over the ruins. Most groups depart camp at 4am or earlier to reach the pass at Machu Picchu and arrive in time for daybreak, around 6:30am. Awaiting them first, though, is a good 60- to 90-minute trek along narrow Inca stone paths, and then a final killer: a 50-step, nearly vertical climb. The descent from Intipunku to Machu Picchu takes about 45 minutes.

Having reached the ruins, trekkers have to exit the site and deposit their backpacks at the entrance gate near the hotel. There, they also get their entrance passes to Machu Picchu stamped; the pass is good for 1 day only. Total distance: 7km (4⅓ miles).

AGUAS CALIENTES (MACHU PICCHU PUEBLO)

Renamed Machu Picchu Pueblo by the Peruvian government—a name adopted by almost no one—Aguas Calientes is quite literally the end of the line, a gringo outpost of *mochileros* (backpackers) outfitted in the latest alpaca and indigenous weave fashions designed to tempt them. Hats, gloves, sweaters—they are walking (if unshaved) advertisements for Peruvian artisanship. Making it Peru's own little Katmandu, the trekkers hang out for a few days after their great journey to Machu Picchu, sharing beers and tales, and scoring a final woven hat or scarf to wear as a trophy back home.

To be honest, there's not much else to do in Aguas Calientes, which might as well be called Aires Calientes, given its sweltering heat and humidity. The town has *baños termales,* or outdoor **hot springs**—the source of the town's name—that are a 10-minute climb up Avenida Pachacútec. Many visitors find them rather hygienically challenged, if not downright nasty, but they're popular with folks who've completed the Inca Trail and are in desperate need of muscular relaxation (not to mention a bath). The one pool with freezing mountain water can be tremendously restorative if you've just finished a long day at the ruins, but the smell of iron is overpowering. The springs are open from 5am to 9pm; admission is S/10. Just be sure to leave your valuables locked up at the hotel.

Adventurous sorts not yet exhausted from climbing might want to climb the sacred mountain **Putukusi ★★**, which commands extraordinary distant views across the river to the ruins of Machu Picchu. The trail begins on the right side of the railroad just out of town. (A signpost reads KM 111.) Veer to the right up stone steps and get ready for an athletic feat, struggling up vertical ladders (several of which aren't in the best of shape) until you reach a clearing and series of stone-carved switchbacks. At the top, Machu Picchu is nestled like an architectural model between its two famous peaks. The trek up takes about 75 minutes; the descent takes 45 minutes. Gazing across the valley at the ancient Inca city? Priceless. Although they've repaired the trail and fixed missing steps, it is still mostly for fit climbers.

Another good trail, particularly for bird-watchers, is the short trail to **Mandor Ravine** and a waterfall found there. From the railroad tracks, walk downstream (beyond the old train station) until you come to the ravine (about 3km/1¾ miles). A short climb takes you to the waterfall.

Mudslides at Machu Picchu

The most recent mudslide at Machu Picchu occurred in January 2010, when five people (including two on the Inca trail) were killed and 2,000 tourists stranded, requiring airlift evacuations by helicopter. Officials said the rains that swelled the Urubamba River were the heaviest in 15 years, and floods affected 80,000 people living in or near Aguas Calientes, leaving many homeless. Train service to Machu Picchu was not restored for more than a month. It was the latest in a series of catastrophic rain-related events near the ancient ruins. In October 2005, an avalanche destroyed part of the train track leading from Cusco to Machu Picchu, stranding 1,400 travelers, and before that, in April 2004, two massive mudslides at the tail end of the rainy season hit Aguas Calientes, killing six local people and stranding as many as 1,500 tourists for the duration of Easter weekend.

Such destructive rains may not be the norm, but they highlight both the dangers of traveling in the highlands during the wet season as well as the precarious infrastructure of Aguas Calientes and its ill-preparedness to handle the explosive growth of tourism in recent years.

In the evening, most folks take to the bars for a few beers. A good spot for music and drinks is **Blues Bar Café,** Av. Pachacútec s/n (© **084/211-125**), an airy, cabinlike two-level place next to the park on restaurant row. In the late afternoon, it's a fine place to chill and gaze out at Putukusi, the mountain across from Machu Picchu.

WHERE TO STAY

At the upper end, hotels in and around Machu Picchu Pueblo have suddenly gotten very expensive—more costly than anything comparable in all of Peru. And it's usually only the very fortunate—those who not only plan far ahead, but who also have very healthy bank accounts—who have the option of staying at the one upscale hotel next to the ruins. For the rest of us, below the ruins in Aguas Calientes, there are scores of *hostales* (inns) aimed at the grungy backpacker crowd, a couple of midrange options, and a couple of self-styled ecolodges (one quite upscale, the other more adventurous).

Although a few new hotels have popped up to take advantage of Machu Picchu's ever-expanding popularity, there are growing concerns about the environmental impact of new construction. Indeed, UNESCO, which named the whole Machu Picchu Historical Sanctuary as a World Heritage Site, has threatened to withdraw the honor if Peru doesn't address growth and environmental concerns.

Very Expensive

Inkaterra Machu Picchu Pueblo Hotel ★★★ (Kids)   This rustic but upscale hotel, tucked into lush gardens near the train station, has real flavor and is easily the best place to stay if you can't get into the fancy hotel next to the ruins (or don't want to pay its exorbitant prices)—though this too has gotten very expensive. It's also the best place for naturalists who want to get a glimpse of some of the extraordinary bird- and plant life in this part of the Machu Picchu Historical Sanctuary; the hotel offers orchid tours, bird-watching, and guided ecological hikes. The compound of charming Spanish colonial, tile-roofed *casitas* (bungalows) is surrounded by 5 hectares (12 acres) of cloud forest beside the Vilcanota River, with a tea plantation and more than 100 species of birds and

Within the map:

To Hot Springs ↗

Tourist Info ⓘ

Colla Raymi

Lloque Yupanqui

Inca Yupanqui

Wiracocha

Yahuar Huaca

Av. Imperio de Los Incas

Colla Suyo

Plaza

ⓘ

Av. Pachacútec

Local Train Station

Sinchi Roca

Mayta Cápac

Cápac Yupanqui

Inca Roca

Bus Station (to Machu Picchu)

Mercado Artesanal

Av. Imperio de Los Incas

Río Urubamba

Estación Machu Picchu Pueblo

Soccer Field

Yahuar Huaca

PERU

Lima ★

Aguas Calientes

Cusco

To Cusco ↓

ACCOMMODATIONS ■

Gringo Bill's Hostal **7**
Hospedaje El Mirador **13**
Hostal Continental **3**
Hostal Don Guiller **11**
Hostal Ima Sumac **16**
Hostal La Cabaña **14**
Hostal Machu Picchu **4**
Hostal Pachacútec **15**
Inkaterra Machu Picchu
 Pueblo Hotel **17**
Machu Picchu Sanctuary Lodge **2**
Rupa Wasi Condor House Ecolodge **5**
Sumaq Machu Picchu Hotel **1**

DINING ◆

Chez Maggy **12**
Indio Feliz **8**
Pueblo Viejo **9**
Toto's House **10**
The Tree House **6**

---

250 species of butterflies. Regular rooms are large and comfortable, and junior suites have fireplaces and small terraces. A pretty spring-water pool makes this a great place to relax while taking in the grandeur of Machu Picchu. It's especially popular with an older set, and the only strike against it is that it sits about a 10-minute, inconvenient walk along the railroad tracks from Aguas Calientes's restaurants and bars—but that's the price to pay for a superior natural setting.

Av. Imperio de los Incas (Km 10 Línea Férrea Cusco, Quillabamba). 🕿 **800/442-5042** in the U.S. and Canada or 084/211-122; 084/245-314 for reservations. Fax 084/211-124. 86 units. $459–$516 double; $569–$960 suite. Rates include breakfast buffet. AE, DC, MC, V. **Amenities:** Restaurant; cafe; bar; outdoor pool; room service; spa; Wi-Fi. In room: Hair dryer.

Machu Picchu Sanctuary Lodge ★★ Back in the 1970s, the Peruvian government built a temporary hotel on the top of the mountain just steps from the entry to Machu Picchu as a way to show off the ruins to international movers and shakers. As the ruins grew in popularity as a destination, the hotel was rewarded with a begrudged permanence. Today the hotel stands as the only major alteration to the ruins' isolated setting, but as hotels go, it is pretty sensitively inserted into the hill and is not visible from the ruins themselves.

Formerly a rather plain but overpriced modern hotel, the rustic inn was taken over by Orient-Express Hotels (which also manages the Hotel Monasterio in Cusco) and transformed into a very pricey luxury lodge, now with a full meal plan program for guests. Without question, it has one of the most dramatic and unique settings in the world, and, as the only hotel perched right next to the ruins, it can pretty much charge what it wants (and does). Guests need very deep pockets to stay here; despite the cost, the hotel remains in high demand most of the year, so advance reservations are absolutely essential. Rooms are not especially large, but they now have a good deal of Peruvian character, with some lovely modern furnishings, and most have small terraces that open to lovely gardens with impressive views of the ruins and the surrounding Andes.

Although some will always decry the hotel as an unwelcome modern intrusion in this mystical and sacred place, it's here to stay. And who can blame travelers for wanting to stay as close to Machu Picchu as possible, waking up to see the sun rise over the ruins and, at night, visiting the ruins in the dark or gazing at the stars from an elevation of 2,400m (7,870 ft.)? If you can afford it as a special treat, you'd be wise to reserve 3 to 6 months in advance during high season (May–Oct). The buffet lunch ($35) is open to all ruins visitors.

Machu Picchu (next to the ruins). *©* **084/246-419.** Fax 084/246-983. www.machupicchu.orient-express. com. 33 units. $1,009 to $1,420 double; $1,584suite. Rates include 3 meals daily. AE, DC, MC, V. **Amenities:** Restaurant; cafeteria; snack bar; room service. *In room:* TV, fridge, hair dryer.

Expensive

Sumaq Machu Picchu Hotel ★ The newest upscale hotel in Aguas Calientes is a sprawling, cantilevered structure—with stonework designed to echo Inca masonry—near the river and a 10-minute walk from the train station, it offers spacious tiled-floor rooms with excellent bedding, soft linens, and Andean motifs in bathrooms and on the headboards. Many rooms have small balconies. Guests who are beat from scaling Machu Picchu will revel in the full-service on-premises Aqlla spa, where they can pick up a relaxing massage or indulge in the steam sauna. The restaurant terrace, with views of the surrounding mountains, is a good spot to celebrate making it to Machu Picchu.

Av. Hermanos Ayar Mz 1 Lote 3. *©* **866/682-0645** in US and Canada, or 01/447-0579. Fax 01/445-7828. www.sumaqhotelperu.com. 60 units. $603 double; $738–$932 suite. Rates include breakfast buffet. AE, DC, MC, V. **Amenities:** Restaurant; cafe; bar; room service; spa. *In room:* Fridge, hair dryer.

Moderate

Gringo Bill's Hostal ★ Gringo Bill's, established by an American expat, is a backpacker's institution that has been around since the early 1980s, when Machu Picchu began to take off. I first stayed here in 1983, at a time when there were very few other options (and it, frankly, was a dump). Tucked into the hillside behind the left corner of the Plaza de Armas, the cheery and plant-filled *hostal* has become quite a bit upscale lately. But it still has a great vibe, with a cool patio, a lounge bar with a fireplace where travelers hang out watching videos, and a pretty good restaurant. The comfortable and clean rooms have good beds, and many have great views of the Upper Amazon tropical rainforest from bedroom windows and balconies. Throughout the inn are trippy cosmic murals painted by the Cusco artist Gonzalo Medina. Visitors headed to Machu Picchu or out on treks can pick up bagged lunches to go. A stay of 2 or 3 nights will earn you a 10% discount, but some backpackers still find it comparatively expensive for budget travel.

Colla Raymi 104, Plaza de Armas, Aguas Calientes. *©*/fax **084/211-046,** or 084/241-545 for reservations. Fax 084/211-046. www.gringobills.com. 86 units. $75 double; $105–$135 suite. Rates include continental breakfast. AE, MC, V. **Amenities:** Restaurant; bar; TV room. *In room:* TV in newer rooms, no phone (in older rooms).

(Tips) More Places to Crash in Aguas Calientes

Aguas Calientes fits the classic definition of a tourist town: It basically exists to accommodate gringos on their way up to or down from Machu Picchu. The town is little more than two main streets crammed with basic hostels, restaurants, and bars. But in the winter months (June–Aug), it gets very crowded, and finding accommodations can be a little complicated if you're the backpacker type arriving on the fly. In addition to the choices reviewed in this section, you might want to check out the following, which are all pretty decent, clean, and moderately priced (ranging from $10–$35 per person) for a double room with a private bathroom).

- **Hostal Don Guiller,** Av. Pachacútec 136 ((*C*) **084/211-128**)
- **Hostal Ima Sumac,** Av. Pachacútec 173 ((*C*) **084/211-021**)
- **Hostal La Cabaña,** Av. Pachacútec 20 ((*C*) **084/211-048**)
- **Hostal Pachacútec,** Av. Pachacútec s/n ((*C*) **084/211-061**)
- **Hospedaje El Mirador,** Av. Pachacútec 135 ((*C*) **084/211-194**)

Rupa Wasi Condor House Ecolodge ★(Finds)   This cool, tree-house-like lodge isn't for everybody. While it's one of the only mid-range options in Aguas Calientes and takes seriously its role in using sustainable materials, alternative energy, and biodegradable products, it's a bit out of the way and up a long flight of about 80 stairs—which, after a visit to Machu Picchu or trekking the Inca Trail, may not exactly be welcome. Located just two blocks from the town's main square, the inn is on the edge of the Machu Picchu protected nature sanctuary and cloud forest. Built from recycled woods, it's surrounded by dozens of species of orchids and native trees. The downside? It can be extremely damp. The three cheery upstairs suites (especially room no. 5) with private balconies and great views of the surrounding Andean peaks are vastly superior to the plain downstairs standard rooms (which are overpriced as basic as they are). The inn features a charming restaurant (The Tree House) and offers terrific cooking classes and boxed lunches.

Jr. Huanacaure 180, Aguas Calientes. (*C*) **084/211-101.** www.rupawasi.net. 5 units. $69–$99 double. Rates include continental breakfast. AE, DC, MC, V. **Amenities:** Restaurant.

Inexpensive

Hostal Continental (Value)   One of the nicer inexpensive *hostales* along the main drag and railroad tracks, this basic hotel is very tidy, and you won't lack for hot water. Rooms aren't large, but they are stylish enough for the price, and the beds are pretty decent—making it a budget backpacker's delight. It used to have great river views, but, sadly, boomtown construction has done away with them. Extras include a library.

Av. Imperio de los Incas 177, Aguas Calientes. (*C*) **084/211-065** or 084/244-598. presidente@terra.com. pe. 12 units. $60 double. Rates include taxes and continental breakfast. No credit cards. **Amenities:** Library. *In room:* No phone.

Hostal Machupicchu   Across from the police station and, in true frontier fashion, right on the train tracks (a better location than it sounds—a balcony on the other side overlooks the Vilcanota River, and the hostel is perfectly positioned for barhopping), this midsize hotel is one of the better less-expensive options in Aguas Calientes, though that's not saying a whole lot. It has very clean, well-furnished, and airy rooms, some painted in funky colors. Its sister hotel next door, the Presidente, has 28 rooms and is pretty similar but slightly costlier.

Av. Imperio de los Incas s/n, Aguas Calientes. © **084/211-065** or 084/244-598. Fax 084/212-034. www. hostalmachupicchu.com. 24 units. $65 double. Rates include taxes and continental breakfast. MC, V. **Amenities:** Cafe; bar.

WHERE TO DINE IN AGUAS CALIENTES

Scores of small and friendly restaurants line the two main drags (okay, the only two real streets) in Aguas Calientes, Avenida Imperio de los Incas and Avenida Pachacútec. There's always a proliferation of cheap pizzerias/pit stops hugging the railroad tracks. If you're looking for an easy meal of wood-fired pizza, almost any spot in town can accommodate you; **El Fogón de las Mestizas** (Avenida Pachacútec) and **Incawasi, Inti Killa, Pizzería Su Chosa,** and **Pachamama** (all on Avenida Imperio de los Incas) are all dependable. Menu hawkers, often the children of the cook or owner, will try to lure you in with very cheap menu deals.

For lunch during visits to the ruins, you have two choices: the expensive buffet lunch at Machu Picchu Sanctuary Lodge or a sack lunch. I recommend the latter, especially because lunchtime is when lots of tourists vacate the ruins (pick one up at Gringo Bill's or assemble one from the breakfast buffet of your hotel).

Moderate

Indio Feliz ★★ (Value) PERUVIAN/FRENCH   A restaurant named "The Happy Indian" might not sound too P.C., especially for a place that sits at the foot of a city abandoned by the Incas sometime before the Spanish invaded, but this is Aguas Calientes's best restaurant. An attractive and friendly two-level place with lots of plants, it's usually jampacked with gringos, save the backpacker set. Even though its fixed-price menu is a great value, the restaurant qualifies as distinctly upscale in this ramshackle town. Nearly everyone opts for the three-course menu because ordering a la carte will get you basically the same thing at higher prices. Starters include quiche Lorraine and *sopa a la criolla* (Peruvian milk-based soup); the standout among main courses is the lemon or garlic trout. The ginger chicken is also quite nice, as are the desserts.

Lloque Yupanqui 4–12 (down an alley to the left off Av. Pachacútec). © **084/211-090.** Reservations recommended in high season. Main courses S/26–S/40. MC, V. Daily noon–midnight.

Pueblo Viejo PERUVIAN   One of the more animated spots on restaurant row (right at the beginning, off the plaza), Pueblo Viejo is fairly large but simple and cozy, with live Andean music and a roaring fire. It specializes in *parrilladas,* or grilled lamb, pork and alpaca, and grilled trout, and it draws plenty of backpackers and families for the low-priced fixed menus: Choose from vegetarian, *menu de la casa,* and *menu turístico* versions. You can also get good pizza.

Av. Pachacútec 108. © **084/211-193.** Reservations not accepted. Main courses S/24–S/39. MC, V. Daily noon–midnight.

Toto's House ★ (Value) PERUVIAN/PIZZA   This large restaurant, perched between the railroad tracks and the banks of the Río Vilcanota, is a terrific addition to Aguas Calientes. It's one of the nicest in town, although the food at Indio Feliz is more sophisticated. Owned by the same people who run Pueblo Viejo, it features an open area overlooking the river with refreshing mountain views. The dining room is dominated by a barbecue pit and, most days, it features live Andean music. The menu is extensive and varied, ranging from a mixed grill and trout to the standby of all restaurants in town, pizza. The lunch buffet is a good deal and popular with folks waiting for the train back to Cusco.

Av. Imperio de los Incas s/n. © **084/211-020.** Reservations not accepted. Main courses S/25–S/40. MC, V. Daily noon–midnight.

The Tree House ★ (Finds NOVO ANDINO   The in-house restaurant of the Rupa Wasi lodge (see above) is literally a cut above most of the restaurants in Aguas Calientes. Indeed reminiscent of a tree house, up a long flight of stairs and surrounded by trees, with indigenous wood paneling on ceilings and walls, a fireplace and communal-style seating, it has a cozy, rustic charm. The chef, who trained abroad, prepares creative Novo Andino dishes, using local ingredients from the inn's garden. For a treat, opt for one of the tasting menus (6, 8 or 10 courses), or try the quinotto (red-quinoa risotto), alpaca tournedos with chimichurri sauce, or spinach, ricotta and quinoa raviolis. If you're a passion-fruit freak like me, save room for the maracuyá pie. While I think it's one of the best options in town, the Tree House is a bit pricey. If you really enjoy your meal, come back for the well-regarded cooking lessons ($30).

Jr. Huanacaure 180, Aguas Calientes. © **084/211-101.** Reservations recommended. Main courses S/32– S/45. AE, MC, V. Daily noon–midnight.

Inexpensive

Chez Maggy (Value PERUVIAN/PIZZA   On the right side of restaurant row, as you walk toward the hot springs, this longtime favorite and branch of the legendary Chez Maggy in Cusco is a good, relaxed place for wood-fired pizzas, pisco sours, and cold beers. You can also get a whole range of Peruvian *comida típica* and Mexican dishes, but everyone I've seen here is always gorging on pizza or pasta.

Av. Pachacútec 156. © **084/211-006.** Reservations not accepted. Main courses S/18–S/36. MC, V. Daily 10am–10pm.

Southern Peru

Southern Peru ranks just behind Cusco and the Sacred Valley on the visitors' circuit. The mountainous desert landscapes are some of Peru's most distinctive, and the region is a beacon to outdoors enthusiasts who enjoy hiking, mountain climbing, and river running. The deep sapphire expanse of Lake Titicaca, the world's highest navigable body of water at nearly 4,000m (13,100 ft.) above sea level, is one of the world's unique sights. The volcanoes and deep canyons near Arequipa hold tremendous opportunities for trekking and viewing the elusive Andean condor, one of the world's great birds, which at one celebrated spot above Colca Canyon soars directly over the heads of spectators every morning. New upscale hotels on the banks of Lake Titicaca, in the historic center of Arequipa, and among the terraced landscapes of Colca Canyon testify to surging interest in the region among travelers once content to leave it to more adventurous sorts.

As cities go, bleak and often brutally cold Puno is not, for most of the year, one of Peru's most interesting or attractive—although its position perched on the banks of Lake Titicaca and as the epicenter of the creative partying at some of the country's legendary folkloric festivals couldn't be more spectacular.

Arequipa, on the other hand, is perhaps Peru's most sophisticated city, a lovely colonial town framed by three snow-capped volcanoes. The people of Arequipa have earned a reputation for thinking themselves different or better than their compatriots to the north (and thus also earned the antagonism of many Peruvians). Certainly the city's elegant historic center, built almost entirely of white volcanic stone, looks quite distinct from the rest of Peru. Behind the thick walls of the Santa Catalina monastery, one of Peru's most glorious sights, you'll almost feel as though you were in southern Spain rather than southern Peru.

---

1 PUNO & LAKE TITICACA ★★★

388km (241 miles) S of Cusco; 297km (185 miles) NE of Arequipa; 1,011km (628 miles) SE of Lima

Puno, founded in the late 17th century following the discovery of nearby silver mines, is a ramshackle town that draws numbers of visitors wholly disproportionate to its innate attractions. A mostly unlovely city on the *altiplano*, a high, wind-swept plateau, it has one thing going for it that no other place on earth can claim: Puno hugs the shores of fabled Lake Titicaca, the world's highest navigable body of water, a sterling expanse of deep blue at 3,830m (12,566 ft.) above sea level. South America's largest lake (8,500 sq. km/3,282 sq mi.), Titicaca is also the largest lake in the world above 2,000m (6,560 ft.). The magnificent lake straddles the border of Peru and Bolivia; many Andean travelers move on from Puno to La Paz, going around or, in some cases, over Lake Titicaca.

Before leaving Puno, though, almost everyone hops aboard a boat to visit at least one of several ancient island-dwelling peoples that seem to have materialized straight out of the pages of *National Geographic*. A 2-day tour takes travelers to the Uros Floating Islands—where Indian communities consisting of just a few families construct tiny islands out of totora reeds—and two inhabited natural islands, Amantaní and Taquile. A special bonus, for travelers who have the time and the funds, is a visit to the lake's only private island, Suasi, home to a luxury ecolodge.

To many Peruvians, Lake Titicaca is a mystical and sacred place. Manco Cápac, the original Inca chieftain believed to be a direct descendant of the sun, is said to have risen from the lake's waters along with his sister to found the Inca Empire. The Uros Indians might remain on their floating islands because they believe themselves to be lake people by birth, the very descendants of the royal siblings.

Puno has one other thing in its favor. Though dry and often brutally cold, the city is celebrated for its spectacular festivals, veritable explosions of *cultura popular.* The unassuming town, where locals largely descended from the Aymara from the south and the Quechua from the north, reigns as the capital of Peruvian folklore. Its traditional fiestas, dances, and music—and consequent street partying—are without argument among the most vibrant and uninhibited in Peru. Among those worth planning a trip around are February's **Festival de la Virgen de la Candelaria (Candlemas)** ★★★ and **Puno Week** ★★, celebrating the birth of the city and the Inca Empire, in early November.

> **(Tips)** **In Juliaca, Hit the Ground Running**
>
> Juliaca, site of the regional airport, is perhaps the most disgraced city in all of Peru. If you are flying into Juliaca on your way to Puno, don't linger. The town is a chaotic and ugly mess of half-finished houses, potholed dirt roads, and trash-strewn streets clogged with sales carts and *ciclotaxis*. If that weren't enough, Juliaca is also reputed to be downright dangerous. The only reason it was awarded an airport is that Puno is boxed in by mountains and local politicians had a stranglehold on Lima's purse strings.

ESSENTIALS
Getting There

BY PLANE   Puno does not have an airport; the nearest is **Aeropuerto Manco Capac** (© 051/322-905) in Juliaca, 45km (28 miles) north of Puno. **LAN** (© 01/213-8300; www.lan.com) flies daily from Lima and Arequipa to Juliaca; flights start at about $139 one-way from Lima. Tourist buses run from the Juliaca airport to Puno (a 1-hr. trip), depositing travelers on Jirón Tacna for S/15. **Rossy Tours** (© 051/366-709) runs inexpensive *combi* taxis to the airport in Juliaca (picking passengers up at their hotels) for S/15 per person.

BY BUS   Puno has a modern, safe bus station, **Terminal Terrestre** (© 051/364-733), Av. Primero de Mayo 703, Barrio Magistral. Road service to Puno from Cusco has been greatly improved in recent years, and many more tourists now travel by bus, which is faster and cheaper than the train. The terrific views during the day are pretty much the same. Most buses drop passengers at Melgar, a few short blocks from downtown.

From Cusco, executive-, imperial-, or royal-class buses make the trip in less than 7 hours (though some services, such as Inka Express, make stop-offs at Inca ruins en route, extending the trip a couple of hours, highly recommended if you have the extra time) and cost about $45. **Imexso** (© 084/240-801; www.perucuzco.com/imexsotours), **Inka Express** (© 084/247-887; www.inkaexpress.com), and **Cruz del Sur** (© 01/311-5050; www.cruzdelsur.com.pe) operate buses with videos and English-speaking tour guides. **Ormeño** (© 01/472-5000; www.grupo-ormeno.com.pe) has daily direct departures between Cusco and Puno (6 hr.). Regular buses are as cheap as S/15, but they are uncomfortable, have no restrooms or videos, and are potentially dangerous—and not recommended.

The trip between Puno and Arequipa by bus is no longer tortuous; the long-awaited highway between the cities has dramatically shortened travel time from 12 hours to just 5. **Cruz del Sur** (© 01/311-5050; www.cruzdelsur.com.pe) and **Ormeño** (© 01/472-5000; www.grupo-ormeno.com.pe) make the trip for around S/40.

BY TRAIN   The Titicaca Route journey from Cusco to Puno, along tracks at an altitude of 3,500m (11,500 ft.), is one of the most scenic in Peru. Though it is slower (10 hr. and prone to late arrivals) and has experienced its share of onboard thievery, it is a favorite of travelers in Peru and preferable to the bus if you've got the time and money. Keep a careful eye on your bags and, if possible, lock backpacks to the luggage rack; keep valuables close to your person. PeruRail's Andean Explorer trains (www.perurail.com) trains from Cusco to Puno depart from **Estación Huanchaq** (© 084/238-722), at the end of Avenida

ATTRACTIONS ●
Central Market **18**
Museo Municipal **12**
Plaza de Armas **14**

DINING ◆
Apu Salkantay **19**
Casa del Corregidor **13**
Colors Lounge **8**
Incabar **9**
Las Casona **19**
Pizzeria El Buho **10**
Restaurant Don Piero **7**
Rico's Pan **21**
Ukuku's **17**

ACCOMMODATIONS ■
Casa Andina Classic Puno
   Plaza **16**
Casa Andina Classi
   Tikarani **2**
Casa Andina Private
   Collection Puno **4**
Hostal El Virrey **22**
Hostal Los Uros **19**
Hostal Q'oñi Wasi **4**

Hotel Colón **20**
Hotel Liberador
   Lake Titicaca **4**
Intiqa Hotel **5**
La Hacienda Hotel **18**
Los Pinos Inn **1**
Posada Don Giorgio **6**
Sonesta Posadas del
   Inca Lake Titicaca **3**

SOUTHERN PERU

10

PUNO & LAKE TITICACA

Sol. Service to Puno is Monday, Wednesday, and Saturday year-round, departing at 8am and arriving at 5:50pm. Fare is $220 one-way in swank coaches and includes lunch in luxurious dining cars. Tickets can be pre-reserved. The Puno train station ((✆ **051/ 351-041**) is at Av. La Torre 224, only a few blocks north of downtown. Inexpensive taxis are widely available; hotels along the banks of Lake Titicaca definitely require a taxi, unless you're staying at Casa Andina Private Collection, which has its own train stop.

Train service from Arequipa to Puno is available by group charter only; see www.peru rail.com for details.

> **Tips** **Take It Easy: You're on Top of the World**
>
> Puno's extreme elevation of 3,830m (12,566 ft.) is even higher than Cusco, so unless you've already spent time in the Andes, you'll almost certainly need to rest for at least a day to acclimatize. See "Health," in chapter 3, for more information on how to address altitude sickness.

Visitor Information

An **iPerú tourist information office** is located at the pedestrian-only main drag of Puno, Jr. Lima 549 (© 051/365-088; at Jirón Deustua, just off the Plaza de Armas). There you can pick up a map and get a couple of hints on sights in town. However, you're better off going to one of the travel agencies that organizes Lake Titicaca–area trips, such as **All Ways Travel** or **Edgar Adventures** (see "Organized Tours," later in this section), for information on Puno's most important attractions, all of which lie beyond the city.

FAST FACTS　You'll find banks and ATMs along Jirón Lima (aka Pasaje Lima), as well as at Hotel Casa Andina, Jr. Independencia 185. Banks include **Banco Continental,** at Jr. Lima 400, and **Banco de Crédito,** on the corner of Jirón Lima and Jirón Grau. Money-changers can generally be found along Jirón Tacna, where most bus stations are located, and at the market near the railway and Avenida de los Incas.

For those crossing into Bolivia, the **Bolivian Consulate** is located at Jr. Arequipa 120 (© 051/351-251). North Americans, Europeans, New Zealanders, and Australians do not need a visa to enter Bolivia, but the border is a historically problematic one (it was closed in 2005 during the widespread strikes that paralyzed parts of Bolivia), so you might need to check on the status of the crossing before traveling to Bolivia.

In a medical emergency, go to **Clínica Puno,** Jr. Ramón Castilla 178–180 (© 051/368-835), or **Hospital Nacional,** Av. El Sol 1022 (© 051/369-696). The **tourist police** are located at Jr. Deustua 538 (© 051/352-720).

Pretty fast Internet connections are available at **Qoll@internet,** Jr. Oquendo 340 (Parque Pino), where you can make inexpensive international calls; rates are S/2 per hour. A nice, quiet spot for surfing the Internet is behind the cafe at **La Casa del Corregidor,** Deustua 576 (© 051/351-921). Other Internet *cabinas* are located along Pasaje Lima. Puno's main **Serpost post office** (© 051/351-141) is at Moquegua 269. The **Telefónica del Perú** office is on the corner of Moquegua and Arequipa.

Getting Around

Few visitors spend more than a day or two in Puno (unless lingering at a festival), and the little getting around that needs to be done in town is either on foot or by taxi to your hotel. The small downtown area is pretty easily managed on foot, although several of Puno's nicest hotels lie several kilometers away, on the banks of Lake Titicaca. The port is only about 10 blocks east from the Plaza de Armas in the center of town. The main pedestrian thoroughfare, Jirón Lima, connects the Plaza de Armas to Parque Pino.

Visits to Lake Titicaca and its islands, as well as the ruins on the outskirts of town, are most conveniently done by organized tour.

BY TAXI　Taxis are inexpensive and plentiful, easily hailed on the street, and best used at night and to get back and forth from the hotels on the banks of Lake Titicaca. Most trips in town cost no more than S/3. Taxis can also be hired for round-trips to nearby

Puno & Lake Titicaca Festivals

Official travel literature rarely tires of labeling Puno the folkloric capital of Peru. Its festivals, celebrated with spectacularly vibrant pre-Columbian dances and costumes, certainly rank among the most spectacular in the country. Festivals in Puno are not just colorful; they're usually wild affairs. (Excessive imbibing seems to be as important a ritual as singing or dancing.) Locals zealously guard their ancestral traditions and cultural expressions, which are known for their unusual variety, singular choreography, and lilting *altiplano* music. The local cultures are responsible for registering more than 360 dances in the National Institute of Culture.

Foremost among local festivals is the **Festival de la Virgen de la Candelaria (Candlemas)**★★★, held during the first 2 weeks of February. The celebration of Puno's patron saint brings bands and more than 200 groups of dancers from villages and towns all over the region. The festival owes its origins to ancient rituals linked to agricultural cycles and harvests. Festivities blend traits associated with the dominant native local groups: the sobriety of the Quechua people and the *joie de vivre* of the Aymara. The principal Candlemas dance is the *diablada,* or devil dance. Dancers wearing spectacular costumes and grotesque masks play panpipes and make offerings to Pachamama, or "Mother Earth." You'll see terrifying devil masks with twisted horns and angelic, sequined "suits of lights." Official functions are held in the stadium, while more popular exercises are on the streets of Puno. The more informal events are a real highlight for most observers. Festival dances are divided clearly between two historical epochs: pre-Columbian dances, celebrated on Saturday, and the post-Columbian dances, which take place on Sunday. On Monday is a grand 12-hour Folkloric Parade throughout Puno. Street dancing is observed every day of the week, so even if you miss the first couple of days, you're sure to get a healthy dose of the Virgen de la Candelaria.

Puno Week★★, celebrated during the first week of November, remembers Manco Cápac, who, according to legend, rose from the waters of Lake Titicaca to found the Inca Empire. A major procession leads from the shores of the lake to the town stadium. Dances and music pervade the city, and things sometimes get pretty wild, with plenty of people staggering and falling down drunk by the end of the evening.

Puno is also well known for its pre-Lenten **Carnaval** celebrations (late Feb to early Mar). Not quite the same as Brazil's hedonistic party, Carnaval here is celebrated with native dances, lots of drinking, and water bombs.

Other lively festivals in and around Puno and Lake Titicaca, worthy of planning your trip around, include **San Juan de Dios** (St. John; Mar 7–8); **Fiesta de las Cruces Alasitas** (May 8); **San Juan, San Pedro, and San Pablo** (St. John, St. Peter, and St. Paul; June 24–29); and **Apóstol Santiago** (St. James; July 25), which is the most enthusiastically celebrated day on Isla Taquile.

SOUTHERN PERU

10

PUNO & LAKE TITICACA

ruins or for half- or full days. Call **Taxi Milenium** (© 051/363-134) or **Taxi Tour Puno** (© 051/369-900).

BY FOOT   Puno is small enough to get around almost entirely on foot, unless you're staying at one of the upscale hotels on the shores of Lake Titicaca several kilometers from the center of town.

BY BOAT   You can independently hire boats at Puno harbor to take you out on Lake Titicaca, but it's simpler to sign up for economical organized tours to the islands (see "Organized Tours," later in this section).

WHAT TO SEE & DO

Most of the year, Puno itself is a rather bleak and unimpressive place if you don't count its enviable geography. The main attractions in Puno are outside the city: the communities of Lake Titicaca and the ancient Sillustani ruins. What there is to see in Puno doesn't delay most visitors for more than a half-day or so. However, if you stumble upon one of Puno's famously colorful festivals, you might want to linger.

Puno Highlights

The large **Catedral** (cathedral), on the west side of the Plaza de Armas at the end of Jirón Lima, is the focal point of downtown Puno. The 18th-century baroque church is large, but no great shakes; the elaborate exterior is much more impressive than the spartan, spacious, chilly interior. Also on the main square is the 17th-century **La Casa del Corregidor,** Deustua 576 (© 051/351-921), purportedly Puno's oldest house, with an impressive Spanish balcony; it now houses a very nice "cultural cafe" and is the best spot in town to take a breather. Nearby, the **Museo Municipal Carlos Dryer,** Conde de Lemos 289, is the town's principal (but small) museum. It has a decent selection of pre-Inca ceramics and textiles, as well as mummies with cranial deformations, but the collection is not very well illuminated. The museum is open Monday through Friday from 7:30am to 3:30pm; admission is S/5.

For a superb view of Lake Titicaca and a vantage point that makes Puno look more attractive than it really is, climb the steep hill to **Mirador Kuntur Wasi** and **Huajsapata Park,** about 10 minutes southwest of the main square. On top is a blazing white statue of Manco Cápac, the legendary first Inca and founder of the empire. Back down below, Jirón (Pasaje) Lima is a pedestrianized mall, chock-full of shops, restaurants, and bars, that runs from the Plaza de Armas to pretty **Parque Pino,** a relaxed square populated by locals just hanging out. Puno's seedy **central market** is 2 blocks east of here, and it spills across several streets. While unattractive, it's a realistic look at the underbelly of the Peruvian economy. Beyond the railroad tracks is a *mercado de artesanía* (artisans' market) targeting tourists with all kinds of alpaca and woven woolen goods, often much cheaper those than found in Cusco and other cities. (Try on the sweaters, though; they rarely seem to fit as well as you'd expect.)

Lake Titicaca

South America's largest lake and the world's highest navigable body of water, Lake Titicaca has long been considered a sacred place among indigenous Andean peoples. The people who live in and around the lake consider themselves descendants of Mama Qota, or Sacred Mother, and they believe that powerful spirits live in the lake's depths. According to Andean legend, Lake Titicaca—which straddles the modern border between Peru and Bolivia—was the birthplace of civilization. Viracocha, the creator deity, lightened a

(Tips) Titicaca's Antique British Steamship

Nowadays, fleets of tourist boats set out daily for the floating and natural islands of Lake Titicaca. The oldest ship to ply the world's highest navigable waterway, the **Yavarí,** built in 1862 in Birmingham, England, today sits inactive on the shore of the lake (outside the Sonesta Posada del Inca hotel). The restored steamship, which was originally shipped as a kit to Arica, Chile (and then carried by mule over the course of 6 years to Lake Titicaca), sailed Titicaca for 100 years. It has now been converted into a small museum and bar. The ship is owned by a foundation, Asociación Yavarí. To arrange a free visit with Capt. Carlos Saavedra and his crew, call ℂ **051/369-329,** visit www.yavari.org, or stop by the ship on most afternoons.

dark world by having the sun, moon, and stars rise from the lake to occupy their places in the sky.

Worthy of such mystical associations, Lake Titicaca is a dazzling sight. Its deep azure waters seemingly extend forever across the altiplano, under the monstrously wide sky. Daybreak and sunset are particularly stunning to witness.

Massive Titicaca has been inhabited for thousands of years. Totora-reed boats roamed the lake as early as 2500 B.C. Titicaca's islands—both man-made and natural—are home to several communities of Quechua and Aymara Indians, groups with remarkably different traditions and ways of life. Visiting them and staying overnight on one of the islands if you can is certainly one of Peru's highlights and one of the most unique experiences in South America.

The most convenient way to visit is by an inexpensive and well-run guided tour, arranged by one of several travel agencies in Puno (see "Organized Tours," later). Although it is possible to arrange independent travel, the low cost and easy organization of group travel don't encourage it. Even if you were to go on your own, you'd inevitably fall in with groups, and your experience wouldn't differ radically. You can go on a half-day tour of the Uros Floating Islands or a full-day tour that includes Taquile Island, but the best way to experience Lake Titicaca's unique indigenous life is to stay at least 1 night on either Taquile or Amantaní, preferably in the home of a local family. Those with more time and money to burn may want to explore the singular experience of staying on private **Isla Suasi,** home to little more than a solar-powered hotel and a dozen llamas and vicuñas.

Uros Floating Islands (Las Islas Flotantes) ★
5km (3 miles) N of Puno

As improbable as it sounds, the Uros Indians of Lake Titicaca live on floating "islands" made by hand from totora reeds that grow in abundance in the shallow waters of the lake. This unique practice has endured since the time of the Incas, and today there are some 45 floating islands in the Bay of Puno. The islands first came into contact with the modern world in the mid-1960s, and their inhabitants now live mostly off tourism. To some visitors, this obvious dependency is a little unseemly.

Many visitors faced with this strange sight conclude that the impoverished islanders can't possibly still live on the 40-odd islands, that it must be a show created for their benefit. True, the islands can seem to be little more than floating souvenir stands; the

> ## (Fun Facts Say What?
>
> The undeniably exotic name Titicaca might cause giggles among some school-children, but the name isn't derived from Spanish: It's a hybrid of the local native languages Aymara and Quechua. To locals, Titicaca might mean "Sacred Lake," but in fact *titi* means "cat" in Aymara, while *caca* means "the sacred rock on the island of the sun" in Quechua.

communities idly await the arrival of tourist boats and then seek to sell handmade textiles and reed-crafted items while gringos walk gingerly about the spongy islands—truly an odd sensation—photographing houses and children. Yet the islands and their people are not just a tourist show. Several hundred Titicaca natives continue to live year-round on the islands, even if they venture to Puno for commercial transactions. The largest island, Huacavacani, has not only homes, but also a floating Seventh-day Adventist church, a candidate for one of the most bizarre juxtapositions you're likely to find in Peru—or anywhere. Others have schools, a post office, public telephone, small hotel, and souvenir shops. Only a few islands are actually set up to receive tourists. The vast majority of the Uros people live in continual isolation and peace, away from curious onlookers and camera lenses.

The Uros, who fled to the middle of the lake to escape conflicts with the Collas and Incas, long ago began intermarrying with the Aymara Indians, and many have now converted to Catholicism. Fishers and birders, they live grouped by family sectors, and entire families live in one-room tentlike thatched huts constructed on the shifting reed island that floats beneath. They build modest houses and splendid gondolas with fanciful animal-head bows out of the reeds and must continually replenish the fast-rotting mats that form their fragile islands. Visitors might be surprised, to say the least, to find some huts outfitted with televisions powered by solar panels (which were donated by the Fujimori administration after a presidential visit to the islands). Incredibly, the Fujimori government also built some solar-powered aluminum houses on several islands, but few if any locals actually dwell in them, because they are very hot during the day and brutally cold at night. For a fee, locals will take visitors on short rides from one island to another in the reed boats, but you should consider it a contribution to the community: At $2 or so a head for a 5-minute jaunt, it's hardly the best deal in Peru, but may be worth it if you're looking for a photo op.

GETTING THERE   Inexpensive tours (normally $12 per person) that go only to the Uros Islands last about 3 hours and include hotel pickup, an English-speaking guide, and motorboat transportation to the islands. Unless you're unusually pressed for time, it's much more enjoyable and informative to visit the Uros as part of a brief stop en route to the natural islands of Amantaní or Taquile. You can go on your own by catching a *lancha* (small boat) at the port. Depending on how many people you or the skipper are able to assemble, the cost will usually be about S/25.

Taquile Island (Isla Taquile) ★★
35km (22 miles) E of Puno

Life on the natural islands of Lake Titicaca is more authentic feeling and less overtly dependent on tourism than on the man-made Uros islands. Taquile is a fascinating and

ACCOMMODATIONS
Casa Andina Private
    Collection Isla Suasi **1**
Kantuta Lodge **2**
Las Cabañas **3**

stunningly beautiful island about 4 hours from Puno. The island is narrow, only a kilometer (½-mile) wide, but about 6km (3¾ miles) long, and it rises to a high point of 264m (866 ft.). The island is a rugged ruddy color, which contrasts spectacularly with the blue lake and sky, and its hillsides are laced with formidable Inca stone agricultural terraces and other Inca and pre-Inca stone ruins.

The island is as serene as the distant lake views. Taquile has been inhabited for 10,000 years, and life remains starkly traditional; there isn't electricity, you won't run into vehicles, and islanders quietly go about their business. Taquile natives, of whom there are still about 3,000 or so, allow tourists to stay at private houses (in primitive but not uncomfortable conditions), and there are a number of simple restaurants serving visitors near the central plaza. Although they're friendly to outsiders, the Quechua-speaking islanders remain a famously reserved and insular community. Their dress is equally famous: Taquile textiles are some of the finest in Peru. Men wear embroidered, woven red waistbands *(fajas)* and embroidered wool stocking caps *(chullos)*—so tightly knitted that they can hold water—that indicate marital status: red for married men, red and white for bachelors. Women wear layered skirts and black shawls over their heads. Taquile textiles are much sought after for their hand-woven quality, though they are considerably more

(Moments) Celebration and Quiet on Taquile

If you are lucky enough to catch a festival on the island, you will be treated to a festive and stubbornly traditional pageant of color, marked by picturesque dances and women twirling in circles, revealing as many as 16 layered, multi-colored skirts. (Easter, Fiesta de Santiago on July 25 and Aug 1–2, and New Year's are the best celebrations.) Any time on the island, though, offers unique experiences—especially once the day-trippers have departed and you have the island and incomparable views of the blue waters framed by stone archways virtually to yourself. Taquile then seems about as far away from modernity and "civilization" as one can travel on this planet. At the top of the island on a clear night, under a carpet of blazing stars, Taquile is more magical still.

Access to the island from the boat dock is either by a long path that wends around the island or by an amazing 533-step stone staircase that climbs to the top, passing through two stone arches with astonishing views of the lake. Independent travelers sign in and pay a nominal fee. Those who want to stay the night can arrange to be put up in a family house. If you stay, expect to rough it a bit without proper showers. Many islanders do not speak Spanish, and English is likely to be met with blank stares.

expensive than mass-produced handicrafts in other parts of Peru. Along with agriculture, textiles are the island's main source of income. A cooperative shop operates on the main plaza, and laid-back stalls are set up during festivals and the high season of tourist travel (June–Sept). Sadly, a hideously modern municipal building now dominates the main square, looking woefully out of place.

Locals are much more resistant to haggling than are artisans in other parts of Peru. (Usually they simply refuse to bargain.) There's very little of the noise and activity that's present at most Peruvian markets. If you go with a group, you're also likely to visit one of the individual communities on the island, and perhaps have a home-cooked meal after a low-key demonstration of their quotidian customs. Buying lunch is one way to contribute money to a community, although many guests also like to tip the head of the community for opening their doors to outsiders.

GETTING THERE   The only feasible way to visit Taquile is as part of an inexpensive and convenient organized tour, which also takes in the Uros Islands ($25 per person). Most single-day tours of the Uros and Taquile islands depart early in the morning and stop at the islands of Uros for a half-hour en route. For most visitors, a day trip, which allows only an hour or two on the island and 8 hours of boat time, is too grueling and insufficient to appreciate the beauty and culture of Taquile Island. A 2- or 3-day visit ($30–$35), with time to spend the night on either Taquile or Amantaní, is preferable.

Amantaní Island (Isla Amantaní) ★★
36km (22 miles) NE of Puno

Amantaní, a circular island located about 4½ hours from Puno (and about 2 hr. from Taquile), is home to a very different, although equally fascinating, Titicaca community. Also handsomely terraced and home to farmers, fishers, and weavers, in many ways

Amantaní is even more rustic and unspoiled than Taquile. It is a beautiful but barren and rocky place, with a handful of villages composed of about 800 families and ruins clinging to the island's two peaks, Pachatata (Father Earth) and Pachamama (Mother Earth). The island presents some excellent opportunities for hikes up to these spots, with terrific views of the lake and the sparsely populated island landscape. The agricultural character of the island is perhaps even more apparent than on Taquile. Long, ancient-looking stone walls mark the fields and terraces of different communities, and cows, sheep, and alpacas graze the hillsides.

The islanders, who, for the most part, understand Spanish, are more open and approachable than natives of Taquile. The highlight of a visit to Amantaní is an overnight stay with a local family. Not only will the family prepare your simple meals, but you will also be invited to a friendly dance in the village meeting place. For the event, most families dress their guests up in local outfits—the women in layered, multicolored, embroidered skirts and blouses, and the men in wool ponchos. Although the evening is obviously staged for tourists' benefit, it is low-key and charming rather than cheesy.

Amantaní islanders also make lovely hand-woven textiles, particularly the show-stopping black shawls embroidered with seven colors. The main festival on Amantaní, Fiesta de la Santa Tierra, is on the third Thursday in January, when the population splits in two—half at the Temple of Pachamama and the other half at the Temple of Pachatata (a perfect illustration of their dualistic male/female belief system). Other good festivals are the anniversary of Amantaní (Apr 9, lasting 3 days) and Carnaval (Feb or Mar).

Amantaní is best visited on a tour that allows you to spend the night (visiting the Uros Islands en route) and travel the next day to Taquile. Tour groups place groups of four or five with local families for overnight stays. The tour price normally includes accommodations, lunch, and dinner on the first day and breakfast the following morning.

It's a good idea to bring small gifts for your family on Amantaní because they make little from stays and must alternate with other families on the island. Pens, pencils, and batteries all make good gifts.

If you want to appreciate the utter quiet and remoteness of the island after the day-trippers depart, a nice place to spend the night is **Kantuta Lodge** (© **051/812-664;** www.punored.com/titicaca/amantani/img/lodge.html), an inn run by the family of Segundino Cari near the port of Comunidad Pueblo. Clean and brightly decorated rooms, featuring local textiles, are $20, which includes three meals a day. Meals only are $5.

GETTING THERE   The only feasible way to visit Amantaní is by organized tour. Almost all tours that go to Amantaní also visit the Uros and Taquile islands, stopping en route at Uros and spending the night on Amantaní before visiting Taquile the following day.

Suasi Island (Isla Suasi) ★★
80km (50 miles) NE of Puno

The only island in private hands on Lake Titicaca, S-shaped Isla Suasi is tiny (just 48 hectares, or 117 acres), isolated, serene, and beautiful. And it makes for a wholly unique getaway, even if it is a long way to go for isolation and relaxation. Though reachable by fast *lancha* (motorized boat) in under 3 hours, most boats take upwards of 5 or 6 to get there (and either way, you'll have to pay close to $300 for the privilege of round-trip transportation). However, once you arrive, you really have traveled far. There are no inhabitants other than the island's owner and part-time resident, the sociologist Martha Giraldo, the few employees of the solar-powered refuge she started (which has since become an upscale ecolodge, administered since 2005 by the Casa Andina hotel chain),

(Fun Facts) Fun with Language & Geography

Lake Titicaca, which covers some 3,200 square miles and is South America's largest lake, is more or less evenly shared by Peru and Bolivia. Yet Peruvians are fond of claiming it is in fact more like a 60/40 breakdown, and there are maps that label the lake with "Titi" covering the Peruvian half and "caca" designating the Bolivian half.

and a dozen alpacas and eight free-ranging vicuñas. There are no cars, no TV, and no electricity. If you're lucky, you'll be one of just a handful of guests to enjoy the stunning high-altitude sunsets, gorgeous panoramic views of Titicaca—which extends in all directions like a sterling, placid cobalt sea—and total peace and quiet. The **ecofriendly lodge ★★★** is luxurious but sensitively designed (rooms have great lake views), its restaurant outstanding, and the personnel friendly. Activities are pretty much limited to reading in hammocks, canoeing around the island (which is small enough that it takes just about an hour to circle), hiking and trying to spot the vicuñas, trekking up to the *cerro* (hilltop) for sunset, and stargazing at night. I can't think of a more peaceful place in all of Peru. Many guests find their sunset visits to the hilltop to be a mystical experience; the sky at 13,000 feet above sea level blazes with unimaginable streaks of violet, red, and gold. At the top of the hill is an *apacheta,* a small tower of stacked, balanced stones, echoing an ancient native practice of leaving stones at high elevations (where one is presumably closer to the *apus,* or gods). You can return to Puno either by boat again or by a very scenic but extremely rough ride in a car or van (the first 38km/24 miles are murder, but then it gets worse; asphalt only arrives after 2 hr.). For additional information, including arranging transportation, see www.casa-andina.com, or call ✆ **01/213-9739** or 051/9513-10070. Rates are $249 to $369 per person.

Other Attractions near Puno
Sillustani Ruins ★
32km (20 miles) NE of Puno

Just beyond Puno are mysterious pre-Inca ruins called *chullpas* (funeral towers). The finest sit on the windswept altiplano on a peninsula in Lake Umayo at Sillustani. The Colla people—a warrior tribe that spoke Aymara—buried their elite in giant cylindrical tombs, some as tall as 12m (39 ft.). The stonemasonry is exquisite (many archaeologists and historians find them more complex and superior even to Inca engineering), and the structures form quite an impression on such a harsh landscape.

The Collas dominated the Titicaca region before the arrival of the Incas. After burying their dead along with foodstuffs, jewels, and other possessions, they sealed the towers. The high-altitude altiplano has a reputation as one of the windiest and coldest places in Peru, so dress warmly for your visit here.

GETTING THERE By far the best way to visit Sillustani is by guided tour, usually in the afternoon around 2 or 2:30pm (see "Organized Tours," below). Tours are inexpensive ($12) and very convenient. Going on your own generally isn't worth it because the site is a pain to reach and, once there, you've no guide to explain the significance of the ruins. If you insist, though, catch a "Juliaca" *colectivo* from downtown Puno and request to be let off after about 20 minutes, at the fork in the road that leads to Sillustani (DESVIO PARA

Chucuito: Fertility Temple
18km (11 miles) S of Puno

On a small promontory on the southern shore of Lake Titicaca, Chucuito, a small Aymara town, is one of the oldest in the altiplano region. The town, capital of the province during colonial times, has a lovely main square and a colonial church, **Nuestra Señora de La Asunción** (built in 1601). Chucuito was also the primary Inca settlement in the region. Another colonial church, **Santo Domino** is a most curious—though many would say dubious—construction, and the town's main attraction. Said to date to pre-Columbian times, Inca Uyo is composed of dozens of large, mushroom-shaped phallic stones, most a few feet high, which locals claim were erected as part of fertility rituals. The anatomically correct stones, which until a few years ago were kept in a sterile museum, leave little doubt as to what their creators were getting at. Some point up at the sun god, Inti, while others are inserted into the ground, directed at Pachamama, or Mother Earth. At the center of the ring, lording over the temple, is the king phallus. Local guides tell tales of the exact rituals during which virgins purportedly sat for hours atop the phalluses to increase fertility. The stones might predate the Incas, but some contend that they, or at least the manner in which they are displayed, are fake, a hoax perpetrated by locals to rustle up tourist business. Spanish missionaries did everything in their power to destroy all symbols and structures they considered pagan, and it is highly unlikely that they would have constructed two churches nearby but left this temple intact.

If you find yourself drawn to the stones at Inka Uyo and want to spend the night, the best option in town is **Las Cabañas ★**, a very smart, comfortable and well-priced inn with pretty gardens, an attractive setting by the lake, and a cute restaurant, at Jr. Tarapacá 538 (✆/fax **051/368-494;** www.chucuito.com). Rooms (some of which have chimneys) have private bathrooms and run S/96 double, while cool duplex bungalows, which sleep six and have chimneys and balconies, are S/168.

GETTING THERE   Acora-bound colectivos leave from Puno's Avenida El Sol. The ride to Chucuito costs S/3 and takes 15 to 20 minutes; tell the driver you want to get off at Chucuito, which lies about halfway between Chimú and Acora.

ORGANIZED TOURS
Most travel agencies in Puno handle the conventional tours of Lake Titicaca and Sillustani, along with a handful of other ruins programs. Two of the best agencies are **All Ways Travel ★★**, Jr. Deustua 576 (in the courtyard of La Casa del Corregidor; ✆ **051/353-979**) and Jr. Tacna 234 (✆ **051/355-552;** www.titicacaperu.com), which is run by the friendly and very helpful Victor Pauca and his daughter Eliana, with good guides and progressive cultural trips in addition to the standard tours (including a library bus that takes tourists to rural communities to donate books and toys to children); and **Edgar Adventures,** Jr. Lima 328 (✆ **051/353-444;** www.edgaradventures.com), which is run by a Peruvian husband/wife team. Both agencies can arrange bus and air travel as well, including travel to Bolivia.

Uros Islands half-day trips cost about $12 per person. Uros Islands and Taquile Island full-day trips cost $25 per person. Uros, Taquile, and Amantaní trips, lasting 2 days and 1 night, cost $30 to $35 per person. Sillustani and Chucuito tours, usually 3 hours long, cost $12 per person.

Although it has very few nice shops on the order of Lima, Cusco, or Arequipa, Puno is one of the better places to load up on inexpensive woolen and alpaca goods, including hats, gloves, scarves, shawls, and blankets. They are cheaper here than in those cities, although you might not encounter the quality found at some upscale shops. The **open-air market** just beyond the railroad tracks (btw. Jirón Melgar and Avenida Titicaca) has a couple dozen stalls specializing in alpaca and woolen goods. There is a cluster of souvenir and clothing shops along **Jirón Lima,** the pedestrian-only main drag, as well on Jirón Grau (just off Lima). A place worth seeking out is the nonprofit **Fair Trade Store (La Tienda de Comercio Justo)** ★ in the patio of La Casa del Corregidor, Jr. Deustua 576 (☎ **051/365-603**). Fifty percent of the purchase price of alpaca and wool scarves, ponchos, and the like here goes directly to the artisans (identified by name on the garments) in rural communities (decidedly not the case in most transactions). It's open 10am to 6pm daily but does not accept credit cards.

WHERE TO STAY

Puno has grown rapidly as a tourist destination in the past few years, and its offer of accommodations is no longer geared almost exclusively toward a budget backpacker crowd. There are a couple of good midrange options in town, but, if you don't mind relying on taxis to get back and forth, the best options are out on the banks of Lake Titicaca (about a 10-min. cab ride). Many of the cheap places in town are very basic, and several of those are dingy, noisy dives with fleeting hot water. If you're looking at the bottom end, check the place out first and ask to see a couple of rooms. Outside high season (June–Sept), most hotels and *hostales* (inns) are more than willing to bargain.

Expensive

Casa Andina Private Collection Puno ★★ Ⓥⓐⓛⓤⓔ The newest hotel presence on the banks of Lake Titicaca is the select but excellent-value hotel of the upstart Peruvian chain Casa Andina, which has two additional, more modest hotels in town. This one, low-slung and attractively rustic, is perched over Titicaca and has marvelous lake views from its deck, dining room, and, especially, the single enormous suite, which has a large Jacuzzi and is the perfect place to splurge (a bit) and feel like a millionaire (a lot). Regular rooms are spacious but not pretentious; they are decorated in a warm, Andean style. (About half the rooms have lake views; be sure to ask for one, as it's well worth the small difference in price.) The gourmet restaurant, which concentrates on local ingredients and lake fish, is as good if not better than anything else in town. While Casa Andina is similar to the nearby Posadas del Inca, it is considerably newer and has a couple of singular amenities, including a pier, with its own floating island a la Uros, extending over the lake, and a private train station—so that if you're coming from Cusco, you can get off right at the hotel without having to go into Puno. After a long train ride, that's a nice little bonus.

Av. Sesquicentenario 1970–72, Sector Huaje, Lake Titicaca (Puno). ☎ **866/220-4434** toll-free in the U.S., or 051/363-992. Fax 051/364-082. www.casa-andina.com. 46 units. $91–$186 double; $318 suite (including pressurized oxygen). Rates include breakfast buffet. AE, DC, MC, V. **Amenities:** Restaurant; bar; concierge. *In room:* A/C, TV, fridge, hair dryer, Wi-Fi.

Hotel Libertador Lake Titicaca ★ Ensconced in serenity and splendid isolation on the shore of a small island 5km (3 miles) from Puno, overlooking the expanse of Titicaca, this large, stark-white hotel, built in the late 1970s, may stick out on the banks of the lake, but it takes full advantage of its privileged or inconvenient location, depending on your perspective. Part of the luxury Libertador chain, the hotel has rooms that are **305** spacious if a little bland, and about half have panoramic views of the lake. Those views, though, are spectacular. Service is excellent and the large, white-block hotel has soaring ceilings, but it doesn't have as much character as the better-value Sonesta Posadas del Inca (below), which has views that are almost as good. The hotel is linked to the mainland by a causeway, and the only way back and forth to Puno is by taxi (about $3 each way).

Isla Esteves s/n, Lake Titicaca. (℃) **877/7782281** toll-free in the U.S. and Canada, or 051/367-780. Fax 051/ 367-879. www.libertador.com.pe. 123 units. $170–$195 deluxe double; $220–$260 suite. Rates include breakfast buffet. AE, DC, MC, V. **Amenities:** Restaurant; bar; concierge; fitness center; sauna. *In room:* A/C, TV, fridge, hair dryer.

Sonesta Posadas del Inca Lake Titicaca ★★ (Kids)   Like the Libertador, Posada del Inca hugs the shores of Titicaca and boasts splendid views, but it fits more sensitively into its enviable surroundings. The hotel is imaginatively designed, with warm colors and Peruvian touches, including bright modern art and folk artifacts. Rooms are large and comfortable, and bathrooms are also large and nicely equipped. The restaurant and many rooms look over the lake; other rooms have views of the mountains. The relaxed lobby has a cozy fireplace. Service is friendly, and the staff can arrange visits to Titicaca's islands. Children will enjoy the miniversion of a floating lake community on the grounds by the lake.

Sesquicentenario 610, Sector Huaje, Lake Titicaca. (℃) **800/SONESTA** [766-3782] in the U.S. and Canada, or 051/364-111. Fax 051/363-672. www.sonesta.com/LakeTiticaca. 62 units. $99–$125 double. Rates include breakfast buffet. Children 8 and under stay free in parent's room. AE, DC, MC, V. **Amenities:** Restaurant; cocktail lounge; concierge. *In room:* A/C, TV, fridge, hair dryer.

Moderate

Casa Andina Classic Tikarani ★ (Value)   This professional Peruvian chain of popular and comfortable midsize hotels with good service and impeccable, if predictably decorated, rooms has two locations in downtown Puno (in addition to one of their signature upscale hotels, Private Collection Puno, just outside town, on the banks of Lake Titicaca); this branch, 5 blocks from the Plaza de Armas, is the larger and quieter of the two. (The other, Casa Andina Classic Puno Plaza, on Jr. Grau 270, is just a short block from the square and one off the main pedestrian drag.) As always, the rooms are good-size, extremely clean, and well-equipped. Those on the second floor in the interior are quietest.

Jr. Independencia 185, Puno. (℃) **866/220-4434** toll-free in the U.S., or 051/367-803. Fax 051/365-333. www.casa-andina.com. 53 units. $87 double. Rates include breakfast buffet. AE, DC, MC, V. **Amenities:** Concierge. *In room:* A/C, TV, fridge, hair dryer, Wi-Fi.

Intiqa Hotel ★★ (Finds)   Exceptionally clean and a particularly good mid-range value, this new small hotel, just one block from Pino Park and Jirón Lima, is a very dependable alternative to the more upscale hotels along the banks of Titicaca. Although not quite luxurious, the large rooms are well appointed, stylishly contemporary and very comfortable for the price, with high-quality bedding and linens, double-paned windows and thermal floors (and hot water bottles warm beds in cold months). Service is friendly and uniformly excellent, with a very accommodating staff eager to help guests with travel, tours and dining suggestions (going as far as ordering pizza and soup for guests who aren't feeling well).

Jr. Tarapacá 272, Puno. (℃) **051/366-900.** Fax 051/355-933. www.intiqahotel.com. 24 units. $70 double; $80 suite. Rates include buffet breakfast. MC, V. **Amenities:** Coffee shop. *In room:* TV, fridge, hair dryer upon request, Wi-Fi.

10

PUNO & LAKE TITICACA

ⓘ Tips   **Additional Hostales**

If you arrive in Puno during festival time and there's a crunch on affordable accommodations, try these modest hotels and budget-backpacker places.

Hostal El Virrey   El Virrey has pretty clean rooms with private bathrooms, TVs, and hot water. Some rooms even have views of Titicaca. Tacna 510. ✆ **051/354-495.** $25 double.

Hostal Q'oñi Wasi   Located across from the train station, this *hostal* has simple rooms with twin beds, private bathrooms, and electric showers. It also has a decent little breakfast room. Av. La Torre 119. ✆ **051/365-784.** $12 double.

Los Pinos Inn ⓥ Value   One of the best values at the budget range, this agreeable and clean place in a modern building has clean bathrooms, ample rooms and good natural light, as well as 24-hour hot showers. Jr. Taracapá 182. ✆ **051/367-398.** $20 double.

Posada Don Giorgio   A step up from the others listed here, this *hostal* is quite a good midrange choice, though perhaps not as good a value as Los Pinos. Its carpeted rooms (all with private bathrooms) are comfortable and nicely decorated for the price. Jr. Tarapacá 238. ✆/fax **051/363-648.** www.posadadongiorgio.com. $40 double.

La Hacienda Hotel ⓥ Value   Built around a pair of sunny courtyards on a busy downtown street, this cheerful midsize hotel, recently remodeled, is pleasant and cozy, impersonating a hacienda-style inn. The lobby has a nice fireplace, and a large, impressive spiral staircase leads to the large rooms, which are carpeted, and on the whole, pretty nice. Half the hotel's rooms were newly constructed just a few years ago; it's certainly a lot brighter and more welcoming than it was in the past. Request one of the newer accommodations because they have much-improved bathrooms (with tubs) and double beds.

Jr. Deustua 297, Puno. ✆ **051/356-109.** Fax 051/365-134. www.lahaciendapuno.com. 40 units. $70 double; $90–$120 suite. Rates include continental breakfast. MC. **Amenities:** Restaurant; cafe; bar; concierge. *In room:* TV, Wi-Fi.

Hotel Colón Inn ★ ⓥ Value   A small and charming Belgian-owned hotel in the heart of Puno, the Colón inhabits a 19th-century republican-era building on a corner. Built around an airy, sky-lit, colonial-style lobby, it has three floors of good-size and comfortably appointed carpeted rooms with desks and marble bathrooms. The cozy top-floor pub is advertised for its panoramic views, but in reality, all you can see are the tops of concrete buildings. The two restaurants, Sol Naciente and Pizzeria Europa, are a couple of the better places in Puno for lunch or dinner.

Calle Tacna 290, Puno. ✆/fax **051/351-432.** www.coloninn.com. 21 units. $60 double; $95 suite. Rates include taxes and breakfast buffet. AE, DC, MC, V. **Amenities:** 2 restaurants; bar; room service. *In room:* TV, fridge.

Inexpensive
Hostal Los Uros   Los Uros is one of the most popular Puno *hostales* targeting backpackers, representing a decent value at the low end. The very basic rooms are clean, beds

are pretty decent, the place is quiet, and if you get chilly, the staff will dole out extra wool blankets. About half the rooms have private bathrooms; the rest have shared bathrooms. Your best bet for hot water is in the evening. Meals are available in the simple cafeteria.

Jr. Teodoro Valcarcel 135, Puno. (℮ **051/352-141.** Fax 051/367-016. www.losuros.com. 24 units. S/50 double with private bathroom; S/40 with shared bathroom No credit cards. **Amenities:** Cafeteria; Internet. *In room:* No phone.

WHERE TO DINE

Chilly, drab Puno isn't a place for particularly sophisticated dining. It's better suited for pizzas from wood-fired ovens and simple, straightforward Peruvian cooking. On those scores, it succeeds. Besides, at this altitude, it's not a great idea to overindulge in eating or drinking. Most of Puno's more attractive restaurants, popular with gringos, are located just off the pedestrian-only main drag, Jirón Lima. In addition to those listed below, check out the two restaurants at **Hotel Colón Inn** (p. 306) and, especially for a light and inexpensive lunch, the attractive cafe **Casa del Corregidor,** Jr. Deustua 576 (℮ **051/351-921**), which serves good salads and sandwiches and has a nice, quiet courtyard.

Moderate

Apu Salkantay INTERNATIONAL/PERUVIAN   This genial restaurant, named for a Quechua mountain god, attracts plenty of travelers for drinks next to the fireplace-stove and occasional live folkloric music. But it's also a good place for Peruvian dishes, like *cuy;* alpaca steak with quinoa; alpaca *piqueo* with fries, onions, tomatoes, and peppers; and standard soups and basic fish (kingfish and trout). The daily *menu* includes a soft drink, bread, and main course.

Jr. Lima 425. (℮ **051/363-955.** Reservations not accepted. Main courses S/21–S/30; daily menu S/25. DC, MC, V. Daily 9am–10pm.

Incabar ★ INTERNATIONAL/PERUVIAN   Awfully stylish and downright funky (as well as relatively expensive) for rough-around-the-edges Puno, this lounge bar/restaurant aims high. The menu is much more creative and flavorful than other places in town (even if dishes don't always succeed), with interesting sauces for lake fish and alpaca steak, curries, and stir fries, and artful presentations. For a recent meal, I had *pescadito crocante*—lake kingfish *(pejerrey)* in quinoa grain, fried and served with apples and blackberry jam. Interesting pastas and big salads, as well as sandwiches and snacks, are served until 5pm, and breakfast is served daily and runs about S/10. Incabar is also a good place to hang out, have a beer or coffee, and write postcards—the colorful back room has comfortable sofas. You might want to check out the owners' other popular restaurant down the street, **Colors Lounge,** Lima 342, too.

Jr. Lima 348. (℮ **051/368-031.** Reservations recommended. Main courses S/22–S/35. AE, DC, MC, V. Daily 9am–10pm.

La Casona ★ (Value INTERNATIONAL/PERUVIAN   Probably puno's most distinguished eatery—not necessarily high praise—calls itself a "museum-restaurant." In a town like Puno, with relatively few attractions, that's fair enough. La Casona ("big house") has traditional, rather old-style Spanish charm, with lace tablecloths. The three dining rooms are filled with antiques and large religious canvasses, but it retains a decidedly informal appeal. Its specialty is Titicaca lake fish, such as trout and kingfish *(pejerrey),* served La Casona style, which means with a kitchen-sink preparation of rice, avocado, ham, cheese, hot dog, apple salad, french fries, and mushrooms. Chicken and beef are prepared the same way. If that's a little overwhelming for you, go with the simple trout served with mashed potatoes. In the evening, make a point about asking for the *menu del día*, which is offered but not advertised; it's a good deal (essentially half-price). Service can be a little slow.

Jr. Lima 517. ⓒ **051/351-108.** Reservations recommended. Main courses S/15–S/36. DC, MC, V. Daily 9am–10pm.

Restaurant Don Piero INTERNATIONAL/PERUVIAN   A longtime standard of Pasaje Lima, the pedestrian boulevard at the heart of Puno, Don Piero now seems a little stale. It still cranks out the same standard Peruvian and international fare in large portions as it always has, but the nondescript, midrange place doesn't appeal much to backpackers, and more interesting competition has cropped up on the street for more discriminating palates. Outside on slow days, bow-tied waiters looking bored halfheartedly appeal to tourists to enter. The menu has barbecued chicken and a long list of Peruvian favorites such as *palta rellena* (avocado stuffed with chicken salad) and *lomo saltado* (beef strips with french fries, onions, and peppers).

Jr. Lima 348-364. ⓒ **051/351-766.** Reservations not accepted. Main courses S/15–S/34. DC, V. Daily 11am–10pm.

Ukuku's ★ PERUVIAN/PIZZA   In a second-story space overlooking Jirón Lima, the main drag, this large pizzeria is a relaxed spot that's good looking enough for Puno, with hardwood floors and wood tables and chairs. It focuses on pizzas from a wood-burning oven, but also offers a full menu of Peruvian specialties, such as alpaca steak cooked in red wine, ceviche, and even *chifa* (Peruvian Chinese cooking). If that's not enough, you can also get a passable plate of pasta. There's a second location at Libertad 216.

Jr. Grau 172 (at Jirón Lima). ⓒ **051/367-373.** Reservations not accepted. Main courses S/12–S/27. MC, V. Daily 11am–10pm.

Inexpensive

Pizzería El Buho Ⓥalue ITALIAN/PIZZA   El Buho's wood-burning oven/chimney kicks out some of Puno's best pizzas. It's extremely popular with both gringos and locals. The menu also lists a good number of pastas and a handful of soups, but I swear I've never seen anyone have anything other than pizza.

Jr. Lima 371. ⓒ **051/363-955.** Reservations not accepted. Main courses S/10–S/25. DC, V. Daily 4:30–11pm.

Rico's Pan BAKERY/CAFE   You know what to expect at a small cafe and bakery with a name like "Tasty Bread," and Rico's Pan doesn't disappoint. Drop by for inexpensive sandwiches, pastries, and cakes. It also serves very good coffees, including espresso and cappuccino, and is a good spot for breakfast or for stockpiling goodies for boat trips on Titicaca. There's now a second, convenient location right on the main drag, Jirón Lima.

Lima 420, Puno. ⓒ **051/354-179.** Reservations not accepted. Main courses S/6–S/12. No credit cards. Daily 7am–11pm.

PUNO AFTER DARK

Though the city is the country's capital of folklore, there's not a whole lot happening in Puno after dark. Outside of festivals, nightlife is pretty much confined to a single street, consisting of a handful of bars and discos strung along (or just off) the pedestrian mall, Jirón Lima. My favorite watering hole, just off Jirón Lima, is **Kamizaraky Rock Pub** ★, Pasaje Grau 148 (no phone). A cozy and cool hangout with a loft space, it looks like a graffiti-filled mountain cabin and serves excellent cocktails to a young, gregarious clientele (with occasional live rock music). Along Jirón Lima itself, the jungle lodge and reggae-themed

Traveling to Bolivia

Plenty of travelers make their way across the Andes to Puno not only to visit Lake Titicaca, but also to continue on to Bolivia, which shares a border with Peru. Several travel agencies (see "Organized Tours," earlier in this section) in Puno sell packages and bus tickets to Bolivia.

The most common and scenic route is from Puno to La Paz via **Yunguyo** and **Copacabana.** You get dropped off at the border and then pick up a colectivo or taxi shuttle across, where you go through Customs and passport control. If you're going on your own, you'll need to catch another colectivo to Copaca-bana, just over a half-hour away. The trip to La Paz takes 7 or 8 hours by bus. Buses also go to La Paz via **Desaguadero.** Or, you can go by a combination of overland travel and hydrofoil or catamaran, a unique but very time-consuming journey (13 hr.).

At the border, visitors get an exit stamp from Peru and a tourist visa (30 days) from Bolivia. Foreigners are commonly tapped for phony departure and entry fees; resist the officials' blatant attempts at corruption.

For more information about Bolivia, pick up a copy of *Frommer's South America.*

Positive Vibrations (no. 378; no phone) and **Apu Salkantay** (no. 425; © **051/363-955**) are among the bars worth a stop for some decent music and hot drinks. **La Hostería** (no. 501) and **Ekeko's** (no. 355, 2nd Floor; © **051/365-986**) often have live bands, and the latter has a large-screen TV showing soccer or videos, and a small dance floor. **Kusillo's Pub,** Libertad 259 (© **051/351-301**), has a nightly happy hour and reggae, jazz, and blues, as well as occasional folklore shows. **Shaman,** Jr. Puno 505 (on the Plaza de Armas; no phone), is a second-floor bar that has free Internet access, pizzas, and drinks.

2 AREQUIPA ★★★

1,020km (634 miles) S of Lima; 521km (324 miles) S of Cusco; 297km (185 miles) SW of Puno

The southern city of Arequipa, the second largest in Peru, might be the most handsome in the country. Founded in 1540, it retains an elegant historic center constructed almost entirely of *sillar* (a porous, white volcanic stone), which gives the city its distinctive look and the nickname *la ciudad blanca,* or "the white city." Colonial churches, mansions, a splendid Plaza de Armas, and the sumptuous 16th-century Santa Catalina convent gleam beneath palm trees and a brilliant sun. Ringing the city, in full view, are three delightfully named volcanic peaks: El Misti, Chachani, and Pichu Pichu, all of which hover around 6,000m (20,000 ft.). And the city's small Museo Santuarios Andinos holds an astounding local discovery: a perfectly preserved Inca teenage maiden sacrificed more than 500 years ago.

Arequipa has also emerged as a favorite base of outdoors enthusiasts who come to climb volcanoes, raft on rivers, trek through the valleys, and, above all, head out to Colca Canyon—twice as deep as the Grand Canyon and the best place in South America to see giant condors soar overhead. Suiting its reputation as an outdoor paradise, Arequipa also

ⓘ **Tips** **The withering snows of Arequipa's volcanoes**

The three volcanoes that encircle Arequipa have, as long as most people can remember, been snowcapped year-round. In recent years, however, that has sadly changed. In 2009, the peaks of Chachani, El Misti, and Pichu Pichu were white with snow for just 3 months (June–Aug). Locals are mystified and heartbroken. The effects of global warming and, presumably, ozone deterioration, have not only altered the look of their city; they also bode ill for future discoveries of Inca sacrifices preserved in icy mountaintops.

enjoys perfect weather: more than 300 days a year of sunshine, huge blue skies, and low humidity.

The commercial capital of the south, Arequipa not only looks different; it feels dissimilar from the rest of Peru. Arequipeños have earned a reputation as aloof and distrusting of centralized power in Lima. Relatively wealthy and home to prominent intellectuals, politicians, and industrialists, Arequipa has a haughty air about it—at least in the view of many Peruvians who hail from less distinguished places—but you'd hardly know it in the evenings, when the historic quarter is alive with bar and restaurant patrons.

As beautiful and confident as it is, Arequipa has a history of natural disaster. The most recent devastating earthquake (which registered 8.1 on the Richter scale) struck the city and other points farther south in 2001. Although international reports at the time painted a picture of a city that had caved in on itself, thankfully, that wasn't the case. The colonial core of the city survived intact, as elegant as ever.

ESSENTIALS
Getting There
BY PLANE There are daily flights to Arequipa from Lima and Juliaca on **LAN** (ⓒ 01/213-8200; www.lan.com) and from Lima on the much cheaper, newly launched **Peruvian Airlines** (ⓒ 01/716-6000; www.peruvianairlines.pe). Flights from Lima and Cusco start at about $109 one-way on LAN; Peruvian Airlines originated its service with offers as low as $59 one-way from Lima.

Aeropuerto Rodríguez Ballón (ⓒ 054/443-464 or 054/443-458), Av. Aviación s/n, Zamácola, Cerro Colorado, is about 7km (4⅓ miles) northwest of the city. From the airport to downtown hotels, transportation is by taxi (S/15) or shared colectivo service (about S/5 per person). See "Getting Around" below for more taxi info.

BY BUS The main **Terminal Terrestre** (ⓒ 054/427-798), Avenida Andrés Avelino Cáceres, at Av. Arturo Ibáñez s/n, is about 4km (2½ miles) south of downtown Arequipa. Nearby is a newer station, **Nuevo Terrapuerto** (ⓒ 054/348-810), Av. Arturo Ibáñez s/n. A huge number of bus companies travel in and out of Peru's second city from across the country, and you'll need to ask if your bus departs from Terminal or Terrapuerto. Taxis are usually present at both stations, though if you had trouble at Terrestre, you'd certainly find one at Terrapuerto; to town it's a 5-minute drive.

From Lima (a 16-hr. ride), recommended companies include **Ormeño** (ⓒ 01/472-5000; www.grupo-ormeno.com.pe), **Cruz del Sur** (ⓒ 01/311-5050; www.cruzdelsur.com.pe), **Civa Transportes** (ⓒ 01/418-1111; www.civa.com.pe), and **Oltursa** (ⓒ 01/708-5000; www.oltursa.com.pe). For service from Puno (5 hr.) and Juliaca, contact **Cruz**

del Sur, Civa, or **Julsa. Ormeño** travels to Arequipa from Puno (as well as Cusco). Other options from Cusco (10–12 hr.) are **Civa Transportes** and **Cruz del Sur.** From Chivay/ Colca Canyon (3–4 hr.), call **Reyna** (© 054/426-549) or **Cristo Rey** (© 054/213-094).

Note: Arequipa's bus stations—and especially the buses themselves—are notorious for attracting thieves. Travelers are advised to pay very close attention to their belongings, even going so far as to lock them to luggage racks. The route between Arequipa and Puno especially has earned a bad reputation. It's best to opt for the more exclusive and safer bus companies recommended above.

BY TRAIN Puno-to-Arequipa trains are now available only by private charter for groups of 40 or more, and there are no trains to or from Lima. However, there's always the possibility that the former trajectory might be reinstated at some point in the future (for updates or charters, visit www.perurail.com). The Arequipa rail station is 8 blocks south of the city center, at Av. Tacna y Arica 201 (© **054/215-640**).

Visitor Information

There's a **tourist information booth** at the Aeropuerto Rodríguez Ballón (© **054/444-564**), open Monday through Friday from 9am to 4pm. The best information office in town is in **Casona de Santa Catalina,** Santa Catalina 210 (across from the convent; © **054/221-227**); it's open daily from 9am to 9pm. There's also an office on the Plaza de Armas across from the cathedral at Portal de la Municipalidad 112 (© **054/223-265**); it's open daily from 8am to 6pm. You can also get information and free maps from the **tourist police,** Jerusalén 315, at the corner of Ugarte (© **054/201-258**).

FAST FACTS You'll find ATMs in the courtyards of the historic Casa Ricketts at San Francisco 108, now the offices of **Banco Continental.** Other banks in the historic center include **Banco Latino,** at San Juan de Dios 112, and **Banco de Crédito,** at General Morán 101. Money-changers can generally be found waving calculators and stacks of dollars on the Plaza de Armas and major streets leading off the main square. There are several *casas de cambio* near the Plaza de Armas and Global Net ATMs in several shops around the plaza; one is **Arequipa Inversiones,** Jerusalén 109.

The general emergency number in Arequipa is © **105.** If you need the police, call the **Policía Nacional** (national police) at © **054/254-020,** or **Policía de Turismo** (tourist police), Jerusalén 315, at the corner of Ugarte, at © **054/201-258.** For fire emergencies, call © **116.** If you need medical attention, go to **Clínica Arequipa,** Avenida Bolognesi at Puente Grau (© **054/253-416**), which has good service and English-speaking doctors. You can also try **Hospital General,** Peral s/n (© **054/231-818**) or **Hospital Regional,** Av. Daniel Alcides Carrión s/n (© **054/231-818**).

Arequipa has plenty of Internet cabinas. Most are open daily from 8am to 10pm, charge S/2 per hour, and have Net2Phone or other programs that allow very cheap Web-based international phone calls. Two of the cheapest and fastest cabinas are **La Red,** Jerusalén 306B (© **054/286-700**), and **TravelNet,** Jerusalén 218 (© **054/205-548**). Another good spot is **Catedral Internet,** in the small passageway behind the cathedral. An only slightly more expensive option that's open a bit later is **Catedral Internet,** Pasaje Catedral 101 (© **054/282-074**), on the pedestrian mall just behind the cathedral.

The main **Serpost** (post office) is located at Moral 118 (© **054/215-247**). A **DHL** office is located at Santa Catalina 115 (© **054/220-045**). **Telefónica del Perú** offices are located at Alvarez Thomas 209 (© **054/281-112**) and Av. Los Arces 200B, in the Cayma district (© **054/252-020**).

> ### (Tips)   A Note about Safety
>
> Arequipa—which on the surface seems to be one of Peru's most placid, easygoing cities—has earned a reputation for rife pickpocketing, although some locals talk about staged tourist robberies and even "strangle muggings." Based on my experience, I've found some citizens to be quite alarmist. Several people have been outspoken about what you should carry on your person (nothing of value, including a camera) and how to conduct yourself (be on guard at all times), even in the daytime, when plenty of police patrol the streets in the old quarter. I've never had a problem in Arequipa, but I do think that late at night you should be especially cautious when exiting bars and restaurants in the historic center; as always, leave your daypack and other unnecessary belongings in your hotel. Some taxi drivers in Arequipa also warn about their colleagues who set tourists up for ambushes. They suggest either calling for a cab or getting into taxis with older drivers because most of the crimes have been perpetrated by younger drivers.

Getting Around

Arequipa is compact, and most of its top attractions can easily be seen on foot and with an occasional taxi. The historic center is built around the stately Plaza de Armas, marked by the cathedral on the north flank and porticoed buildings on the other three sides. Most sites of visitor interest, including most hotels and restaurants, are found in the blocks immediately north of the plaza. A few blocks west of the main square is the Río Chili and, beyond it, the residential neighborhood Yanahuara and La Recoleta monastery. Two bridges, Puente Grau and Puente Bolognesi, lead from the center to these areas. A double-decker bus offering tours of the city and countryside is the imaginatively named **Bustour,** Portal de San Agustín 111, Plaza de Armas (✆ 054/203-434; www.bustour.com.pe); with daily departures ranging from 2½ to 4 hours in length (S/25–S/40).

BY TAXI   Taxis are inexpensive and plentiful, easily hailed on the street, and best used at night. Most trips in town cost no more than S/4. To call a taxi at night, try **Taxi Seguro** (✆ 054/450-250), **Taxi Sur** (✆ 054/465-656), **Master Taxi** (✆ 054/220-505), or **Ideal Taxi** (✆ 054/288-888). An excellent private driver for trips to Colca and elsewhere is Manuel Pino Torres of **Privatour** (✆ 054/952-6495).

BY CAR   A car isn't necessary in Arequipa unless you want to explore the countryside, especially Colca and/or Cotahuasi canyons, independently. Try **Lucava Rent-a-Car,** Aeropuerto Rodríquez Ballón (✆ **054/650-565**) and Centro Comercial Cayma no. 10 (✆ **054/663-378**); and **Avis,** Aeropuerto Rodríquez Ballón (✆ **054/443-576**) and Palacio Viejo 214 (✆ **054/282-519**).

WHAT TO SEE & DO
The Top Attractions
Monasterio de Santa Catalina ★★★ (Kids)   Arequipa's serene Convent of Santa Catalina, founded in 1579 under the Dominican order, is the most important and impressive religious monument in Peru. The 16th-century convent remained a mysterious world unto itself until 1972, when local authorities forced the sisters to install modern infrastructure, a requirement that led to opening the convent for tourism. Today only 19 cloistered nuns, ages 20 to 90 remain, mostly out of sight of the hundreds of tourists

Casa Arango **11**

Casa Arróspide **5**

Casa del Moral **4**

Casa Goyeneche **10**

Casa Ricketts **15**

Casano Flores del Campo **14**

Catedral **8**

Convento de Santa Teresa **17**

Iglesia de La Merced **12**

Iglesia de San Agustin **6**

Iglesia de San Francisco **16**

Iglesia de Santo Domingo **18**

La Compañía **13**

Monasterio de la Recoleta **1**

Monasterio de Santa Catalina **3**

Museo Santuarios Andinos **9**

Plaza de Armas **7**

who arrive daily to explore the huge and curious complex. Although the nuns, all from wealthy Spanish families, entered the convent having taken vows of poverty, in the early days they lived in relative luxury, having paid a dowry to live the monastic life amid servants (who outnumbered the nuns), well-equipped kitchens, and art collections.

Behind tall, thick *sillar* fortifications are walls painted sunburned orange, cobalt blue, and brick red, hiding dozens of small cells where more than 200 sequestered nuns once lived. Santa Catalina is a small, labyrinthine village, with narrow cobblestone streets, plant-lined passageways, and pretty plazas, fountains, chapels, and secret niches and quiet corners. Not by accident does it look and feel like a small village in southern Spain, with its predominantly *mudéjar* (Moorish-Christian) architecture and streets named for Spanish

The Discovery of Juanita, the Ampato Maiden

The mummy of the teenage Inca maiden, now christened Juanita, is one of the most important archaeological finds of the last few decades in the Americas. The first frozen female found from the pre-Columbian era in the Andes, her body, packed in ice and thus not desiccated like most mummies, preserved a wealth of information about her culture and life.

Juanita was discovered at the summit of the Ampato volcano in September 1995 by the American anthropologist Dr. Johan Reinhard, the *National Geographic* explorer-in-residence. She immediately became news around the world. Reinhard, who had spent 2 decades looking for clues in the volcanoes of the western Andes near Arequipa, was working on a project co-sponsored by Arequipa's Catholic University of Santa María and was accompanied by Carlos Zárate, a locally famous mountaineer who for years has run one of the best mountain-climbing-expedition tour companies in Peru. Juanita had been remarkably preserved in ice for more than 500 years, but hot ashes from the eruption of the nearby Mount Sabancaya volcano melted the snowcap on Ampato and collapsed the summit ridge, exposing what had been hidden for centuries. Reinhard and Zárate at first saw only the feathers of a ceremonial Inca headdress. It took the two men 2 days to descend the peak with the 80-pound mummy, fighting against time to conserve her frozen body and get her back to Arequipa and the Catholic University labs.

Juanita was selected by Inca priests to be sacrificed as an appeasement to Ampato, whose dominion was water supply and harvests. The offering was almost certainly a desperate plea to stave off drought and starvation. Reinhard and his team later discovered two additional mummies, a girl and a boy, several thousand feet below the summit—probably companion sacrifices leading to the more important sacrifice of the princess on Ampato's summit.

The mummy's incredibly well-preserved corpse allows scientists to examine her skin, hair, blood, and internal organs, and even the contents of her stomach. Her DNA makeup is being studied. Juanita was dressed in superior textiles from Cusco, clues to her probable nobility. Incredibly important was the fact

cities. In all, it contains 3 cloisters, 6 streets, 80 housing units, art gallery, and a cemetery. The interplay of intense sunlight and shadows, tiny white-stone windows suddenly framing brilliant bursts of color, and sense of splendid isolation from the city beyond make for an incredible aesthetic experience. No less an expert than the great Portuguese architect Alvaro Siza called Santa Catalina a "magnificent lesson in architecture." Yet, alarmingly it is on World Monuments Watch list of Most Endangered Monuments; experts say the great convent is threatened by structural damage caused by pollution and earthquakes.

Among the convent's highlights are the Orange Tree Cloister, with mural paintings over the arches; Calle Toledo, a long boulevard with a communal *lavandería* at its end, where the sisters washed their clothes in halved earthenware jugs; the 17th-century kitchen with charred walls; and the rooms belonging to Sor Ana, a 17th-century nun at the convent who was beatified by Pope John Paul II and is on her way to becoming a that the ceremonial site was undisturbed, with all ritual elements in place, allowing anthropologists to essentially re-create the ceremony.

The peak of Apu Ampato was sacred to the Incas, and only priests were allowed to ascend to it. It is most extraordinary that the Incas were able to climb 6,000m (20,000-ft.) peaks without the assistance of oxygen or other modern climbing equipment. Juanita's transfer and sacrifice there, at the age of 13, was part of an elaborate ritual. Having first met with the Inca emperor in Cusco, she must have known her fate: an imminent journey to meet the mountain gods so revered by the Incas. Sacrifice was the greatest honor bestowed upon an individual. Led up the frozen summit by priests, in sandals and surely exhausted, she was probably made to fast and might have been given drugs or an intoxicating beverage before she was killed by a swift blow to her right temple. Scientists at Johns Hopkins University in Baltimore examined the mummy with a CT scan that revealed a crack in the skull, just above the right eye, and internal bleeding.

More than 100 sacred Inca ceremonial sites have been found on dozens of Andes peaks, although no mummies have been uncovered in the frozen condition of Juanita. Anthropologists believe that hundreds of Inca children might be entombed in ice graves on the highest peaks in South America from central Chile to southern Peru. The Incas believed that they could approach Inti, the sun god, by ascending the highest summits of the Andes. The mountain deities they believed to live there were considered protectors of the Inca people. Sacrifices were frequently responses to cataclysmic events: earthquakes, eclipses, and droughts.

Juanita and many of the ritualistic elements found at the ceremonial site are now exhibited at the Museo Santuarios Andinos (p. 316). More information about the Mount Ampato expedition can be found at www.national geographic.com.

saint. Visitors can enter the choir room of the church, but it's difficult to get a good look at the main chapel and its marvelous painted cupola. To see the church, slip in during early morning Mass (daily at 7:30am); the cloistered nuns remain at the back, in view behind a wooden grille. Visitors are advised to take an informative guided tour (in English and other languages, available for a tip of about S/20), though it's also fun just to wander idly around discovering its myriad spaces, especially before or after the crowds arrive. For an especially transfixing experience, visit at night, when cells and the huge kitchen are illuminated by wood fires and flickering candles (come in the early evening as the sun sets). Allow at least a couple of hours to see the convent in all its glory.

Santa Catalina 301. ℂ 054/608-282. www.santacatalina.org.pe. Admission S/30. Fri–Mon 9am–5pm; Tues–Thurs 8am–8pm.

> ### (Tips) Photo Op: Yanahuara
>
> One of the best views in Arequipa is from the elevated *mirador* (lookout point) in the tranquil suburb of Yanahuara ★★ just across Puente Grau. Next to the delightful Plaza de Yanahuara, with its tall palm trees and lovely gardens, a series of *sillar* stone arches beautifully frames the volcanic peaks of El Misti and Chachani. Across from the mirador is the Iglesia de Yanahuara, also built of *sillar* in the mid–18th century and featuring a splendid baroque carved facade and bell tower. The Plaza de Yanahuara, about a 25-minute walk up to Avenida del Ejército from downtown Arequipa, makes a very pleasant place to duck out of Arequipa's intense sun. A bar-restaurant on one side of the square, **Tinto & Asado,** Calle Cuesta del Olivo 318 (☎ **054/272-380**), has a relaxing terrace with superlative views of El Misti and happy-hour drinks. Or visit the mirador after lunch at **Sol de Mayo** (p. 325), just a few blocks south.

Museo Santuarios Andinos ★★ (Kids) The small Museum of Andean Sanctuaries features a collection of fascinating exhibits, including mummies and artifacts from the Inca Empire, but it is dominated by one tiny girl: Juanita, the Ice Maiden of Ampato. The victim of a ritualistic sacrifice by Inca priests high on the volcano Mount Ampato and buried in ice at 6,380m (20,932 ft.), "Juanita"—named after the leader of the expedition, Johan Rhinehard—was discovered in almost perfect condition in September 1995 after the eruption of the nearby Sabancaya Volcano melted ice on the peak. Juanita had lain buried in the snow for more than 550 years. Only Inca priests were allowed to ascend to such a high point, where the gods were believed to have lived. Juanita, who became famous worldwide through a *National Geographic* report on the find, died from a violent blow to the head; she was 13 at the time of her death. Her remarkable preservation has allowed researchers to gain great insights into Inca culture by analyzing her DNA. Today, she is kept in a glass-walled freezer chamber here, less a mummy than a frozen body, in astoundingly good condition, nearly 600 years old—visitors should leave feeling truly privileged at the chance to observe such a monumental discovery and window onto the legacy of the Inca people. Displayed nearby and in adjacent rooms are some of the superb doll offerings and burial items found alongside Juanita's corpse and those of three other sacrificial victims also found on the mountain. Guided visits, which begin with a good *National Geographic* film, are mandatory. Allow about an hour for your visit.

La Merced 110. ☎ **054/200-345.** Admission S/15 adults, S/5 children, free for seniors. Mon–Sat 9am–6pm; Sun 9am–3pm.

Plaza de Armas ★★

Arequipa's grand Plaza de Armas, an elegant and symmetrical square of gardens and a central fountain lined by arcaded buildings on three sides, is the focus of urban life. Dominated by the massive, 17th-century neoclassical **Catedral** ★, it is perhaps the loveliest main square in Peru, even though its profile suffered considerable damage when the great earthquake of 2001 felled one of the cathedral's two towers and whittled the other to a delicate pedestal. The cathedral, previously devastated by fire and other earthquakes, has now been fully restored to its original grandeur and you'd never know an earthquake struck. The interior is peach and white, with carved arches and a massive pipe

House Tour: Arequipa's Colonial Mansions ★★

Arequipa possesses one of the most attractive and harmonious colonial nuclei in Peru. Several extraordinary seigniorial houses were constructed in white *sillar* stone. They are predominantly flat-roofed, single-story structures, a construction style that has helped them withstand the effects of frequent earthquakes that would have toppled less solid buildings. Most of these houses have attractive, though small, interior patios and elaborately carved facades. Best equipped for visitors is the restored **Casa del Moral** (p. 318), but several others are worth a look, especially if you have an interest in colonial architecture.

Just off the main square at San Francisco 108, **Casa Ricketts** (also called **Casa Tristán del Pozo**), a former seminary and today the offices of Banco Continental, is one of the finest colonial homes in Arequipa. Built in the 1730s, it has a beautiful portal, perhaps Arequipa's finest expression of colonial civil architecture, with delicate representations of the life of Jesus. Inside are two large, beautiful courtyards with gargoyle drainage pipes.

On the other side of the cathedral at the corner of Santa Catalina 101 at San Agustín, **Casa Arróspide** (also called **Casa Iriberry**), from the late 18th century, is one of the most distinguished *sillar* mansions in the city. Now the Cultural Center of San Agustín University (✆ **054/204-482**), its several *salas* host temporary exhibits of contemporary art and photography; you'll also find an art shop and nice little cafe with a terrace and great views over the top of the cathedral.

Other colonial houses of interest include **Casa Arango,** a squat and eclectic 17th-century home located on Consuelo at La Merced; **Casa Goyeneche,** La Merced 201, today the offices of Banco de Reserva; and **Casa de la Moneda,** Ugarte at Villaba.

About a 15-minute cab ride outside of town, in Huasacache, is the **Mansión del Fundador** (✆ **054/442-460**), one of the most important *sillar* mansions in Arequipa. It is said to have been constructed by the founder of Arequipa, Manuel de Carbajal, for his son. It features terrific vaulted ceilings and a large interior patio. The house is open daily from 9am to 5pm; admission is S/10.

Parroquia de Yanahuara, a stunningly carved church with a long, single nave and vaulted ceiling, dates to 1730 and is the centerpiece of the Yanahuara main square overlooking Arequipa.

organ. The cathedral is open Monday to Saturday from 7 to 11:30am and 5 to 7:30pm, Sunday from 7am to 1pm and 5 to 7pm.

La Compañía ★, just off the plaza at the corner of Alvarez Thomas and General Morán, opposite the cathedral, is a splendid 17th-century Jesuit church with an elaborate (Plateresque) facade carved of *sillar* stone. The magnificent portal, one of the finest in Peru, shows the end date of the church's construction, 1698—more than a century after work began on it. The interior holds a handsome carved-cedar main altar, bathed in gold leaf, and two impressive chapels: the Capilla de San Ignacio, which has a remarkable

Tips Arequipa's Colonial Churches

Arequipa has a wealth of colonial churches that are well worth a visit if you have the time. They include **Iglesia de San Francisco** (Zela 103), built of *sillar* and brick in the 16th century with an impressive all-silver altar and a beautiful vaulted ceiling; **Iglesia de San Agustín** (at the corner of San Agustín and Sucre), with a superbly stylized baroque facade, an excellent example of 16th- and 17th-century mestizo architecture (it was rebuilt in 1898 after earthquake damage and was restored, with an unfortunate new bell tower, again in October 2005); **Iglesia de Santo Domingo** (at Santo Domingo and Piérola), with handsome 1734 cloisters; **Iglesia de La Merced** (La Merced 303), built in 1607 and possessing a lovely carved *sillar* facade and an impressive colonial library; **Convento de Santa Teresa** (Melgar at Peral), of brilliant sillar and newly restored, with a museum and lovely outdoor terrace; and **Iglesia de Yanahuara** (see p. 316).

painted cupola, and the Capilla Real, or Royal Chapel. Painted murals in the sacristy feature a jungle motif in brilliant colors. Next door to the church are the stately Jesuit cloisters, of stark *sillar* construction, now housing upscale boutiques (enter on Calle Morán). Climb to the top for good views of the city's rooftops and distant volcanoes. The church is open Monday through Saturday from 9 to 11am and 3 to 6pm; admission is free.

On the east side of the plaza at Portal de Flores 136 is the **Casona Flores del Campo** (© 054/244-150), the oldest house in Arequipa. Begun in the late 1500s but not finished until 1779, today it is in deplorable condition, having suffered through earthquakes and a lack of funds that have left it barely standing, and is now closed to the public for safety considerations.

More Attractions

Casa del Moral ★★ An extraordinary *mestizo* baroque mansion, built in 1733 by a Spanish knight and nicely restored with period detail in 1994, Casa del Moral offers one of the best windows onto colonial times in Arequipa. Named for an ancient mulberry tree—the *moral* found in the courtyard—the home is also distinguished by a magnificent stone portal with heraldic emblems carved in *sillar*. Handsome furnishings, carved wooden doors, and Cusco School oil paintings decorate large salons, built around a beautiful courtyard, the largest of the colonial residences in the city. Look for 17th-century maps that depict the borders and shapes of countries quite differently from their usual representations today. A second courtyard, painted cobalt blue, was used as the summer patio. Climb to the rooftop for a great view of Arequipa and the surrounding volcanoes. Visits are by guided tour (at no extra cost).

Moral 318 (at Bolívar). © 054/210-084. Admission S/5 adults, S/3 students. Mon–Sat 9am–5pm; Sun 9am–1pm.

Monasterio de la Recoleta ★ A 10-minute walk from the Plaza de Armas across the Río Chili, distinguished by its tall brick-red-and-white steeple, is the Recoleta convent museum. Founded in 1648 and rebuilt after earthquakes, the peaceful Franciscan convent contains impressive cloisters with *sillar* columns and lovely gardens; today just four of the original seven remain. The convent museum includes several collections. In one room is a collection of pre-Inca culture artifacts, including funereal masks, textiles, and totems; in another are mummies and a series of paintings of the 12 Inca emperors. At the rear of the convent is a small Amazonian museum, stocked with curious items collected by Franciscan missionaries in the Amazon basin. The missionaries were understandably fascinated by prehistoric-looking fish, crocodiles, piranhas, and the clothing of indigenous communities. These souvenirs pose an interesting contrast to the Dominicans' fine library containing some 20,000 volumes, including rare published texts from the 15th century. Guides (tip basis) are available for 1-hour tours in English, Spanish, and French.

Recoleta 117. (C) **054/270-966.** Admission S/5 adults, S/3 students, free for seniors. Mon–Sat 9am–noon and 3–5pm.

SHOPPING

Arequipa is perhaps the number one spot in Peru—better even than Cusco and Lima— to shop for top-quality baby alpaca, vicuña, and woolen goods. Although many items are more expensive than the lesser-quality goods sold in other parts of Peru, in Arequipa you'll find nicer designs and export-quality knit sweaters, shawls, blankets, and scarves. In many parts of Peru, what is sold as alpaca or baby alpaca is often a mix of alpaca and synthetics. Many of the finest pure alpaca woven items in Peru come from Arequipa. Vicuña wool, which is softer, rarer, and more expensive than alpaca, is also now found at a couple of shops, but keep in mind that a simple shawl runs about $1,600. The city also produces very nice leather goods, and several excellent antiques shops feature colonial pieces and even older items (remember, though, that these antiques cannot legally be exported from Peru; see "Entry Requirements," in chapter 3, for regulations). **Casona de Santa Catalina,** Santa Catalina 210 ((C) **054/281-334**) and **Patio del Ekeko,** Mercaderes 141 ((C) **054/215-861**), are two small shopping malls near the Plaza de Armas with several good, upscale shops, including alpaca goods, handicrafts, jewelry, and food shops. Calle Mercaderes is newly pedestrian-only and more than ever the city's top shopping avenue.

ALPACA GOODS Three general areas are particularly good for alpaca items. One is the **cloisters** next to La Compañía church, where you'll find several alpaca boutiques and outlets. Another good place is **Pasaje Catedral,** the pedestrian mall just behind the cathedral, and a third is **Calle Santa Catalina.** Shops with fine alpaca items include **Kuna** ★★, Santa Catalina 210 and Calle Mercaderes 141 ((C) 054/282-485 and 054/225-550); **Millma's Baby Alpaca,** Pasaje Catedral 177 ((C) 054/205-134); **Baby Alpaca Boutique,** Santa Catalina 208 ((C) 054/206-716); **Anselmo's Souvenirs,** Pasaje Catedral 119 (no phone); **Wari,** San Francisco 311 ((C) 054/223-301); **Alpaca Azul,** Moral 223–225 ((C) 054/228-331); and **Alpaca 111** ★, Zela 212 ((C) 054/223-238). Two **Incalpaca** (Grupo Inca) ★ factory outlets are good spots to get last season's items at discounted prices: One is in town, within the courtyard of La Compañía, on General Moran and Álvarez Thomas ((C) 054/205-931); the other is about 10 minutes outside of town, Av. Juan Bustamante s/n, in the Tahuaycani district ((C) 054/251-025). The latter also has a small zoo of camelids to entertain the kids while parents shop for alpaca and hard-to-find and expensive vicuña items.

ANTIQUES Calle Santa Catalina and nearby streets have several antiques shops. I found lots of items I wished I could have taken home at the following three stores: **Curiosidades,** Zela 207 ((C) **054/952-986**); **Álvaro Valdivia Montoya**'s two well-stocked shops at Santa Catalina 204 and Santa Catalina 406 (② **054/229-103**); and **Arte Colonial,** Santa Catalina 312 (② **054/214-887**).

BOOKS   A very good and friendly bookstore with art books and English-language paperbacks is **Libería El Lector,** San Francisco 221 (② **054/288-677**).

HANDICRAFTS   A general handicrafts market *(mercado de artesanía)* with dozens of stalls in the old town jail, is next door to the Plazuela de San Francisco (btw. Zela and Puente Grau). For handmade leather goods, stroll along Puente Bolognesi, which leads west from the Plaza de Armas, and you'll find numerous small stores with handbags, shoes, and other items.

WHERE TO STAY

Arequipa has an ample roster of hotels and *hostales* (inns) at all levels. A number of them occupy historic houses in the old quarter, within very easy walking distance of major sights, restaurants, and bars. Even budget travelers can do very well in Arequipa—it's a good place for a significant step up in comfort and style (but not price) from the usual backpacker dregs. Indeed, even travelers not accustomed to looking at hotels in the inexpensive or moderate range may well find a very welcome surprise in here in terms of comfort and value. The area north of the Plaza de Armas is nicer and less chaotic (though full of restaurants and bars) than the streets south of the square.

Note: If you hop in a taxi from the airport or bus station, insist on going to the hotel of your choice; local taxi drivers often claim that a particular hotel is closed in order to take you to one that will pay them a commission.

Expensive

Casa Andina Private Collection Arequipa ★★★   Inaugurated in 2008, this upscale midsize hotel, in one of Arequipa's emblematic colonial buildings, the storied Mint House—a national historic monument—is a splendid addition to the city's few true luxury options. Just 3 blocks from the Plaza de Armas, around the corner from the Santa Catalina convent, it's ideally located. It features beautiful *sillar* walls, two lovely interior courtyards, an elegant gourmet restaurant, and even a small on-site museum depicting the minting of old coins. Accommodations in the modern wing are elegantly understated and spacious, with nice bathrooms, while the sprawling suites in the historic main house are downright sumptuous. Intimate, with a boutique feel but all the services of a larger luxury hotel, and prices that, while not inexpensive, seem merited, it has immediately become Arequipa's top place to stay, and one of the top hotels in Peru.

Ugarte 403, Arequipa. ② **866/220-4434** toll-free in the U.S., or 054/226-907. Fax 054/226-908. www. casa-andina.com. 41 units. $124–$208 double; $263–$494 suite. Rates include breakfast buffet. AE, DC, MC, V. **Amenities:** Restaurant; bar; concierge. *In room:* A/C, TV, fridge, hair dryer, Wi-Fi.

Hotel Libertador Arequipa ★ (Kids)   Arequipa's swankest large hotel within reach of the historic center is in this handsome, sprawling 1940s colonial-style building. In the midst of quiet Selva Alegre, the largest park in Arequipa, the midsize hotel, recently renovated and part of a small upmarket Peruvian chain, is about a 15-minute walk from the main square. It maintains a colonial theme throughout, with soaring ceilings, historical murals, and older-style dark-wood period furnishings in expansive, elegantly appointed rooms. Accommodations, equipped with marble bathrooms, are about as large as you're likely to find. The hotel has a lovely, large outdoor pool among nice gardens and tall palm trees. Families will appreciate the outdoor recreation and game area for children.

ACCOMMODATIONS ■

Casa Andina Classic Arequipa **3**

Casa Andina Classic Arequipa
Convento **14**

Casa Andina Private
Collection Arequipa **16**

Casa Arequipa **25**

Colonial House Inn **7**

Hostal Núñez **5**

Hotel Libertador Arequipa **2**

Las Casa de Mi Abuela
Hostal **4**

La Reyna **10**

Los Balcones de Moral y
Santa Catalina **18**

Sonesta Posada del
Inca **23**

Tambo Viejo **26**

DINING ◆

Ary Quepay **6**

El Cerrojo **19**

El Turko II **14**

El Viñedo **13**

Govinda **17**

La Canasta **22**

La Trattoria del
Monasterio **12**

La Truffa **20**

Los Leños **8**

Sol de Mayo **18**

Tradición
Arequipeña **25**

Zig Zag **11**

Plaza Bolívar, Selva Alegre, Arequipa. ✆ **054/215-110.** Fax 054/241–933. www.libertador.com.pe. 88
units. $125–$160 deluxe double; $185 suite. Rates include buffet breakfast. AE, DC, MC, V. **Amenities:** 2
restaurants; bar; concierge; fitness center; Jacuzzi; large outdoor pool; sauna. *In room:* A/C, TV, fridge.

Sonesta Posadas del Inca Arequipa ★   Now that it's been acquired by the Sonesta chain, things are looking up for this hotel with perhaps the most coveted location in
Arequipa, right on the stately Plaza de Armas. Even if that's the best thing about this large
hotel, it's still plenty. It's perfectly located to allow you to see and do everything in Arequipa with ease. The hotel has gotten a partial but not yet full makeover, so the dated
casino lobby decor, an awkward step back into the 1970s, is thankfully gone. Rooms are

spacious and comfortable, if not luxurious, with a retro feel to them; the desirable executive rooms on upper floors have attractive terraces under the porticoes with plaza views. There's also a nice little rooftop pool framed by flower beds and sweeping views of the cathedral and volcanoes in the distance, and the restaurant bar has seats overlooking the plaza. Look for Web-only specials that can be as little as half the rack rate.

Portal de Flores 116, Plaza de Armas, Arequipa. © **054/215-530.** Fax 054/234-374. www.sonesta.com/ Arequipa. 58 units. $125 standard double; $140 deluxe double; $155 suite. Rates include taxes and buffet breakfast. AE, DC, MC, V. **Amenities:** Restaurant; bar; concierge; outdoor rooftop pool. *In room:* A/C, TV, fridge.

Moderate

Casa Andina Classic Arequipa Convento ★★ (Value)

Directly across the street from Santa Catalina convent—in fact, occupying an 18th-century manor house that once belonged to the sequestered nuns and was more recently a less distinguished hotel—this new property, inaugurated in 2010 by Casa Andina, which already has two others in Arequipa—is a terrific midrange choice. The soaring, vaulted *sillar* ceilings of common rooms are spectacular, as is the pretty central patio, very reminiscent of Santa Catalina. Rooms have been very nicely refurbished, and they feature flatscreen TVs and excellent bedding. Other bonuses are a nice outdoor pool with sundeck and Café Sama, a cool little coffee shop outfitted with travel guides and books, a great place to plan the rest of your Peru trip.

Santa Catalina 300, Arequipa. © **866/220-4434** toll-free in the U.S., or 054/226-907. Fax 054/226-908. www.casa-andina.com. 47 units. $79–$119 double; $149 suite. Rates include breakfast buffet. AE, DC, MC, V. **Amenities:** Cafe; concierge. *In room:* A/C, TV, hair dryer upon request, Wi-Fi.

Casa Arequipa ★★ (Value)

This intimate inn, akin to a European boutique hotel—something very unusual for Peru—is one of the most surprisingly luxurious places to stay in the country and boasts bargain prices. It occupies a beautifully restored, pink 1950s mansion in the quiet Vallecito residential district, a short walk or cab ride from the Plaza de Armas (which some may find a bit inconvenient; others will appreciate being removed from the hubbub). The inn features elegantly designed guest rooms, with nicely chosen furnishings (including many antiques), very comfortable beds, and the finest towels and bed linens you'll find in Peru. Photographs of the Andes, taken by the owner (who splits his time between Arequipa and Washington, D.C.), decorate the rooms, and fresh flowers are placed in every room and throughout the house. The excellent bathrooms, several of which have tubs, are of gleaming marble. The breakfast buffet and personal attention are worthy of a five-star hotel.

Av. Lima, Vallecito, Arequipa. © **054/284-219** or 202/518-9672 for reservations in the U.S. Fax 054/253-343. www.arequipacasa.com. 10 units. $65–$99 double. Rates include taxes. AE, DC, MC, V. **Amenities:** Concierge; CD library. *In room:* A/C, TV, CD player, fridge.

La Maison d' Elise ★ (Finds)

This small gem of a hotel is hidden behind a nondescript, rather unappealing facade. Across from the park on the other side of Puente Grau, just beyond the historic center, this 14-year-old hotel is like a small Mediterranean village. Ocher-and-white villas are clustered around courtyards ripe with cactus and colorful flowering plants. Double rooms are very large and comfortably furnished; matrimonial suites have a lower-level sitting room. There are also apartments with private terraces. The hotel has a small pool with a rock waterfall, and a notable and nicely decorated restaurant. Deals are sometimes available. The hotel is less luxurious overall than the Libertador (above), but it's got a quirkier charm and is much more affordable.

Av. Bolognesi 104, Yanahuara, Arequipa. © **054/256-185.** Fax 054/253-343. www.aqplink.com/hotel/maison. 88 units. $70 double; $78–$96 suite. AE, DC, MC, V. **Amenities:** 2 restaurants; bar; pool. *In room:* A/C, TV.

Inexpensive

Colonial House Inn (Finds) A rambling 200-year-old house—continually owned by the same family—in the old quarter, this friendly, eclectic inn is perfect for backpackers or budget travelers in search of some local flavor. It has a great rooftop terrace; nice large rooms, all with a private bathroom; a comfortable covered patio; a library and book exchange; and good breakfasts in a little cafe area. Book in advance, as it is frequently full.

Puente Grau 114, Arequipa. ℂ/fax **054/223-533.** www.colonialhouseinn-arequipa.com. 7 units. $18 double. No credit cards. **Amenities:** Restaurant.

Hostal Núñez (Value) This colonial inn is attractive and affordable—and thus popular. Friendly and family-owned, it's on a street in the old quarter loaded with travel agencies. Rooms aren't anything special, but they are ample and have hardwood floors and cable TV, and they're decorated with actual color schemes, a rarity at these prices. Public rooms are very congenial and loaded with plants. A huge rooftop terrace has excellent views of the city, and there are other unusual amenities at this level, including an on-site salon. Breakfast on the terrace is a great perk. Couples or friends sharing a room are best off: Single rooms are pretty small.

Jerusalén 528, Arequipa. ℂ/fax **054/218-648.** www.hotel-nunez.de. 7 units. $30 double. Rates include continental breakfast. No credit cards. **Amenities:** Restaurant; bar. *In room:* TV.

La Casa de Melgar Hostal ★★ (Finds) A handsome colonial house made of white *sillar* (volcanic stone), this charming small hotel is one of the nicest and most relaxed in Peru, as well as one of the best values. Just 3 blocks from the Plaza de Armas, the lovingly restored 18th-century mansion—the former residence of the bishop of Arequipa—has thick, massive walls and three interior courtyards. It echoes the rich, brick-red and royal-blue tones of the Santa Catalina Monastery and is the perfect place to stay if you're a fan of colonial architecture. The ample rooms have good beds. Some rooms—especially those on the ground floor that have high vaulted brick ceilings—exude colonial character; if the hotel isn't full, ask to see a couple. A newer wing of rooms, also in a colonial building with *sillar* walls at the rear, behind a nice garden and terrace, are also lovely; some have incredibly high ceilings.

Breakfast is served in the neat little cafe next door in one of the courtyards. Advance reservations are a must in high season, as the inn is justifiably popular.

Melgar 108, Cercado, Arequipa. ℂ/fax **054/222-459** or 01/446-8343 for reservations. www.lacasademelgar. com. 30 units. $45 double. Rates include breakfast. V. **Amenities:** Restaurant; bar.

La Casa de Mi Abuela Hotel ★ One of the best-run small hotels in Arequipa, "my grandmother's house" is tucked behind a security gate but welcomes everyone with an easygoing atmosphere. An organic, quirky place that has grown from a tiny B&B operation into a very popular 50-room hotel, it is still family run. Today it's a self-contained tourism complex and miniresort, with a live-music peña bar, book exchange, travel agency, and beautiful, relaxing gardens with views of El Misti. Some rooms have roof terraces; others have balconies. Many rooms are plainly decorated and cramped, but the *hostal* compensates with services, facilities, and security. The inn is about a 10-minute walk (6 blocks) north of the main square; it's often filled, so make advance reservations. Nice breakfasts are served in the garden (extra charge).

Jerusalén 606, Cercado, Arequipa. ℂ **054/241-206.** Fax 054/242-761. www.lacasademiabuela.com. 50 units. $54 double; $66 suite. DC, MC, V. **Amenities:** Restaurant; bar; outdoor pool. *In room:* TV, fridge.

La Reyna A popular backpacker inn in town, La Reyna is smack in the middle of the historic center, just a block from the famed Santa Catalina monastery and paces away from plenty of bars and restaurants. The *hostal's* many rooms feed off a labyrinth of narrow staircases that climb up three floors to a roof terrace, a popular spot to hang out and write postcards and plan hiking expeditions, or to veg out and stargaze late at night. There are simple, rock-bottom dormitory rooms for zero-budget travelers and a couple of rooftop casitas that, although basic in their decoration, have private bathrooms and their own terraces with awesome views of the mountains and the monastery below—something akin to backpacker penthouse suites. (Number 20 is worth reserving, if you can.) The *hostal,* though a little haphazardly run, organizes lots of canyon treks and volcano-climbing tours, and even offers Spanish classes.

Zela 209, Arequipa. ℂ/fax **054/286-578.** 20 units. $10 double without bathroom, $12 double with bathroom. No credit cards.

Los Balcones de Moral y Santa Catalina ★ (Value This inviting small hotel is very comfortable and decently furnished, a nice step up from budget hostels for not too much more money. In the heart of the old quarter, it's only a couple of blocks from the Plaza de Armas. Half of the house is colonial (first floor); the other is republican, dating from the 1800s. The house is built around a colonial patio with a sunny terrace. Furnishings are modern, with wallpaper and firm beds. Eleven of the good-size rooms have hardwood floors and large balconies with nice views looking toward the back of the cathedral; the other rooms are carpeted and less desirable (though quieter). All have good, tiled bathrooms.

Moral 217, Arequipa. ℂ/fax **054/201-291.** www.balconeshotel.com. 17 units. S/135 double. MC, V. **Amenities:** Restaurant. *In room:* TV.

Tambo Viejo (Finds This quirky and charming budget *hostal,* occupying an old colonial family home, is a 15-minute walk south of the Plaza de Armas, but it's popular and usually full of backpackers drawn by good word of mouth about the tranquil and genial atmosphere. There are rooms with shared and private bathrooms, a big garden with sun terraces and volcano views, a cafe serving veggie breakfasts and other meals, a book exchange, a TV lounge, and hot water all day.

Av. Malecón Socabaya 107, Arequipa. ℂ **054/288-195.** Fax 054/284-747. www.tamboviejo.com. 20 units. S/55–S/92 double. Rates include American breakfast and bus station pickup (with 2-night stay). DC, MC, V. **Amenities:** Cafe; bike rental; Internet (in lobby).

WHERE TO DINE

Arequipa ranks just behind Lima for gastronomic adventures, and at very reasonable prices. Arequipeño cooking is famous throughout Peru, and several restaurants specialize in traditional regional specialties, a couple of them with fabulous outdoor seating and excellent views of the volcanoes. Several restaurants in the historic quarter—the two streets leading north from the Plaza de Armas, Santa Catalina, and San Francisco are the main hub of nighttime activity—specialize in traditional Arequipeño cooking, though two of the best are a short taxi ride beyond downtown.

Expensive

Chi Cha ★★★ (Value AREQUIPEÑO The full name of this stylish new restaurant is "Chi Cha por Gastón Acurio," which, for anyone who's been following Peruvian cuisine, is pretty much all you need to know. Acurio hit it big in Lima with Astrid & Gastón and La Mar and then expanded to other parts of South and North America. His latest

venture is Chi Cha in both Cusco and Arequipa, taking on regional Peruvian cuisines. **325**
Especially here, it's a hit. In a handsome, inviting massive space with vaulted ceilings and
divided into several dining rooms with different ambiences (from an open patio with a
picnic table at the center and a view of the long open kitchen to a stylish bar room).
While several of Acurio's signature dishes from his *cevichería* and other restaurants are on
the menu, go for his local-accented fare labeled "la tradición." Those plates include
escribano, a tangy, spicy potato salad; and rocoto relleno, a spicy pepper stuffed with
minced meat. The excellent pisco cocktails, with local fruit juices and named for Arequipa landmarks, such as the Chachani, are superb. While the restaurant is not inexpensive
by Peruvian standards, by international comparisons, it's a downright bargain for top-
flight, creative cooking using indigenous ingredients and advancing local cuisine.

Santa Catalina 210 (interior). © **054/287-360.** Reservations recommended. Main courses S/18–S/39. AE,
DC, MC, V. Mon–Sat 1pm–midnight; Sun noon–5pm.

Sol de Mayo ★★ (Value) AREQUIPEÑO/PERUVIAN   A 5-minute taxi ride from
the *centro* in Yanahuara, the city's nicest residential neighborhood, this longtime stalwart
(it's been around for more than a century) is the standard-bearer for Arequipeño cooking.
A favorite of upscale locals and tourists alike, it has the most delightful setting of the city's
restaurants. The colonial tables are set around the edges of a breezy, picture-perfect courtyard with thick grass, geraniums, a small pool and cascading waterfall, and strolling
altiplano musicians. There are also indoor dining rooms inside the brick-red and yellow
sillar stone building, but nothing beats eating outdoors here. Peruvian specialties are Sol
de Mayo's calling card: *chicharrón de chancho* (fried pork), ostrich, fresh shellfish, and a
tantalizing lineup of ceviche. Starters include a yummy mixed salad of *choclo* (white
corn), tomato, and avocado. Good pisco sours are a must to start off your meal. Even for
budget-oriented backpackers, this is one of the best places in Arequipa to splurge and get
a taste of local cuisine, though splurging here means no more than about $15 a head.

Jerusalén 207, Yanahuara. © **054/254-148.** Reservations recommended. Main courses S/15–S/48. AE,
DC, MC, V. Daily 11am–10pm.

Zig Zag Restaurant ★★ GRILL/SWISS   Calling its cuisine "Alpandino," Zig Zag
has an awful lot going for it. Occupying a cool two-level, *sillar*-walled space with a fantastic, twisting iron staircase, it's chic enough to appeal to young people on dates and
comfortable enough for families and small tourist groups. If you're in need of a meat fix,
this is the place. The house specialty is stone-grilled meats, including ostrich and alpaca,
ordered by quantity (10–250 grams) and served either unadorned on a sizzling stone or
with a variety of sauces. The owners like to educate their customers about these lean
meats as a healthy alternative to other meats. Try the ostrich carpaccio in lemon or ostrich
stone-grilled with Swiss-style hash browns. If you're not a carnivore, other favorites are
trout and shrimp, or fondues and pastas (such as the interesting Peruvian-Italian quinoa
gnocchi). The two-level restaurant plays hip music and has attentive service, and a couple
of tables upstairs are perched on a ledge overlooking the attractive Plazuela San Francisco.

Zela 210. © **054/206-020.** www.zigzagrestaurant.com. Reservations recommended. Main courses
S/25–S/48. AE, DC, MC, V. Daily 6pm–midnight.

Moderate
Arte y Comida ★ MEDITERRANEAN/TURKISH   Turkish and Middle Eastern
specialties are a find in Peru, but this handsome little joint boasts a prime spot on restaurant row in Arequipa, in a long space carved out of *sillar* and opening onto a relaxing

SOUTHERN PERU

10

AREQUIPA

courtyard, where tables are set up. It serves up vegetarian Turkish dishes such as *Tübyaz* (zucchini stuffed with tomatoes, cheese, egg, and coconut and served with Turkish rice), Turkish grilled meats, excellent Mediterranean salads and Arequipeño dishes. But the reason to stop by is to get your hands on *sis kebaps* and other hard-to-come-by dishes. Happily, this isn't one of those austere falafel joints; it's pretty nice looking, with contemporary art, good music, and attractive lighting, making it ideal for a sunny lunch or surprisingly chic dinner.

San Francisco 315. ℂ **054/215-729.** Reservations not accepted. Main courses S/15–S/38. MC, V. Daily 8am–midnight.

Ary Quepay ★ (**Value** AREQUIPEÑO/PERUVIAN   A relaxed and friendly, family-owned restaurant with a gardenlike dining room under a bamboo roof and skylights, Ary Quepay, a longtime favorite of both locals and in-the-know visitors, specializes in authentic, traditional Peruvian cooking. It's less fancy than a couple of the better-known restaurants specializing in Arequipeño cooking, but the others are on the outskirts of the city, and a tad bit more expensive. Starters include *choclo con queso* (corn on the cob with cheese), *palta rellena* (stuffed avocado), and *sopa a la criolla* (with beef, noodles, and eggs). Main courses are classic: *rocoto relleno* (stuffed spicy red peppers), *adobo* (pork stew with *ají*), and *escabeche de pescado* (spicy fish stew). The menu also features a number of dishes for vegetarians, and good breakfasts, juices, and milkshakes. In the evenings, there's often live folkloric music.

Jerusalén 502. ℂ **054/672-922.** Main courses S/16–S/30. DC, MC, V. Daily 10am–11pm.

El Viñedo ARGENTINE/GRILL   I can't say whether this Argentine restaurant would satisfy the purist carnivore instincts of friends from Buenos Aires, but at least in Peru, this rustic yet refined spot on Arequipa's restaurant row is a winner. It does a good enough job with its *parrilladas* (mixed grills) to convince this gringo. For those who can eat only so much meat, there's a free salad bar. There are also "Argentine" pizzas (topped with ingredients such as grilled chorizo and served on wood boards) and the old standby, pastas. The interior is sprawling, cozy, and candlelit, with a tango music soundtrack, a half-dozen separate dining rooms, and a garden courtyard that a waiter told me is perfect for couples. Although the ceilings are bamboo and the walls are wood-paneled, waiters wear white gloves and tuxedo shirts. The wine list might not earn the restaurant's name ("the Vineyard"), but it's a decent list. Connected to the restaurant is El Jayari, a restaurant serving Peruvian dishes (and sharing the same chef and kitchen).

San Francisco 319-A. ℂ **054/205-053.** Reservations recommended Fri–Sat. Main courses S/10–S/33. AE, DC, MC, V. Daily 1pm–midnight.

La Trattoria del Monasterio ★★ (**Value** ITALIAN   Cleaved into the outer *sillar* wall of the splendid Santa Catalina monastery, this chic but unassuming Italian eatery—a fairly new addition to the Arequipa dining scene—is an excellent spot for lingering over an intimate dinner. It's considerably quieter than the hopping restaurant row just 1 block over on San Francisco. Spilling into three elegant, small, and whitewashed dining rooms, it specializes in Italian favorites like risottos, lasagnas, ravioli, and *osso buco*. For cognoscenti, it features both long and short pastas. The menu was prepared by the hot chef of the moment in Peru, Gastón Acurio of Astrid & Gastón, La Mar, and others in Lima and up and down South America. You'll also find a good selection of wines, great desserts and fine, attentive service.

Santa Catalina 309 ℂ **054/204-062.** Reservations recommended. Main courses S/22–S/32. AE, DC, MC, V. Mon–Sat noon–3pm and 7–11pm; Sun noon–4pm.

La Truffa (Value) ITALIAN   A charming little restaurant tucked behind the cathedral on a pedestrian-only *pasaje* lined with alpaca boutiques and a couple of cafes, La Truffa (the truffle) is decorated like someone's cozy house, with oil paintings and local artifacts. The menu specializes in homemade pastas and good pizzas, but it's also a great place to get well-prepared fish dishes such as *delicia de corvina* (sea bass served with cheese, shrimp, and mushrooms). There are only a handful of tables in two rooms, and it's popular with gringos and locals, so don't be surprised if you have to wait. The rooftop tables are the most sought-after during nice weather.

Pasaje la Catedral 111. (℄ 054/242-010. Reservations recommended. Main courses S/12–S/30. DC, MC, V. Mon–Sat 11am–11pm.

Tradición Arequipeña ★★ (Value) AREQUIPEÑO/PERUVIAN   It's a few kilometers outside town on a busy avenue in the district called Paucarpata, so you'll need to grab a taxi to get to this classic open-air restaurant. Elegantly set amid beautiful gardens and stunning views of snowcapped El Misti from the upper deck, it's open only for lunch (although you could also squeeze in an early dinner at 5 or 6pm). Most encouraging is how popular it is not only among tourists, but also among locals. In fact, it's the restaurant that seems most highly recommended to foreigners by Arequipeños. It serves large portions of classic Peruvian and Arequipeño dishes, such as *cuy, adobo,* and ceviche, but they're more carefully prepared here than in many other *comida típica* restaurants. A good starter is combination fried cheese and fried *yuca* with picante sauce and salsa verde. The prices are very affordable for such an elegant place.

Av. Dolores 111, Paucarpata. (℄ **054/426-467.** Reservations recommended Fri–Sat. Main courses S/15– S/39. AE, DC, MC, V. Daily noon–7pm.

Inexpensive

Crepisimo (Value) CREPES   Owned by the folks who operate the excellent Zig Zag, this laid-back little restaurant looks more like a bar or cafe. It's a great spot for lunch, especially if you nab one of the tables on the interior courtyard and opt for the superb-value *menu,* which for about $7 gets you a great salad, choice of savory crepe, dessert and a drink. Or go a la carte and pick any of a long roster (more than 100 varieties) of sweet and savory crepes.

Santa Catalina 208 (℄ **054/206-620.** www.crepisimo.com. Reservations recommended. Main courses S/12–S/22. AE, DC, MC, V. Daily noon–11pm; Sun noon–5pm.

Govinda (Value) VEGETARIAN   A good all-around vegetarian restaurant, Govinda— part of a chain across Peru, with the original in London—has a pleasant outdoor garden dining area and good-value menus and dishes. It serves vegetarian Italian, Asian, and Peruvian items, as well as pizzas, pastas, soups, salads, and yogurt dishes, a nice reprieve from many travelers' overdose of chicken, pork, and alpaca in Peru. The daily menus are very cheap, although the self-service buffet is not all-you-can-eat and its lineup of vegetarian dishes isn't the most creative you've ever seen. It's a good place for breakfast, with muesli, brown bread, fruit salads, and juices.

Santa Catalina 120. (℄ **054/285-540.** Reservations not accepted. Main courses S/6–S/20. No credit cards. Daily 7am–9:30pm.

La Canasta BREAKFAST/BAKERY   A charming bakery and lunch and breakfast nook, hidden away inside the courtyard of a massive colonial mansion on a heavily trafficked street, La Canasta only has a couple of tables on the patio. You can get pizzas, *empanadas* (stuffed pastries), sandwiches, and hamburgers, as well as some of the best breakfasts you're likely to come across in Peru.

Jerusalén 115. (℗ **054/287-138.** Reservations not accepted. Main courses S/5–S/9. No credit cards. Mon–Sat 7am–8:30pm.

Los Leños (Value) PIZZERIA   At this charming cave of a pizza place, diners share long wooden tables, and the footprints of many hundreds of travelers carry on in the graffiti that covers every square inch of stone walls up to a vaulted ceiling. It looks and feels like a college tavern. The house specialty is pizza from the wood-fired oven; among the many varieties, the Leños house pizza is a standout: cheese, sausage, bacon, ham, chicken, and mushrooms. Those who've had their fill of pizza can opt for other standards, such as lasagna and a slew of other pastas. Los Leños opens early, and you can choose from among 20 different "American breakfasts" offered here.

Jerusalén 407. (℗ **054/289-179.** Reservations not accepted. S/8–S/18. No credit cards. Daily 7am–11pm.

AREQUIPA AFTER DARK

Arequipa has a pretty hopping nightlife in the old quarter, with plenty of bars, restaurants, and discos catering to both gringos and locals. On a busy night, Arequipa does its best impression of the Cusco bar scene, and the alleyway just behind the Cathedral (Pasaje de la Catedral) is Arequipa's version of Cusco's "gringo alley," though more respectable. Just as in Cusco many bars are housed in impressive colonial digs, in Arequipa you're likely to do your drinking in a bar with vaulted *sillar* ceilings. Sunday through Wednesday is usually pretty quiet, with things heating up beginning on Thursday night. Virtually every bar in town advertises elastic happy hours, with basic cocktails going for as little as three for S/12. Calles San Francisco and Zela are the main hot spots, while there are also a number of bars along Santa Catalina.

Las Quenas ★, Santa Catalina 302 (℗ **054/281-115**), is a peña bar and restaurant featuring live Andean music Monday through Saturday from 9pm to midnight, and special dance performances on Friday and Saturday nights. It's a cozy little place that serves pretty good Peruvian dishes. You can also catch peña music most evenings at **El Tuturutu,** Portal San Agustín 105 (℗ **054/201-842**), a restaurant on the main square, and Afro-Peruvian and folkloric music at **La Troica,** Jerusalén 522 (℗ **054/225-690**), a tourist-oriented restaurant in an old house.

As for pubs and bars, **Siwara ★**, Santa Catalina 210 (℗ **054/626-218**) is a great-looking beer tavern that spills into two patios in the building of the Santuarios Andinos museum, across from the Santa Catalina monastery. **Farrens Irish Pub,** Pasaje Catedral 107 (℗ **054/238-465**), very popular with visiting gringos, is a cool two-level joint with good drink specials and a rock and pop soundtrack. A cozy little watering hole with good drink specials is **Brujas,** San Francisco 300 (no phone). Another good spot for a drink is **Montreál Le Café Art ★**, Ugarte 210 (℗ **054/931-2796**), which features an eclectic variety of live music Wednesday through Saturday and has happy hours between 5 and 11pm. **La Casa de Klaus,** Zela 207 (℗ **054/203-711**), is a simple and brightly lit tavern popular with German, British, and local beer drinkers.

For a little more action, check out **Forum Rock Café ★★**, San Francisco 317 (℗ **054/202-697**), a huge place that is equal parts restaurant, bar, disco, and concert hall. It sports a rainforest theme, with jungle vegetation and "canopy walkways" everywhere. Live bands (usually rock) take the stage Thursday through Saturday. The upstairs grill has great panoramic views of the city. Just down the street, **Déjà Vu ★**, San Francisco 319 (℗ **054/221-904**), has a good bar with a mix of locals and gringos, a lively dance floor, and English-language movies on a big screen every night at 8pm. It also has a spectacular rooftop terrace, which is a good spot for dinner or even breakfast after a long night partying. **Kibosh,** Zela 205 (© **054/626-218**), is a chic, upscale pub with four bars, wood-oven pizza, a dance floor, and live music Wednesday through Saturday (ranging from Latin to hard rock).

SIDE TRIPS FROM AREQUIPA

Easy day trips from Arequipa include jaunts to the relaxed small towns of **Paucarpata** and **Sabandía,** in the beautiful countryside surrounding the city. But the excursions of primary interest to visitors—for many, the main reason for a visit to Arequipa—is **Colca Canyon,** where the highlight is **Cruz del Cóndor,** a lookout point where giant South American condors soar overhead; see "Colca Valley," below, for more information. The region around Arequipa is unimaginably blessed by nature. It has soaring, active volcanoes, perfect for experienced mountaineers and trekkers; the two deepest canyons in the world, Colca and Cotahuasi; and chilly rivers that lace the canyons. The opportunities for trekking, rafting, and mountaineering expeditions through the valley are some of the finest in Peru. Out in the desert are ancient petroglyphs at **Toro Muerto.**

Tour agencies have mushroomed in Arequipa, and most offer very similar city and countryside *(campiña)* highlight trips (about $30 per person). Going with a tour operator is economical and by far the most convenient option for visitors with limited time and patience—public transportation is poor and very time-consuming in these parts. Of the many agencies that crowd the principal streets in the old quarter, only a handful of tour operators in Arequipa are well run, and visitors need to be careful when signing up for guided tours to the valley. Avoid independent guides who don't have official accreditation; see p. 303 for recommendations.

The Outskirts (Campiña Tours)

Paucarpata, 7km (4⅓ miles) southeast of Arequipa, is a pretty little town surrounded by Inca-terraced farmlands and El Misti volcano in the distance. About a kilometer down the road, the peaceful village of **Sabandía** is where many Arequipeños visit on weekends to dine at country-style restaurants. For out-of-town visitors, the highlight of the village is a large, early 17th-century stone *molino,* or water-powered mill. There are several nice colonial estates in the surrounding countryside. One of the nicest is **La Mansión del Fundador** ★ (© **054/213-423;** www.lamansiondelfundador.com), a handsome colonial mansion in the suburb of **Huasacache,** 10km (6¼ miles) from Arequipa. The house, once the property of the founder of Arequipa, Don García Manuel de Carbajal, is nicely outfitted with original antique paintings and furnishings. It's open daily from 9am to 5pm; admission is S/10.

GETTING THERE If you are one of the few who decides not to go with an organized tour, you can catch a Sabandía colectivo from San Juan de Dios or Independencia, a few blocks from the Plaza de Armas, but it's much simpler to take a taxi for S/10. The molino is on the same road as the **El Lago Resort** at Camino al Molino s/n, Sabandía (© **054/448-383**), a good spot for lunch.

Toro Muerto

About 3 hours from Arequipa, near the town of Corire, is **Toro Muerto,** touted as the world's largest field of petroglyphs. Whether it is actually the world's largest number of petroglyphs in one place is hard to say; many contend that other places have more. But the site is certainly exceptionally big, unique, and fascinating: Carved on hundreds of

10

AREQUIPA

volcanic boulders, the glyphs lie scattered in an area at least a couple kilometers long. Most historians believe that they were created by the Huari culture more than 1,000 years ago (and perhaps added to by subsequent peoples such as the Incas).

The enormous scale and the beautiful desert setting, more so than the individual drawings, are what most impress visitors to the site. The carvings comprise somewhat crude animal, human, and geometric representations. Although some estimates claim that there are 6,000 engraved stones at Toro Muerto, many more stones are not carved, so walking among the boulders in the sand and under a hot desert sun in search of the engraved stones requires considerable effort. The site draws very few tourists. Its distance from Arequipa and the difficulty getting there (and, no doubt, the competing popularity of Colca Canyon) preclude many groups from going to Toro Muerto.

GETTING THERE General-service tour agencies in Arequipa arrange group trips to Toro Muerto; see "Getting There: By Organized Tour" under "Essentials" in the "Colca Valley" section, below. You can also hire a taxi from Arequipa at a cost of $35 to $40.

---

3 COLCA VALLEY ★★★

165km (103 miles) N of Arequipa

Mario Vargas Llosa, the Peruvian novelist and most famous Arequipeño, described Colca as "The Valley of Wonders." That is no literary overstatement. Colca is one of the most scenic regions in Peru, a land of imposing snowcapped volcanoes, narrow gorges, artistically terraced agricultural slopes that predate the Incas, arid desert landscapes and vegetation, and remote traditional villages, many visibly scarred by seismic tremors common in southern Peru. Some of Peru's most recognizable wildlife, including llamas, alpacas, vicuñas, and the celebrated giant Andean condors, roam the region.

The Colca River, one of the sources of the mighty Amazon, slices through the massive canyon, which remained largely unexplored until the late 1970s, when rafting expeditions descended to the bottom of the gorge. Reaching depths of 3,400m (11,150 ft.)— twice as deep as the Grand Canyon—*el Cañón del Colca* forms part of a tremendous volcanic mountain range more than 100km (62 miles) long. Colca, though, is no longer considered the world's, or even southern Peru's, deepest canyon; Cotahuasi, at the extreme northwest of the Arequipa department, has wrested away that honor. Among the region's great volcanoes, several of which are still active, are Mount Coropuna (6,425m/ 21,079 ft.), Peru's second-highest peak, and Mount Ampato (6,310m/20,702 ft.), where a sacrificed Inca maiden, known to the world as Juanita, was discovered frozen in 1995 (see "The Discovery of Juanita, the Ampato Maiden" on p. 314). The valley and its summits are a rapidly growing extreme-sports destination for hiking, mountain climbing, river rafting, and mountain biking.

Dispersed across the Colca Valley are 14 Colonial-era villages, which date to the 16th century and are distinguished primarily by their small but often richly decorated churches. Local populations in the valley, descendants of the Collaguas and Cabanas, pre-Inca ethnic communities that have lived in the region for some 2,000 years, preserve ancient customs and distinctive traditional dress. They speak different languages and can be distinguished by their hats; Collagua women wear straw hats with colored ribbons, while the Cabanas sport elaborately embroidered and sequined felt headgear. (The men once wore distinctive dress as well but today are decidedly less colorful.) Colca villages are also celebrated for their vibrant festivals, which remain as authentic as any in Peru, throughout the year. The valley's meticulous agricultural terracing, even more extraordinary and extensive than the Inca terraces seen in the Sacred Valley near Cusco, were first cultivated more than 1,000 years ago.

Travelers are now spending more time in the Colca Valley, lapping up its extraordinary beauty, quiet traditional life, and opportunities for outdoor adventure sports, but the number-one draw remains the almost ineffable wonder of seeing majestic, giant condors with massive wingspans soar overhead at Cruz del Cóndor lookout point over Colca Canyon and head out along the river.

The Colca Valley is lush and emerald green just after the heavy rains from January to March, but most of the rest of the year it is arid and dusty. Apart from that, the best time to visit Colca is during the dry season, May through November. The condors put on their best show from June to September, although recent reports of dwindling number of Andean condors in the canyon, perhaps due to continuing development in the region, are certainly cause for concern. Though sunny during the day, it can also get quite cold (below freezing) at night—which is not unexpected, since Chivay is higher than Cusco.

> ## ⓘ Tips   The Air up There
>
> The road from Arequipa to the Colca Valley climbs impressively, reaching 4,910m (16,100 ft.) at the Patapampa lookout point. The air is very thin at this altitude, and breathing is not at all easy. The main town in the valley, Chivay, sits at an altitude of nearly 3,600m (11,800 ft.), and nights can be brutally cold. Travelers who haven't yet spent time in either Cusco or Puno/Lake Titicaca should take it easy for a couple of days in Arequipa before heading out to Colca. *Soroche,* or acute altitude sickness, is common. See "Health," in chapter 3, for additional information on how to combat it.

ESSENTIALS
Getting There

Colca Valley is a long half-day (3–4 hr.) trip from Arequipa along dusty roads that climb steadily, passing through the **Reserva Nacional Salinas y Aguada Blanca,** populated only by a collection of grazing alpacas and vicuñas, en route. The road poses less suffering than it did just a few years ago; the section of unpaved and bumpy travel is down to just 23km (14 miles), from 120km (75 miles). The **Mirador de los Andes** (also called Patapampa), 27km (17 miles) outside Chivay, is the highest point in the valley, ringed by eight snowcapped volcanoes and a small army of *apachetas,* tiny towers of piled stones, marks the spot locals considered closest to mountain *apus* (gods). (Originally *apachetas* were offerings to the gods, but most if not all of these have been left behind by tourists.)

The great majority of visitors to the Colca Valley and the canyon do so on guided tours, arranged in Arequipa. Entry to Colca is $7 per person; you'll get a *boleto turístico* that serves for admission to a half-dozen sights in the region, including churches and the Cruz del Cóndor.

BY ORGANIZED TOUR   Conventional travel agencies offer day trips to Cruz del Cóndor, usually leaving at 3 or 4am, with brief stops at Chivay before returning to Arequipa—it's an awful lot to pack into a single day, especially at a high altitude, and it leaves no time to enjoy what makes the region unique (though you do arrive in time to see the condors at 8 or 9am). Expect to pay about $30 per person. Two-day "pool" (grouped) tours are much more enjoyably paced and cost $50 to $130, depending on hotel arrangements (they include transportation, a guide, hotel accommodations, and breakfast; other meals are extra). Other campiña tours offered by many agencies include the Toro Muerto petroglyphs; Mejía lagoons, a bird sanctuary; Laguna Salinas, a saltwater lagoon populated by flamingos; Aguada Blanca Nature Reserve; and the remote Valley of the Volcanoes, a lunar landscape located more than 13 hours from Arequipa. The best all-purpose agencies in Arequipa, which offer everything from city tours to general and private tours of Colca, as well as hard-core adventure, are **Giardino Tours ★**, Jerusalén 604-A (© **054/241-206;** www.giardinotours.com); **Colonial Tours,** Santa Catalina 106 (© **054/286-868;** www.helloarequipa.com/colonial_tours); **Illary Tours,** Santa Catalina 205 (© **054/220-844**); **Ideal Tours,** Urbanización San Isidro F-2, Vallecito (© **01/9883-5617;** idealperu@terra.com.pe); and **Santa Catalina Tours,** Santa Catalina 219 (© **054/216-994;** santacatalina@star.com.pe). All of these agencies are also equipped to organize private transportation and hotel packages, which range from $95 per person for

1-day trips to $400 per person with accommodations at one of the top lodges in the region, such as Colca Lodge or the Las Casitas del Colca.

BY BUS Local buses travel from Arequipa to Cabanaconde (6 hr.), near Cruz del Cóndor, with stops in Chivay (4 hr.). Two companies that make these runs are **La Reyna,** Terminal Terrestre, Arequipa (© **054/426-549**), and **Cristo Rey,** San Juan de Dios 510, Arequipa (© **054/213-094**). The ride costs S/15. Unless you have plenty of time and patience, or a real need to be on your own, your best bet for getting to Colca is to go with an organized group.

Visitor Information

A **Centro de Visitantes (Visitor's Center),** open daily 8am to 5pm, with maps and a small exhibit on the region, is located within Aguada Blanca National Reserve, 45km (28 miles) outside of Arequipa. The office of the local **Tourist Police** (© **054/488-623**) can be found on the Plaza de Armas in Chivay. It's open daily in the afternoon and should be able to provide hiking information. You can also pick up information in Arequipa from the tourist information office or one of the travel agencies that organize Colca trips.

WHAT TO SEE & DO
Main Colca Villages: Chivay & Cabanaconde

The Valle del Colca is generally thought of in terms of left (south) and right (north) banks of the canyon, with villages and hotels of interest on either. Villages aren't separated by many kilometers, but the roads on both sides are rocky, dusty, and meandering, making for arduous and time-consuming driving. The left bank, which leads to Cruz del Cóndor, sees most of the tourists.

Although **Chivay,** on the left bank, is the valley's main town, it is still a largely sleepy little place that not long ago got on just fine without electricity. For many travelers on their way to Cruz del Cóndor and other spots in the valley, Chivay, which has the lion's share of restaurants and affordable hotels in the region, amounts to little more than a stopover. For those adhering to a leisurely pace, though, Chivay can be an enjoyable place to hang out; it benefits from an extraordinarily scenic natural setting. The attractive, low-key Plaza de Armas is the focus of attention in town and the site of several restaurants and *hostales.*

Most visitors hit the soothing and clean **La Calera hot springs** ★ while in town. Though they can't compare with the thermal baths of Colca Lodge (see later in this chapter), they're enjoyable and easy to get to, just a 4km (2½-mile) walk or a colectivo ride from town, and inexpensive (S/10); they're open daily from 8am to 8pm.

The first village past Chivay (10km/6¼ miles) is **Yanque,** a modest town with a baroque 18th-century church. In **Maca** ★, a village on the way to Cruz del Cóndor that was destroyed by a 1979 earthquake, you'll find Santa Ana, a restored, brilliant white church with a surprising gilded interior. Nearby, perched overlooking the river, is the **Choquetico stone,** a pre-Inca carved-stone scale model of the mountains across the canyon, as well as a handful of Inca tombs carved out of the cliff face.

The remote, reserved village of **Cabanaconde,** the last town in the Colca Valley, is a couple of hours from Chivay. Some independent travelers prefer to stay here because it is within (hearty) walking distance, 15km (9⅓ miles), or a 15-minute drive, from the Cruz del Cóndor lookout point, and it's well positioned for other hikes in the canyon and throughout the valley. The views of the canyon are tremendous, and short walks take you to excellent vantage points overlooking some of the most brilliant agricultural terracing in the area. The locals are descendants of the Cabanas people, and they maintain

A Typical Guided Tour of Colca Valley

Most organized tours of the region are very similar, if not identical. The road that leads out of Arequipa and into the valley, bending around the El Misti and Chachani volcanoes, is poor and unbearably dusty. It passes through the **Laguna Salinas** and **Aguada Blanca Nature Reserve,** where you'll usually have a chance to see rare vicuñas, llamas, and alpacas from the road. The altiplano landscape is barren and bleak. Most tours stop at volcano and valley lookout points along the way before heading to Chivay.

From **Chivay,** the valley's main town and the gateway to the region, many organized tours embark on short hikes above the canyon and visit the wonderfully relaxing hot springs of **La Calera** (p. 333). Evening visits to the hot springs allow visitors to bathe in open-air pools beneath a huge, starry sky; artificial light in the valley is almost nonexistent. Charming colonial villages in the valley that are often visited by tours include Yanque, Coporaque, Maca, and Lari. Most 2-day tours head out early the following morning for **Cruz del Cóndor** to see the Andean condors begin to circle around 9am.

Organized tours generally include transportation, an English-speaking guide, hotel accommodations in Chivay or a nearby village (with breakfast), and park entrance fees to Colca and Cruz del Cóndor. Additional meals are extra.

traditional dress and customs; women wear hats embroidered with flowers and wide skirts. There is a good small hotel and a couple of inexpensive *hostales* in the village (see "Where to Stay & Dine," below).

The right (north) side of Colca Canyon is less visited. **Coporaque** ★, just across the river from Chivay, is a sleepy village with the oldest church in the valley, the charming **Templo de Coporaque,** built in 1569 with twin bell towers. Just outside the village, and on the way to Colca Lodge, is the stunning **Mirador de Ocolle** ★★, an amphitheater formed by agricultural terraces of varying shades of green. A new bridge from **Pinchollo** to **Lari** leads across a gorgeously terraced valley of pink rock and abundant cacti. Lary's primary attraction is its splendidly simple 1886 church, **Templo de la Purísima Concepción de Lari** ★. White with red trim, an orange and green portal, and double bell towers, it looks like a rural Mexican church or something that would decorate the top of a cake. It has recently been restored, and the interior is full of colorful murals and paintings, while the entire altar is adorned with brilliant baroque murals and painted columns. If you're not on a tour, you may have to ask at the shop next door for the key.

Cruz del Cóndor ★★★

Cruz del Cóndor, or Condor Cross, about 50km (31 miles) west of Chivay, is nothing more than a lookout point on one side of Colca Canyon that has become famous throughout Peru for its spectacular inhabitants, graceful Andean condors *(Vultur gryphus)*. At a spot 1,200m (3,937 ft.) above the canyon river, large crowds gather every morning, zoom lenses poised, to witness a stunning wildlife spectacle. Beginning around 9am, the condors—the largest birds in the world, with awesome wingspans of 3.5m (12 ft.)—suddenly begin to appear, theatrically circling far below in the gorge and gradually

On Those Camelids

You'll likely have a chance to see three types of South American camelids common to the Andes: the domesticated llama and alpaca, and the considerably rarer wild vicuña. Llamas have been domesticated in the Andes for more than 5,000 years, used for meat, clothing, shelter, and fertilizer. Pre-Columbian civilizations also sacrificed llamas and alpacas as offerings to gods. Vicuñas are the smallest members of the camelid family, as well as the most prized and endangered. These camelids are native to the high plains of the Andes Mountains in Bolivia, Chile, and, primarily, Peru.

Alpacas and llamas differ in size and fiber quality. Adult alpacas are usually about a foot shorter than llamas, and the former produces 10 pounds a year or more of high-quality fiber in a single fleece. Alpaca hair is extremely fine, soft, smooth, and lightweight. It is stronger, warmer, and longer lasting than wool. "Baby alpaca" is the first clipping of the shearling, and, extraordinarily soft, it is universally prized and expensive. Llamas, on the other hand, have a less fine dual fiber fleece, and the animals are better equipped to serve as excellent beasts of burden, perfect for mountain-trekking expeditions. Both llamas and alpacas graze at elevations of 3,000m (9,800 ft.) and higher. Llamas and alpacas are intelligent and gentle animals, but they have a reputation for a nasty habit: spitting. They usually spit at each other over food, but female llamas also spit at male llamas to ward off advances.

The vicuña is a national symbol in Peru, which is home to more than half the world's vicuña population. The Incas dressed their nobility in its ultrasoft fibers, considered the finest and warmest in the world, considerably lighter even than cashmere. Vicuña fleece sells for as much as $1,600 a pound; a man's sport coat made of vicuña costs at least $5,000. Poaching nearly rendered the vicuña extinct; it was declared endangered, and trade in vicuña products was banned internationally in 1975. With the vicuña community back up to approximately 200,000 animals throughout the Andean highlands, the animal is now considered threatened rather than endangered, and control over the harvesting of vicuña coats was placed under the ownership and management of Peru's Indian communities in the 1990s. Limited vicuña trade is now allowed; only garments stamped with the "Vicuñandes" trademark or "Vicuña" and the country of origin are deemed legal.

gaining altitude with each pass, until they literally soar silently above the heads of awe-struck admirers before heading out along the river in search of prey. Condors are such immense and heavy creatures that they cannot simply lift off from the ground; instead, they take flight from cliff perches. The condors return late in the afternoon, but only a small group of people attends the show then. Witnessing the condors' majestic flight up close is a memorable and mesmerizing sight, capable of producing goose bumps on even the most jaded travelers (though photographing the condors in flight demands skill, patience, and a substantial zoom lens). It's little wonder that the Incas believed them to be sacred creatures.

The dry months of June through September are when you're likely to see the largest group of condors in flight, and that's when they tend to circle and circle just over spectators' heads as they gain altitude, catch hold of a current, and set off down the river. The smallest number of condors is visible during the wet months of January through April and even October to December. On one trip to Colca in the last decade, I saw at least two dozen condors take off over the canyon, and a guide I spoke with claimed he once saw 54 in a single morning. On my most recent visit, however, I saw just three. There is great concern that the number of resident Andean condors has decreased dramatically, likely in response to the rapid hotel development and increased traffic near the canyon.

Independent Hiking in Colca

Those looking to spend some quality hiking time in the valley and canyon can get to the region by public transportation or rental car from Arequipa and go out on their own. The largest number of inexpensive hotel accommodations is in Chivay. You can also camp throughout the canyon and valley, with the exception of Cruz del Cóndor.

The region is loaded with excellent hikes that can be done independently if you have suitable gear and camping equipment. Unless you're an experienced hiker, however, it's best to go with a guide (see "Tour Agencies for Rafting, Trekking & Mountaineering Expeditions," below).

Among the best hikes is a 2- to 3-hour, 1,300m (4,265-ft.) **descent into Colca Canyon** from the Cruz del Cóndor lookout. Because of the arduous, lengthy 5- or 6-hour climb back out, most travelers who do this hike end up camping down below near the **Sangalle oasis** with palm trees and water suitable for swimming. Hikes down to the canyon floor require good physical conditioning and preparedness (plenty of water, food, sunscreen, and so on). The trails are quite difficult in sections, and the altitude complicates the trek—the drop is more than 1,000m (3,281 ft.). An even longer and more demanding hike is to the village of **Tapay,** beginning at Cabanaconde and following a good trail from the oasis via the Río Colca (about 6 hr. each way). The path is very steep.

Less taxing hikes are possible by simply walking from one village to another in the region. From **Chivay** to **Yanque** along the main road is about 7km (4⅓ miles). You can continue from Yanque to the villages of **Achoma** (another 7km/4⅓ miles), **Maca** (12km/7½ miles), and **Pinchollo** (10km/6¼ miles). From there, on the way to Cabanaconde, it's about an hour to the **Colca Geyser (Hatun Infiernillo).**

EXTREME COLCA VALLEY: RAFTING, TREKKING & VOLCANO CLIMBS

The countryside around Arequipa, laced with canyons and volcanoes, is one of the best in Peru for outdoor adventure travel. Trails crisscross the Colca Valley, leading across mountain ridges, agricultural terraces, and curious rock formations, and past colonial towns and fields where llamas and vicuñas graze. The most common pursuits are river running, treks through the canyon valleys, and mountain climbing on the volcanoes just beyond the city. Many tour agencies in Arequipa offer conventional 2- and 3-day visits to Colca Canyon, as well as longer, more strenuous treks through the valley and to Cotahuasi Canyon. Some of the most interesting (but most time-consuming and difficult) expeditions combine rafting and trekking. Your best bet for organizing any of these activities is with one of the tour operators mentioned below; several in Arequipa focus solely on eco- and adventure tourism.

(Tips) **Cotahuasi Canyon**

Reputedly the deepest canyon in the world, Cotahuasi (3,354m/11,000 ft. at its deepest point) was only explored by rafting teams a few years ago. As enticing as trekking or rafting in the world's deepest canyon no doubt is to many, the effort required to get to Cotahuasi is substantial. It's a full 12 to 15 hours from Arequipa by bus, more than 400km (250 miles) on pretty difficult roads. Although some adventurers do go independently, trekking or rafting in the Cotahuasi is much better and more safely organized by a professional outfit such as Zárate Aventuras (see "Tour Agencies for Rafting, Trekking & Mountaineering Expeditions," below).

River Rafting

The rivers and canyons around Arequipa pose some excellent river-running opportunities for both novices and experts. The best months for rafting are May through September, when water levels are low. (In the rainy season, when water levels are high, the canyon rivers can be extremely dangerous.) The most accessible rafting, suitable for first-timers, is on the **Río Chili,** just 15 minutes from downtown. It offers Class III and IV runs, and is a great way to get your feet wet during a half-day trip. Year-round runs of similarly moderate difficulty and scenic beauty can be arranged on day trips to the **Río Majes** (the Río Colca beyond the gorge). Rafting in Cotahuasi and Colca canyons is serious stuff for confident rafters; there are 3-day rafting trips to Colca (about $175) for those with moderate experience, and longer, 10- to 12-day trips to either canyon for serious white-water runners. The **Río Colca** (Class IV–V) is extremely technical, although some upriver sections are less dangerous and difficult. **Río Cotahuasi** was first explored only in 1994; it has 120km (75 miles) of Class IV and V rapids (and some Class VI). A few agencies offer annual trips that combine trekking with hard-core white-water rafting in Cotahuasi. These organized trips are expensive ($2,000 and up) and lengthy, usually 12 to 14 days total.

Mountain & Volcano Climbing

At the foot of the western Andes, Arequipa is ideally positioned for a variety of ascents—many of them not technically challenging—to volcano summits and mighty Andes peaks. Climbers in good physical condition can bag 5,000m (16,400-ft.) summits on ascents of 2 days or less. The best months for climbing are July through September, although some peaks can be climbed year-round. Climbers should be sufficiently acclimatized before making any ascents; if you've spent several days in Cusco or Puno before arriving in Arequipa (and are in good physical shape), you should be fine. Adventure travel operators in Arequipa provide logistical support, porters, and guides, but you must provide your own sleeping bag and boots. Be sure to ask plenty of questions about weather conditions, equipment, and experience before setting out with any guide.

El Misti, a nearly 6,000m (19,680-ft.) volcano, dominates the Arequipa landscape from a distance of about 20km (12 miles). The most popular climb among both locals and visitors, Misti is a demanding 2- or 3-day trek with few technical challenges. It is suitable for inexperienced climbers accompanied by professional guides. Most climbers stay the first night at the base camp Nido de Aguilas (Eagle's Nest) and reach the summit after about 7 hours of climbing on the second day. Arequipa's other major volcano, **Chachani** (6,075m/19,931 ft.), also presents an excellent and technically straightforward climb, a good opportunity for inexperienced climbers to brag about reaching a 6,000m (19,680-ft.) summit.

The Colca Valley has a number of peaks that draw serious climbers, including the **Ampato** volcano (6,288m/20,630 ft.), a 3- or 4-day climb, and the **Hualca Hualca** glacier (6,025m/19,767 ft.). **Coropuna** (6,425m/21,079 ft.), perhaps the most stunning mountain in the Cotahuasi Valley, requires a couple of days of travel from Arequipa to begin the difficult climb.

Tour Agencies for Rafting, Trekking & Mountaineering Expeditions

The best general agencies in Arequipa (see "Getting There," earlier) arrange entry-level rafting and trekking itineraries. Almost all are located on just two streets in Arequipa, Jerusalén and Santa Catalina, so it's pretty simple to browse up and down and get a feel for an agency.

Apumayo Expediciones ★★, Jirón Ricardo Palma, N-5 Santa Monica, Wanchaq, Cusco (℃ **084/246-018;** www.apumayo.com), is excellent for adventure trips in the region, including long trekking/rafting expeditions to Cotahuasi and Colca, as is **Amazonas Explorer** ★★, Zela 212, Cusco (℃ **054/252-846;** www.amazonas-explorer.com), an international company that organizes hardy multisport trips to Cotahuasi and Colca (which can be combined with tours to Cusco, the Inca Trail, and Machu Picchu). **Cusipata Viajes y Turismo** ★, Jerusalén 408-A (℃ **054/203-966;** www.cusipata.com), is the local specialist for Chili and Colca rafting and kayaking (including courses), and its guides, led by Gianmarco Vellutino, frequently subcontract out to other agencies in Arequipa. **Ideal Tours,** Urbanización San Isidro F-2, Vallecito (℃ **054/244-439**), handles Chili and Majes rafting, as well as Colca and other standard tours.

Colca Trek ★, Santa Catalina 204 (℃ **054/202-461;** www.colcatrek.com), offers canyon treks of 3 to 5 days or more and a number of other adventure activities, such as horseback riding, mountain biking, rafting, and climbing.

For hard-core mountain climbing and trekking, one agency stands out: **Carlos Zárate Aventuras** ★★, Santa Catalina 204, no. 3 (℃ **054/202-461;** www.zarateadventures. com), is run by Carlos Zárate, the top climbing guide in Arequipa (a title his dad held before him). He can arrange any area climb and has equipment rental and a 24-hour mountain-rescue service. Climbing expeditions (per person) start at: El Misti, $50; Chachani, $70; and Colca Canyon, $75. Mountain biking and rafting trips are also arranged.

For specialized birding programs (as well as other nature tours), **Tanager Tours,** La Estrella F-9, in the J. L. Bustamante y Rivero district (℃ **054/426-210;** www.tanager tours.com), is the top choice in Arequipa.

WHERE TO STAY & DINE

Most agencies offering 2- and 3-day trips to Colca Canyon put passengers up at modest hotels in the village of Chivay. If you can afford to step up a notch from budget accommodations, the following rustic inns in and around the canyon—primarily between Chivay and Cabanaconde—are the most comfortable and atmospheric places to stay in Colca. Comparatively luxurious, they are by far the best choices if offered by tour operators (often at bargain rates) or if you're traveling to Colca independently.

In the center of Chivay, **Casa Andina Classic Colca** ★ (Value), Huayna Cápac s/n,
Chivay ((C) **866/220-4434** toll-free in the U.S., or 054/531-020; fax 054/531-098;
www.casa-andina.com), is the latest entry into the Colca rustic hotel category and an
indication that many people in the industry are betting on Colca's further development.
It's easily the nicest place in the hub of Chivay. It recently expanded to 52 accommodations in the style that has become so popular in the region: stone walls, thatched roofs,
and cozy furnishings with thick wool blankets. The new bungalow-style rooms are
slightly larger and have higher ceilings. A double room costs $87. The restaurant features
folk music and dance shows as well as a cool planetarium and telescope.

Las Casitas del Colca ★★, Parque Curiña s/n, on the outskirts of Yanque
((C) **01/610-8300** or 054/959-672-480; www.lascasitasdelcolca.com), part of the upscale
Orient Express chain that owns the Hotel Monasterio in Cusco and Machu Picchu
Sanctuary Lodge, is easily the most exclusive inn in the valley. All-inclusive and the
height of country luxury, it has undergone a stunning transformation in recent years. Its
extraordinary casitas (individual thatched-roof bungalows) were inaugurated in 2008.
Elegantly decorated and nestled about the property, the 20 casitas have private terraces
and plunge pools. They're joined by a spectacular spa and free-form swimming pool.
Perched on the lip of the canyon, the ecolodge features solar energy and electricity, a
breakfast terrace with gorgeous valley views of extensive gardens, terraced fields, and the
river. The kitchen turns out wonderfully fresh dinners and excellent breakfasts using
ingredients from the garden, and the lodge also offers horseback riding. Although the
place was once an incredible bargain, those days are gone, as is much of the old charming
rustic simplicity. Handsome and studiously perfect as the new place is, I miss what it used
to be—as well as the old tariffs! A night in a private casita, with all meals and activities
(such as horseback riding, cooking lessons and fly-fishing) included, runs $1,000 double
(though much-cheaper deals are usually available online).

Colca Lodge ★★★, about 10km (6¼ miles) from Chivay ((C) **054/531-191;** fax 054/
220-407; www.colca-lodge.com), is beautifully situated across the river from Yanque and
has one feature no other lodge can match: its own private thermal baths, carved in stone
and secluded along the banks of the river. The continually expanding lodge is a very
comfortable, eco-style hotel with adobe, stone, and thatched-roof architecture, solar
power, and a swank new spa. Its level of luxury is just a small step down from the Las
Casitas del Colca (above), the fanciest lodge in the region (although those hot springs
make it a close call). The views of the valley are excellent from nearly everywhere. The
hotel also has a sophisticated lodge-style restaurant serving fairly expensive lunches and
dinners. The lodge's 29 rooms cost $181 per double (suites from $284). If you're not a
guest, you can experience the thermal pools for $10.

Giardino Tours books its Colca tour guests at one of the newer country inns in the
Colca Valley, **La Casa de Mamayacchi** ★ (Value), Coporaque ((C) **054/241-206;** fax 054/
242-761; www.lacasademamayacchi.com). Located just outside the village of Coporaque,
it has 50 very comfortable rooms with exposed beams, great views, a fireplace lounge, and
an attractive rustic restaurant featuring good local preparations. It's owned by the same
folks who run La Casa de Mi Abuela Hotel in Arequipa. Rooms cost $70 per double.

There are just a few *hostales* and one hotel in quiet Cabanaconde, which will appeal to
those who spend a couple of days hiking in the canyon. The top spot is **Hotel Kuntur
Wassi** ★, La Ladera 360 ((C) **054/812-166** or 054/812-166; www.kunturwassi.com).
On a hill above the village, this rambling small hotel, built of adobe and stone, has nicely
decorated rooms with high ceilings, faux stone bathrooms, and lots of plants lining the

walkways along the property. With a good restaurant and bar overlooking town, it's a nice place to relax after a long hike. The 25 rooms are $55 for doubles, $70 to $100 for suites. Ask about special multi-night package deals. **La Posada del Conde,** San Pedro at Bolognesi (℗ **054/440-197**), is the next best choice in the village: a decent, clean place, with private bathrooms; doubles are a value at $25.

Although most visitors eat all meals at their hotels, several restaurants, mostly in Chivay, host the lunchtime tourist groups that come through town. **Witite,** Calle Siglo XX 328 (℗ **054/531-036**), named for a locally famous dance competition, serves a general Andean menu. **Solar Rosario,** Calle Arequipa 504 (℗ **054/531-133**), is a good-looking spot that offers a pretty good buffet lunch, and **Casablanca,** Plaza de Armas 705 (℗ **054/521-019**), serves a good-value *menu* and boasts a handful of vegetarian dishes. If you stay the night, you may want to check out a little peña action (served up with dinner) at **El Encanto del Colca,** Calle Mariscal Castilla 500 (no phone), down a little side street. Good folkloric peña music can also be found at **El Nido,** Zarumilla 216 (℗ **054/531-010**), around the corner from El Encanto.

Amazonia

Nearly two-thirds of Peru is Amazon rainforest, which thrives with some of the richest biodiversity on the planet. Covering 6,475,000 sq. km (2,500,000 sq. miles), the Amazon basin represents 54% of all remaining rainforest on the planet. This vast, largely impenetrable region, with the smallest human population in the country and few towns of any significant size, clearly is not the Peru of great pre-Columbian civilizations and Inca ruins. It stands in stunning contrast to the country's rugged Andean peaks and arid desert coasts. The humid frontier towns of the jungle, well past stages of oil and rubber booms and now hell-bent on ecotourism, are worlds removed from the historic cities Cusco and Arequipa and the modern madness of Lima.

Many naturalists and biologists believe that Peru's Amazon rainforest holds the greatest diversity in the world. It teems with a staggering roster of wildlife: 400 species of mammals, 2,000 species of fish, 300 reptiles, 1,800 birds, and more than 50,000 plants. Recent studies have shown that a region just south of Iquitos has the highest concentration of mammals anywhere in the world.

Not surprisingly, jungle ecotourism has exploded in Peru, as it has in several other Latin American countries. Peru's jungle regions are now much more accessible than they once were—which is both a good and a bad thing, of course—and there are more lodges and eco-options than ever. Remote as the Amazon jungle surely seems, it is possible to find yourself at an ecolodge in as little as 12 hours after boarding a flight in the U.S. Still, accessibility is a crucial factor in jungle trips: The more remote a lodge or camping trek is, and the more pristine and unspoiled the

environment is, the more it's going to cost you to get there in terms of both time and money. Rivers define life in the jungle even more than do the forests; for both locals and visitors, almost all transport along the vast river system that stretches across the whole of eastern Peru is by dugout canoe, motorboat, or large riverboats *(lanchas)*.

The southern Amazon region, which extends to the Bolivian and Brazilian borders, is concentrated in the Madre de Dios department, the least populated area in Peru. Although it is accessible by land from Cusco, it is an exceedingly difficult route. Most travelers fly to Puerto Maldonado (the gateway to the Tambopata National Reserve) and travel overland to the Manu Biosphere Reserve, returning by small aircraft.

The northern Amazon reaches all the way to Peru's borders with Colombia and Brazil. The gateway to Peru's northern Amazon basin is Iquitos. As an example of how huge the Amazon is, Iquitos lies nearly 3,220km (2,000 miles) from the mouth of the great Río Amazonas, the second-longest river in the world. Other than an arduous journey by boat, the only way to get to Iquitos is by airplane (usually from Lima).

The best time to visit the Amazon is during the dry season, May through the end of October. During the rainy season in the southern Amazon, parts of the jungle are flooded and impassable. The northern jungle does not have a rainy season, per se, and travel there is less restricted during the winter. However, water levels can rise from 7.5m (25 ft.) to more than 15m (50 ft.) from December to May, and some jungle villages become flooded. Many naturalists find high-water months best for wildlife observation.

1 THE SOUTHERN AMAZON JUNGLE ★★★

Easily accessible from Cusco, the southern jungle boasts some of Peru's finest and least spoiled Amazon rainforest. The area has been less penetrated by man than has the northern Amazon; indeed, the southern jungle remained largely unexplored until expeditions into the remote rainforest were undertaken in the 1950s. Two of Peru's top three jungle zones—and two of the finest in South America—dominate the southeastern department of Madre de Dios. The region's two principal protected areas, the **Manu Biosphere Reserve** (which encompasses the Parque Nacional del Manu, or Manu National Park) and the **Tambopata National Reserve (Reserva Nacional de Tambopata),** are both excellent for jungle expeditions, although they differ in terms of remoteness and facilities.

Manu, one of the largest protected natural areas in the Americas and considered to be one of the most pristine jungle regions in the world, remains complicated and time-consuming to visit. Flights in and out of Boca Manu are now handled by the National Air Force rather than commercial carriers, and travel is possible only with one of eight officially sanctioned agencies. Expeditions last a minimum of 5 or 6 days (and most are a week or more), involve both significant overland and air (not to mention extensive river) travel, are expensive, and are very rustic, with the focus much more on contact with nature than creature comforts. Access is easiest from Cusco, although it involves a (spectacular) day's travel overland (or a half-hour flight), followed by a couple of days by boat.

Travelers without the time or budget to reach Manu often find Tambopata a most worthy alternative: Its wildlife and jungle vegetation are nearly the equal of Manu in some parts. Most lodges in Tambopata are considerably easier to get to and cheaper than those in Manu, although a couple require up to 8 or even 12 hours of travel by boat from Puerto Maldonado. The jungle frontier city of Puerto Maldonado, which is the capital of Madre de Dios department and just a half-hour flight from Cusco, is the jumping-off point to explore Tambopata. Travelers interested in the least time-consuming and least expensive way to see a part of the Peruvian jungle can visit one of the lodges on Madre de Dios River or Lago Sandoval, the latter an oxbow lake within a couple of hours of Puerto Maldonado.

In travel packages to both destinations, round-trip airfare from Cusco to Puerto Maldonado or Boca Manu (the gateway to the Manu Biosphere Reserve) is usually extra. Cheaper tours travel overland, stay at lesser-quality lodges (or primarily at campsites), and might travel on riverboats without canopies. Independent travel to Tambopata and two-way overland travel to either are options only for those with a lot of time and patience on their hands. Independent travelers not only find it complicated to enter many parts of the jungle, but they are also not permitted to enter the most desirable section of Manu, the Reserve Zone. Organizing a trip with one of the lodges or specialized tour operators listed below is highly recommended, in terms of both access and convenience. Most have fixed departure dates throughout the year. Do not purchase any jungle packages from salesmen on the streets of Cusco; their agencies might not even be authorized to enter restricted zones, and last-minute "itinerary changes" are likely.

Searing heat and humidity are year-round constants in the jungle (though in the southern jungle, occasional cold fronts called *friajes* are common). Appropriate gear for steamy tropical conditions is a must. Dry season (May–Oct) is the best time for southern jungle expeditions—during the rainy season, rivers overflow and mosquitoes gobble up everything in sight. Be careful to note when a tour operator's fixed departures leave (some are every Wed, others every Sun, and so on). Most lodge visits include boat transportation and three meals daily, as well as guided visits and activities (some, such as canopy walks and distant clay-lick outings, entail additional fees).

PUERTO MALDONADO
Founded in 1902 and once a prosperous rubber town, Puerto Maldonado is a humid, scruffy, and fast-growing place, a frontier market town that has gone through several phases of boom and bust, as have most jungle outposts. After the rubber boom came the game hunters and loggers. It's the kind of place where streets just off the main square are still unpaved and full of muddy potholes. Today the town's primary industries continue

ⓘ Tips Preventive Medicine for the Jungle

Yellow fever vaccinations are a wise idea before visiting the jungles of southeastern Peru. Even though the only reported outbreaks of yellow fever in the last couple of years have been in the northern Amazon around Iquitos, local authorities in Puerto Maldonado make sure that visitors who want to be protected are. At the airport arrival terminal, yellow fever shots are administered by Health Ministry nurses.

Other vaccinations worth considering are those for Hepatitis A and typhoid. Malaria pills are also a good idea, especially if you're planning to venture deep into the jungle. You should carry your vaccination records with you while traveling in Peru. For more information on health issues, see p. 56; also speak to your doctor or consult the World Health Organization or Centers for Disease Control and Prevention websites.

to be based on exploiting the rainforest that surrounds Puerto Maldonado: gold prospecting, Brazil-nut harvesting, and ecotourism. For most travelers, Puerto Maldonado is merely a gateway to the jungle, and groups booked on Tambopata package tours often blow through town with little notice, ferried directly from the airport to waiting riverboats. For some visitors, it's a stiflingly hot one-horse (and motor-scooter) town, but the frontier atmosphere, which continues to draw dreamers from across Peru, proves interesting to others, at least for a day or two before they push on into the jungle.

Essentials

GETTING THERE   The **Aeropuerto Internacional Padre Aldamiz Puerto Maldonado** (☎ 082/571-531) is 8km (5 miles) outside of the city. Flights arrive daily from Cusco and Lima on **LAN** (☎ 01/213-8200; www.lan.com) and **Star Perú** (☎ 01/705-9000; www.starperu.com) starting from $105 one-way from Cusco, $135 one-way from Lima. Health Ministry nurses are on hand to vaccinate visitors against yellow fever *(fiebra amarilla)*. To get from the airport to town, the best bet is a *motocarro* (a motorcycle rickshaw), which costs S/5 to S/7.

Adventurous budget travelers with bountiful patience and perseverance, particularly those looking for a new warrior experience and the bragging rights that go with it, can travel by truck to Puerto Maldonado from Cusco. The journey takes at least 3 days in the dry season and up to 10 days in wetter conditions, and the route traverses more than 500km (310 miles) with zero comfort to speak of; it's certainly one of the worst (if not *the* worst) roads in Peru connecting two points of obvious interest. It costs about $15 and will provide you with stories for months, but you will definitely suffer for the dubious privilege. Trucks leave from Plaza Tupac Amaru in Cusco and arrive in Puerto Maldonado at the Mercado Modelo on Calle Ernesto Rivero. Take the challenge at your own risk; though the scenery is said to be astounding, the trip is not something I can recommend.

VISITOR INFORMATION   In Puerto Maldonado, there's a small booth at the airport that can give very limited information on the city and jungle lodges. Most visitors leave for the southern jungle from Cusco, so if you spend a few days there first, it's worthwhile to pick up more complete information on Puerto Maldonado and the rest of the jungle

Cock-of-the-Rock Lodge **12**
EcoAmazonia Lodge **1**
Explorer's Inn **6**
Heath River Wildlife Center **4**

Libertador Tambopata Lodge **7**
Manu Cloud Forest Lodge **11**
Manu Lodge **9**
Manu Wildlife Center **8**

Pantiacolla Lodge **10**
Posada Amazonas **5**
Reserva Amazonica Lodge **2**
Sandoval Lake Lodge **3**

at the main **Tourist Information Office** at Mantas 117-A, a block from the Plaza de Armas (℃ **082/263-176**). Anyone traveling to Manu or Tambopata with an organized expedition should be able to get all the necessary information from the tour organizer.

FAST FACTS   Banks on the Plaza de Armas include **Banco de la Nación,** Jr. Carrión 233 (℃ **082/571-064**), and **Banco de Crédito,** Arequipa 334 (℃ **082/571-001**). Only Banco de Crédito changes traveler's checks. There are also *casas de cambio* along Jirón Puno. Credit cards are not widely accepted in Puerto Maldonado, so you should plan on bringing cash for incidentals if you've already booked a lodge or tour program.

For required exit stamps to travel to Bolivia via Puerto Heath (a trip of 3–4 days by boat), visit the **Peruvian Immigration Office** at 26 de Diciembre 356, a block from the Plaza de Armas. It's open Monday through Friday from 9am to 1pm.

For medical attention, go to **Hospital Santa Rosa,** Jr. Cajamarca 171, at Velarde (℃ **082/571-019**). The **police** can be found at Jr. Carrión 410 (℃ **105** or 082/571-022). The **post office** is on Av. León Velarde 675 (℃ **082/571-088**). There's a **Telefónica del Perú** office at Jr. Puno 670 (℃ **082/571-600**).

GETTING AROUND   Quick, easy, and cheap, *motocarros* are everywhere; most rides in town cost S/2. Ferries cross the Ríos Madre de Dios and Tambopata daily. If you just want to cruise across the river you'll have to negotiate the price, but expect to spend about S/20 per person.

What to See & Do Near Puerto Maldonado

Good jungle experiences, with possibilities of some fauna sightings and attractive walks in primary and secondary forest, are within easy reach of Puerto Maldonado. However, your experience will be vastly improved if you go farther from the city, particularly for stays of 2 nights or more at one of the lodges discussed below. Still, a couple of easy and inexpensive day trips from the regional capital—vastly better than comparable close-in trips from Iquitos—can be arranged.

LAGO SANDOVAL ★★   Sandoval Lake is about 5km (3 miles), or an hour by boat, from Puerto Maldonado. Even if you don't stay at the lodge on the lake or one of those nearby along the Río Madre de Dios (see "Tambopata Lodges," below), this pretty and serene oxbow lake, ringed by palm trees, makes an excellent day trip downriver from Puerto Maldonado. It boasts a surprising diversity of wildlife, including macaws, parrots, herons, kingfishers, caimans, turtles, and even a family of giant river otters that can frequently be spied in the lake. The best way to get here is to catch a canoe or motorboat at the port. You'll then have to walk a couple kilometers along a path through the jungle, but it's a beautiful (if very hot) hour-long trek. Most jungle lodges along the Madre de Dios offer excursions to Lago Sandoval among their activities, though they usually arrive in the heat of the day, when wildlife activity is least observable (birds, monkeys, and the lake's caimans and resident river otters are much more active in the early morning and early evening hours).

Where to Stay & Dine

Most people who stay overnight in Puerto Maldonado are either resting up from a trip to the jungle or trying to arrange one. In town, there are only a couple of decent and comfortable hotels, in addition to about a dozen very basic hostels.

The best place to stay in Puerto Maldonado is **Wasaí Maldonado Lodge ★**, Jirón Guillermo Billinghurst (℃ **01/436-8792;** www.wasai.com). Although it's only a block from the main square in town, this inn is built much more like a mini–jungle lodge, with

Río Madre de Dios

Port

Trail

Jr. Billinghurst

Jr. Loreto

Jr. Carrión

PLAZA DE ARMAS

Jr. Cusco

Jr. Puno

Av. 2 de Mayo

← To Airport

Jr. González Prada

Jr. J. Troncoso

Jr. Tacna

Jr. Ernesto River

Jr. Moquegua

Av. León Velarde

Jr. Arequipa

Jr. 26 de Diciembre

PERU

Lima

Puerto Maldonado

Cusco

0   1/5 mile
0   200 meters

ACCOMMODATIONS■
Don Carlos Hotel **3**
Hostal Residencial Cabañaquinta **2**
Wasaí Maldonado Lodge **6**

DINING◆
El Califa **1**
Hostal Residencial Cabañaquinta Restaurant **2**
Pizzeria El Hornito **4**
Pollos a la Brasa La Estrella **5**
Wasaí Maldonado Restaurant **6**

6 of the 18 bungalows perched on stilts. The location is quite stunning, overlooking the Madre de Dios River. The spacious and comfortable bungalows are cabinlike paneled rooms with refrigerators, private bathrooms with hot water, air-conditioning (or fan), and TV. The small swimming pool, which looked abandoned on my last visit, overlooks the river. The lodge restaurant, the best and most upscale in town, is in a gazebo that sits above the riverbank; on the second floor is a new bar with good river views. Doubles in bungalows with river views cost $52. Ecotours and jungle expeditions with stays at the **Wasaí Tambopata Lodge,** 120km (75 miles)—about 6 hours—upriver on the Río Tambopata, and visits to Sandoval Lake (4 days/3 nights; $448 per person), as well as other jungle junkets, can be arranged.

Don Carlos Hotel, Velarde 1271 (© **082/571-029;** www.hotelesdoncarlos.com), sits above the banks of Tambopata River about 5 blocks south of the center of town and is surrounded by native flora. Smaller, more rustic, and more low-key than the chain's other hotels, this inn nonetheless has a host of services and amenities, including a restaurant, laundry, 24-hour room service, an outdoor swimming pool, and air-conditioning. The 15 rooms are nice enough, but hardly a steal, at $60 for a double. **Hostal Residencial Cabañaquinta,** Cusco 535 (© **082/571-045;** perutourytravel@hotmail.com), is a

(Fun Facts) Native Foods

Local jungle dishes worth a try include *patarashca,* a steamed river fish wrapped in banana leaves; *timbuche,* a thick soup made with local fish; and *tacacho,* or bananas cooked over coals and served with fried pork and chopped onions. Locals also eat *motelo* (turtle soup served in its shell) and *muchangue* (turtle eggs with steamed bananas), but, given that river and sea turtles are endangered species protected by Peruvian law, it seems especially criminal for gringos to indulge this custom. *Mazato* is a local beverage of fermented *yuca,* bananas, and milk.

comfortable inn with 50 pretty decent rooms with private bathrooms, a nice garden, and one of the better restaurants in town. Double rooms cost $25.

The top restaurant in town is the one at **Wasaí Maldonado Lodge.** The hotel restaurants at **Don Carlos** and **Cabañaquinta** are also frequented by visitors to town, but there are a slew of basic eateries, *chifas,* and cafes clustered near the Plaza de Armas and lining León de Velarde, the main street. **Pizzería El Hornito,** Jr. Carrión 271, Plaza de Armas (© 082/572-082), is a good and cozy pizza joint and pub serving wood-fired pies. It's open daily until midnight and accepts credit cards. Next door, down a long passageway, is **Bulevard Video-Pub** (no phone), which has a large screen playing music videos; you can get a pizza and beers there, but El Hornito is far more agreeable. **El Califa,** Piura 266 (© 082/571-119), on a small side street, is a local, open-air joint that, with bright green paneling, ceiling fans, a tin roof, and verdant garden, very much looks the part of small-town tropical eatery. It serves local jungle cuisine and good Peruvian meals, including ceviche, at lunch. Grilled and rotisserie chicken, always a good bet in Peru, can be had at **Pollos a la Brasa La Estrella,** Velarde 474 (© 082/573-107).

TAMBOPATA NATIONAL RESERVE ★★
650km (404 miles) NE of Cusco; 37km (23 miles) SW of Puerto Maldonado

Upstream from Puerto Maldonado, jungle lodges in and around the **Tambopata National Reserve (Reserva Nacional de Tambopata)**—a massive tract of humid subtropical rainforest in the department of Madre de Dios—are located either along the Tambopata or Madre de Dios rivers. The National Reserve covers 275,000 hectares (nearly 680,000 acres), while the entire area, including the Bahuaja-Sonene National Park, encompasses some 1.5 million hectares (3.7 million acres) of Amazonian jungle. The Peruvian government prohibited hunting and logging in the area in 1977 and created the reserve, then called the Tambopata-Candamo Reserve Zone, in 1990. Nearly one-third the size of Costa Rica, Tambopata has more species of birds (595) and butterflies (more than 1,200) than any place of similar size on earth.

Visits to lodges here are considerably more accessible than those in Manu. Most trips involve flying a half-hour from Cusco and then boarding a boat and traveling by river for 45 minutes up to 5 hours to reach a jungle lodge. Primary lodges are those that travelers can get to the same day they arrive by plane in Puerto Maldonado. Although mankind's imprints are slightly more noticeable in the Tambopata region, the area remains one of superb environmental diversity, with a dozen different types of forest and several gorgeous oxbow lakes. Environmentalists claim that Tambopata's great diversity of wildlife is due to its location at the confluence of lowland Amazon forest with three other ecosystems. At least 13 endangered species are found here, including the jaguar, ocelot, giant armadillo, harpy eagle, and giant river otter. The farther one travels from Puerto Maldonado, the greater the chances of significant wildlife viewing.

The Tambopata Macaw Clay Lick *(collpa de guacamayos)* within the reserve is one of the largest natural clay licks in the country and one of the wildlife highlights of Peru. Thousands of brilliantly colored macaws and parrots arrive daily at the cliffs to feed on mineral salts.

Most visitors prearrange tours to Tambopata in Cusco or in their country of origin, although one could also book a lodge visit by stopping in the local offices of travel agents and tour operators in the center of Puerto Maldonado or at the airport (though you will have less information and opportunity to compare offerings). Access to Tambopata is by boat from Puerto Maldonado. Packages begin with 2-day/1-night arrangements, but 3-day/2-night packages are preferable. Lodge stays generally allow visitors to see a large variety of trees, plants, and birds, but sightings of wild mammals, apart from monkeys and otters, are rare. Large and rare species such as jaguars and tapirs are infrequently seen, though visitors to Lago Sandoval, an oxbow lake, have the exciting opportunity to see an extended family of resident giant river otters (known in Spanish as *lobos de río*).

Lodges are located predominantly either along the Río Tambopata, which extends south of Puerto Maldonado, or the Río Madre de Dios, east of the city. The area around the Río Tambopata, with greater primary forest, is generally considered better for wildlife viewing.

East of Puerto Maldonado: Along the Rio Madre de Dios

Lodges within a couple of hours by boat from Puerto Maldonado are generally cheaper (and, of course, less time-consuming to get to) than those deeper in the Tambopata National Reserve. Because they are located in secondary jungle and are not nearly as remote, they best serve as introductory visits to the Amazon. The forest along the Madre de Dios is generally not as pristine as that found along the Tambopata River. The following lodges are several of the best that are easily accessible from Puerto Maldonado (as little as a half-hour by boat).

• **Sandoval Lake Lodge** ★★, Calle Ricardo Palma N J1, Urb Santa Monica, Cusco (© 01/440-2022, or 877/870-7378 in the U.S. and Canada; www.inkanatura.com). This pioneering lodge, on high bluffs overlooking lovely Sandoval Lake (p. 346) and surrounded by palm trees and thick forest, is the best option close to Puerto Maldonado if you're more into wildlife than plush accommodations. It is one of just three in the Amazon in a nationally protected zone, and by far its greatest advantage is its unique location on one of the jungle's prettiest oxbow lakes. The journey to the lodge

---

Tips **¿Qué Frío?**

The weather in the Madre de Dios region is usually extremely hot and sticky, as you would expect. But the southern jungle's proximity to the Andes produces periodic cold spells called *friajes*, which originate in the South Pole, from June through September. When they hit, *friajes* drop the temperature to 48°F (9°C) for a period of 2 or 3 days. It's a good idea to pack a jacket and even some gloves on the off chance that the jungle turns cold on you.

is part of the experience; after a 45-minute boat ride, you walk a couple kilometers (another 45 min.) through secondary forest, then you hop in a wooden canoe and paddle along a canal and then across the lake. The rustic, spacious facility consists of a large main dining room and lounge, and two wings of rooms with private bathrooms (but open ceilings). Visitors have their choice of wildlife-viewing centers and leisurely paddled catamaran and canoe trips on the lake at prime viewing hours; most visitors not only see a wealth of aquatic and jungle birds, including macaws, but several species of monkeys, caimans, and the elusive, highly prized community of giant river otters (on my last trip here I witnessed the complete group of 10 playing and lounging on a log in the lake). Prices range from $178 to $438 for 3- to 4-day stays. InkaNatura's newest lodge is the remote **Heath River Wildlife Center,** situated another 3 hours downriver near the Bolivian border, within easy reach of a large macaw clay lick and owned and staffed by the indigenous Ese'Eja Sonene people; it is possible to combine a couple of nights at either lodge. Heath River prices range from $575 for 4 days to $855 for 6 days. InkaNatura, which administers the lodge, is the Peruvian partner of the American environmental organization Tropical Nature (which handles international marketing). Outside Peru, trips can be organized through **Tropical Nature Travel,** P.O. Box 5276 Gainesville, FL 32627-5276 (© **877/827-8350** toll-free in the U.S. and Canada; www.tropicalnaturetravel.com).

- **Reserva Amazónica Rainforest Lodge ★★**, Plaza Las Nazarenas 211, Cusco (© **800/442-5042** in the U.S. and Canada, 800/458-7506 in the U.K., 084/245-314 in Cusco, or 01/610-0400 in Lima; www.inkaterra.com). Although one of the oldest lodges in the Peruvian Amazon, this completely upgraded place—operated by the folks behind the swanky Machu Picchu Pueblo Hotel—just 15km (9⅓ miles), or 1 hour down the Madre de Dios from Puerto Maldonado, is also one of the plushest. In other words, it is *the* place for an upscale jungle experience and creature comforts. Its large main house, stylishly designed like an Indian roundhouse, features a dining room and upstairs lounge, perfect for swilling drinks after a day in the jungle. The 43 thatched-roof, African-style bungalows, attractively strewn about the riverside property, are a model of rustic chic, a fancy step up from most accommodations in the jungle. Rooms have private bathrooms and terraces with hammocks. Though there's no electricity in the rooms, the kerosene lamps left at the door add to the romance of the place. The superior cabanas and suites are particularly luxurious. Food is excellent, and the guides are very professional (they even wear matching Disney-like eco-outfits). Although the surrounding forest doesn't teem with wildlife (except for sonorous russet-backed Oropendula birds that make waking up a treat), there's a good system of trails nearby, as well as an island that is home to a dozen or so rescued monkeys and a terrific canopy walk. An unusual bonus in the Amazon, the lodge's expanded ENA spa, overlooking the river, offers Reiki, cold stone massage, reflexology, and other types of massage services. Rates range from $337 per night in a standard cabaña to $573 for 3 nights in a swanky Amazonia suite.

- **EcoAmazonia Lodge,** Calle Garcilazo 210, Of. 206, Cusco (© **084/236-159;** www.ecoamazonia.com.pe). About an hour by boat from Puerto Maldonado, this large lodge features long rows of basic bungalows and trails that lead to a canopy-viewing platform. It's a friendly and comfortable place that primarily caters to large groups, and it offers *ayahuasca* ceremonies (see "Trippin' Amazon Style" on p. 369). Prices range from $160 for an easy 2-day, 1-night stay to $2,800 for 4 days and 3 nights.

Tambopata Lodges
South of Puerto Maldonado: Along Río Tambopata

- **Explorer's Inn ★★★**, the only lodge located within the Tambopata National Reserve, is a comfortable 30-year-old lodge that hosts both ecotourists and scientists. It's a little over 3 hours upriver from Puerto Maldonado along the Tambopata River, and is excellent for viewing fauna, including otters, monkeys, and particularly jungle birds. Accommodations are in rustic, thatched-roof bungalows. The inn is excellent for fauna, particularly jungle birds. (It's probably the top spot in Tambopata for birding.) Established in 1976, the complex has seven thatched-roof bungalows and 30 rooms with private bathrooms. The lodge has a good network of nearly 32km (20 miles) of trails, including several to nearby oxbow lakes. Guides are Peruvian and international biologists (or biologists in training). Trips are arranged through **Peruvian Safaris,** Alcanfores 459, Miraflores, Lima (✆ **01/447-8888;** www.explorersinn. com or www.peruviansafaris.com); or Plateros 365, Cusco (✆ **084/235-342**). Prices range from $198 for 2 nights to $450 for a 4-night Macaw Clay Lick program.

- **Posada Amazonas ★**, about 2 hours up the Tambopata River from Puerto Maldonado, is owned jointly with the Infierno indigenous community and is quite good for inexpensive, introductory nature tours. It has an eagle nest site and a canopy observation tower, and two parrot clay licks are located within a kilometer of the lodge. The lodge, inaugurated in 1998, featuring 30 rustic rooms and a wall open to the forest, is operated by the award-winning **Rainforest Expeditions ★★**, Portal de Carnes 236, Cusco (✆ **877/870-0578** in the U.S., or 084/232-772 or 01/421-8347), and Jr. Arequipa 401, Puerto Maldonado (✆ **082/571-056;** www.perunature.com). This veteran ecotourism company promotes tourism with environmental education, research, and conservation, and operates two Tambopata lodges. The prices are $295 to $565 for 3- to 5-day trips. The 13-room **Tambopata Research Center ★★★** is more remote (8 hr. upriver from Puerto Maldonado), just 500m (1,640 ft.) from the jungle's largest and most famous Macaw Clay Lick. Just one of three Peruvian lodges in a protected national nature reserve, it is the best lodge in Tambopata for in-depth tours and viewing wildlife, including several species of monkeys. It's certainly *the* place to see flocks of colorful macaws and parrots. Trips usually entail an overnight at Posada Amazonas before continuing on to the Research Center. Prices are $745 to $945 for 5- to 7-day trips.

- **Libertador Tambopata Lodge,** Nueva Baja 432, Cusco (✆ **084/245-695;** www. tambopatalodge.com). Operated by an upscale Peruvian hotel chain, this private

---

(Fun Facts) What's an Oxbow Lake?

An oxbow lake is a natural lake formed by the normal shifting of river waters, which have fashioned a new streambed in the riverbanks. The old riverbed fills with water and forms a lake. Oxbow lakes are essentially designed to become extinct. After forming, they have life expectancies of perhaps 400 years; they expand but then become shallower as river flooding and runoff deposits sediment, sand, and leaves and then begin to dry up as grasses and trees take root. Oxbow lakes, which can be very large and superb spots for wildlife viewing, are so named because they are shaped like an old-fashioned U-shaped yoke.

> **Tips** **Birds, Plants? Check. Monkeys and Macaws? Check. Caimans? Check. Jaguars? Not So Fast!**
>
> Peru's Amazon jungle regions have some of the greatest recorded biodiversity and species of plants and animals on earth. However, you may be disappointed if you go expecting a daily episode of *Wild Kingdom*. An expedition to the Amazon is not like a safari to the African savanna. Many mammals are extremely difficult to see in the thick jungle vegetation, and though the best tour operators employ guides skilled in ferreting them out, there are no guarantees. Even in the most virgin sections, after devoting several patient days to the exercise, you are unlikely to see a huge number of mammals, especially the rare large species such as tapirs, jaguars, and giant river otters. If you spot a single one of these prized mammals, your jungle expedition can be considered a roaring success. (Your best shot at seeing jaguars is in Manu during the months of May and June.) However, in both Manu and Tambopata you are very likely to see a wealth of jungle birds (including the region's famous and fabulous macaws), several species of monkeys, black caimans, butterflies, and insects.

reserve lodge is about 3 hours upstream from Puerto Maldonado along the Río Tambopata. The lodge, with a handsome dining room and bar, is more luxurious than most and has more of a jungle hotel feel than others; newer bungalows are constructed of cement rather than wood. The lodge has 25km (16 miles) of trails nearby, including trails to lake systems on the opposite bank of the Tambopata River, in about 100 hectares of secondary forest, and offers overnight trips to the Macaw Clay Lick. Prices range from $307 for 3 days to $998 for 5 nights, including a visit to the Macaw Clay Lick, in a "superior" double.

MANU BIOSPHERE RESERVE ★★★
242km (150 miles) NE of Cusco

Manu, a UNESCO World Biosphere Reserve and World Heritage Site, certainly doesn't lack for distinctions and accolades. The Biosphere Reserve encompasses the least accessible and explored jungle of primary and secondary forest in Peru, and it is about as close as you're likely to come to virgin rainforest anywhere in the world. In fact, it's so remote that not only did the Spaniards, who found their way to virtually every corner of Peru except Machu Picchu, never enter the jungle, but the Incas, who created an empire that stretched from Ecuador to Chile, never conquered the region, either. The forest wasn't really penetrated until the late 1800s, when rubber barons and loggers set their sights on it. Peru declared it a national park in 1973.

Only slightly smaller than the Pacaya-Samiria National Reserve (see "Into the Wild: Farther Afield from Iquitos" on p. 370), Manu—about half the size of Switzerland—is one of the largest protected areas in South America, with just less than 2 million hectares (nearly 5 million acres). Its surface area of varied habitats includes Andes highlands, cloud forests, and lowland tropical rainforests. The park encompasses an area of almost unimaginable diversity, climbing as it does from an altitude near sea level to elevations of 3,500m (11,480 ft.).

A single hectare of forest in Manu might have 10 times the number of species of trees 353 that a hectare of temperate forest in Europe or North America has. Manu, which contains the highest bird, mammal, and plant diversity of any park on the planet, offers visitors perhaps their best opportunity for viewing wildlife that has been pushed deep into the rainforest by man's presence. It boasts nearly 1,000 species of birds, 1,200 species of butterflies, 20,000 plants, 200 species of mammals, and 13 species of primates. Species in danger of extinction include the spectacled bear, giant armadillo, and cock-of-the-rock.

Birders thrill at the prospect of glimpsing bird populations that account for 10% of the world's total, more than what's found in all of Costa Rica. Hugely prized among wildlife observers are giant river otters, parrots, and macaws at a riverbank clay lick; preening and bright red cocks-of-the-rock; and lumbering lowland tapirs gathering at a forest clay lick. Scientists estimate that perhaps 12,000 to 15,000 animal species remain to be identified. Manu is also home to dozens of native Amerindian tribes, some of which have contact with the modern world and others that remain secluded.

Going with a group tour to Manu is the only realistic way to visit the park, and only a handful of travel agencies in Cusco are authorized to organize excursions to the Manu Biosphere Reserve. The Reserve comprises three zones: **Manu National Park,** an area of dedicated conservation reserved for scientific study (the largest zone, it occupies 3.7 million hectares/9.1 million acres, or about three-fourths of the entire reserve); the **Reserve Zone,** up the River Manu northwest of Boca Manu, accessible by permit and accompanied by an authorized guide only for ecotourist activities; and the Multiuse or **Cultural Zone,** home to traditional nomadic groups and open to all visitors. Traveling independently to the Cultural Zone is possible but extremely demanding and time-consuming—too much so for all but the hardiest ecoadventurers with plenty of time.

Most trips to Manu visit jungle trails and lakes Cocha Salvador and Cocha Otorongo. Both are uniquely endowed with wildlife, including several types of caimans and wild monkeys. Cocha Otorongo is home to a prized, endangered group of giant otters. Virtually all tours make stops at key observation piers, platforms, and towers for wildlife viewing. Many longer Manu trips include visits to a macaw clay lick.

Getting to Manu is itself an ecoadventure. Overland access to the Manu Reserve Zone from Cusco (from Puerto Maldonado is much more difficult) is a stunning (and stunningly beautiful) 2-day journey through 4,000m (13,120-ft.) mountains and cloud forest before descending into lowland rainforest. The scenery along the narrow road, full of switchbacks and great panoramic views of glaciers and the eastern Andes, is so extraordinary that many lodges and tour operators travel overland and return to Cusco by small aircraft (a 25-min. flight from Boca Manu). The trip passes through Paucartambo (see chapter 8) and travels along roads whose steep descents are thrilling—though unsettling

---

ⓘ Tips   Manu Tour Considerations

The best deals are usually available by arranging your trip on-site in Cusco rather than your home country. However, doing so carries some risks. Your chosen tour operator might not have space available. Another warning worth heeding is that previous travelers have gone to Manu but had their returns delayed (by weather conditions and mechanical and other mishaps) by several days. It's wise to schedule a Manu expedition in the middle of your trip, with a few buffer days before your scheduled departure.

> ## Tips · All Alone in the Forest . . . with a Few Good Friends
>
> As remote and huge as the Manu Reserve Zone is, don't expect to find yourself enveloped and alone in the quiet of the jungle during high season. The few lodges and tour operators with a presence in the zone are very busy during the months of June, July, and August, and travelers' contact with each other might greatly outdistance their contact with species native to the rainforest. This is the case despite the official limits of 30 travelers per agency per week. (If all 10 agencies have full loads, that's still 300 people traveling many of the same waterways and racing to arrive first at primary observation points.)

to some travelers—on the way to high jungle. Bus or plane travel to Boca Manu is followed by up to a couple of days of river travel to lodges, campsites, and principal points of interest in the reserve. Because Manu is so isolated and access is so restricted, reserve visits are expensive and plainly beyond the scope of most budget travelers ($700 to more than $2,500 or more per person for a 5- to 8-day trip). Most visits to Manu require about a week.

Manu Tour Operators

Only eight tour companies are permitted to run organized expeditions to Manu, and the number of travelers they can take there each week is strictly limited. The best firms listed below are closely involved with conservation efforts and local development programs. The least expensive expeditions bus travelers in and out or return by small plane. Land (and river) travel is very time-consuming, but it makes for an excellent opportunity to experience the diverse terrain and types of forest that comprise Manu. Note that most companies operate with fixed departure dates only in the dry season, from May to November. The prices below do not include air transportation from Cusco.

Most of the tour operators below post detailed itineraries and information about their Manu trips on their websites.

- **InkaNatura** ★★★, Calle Ricardo Palma N J1 Urb., Santa Mónica, Cusco (② **084/255-255;** www.inkanatura.com): Perhaps the most serious and sophisticated outfit operating ecotourism trips in the Peruvian Amazon, InkaNatura, associated with the Peruvian conservation group PerúVerde and the American organization Tropical Nature, organizes stays at the famed **Manu Wildlife Center** ★★ (of which InkaNatura is a joint owner). The lodge, opened in 1996, is located near the world's largest tapir clay lick, as well as the Blanquillo macaw clay lick, and it features 48km (30 miles) of nature trails and two canopy-viewing platforms. Accommodations are in 22 spacious, private bungalows with tiled bathrooms. Packages at the Manu Wildlife Center range from 4 days/3 nights for $1,285 to 5 days/4 nights for $1,475. InkaNatura also operates shorter trips to the **Cock-of-the-Rock Lodge** (in the Selva Sur Nature Reserve at an elevation of 1,600m (5,250 ft.), excellent for birders), several lodges in Tambopata (above), and multilodge sojourns that include Cusco and Machu Picchu. Outside Peru, trips can be organized through **Tropical Nature Travel,** P.O. Box 5276, Gainesville, FL 32627-5276 (② **877/827-8350** toll-free in the U.S.; www.tropicalnaturetravel.com).

- **Manu Adventures,** Plateros 356, Cusco (℗ **213/283-6987** in the U.S. and Canada, or 084/261-640; www.manuadventures.com): This 8-year-old agency offers some of the most affordable trips, ranging from 5 days/4 nights (in and out by plane, $724 per person) to 8 days/7 nights (overland, $550), with 2 nights in open-air lodges and the rest in campsites. A 4-day visit to the Cultural Zone is $300 (overland).

- **Manu Expeditions** ★★★, Urb. Magisterio, segunda Etapa G-5, P.O. Box 606, Cusco (℗ **084/226-671;** www.manuexpeditions.com): One of the pioneering eco-tourism operators in southern Peruvian Amazon, Manu Expeditions—run by an ornithologist who is the British Consul in Cusco—has been organizing rainforest tours for more than 2 decades. Tours include stays at the **Manu Wildlife Center,** of which the group is part owner (above), near the famed macaw clay lick, and a safari camp facility deep at Cocha Salvador within the Manu Biosphere Reserve. The Wild-life Center is considered the best lodge in Peru for birding. The longer tours include initial stays at the **Cock-of-the-Rock Lodge** in cloud forest. Four-, six-, and nine-day fixed-departure tours range from $1,180 to $1,895 per person.

- **Manu Nature Tours** ★★★, Av. Pardo 1046, Cusco (℗ **084/252-721;** www.manu peru.com): A highly professional, prizewinning outfit with 20 years' experience in Manu—it was one of the first to send expeditions to the reserve—Manu Nature Tours operates the well-known and comfortable **Manu Lodge,** situated next to a pristine oxbow lake and the only full-service lodge within Manu National Park itself (5-day/4-night trips, $1,029–$1,500 per person), and the excellent **Manu Cloud Forest Lodge,** the first of its kind in Peru, overlooking a waterfall (3-day, 2-night trips; $849 per person). The agency claims that the oxbow lake is one of the best spots anywhere in the jungle to view giant river otters. Add-on options include mountain biking, rafting, and tree canopy climbs. The office in Cusco is attached to a Patagonia outdoor gear shop and a rainforest cafe, in case you needed any reassurance of their commitment. The agency has expanded its activities to include trekking programs in the southern and central highlands, as well as more traditional tourist trips throughout Peru.

- **Pantiacolla** ★, Saphy 554, Cusco (℗ **084/238-323;** www.pantiacolla.com): An ini-tiative of a Dutch biologist and Boca Manu-born conservationist, this agency operates the small **Pantiacolla Lodge,** with double rooms in bungalows, on bluffs overlooking the Madre de Dios River at the edge of Manu National Park. The organization also operates a community-based ecotourism project with the Yine Indians of the Manu rainforest, with a lodge that will be entirely turned over to the community in 2011. Pantiacolla is favored by ecotravelers on a budget, offering camping and lodge trips ranging from $990 for 5 days to $1,064 for / days.

Other reputable Manu tour companies and lodges, which run economical camping-based trips, especially for budget travelers, include:

- **Expediciones Vilca,** Plateros 359, Cusco (℗ **084/253-773;** www.cbc.org.pe/manu vilca): Vilca has been organizing Manu expeditions for a decade, with trips that split time between lodges and campsites. It has earned a sturdy reputation among budget-minded travelers.

- **Mayuc,** Portal de Confiturías 211, Plaza de Armas, Cusco (℗ **084/242-824;** www. mayuc.com): Mayuc is a traditional tour operator with programs across Peru, plus good budget-camping programs to Manu.

- **SAS Travel,** Garcilaso 270, Plaza San Francisco (℗ **084/249-194;** www.sastravelperu. com): This well-run and popular all-purpose agency offers varied programs to both Manu and Tambopata, and stays at various lodges.

356

AMAZONIA

11

IQUITOS & THE NORTHERN AMAZON

Bird-Watching and Macaw Clay Licks

While Tambopata is superb for bird-watching, with nearly 600 species, Manu enjoys a nearly mythic reputation among birders. And it should: It has the highest concentration of birdlife on the planet. In addition to its many thousands of species of plants, more than a dozen species of monkeys, and hundreds of mammals, the Manu Biosphere Reserve contains some 1,000 species of birds, including seven species of colorful macaws. That's more than half the bird species in all of Peru—one of the top countries in the world (along with Colombia and Indonesia) for recorded bird species within its borders. That's more species than are found in all of Costa Rica, and it's one of every nine birds in the world! The forests of the western Amazon enjoy the highest density of birds per square mile of any on earth.

The immense variety of birds is due to the diversity of altitudinal zones, habitats, and ecosystems spread across Manu, which encompasses cloud forest and upper and lowland tropical forest. In addition, Manu shimmers with vastly different types of forests, lakes, and microclimates. From the Andes Mountains surrounding Cusco, the road to Manu plummets an amazing 4,000m (13,120 ft.) down to the dense tropical forests of the Amazon basin. For every 1,000m (3,280 ft.) of change in elevation, the indigenous bird life changes just as dramatically. The twisting road near the Cock-of-the-Rock Lodge has been called "the best road in the world" by leading bird-tour companies.

In visits of just 2 to 3 weeks in Manu, dedicated birders have recorded a staggering 500 species. Birders can expect to come into contact with quetzals, toucanets, tanagers, and the famed, blazing-red Andean cocks-of-the-rock at their numerous leks. Also of interest to birders, among many dozens more, are the blue-headed macaw, white-cheeked tody-tyrant, bamboo antshrike, and Manu antbird.

2 IQUITOS & THE NORTHERN AMAZON ★★

1,860km (1,156 miles) NE of Lima

Iquitos, the gateway to the northern Amazon, is Peru's largest jungle town and the capital of its largest department, Loreto, which occupies nearly a third of the national territory and is nearly the size of Germany. You must fly to get here—unless you have a week to kill for hot and uncomfortable river travel—but the pockets of jungle down- and upriver from Iquitos are among the most accessible of the Peruvian Amazon basin. Some of the best jungle lodges in the country, some of which are well into their fifth decade of ecotourism, are located just a few hours by boat from Iquitos. Because the region is the most trafficked and developed of the Peruvian Amazon, costs are lower for most jungle excursions than they are in the more exclusive Manu Biosphere Reserve in southeastern Peru.

The most important port city of the Amazon lies at the confluence of the Nanay and Itaya rivers. The city was founded in 1754 by Jesuit missionaries, although some continue

For most visitors, the spectacle of viewing hundreds of *guacamayos*, or macaws, and other birds feeding at a *collpa* (clay lick) in Tambopata or Manu remains the holy grail of Amazon bird-watching. Many birds and mammals (such as tapirs) supplement their diets with minerals found in clay, which is loaded with minerals and salts. Early in the morning, parrots gather in trees above the river. They then descend in large numbers and feed at the clay. Gorgeously colored and noisy macaws arrive next. Visitors often view the scene from a small catamaran. **Blanquillo Macaw and Parrot Lick,** the subject of a 1994 *National Geographic* report and subsequent TV special on macaws, is the most famous *collpa* in Manu. *Collpa* viewings are during the dry season only and are best from July to September; macaws do not feed at the clay licks during the month of June, for reasons unknown.

All the Manu tour operators focus to some extent on birding, of course, but for specialists, the **Manu Wildlife Center ★★★** (www.manu-wildlife-center. com), jointly owned by Manu Expeditions, itself run by a well-known ornithologist, is perhaps best suited for enthusiastic birding in Manu. Also recommended by birders is **Pantiacolla Lodge ★** (p. 355) where birders have recorded 500 birds in a month's time. **Tanager Tours ★**, La Estrella F-9, J. L. Bustamante y Rivero, Arequipa (✆ **054/426-210;** www.tanagertours.com), organizes birding trips to Manu, Puerto Maldonado, and many other spots in Peru; the Dutch-owned group also has a branch in Cusco.

Birders and would-be birders should check out **Birding Peru** (www.birding peru.org) and **Ornifolks** (www.ornifolks.org) for additional bird-watching trips to Peru. **WorldTwitch** (www.worldtwitch.com) has helpful links to birding lodges, tour operators, and organizations throughout Peru, as well as the Americas and the Caribbean.

to claim that it actually was not founded until nearly a century later. The city's proximity to South America's greatest rainforest and its isolation from the rest of Peru have created a unique tropical atmosphere. In the late 1860s and 1870s, pioneering merchants got rich off the booming rubber trade and built ostentatious mansions lined with glazed tiles along the river. Iquitos rivaled Manaus in Brazil for leadership of the rubber trade. The city went from boom to bust, although oil exploration, shipping, logging, and other export trade later revived and sustained the city's fortunes. Today tourism is quite evidently among Iquitos's most important industries.

Iquitos is far from the grand port of old. The modern city of nearly a half-million is composed of descendants of original ethnic groups such as the Yaguas, Boras, Kukama, and Iquitos, as well as significant populations of immigrant groups from Europe and Asia. Those great homes along the *malecón* are now faded monuments to the city's glory days, and just blocks from the main square lies the fascinating Belén district, where families live in a squalid pile of ramshackle wooden houses on the banks of the river. Some are propped up by spindly stilts, while others float, tethered to poles, when the river rises 6m (20 ft.) or more.

The Amazon in Danger

Could the vast Amazon rainforest disappear from the face of the earth during our lifetimes? Some scientists now maintain that the forest itself—not to mention the many thousands of plant, animal, bird, and insect species that call it home—is in imminent danger of extinction. A mathematical model by an American researcher, presented at a 2001 Geology Society conference in Scotland, suggests that the destruction of Amazonian rainforests could be irreversible in a few years, and forecasts the wholesale destruction of Brazil's rainforest in about 40 years.

Peru, the origin of the great Amazon River, boasts some of the largest and most biologically diverse rainforests in the world. The country counts 84 of 103 existing ecosystems and 28 of the 32 climates on the planet among its remarkable statistics. Peru has 72 million hectares (178 million acres) of natural-growth forests—70% in the Amazon jungle region—that comprise nearly 60% of the national territory. But it's losing nearly 300,000 hectares (740,000 acres) of rainforest annually. In other Amazon basin countries, the picture is even bleaker. Half the world's known plant and animal species live in rainforests, but according to the World Resources Institute, more than 100 species become extinct in the world every day due to tropical deforestation. The destruction of their habitats is estimated at 81,000 hectares (200,150 acres) each day—an area larger than New York City. Less than 50 years ago, 15% of the earth's land surface was rainforest. Today that total has been reduced to a mere 6%.

The primary threats to Peru's tropical forests are deforestation caused by agricultural expansion, cattle ranching, logging, oil extraction and spills, mining, illegal coca farming, and colonization initiatives. Deforestation has shrunk territories belonging to indigenous peoples and wiped out more than 90% of the population. In the southern Amazon's Madre de Dios department, 3 decades of gold prospecting have pushed isolated tribes to the edge of extinction. Along with the threats to communities comes cultural extinction: Knowledge of plants and natural medicines, traditional ways of life, and even languages are lost. In Peru's Amazon jungle, new languages are being discovered even as others become extinct. Once-isolated communities in the jungle spoke up to 150 languages; today, only 53 survive and 25 of them are in danger of extinction, according to the Summer Institute of Linguistics.

Governments in developing countries have traditionally been reluctant to adopt tough measures to halt deforestation, bowing to the need for "economic development" and offering inducements to industry and extraction practices that have ranged from rubber extraction to logging and oil drilling. Slash-and-burn clearing of land, unproductive farming, and overhunting by marginalized people living in and around the jungle have further denuded the landscape of vegetation and animals. And, 500 years ago, an estimated 10 million indigenous people inhabited the Amazon rainforest; by the 21st century, that population had dropped to less than 200,000.

Can anything be done to save the Amazon and its people, plants, and animals? Leaving the rainforests intact, with their wealth of nuts, fruits, oil-producing plants, and medicinal plants, has greater economic value than destroying them for unsustainable short-term interests. More than six times as much can be earned from sustainable harvests of fruit, cocoa, timber, and rubber from the rainforest tract than commercial logging produces. Slash-and-burn practices, which involve no preparation of the land and no safeguards to make its yield sustainable, destroy the land's capacity to produce: A plot can be burned just twice before a farmer must abandon it and search for another, uncultivated piece of land.

For most of the 20th century, Peru gave carte blanche to oil and gas exploration by multinationals in the Amazon basin, and the government looked the other way with regard to invasive gold mining in Indian communities. However, Peru has done a slightly better job of setting aside tracts of rainforest as national park reserves and regulating industry than have some other Latin American and Asian countries. The Manu Biosphere Reserve, the Tambopata National Reserve, and the Pacaya-Samiria National Reserve are three of the largest protected rainforest areas in the world, and the government regulates entry of tour groups. Peru augmented the Bahuaja-Sonene National Park, which was created in 1996, by 809,000 hectares (nearly 2 million acres) in 2001. INRENA, Peru's Institute for Natural Resource Management, enforces logging regulations and reseeds Peru's Amazon forests. A handful of international and Peruvian environmental and conservation groups, such as ProNaturaleza and Conservation International are active in Peru, working on reforestation and sustainable forestry projects.

Many conservationists have mixed feelings about promoting ecotourism in endangered habitats. Responsible tourism has the potential to educate people about the rainforest and its threats and could spur much-needed activism. The income produced by ecotourism is vital to local communities—many of whom are increasingly dependent upon tourists to buy their handicrafts or to lead on treks into the jungle—and to countries, as an incentive to protect the very things tourists come to see. A small handful of lodges in the rainforest have successfully integrated local tribes into the running of the lodges. The lodges and tour operators I've recommended for travel in the Amazon all profess to practice responsible, low-impact tourism. Please do your utmost to follow suit. If you witness a tour group or lodge practicing unsafe ecotourism, by all means report it to either **INRENA** (✆ **01/224-3298**) or **PromPerú** (✆ **01/224-3279**), or to the tourist information offices in Cusco (✆ **084/263-176**) or Iquitos (✆ **065/235-621**).

> ## (Tips) Malaria & Yellow Fever in Northern Peru
>
> According to the Centers for Disease Control and Prevention, epidemic malaria rapidly emerged in the northern Amazon most recently in the 1990s. Peru has the second-highest number of malaria cases in South America (after Brazil), with the majority of cases from the Loreto department. From 1992 to 1997, malaria increased 50 times in Loreto, a rate more than 10 times greater than in the rest of the country. Malaria around the city of Iquitos accounts for the greatest number of cases in Loreto.
>
> In 2001, the Peruvian Ministry of Health also reported an outbreak of yellow fever in the Loreto department in three districts, including Iquitos. Eight cases of yellow fever were confirmed, with two deaths. In 2003, the Pan American Health Organization recorded 22 cases and 13 deaths in Peru, just one of five Latin American nations grappling with an outbreak that claimed 99 lives by the end of the year.
>
> These outbreaks should not deter most travelers from visiting the Amazon of northern Peru, but they should emphasize the need for proper vaccinations and medication before (and during) traveling to the region. See "Health" in chapter 3, for more information.

The Belén district looks distinctly Far Eastern, and Iquitos has more in common with steamy tropical Asian cities than the highlands of Peru. Like a South American Saigon, the air is waterlogged and the streets buzz with unrelenting waves of motorcycles and *motocarros*. Locals speak a languid, mellifluous Spanish unmatched in other parts of the country, and pretty prostitutes loll about the Plaza de Armas. Locals dress not in alpaca sweaters and shawls, but in flesh-baring tank tops and short skirts.

Iquitos has a relaxed, intoxicating feel that's likely to detain you for a couple of days at least. But for most visitors, the lure of the Amazon rainforest is the primary attraction. Virgin rainforest, though, is hard to find. To lay eyes on exotic wildlife, such as pink dolphins, caimans, and macaws, you have to get far away from Iquitos, at least 80km (50 miles) out and onto secondary waterways. Options for rainforest excursions include lodge visits, river cruises, and, for the adventurous, independent guided treks.

ESSENTIALS
Getting There
Water-locked Iquitos can be reached only by airplane or boat. For most travelers, air is the only practical option.

BY PLANE   Iquitos's **Aeropuerto Francisco Secada Vigneta,** Avenida Abelardo Quiñones, Km 6 (© **065/260-147**), was once an international airport, receiving flights from Miami, but those were suspended several years ago. **LAN** (© **01/213-8200;** www.lan.com), and **Star Perú** (© **01/705-9000;** www.starperu.com) fly daily to Iquitos from Lima and from Pucallpa and Tarapoto, other cities in the Loreto department. Flights from Lima start at $112 one-way.

The airport is usually chaotic when flights arrive, with dozens of representatives of tour operators, and countless touts and con men competing for your attention. Do not let anyone take your bags, and don't let anyone you don't know hop in a cab with you.

Ceiba Tops **3**
Explorama Inn **2**
Explornapo **1**
Sinchicuy Lodge **4**
Tambo Amazonico Lodge **5**
Tahuayo Lodge **7**
Yacumama Lodge **8**
Yarapa River Lodge **6**

Definitely wait before even discussing Amazon lodge packages. To downtown Iquitos, an automobile taxi costs about S/10; a *motocarro* costs S/7. If a taxi driver offers to take you for less, he will certainly take you directly to a hotel where he can earn commission, not where you necessarily want to go. (The difference could be a lot more than the few soles you save on the taxi fare.) City buses (S/1) are available outside the gates of the airport on the main road (they travel along Ocampo/Tacna/Grau), but unless you have a very manageable backpack as your only luggage, it's not worth the hassle.

BY BOAT   Arriving by boat is an option only for those with the luxury of ample time and patience. It takes about a week when the river is high (and 3–4 days in the dry season) to reach the capital city of Loretos upriver along the Amazon from Pucallpa or Yurimaguas.

To travel to Colombia or Brazil (Manaus, Santarém, and Belém) by boat, your best bet is by river cruise. The Iquitos port, Puerto Masusa, is about 3km (1¾ miles) north of the Plaza de Armas. See "Cruises," below, for more details.

Visitor Information

A municipal **tourism information booth** (✆ 065/260-251) is at the arrivals terminal baggage claim at the airport. It maintains a chart of hotels and costs, and the staff is happy to dispense information (and frequently opinions) about the various jungle-tour and lodge operators.

One of Peru's most helpful tourism information offices is on the north side of the Plaza de Armas at Napo 232 (✆ 065/236-144). The English-speaking staff has free maps and lists of all recommended hotels and tour operators (including photo albums of lodges), and will try to sort through the (often intentionally) confusing sales pitches of jungle-tour companies. The office is open Monday through Saturday from 8am to 8pm, as well as occasional Sunday mornings.

FAST FACTS   ATMs and banks are located along Putumayo and Próspero, on the south side of the Plaza de Armas. Two banks that exchange traveler's checks and cash are **Banco de Crédito,** Putumayo 201, at Próspero, and **Banco Continental,** Sargento Lores 171. Money-changers can usually be found hanging around the Plaza de Armas and along Putumayo and Próspero, but calculate the exchange beforehand and count your money carefully.

If you're looking to cross into Brazil or Colombia, the **Brazilian Consulate** is located at Sargento Lores 363 (✆ 065/232-081), and the **Colombian Consulate** is at Callao 200 (✆ 065/231-461). You should make contact with the embassies in Lima or even at home before traveling to Peru. For questions about border-crossing formalities for jungle travel to and from Brazil and Colombia, visit or call the **Migraciones** office at Malecón Tarapacá 382 (✆ 065/235-371).

In an **emergency,** call ✆ 105. You can also call **Cruz Roja (Red Cross)** at ✆ 065/241-072 for medical emergencies, and ✆ 065/267-555 for **fire emergencies.** For medical attention, go to one of the following hospitals or clinics: **Clínica Ana Stahl,** Av. la Marina 285 (✆ 065/252-535); **EsSalud,** Av. la Marina 2054 (✆ 065/250-333); or **Hospital Regional de Loreto,** Av. 28 de Julio s/n, Punchana (✆ 065/252-004). The **tourist police** office is located at Sargento Lores 834 (✆ 065/242-081). There's also a **Tourist Protection Service** office at Huallaga 311 (✆ 065/243-490).

Most Internet *cabinas* in Iquitos stay open late, and rates are about S/2 per hour. One to try is **Estación Internet,** Fitzcarrald 120 (✆ 065/223-608). Several other cabinas are

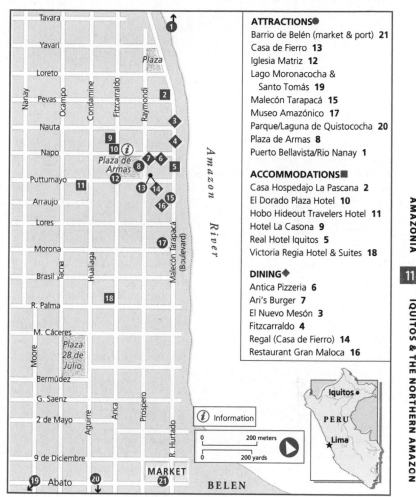

ATTRACTIONS●
Barrio de Belén (market & port) 21
Casa de Fierro 13
Iglesia Matriz 12
Lago Moronacocha &
   Santo Tomás 19
Malecón Tarapacá 15
Museo Amazónico 17
Parque/Laguna de Quistococha 20
Plaza de Armas 8
Puerto Bellavista/Rio Nanay 1

ACCOMMODATIONS■
Casa Hospedajo La Pascana 2
El Dorado Plaza Hotel 10
Hobo Hideout Travelers Hotel 11
Hotel La Casona 9
Real Hotel Iquitos 5
Victoria Regia Hotel & Suites 18

DINING◆
Antica Pizzeria 6
Ari's Burger 7
El Nuevo Mesón 3
Fitzcarraldo 4
Regal (Casa de Fierro) 14
Restaurant Gran Maloca 16

AMAZONIA

11

IQUITOS & THE NORTHERN AMAZON

located near the Plaza de Armas, particularly on Próspero and Putumayo. The small cabina (no name) next to the entrance to the Casa de Fierro is pretty dependable.

Iquitos's **post office** is at Arica 403, on the corner of Morona (© **065/223-812**). The **Telefónica del Perú** office is at Arica 276.

Getting Around

For all practical purposes, Iquitos is an island city, defined by water—not just the mighty Amazon, which borders it to the west, but also a complex network of smaller rivers and streams, and a series of lakes just outside the city. The riverfront along the Amazon is a long boulevard, Malecón Tarapacá, with a pedestrian walkway. It reaches all the way from

> **(Tips) Biblioteca Amazónica**
>
> The Iquitos municipal library, Biblioteca Amazónica (Malecón Tarapacá 354, 2nd
> Floor; ✆ 065/242-353), is a handsome public space inhabiting an old rubber
> baron's mansion and overlooking the *malecón* and Río Amazonas. The reading
> room features lots of carved wood and colorful tiles. If a visit to the Amazon has
> whetted your appetite for old maps or information on the jungle, you can find it
> here, in the largest collection of historical documents on the Amazon basin in
> Peru. It's open Monday through Friday from 9am to noon.

the focal point of downtown to the shabby but picturesque Belén district. Próspero is the
main avenue of communication from the main square to residential zones south.

BY MOTOTAXI & TAXI *Motocarros* are everywhere in Iquitos; if you don't mind the
noise and wind in your face (and aren't worried about accidents), it's a great way to get
around. In-town fares are S/2. Regular car taxis are only slightly less ubiquitous; most
trips in town cost S/3.

BY BUS *Combis* and *omnibuses* (buses) travel principal routes but are much less comfortable and not much less expensive than more convenient *motocarros*. The fare is S/1.

BY MOTORCYCLE If you want to travel around town as Iquiteños do, rent a small
moto, or motorcycle. Try **Visión Motos,** Nauta 309 (✆ 065/234-759). Rates are about
$45 per day or $5 per hour.

BY FOOT Although the city is spread over several square miles, the core of downtown
Iquitos is compact and easy to get around on foot, and even the waterfront Belén district
is easy to walk to. Some hostels and hotels are a distance from the main square, though,
requiring at least the occasional use of inexpensive *motocarros*.

WHAT TO SEE & DO
In Iquitos

Although the **Plaza de Armas** is perhaps not Peru's most distinguished, it is, as always,
one of the focal points in town. It is marked by the early-20th-century neo-Gothic **Iglesia Matríz** (parish church), built in 1919. Many of the church's most attractive elements,
such as the tower, were later additions. Across the square stands the **Casa de Fierro,** or
Iron House, which was designed by Gustave Eiffel for the 1889 Paris Exhibition. The
walls, ceiling, and balcony are plastered in rectangular sheets of iron. Said to be the first
prefabricated house in the Americas, it was shipped unassembled from Europe and built
on-site where it currently stands.

One block back from the plaza, facing the Amazon River, the riverfront promenade
Malecón Tarapacá was enlarged and improved a few years back with fountains (one a
giant pink dolphin), benches, and street lamps, making it the focus of Iquitos urban life.
The *malecón* is lined with several exquisite 19th-century mansions, relics from the rubber
heyday, lined with Portuguese glazed tiles, or *azulejos*. The most spectacular is probably
Casa Hernández, nos. 302–308. Other houses worth checking out along the boulevard
are **Casa Fitzcarrald,** Napo 200–212, an adobe house belonging to a famed rubber
baron; **Casa Cohen,** Próspero 401–437; **Casa Morey,** Brail, on the first block off the
malecón; and the **Logia Unión Amazónica,** Nauta 262.

The **Museo Amazónico,** Malecón Tarapacá 386 (© **065/231-072**), occasionally has
interesting exhibits of Amazon folklore and tribal art, and a curious collection of 76
Indian statues made of fiberglass but fashioned as if they were bronze. Reportedly, some
of the mothers whose children served as models for the works freaked out when they were
covered in plaster for the moulds, thinking the children would be buried alive. The
museum building, which dates to the mid–19th century, is a nicely restored example of
the *malecón's* period mansions. The museum is open Monday through Friday from 8am
to 1pm and 3 to 7pm, and Saturday from 9am to 1pm. Admission is S/3.

The waterfront **Barrio de Belén ★**, about a 15-minute walk south along the *malecón,*
is Iquitos's most unusual quarter. Known for its sprawling, colorful, and odiferous open-
air market, where you'll find a bounty of strange and wonderful Amazon fish, fauna, and
fruits, Belén's residential district is a seedy and extremely poor but endlessly fascinating
shantytown. Houses are constructed above the waters of the Amazon, and when the river
is high, transportation is by canoe. Visitors are free to walk about in dry season (or, for
much of the year, to take a locally arranged canoe trip) and see the houses—some on
stilts, others floating during the rainy season; for safety's sake, though, go in a group and
during the day only. It's an atmospheric and photogenic place, akin to Calcutta—you'll
see scrappy kids tumbling out of clapboard houses and playing with pet monkeys, and a
few houses proudly outfitted with cable TV and other modern conveniences. Exercise
some caution and restraint if walking around the area with expensive camera equipment.
Most residents of the neighborhood, while perhaps puzzled at foreigners' interest in the
aesthetics of their dilapidated streets, are more than approachable for photos, if you ask
respectfully. The animated market, which extends over several blocks, is itself a wild place
to visit, with all sorts of extraordinary exotic items for sale, including potions used by
faith healers, *paiche* fish, and yummy Amazonian fruits such as *maracuyá* (passion fruit),
aguaje, cocona, and others. Look for the stands set up with blenders, cranking out fruit
juices and smoothies (*refrigerios* and *jugos*).

Attractions near Iquitos

PUERTO BELLAVISTA & RIO NANAY   This Río Mañon port and suburb, a couple
kilometers from downtown at the northern edge of Iquitos, has a pretty white-sand beach
(Playa Nanay) that locals enjoy and that is safe for swimming during summer months.
It's also a good spot to hire a boat and cruise down to the confluence of the Amazon and
Nanay rivers, where you can appreciate the difference in water colors (muddy brown and
black), passing beaches, and a handful of local communities—among them the Boras and
Yaguas—along the way. To get there, take a *colectivo* marked BELLAVISTA/NANAY, which
leaves from points along Próspero.

PARQUE/LAGUNA DE QUISTOCOCHA   A resort complex about 13km (8 miles)
south of Iquitos, the Quistococha Lagoon and Tourist Park has a nice beach and swimming area. It's mostly a spot for local families to hang out on weekends. Attractions
include picnic grounds, paddleboats, an aquarium, a walking path around the lagoon, a
zoo with exotic jungle animals and fish, including monkeys, serpents, jaguars, and
pumas, and a fish hatchery that's populated by giant *paiche* fish. There's a restaurant on
the grounds, as well as informal food stalls set up near the entrance to the park. To get
there, you can take a 20-minute ride in a *motocarro* (about $3) or catch a colectivo
marked QUISTOCOCHA (S/2) on the corner of Moore and Bermúdez.

LAGO MORONACOCHA & SANTO TOMAS   Southwest of Iquitos, the lake at Moronacocha is little more than a place to relax at a couple of bars by the water, although locals

11

IQUITOS & THE NORTHERN AMAZON

head out there to swim and water-ski. Another 16km (10 miles) or so south of Moronacocha is another lake complex, Rumococha, and the small fishing village of Santo Tomás, known for its pottery artisans. It also has a lake (Lago Mapacocha) and resortlike activities, such as paddleboats and dugout canoes. To get there, board a colectivo marked AEROPUERTO on Tacna/Grau; ask to be let off at the turnoff to Santo Tomás. There are colectivos waiting at the intersection that ferry people back and forth to Santo Tomás. You can also get there by *motocarro;* the 20-minute ride is about $4.

Shopping in Iquitos

The most intriguing shopping option is the Belén open-air market (above), although you'll likely find more to photograph and smell than to actually buy. For local artisans' goods, there aren't many options; try **Centro Artesanal Anaconda,** Malecón Tarapacá-Boulevard, the sparsely populated market downstairs from the *malecón,* or **Mercado Artesanal de San Juan,** the larger market with wooden outdoor stalls selling hammocks, woodcarvings, and paintings. The market's on Avenida Quiñones, Km 4.5, on the way out to the airport (about 3km/1¾ miles from downtown). Unlike most markets in Peru, here many of the sellers are also the craftspeople behind the work. Some of the best crafts, including textiles and pottery, come from the Shipibo Indian tribe of the Amazon.

Art Gallery Camu-Camu, Trujillo 498 (© **065/253-120**), showcases the work of the most famous local artist, Francisco Grippa, whose colorful paintings evoke Amazonian themes, including jungle flora and fauna. Grippa's exuberant and expressive style, known in the United States and Europe, has been labeled "grippismo." He uses local materials, including a canvas made from tree bark. The gallery is open daily from 10am to 1pm and 4 to 7pm. Tour groups often visit the Grippa's home/gallery in Pevas, the oldest town in the Peruvian Amazon, about 150km (93 miles) downriver from Iquitos.

JUNGLE TOURS, LODGES & RIVER CRUISES

The mighty Amazon reaches widths of about 4km (2½ miles) beyond Iquitos, and the river basin contains 2,000 species of fish (among them, everyone's favorite, piranhas); 4,000 species of birds (including 120 hummingbirds); native mammals such as anteaters, tapirs, marmosets, and pink dolphins; and 60 species of reptiles, including caimans and anacondas.

Although the town itself holds a kind of sultry fascination, ecotourism is the primary draw for visitors to Iquitos, and the giant Amazon river system just beyond the city holds a wealth of natural wonders: rustic jungle lodges, canopy walks, and opportunities for bird-watching, piranha fishing, visits to Indian villages, and wildlife spotting (as well as less-standard activities, such as shaman consultations and *ayahuasca* drug ceremonies). Your options for exploring the jungle are **lodge stays,** which include jungle activities such as treks and canoe excursions; **river cruises;** or more adventurous **camping treks** with private guides. Most people head for lodges of varying degrees of rusticity and distance from Iquitos. The jungle is immense, and most parts of it are inaccessible. Immersing yourself in anything resembling pristine jungle is both costly and time-consuming. The northern Amazon basin within reach of Iquitos has been explored and popularly exploited far longer than the more remote southern jungle areas of Manu and Tambopata.

Don't expect to spend your time in the jungle checking off a lengthy wildlife list of sightings; no matter where you go, your opportunities for viewing more than a couple of species of birds, fish, and mammals will be severely limited. You'll see lots of birds and, if you're lucky, perhaps a few monkeys, caimans, and pink dolphins. (For deeper and

For a quick and simple experience, you can stay at a lodge only an hour or two (within a 50km/31-mile radius) by boat from Iquitos, in secondary jungle. You're likely to see more fauna and have a more authentic experience in primary rainforest, but you'll have to travel much farther (beyond a radius of 80km/50 miles; up to 4 hr. by boat) and pay quite a bit more for the privilege. Generally, you must trade comforts for authenticity. Very short trips (2–3 days) are unlikely to produce much in the way of wildlife, although you can still expect enjoyable contact with the Amazonian habitat. A true foray into virgin jungle, far from the heavy footsteps of thousands of guides and visitors before you, requires at least a week of demanding camping and trekking. Hard-core eco-types might want to contract private guides to go deep into the *selva* and camp. (Ask at the tourism information office for a list of licensed, official guides; the office also has a list of black-listed guides.)

Prices for lodges and tours vary tremendously. For conventional, easy-to-reach lodges contracted in Iquitos, lodge tours average around $50 to $65, and $175 or more per person per day for lodges located farthest from the city. Some budget lodges offer bargain rates, as little as $30 a day (although, in most cases, you get what you pay for), and independent guides might charge as little as $15 a day. Costs are directly related to distance from Iquitos; the farther they are, the more expensive they are. Costs include transportation, lodging, buffet-style meals, and guided activities (beverages cost extra).

Be careful: There are lots of lookalike lodges and tours. Lodges and ecotourism companies come and go, and everyone's competing for your dollars. Hustlers, con artists, and all manner of disreputable touts abound in Iquitos, and you need to exercise a certain amount of caution before handing over money for a promised itinerary. The local tourism office (© **065/260-251**) works hard to ferret out guides, tours, and lodges with bad reputations. The office has photo albums of lodges and a thick book of travelers' comments, with pages and pages of frank opinions on virtually every lodge and tour. If you're making a tour decision on the ground in Iquitos, it's a good idea to visit the office first for the most up-to-date information.

(Tips) Eco-nomizing

Although the prices of some lodges might seem steep to backpackers accustomed to dropping $10 for a place to sleep in other parts of Peru, getting by on $50 a day or a little more is really a pretty decent bargain, considering that food, river transportation, English-speaking guides, fishing and wildlife trips and treks, and shelter are all included. That said, you can almost certainly get a better deal when signing up with a lodge or tour on the ground in Iquitos by going door-to-door to the sales offices and comparing programs and prices than you would contracting one in Lima or from your home country before stepping foot in Peru. Especially during the off season, lodges are willing to negotiate. However, you risk not getting the tour you want when you want it. For many travelers, the extra hassle and uncertainty might not be worth the dollars saved. Prices quoted on websites and through travel agents might be quite negotiable if you contact operators directly, depending on season and occupancy levels.

Most jungle lodges feature either individual rustic thatched-roof bungalows or main buildings with individual rooms, beds with mosquito netting, communal dining areas, hammock lounges, covered plank walkways, toilets, and either hot- or cold-water sinks and showers. A few lodges have extras such as swimming pools, lookout towers, canopy walkways, and electricity. Guests are taken on guided day- and nighttime excursions, including jungle walks, piranha fishing, and canoe and motorboat trips to spot birds, caimans, and dolphins. Many lodges offer artificial, even cheesy, visits with local Indian tribes, staged for your pleasure, and some host *ayahuasca* rituals (see "Trippin' Amazon Style" on p. 369).

Jungle Lodges

The following are tour operators and lodges with good reputations in the area. The list is not by any means exhaustive; there are dozens more agencies and lodges, but reports on many of them are less than stellar.

- **Explorama Lodge ★**, Av. la Marina 340, Iquitos (© 065/252-530, or 800/707-5275 in the U.S. and Canada; www.explorama.com). The longest-established jungle-tour company in Iquitos (now into its 5th decade) and owned by an American, Explorama operates three lodges and a campsite, ranging from 160km (100 miles) to 40km (25 miles) downriver from Iquitos. The company has one of the best reputations of the Northern Amazon lodge operators, bolstered by good guides, very good facilities and food, and a range of flexible activities. The company's first lodge, **Explorama Inn** (80km/50 miles from Iquitos), is large and attractive, with two long wings and a lovely restaurant/bar and communal area. Explorama owns the jungle's most luxurious lodge, **Ceiba Tops** (40km/25 miles from Iquitos), a jungle resort hotel with air-conditioning, a spectacular pool with a slide, and a Jacuzzi. There are trails nearby, and boats can take you out onto the river for dolphin-spotting and fishing, but Ceiba Tops is much more about relaxing in style surrounded by jungle. Near **Explornapo** (the Explorama lodge deepest in the jungle), there's a splendid **canopy walkway ★**, one of the longest in the world. At a height of 36m (118 ft.) and a rambling length of 500m (1,640 ft.), it alone is one of the highlights of a visit to this part of the Peruvian Amazon. It's possible to mix and match lodges; a popular plan for many travelers is several days at Explornapo (or, more adventurous still, the rustic Explortambos campsite) followed by a couple days of relative luxury at Ceiba Tops. Prices range from $270 for a 2-day/1-night trip to Ceiba Tops to $890 for a 5-day/4-night trip to Explornapo. Web specials as well as special programs are frequently available.
- **Paseos Amazónicos,** Pevas 246, Iquitos (© 065/231-618 or 01/417-576 in Lima; www.paseosamazonicos.com). This company operates three well-run lodges, **Tambo Amazónico, Sinchicuy,** and **Yanayacu.** The farthest, Tambo Amazónico, is 180km (112 miles) upriver from Iquitos on the Yarapa River; the other two are much closer and focus on quick in-and-out tours. The Sinchicuy (30km/19 miles from Iquitos) is one of the oldest established lodges in the zone. Yanayacu lodge is 60km (37 miles) from the city. The company is honest and professionally run, and offers good and clean budget- to midrange standard tours in rustic shared lodges. The lodges are offered by several Peruvian and international travel agents and tour operators. Adventurers might be interested in the company's camping trips to the Pacaya-Samiria National Reserve, one of the best opportunities to rough it and catch glimpses of Amazonian wildlife (see "Into the Wild: Farther Afield from Iquitos" on p. 370). A 4-day/3-night trip to the Amazon Sinchicuy and Tambo Yanayacu lodges starts at $311, while 2-night trips to the nearer lodges cost $168.

(Fun Facts Trippin' Amazon Style

Several Amazon lodges offer *ayahuasca* ceremonies, which involve the privilege of taking a natural hallucinogenic potion prepared by an "authentic" Indian shaman, at $15 a shot. It's the local version of taking peyote with Don Juan, but at some joints, it teeters on the edge of spring break at the ecolodge. *Ayahuasca* is an authentic ritual and herbal drug with deep roots in local communities. A shaman boils diverse Amazonian plants and roots for up to 6 hours, and the resulting potion can indeed be very hallucinogenic. It is taken as part of a cleansing ritual, to purify the body and mind. The ceremony is not to be taken lightly, although some lodges seem to do just that, for the sake of selling a cool Amazon experience. Reports circulate about some travelers losing their minds, but it's hard to say if they should be taken seriously. At a minimum, *ayahuasca* is a cultural practice that should be respected and not abused by gringos.

- **Tahuayo Lodge** ★★★, Amazonia Expeditions, 10305 Riverburn Dr., Tampa, FL 33647 (© **800/262-9669;** www.perujungle.com). One of the most outstanding Amazon ecolodges in Peru, this low-impact ecoproperty, associated with the Rainforest Conservation Fund, lies on the shores of the River Tahuayo, about 4 hours from Iquitos. *Outside* magazine has touted it as one of the top-10 travel finds in the world. It is the only lodge with access to the Tamshiyacu-Tahuayo Reserve, a splendid area for primate and other wildlife viewing (it counts 500 species of birds). Because of its remoteness, it recommends visits of at least a week; programs are individually tailored. The 15 cabins are open year-round, and the lodge offers an excellent schedule of excursions ranging from rugged (jungle survival training) to relaxed; most enticing are zip-line canopy ropes for treetop viewing. An 8-day/7-night trip is $1,295 per person (additional days $100).
- **Yacumama Lodge** ★★, Sargento Lores 149, Iquitos (© **065/235-510**, or 800/854-0023 in the U.S. and Canada; www.yacumamalodge.com). Yacumama is an American-owned, first-class lodge with a handsome main house, private bungalows, solar power, and ecosensitive flush toilets deep in the Amazon—186km (116 miles) upriver on Río Yarapa (a tributary of the Río Ucayali). It's on an excellent 7,000-hectare (17,290-acre) forest reserve with a cool 10-story canopy tower; the treetop perspective is nearly as spectacular as the Explorama canopy walkway, although you miss the possibility of walking above the trees. In operation since 1993, Yacumama has built a solid reputation with its environmentally sound engineering, good jungle treks, and possibilities for dolphin sightings, and the company dedicates a percentage of its profits to conservation efforts. The company offers Machu Picchu/Cusco program extensions. A 4-day/3-night stay starts at $750.
- **Yarapa River Lodge** ★★★ (© **065/993-1172**, or 315/952-6771 in the U.S. and Canada; www.yarapa.com). Associated with Cornell University (which built a tropical biology field lab for students and faculty here), this terrific conservation-minded lodge—two-time winner of a World Travel Award as the top resort in Peru—is 177km (110 miles) upriver on the Yarapa River, an Amazon tributary, near the Reserva Nacional Pacaya-Samiria. Surrounded by pristine jungle and oxbow lakes that teem with wildlife, the beautiful lodge features full solar power, composting, and flush toilets

Into the Wild: Farther Afield from Iquitos

The opportunities for enjoying spectacular wildlife sightings and experiencing how locals truly live in the Amazon are severely diminished in most areas where the jungle lodges are located. For primary rainforest and more authentic native villages, you have to be willing to rough it more than traditional lodges force you to. However, as jungle tourism in Peru continues to grow, several midrange and luxury cruise operators are now organizing river cruises to one of Peru's greatest jungle zones.

About 300km (190 miles) south of Iquitos, a couple days removed by boat and sandwiched between the Marañon and Ucayali rivers, is the **Pacaya-Samiria National Reserve ★★**, the largest protected area in Peru and one of the most pristine in the world. Established in 1982, it contains 2,080,000 hectares (5,139,800 acres) of thick, untouched rainforest and wetlands. Incredibly, that accounts for 1.5% of Peru's total surface area. Riddled with rivers and 85 lakes, it's huge and daunting, and should be explored only with an experienced guide. Some of the Amazon's finest and most abundant wildlife resides in the reserve, such as pink dolphins, macaws, black caimans, spider monkeys, and giant river turtles. The reserve's numbers are staggering: It is home to 539 species of birds, 101 species of mammals, 256 kinds of fish, and 22 species of orchids. Guides typically take visitors by dugout canoe from **Lagunas** (upstream from Iquitos) through the reserve. Villages on the outskirts of the reserve worth visiting are **San Martín de Timpishia** and **Puerto Miguel.** To enter the reserve, officially you need permission from **INRENA,** the Peruvian parks authority. Contact its office in Iquitos (Pevas 350; ✆ **065/231-230**) or in Lima (Los Petirrojos 355, Urbanización El Palomar; ✆ **01/224-3298**) for additional information. You'll need a minimum of 4 or 5 days to do the trip from Iquitos. Jungle Expeditions, Amazon Tours and Cruises, and Paseos Amazónicos all organize Pacaya-Samiria National Reserve river cruises and, in the case of the latter, camping trips (for contact information, see "Jungle Lodges" and "Cruises," above).

The Cocamas native community at San Martín de Tipishca, in the northern edge of the Pacaya-Samiria National Reserve, has an American woman working with a waste-management system. Both lodge facilities and guides are first-rate and among the finest in the Peruvian Amazon; spacious private bungalows are almost luxurious. A 4-day/3-night trip (with private bathroom) runs $1,020 per person; a 7-day/6-night trip is $1,575 per person. Travelers can opt for an overnight in the remote Pacaya-Samiria National Park Reserve, 4 hours away by boat.

Cruises

Riverboat cruises down the Amazon and along its tributaries don't allow you to see much in the way of fauna or pristine jungle, although you will likely spot lots of birds and dolphins. Cruises are best for people who don't want to rough it too much and who like the romance of traveling the Amazon by boat, although varying degrees of rusticity and

with it as an interpreter and is reaching out to travelers who want an experience of close contact with the people of an Amazon village. Reports are that the trips are extremely professional in character. Contact **Virginia Blum,** care of her office at Piura 1072, in Iquitos (© **065/251-185;** virginiablum@yahoo.com). The community charges $40 per day per person, plus the $19 permit to enter the preserve. Trips usually last 4 to 5 days and are limited to groups of 12 to 15 people (although as few as two people can arrange a trip). Other, less involved visits to local native communities, such as the Huitotos, Boras, and Yaguas, can also be arranged. Inquire about independent trips at the tourism office on the Plaza de Armas in Iquitos.

Another option for down-and-dirty exploration of Amazon culture and sights is to cruise the rivers not on (relatively) pampered boats that take tourists out to lodges, but aboard the **three-decked riverboats** that form the transportation backbone of the region, ferrying people back and forth from villages on Amazon tributaries to Iquitos and other towns. The boats are rough going, stuffed with animals and densely packed families and their household goods, and are almost entirely absent of comforts. You should take along plenty of bottled water, a hammock, and foodstuffs such as fruit and canned items. Journeys can last several days, but slinging yourself into a hammock on the top deck and floating slowly down the Huallaga or Ucayali will certainly win points among your friends when it comes to regaling them with vacation heroics. For budget travelers, it's a perfect antidote to high-priced lodges and river cruises: It's virtually impossible to spend more than $15 a day, including transportation.

For more details about how to organize trips to Pacaya-Samiria or simple river transport along the rivers, contact the helpful folks at the tourist information office on the Plaza de Armas in Iquitos for up-to-the-minute suggestions. See also "Independent Guides," below, for information on treks with independent guides.

luxury are available. Many cruises stop off at reserves for jungle walks and visits to local villages. Some of the best cruises are those to the Pacaya-Samiria National Reserve; see "Into the Wild: Farther Afield from Iquitos," above, for details.

- **GreenTracks Amazon Tours & Cruises,** Requena 336 (© **800/892-1035** in the U.S. and Canada, or 065/231-611; www.amazontours.net). This American-owned company has been active in the northern Amazon for more than 4 decades. Its midlevel cruises are aboard older, air-conditioned fleets that aren't quite as nice or as expensive as those of Jungle Expeditions (see below). Four-night riverboat cruise on the Delfin II is $1,808 per person in a double room; a 7-night cruise on a rubber boom–era riverboat to the Pacaya-Samiria National Reserve is $2,500 per person.

• **Aqua Expeditions** ★★★ (© 866/603-3687 in the U.S. and Canada, or 065/601-053 in Peru; www.aquaexpeditions.com) has blown the old concept of creaky, uncomfortable Amazon cruises out of the water. Its luxury river cruises are aboard the gorgeous, modern 130-foot MV *Aqua,* designed by the well-known Peruvian architect Jordi Puig, and the menu is overseen by a fashionable Lima chef, Miguel Schiaffino. Sleeping quarters are sleekly contemporary, with swank indoor and outdoor lounge spaces, 12 air-conditioned rooms with high-quality bedding, and large, panoramic windows that make it look like you're watching a big-screen movie of the Amazon. Cruises depart from Iquitos and go through the Pacaya-Samiria National Reserve. Prices range from $2,250 to $5,250 per person for 3-, 4- and 7-day cruises.

• **Jungle Expeditions** ★, Av. Quiñones 1980 (© 065/261-583; www.junglex.com). This company offers luxury river cruises on a fleet of six very elegant, 19th-century style boats, and cruises upriver along the Río Ucayali. Prices are about $2,700 for 7-day and $3,300 for 10-day expeditions. The company also accepts passengers through their Lima booking office (© 01/241-3232) or **International Expeditions** (© 800/633-4734; www.internationalexpeditions.com) in the United States, which offers air-inclusive packages and programs with Cusco and Machu Picchu extensions.

Independent Guides

For travelers who want to get away from the lodges and groups and riverboats, more flexible independent treks into the jungle could be the way to go. You'll see more fauna, and especially flora, than will other travelers, and you'll get to visit native communities that aren't merely putting on a show for your benefit. You'll rough it in varying degrees (everything from eating cans of tuna and rice and beans cooked over an open fire, to enjoying fresh-caught fish straight from the river, to camping in makeshift sites along the way). To immerse yourself in the dense Amazonian jungle, you need an experienced, reliable wilderness guide. Scores of independent guides operate in the jungle around Iquitos and scout for tourists in the city. Their quality and professionalism vary tremendously, however, and many plainly are not to be trusted. Several guides in Iquitos have criminal records for robbing the very tourists who trusted them. The local tourism office maintains a book of disreputable, blacklisted guides.

Because you're going to be spending all your time in the jungle with the guide, depending on him to lead you, communicate with you, cook for you, and build good campsites, selecting a competent guide is of the utmost importance. Most guides are "extralegal"; only a couple of guides in Iquitos are officially licensed to operate as full-fledged independent jungle guides (possessing a license, an expensive bureaucratic requirement out of reach of most guides, isn't the only determination, however). No matter what you hear from other travelers, if you're considering hiring a guide for a solo or small-group trek into the jungle, visit the tourism information office in Iquitos before exchanging moneys; ask for the office personnel's recommendations—which they're usually happy to dispense—and take a look at the review books of comments about guides. Rates depend on the number of travelers and length of trips; they can range from $40 to $50 a day per person to more than $100 per day.

If you manage to locate a guide for an independent trip, never pay upfront before your arrival in Iquitos; some travelers have been scammed.

WHERE TO STAY

For many visitors, Iquitos amounts to little more than a way station on their journey to the Amazon. As a result, the city has fewer good hotels than its environs have attractive jungle lodges. Things are improving, though, and Iquitos finally got its first high-end **373** hotel a couple years back. Midrange hotels are more expensive than similarly equipped hotels in many other parts of the country, but discounts are frequently available at most top-level and midrange hotels.

All but the cheapest *hostales* (inns) will usually arrange for a free airport transfer if you pass on your arrival information ahead of time. Even so, be careful whom you tell at the airport that you're expecting a certain hotel to pick you up; always make sure that the driver already knows your name before going anywhere with him.

Expensive

Hotel El Dorado Plaza ★ Occupying a privileged place on the Plaza de Armas, the El Dorado Plaza fills a gaping hole in the Iquitos hotel scene—the city's first bona fide high-end hotel. A modern high-rise building, with a soaring lobby, a good restaurant, and an excellent outdoor pool, this is clearly the finest hotel in town. Rooms are large and nicely outfitted, if not quite at the upper-echelon levels found in Lima or Cusco. Guests have a view of either the main square or the pool. The hotel has quickly become popular with foreigners who come to Iquitos for top-of-the-line jungle tours. See the website for frequent deals—occasionally as much as half the rack rate.

Napo 258 (Plaza de Armas), Iquitos. (℗ **065/222-555.** Fax 065/224-304. 65 units. $242–$297 double; $385–$660 suite. Rates include breakfast buffet. AE, DC, MC, V. **Amenities:** Restaurant; 2 bars; coffee shop; concierge; fitness center; Jacuzzi; outdoor pool; sauna. *In room:* A/C, TV, fridge, hair dryer.

Moderate

Real Hotel Iquitos The former (and formerly grand) state-owned Hotel de Turistas is now a curious hotel with a throw-back appeal to those who shy away from internationally flavored but anonymous chain hotels (and a good deal of comfort). This midsize hotel, overlooking the Amazon, seems even larger and emptier than it is; its semi-abandoned, somewhat run-down feel reminds me of grand old hotels in Cuba. Admittedly, that has limited appeal for most travelers. Some rooms are surprisingly expansive, and a few have enviable balconies overlooking the *malecón* and the river. If you score such a room (ask to see a few first), you'll have yourself a deal (no. 312 is huge and has its own terrace). They're simply furnished, with some unique touches, such as red curtains and green walls (kind of cool in a Lynchiam, offbeat way), but it's not the place for folks in search of great air-conditioning and top-shelf service. No other hotel can boast its river views, though.

Malecón Tarapacá s/n, Iquitos. (℗)/fax **065/231-011.** 54 units. $45 double with view; $23 double without view; $80 suite. Rates include continental breakfast. MC, V. **Amenities:** Restaurant; bar. *In room:* A/C, TV.

Victoria Regia ★ (Value) A comfortable, friendly midsize hotel, the Victoria Regia—named for the lily found throughout the Amazon—is a good choice for both independent travelers and business execs with long-term affairs to attend to in Iquitos. A modern block hotel on a busy residential street about 10 minutes from the main square, the hotel's rooms, with air-conditioning that really cranks, are built around an attractive indoor pool and are just a notch below the Hotel El Dorado Plaza in terms of comfort. The Victoria Regia is part of a small, local, family-owned chain of hotels, which includes the Hotel Acosta and the Heliconia and Zungarococha lodges.

Av. Ricardo Palma 252, Iquitos. (℗ **01/442-4515** for reservations, or (℗)/fax 065/231-983. www.victoria regiahotel.com. 5 units. S/264 double; S/396–S/495 suite. Rates include breakfast buffet. AE, DC, MC, V. **Amenities:** Restaurant; bar; outdoor pool. *In room:* A/C, TV, fridge.

Casa Hospedaje La Pascana (Value) One of the better basic budget inns in Iquitos, the Pascana is a friendly, small place with rooms built around a long, plant-lined, and open-air courtyard. Rooms are very simple, even plain, but not uncomfortable, and they have fans rather than air-conditioning. The place is quiet and peaceful, and just a 2-minute walk from the *malecón* and the Plaza de Armas—reasons why it's often full and popular with small budget-level groups. Don't expect much hot water at this price, although you probably won't care in the sweltering heat.

Pevas 133, Iquitos. © 065/231-418. Fax 065/233-466. 18 units. S/40 double. Rates include taxes and continental breakfast buffet. MC, V. **Amenities:** Cafeteria.

Hobo Hideout Travelers Hotel Jimmy and Sandra opened this quirky budget *hostal*, run in tandem with a small ecotour operator, Great Amazon Safari & Trading Company, and gave it a jungle feel in the city. It was built with native materials, including palm leaves and native woods, and the rooms are well maintained and comfortable for the low prices. It's just 1 block from the main square, and particularly good for backpackers who don't mind sleeping in dorm rooms without air-conditioning. (But the collection of animal skins will turn off anyone with a soft spot for PETA.) Besides a kitchen, it has common reading and TV rooms, a laundry area, and a small swimming pool. The space is replete with jungle plants and a true jungle feel, which sets it apart from its more austere competitors at the budget level.

Jr. Putumayo 437, Iquitos. © 065/234-099. 30 beds. $7 per person in dormitory rooms; $11 double. Rates include taxes and continental breakfast buffet. No credit cards. **Amenities:** Bar; outdoor pool. *In room:* No phone.

Hotel La Casona ★★ (Value) A significant cut above other budget inns in Iquitos, this family-owned small hotel just off the Plaza de Armas is amiable, safe, well-equipped and a superb value. Though it doesn't look like much from the street, it's a better bet than most hotels double its price. Rooms are simply decorated but spacious, and very clean, equipped with either fans or air-conditioning. And they count with several amenities hard to find at this price: wireless (albeit slow) Internet, cable TV and guaranteed hot water. You'll also find a communal kitchen and leafy little patio. Add to that excellent, friendly service, and you've got a winner. It's the kind of place that people come back to time and again.

Calle Fitzcarraldo 147, Iquitos. © 065/234-394. www.hotellacasonaiquitos.com. 23 units. S/60–S/65 with fan; S/75–S/85 with A/C. MC, V. *In room:* A/C (some rooms), TV, Wi-Fi.

WHERE TO DINE

Easygoing restaurants in Iquitos are a good place to sample dishes straight out of the Amazon, such as *paiche* (Amazon river fish), hearts of palm salad, and *juanes* (rice tamales made with minced chicken, pork, or fish, prepared with black olives and egg and wrapped in *bijao* leaves). Although protected species are not supposed to appear on menus, they often do. You might want to think twice before encouraging restaurateurs by ordering turtle-meat soup or alligator. If you venture into the Belén market, be prepared for even more exotic foodstuffs, such as monkey and lizard meat.

Moderate

Antica Pizzeria ★ ITALIAN/PIZZA A sister to several popular branches in Lima's coolest neighborhoods, this stylish, modern Italian restaurant, a half-block from the Plaza de Armas, is a very welcome addition to Iquitos' more local dining scene. Though you

(Tips) Amazonian Delicacies

Throughout South America, the Amazon region is famed for its exotic fruits. In Iquitos, check out stands around the Plaza de Armas for natural fruit juices and ice creams made from stuff hard to get at home, such as *aguaje, maracuyá,* and *cocona.*

can feast on very good thin-crust pizzas from the wood-burning stove or straightforward pastas, chef Juan Seminario's "fusioini" menu also includes more sophisticated fare, such as tuna tartare, octopus salad, and porcini mushroom risotto, as well as *maracuyá* (passion fruit) cheesecake for dessert. The place has a cool, relaxed atmosphere, with a reggae and pop soundtrack and young clientele.

Jr. Napo 159. ⓒ **065/241-988.** Reservations recommended for groups. Main courses S/15–S/35. AE, MC, V. Daily noon–midnight.

El Nuevo Mesón PERUVIAN   Open to the passing parade of people, souvenir sellers, and curious locals on the *malecón,* this lively restaurant is a good place for an introduction to regional specialties and the city itself. If you come on a weekend night, you'll be entertained not only by *altiplano* musicians inside, but also by all kinds of locals hovering about the sidewalk tables, some gawking at your meal. (Several kids jostled for the rights to my leftovers; disadvantaged people occasionally hang around outside restaurants hoping for part of a meal.) Service can be a little haphazard, but most dishes are pretty well prepared. Try dishes such as the regional favorite *pescado a la loretana* (fish filet with *yuca,* fried bananas, and palm-heart salad), and freakier fare such as alligator crisps with fried manioc or curried turtle. There are also steaks, and a long list of fish, dominated by *dorado* (a kind of flaky white catfish).

Malecón Tarapacá 153. ⓒ **065/231-837.** Reservations recommended for groups. Main courses S/18–S/33. MC, V. Daily noon–midnight.

Fitzcarraldo ★ INTERNATIONAL   This popular joint right on the *malecón* has a diverse menu to appeal to travelers of all stripes and appetites. You can go light, choosing from a number of salads, such as *chonta* (palm-heart salad) with avocado and tomato; or regular dinners, including turtle in ginger sauce with manioc. There are also excellent pizzas, sandwiches, and hamburgers, as well as large salads. The restaurant is a convivial place in an open-air house (which once belonged to a British rubber company) featuring updated colonial touches and views of the Amazon, along with good music and sidewalk tables and, unfortunately, underpowered ceiling fans.

Napo 100 (at Malecón Tarapacá). ⓒ **065/243-434.** Reservations recommended for groups. Main courses S/13–S/40. MC, V. Daily noon–midnight.

Regal (Casa de Fierro) INTERNATIONAL/PERUVIAN   In the famed Iron House on the Plaza de Armas, this British pub and hangout is also a reputable restaurant exuding a desultory colonial atmosphere. There are great views from the wraparound iron balcony, with its slowly rotating old-style ceiling fans. It's a good place to try local dishes such as *paiche* (Amazon river fish), which is served any number of ways, or the house specialty, Regal *lomo fino* (beef tenderloin in port-wine sauce), served with salad, Greek rice, a peach stuffed with Russian salad, and french fries. Some find that the food suffers

AMAZONIA

11

IQUITOS & THE NORTHERN AMAZON

| Tips | Chifas in Iquitos |

To some observers, there's something distinctly Asian-feeling about hot, humid, and motorcycle-crazed Iquitos. Waves of Chinese immigrants came as laborers to Iquitos throughout the 20th century, which is the biggest reason there are so many *chifas* (Peruvian-Chinese restaurants) in town. Eating Chinese food at the edge of the Amazon instead of exotic jungle fruits and fish might not be your first impulse in Iquitos, but *chifas* are plentiful and reasonably priced—perfect fallback dining options. Try **Wai Ming,** San Martín 464 at Plaza 28 de Julio (℡ 065/234-391); **Chifa Chong,** Huallaga 165 (no phone); **Hueng Teng,** Nauta at Pucallpa (no phone); and **Chifa Can Chau,** Huallaga 173 (no phone). Other *chifas,* cheaper still, line Avenida Grau, near Plaza 28 de Julio.

in comparison with the general ambience, so you might opt just to kick back with the expat Brits around the bar for a pint.

Putumayo 182, Plaza de Armas (2nd Floor). ℡ 065/222-732. Reservations recommended. Main courses S/18–S/36. AE, DC, MC, V. Daily noon–10pm.

Restaurant Gran Maloca (Value) AMAZONIAN/PERUVIAN   One of Iquitos's most celebrated traditional restaurants, in a grand, tile-covered (and air-conditioned!) 19th-century house, Gran Maloca serves both *platos de la selva*—jungle dishes—and standard upscale fare. Try Amazon-style venison (with cilantro, coconut, and *yuca*), tropical alligator, or less risky items such as filet mignon or tenderloin with mushroom risotto. The split personality of the restaurant is present in the decor: The would-be formal trappings and pastel color scheme coexist with a large collection of colorful butterflies adorning the walls. (If you like those, wait until you get a load of the framed Amazonian bugs, tarantulas, and other creepy crawlers in the bathrooms.) Gran Maloca serves a cheap three-course daily lunch special for just S/12.

Sargento Lores 170. ℡ 065/233-126. Reservations recommended. Main courses S/18–S/36. AE, DC, MC, V. Daily noon–10pm.

Inexpensive

Ari's Burger AMERICAN   A quintessential gringo (and local) hangout right on the Plaza de Armas, this brightly lit fast-food joint is open to the street on two sides—great for people-watching. It seems nearly every visitor to the city hits Ari, called "Gringolandia" by locals both for its clientele and American-style menu, at least once for a burger and fries, ice cream, or fresh-squeezed juice or a milkshake. It's open late and is very popular with folks after rounds at the bars and discos.

Próspero 127 (at the corner of Napo). No phone. Reservations not accepted. Main courses S/5–S/18. MC, V. Daily 8am–3am.

IQUITOS AFTER DARK

More locals than gringos usually make it to the coolest spot in Iquitos, **Café-Teatro Amauta** ★★, Nauta 250 (℡ 065/233-366), a bar-cum-theater with great bohemian flavor and a romantic interior with thick, red curtains framing a small stage that opens to sidewalk tables. Calling itself "El Rincón de los Artistas" (Artists' Corner), it supports live Peruvian, Latin, and Amazon music Monday through Saturday from 10pm until

3am. Try some of the funky *aguardientes* ("fire waters") made from Amazonian herbs. Along the *malecón* are a couple of lively bars with good views of the river. **Arandú Bar,** Malecón Tarapacá 113 (© **065/243-434**), is particularly hopping, a good place for sharing a pitcher of sangria and loud rock 'n' roll. You can also grab a drink at the **Yellow Rose of Texas,** Putumayo 180 (© **065/241-010**), a spot owned by the (controversial and Texan) former head of the local tourist office. Locals hang out at **Noa-Noa,** Pevas 298, at Fitzcarraldo (© **065/232-902**), a disco and rock bar near the Plaza de Armas. When the two-level dance floor is happening, the smoke machines crank and the sound system pumps out salsa and Latin rock.

Northern Peru

Northern Peru is sadly underap-preciated as compared to the vastly more popular south. In fact, most of the region—with the exception of the north-central Cordillera Blanca and Callejón de Huaylas, beacons to international mountain climbers and trekkers—is virtually unknown to most foreigners who travel to Peru. The few who make the effort to get to know the north are mainly those with a specific interest in ancient Peruvian cultures, or hikers and adventurous travelers (including surfers) looking to get out into the rugged country, beyond the reach of the majority of gringos who trod well-beaten paths in the Andes and southern Peru. If you make it to this part of Peru, you might be in for the not unwelcome treat of being one of the few.

You wouldn't know it from the paucity of foreign visitors, but the northern coastal desert of Peru holds some of the country's greatest archaeological treasures: Chan Chan, the great adobe city of the Chimú civilization; 1,500-year-old Moche temples; and the royal tomb that brought the great Lord of Sipán to the world's attention in 1987—Peru's very own King Tut. And the region continues to make news: In 2007, a 4,000-year-old temple and

mural—among the oldest discoveries of their kind in the Americas—were uncovered in the Lambayeque Valley. If archaeology isn't your thing, northern beaches along the vast Pacific coastline—particularly those in and around Máncora, the coast's hot new destination—draw surfers to some of the best waves off South America, and nestled in the *sierra* is one of the country's most charming and beautiful mountain towns, Cajamarca, which could fairly be called the Cusco of the north.

Gringos of a rugged ilk and style of outdoor performance gear do make it in significant number to the Cordillera Blanca, which boasts some of the most beautiful peaks in South America and some of the finest and most challenging trekking and mountain climbing on the continent. Huaraz is the primary base in the Callejón de Huaylas for excursions into the valleys and mountain ranges of the northern Andes. For years, the destination has been favored principally by sports and adventurer travelers, especially hardcore hikers, but the range of trekking destinations and activities is opening up and appealing more to other travelers who also want a taste of Peru's great outdoors.

---

1 TRUJILLO ★

561km (349 miles) N of Lima; 200km (124 miles) S of Chiclayo; 298km (185 miles) SW of Cajamarca

Trujillo, the capital of La Libertad department, is the third-largest city in Peru and one of only two of commercial importance on the entire north coast. Yet the town, founded in 1534 by Diego Almagro on the orders of Francisco Pizarro, retains the Spanish colonial feel of a much smaller town. Locals saunter along the grandly laid-out Plaza Mayor, and the downtown area is a handsome grid of streets lined with elegant, pastel-colored colonial mansions embellished by wrought-iron window grilles.

The importance of the region greatly predates the arrival of the Spaniards, however, and Trujillo is celebrated mostly for a stunning collection of pre-Columbian sites that abound on the outskirts of the city. Looming in the desert are five major archaeological sites, including two of the richest ensembles of Moche temples and ruins of the Chimú culture in Peru. Chan Chan, a monumental adobe complex of royal palaces covering more than 52 sq. km (20 sq. miles), is the primary draw for visitors, but archaeological tours also visit the fascinating Temples of the Moon and Sun (Huacas del Sol y de la Luna), built by the Moche culture around A.D. 500. Several of these sites have been partially restored, but they still require some imagination to conjure a sense of their immensity, the busy daily activity, and the grandeur of the ceremonies once held there.

Just northwest of Trujillo is Huanchaco, a laid-back beach resort that serves as a virtual bedroom community for many visitors, particularly younger travelers with an interest in surfing. Ideally positioned for ruins visits, Huanchaco is also a lot less hectic than Trujillo and has a better roster of cheaper small hotels, budget *hostales* (inns), and seaside seafood restaurants.

Getting There

BY PLANE Trujillo is well connected to the rest of the country, but by far the easiest way to get here is to fly. **LAN** (℡ 01/213-8200; www.lan.com), **AeroCondor** (℡ 01/614-6014), and **Star Perú** (℡ 01/705-9000; www.starperu.com) fly daily to Trujillo from Lima (1 hr.). Flights arrive at the **Aeropuerto Carlos Martínez de Pinillos** on Carretera Huanchaco in the Huanchaco district (℡ 044/464-013). The airport is about 20 minutes northwest of downtown.

A taxi to downtown Trujillo costs about S/20. Huanchaco-Trujillo buses and *colectivos* pass in the general direction of the airport, but at a distance of about a mile from the entrance, making public transportation to and from the airport impractical for anyone with luggage.

BY BUS Like most big cities, Trujillo is serviced by several domestic bus companies from Lima and most major points along the north coast and northern highlands. Many long-distance buses travel at night only. There is no central bus station in Trujillo. Most individual company terminals are near downtown, located to the northwest by the Estadio Mansiche, to the southwest near Avenida España, or to the east near Avenida El Ejército.

The major companies making the 8-hour trip from Lima are **Ormeño** (℡ 01/472-5000; www.grupo-ormeno.com.pe), **Cruz del Sur** (℡ 01/311-5050; www.cruzdelsur.com.pe), and **Oltursa** (℡ 01/708-5000; www.oltursa.com.pe). For the 6-hour trip from Cajamarca, **Transportes Línea** (℡ 044/286-538 in Trujillo, or 076/823-956 in Cajamarca; www.transporteslinea.com.pe) has two classes of service, *económico* and *especial,* which is slightly faster, a bit more comfortable, and a tad more expensive than *económico* class. Transportes Línea (℡ 074/233-497) is also the major company for the 3-hour journey from Chiclayo and the 8-hour journey from Huaraz. **ITTSA** (℡ 044/222-541) runs from Lima, Chiclayo, and Piura. Note that night buses especially have a reputation for being unsafe. In Trujillo, **Ormeño** is at Av. Ejército 342, **Cruz del Sur** at Amazonas 437, **Línea** at Av. América Sur 2857, and **ITTSA** at Mansiche 145.

Visitor Information

The **iPerú** offices are located at the airport (℡ 044/464-226) and downtown at Jr. Diego de Almagro 420, on the Plaza Mayor (also called the Plaza de Armas; ℡ 044/294-561); the downtown office is open Monday through Friday from 9am to 1pm and 2 to 5pm. A small and friendly (although not very well equipped) tourist information office belonging to the **Cámara Regional de La Libertad** is located at Independencia 628, 1 block north of the Plaza de Armas (℡ 044/938-922). The office is open Monday through Saturday from 9am to 6pm. It has free maps, and the staff can advise you on the easiest way to visit Chan Chan and the other major archaeological sites beyond the city.

FAST FACTS Banks that exchange traveler's checks and cash and that have ATMs are **Banco de Crédito,** Jr. Gamarra 562 (℡ 044/242-360); **Banco Latino,** Jr. Gamarra 572 (℡ 044/243-461); and **Banco Continental,** Pizarro 620, in the colonial Casa de la Emancipación. **Interbanc,** located at Pizarro and Gamarra, has a Cirrus/PLUS ATM. Money-changers can usually be found hanging about the Plaza de Armas or along Gamarra.

In case of emergency, call ℡ 105. The helpful **tourist police** are located at Independencia 630, in the Casa Ganoza Chopitea (℡ 044/291-705). For complaints, you can also call the **Tourist Protection Service** at ℡ 044/204-146.

ACCOMMODATIONS ■
Gran Hotel El Golf **22**
Hostal Colonial **8**
Hotel Americano **12**
Hotel Libertador Plaza
Mayor Trujillo **4**
Los Conquistadores
Hotel **20**

DINING ◆
El Mochica **18**
Il Valetino **2**
Restaurant Colonial **7**
Restaurant Demarco **10**
Restaurant Romano **11**

ⓘ Information

ATTRACTIONS ●
Casa Bracomonte **3**
Casa del la
Emancipacion **14**
Casa del Mayorazgo
de Facala **21**
Casa Ganoza Chopitea **9**
Casa Garcia Holguin **5**
Casa Orbegoso **16**

Casa Urquiaga **17**
Catedral/Museo
Catedratico **6**
Iglesia de la Merced **15**
Museo Arqueologico
Casinelli **1**
Museo de Arte
Moderno **19**
Palacio Iturregui **12**

NORTHERN PERU

12

TRUJILLO

If you need medical attention, you're likely to find English-speaking doctors at **Clínica Peruana-Americana,** Av. Mansiche 702 (℡ **044/231-261**). Other hospitals are **Hospital Regional Docente de Trujillo,** Av. Mansiche 795 (℡ **044/231-581**), and **Hospital Belén,** Bolívar 350 (℡ **044/245-281**). In Huanchaco, a clinic *(posta médica)* is located at Atahualpa 437 (℡ **044/461-547**).

For Internet access, two *cabinas* to try are **Cibercafé Internet,** Manuel María Izaga 716 (℡ **044/228-729**), and **Deltanet/Telecom,** Orbegoso 641 (℡ **044/294-327**). Both charge about S/2 per hour.

Trujillo's **post office** is at Independencia 286 (℡ **044/245-941**). A **DHL/Western Union** branch is at Almagro 579 (℡ **044/203-686**). The **Telefónica del Perú** office is at Pizarro 561. A *locutorio* (public calling place) is located at Gamarra 454.

Getting Around

Downtown Trujillo is a grid of relatively short blocks ringed by Avenida España. At the heart of the *centro* is the Plaza de Armas, and the main sights are all nearby on the major streets leading off the square. Getting around the small *centro* is thus best managed on foot. However, you'll need to take either a taxi or a public bus to visit the major archaeological sites outside Trujillo, or the beachside suburb, Huanchaco.

> **Tips** **Guided Tours**
>
> Agencies offering standard city and archaeological tours include **Guía Tours,** Jr.
> Independencia 580 (𝄢 044/245-170); **Chacón Tours,** Av. España 106
> (𝄢 044/255-212); **Consorcio Turístico del Norte,** Jr. Pizarro 478 (𝄢 044/205-
> 645); and **Trujillo Tours,** Diego de Almagro 301 (𝄢 044/233-091). Most standard
> tours cost S/45 to S/60 per person. Tours to El Brujo are generally S/90 to S/120.

Confusing as can be are Trujillo's street names: Nearly every street and avenue has two names and two corresponding signs, one a smaller printed version and the other a fancier painted sign. Most maps go by the smaller, printed name, which is what I give in this chapter.

Several *urbanizaciones,* or residential districts, lie just beyond Avenida España. Urbanización El Recreo, where several resort-style hotels are located, is just west of Av. 28 de Julio. Chan Chan is just 5km (3 miles) northwest of the city, on the way to the airport and Huanchaco. The Huacas de Moche are 8km (5 miles) south of town beyond the Carretera Industrial.

BY TAXI   Taxis are plentiful in Trujillo. Most in-town fares, inside the Avenida España ring, are about S/4. A taxi ride to Chan Chan or Huanchaco costs about S/15. You can hire taxis by the hour (S/20) or by the day S/100 to S/125 to tour archaeological sites in the environs. Be sure to negotiate or ask first in the tourist office to determine the fare.

BY BUS   *Combis* and *ómnibuses* cost S/1. Somewhat rickety buses will take you to Huanchaco for S/3.

BY CAR   If you want to rent a vehicle to make trips to Chan Chan and other sites, or even to travel around the northern region, try **Global Car Rental,** Ecuador 122, Of. 201, Urbanización El Recreo (𝄢 **044/295-548**).

WHAT TO SEE & DO
Colonial Trujillo

Trujillo has an impressive collection of elegant colonial- and republican-era houses *(casas antiguas)* and baroque churches, as well as one of Peru's odder museums of ancient ceramics. A tour of Trujillo rightly begins with the graceful **Plaza de Armas,** where vendors hang out and families in their Sunday finery pose for pictures in front of the Libertad monument. On the square is the **Catedral,** built in the mid–17th century but rather sober and uninteresting, although it has a **Museo Catedrático** (𝄢 **044/235-083**) with silver and gold chalices and bishops' vestments. The museum is open 9am to 1pm and 4 to 7pm Monday to Friday, 9am to 1pm Saturday; admission is S/5. The plaza is ringed by colorful examples of fine colonial-era mansions, including the one that is now home to the Hotel Libertador. Trujillo's pastel colonial buildings are distinguished by their ornamental wrought-iron window grilles, unusual in Peru.

Casa Ganoza Chopitea ★   Better known in Trujillo as La Casa de los Leones (House of the Lions) because of the lions crowning the main door, this 17th-century house is one of the most splendid of the colonial era. Opposite the San Francisco church, the entrance is loaded with baroque and rococo details, including river stones *(canto rodado)* on the ground. A *concha venera,* or welcoming shell, is placed above the door.

Inside the house, you'll pass through the Salón de Varones (Men's Hall), with a high **383**
wooden ceiling, followed by the Salón de Damas (Women's Hall). Look for the curious
air holes in the latter—they go all the way to the roof to allow fresh air to circulate.
Jr. Independencia 630. No phone. Free admission. Mon–Fri 9am–1pm and 3–5pm.

Casa Orbegoso ★ This huge yellow-and-brown mid-18th-century house, once the
property of former president Luis José de Orbegoso, stretches around the block and has
its own plaza facing the San Agustín church. In the entrance are Moorish-Christian
mural paintings that were buried beneath successive baroque, rococo, and finally neoclassical murals. Inside are some original furnishings and mural paintings that can still be
seen around the lower sections of some rooms. The front part of the house still belongs
to descendants of the original owners. Orbegoso, who fought alongside Bolívar in the
War of Independence, is buried in a mausoleum in the house.
Orbegoso 553. ℂ **044/234-950.** Free admission. Tues–Sun 9am–7pm.

Casa Urquiaga (Casa Calonge) ★★ This grand colonial mansion, royal blue with
white window grilles, conserves the 18th-century desk of Simón Bolívar, who lived here
for 2 years after proclaiming Peru's independence in 1824. The home, with three lovely
interior courtyards, is one of Trujillo's most magnificently restored and most historic. It
hosted the first viceroy of Peru in 1604 and was the headquarters of the first bank in
Trujillo. The dining room features spectacular French porcelain, and throughout there
are beautiful chandeliers and mirrors. In a second patio is an exhibit of Moche and Nasca
ceramics. Look for the gold Chavín necklaces and several Chimú ornamental pieces, also
in gold. Today the mansion is owned by the Banco Central.
Jr. Pizarro 446 (Plaza Mayor). No phone. Free admission; passport or other identification required. Mon–
Fri 9am–3pm; Sat–Sun 10am–1pm.

Iglesia de La Merced On a small square set back from the street and next to the
Corte Superior de Justicia (itself worth a peek), La Merced, one of Trujillo's most impressive churches, dates to 1636. It's especially notable for the colorful carved figures in relief
around the cupola, including alternating series of small angels and cherubs supporting
the top section—perhaps 100 in all. Inside, the church is salmon and white, with white
stone arches. At the rear, apparently jammed into the organ loft, is a massive rococo pipe
organ.
Jr. Pizarro 550. No phone. Free admission. Daily 8am–6pm.

Ⓣ **Trujillo's Other Casas Coloniales**

Besides the colonial and republican houses that allow visitors, other houses
worth a look from outside (and occasionally inside, if they're public buildings) are
the bright yellow **Casa de la Emancipación** (now Banco Continental), Pizarro
610, where independence from Spain was proclaimed on December 29, 1820;
Casa Bracamonte, Independencia 441; **Casa Lynch,** on the Plaza de Armas
opposite the cathedral; **Casa Aranda,** Bolívar 621; **Casa del Mayorazgo de
Facalá,** Pizarro 314; and **Casa García Holguín,** Independencia 527 on the Plaza
de Armas.

NORTHERN PERU

12

TRUJILLO

Iglesia y Monasterio El Carmen ★   This lovely church and monastery, founded in 1724 and occupying an entire city block, has the most important collection of colonial art in Trujillo. Its Carmelite museum (Pinacoteca Carmelita) possesses 150 baroque and rococo paintings, the majority of them from the 17th and 18th centuries, as well as paintings of the Quito Art School. The final room shows the process of restoration of paintings, although explanations are in Spanish only. The church's central gilded altar is marvelous. The main *retablo* (altar) was created by Master Fernando Collado de la Cruz, a free black Peruvian. Floral murals in soft pastels line each side of the church. The monastery has two cloisters (and 10 cloistered nuns) and contains a fair portion of the convent's art collection, but it cannot be visited.

Jirón Bolívar (at Colón). ✆ **044/233-091.** Admission to church and museum S/3 adults, S/1 children. Mon–Sat 9am–1pm.

Museo Arqueológico Casinelli ★ (Finds)   One of the most curious places you'll ever see fine ceramics exhibits is this private museum, about a 10-minute walk from the Plaza de Armas, housed in a dumpy space beneath a Mobil gas station. What are the odds of a gas-station and car-wash owner devoting all his money, time, and attention to assembling and displaying one of the largest private collections of ancient ceramics? Going on over 40 years of existence, with dreams of greater recognition and expansion, Señor Casinelli's superb collection of the Moche, Nasca, Chavín, Huari, and Chimú cultures (among others) holds about 4,000 pieces (although Casinelli says only 2,000 can be displayed "for lack of space and lack of support from the Peruvian government") and spans more than 2,500 years. There are some excellent examples of all those cultures displayed on pressboard shelves, including, behind a wall meant to protect innocent eyes, the famed erotic ceramics of the Moche. (You might have to ask the old guy to open the case, a feeling akin to asking the pharmacist for condoms.) Casinelli owns the gas station upstairs and has an architect's model of the much larger museum, along with a hotel, he'd like someday to build (but he's now in his 80s, so that dream is growing dim). Guided tours are in Spanish only.

Av. Nicolás de Piérola 607 (at intersection of Huanchaco and Ctra. Panamericana). ✆ **044/246-110.** Admission S/7. Mon–Sat 9am–12:30pm and 3–6:30pm.

Museo de Arte Moderno de Trujillo ★ (Finds)   Unusual for this city that celebrates its colonial past is its relatively new Museum of Modern Art. The private collection of the *Trujillano* painter and sculptor Gerardo Chávez includes, in addition to his own pieces, the contemporary works of renowned international artists such as Alberto Giacometti, Paul Klee and the celebrated Latin American painters Roberto Sebastián Matta, Wifredo Lam, Joaquín Torres-García, Oswaldo Guayasamin and Rufino Tamayo. The small, handsome museum (with fewer than 100 works) is located about 4 km (2 miles) outside Trujillo.

Ctra. Industrial s/n. ✆ **044/215-668.** Admission S/10. Mon–Sat 9:30am–5:30pm.

Tips   Catch Some Ondas

If you want to check out some waves along Peru's north coast, check the "Spot Atlas" at **www.wannasurf.com**. If you can read Spanish, another good surfing site is **www.peruazul.com**.

Palacio Iturregui This bright yellow mansion, an excellent example of neoclassical civil architecture that dates to the 19th century, is home to the Club Central, Trujillo's traditional social club. Although the club continues to be members-only, visitors can tool around for a view of an only slightly dilapidated exclusivity. The two-story mansion, with a large central courtyard, is outfitted with window grilles, thin columns, and Italian marble statues. Upstairs is a small museum containing Moche ceramics. Members in semiformal dress still drop by for lunch or dinner at the club, followed by a game of cards.

Jr. Pizarro 688. $(\mathcal{C})$ **044/234-212.** Admission (guided tour) S/5. Mon–Sat 8–11am (before 10am, ring bell for entrance).

Huanchaco ★

Huanchaco, 13km (7½ miles) northwest of Trujillo, is a tranquil and traditional fishing village now doubling as a pretty low-key resort. On summer weekends, though, it gets jumping with folks from Trujillo and vacationing Peruvians. Huanchaco is a very good alternative to Trujillo as a base for exploring the archaeological sites of the Chimú and Moche (and a day's visit to the capital city is easily accomplished from Huanchaco).

The town's fishing character is apparent in the long jetty that juts out over the water and the pointy handcrafted boats called *caballitos del mar* (or *caballitos de totora*), for which Huanchaco has become famous and which remain the photogenic vessel of choice for fishers. These small boats, made of bound totora reeds, have been used by fishermen for more than 1,000 years, since the reign of the Moche. The area around Huanchaco is one of the few places in Peru where this ancient sea-vessel tradition has not disappeared from use. When not out on the water, they're parked on the beach in groups like slender tepees.

Besides a stroll on the beach and visit to Huanchaco's pleasant *artesanía* market, there's not too much to see or do. A 16th-century colonial church clings to a cliff, but it's a long walk uphill from town. More than anything else, Huanchaco's easy pace and proximity to the sea are its main attractions. It has several agreeable resort hotels, seafood restaurants, and nice stretches of beach. The big waves here attract local surfers and a few board-carrying tourists, although the biggest and best waves are at **Puerto Chicama** (also known as **Malabrigo**), about 80km (50 miles) farther up the coast. Waves there can be ridden up to a half-mile, and it's the site of the largest left wave in the world. (Another good spot in the far north is **Cabo Blanco,** about 110km/68 miles south of Tumbes.) La Casa Suiza *hostal* (p. 391) rents out body boards.

GETTING THERE Pick up a Huanchaco bus (S/3) along Independencia in Trujillo; the buses go along the first part of the beach before turning on Los Ficus. You can get to Puerto Chicama by colectivos, which depart hourly from the Terminal Interurbano on Calle Santa Cruz in Trujillo; the journey takes about 90 minutes. A taxi from Trujillo is about S/20.

Archaeological Sites near Trujillo ★★

Chan Chan ★★ One of the most important archaeological sites in Peru (although, in its present state it might not seem as "complete" to the layman observer as some of the Inca stone ruins in the highlands), Chan Chan is an enormous adobe city in the Moche valley, just 5km (3 miles) from Trujillo. The great capital of the Chimú Empire, which stretched some 966km (600 miles) along the northern coast of Peru from Lima to the Ecuadorian border, is the largest complex of its kind from pre-Columbian America. The urban Chimú was the chief state in Peru before the continental conquest of the Inca

(Tips) **Chan Chan Crime Report**

Chan Chan is spread out over several kilometers, and some visitors walking alone among the component parts have reported robberies and attacks. To be safe, stick to the main paths between major sites and avoid wandering along smaller paths in the open fields around Tschudi Palace. Chan Chan is just a couple of kilometers from the beach, but the route to the water has a very bad reputation and should be avoided; too many reports of muggings and worse have been registered over the years to risk it. There have also been crime reports in the neighborhoods around Huaca Arco Iris and Huaca Esmeralda; it's best to take a taxi there from the Museo de Sitio de Chan Chan.

Empire. Begun around 1300, it reaches all the way from Huanchaco port to Campana Mountain, an area covering more than 25 sq. km (9¾ sq. miles) of desert floor.

First excavated in the mid-1960s, the crumbling mud city was once home to perhaps as many as 60,000 inhabitants. In all, the UNESCO Cultural Mankind Heritage Monument comprises more than a dozen citadels and a maze of living quarters, thick defensive walls, ramps, plazas, gardens, workshops, warehouses, narrow streets, a huge reservoir, a royal cemetery, and pyramidal temples. Nine palaces were the personal domains of Chimú chieftains; when one died, he was buried in an elaborate ritual in the palace and a new royal compound was built for his successor. These were almost certainly overflowing with gold and silver riches, and were later ransacked not by the Incas, but by the Spaniards and subsequent *huaqueros* (grave robbers, or treasure hunters). The fragile buildings themselves have fallen victim to erosion caused by recurring El Niño floods; in 1986, Chan Chan was listed on World Heritage Sites in Danger due to both physical erosion and acts of continued pillaging.

The Chimú kingdom began around A.D. 1000 and reached its apex in the 15th century before succumbing to the Incas in 1470 and 1471, after more than a decade of resistance. Today one can only imagine what this massive complex looked like and the sophisticated society that once inhabited it. Unfortunately, no written records or documents aid our understanding of the establishment of the city or reconstruct the daily activities that took place there. Long walls are embellished with friezes of geometric figures, stylized birds and fish, ocean motifs, and mythological creatures—although some might be considered a bit too impeccably restored. There are no doors or arches in the entire complex, and there are no stairs—only ramps.

There are four main sites at Chan Chan, all spread over a large area that requires either a lot of walking or a couple of taxi rides. The principal complex, named the **Tschudi Palace** for a 19th-century Swiss explorer, has been partially restored, and a walking tour is indicated by painted arrows. The royal palace was home to a noble population of 500 to 1,000. The first area of interest is a ceremonial courtyard decorated with aquatic-themed friezes. The original walls were 18m (59 ft.) high. Just beyond the courtyard are walls with interesting friezes of fish and seabirds. The most fascinating component of the palace is the large area known as the Sanctuary, whose walls are textured like fishing nets. Although Chan Chan contains the ruins of an additional eight royal compounds, none has been restored like Tschudi, and very little can be seen or understood from viewing them.

The **Museo de Sitio de Chan Chan,** along the road back toward Trujillo, has a small collection of ceramics from Chan Chan and some exhibits about the nature of the city and its history. The museum is equipped with an auditorium and models of Chan Chan; an audio and light presentation is given in English as well as Spanish. The museum is at least a 20-minute walk from Tschudi Palace.

Huaca Esmeralda and Huaca Arco Iris are two smaller pyramidal temples that are rather removed from the main palace. They are included in the Chan Chan ticket, but one must go to either the museum or Tschudi Palace first. **Huaca Esmeralda** is in the Mansiche district, midway between Chan Chan and Trujillo (several blocks behind the church, to the right). The *huaca* consists of a couple platforms and some friezes that have not yet been restored; although they are less impressive than others, at least visitors get a clear chance to see original reliefs.

Huaca Arco Iris (Rainbow Temple, also called **Huaca El Dragón**), lies in the La Esperanza suburb a couple kilometers from Trujillo, west of the Pan-American Highway. It is in much better condition than Huaca Esmeralda, having been excavated only in the 1960s, and its well-conserved rainbow-shaped friezes are fascinating. Some have interpreted the central motif to be that of a dragon. Outer walls have reliefs of snakes and peculiar lizards. The fairly large structure has several ramps, and visitors can climb to platforms at the top of the temple.

To visit all the sites, you'll need the better part of a day. Many people choose to break up the visit over 2 days. A visit can begin at either Tschudi Palace or at the Museo de Sitio, transferring between them by bus or taxi, and then going to the adjunct temple sites by taxi.

Valle de Moche. (Huaca Arco Iris: Jr. Pedro Murillo 1681, La Esperanza, Trujillo, Panamericana Norte). Admission S/11; ticket is good for 48 hr. and all 4 sites of the complex. Guides are available at the entrance to Tschudi Palace for S/35 per group. Daily 9am–4pm. Catch the Huanchaco bus (S/4) on Av. España (at the corner of Independencia/Ejército) and ask to be let off at the turnoff to Chan Chan. Occasionally, there are taxis waiting here; otherwise, walk nearly a mile down a dirt road to the left, to the Tschudi Palace. For the Museo de Sitio, catch a bus returning to Trujillo. Taxis from Trujillo cost about S/20. Because transportation among the 4 sites is not always available, it might be worthwhile to contract a taxi to take you to the sites and wait for you (round-trip, S/60–S/75).

El Brujo ★   Difficult to get to and explore without a private guide, the remote Moche complex of El Brujo nonetheless makes a very worthwhile visit for those intrigued by what they've seen at Chan Chan and the huacas near Trujillo. Because it is so little explored—until recently, it was closed to the public—many visitors enjoy El Brujo even more than those other sites. (Because of ongoing excavations, some groups are reportedly still occasionally turned away.)

El Brujo lies in the Chicama Valley, about 60km (37 miles) north of Trujillo along the coast, or 1½ hours by car. A number of cultures developed in the Chicama Valley region since the pre-ceramic period, and at least one of the three temples here, **Huaca Prieta,** is about 5,000 years old. Oddly enough, it's essentially a giant, prehistoric garbage dump—not much to see for nonspecialists, but containing a wealth of nonbiodegradable information for archaeologists researching the ancient people of the same name. (The Huaca Prieta civilization inhabited the area from around 3500–2200 B.C.) The main temple of interest at El Brujo is **Huaca Cao,** a leveled-off pyramid with terrific and huge multicolored friezes—some of the finest in northern Peru. They depict figures of warriors, priests, and sacrificial victims. Nearby, **Huaca Cortada** has some cool and menacing figures in high relief brandishing a knife in one hand and a recently decapitated head in the other.

Near Magdalena de Cao, Valle de Chicama. Admission S/20. Daily 9am–4pm. Several tour agencies in Trujillo organize excursions to El Brujo; be sure to ask about the status of the current admissions policy at the site. Private guides who frequently take individuals and small groups are Michael White and Clara Luz Bravo (© **044/243-347**). Ask at the Tourism Information Office (© **044/938-922**) about other guides.

Huacas de Moche ★   About 8km (5 miles) south of Trujillo in the desert Valle de Moche, this complex of Moche ruins is enigmatic from a distance. Two imposing rounded-off and weathered adobe pyramids, partially eroded, sit in a dusty open field at the foot of Cerro Blanco. Built by the Moche people around A.D. 500, they are about 7 centuries older than the ruined city of Chan Chan. The two masses constituted a religious center and an urban settlement.

The first pyramid, the **Huaca del Sol (Temple of the Sun),** is nearly 20m (66 ft.) high, although it was once bigger by perhaps two-thirds, and it was very likely the largest man-made structure in the Americas in its day. Heavy rains of the El Niño phenomenon, and the Spaniards' diversion of the nearby Moche River, precipitated the erosion. It is said to have been built by 250,000 men and 140 million adobe bricks. The pyramid once surely was composed of multiple staircases and platforms. The huaca remains unexcavated, and it looks very fragile, as though a major rainstorm could easily take it out. Signs warn visitors against climbing on the ruins (NO ESCALAR), but plenty do climb up to the top along steep trails. Additional foot traffic only furthers the erosion, though, and the views are equally good from the Huaca de la Luna across the way. Some visitors inevitably find this lumped mass a bit of a disappointment, just a massive mound of muddy earth; if you find yourself in that camp, hurry over to the neighboring huaca.

Across the open field, where burial sites have been found and living quarters were once erected, is the smaller but more interesting **Huaca de la Luna (Temple of the Moon).** It is better preserved than the Temple of the Sun and has been excavated; many of the most important finds took place in the 1990s, and excavations are ongoing. The structure consists of five independent levels, with no communication among them—perhaps a result of the fact that the *huaca* (pyramid) was constructed in major phases over 600 years. Inside the adobe walls (at the top of an entrance ramp) are polychromatic friezes of large rhomboids, featuring a repeated motif of the fearsome anthropomorphic figure Ai-Apaek, known as *El Degollador* (the decapitator), and several secondary figures. The yellow, red, white, and black designs are quite remarkable; the god is said to have the hair of the sea and eyes of an owl. From the top of the Huaca de la Luna, there are excellent

---

Fun Facts   The Hairless Peruvian Dog

Near the Chan Chan site museum and elsewhere in northern Peru, you might spot a peculiar smooth, black-skinned creature, often with blotches. This less than blessed creature is the *biringo,* or Peruvian hairless dog. Ancient and—to my Labrador-loving tastes—ugly as all get out, these dogs were kept by several of the pre-Inca cultures of the region, and they're still around and kept as pets. These dogs are hot to the touch, and it is said that ancient nobles kept them as portable heaters. The Lambayeque and Chimú not only domesticated the animal, though; they also made it part of their diets. Eeww.

Moche Culture

Anyone who has spent time in a small museum room crammed with the famed erotic ceramics of the Moche culture might feel that we know almost too much about this ancient civilization, certainly more than plenty of people are comfortable seeing depicted on vases and other vessels. But our knowledge isn't limited to the Moche's sexual mores. The Moche, who inhabited the northern coastal desert of Peru from A.D. 100 to 700, left detailed information about their entire civilization in their finely detailed ceramics, which are some of the finest produced in pre-Columbian Peru. The Moche are, along with the contemporary Nasca people from the desert coast south of Lima, the best-documented culture of the Classical period.

The apogee of Moche society was A.D. 500 to 600. Although they possessed no written language, their superior painted pottery presents evidence of nearly all elements of their society, from disease and dance to architecture, transportation, agriculture, music, and religion. The Moche (also referred to as "Mochica," although the latter term is losing some currency) were a strictly hierarchical, elite-dominated society that developed into a theocracy. They also constituted one of the first true urban cultures in Peru. Religious temples or pyramids, called huacas, were restricted to nobles, warriors, and priests; common citizens—farmers, artisans, fishers, and slaves—lived in areas removed from the temples.

The finest selection of Moche ceramics in the country is found at the Museo Arqueológico Rafael Larco Herrera (p. 136) in Lima, the largest private collection of pre-Columbian art in the world. The founder of the museum is the author of the classic study *Los Mochicas*. The Museo de Arte Precolombino (p. 217) in Cusco also has a fine, although small, collection of Moche artifacts.

NORTHERN PERU

12

TRUJILLO

views of Huaca del Sol and the surrounding countryside. Near the ticket booth, where you can arrange for a guide, is a small refreshment stand and souvenir shop.

Valle de Moche. ⓒ **044/291-894.** Admission S/10; cost includes a Spanish- or English-speaking guide (tip expected). Daily 9am–4pm. Catch the yellow "Campiña de Moche" colectivo (S/2) on Suárez (at Av. Los Incas), several blocks northeast of the Plaza de Armas. Otherwise, you can take a taxi there for about S/20. In high season, you won't need to have the driver wait because there are frequent buses and taxis returning to Trujillo. If there are few people around, however, you can usually get the driver to wait an hour or so to take you back to Trujillo for around S/35.

SHOPPING

Trujillo doesn't have much to interest potential shoppers, unless you need eyeglasses; Calle Bolívar is loaded with opticians. For a taste of what shopping means to most Trujillo natives, check out the sprawling **street mercado** that operates daily along Avenida Los Incas. It's one of the more unruly (and headache-inducing) markets in Peru, with vendors struggling to be heard over the incessant sounds of car horns. The market stretches across several blocks and spreads out into the street, selling an unending variety of vegetables, fish, and household items; there are even carts full of charcoal.

Most visitors will be better off shopping in Huanchaco. **Artesanía del Norte,** Los Olivos 504 (**© 044/461-220**), has some of the coolest exclusive ceramics designs in Peru. They'll ship pieces to your home if you can't limit yourself to just one. The *mercado de artesanía* fronting the beach in Huanchaco has a number of stalls and is also an excellent place for jewelry, including pieces made with the sought-after blue stone lapis lazuli.

WHERE TO STAY

Visitors have the option of staying in downtown Trujillo, which despite its nice colonial feel can be rather noisy and harried—and truth be told, not exactly possessing of a stellar roster of hotels—or staying in the less expensive and more relaxed beachside town of Huanchaco, just 12km (7½ miles) away, where there are several laid-back resort hotels and some good budget *hostales.* Because the focus of many travelers' attentions is Chan Chan, which is located northwest of the city toward Huanchaco, staying beachside is a very practical option.

Downtown Trujillo
Expensive

Gran Hotel El Golf (Kids) This modern resort hotel, the largest in the north of Peru, is built around a large circular swimming pool and is close to a golf country club in one of the most upscale residential districts of Trujillo (5 min. driving from the Plaza de Armas). However, the hotel certainly doesn't have the character of the Hotel Libertador on the main square, which beats it with its location and historic building. Rooms are spacious, as are bathrooms, but I wouldn't call them luxurious. The Golf's two-story units overlook the pool and nice gardens. For those (particularly families) looking for some relaxation and space for the kids to run around in, it's not a bad bet. Additional distractions include tennis courts, a spa, children's games, and nearby beaches.

Los Cocoteros 500, Urbanización El Golf, Trujillo. © **044/484-150.** Fax 044/282-231. www.granhotel.pe. 120 units. $110–$123 double; $200–$275 suite. Rates include breakfast buffet. AE, V. **Amenities:** Restaurant; bar; concierge; *frontón;* nearby golf course w/guest privileges; outdoor pool; spa; 2 tennis courts. *In room:* A/C, TV, fridge, hair dryer.

Hotel Libertador Plaza Mayor Trujillo ★★ The top place to stay in Trujillo, and not a bad value given its superb location and amenities, is right on the Plaza de Armas, in a beautiful salmon-colored colonial mansion with a courtyard patio and a nice pool with palm trees and lots of vegetation. The place has a fair amount of colonial elegance and flavor. Rooms are not spectacularly luxurious, but they are certainly comfortable and well outfitted with somewhat dated furnishings. Rooms on the interior are quieter and have views of the pool. Other rooms look out onto the busy but pretty plaza, and some have small balconies that are perfect for people-watching (but be prepared for the trade-off: street noise until late). The hotel has a handsome bar, a good restaurant, and both dry and steam saunas. On Sunday, there's a big-time brunch starting at noon, with both Peruvian and international foods.

Jr. Independencia 48, Plaza de Armas, Trujillo. © **044/232-741,** or 01/518-6500 for reservations. Fax 044/235-641. www.libertador.com.pe. 78 units. $125 double; $165–$1,950 suite. Rates include breakfast buffet. AE, DC, MC, V. **Amenities:** Restaurant; bar; concierge; gym; excellent outdoor pool; sauna. *In room:* A/C, TV, fridge, hair dryer.

Moderate

Los Conquistadores Hotel (Value) On a busy street just a couple blocks from the Plaza de Armas, this clean midsize independent hotel is your best bet in this price range, even if it's hardly an exciting option. With nice-looking public rooms set way back from the street and its hubbub, it counts with a welcoming atmosphere and good service. Accommodations are quiet, large and carpeted, with outmoded, almost retro hotel décor; beds are decked out in flowery bedspreads. Suites are especially large, with separate sitting areas. Walk-in discounts are frequently available.

Jr. Diego de Almagro 586, Trujillo. ℂ **044/481-650.** Fax 044/235-917. www.losconquistadoreshotel.com. 50 units. S/343 double; S/473–S/563 suite. Rates include continental breakfast. AE, DC, MC, V. **Amenities:** Restaurant; bar. In room: A/C, TV.

Inexpensive
Hostal Colonial ★ (Finds)   My taxi driver turned me on to this small, simple, Belgian-owned hotel, and for once, the driver wasn't just trawling for a commission—he was right. A handsome and recently restored colonial house just a block from the Plaza de Armas, it represents good value for Trujillo. Some of the rooms, though large, are rather plain. The rooms looking over the interior patio are best; a couple of them have balconies with chairs. If you don't mind a bit of street noise, the rooms facing the street are also good bets. Attached to the hotel is a genial little cafe that's a good, cheap place for lunch.

Jr. Independencia 618, Trujillo. ℂ **044/258-261.** Fax 044/223-410. hostcolonialtruji@hotmail.com. 24 units. S/70 double. Rates include taxes and breakfast. No credit cards. **Amenities:** Restaurant; room service. In room: TV.

Huanchaco
Moderate
Hostal Bracamonte (Value) (Kids)   A miniresort tucked behind a high gate and a couple of blocks from the beach, this relaxed *hostal* has a bit of a motel atmosphere. Rooms and bungalows are positioned around a large pool, and the hotel has a playground and gardens for kids to run around, as well as several terraces, a barbecue grill area, and a game room. Bungalows have room for three or four guests each. Rooms have a beachy, unadorned feel, with tile floors but comfortable beds. Overall, it's a pretty good, if not outstanding, value, and it's an especially welcome retreat for those traveling with children.

Jr. Los Olivos 503, Huanchaco. ℂ **044/461-162.** Fax 044/461-266. www.hotelbracamonte.com.pe. 28 units. S/117–S/185 double; S/190–S/285 suite. AE, DC, MC, V. **Amenities:** Restaurant; cafeteria; bar; outdoor pool. In room: A/C, TV.

Huanchaco International Hotel ★ (Kids)   This Belgian-owned modern beach resort hotel, positioned right on the beach but a bit out of town, on the road to Huanchaco, is a welcoming place, particularly for families. Popular with vacationing Peruvians, it has a huge pool, yellow and white bungalow accommodations dotting the property, and gardens with sea views. Breakfast is served on a terrace overlooking the beach. Rooms are large and very clean; many of the little houselike bungalows—which can house four adults—are attractively positioned up stone steps. If you're staying for a few days, ask about package deals that include area visits.

Autopista a Huanchaco, Km 13.5, Playa Azul, Huanchaco. ℂ/fax **044/461-754.** www.huanchacointernational.com. 40 units. $49 double; $69–$89 bungalow. Rates include breakfast. AE, DC, MC, V. **Amenities:** Restaurant; bar; cafe; large outdoor pool; solarium. In room: TV.

Inexpensive
La Casa Suiza ★ (Value)   A favorite of backpackers for more than a quarter of a century, this inn run by a Swiss-Peruvian family—still referred to as "Heidi's house" by longtime vets—is an extremely friendly place to hang out and meet up with other travelers.

The large and comfortable rooms have been remodeled, with colorful (some might say garish) murals of local sights above the beds, but the star at this *hostal* is the great rooftop terrace, where guests line-dry their laundry and write in their journals. The terrace is topped by a tile table and glowing red Swiss lamp. There's a cable TV room, a book exchange, and Internet access (and even a laser printer). Would-be surfers are well cared for here; the *hostal* has gear (including wet suits and boards) for rent. Breakfast is prepared by Wendy, a Swiss woman who's practically an institution at this friendly joint.

Los Pinos 451, Huanchaco. © **044/461-285.** www.lacasasuiza.com. 16 units. S/50–S/75 double with private bathroom; S/20–S/25 per person in shared room with shared bathroom. No credit cards. **Amenities:** Breakfast room. *In room:* No phone, Wi-Fi.

WHERE TO DINE

Dining out is a pretty low-key affair in Trujillo. Even though it's Peru's third-largest city, it doesn't have many sophisticated restaurants—though a branch of Gastón Acurio's **Chi Cha** ★★★, which the celebrated Lima chef has already inaugurated with success in Cusco and Arequipa (p. 324), is on its way and should immediately be the finest restaurant Trujillo has seen. One hotel restaurant that's worth a visit even if you're not staying there—especially for brunch on the weekend—is the **Las Bóvedas** restaurant at the Hotel Libertador (p. 390). Most visitors also enjoy eating out in Huanchaco, which has one truly excellent luxury restaurant, **Club Colonial,** and a number of simple seafood places along the beach.

Trujillo
Moderate

El Mochica ★ PERUVIAN The one restaurant that it seems everyone in Trujillo recommends is a bit of a surprise. From the outside, it looks to be a pretty sophisticated joint: It's housed within a beautiful colonial building with an impressive carved-wood balcony. Inside, though, the dining room is a little jarring, with white plastic chairs and a large TV blaring videos in the front room. A second room has a bar and a stage for live music on weekends. Despite the inauspicious surroundings, service is good—waiters are even dressed in black tie. El Mochica also produces well-prepared and good-value *criollo* cooking and classic dishes such as roasted guinea pig and *parrilladas* (mixed grilled meats), in addition to fresh fish such as *corvina* (sea bass).

Bolívar 462. © **044/293-441.** Reservations recommended for live music Fri–Sat. Main courses S/12–S/34. AE, DC, MC, V. Daily 8pm–1am.

Il Valentino ★ ITALIAN Across from Trujillo's jampacked Cine Primavera is the city's classiest-looking restaurant. An attractive, somewhat Mediterranean-style place, it has yellow walls and arched doorways, subdued lighting, and tables on two levels with tablecloths and fake flowers. The menu is dominated by pizzas and pastas of the upscale variety, plus a few steaks. It's perfectly located for dinner before or after a movie (Cine Primavera shows films in their original language), although service here can be a bit slow, so I recommend going to the movie first and having dinner afterward.

Orbegoso 224. © **044/246-643.** Reservations recommended on Fri–Sat. Main courses S/15–S/35. AE, DC, MC, V. Tues–Sun noon–11pm.

Restaurante Demarco ⓥ Value INTERNATIONAL/ITALIAN A pleasant-enough, cafe-style restaurant, which resembles an ice-cream parlor crammed with small tables and ceiling fans, Demarco has something for just about everyone and every time of day. It

draws a consistent crowd of locals for its good breakfast selection, its sandwiches, pizza,
pastas, and other Italian fare, as well as its excellent cakes and ice creams. The extensive
menu also has *criollo* specialties such as *asado de res con puré y arroz* (roast beef with
mashed potatoes and rice), *churrasco con tacu tacu* (grilled meats served with rice and
beans), and the classic *lomo saltado* (strips of beef with onions, tomatoes, and french fries
over rice). Though it boasts a daily lunch *menu* (inexpensive set-price meal), it's just as
good for a midafternoon snack or late dessert.

Pizarro 725. ℭ **044/234-251.** Reservations not accepted. Main courses S/12–S/30. AE, DC, MC, V. Daily
8am–midnight.

Restaurante Romano ⟨Value⟩ INTERNATIONAL/ITALIAN   Located on one of the
city's main thoroughfares, this uncomplicated and cheery restaurant is a good, easygoing
place for pizzas, rice dishes, salads, and omelets, as well as more substantial items such as
steak, pork loin, and filet mignon with mushrooms. There are also homemade pastas,
including ravioli, lasagna, and cannelloni. The weekday set-price menu is a very good
value; it might be a tuna and vegetable salad to start, followed by baked chicken with rice
and mashed potatoes, plus juice and bread. Romano is open for breakfast and has a nice
selection of desserts and excellent coffees, including cappuccino and espresso. It's very
popular with local regulars, especially at lunch. Waiters bring the food through the front
door, which looks odd, as if they are going out to the street to fetch your meal. (The
kitchen is around the other side of the restaurant.)

Pizarro 747. ℭ **044/252-251.** Reservations not accepted. Main courses S/12–S/29. AE, DC, MC, V. Daily
8am–midnight.

Inexpensive

Restaurant Colonial PERUVIAN   This cute and relaxed cafe, with just six tables, is
attached to the Hostal Colonial (and shouldn't be confused with the recommended Club
Colonial in Huanchaco). It has floor-to-ceiling wall murals of colonial Trujillo and
Moche motifs from Las Huacas and other sites in the area. It offers simple Peruvian fare,
but it's perfect for a good and cheap midday menu, which might include a soup or *papa
a la huancaína* (boiled potato with a creamy cheese sauce) and a main course of *churrasco*
(barbecued meats) or *arroz con pollo* (chicken and rice). The menu also has pork, Chi-
nese-style fried rice, spaghetti, and omelets, as well as three breakfast options.

Jr. Independencia 618. ℭ **044/258-261.** Reservations not accepted. Main courses S/12–S/19. No credit
cards. Daily 8am–9pm.

Huanchaco
Moderate

Club Colonial ★★ ⟨Finds⟩ BELGIAN/FRENCH   A romantic and magnificently
inviting restaurant occupying a renovated 1790s mansion on a quiet square, this is the
most refined place to dine in northern Peru. Enter through a small courtyard and stunning Art Nouveau stained-glass doors. The warm dining salon is straight ahead, and off
to the right is a small bar with well-chosen cafe tables and chairs. The colorful decor lives
up to the restaurant's name and reeks of French colonial atmosphere—walls are bright
blue, orange, red, and yellow, and the place is brimming with large mirrors, antiques,
fresh flowers, and dark wood. It looks like some cool expat's house (and in fact, is owned
by a Belgian woman).

The menu is an interesting mix of Peruvian and Franco-Belgian items. Starters include
excellent salads, ceviches, and homemade pastas. Main courses include French brochette

in three sauces, *cordon bleu,* and pork loin with curry pineapple sauce. But for my money, the stars are the exquisitely prepared fish dishes, such as *corvina a la vasca* (Basque-style sea bass) and lobster. Desserts, such as *crêpes suchards* (crepes with ice cream and chocolate), are also outstanding. Service lags in comparison to the food and surroundings, but you're unlikely to care. After you've dined, wander out to the courtyard past the bar to see the 12 penguins and two small caimans. Club Colonial is more expensive than other restaurants in northern Peru but is definitely worth it.

Grau 272. © **044/761-639.** Reservations recommended. Main courses S/18–S/42. AE, DC, MC, V. Daily noon–10pm.

Inexpensive

El Peñón (Value) SEAFOOD   Huanchaco, a fishing village, is rightly famous for its fresh fish. And there are few better places to plunge into the local catch than this casual and comfy place, one of the first tourist-oriented restaurants in Huanchaco. It couldn't be simpler: white plastic chairs, tables with green tablecloths, and the roar of the sea. (Indoor seating is also available, but the best spot is on the small terrace.) Located right across the street from the surf, this family-run restaurant is a favorite of locals, and the amiable owner seems to know everyone. Try one of the excellent ceviches, seafood omelets, or main courses such as *arroz con mariscos* (shellfish rice), *calamares* (squid), or *pulpo* (octopus).

Corner of Av. Víctor Larco and Raymondi. © **044/461-549.** Reservations recommended in high season. Main courses S/8–S/27. DC, MC, V. Daily noon–10pm.

La Barca SEAFOOD   A popular, homey little place with basic tables and chairs and little fuss, "The Boat" serves up very good and reasonably priced fresh seafood dishes, as well as some *criollo* standards. I'd stick to the fish: succulent ceviche, *langostinos* (prawns), or *cangrejo* (crab). A daily set menu is offered Monday through Friday, and on Saturday evening, there's a piano bar. There's a second, similar branch (© **044/461-052**) at Av. Víctor Larco 514, just a couple blocks away, facing the beach.

Jr. Unión 209. © **044/461-549.** Reservations recommended in high season. Main courses S/11–S/28. DC, MC, V. Daily noon–10pm.

TRUJILLO AFTER DARK

Trujillo is pretty quiet except on weekends, when it springs to life. A few nightclubs and peñas are clustered in the *centro,* but most of the hopping discos that go all night are very local and young affairs, on the outskirts of the city. Trujillo has a surprising roster of casinos and movie houses (including two multiplexes showing recently arrived English-language films), and those are as good as any destination for an evening out.

Las Tinajas, Pizarro 383 (© **044/296-272**), with a balcony overlooking the Plaza de Armas, is a pretty chic and popular bar with a downstairs disco, good for drinks midweek. On weekends, it features live rock and pop; the cover is usually S/5. **El Estribo,** San Martín 810, is a lively and large open music hall with peña music and Mariah Carey wannabes occasionally performing. The cover charge is about S/10. **La Canana,** San Martín 791 (© **044/232-503**), is another nearby peña with a good restaurant and live music and dancing on weekends. The cover is usually about S/10.

Luna Rota, at América Sur 2119 in the Santa María district at the end of Huayna Cápac (© **044/228-877**), is an all-in-one complex with a thumping disco for teenagers, a pub, and a casino for slightly more mature folks. The cover in the disco and pub is usually S/10.

Cine Primavera, Orbegoso 239, near the Plaza de Armas ((C) **044/241-277**), has first-run American and European films in their original languages and draws long lines of moviegoers. Among the collection of casinos along Orbegoso and Pizarro is **Casino Solid Gold,** Orbegoso 554 ((C) **044/207-662**). Open daily 24 hours, the club features cocktail waitresses in flashy short skirts and has a low-rent Vegas feel to it.

---

2 CHICLAYO ★

770km (478 miles) N of Lima; 200km (124 miles) N of Trujillo; 235km (146 miles) NW of Cajamarca

Although it's Peru's fourth-largest city, with a population of just under a half-million, Chiclayo would be just another busy commercial town, generating little notice among travelers, were it not for the city's strong associations with Peru's ancient cultures. The primary draw is Chiclayo's proximity to the archaeological sites Sipán and Túcume, two of the most important related to the Moche and Lambayeque cultures, and the spectacular Museo Tumbas Reales de Sipán, which houses one of the country's most remarkable finds of the past several decades: the tomb of the Lord of Sipán.

Chiclayo is a modern and relatively new city. Although it was founded in the mid–16th century, most of its real development dates to the late 1800s and early 1900s. (The Parque Principal, or main square, didn't come into existence until 1916.) Today Chiclayo is a sprawling, bustling place; the city itself holds little interest for most visitors. Frankly, most people come here to get out of town. The capital of the Lambayeque department, Chiclayo calls itself "La Ciudad de la Amistad"—the City of Friendship. There's no real reason for such a distinction as far as I can see, but why not? It's not Peru's prettiest, biggest, or most fascinating city, but it is an agreeable, down-to-earth place.

About 12km (7½ miles) northwest of Chiclayo, Lambayeque, site of the distinguished archaeological museums, Museo Tumbas Reales de Sipán and Museo Brüning, was once the more important of the two towns. Today that is true only from the traveler's perspective. It is a slow-moving, rather dilapidated town with a smattering of interesting colonial buildings, none of which is particularly well restored or open to visitors. Except for the draw of the Lord of Sipán, the town lives in the shadow of Chiclayo's ever-growing commercial importance.

ESSENTIALS

Getting There

BY PLANE Star Perú ((C) **01/705-9000;** www.starperu.com) and **LAN** ((C) **01/213-8200;** www.lan.com) fly daily from Lima to Chiclayo, with flights starting at around $95 one-way. There are also flights north to and from Piura.

Flights arrive at **Aeropuerto José Quiñones González,** Av. Bolognesi s/n ((C) **074/233-192**), just 2km (1¼ miles) east of downtown. To the center of Chiclayo, a taxi costs S/5.

BY BUS Chiclayo is serviced by several domestic bus companies from Lima and most major points along the north coast and northern highlands. Many long-distance buses travel at night only. There is no central bus station in Chiclayo; most companies have their own terminals at offices on Avenida Bolognesi, 5 blocks south of the Parque Principal.

The major carriers making the 8-hour trip from Lima are **Ormeño** ((C) **01/472-5000;** www.grupo-ormeno.com.pe), **CIVA Transportes** ((C) **01/418-1111;** www.civa.com.pe),

Cruz del Sur (© 01/311-5050; www.cruzdelsur.com.pe), and **Oltursa** (© 01/708-5000; www.oltursa.com). **Transportes Línea** (© 044/297-000 or 076/222-221; www. transporteslinea.com.pe) and **ITTSA** (© 044/222-541) make the 3-hour trip from Trujillo to Chiclayo, as do a number of colectivos and combis. **Transportes Línea** is also the major carrier from Cajamarca (© 076/366-100).

Visitor Information

Chiclayo has two accessible tourist information kiosks, run not by the municipal government, but by two related restaurants. One is on the Parque Principal, or the main plaza. Another is on Avenida José Balta Sur (at Manuel María Izaga), in front of the Hebrón restaurant. Both kiosks give out maps of the city and the area, and they'll give you some basic information about how to get around (and they'll put in a plug for barbecue chicken, to boot).

The **iPerú** tourism information office is located on Av. Sáenz Peña 838 (© 074/205-703). **Sipán Tours,** 7 de Enero 772 (© 074/229-053), is willing to dispense information without giving you the hard sell for package tours (but if you're interested, it's one of the most reputable agencies in town offering city and archaeological tours). Another excellent agency, which has specialized in archaeology tours and independent travel in northern Peru and offers bilingual guides in several languages, is **Indiana Tours,** Colón 556 (© 074/222-991 or 01/9883-5617; www.indianatoursperu.com).

FAST FACTS Most banks are clustered around the Parque Principal, including **Banco de Crédito,** José Balta 630, and **Interbanc,** Elías Aguirre 680. Money-changers usually hang around in front of banks.

In an **emergency,** call © 105. The helpful **tourist police** are located at Sáenz Peña 830 (© 074/236-700). For medical attention, go to **Hospital Las Mercedes,** González 635 (© 074/237-021); **Clínica Lambayeque,** Vicente de la Vega 415 (© 074/237-961); or **Clínica Santa Cecilia,** González 668 (© 074/237-154). In Lambayeque, head to **Hospital Belén de Lambayeque,** Ramón Castilla 597 (© 074/281-190).

For Internet access, try **Sic@n Internet,** Vicente de la Vega 204 (© 074/227-668), or **Efenet,** Elías Aguirre 181 (no phone). There are also Internet cabinas clustered around the Parque Principal and on Manuel María Izaga near Avenida Balta.

Chiclayo's **post office** is at Elías Aguirre 140 (© 074/237-031), about 6 blocks from the Parque Principal. The **Telefónica del Perú** office is behind the cathedral at Elías Aguirre 631 (© 074/232-225).

Getting Around

Chiclayo is a busy and fairly congested city. The center of town is, as always, the Plaza de Armas—although, in Chiclayo, it more often goes by the name Parque Principal. About 4 blocks north of the main square is the other focal point in the city: the Mercado Modelo, a sprawling, spirited open street market with stalls spread across several blocks. The main axis in town is Avenida José Balta, which runs north to south and extends on either side of the Parque Principal (with designations Sur [south] and Norte [north]). Lambayeque is 12km (7½ miles) due west of Chiclayo; the airport and Sipán are to the east of Chiclayo.

Walking around the *centro* is easy enough, but you'll need public or private transportation to get to Lambayeque or the major archaeological sites.

BY TAXI Inexpensive *mototaxis* buzz about downtown, as do regular taxis. You can hire the latter by the hour (S/25) or by the day (S/120–S/150) to tour archaeological sites or to visit Lambayeque. A round-trip taxi ride to Túcume from Chiclayo costs about S/70.

NORTHERN PERU

12

CHICLAYO

ACCOMMODATIONS ■
Costa del Sol **5**
Gran Hotel Chiclayo **2**
Hostal Royal **3**
Las Musas Hotel y
   Casino **10**
Los Horcones de
   Túcume **11**

DINING ◆
Fiesta Restaurant Gourmet **1**
La Parra **7**
Jhon **6**
Pueblo Viejo **8**

ATTRACTIONS ●
Catedral **4**
Paseo de las Musas **9**

BY BUS   Combis and omnibuses are most useful for getting to Lambayeque and several archaeological sites outside Chiclayo. There are several terminals around the city serving different destinations. The fare is S/2.

BY CAR   If you want to rent a car to make trips to Lambayeque, Sipán, Túcume, and other sites, try **Chiclayo Rent a Car** in the Gran Hotel Chiclayo at Av. Federico Villarreal 115 (© 074/237-512). It rents four-wheel-drive vehicles.

WHAT TO SEE & DO
In Chiclayo
A brief look around Chiclayo should be sufficient. Start at the **Parque Principal,** the attractive and overwhelming focal point of life in the city. People camp out on park benches and slurp on ice-cream cones, shoeshine boys scurry from one pair of scuffed-up loafers to the next, and pigeons flutter from treetops to sidewalks to rooftops. The white, twin-domed neoclassical **Catedral** that dominates the square dates to 1869. About 10 long blocks south of the plaza, the **Paseo de las Musas** is an attractive park area rather inexplicably outfitted with neoclassical statuary of mythological figures.

The fascinating **Mercado Modelo** ★, 5 blocks north of the Parque Principal, is one of Peru's most raucous open street markets. Open daily from dawn to dusk, it carries virtually everything under the sun, but it's famed for the section of small stalls crammed with the elixirs and potions of shamans and faith healers. The so-called *mercadillo de brujas* (witches' little market), near Calle Arica, is redolent with exotic spices and drying herbs, wild with visual overload: hanging shells, small altarpieces and bottles filled with hooves and claws, snake skins, miniature desiccated crocs, claws, skunks, and fish eggs. Echoing throughout are the distinctive come-ons of vendors. This city of stalls is about as close as you'll get to India or Morocco in Peru, but it's nonetheless a primer on the country's extensive informal economy. You'll find luggage, natural Viagra substitutes, baskets, guitars, hats, calf brains, children's clothes, vats of peanut butter, stuffed animals, shops of canned goods, machetes, and butcher knives, plus dozens of beauty salons and shoe and electronics repair headquarters.

In Lambayeque

The **Museo Tumbas Reales de Sipán** (below) is the undisputed highlight of this small, quiet, and dusty town that was once considerably more important than its bigger neighbor but which has long since been overtaken, at least in terms of commercial importance, by it. The new museum has stolen quite a bit of the thunder of the **Museo Arqueológico Brüning** (below), where the Lord of Sipán used to reside. A few clues to Lambayeque's former status are evident in a number of colonial houses and the baroque **Iglesia de San Pedro** (daily 8am–4pm), a large and impressive yellow-and-white church built in 1700 and located on the main square. It's worth a look inside to see the impressive mural paintings on the ceiling of the central nave and the cupola. Columns are painted to look like real marble, which I suppose they do if you squint hard enough. The rest of the church is done up in pastel hues of green, blue, and yellow.

On the corner of Dos de Mayo and San Martín is Lambayeque's other building of import, **Casa de la Logia** ★ (also known as **Casa Montjoy**). Erected in the 16th century, it claims the longest colonial balcony in Peru, a splendidly carved wooden wraparound structure 67m (220 ft.) long. It can be viewed only from outside.

Lambayeque really springs to life on market day, Sunday. Otherwise, there's little to detain visitors. If you're looking for a bite to eat after visiting the Brüning Museum, check out Dos de Mayo, where there are several *cevicherías* and other restaurants.

Museo Nacional de Arqueología y Etnografía Heinrich Brüning ★ Until its
Sipán treasures were removed and transferred to the new Tumbas Reales Museum 2 blocks away (below), this was the preeminent museum in northern Peru. Without its star attraction, the museum, founded in 1966, no longer draws crowds, but it still retains some important archaeological finds, such as Sicán masks from Batán Grande, excellent Moche ceramics, and an assortment of artifacts found at Tucumé. The collection includes some 1,500 items from the Lambayeque, Moche, Chavín, Vicus, and Inca civilizations. Some pieces date back 10,000 years.

Av. Huamachuco (Block 7), Lambayeque. ✆ **074/282-110.** Admission S/10 adults, S/3 students. Guides available for S/10. Daily 9am–5:30pm. Colectivos to Lambayeque depart Chiclayo from the corner of Avenida Angamos and Vicente de la Vega, and pass right in front of the Brüning Museum about a half-hour later. The main plaza is a couple blocks from the museum (across the street).

Museo Tumbas Reales de Sipán ★★★ This stunningly modern museum certainly stands out in northern Peru, land of dusty archaeological pyramids and colonial towns. Its daring architecture of bold angles, glass, and orange concrete makes a statement

by echoing the ancient Moche pyramids of the region, but the principal attraction is within. It holds one of Peru's most spectacular exhibits, the tomb of the **Lord of Sipán**, discovered in 1987, which ranks as one of the most important archaeological discoveries in Peru of the past 50 years. Unearthed at the Huaca Rajada at Sipán, the multilevel royal funeral tomb of El Señor de Sipán, a Moche royal figure buried more than 1,700 years ago, was remarkable for its undisturbed, methodical layers and wealth of ceremonial ornaments and treasures that provided key clues to Moche culture. Buried along with the king, who was presumed to be a sort of living deity, were companions joining him on his journey to the afterlife: a Moche warrior, a priest, three female concubines, a dog, two llamas, a child, 212 food and beverage vessels, and a guard with a copper shield, gold helmet, and amputated feet—symbolic of his everlasting protection over the king's tomb.

The space dedicated to the Lord of Sipán is one of the most impressive and unforgettable sights under a roof in Peru—a revelation for visitors who've visited several of the archaeological sites in northern Peru and been disappointed to find little more than difficult-to-decipher colossal piles of clay. In this marvelously designed three-level museum, the spectacular Sipán finds articulate the grandeur and achievements of pre-Inca cultures and help us comprehend their religious beliefs, social structure, and sophistication. On display from the main funerary chamber—amazingly, never looted—are headdresses, garments, and breastplates of gold, silver, and precious stones that tell an intricate story of power and rank. Several pieces, such as the royal necklace of 20 peanuts, half gold and half silver, are stunning. Other tombs uncovered and re-created here are those of the priest, the mythical "Bird-Man" and top-ranking religious official, and the Viejo Señor de Sipán (or Old Lord of Sipán), a Moche spiritual dignitary whose death preceded that of the newer lord's and whose remains were found buried farther below.

The Tumbas Reales Museum is one of the best organized and best designed in Peru, an eminently worthy resting place for this monumental discovery. You'll need at least a couple of hours to explore it fully.

Juan Pablo Vizcardo y Guzman s/n, Lambayeque. (© **074/283-977.** www.museotumbasrealessipan.pe. Admission S/10 adults, S/4 seniors, S/1.50 students. Guides available for S/15. Tues–Sun 9am–5pm. Colectivos to Lambayeque depart Chiclayo from the corner of Av. Angamos and Vicente de la Vega, and pass right in front of the Tumbas Reales Museum about a half-hour later.

In Ferreñafe

Museo Nacional Sicán ★★   Although not quite as celebrated as the Museo Tumbas Reales, this handsome, modern, and excellent museum, inaugurated in 2001, is very much worth a visit to round out an understanding of the region's ancient civilizations. Like its better-known sibling, it too is pyramid-shaped and a study in cement and glass, but it focuses on the Sicán culture (also called Lambayeque) that succeeded the Moche and thrived until the 14th century. The Sicán (which means "Temple of the Moon"), who were the first to discover bronze in northern Peru, buried their dead in unique vertical rooms and surrounded them with large collections of valuable metals. Those graves provided looters throughout Peru with a wealth of sought-after gold objects. Sicán masks with *ojos alados*, or "winged eyes," are very prized among institutions and collectors, and some excellent examples are on view here. The museum is located in Ferreñafe, 20km (12 miles) north of Chiclayo, along the road that leads to Batán Grande (below).

Av. Batán Grande (Block 9), Carretera a Pítipo, Ferreñafe. (© **074/286-469.** Admission S/10 adults, S/4 seniors, S/1.50 students. Guides available for S/15. Tues–Sun 9am–5pm. Colectivos to Ferreñafe depart Chiclayo from the Terminal de Epsel, Av. Oriente at Nicolás de Piérola.

Colectivos (buses) to the archaeological sites Batán Grande, Templo de Sipán, and Zaña leave from the Terminal de Epsel at the corner of Avenida Oriente and Nicolás de Piérola in Chiclayo, a somewhat unsavory area. It's more convenient to visit these sites by organized tour; contact **Sipán Tours** at 🕐 **074/229-053.**

Batán Grande   The Batán Grande archaeological complex is a set of ruins from the Sicán culture that comprises some 50 adobe pyramids and a network of tombs from the middle Sicán period (A.D. 900–1000). Some of the finest pre-Columbian artifacts in Peruvian museums were found by archaeologists here, including a nearly 7-pound gold Tumi (ceremonial knife) figure and an estimated 90% of all gold pieces from the Lambayeque civilization. Set amid a large nature reserve of mesquite forest (El Bosque Seco de Pómac), there's an on-site interpretation center for visitors, but the pyramids are not as established on the tourist circuit as are those at Túcume.

Located 57km (35 miles) SE of Chiclayo, and 5km (3 miles) NE of Túcume. 🕐 **074/201-470.** Admission S/10 adults, S/4 students. Guides available for S/10. Daily 7am–4pm. Colectivos leave from the Terminal de Epsel at the corner of Av. Oriente and Nicolás de Piérola in Chiclayo. It's more convenient to visit Batán Grande by organized tour; contact Sipán Tours at 🕐 **074/229-053.**

Templo de Sipán   The site where the Lord of Sipán was discovered in 1987, this Moche burial ground 35km (22 miles) from Chiclayo was overlooked by archaeologists for decades. Grave robbers, who'd beaten scientists to countless other valuable sites in Peru, had just begun to loot the ones here, tipping off Peruvian archaeologist Dr. Walter Alva to the presence of the tomb in time to save it. The Sipán sarcophagus held greater riches than any other found to date in Peru and, today, is recognized as one of the most outstanding of the Americas. The twin adobe pyramids, connected by a platform, held five royal tombs. The most elaborate was that of El Señor de Sipán; deeper still was the tomb of an older spiritual leader, now referred to as El Viejo Señor. The remains of both are exhibited at the Museo Tumbas Reales in Lambayeque. Near the original site, Huaca Rajada ("Cracked Pyramid") is a small site museum with photos of the excavations and some replicas of tombs. Although it's interesting to see where the tombs were found, and the views from the top of the large pyramid across from the Sipán excavation site are excellent, Templo de Sipán is no substitute for the splendor of jewels and ornaments now housed at the Museo Tumbas Reales.

Complejo Arqueológico de Huaca Rajada, Sipán. 🕐 **074/800-048.** Admission S/5. Guides available for S/10. Daily 8am–6pm. Colectivos leave from the Terminal de Epsel at the corner of Av. Oriente and Nicolás de Piérola in Chiclayo, and take about 45 min.

Túcume ★★   Located 33km (20 miles) north of Chiclayo, this magnificent, massive complex of 26 adobe pyramids (not for nothing do locals call it "El Valle de las Pirámides") was constructed by the Sicán civilization around A.D. 1000 and developed over a period of nearly 500 years. The site was settled and enlarged by the Chimú culture in the 14th century and, finally, occupied by the Incas. Túcume was the most important elite urban center of the region and is considered the last great capital of the Lambayeque culture.

You can wander freely around the maze of courtyards and pyramids, and even scale several of them, which are still being excavated and together present an enigmatic desert ensemble. Walking around sites such as these is almost more evocative of what a contemporary archaeologist's life is like than of the lives of those ancient cultures that lived there. The Túcume complex's stunning size, more than a mile long in each direction (a total of 32 hectares/79 acres), is more impressive than any individual structure. The pyramid

The Sicán Civilization

The Sicán culture (often designated the Lambayeque civilization, referring to the region where it grew to prominence) developed on the north coast of Peru in the 7th century following the collapse of the Moche civilization. A sophisticated culture whose economic mainstay was agriculture, the Sicán specialized in irrigation engineering. The society reached its apogee between A.D. 900 and 1100, and established religious and administrative headquarters at Batán Grande in the Pómac forest, near the Leche River. The site there is known as the "Temple of the Moon" in the ancient local dialect, Muchik. Around 1100, the Sicán abandoned Batán Grande, which they appear to have set fire to, and moved their capital across the valley to El Purgatorio, a hill in the midst of what are now the Túcume ruins. There they built a splendid urban center, the most important in the region, but the civilization was eventually conquered by the Chimú in 1375.

toward the back of the complex, known as **Huaca Larga,** is reputed to be the largest adobe brick structure in South America. It measures (even after erosion) 700m (2,297 ft.) long, 280m (919 ft.) wide, and 30m (98 ft.) high. A massive platform with several patios and courtyards connected by ramps and corridors, the huaca has walls covered in red, white, and black murals. Archaeologists have uncovered evidence of the three major stages of construction in Huaca Larga, from the original Lambayeque to Chimú, whose "Temple of the Mythical Bird" dates to 1375, and finally an Inca structure built on top of the Chimú building at the end of the 15th century. Inside the Inca room was a burial tomb, where 22 bodies were discovered, including a local ruler and warrior, interred along with two other males and 19 females.

An interestingly conceived site museum exhibits photographs of the excavations and discusses the involvement of a Norwegian explorer, the late Dr. Thor Heyerdahl, who sought to connect ancient Peruvian culture to that of Polynesia. (He sailed a balsawood craft called the *Kon Tiki* from Peru to the Polynesian islands.) Heyerdahl was the director of the 1989 to 1994 Túcume Project, which carried out excavations at the site. Also onsite are a handicrafts-and-ceramics workshop and a snack shop. You'll often find women cooking out in the open on the grounds.

Complejo Arqueológico, Caserío La Raya, Campo. ☎ **074/422-027,** or 074/800-052 site museum. Admission S/10 adults, S/4 students. Guides available for S/10. Daily 8am–4:30pm. Colectivos leave from Av. Angamos, btw. Naturaleza and Pardo in Chiclayo (a 45-min. ride), although they leave travelers a good mile or so from the site. Look for a taxi or *mototaxi,* or walk along the road. A good idea is to visit the Museo Arqueológico Brüning in the morning and head out to Túcume in the afternoon. Buses leave for Túcume from very near the museum in Lambayeque; the ticket office can indicate exactly where. Tell the driver you'll be getting off at Túcume.

Zaña Ruins of an entirely different sort, this 16th-century ghost town was once an important and wealthy colonial outpost, loaded with churches and monasteries. On the fast track toward becoming the Peruvian capital, it underwent a turbulent period of slave rebellion and pirate attacks. Wealthy families fled to Lambayeque city, and Zaña was soon afterward wiped out by a massive flood in 1720. The overflowing Río Zaña caused

Finds The Ruins of Kuélap ★★

Everyone—at least everyone on his or her way to Peru—has heard of Machu Picchu. Very few have heard of Kuélap, though. Yet it's one of the archaeological wonders of Peru, a formerly lost city that stands as the true adventurer's alternative to Machu Picchu, which today is easily accessible and exceedingly popular. Tucked in highland cloud forest on top of an Andean mountain ridge at an altitude of 3,000m (9,840 ft.), Kuélap is a stupendous and titanic set of ruins that in fact predates the Incas—it's more than 800 years old. Though ripe for discovery by a wider swath of visitors to Peru, Kuélap is still primarily a destination for independent travelers with plenty of time and a keen sense of adventure.

Located northeast of Cajamarca, near the small town of Chachapoyas (itself something of a poor man's Cusco, given the assortment of ruins littered about it), and discovered in the mid–19th century, the site is said to have employed more stone during its 200-year construction than even the Great Pyramids of Egypt. A fortress complex of nearly 400 buildings, most of them round, and surrounded by a 30m-high (98-ft.) defensive wall, Kuélap was home to 2,000 people from A.D. 1100 to 1300. Very little is known about its builders and inhabitants, though. They were most likely the Chachapoyans or Sachupoyans, both

such structural damage that the population abandoned the city. Today it's a curious sight of ornate columns, church arches, and the remains of the once-grand Gothic Convento de San Agustín (as well as three other convents). A small, inhabited village (also called Zaña) is nearby.

46km (29 miles) SE of Chiclayo. Admission by organized tour only. Colectivos leave from the Terminal de Epsel on the corner of Av. Oriente and Nicolás de Piérola in Chiclayo. Numerous tour agencies also include Zaña in organized outings, probably the most efficient way of visiting the town; try Sipán Tours at ✆ 074/229-053.

Nearby Beaches: Pimentel & Santa Rosa
Pimentel is a beach resort 14km (8¾ miles) west of Chiclayo, with a nice enough beach that's very popular in summer and a small fishing community that still employs the *caballitos de mar* (totora-reed boats) seen in Huanchaco, near Trujillo. Just 6km (3¾ miles) south of Pimentel is **Santa Rosa,** a more attractive beach and fishing village with totora-reed and gaily painted wooden fishing boats. It has a handful of good seafood restaurants. Both beaches are low-key and a good antidote to touring archaeological sites.

Buses and colectivos run from Vicente Vega and Angamos in Chiclayo to Pimentel. In summer, they continue along a "circuito de playas" to Santa Rosa, Puerto Etén, and Monsefú, none of which is spectacular.

WHERE TO STAY
Chiclayo is hardly brimming with good, interesting hotel options. The best among the bunch are merely functional. Travelers used to a high level of comfort and style won't find much to their liking in Chiclayo, and the paucity of good hotels extends down to the budget level.

groups that were later brought into the Inca fold that unified the highlands. Unlike other ruins in Peru, most of what exists at Kuélap is original, although some reconstruction has been initiated.

The ruins are open daily from 8:30am to 5pm; admission is S/10. Getting to Kuélap independently remains a laborious endeavor, involving buses to Chachapoyas and/or Tingo, plus a long and very difficult 5- to 6-hour hike. (It's a scenic but wearying 18- to 24-hour bus ride from Cajamarca, or a less exciting 9- to 10-hour journey from Chiclayo.) Organized visits from Cajamarca might not suit modern-day Hiram Binghams, but they are by far the most convenient way to get to what remains a very remote outpost. Group trips usually cost $250 or more per person and last 5 days round-trip. If you've got the time and money to spare, and a sense of adventure, check with **Cumbe Mayo** and **Inca Baths Tours** (see "Getting Around" in "Cajamarca," below) or **Chachapoyas Tours,** Jr. Grau 534, Chachapoyas (© **041/478-078,** or 866/396-9582 in the U.S.; www.kuelapperu.com), which specializes in tours of Kuélap (from comfortable to rugged) leaving from Chachapoyas. There's a small Institute of National Culture albergue with dorm-style sleeping arrangements available.

Expensive

Gran Hotel Chiclayo   Several blocks removed from the heart of downtown, Chiclayo's largest and most luxurious hotel is a modern, massive concrete block with mainstream corporate style. Rooms are large and well equipped, if without much personality. This hotel has all the amenities and services that business travelers demand, as well as a nice round pool for leisure visitors. The El Caballito disco and the happening "Karaoke Solid Gold" casino draw plenty of locals throughout the week.

Av. Federico Villarreal 115, Chiclayo. © **074/234-911.** Fax 074/223-961. www.granhotelchiclayo.com.pe. 129 units. S/300 double; S/345–S/560 suite. Rates include breakfast buffet and airport transfer. AE, DC, MC, V. **Amenities:** Restaurant; bar; concierge; outdoor pool. *In room:* A/C, TV, fridge, hair dryer, Wi-Fi.

Moderate

Costa del Sol ★ (Value   A miniature high-rise building on Chiclayo's most important and busiest street, this midsize hotel offers a good mix of amenities and easygoing charm. The remodeled, newly sedate rooms are spacious and comfortable, and bathrooms are also of a good size. Unexpected features are the cute rooftop pool and the Jacuzzi with a dry sauna. All in all, it's a good value with enough personality to set it apart from the more expensive and more standard Gran Hotel Chiclayo.

Av. José Balta 399, Chiclayo. © **074/227-272.** Fax 074/209-342. www.costadelsolperu.com. 40 units. S/329 double; S/503 suite. Rates include continental breakfast buffet. AE, DC, MC, V. **Amenities:** Restaurant; bar; concierge; Jacuzzi; outdoor pool; sauna. *In room:* A/C, TV, fridge.

Las Musas Hotel & Casino (Value   Formerly the Hotel María Alejandra, now revamped as a casino and hotel, Las Musas is pleasant and one of Chiclayo's better values, though for a few dollars more, I think the Costa del Sol is preferable. Las Musas's modern exterior doesn't do much for me, but it has pretty good services, a casino, and a nice view of the city from a fairly calm residential area. The rooms aren't luxurious but they are quite nicely decorated in subdued colors, and all have nice, large bathtubs—which is an unexpected luxury.

Los Faiques 101 (facing Paseo de las Musas), Urbanización Santa Victoria, Chiclayo. © **074/273-445.** Fax 074/273-450. www.lasmusashotel.com.pe. 42 units. $70 double; $100 suite. Rates include continental breakfast. AE, DC, MC, V. **Amenities:** Restaurant; bar. *In room:* A/C, TV, fridge.

Inexpensive

Hostal Royal (Finds)   This large, rambling old colonial hotel, with a formerly grand, winding central staircase, sits right on the Parque Principal. The place is a bit run-down, although some travelers will find it full of local character. Rooms are large and spartan, with hardwood floors. Beds are a bit soft, though, and bathrooms are tucked behind cheapo partitions, which makes privacy a problem. The best rooms, although surely not the quietest, are those with balconies overlooking the plaza.

San José 787, Chiclayo. © **074/233-421.** Fax 074/228-171. 30 units. S/45 double. No credit cards. *In room:* No phone.

WHERE TO STAY OUTSIDE CHICLAYO

Los Horcones de Túcume ★★ (Finds)   The best place to stay in the Chiclayo area—especially for anyone interested in visiting the region's archaeological sites—is this stylish rural lodge in the shadow of the Túcume pyramids, about 30km (19 miles) outside of town. This relaxing inn, constructed of adobe and local *algarrobo* beams and designed by the owner, an architect, sits in an open area of corn fields, and it has peaceful private and common terraces swathed in trees and flowers. Rooms are airy and colorfully decorated, and there's a nice little, affordable restaurant on-site. The inn offers horseback riding in the valley, making it the perfect place to enjoy the sunny valley of the pyramids.

Antigua Panamericana Norte Lambayeque-Túcume. © **01/242-1866.** Fax 01/445-5186. http://los horconesdetucume.com. 12 units. $50 double. Rates include breakfast. MC, V. **Amenities:** Restaurant. *In room:* A/C, no phone.

WHERE TO DINE

Fiesta Chiclayo Gourmet ★★★ NORTHERN PERUVIAN   This terrific restaurant, where all the clients seem to be regulars and even friends, specializes in a very underrated cuisine, that of Lambayeque. Chiclayo is definitely the best place to indulge in its distinctive, hearty fare (although there's a Fiesta branch in Lima). Behind an unassuming facade with a mural representation of the region's rich ancient cultures and archaeology is one of the north's best restaurants. Have an excellent cocktail in the cozy Bar Sipán before moving on to the straightforward dining room, with parquet wood floors, straw window treatments and simply framed photographs on the walls. Start with the pork or corn *humitas* (tamales) or grouper *causa* (with mashed potatoes), a dish that in Chiclayo is typically eaten only on Sundays (but here is served daily), followed perhaps by succulent barbecued goat ribs. Service is impeccable and friendly. Just be sure to bring your appetite, as this is rich and filling food.

Salaverry 1820. © **074/201-970.** www.restaurantfiestagourmet.com. Reservations recommended. Main courses S/22–S/46. AE, DC, MC, V. Daily noon–11pm.

Jhon (Finds) CEVICHE/SEAFOOD   A tiny neighborhood place with just 10 tables, this informal *cevichería* specializes in fish, shellfish, and, of course, several types of ceviche. Among the latter, try the *conchas negras* (black scallops) or *mixto a la Jhon* (with octopus, white fish, shrimp, and conchas). A more substantial entree is one of the *arroces* (rice dishes) with fish or shellfish. There are also several preparations of fish, such as *mero* (grouper) and a nice *picante de camarones* (spicy shrimp). Note that Jhon, which is a local favorite, is open only for lunch or a very early dinner.

Colón 276 (at Tacna). © **074/208-593.** Reservations not accepted. Main courses S/12–S/30. No credit cards. Daily 10am–6pm.

La Parra ★ (Kids) GRILL   At the entrance of this restaurant is a busy, open grill—an indication of the meat-dominated menu inside. This comfortable, relaxed restaurant is nice, if a tad nondescript, with a vaulted wood ceiling, wood paneling, stucco walls, and hardwood floors—and odd incongruous touches such as a framed portrait of Jesus and a deer head. Everyone chows down on grilled meats, served with fries and a salad, not just because it's the house specialty, but also because it's the only thing La Parra serves. *Lomo fino* (sirloin), shish kabob, sausage, and chicken are among the excellent choices from the grill. Shareable menu options like the *parrillada* for four make this place popular with families. Next door is a good *chifa* (Peruvian Chinese restaurant) by the same owner.

Manuel María Izaga 752. © **074/227-471.** Reservations recommended Fri–Sat. Main courses S/11–S/32. AE, DC, MC, V. Daily noon–11pm.

Pueblo Viejo ★★ (Value) PERUVIAN   Chiclayo's most chic and best restaurant, this relaxed and attractive two-story place serves traditional Chiclayano cooking and *comida criolla,* but only for lunch. The menu is interesting and creative, derived from old recipes from the surrounding area. Especially good are the fish and shellfish dishes, such as *tiradito de la casa* (sliced fish with lemon, chilies, corn, and onions), ceviche, and *tollito a la panca* (dogfish with *chicha,* cilantro, and corn, served in a clay pot). Other options are fish soup, tender goat, and dried roasted beef. A tasty appetizer is the *humitas de la abuela,* a white-corn tamale stuffed with pork. The nicest area is upstairs under the colored skylights, with lots of plants and wooden walkways, which give it the feel of a well-equipped tree house. (Okay, that might be a stretch, but it's head and shoulders above the norm of plain Peruvian eateries in the north.)

Manuel María Izaga 900 (at Calzoncillo). © **074/228-863.** Reservations recommended Fri–Sat. Main courses S/12–S/36. No credit cards. Daily noon–5pm.

3 CAJAMARCA ★★

855km (531 miles) NE of Lima; 298km (185 miles) NE of Trujillo; 235km (146 miles) SE of Chiclayo

Delightful and historic Cajamarca, the jewel of Peru's northern highlands, deserves to be more widely appreciated. Those who know the city often call it "the Cusco of the north," and comparisons to that tourist magnet farther south are not illegitimate. This graceful and traditional mountain town possesses some of the same attributes as Cusco, but it is refreshingly free of many of the hassles associated with the gringo capital of South America. Although it's surrounded by the Andes at an altitude of nearly 2,700m (8,900 ft.) above sea level, Cajamarca is a down-to-earth and unassuming place that doesn't get caught up in its colonial beauty and Andean grace. Townspeople, nearly all of them decked out in marvelously distinctive *sombreros de paja* (straw hats), merely go about their business.

Cajamarca is the largest city in a fertile agricultural region (though see the box on p. 411 for info on the growing mining industry here) that is virtually unsurpassed in Peru

Caxamarca: A Brief History

The Cajamarca Valley was the epicenter of a pre-Inca culture called Caxamarca (as it was spelled pre-conquest) which reached its apex between A.D. 500 and 1000. Cajamarca was part of a small northern highlands kingdom called Cuis-mango, which was influenced by two great cultures, Chavín and Huari. The Incas, led by Cápac Yupanqui, conquered Caxamarca around 1465, annexing the territory and solidifying the empire's hold on the northern Andes. Caja-marca soon became an important administrative, political, and religious center and a major link in the transcontinental Andes highway; the Incas constructed great palaces and temples in the city.

Francisco Pizarro and a small band of troops, numbering around 160, reached the Cajamarca Valley in November 1532. November 16 shook the very foundations of the Inca Empire and changed Spanish-American and Peruvian history. Pizarro's men ambushed Atahualpa, the last Inca emperor, and held him prisoner. Inca troops, numbering more than 50,000 but already in the midst of civil war, offered no resistance. Atahualpa proposed a huge ransom to win his release, but the Spaniards killed him anyway, 7 months after a staged trial condemning him for attempting to arrange his rescue. The end of the Inca Empire was near, as the Spanish moved south toward Cusco. Cajamarca became a colonial city in 1802. Besides a few stone foundations, only Atahual-pa's Cuarto de Rescate (Ransom Room) remains of the grand Inca masonry that once distinguished Cajamarca. But the city's post-Inca colonial roots are very much evident in Spanish-style architecture throughout Cajamarca.

for its luxurious, verdant countryside. (The climate is pleasantly springlike, with clear blue skies, most of the year.) It's also known for its splendid dairy products, so any visit here should involve stops at some of the many ice-cream and cheese shops. And Caja-marca is ringed by archaeological sites and handsome hacienda estates, which make get-ting out to the country a must.

ESSENTIALS
Getting There
BY PLANE   There are daily 2-hour flights from Lima on LAN (✆ **01/213-8200;** www.lan.com) and **LC Busre** (✆ **01/619-1313;** www.lcbusre.com.pe). Flights start at $113 one-way.

The **Armando Revoredo Aeropuerto de Cajamarca** (✆ **076/362-523**) is just 3km (1¾ miles) east of the Plaza de Armas. To downtown Cajamarca, a taxi costs S/5.

BY BUS   **Cruz del Sur** (✆ **01/311-5050;** www.cruzdelsur.com.pe) and **Expreso Cia** (✆ **01/428-5218**) make the 12-hour trip from Lima to Cajamarca. **Transportes Línea** (✆ **076/222-221** or 044/297-000; www.transporteslinea.com.pe) travels from Lima, Trujillo (6 hr.), and Chiclayo (5–6 hr.). The bus terminals are located mostly on Avenida Atahualpa and Avenida Zavala, about 3km (1¾ miles) from the center of town.

NORTHERN PERU

12

CAJAMARCA

ACCOMMODATIONS ■
El Cabildo Hostal **13**
El Portal del Marqués **10**
Hacienda San Vicente **17**
Hostal Plaza **5**
Hostal Portada del Sol **1**
Hotel Costa del Sol **12**
Hotel & Spa Laguna
  Seca **20**
Hotel Posada del Puruay/
  Hostal Portada del Sol
  Hacienda **2**
Los Balcones de
  la Recoleta **19**

DINING ◆
Cascanuez Café-Bar **4**
El Batán **3**
El Querubino **7**
La Casa de la Abuela **15**
La Vaca Loca **14**
Om-Gri **16**
Restaurant Salas **6**

ATTRACTIONS ●
Catedral **11**
Conjunto Monumental
  de Belén **18**
El Cuarto de Rescate **9**
Iglesia de San Francisco **8**

Visitor Information

There's a branch of the **Regional Tourism Office** within the massive Conjunto Monumental de Belén complex at Jr. Belén 600 (© 076/362-997). It's open Monday through Friday from 8:30am to 1pm and 2:30 to 6:30pm. The office has a handful of photocopied materials and some brochures for sale, including a self-published tourist information guide. There's another small **Oficina de Información Turística,** associated with the university, at Batán 289 (© 076/361-546), which is very helpful and gives out free city maps. It's open Monday through Friday from 8:30am to 1pm.

FAST FACTS Two banks are **Interbank,** 2 de Mayo on the Plaza de Armas (© 076/362-4600), and **Banco de Crédito,** Jr. del Comercio 679 (© 076/362-742). Neither of these banks exchanges traveler's checks. There are generally money-changers on the Plaza de Armas and Jirón del Batán; there are also several small *casas de cambio* in the same area.

In an **emergency,** call © 105. The **police** are located at Amalia Puga 807 (© 076/362-832). For medical attention, go to **Hospital Regional,** Mario Urteaga 500 (© 076/362-156); **Clínica San Francisco,** Avenida Grau (© 076/362-050); or **Clínica Limatambo,** Puno s/n (© 076/364-241).

(Moments) Carnaval in Cajamarca

Cajamarca is a very traditional Andean highland city, but it lets loose once a year during Carnaval. Its pre-Lenten festivities are said to be the wildest in Peru. Full of music and dance, it also takes on aspects of a high-school locker room. Paint, water, and even bodily fluids (!) are flung around with abandon, so wear a raincoat. If you want to experience (or subject yourself to?) Cajamarca's Carnaval, plan ahead. It's very popular with Peruvians, and hotels sell out. Another festive time in Cajamarca, formerly Peru's grandest Inca celebration, is Corpus Christi (May or June), which includes lots of processions, music, bullfights, and horse shows.

For Internet access, try **Efenet,** Jirón Dos de Mayo, **CyberNet,** Comercio 924, or **Atajo,** Jr. del Comercio 716 (© **076/362-245**). Atajo is open until 1am and offers cheap international Internet calls.

Cajamarca's **Serpost** (post office) is at Amalia Puga 778 (© **076/364-065**). There's a **DHL/Western Union** office at Dos de Mayo 323 (© **076/364-674**), within the Cajamarca Tours office. The **Telefónica del Perú** office is at Dos de Mayo 460 on the Plaza de Armas (© **076/364-008**).

Getting Around

The major sights of interest in Cajamarca are all around the Plaza de Armas or within easy walking distance of it. Except for the Inca Baths, you're unlikely to require transportation unless you're staying at one of the country hotels on the outskirts of town, which are serviced by taxi and, to a lesser extent, colectivo.

BY TAXI Taxis are easy to come by in the center of Cajamarca. They circulate around the Plaza de Armas and the streets leading off it. Most in-town fares are about S/3. To call a cab, try **Taxi Seguro** (© **076/365-103**) or **Taxis Unidos** (© **076/368-888**).

BY ORGANIZED TOUR Reliable tour agencies include **Inca Baths Tours,** Jr. Amalia Puga 653 (© **076/362-938**); **Cumbe Mayo Tours,** Jr. Amalia Puga 635 (© **076/822-938**); and **Cajamarca Travel,** Jr. Dos de Mayo 570 (© **076/365-651**). These companies offer city tours and inexpensive, pooled half- and full-day tours to sights in the countryside around Cajamarca (including Cumbe Mayo, Otuzco, Colpa, and Inca Baths). Most standard tours cost S/25 to S/35. Several agencies also offer long-distance tours to the famed but remote Kuélap ruins for around $600 per person. All agencies advertise English-speaking guides, but fluency is a relative term. The best bets are Inca Baths Tours and Cumbe Mayo Tours.

WHAT TO SEE & DO

In Cajamarca

Colonial Cajamarca has several sights of interest, although the town's principal appeal might lie in its relaxed and proudly traditional air, as yet undisturbed by a tourist onslaught. Many of Cajamarca's premier tourist attractions are just outside the city in the beautiful pastoral countryside, within easy reach for day trips. Most are best visited by convenient organized tour (see "Getting Around," above).

Plaza de Armas ★★

The heart of city life, Cajamarca's peaceful Plaza de Armas is one of the loveliest in Peru. In the days of the Incas, it was also the focal point of town, but it was a triangular court-yard rather than a square, per se. The plaza was taken in dramatic fashion by Pizarro's small band of invading troops in 1532, and the Inca Emperor Atahualpa was killed there after a mock trial. The fountain at the center of the square dates back more than 300 years, and the plaza is marked by handsome topiaries and low trees. Two grand churches front the square, and it can be difficult to determine which one is the cathedral. On one side is the **Catedral** (cathedral), built in the 17th and 18th centuries. Its baroque facade is ornately carved from volcanic stone. The gloomy interior features a bold, amazingly carved main altar and a pulpit of carved wood and gold leaf. If the cathedral looks a bit squat and unfinished, it's because its belfry was never completed, a drastic measure to avoid payment of a Spanish tax on finished ecclesiastical buildings. As seen in colonial churches in Cusco, the cathedral is built upon original Inca stonework.

The grander of the two churches, though, is directly across the plaza. The **Iglesia de San Francisco** ★, which once formed part of the San Francisco Convent, is entirely wrought from volcanic rock. Built in the first half of the 18th century, the parish church did not add the two bell towers until 1951. Covering every inch of the facade is terrific stone sculpting. Inside is a **Museo de Arte Religioso Colonial,** Jr. Dos de Mayo 435 (✆ 076/322-994); it's open Monday through Saturday from 3 to 6pm and admission is S/3. The collection of colonial art includes interesting icons and paintings. Beneath the museum are the church's catacombs, good for an eerie visit. Next door to the church is the small and beautiful Santuario de la Virgen de Dolores, or the chapel of **La Dolorosa,** named for the patron saint of Cajamarca. The 18th-century facade is one of the greatest examples of stone carving in the city.

Conjunto Monumental de Belén ★★★

On block six of Belén is the city's most important and historic architectural complex, almost entirely constructed of volcanic stone. Dating to the 18th century, it includes a church and colonial women's and men's hospitals, now housing ancient medical and archaeological exhibits. The entire complex is run by the National Institute of Culture. On a small and pretty square, the **Iglesia Belén** might be the most extraordinary work of colonial architecture in Cajamarca. The church, which replaced a primitive adobe-and-wood church on the spot, was begun in 1699 and completed a half-century later. Its decorative baroque stone facade is one of the finest in Peru. The interior is replete with delightful and large, carved polychromatic figures of angels and warriors; the carved pulpit is particularly impressive. The richly decorative cupola, supported by eight almost cartoon-like cherubs, was painted by high-land natives.

The **Hospital de Hombres (Men's Hospital)** is located on a lovely courtyard marked by a fountain. The austere hospital, run by Franciscans, began receiving patients in 1630. So that they could focus on prayer, the patients' beds faced the altar and the Virgen de la

---

Ⓣⓘⓟⓢ **Get Out of Town on Tuesday**

Most of Cajamarca's top sights are closed on Tuesday. If you're in town that day, it would be wise to schedule a visit to the Inca Baths or another out-of-town excursion, such as Cumbe Mayo or Otuzco.

Cajamarca's Colonial Mansions & Churches

In the center of Cajamarca are several notable large houses that feature carved stone porticoes, slanted roofs, long wooden balconies, and the type of pretty garden courtyards favored by Spanish colonialists. Visitors with an interest in 17th- and 18th-century colonial and republican architecture should check out the following *casonas* and churches, in addition to those discussed elsewhere in greater detail.

- **Casa Toribio Casanova,** Jr. José Gálvez 938.
- **Casa Santiesteban,** Junín 1123.
- The **house** at Cruz de Piedra 613. Now the property of the municipal government, the house has another excellent carved portico. Also on Cruz de Piedra is a stone cross, which supposedly marks the spot where Simón Bolívar, the Great Libertador, swore to avenge the death of Atahualpa.
- **La Recoleta,** a church about 6 blocks south of the Plaza de Armas, at the end of Amalia Puga.
- **Palacio de los Condes de Uceda** (now the Banco de Crédito), Apurímac 717. A splendid yellowish-orange, well-restored noble house with a carved stone portico.
- **Palacio del Obispo,** next to the Cathedral.
- **San Pedro,** a church at the corner of Gálvez and Junín.

Piedad. To the right of the entrance is a gallery of vibrant paintings, several of them portraits of highlands *campesinos,* by Andrés Zevallos. Across the street is the **Hospital de Mujeres (Women's Hospital);** on the facade, note the woman with child above the portal and, on either side of it, female figures with four breasts, symbols of the valley's super-potent fertility. Today the building houses perhaps the most interesting component of the Belén complex, a **Museo de Arqueología y Etnografía,** well laid out and exhibiting textiles and ceramics dating from as far back as 1500 B.C., replicas of Moche vessels, and local artisanship, dress (including Carnaval costumes), and silver *milagros* (prayer fetishes).

Jr. Belén s/n (at Junín). (© 076/322-601. Admission is by *boleto* (S/7.50; S/4 students), which also admits visitors to El Cuarto de Rescate (below). Mon and Wed–Fri 9am–1pm and 3–6pm; Sat–Sun 9am–1pm.

El Cuarto de Rescate ★ Across the street from La Dolorosa Chapel is the most famous building in Cajamarca. When Atahualpa was taken prisoner by Pizarro and his band of men in 1532, the Inca emperor was held in a cell, which he promised to fill with gold and silver many times over if the Spaniards would spare his life. The so-called "Ransom Room" is a small, rectangular stone room, set in the back of a colonial courtyard, once part of Atahualpa's palace. It is made of unadorned Inca masonry—the last intact example of Inca architecture in the city—and is barren except for a red line drawn across one wall, supposedly the very line Atahualpa drew to demonstrate to the Spanish how high his men would fill the cell with treasures. No one knows for sure whether this was simply Atahualpa's prison cell or if it was indeed a ransom room. What we do know is that the Inca chief was later executed by Pizarro's men, presumably on a stone right here, even before the Incas had surrendered all of the promised riches. The Cuarto de Rescate represents a crucial moment in Peruvian history, a clash in cultures with ramifications for the entire continent, but it might take some imagination to conjure the drama of the moment. The large painting at the entrance near the ticket booth, of Atahualpa being burned at the stake by the Spanish, is not entirely accurate; after accepting baptism, Atahualpa was merely strangled to death.

Amalia Puga 750 ($\frac{1}{2}$-block from Plaza de Armas). 076/322-601. Admission by *boleto* (S/7.50 adults; S/4 students), which admits visitors to the component parts of the Conjunto Monumental de Belén (above). Mon and Wed–Fri 9am–1pm and 3–6pm; Sat–Sun 9am–1pm.

On the Outskirts of Cajamarca

Baños del Inca (Kids) Just beyond Cajamarca lies the Inca Baths complex of gardens and pools with Cajamarca's famed thermal waters. In use since the time of the Incas (supposedly, Atahualpa had to be roused from his beloved bath when Pizarro and his troops entered the city), the baths are a wonderful respite of clean air and hot waters, ideal for relaxing after days of travel in the highlands. Set in a serene valley, at an elevation of nearly 2,650m (8,700 ft.) with wonderful mountain views, the park's thermal waters are said to be medicinal and effective for treating bronchial and rheumatic conditions. The waters, which reach temperatures of 165°F (74°C, but you can control the temperature with spigots in private pools), come from two different sources, Los Perolitos and El Tragadero. The open pools with rising steam make clear the scalding nature of the waters. The modern complex is extremely popular with locals and visitors alike. You can either opt for a private, indoor bath, in which you wait for a room to be vacated and cleaned and the deep pool filled with fresh sulfurous spring waters, or the sauna or outdoor pool. Take a bathing suit and towel with you. Bath products are for sale at the entrance.

6km (3$\frac{3}{4}$ miles) from Cajamarca. 076/821-563. Admission to the tourist complex (individual bathing cabins) S/5; to the communal baths S/3. Outdoor pool has assigned entrance times. Daily 5am–7pm. Colectivos labeled BAÑOS DEL INCA leave from Calle Amazonas and take about 15 min.; virtually everyone gets off at the same stop, across the street from the complex. A taxi costs about S/8.

Cerro Santa Apolonia A steep but lovely climb up the stairs at the southeast end of the Dos de Mayo leads to Santa Apolonia hill. On the way to the top is a small white chapel, the Virgen de Fátima, built in 1854. Often locked, the interior can still be glimpsed through the doorway. Up more paths, through terraced gardens where there are also a handful of caged animals, is a mirador with splendid panoramic views of Cajamarca

Mining Gold—and Digging Up Controversy

Cajamarca's rural roots and agriculture-based economy have been given a jolt with the discovery in the late 1980s of one of the world's largest and most productive gold mines, Yanacocha. The mine, about 48km (30 miles) north of Cajamarca, has quickly become the region's largest employer and brought an influx of foreign executives and their families, as well as controversy and conflict. Newmont Mining Corporation, with headquarters in Denver, Colorado, gained majority control of the Peruvian mine in 2000 through reported dealings with some of the Fujimori government's more unsavory officials. Since then, the firm has been engulfed in charges of contaminating local water supplies and protests over its proposed expansion to a nearby mountain, Cerro Quilish.

laid out at your feet. Rocks at the top, carved with petroglyphs, are believed to date to the Chavín civilization (1000–500 B.C.). Nearby, to the right of the white cross (if you're looking down at Cajamarca), sits a stone altar that has earned the popular name "the Inca's Throne." At this altar, carved like a chair, the Inca chief reportedly sat and gazed down on his city and troops. There's also a small tunnel that, according to legend, went all the way from Cajamarca to Cusco.

Reached by stairs at the end of Dos de Mayo. Park admission S/1. Daily 8am–6pm.

Attractions Beyond Cajamarca ★★

The countryside *(campiña)* around Cajamarca is extraordinary: a luxuriant expanse of rolling hills, eucalyptus trees, and meadows. If you're not staying at one of the country-style hacienda hotels outside of Cajamarca, a visit to the country is highly recommended to see this gorgeous, fertile region.

Among the standard organized campiña visits are excursions to several rural haciendas, including the worthwhile **Granja Porcón** (✆ **076/365-631**), a huge cooperative farm and agrotourism experiment supported by the Peruvian government and the European Union. It's about 30km (19 miles) north of Cajamarca. The community runs entirely on hydroelectric power, and hilltop forests have been planted at an altitude of 3,700m (12,139 ft.) to provide paper and wood products without harming the area's natural forests. There is a small *albergue* (lodging) and a restaurant on the premises. In **Lower Porcón,** the Festival of the Crosses (on Palm Sunday at the beginning of Easter week) is a famous expression of local folklore. Huge wood and cane crosses, adorned with images of Jesus and saints, flowers, and palm fronds, are carried in devout processions.

Other area cooperatives have not been well maintained and are less worthy of a visit. They include **La Colpa** (no phone), a cattle ranch and manor house in a beautiful setting; **Llacanora** (no phone), a small mountain village with ancient cave paintings and hikes to a pretty waterfall; and **Tres Molinos** (no phone), an agricultural center and gardens, where dairy products are sold.

The best way to visit one or more of the archaeological sites beyond Cajamarca is to sign on with one of the tour operators in town. Several of the sites are not accessible by public transportation; going with a guide in a small private colectivo is economical and convenient. Most agencies charge S/20 for standard day trips. Many combine visits (for example, to the Inca Baths, Colpa, and Llacanora; or to Otuzco and Tres Molinos).

Cumbe Mayo ★★   A stunning natural spot of huge and fascinating rock formations set amid rolling green hills at an elevation of 3,400m (11,150 ft.), Cumbe Mayo has been called a stone forest. Equally remarkable, if not more so, is the evidence of human intervention here, first discovered in 1937: caves etched with petroglyphs and a pre-Inca **aqueduct** that is a marvel of hydraulic engineering. The remarkable open canal, carved out of volcanic stone in perfect, polished lines, served to collect and redirect water from various sources on its way to the Pacific Ocean. At points, the canal narrows and introduces right angles to slow the flow of water and lessen the effects of erosion. In all, the aqueduct stretches more than 9km (5½ miles). Created, incredibly, around 1000 B.C., it is perhaps the oldest known man-made structure in South America.

Elsewhere in the park is a cliff referred to as the **sanctuary,** which looks like a human head from the outside; a grotto inside is adorned with enigmatic petroglyphs and is said to have been a place of ritual. Stairs carved in stone lead to sacrificial altars (llamas, not humans) and platforms, signs of the ceremonial importance of the zone. As guides lead groups through the "stone forest," they point out figures that can be seen in the stones, such as a group of monks as well as phalluses, breasts, a dog climbing a hill, a tortoise, a pirate's head, and mushrooms. Some are clear, amusing likenesses; others are like trying to identify someone else's images in cloud formations.

20km (12 miles) SW of Cajamarca. Daily 8am–5pm. To get there, take an organized tour (S/30). It is also possible to take a colectivo that leaves from behind Cerro de Santo Apolonia; it leaves passengers a short walking distance from the entrance to Cumbe Mayo.

Kunturwasi Three to 4 hours away from Cajamarca, in the province of San Pablo, these ceremonial stone ruins date to 1100 B.C. Besides a series of courtyards, plazas, and platforms, many marked with large petroglyphs, burial sites were discovered here. The gold treasures from the tombs are now exhibited in a small museum in the nearby town of San Pablo.

110km (68 miles) from Cajamarca. Tours to Kunturwasi cost about S/50 per person and last a full day. Daily 8am–5pm.

Ventanillas de Otuzco ★ A large necropolis whose gravesites are small square window niches carved out of a hillside, Otuzco was created by the Caxamarca culture, probably around 500 B.C. The niches were funereal tombs for elites. Many held just one body; others housed several corpses. Another 20km (12 miles) beyond Otuzco are the even more impressive (and better preserved) burial niches of **Ventanillas de Comboyo**. More extensive than Otuzco, they are holed out of a sheer volcanic cliff.

7km (4¹/₂ miles) NW of Cajamarca. Admission S/3. Daily 8am–5pm. To get there, take an organized tour (S/30), which combines visits with stops at a hacienda. You can also hop on a colectivo along Batán, a few blocks from the Plaza de Armas.

SHOPPING

Relaxed and untouristy Cajamarca isn't brimming with chic shops and merchants hawking *artesanía* to visitors. Yet its colorful central market is an enjoyable place to absorb the flavor of an authentic Andean town market and pick up a regional specialty: Cajamarca has excellent handicrafts, including ceramics and Cajarmarquiña mirrors with decorative glass frames. The **Mercado Central ★★** on Amazonas, which sprawls among several streets daily 7am to 5pm, is a great place to score one of those amazing, finely woven tall straw hats that virtually all natives wear. Those *sombreros de paja* are famous throughout Peru, but some are so finely made that you might be shocked at the prices. I'm told that some campesinos spend up to $400 for their hat, which is their most prideful article of clothing. As you'll see, the hats beg all sorts of individual style; forming and wearing the hat according to one's taste is part of the fashion. I own two, and they're certainly conversation pieces back home—perfect for gardening—though finding ones to fit large, non-Andean heads can be trying. Ask the seller to show you how to roll up the hat for easy packing. Other items of interest include saddlebags *(alforjas)*, decorative glass-and-silkscreen mirrors, and dairy products.

WHERE TO STAY

Like the mini-Cusco it appears to be, Cajamarca has a very nice selection of affordable small hotels, many of them in converted colonial mansions, all quite close to the main square. The finest and most relaxing hotel, however—one of the nicest in Peru—is in the countryside on the outskirts of town.

Hotel & Spa Laguna Seca ★ (Kids   A luxurious country-style hotel renowned for its proximity to the Baños del Inca, this spa resort hotel is where to stay if you're looking for things you don't typically find in Peru: aerobics, massages, and in-room thermal baths. It also features thermal pools (two for adults, one for children), Turkish baths, and a host of outdoor activities (including horseback riding). Rooms are large and nicely equipped, but not nearly as luxurious as those at the similarly priced Hotel Posada del Puruay (below).

Av. Manco Cápac 1098, Baños del Inca, Cajamarca. ⓒ **076/584-300.** Fax 044/584-311. www.lagunaseca. com.pe. 40 units. $120–$135 double; $144–$170 suite. Rates include breakfast buffet. AE, DC, MC, V. **Amenities:** Restaurant; cafeteria; bar; concierge; Jacuzzi; 3 thermal-water pools; aerobics, massage room; spa. *In room:* A/C, TV/VCR, fridge, hair dryer.

Hotel Costa del Sol ★★ (Value   An excellent hotel in a handsome colonial building next to the cathedral on the Plaza de Armas—hands-down the most enviable location in town—and part of a small Peruvian chain with several properties in northern Peru, this is the best, and really only, upscale place to stay if you want to be right in town. For visiting business travelers, including those who come to oversee operations in the mines outside town, it's the top choice. It has very comfortable, good-size, and nicely decorated rooms, as well as the most complete menu of amenities and services in Cajamarca, including a pool, spa, casino, and a very nice glass-enclosed restaurant. Given all it offers, it's an excellent value.

Jr. del Comercio 773, Cajamarca. ⓒ **076/343-434.** www.costadelsolperu.com. 71 units. S/329 double; S/461–S/695 suite. Rates include continental breakfast. V. **Amenities:** Restaurant; bar; exercise room; outdoor pool; sauna; spa. *In room:* A/C, TV, fridge, hair dryer, Wi-Fi.

Moderate

El Portal del Marques ★ (Value   An attractively furnished colonial *casona* located a block and a half from the main square, this comfortable and friendly hotel is a good midrange option. The carpeted rooms, placed around the brightly painted central court-yard and interior garden, are good-size and feature very clean bathrooms. Public rooms are inviting and warm, with wood-beam ceilings, stone portals, original paintings, local ceramics, and cozy armchairs and sofas. El Real Gourmet, the good-looking bar and renovated restaurant on the premises, is one of the better spots for dinner in town, and it features a happy hour every afternoon from 6 to 8pm.

Jr. del Comercio 644, Cajamarca. ⓒ/fax **076/368-464,** or ⓒ 01/9880-5440 for reservations. www. portaldelmarques.com. 20 units. $30 double; $75 family suite. Rates include continental breakfast. V. **Amenities:** Restaurant; bar. *In room:* TV/DVD, Wi-Fi.

Hacienda San Vicente ★ (Finds   Hands down the funkiest hotel you'll find in Peru, this old hacienda is perched on a hill up above Cajamarca—a taxi ride or long trek from downtown. It proclaims itself a *"refugio ecológico";* it could just as easily be called a "refu-gio funkadelico." The seven unique rooms overflow with an oddball, rustic sense of style; some are like caves carved out of the rock. The whole place slides down the hill with unexpected niches, tight stone stairways, peculiar spaces, and great views from the gardens. Clearly, this isn't for everyone, and it could use a little updating in linens and bedding. Rooms have wood-beam ceilings and skylights for views of the moon and stars. Room C has a round bed under the skylight. Others have headboards carved right into the stone walls. There is also a group room, where guests stay dorm-style in bunk beds—perfect for trekking groups. For families, there's an apartment. On-site is a little chapel.

Jirón Revolución (above Cerro Santa Apolonia), Cajamarca. ⓒ/fax **076/362-644.** www.sanvicentelodge.
com. 7 units, $45 double; $10 per person group room. Rates include continental breakfast and airport
pickup. Weekend deals available. MC, V. **Amenities:** Restaurant; bar; courtesy car to Cajamarca. *In room:*
TV, fridge.

Posada del Puruay ★★★ ⟨Value⟩ ⟨Kids⟩
An extraordinary country hotel housed in an
impeccably restored, elegant 1830 salmon-colored hacienda, this is one of the most
refined and relaxing hotels in Peru. And it's also a flat-out bargain. Set amid more than
202,350 hectares (500,000 acres) of land, with eucalyptus forest, beautifully landscaped
gardens, and views of the verdant, mountainous countryside, the hotel feels light-years
removed from any city, yet it's only 7km (4½ miles) from downtown Cajamarca. The
lovely house, built around a pretty courtyard, has rooms with names such as La Mansión
and La Prisión. The first couldn't be truer: Rooms are gigantic and extremely well
equipped, with large, luxurious bathrooms. The second room name, though, is misleading: If this is prison, I want to be thrown in the slammer. The restaurant and public
rooms are decorated with well-chosen antiques. Outdoors, horses beckon, as does the
trail up the hill to a small structure with stupendous panoramic views. The charming and
loquacious owner, Nora, and her husband and daughter live on the premises and couldn't
be more gracious. The terrific restaurant and vast video-rental library make this a perfect
spot to kick back for several days in the northern highlands.

Ctra. Porcón-Hualgayoc, Km 4.5, Cajamarca. ⓒ **076/367-928** or 01/336-7869 for reservations. www.
posadapuruay.com.pe. 14 units. S/191 double; S/207–S/280 suite. Rates include breakfast buffet. AE, DC,
MC, V. **Amenities:** Restaurant; bar; concierge. *In room:* A/C, TV/VCR, fridge, hair dryer, Wi-Fi.

Inexpensive

El Cabildo Hostal ⟨Kids⟩   One block from the Plaza de Armas, this charming small
hotel has the swankest colonial courtyard in town: It's sunny, with a central fountain,
arches, and balconies on all four sides—a perfect spot to relax. Rooms have a cozy,
comfortable vibe, and the beds have carved-wood headboards. Four of the rooms are
loft-style, which is perfect for families. Furnishings aren't plush, and the brown-carpet-
and-orange-bedspread look could probably do with an update, but given the friendly
services and pedigree of the building, it's not a bad deal.

Jr. Junín, Cajamarca. ⓒ/fax **076/367-025.** cabildoh@latinmail.com. 22 units. S/90–S/100 double. Rates
include taxes and continental breakfast. DC, MC, V. **Amenities:** Restaurant; bar; small gym; spa. *In room:*
TV, fridge.

Hostal Plaza   This large and rambling old colonial wooden house, a favorite of backpackers, is loaded with character, even if the rooms are dormlike and completely
unadorned. It's not uncomfortable, though, and it certainly has a great location—right
on the Plaza de Armas—for the cheap price. The hotel is spread across two interconnected wings that are built around a pair of courtyards. Hot water comes and goes. The
rickety wooden floors and varied levels have their own kind of charm for travelers looking
for a bargain but who need little in the way of creature comforts.

Plaza de Armas, Cajamarca. ⓒ **076/362-058.** 22 units. S/50 double with private bathroom; S/25 double
with shared bathroom. No credit cards. *In room:* No phone.

Hostal Portada del Sol ★ ⟨Value⟩   A cozy family inn occupying a beautiful colonial
house about 5 minutes from the Plaza de Armas, this is one of the best affordable hotels
in town. Rooms have wood-beam ceilings, older-style furnishings, and small bathrooms.
Some rooms have upstairs loft areas. The small, covered central courtyard has a marble
fountain and is set up with tables beneath the wooden balcony on three sides. El Sol

Grill, a charming restaurant with a wood-burning stove, is on the premises, and service is personal and accommodating. The hotel owns the handsome hacienda hotel of the same name in the countryside outside Cajamarca (below).

Jr. Pisagua 731, Cajamarca. ☏/fax **076/365-395** or 01/225-4306 for reservations. portasol@amet.com.pe. 20 units. $35 double. MC, V. **Amenities:** Restaurant; bar. *In room:* TV.

Hostal Portada del Sol Hacienda ★ Ⓥalue Ⓚids A great-value country hacienda, only 6km (3¾ miles) from the Plaza de Armas in Cajamarca, this pretty house with beautiful gardens and comfortable, nicely decorated but simple rooms is an excellent option for a relaxed stay. Owned by the same people who run a similarly named inn in town (above), this cozy Spanish-style hacienda doesn't have the funky character of San Vicente or the classy luxury of Puruay, but it's a great middle-of-the-road choice. Almost unheard of at this price, the hotel has tennis courts, football fields, games for children, horseback riding, and trails for walking.

Camino al Cumbe Mayo Km 6, Cajamarca. ☏ **076/365-395** or 01/225-4306 for reservations. portasol@ amet.com.pe. 15 units. $35 double. MC, V. **Amenities:** Restaurant; bar; tennis courts. *In room:* TV.

Los Balcones de la Recoleta Yet another charming 19th-century house in Cajamarca, this small inn, a 5-minute walk from the Plaza de Armas, is named for its handsome balconies, which drip with vines. The nice central courtyard is similarly overflowing with plants and flowers. Rooms are a little dank, but they live up to the colonial character of the place, with hardwood floors and thick ceiling beams. The restaurant is recommended for Spanish specialties and the good-value lunch menu.

Jr. Amalia Puga 1050, Cajamarca. ☏/fax **076/363-302.** 12 units. S/90 double. Rates include continental breakfast. DC, MC, V. **Amenities:** Restaurant; bar. *In room:* TV, minibar.

WHERE TO DINE

Cajamarca's dining scene pretty fairly matches its roster of hotels: a laid-back selection of excellent-value restaurants, all within easy walking distance of the Plaza de Armas. The city is famous for its desserts and ice cream, and bakeries and cafes stuffed with cakes line the streets. In addition to the restaurants below, **Cascanuez Café-Bar,** Amalia Puga 554 (☏ **076/366-089**) is terrific for either dessert or a full, quick meal. For ice cream, the two best spots are **La Cremería,** Comercio 964 and Amazonas 741 (☏ **076/362-235**), and **Heladería Holanda,** Amalia Puga 657 (☏ **076/340-113**).

El Batán Ⓥalue PERUVIAN A sophisticated restaurant, with perhaps the most elevated reputation in town, El Batán uses the tag line "buffet de arte." In fact, the place is part art gallery upstairs. Elegant but relaxed, inhabiting a handsome 18th-century colonial house entered through the courtyard, it offers a series of relatively expensive fixed-price menus, but there's also a bargain hunter's *menu ejecutivo* for just S/15. You can mix and match appetizers with main courses. You might have a stuffed avocado to start, followed by chicken in mushroom sauce. The menu is meat-heavy, as seems typical in Cajamarca. Meat eaters will appreciate dishes such as stuffed tenderloin with peppercorns or filet mignon in whiskey sauce. On weekends, there's peña music. You can dine in either the covered courtyard or the relaxed, art-filled interior.

Jr. del Batán 369. ☏ **076/366-025.** Reservations recommended. Main courses S/12–S/25. AE, DC, MC, V. Daily noon–midnight.

El Querubino ★ PERUVIAN An elegant place a half-block off the Plaza de Armas, El Querubino has quickly become one of Cajamarca's trendsetters. With mustard-yellow walls, decorative tiles, and a live music duo playing *altiplano* tunes, it's bright, cheery, friendly, and intimate, and just a few paces from the cathedral. The restaurant qualifies as upscale for low-key Cajamarca, but it's quite popular with locals. House specialties include *mollejas al ajillo* (sweetbreads in garlic) and mustard chicken. Other options among meat dishes are also nice: beef stroganoff, filet mignon, and pork chops. There's a daily list of bargain specials such as lemon chicken written on a board at the entrance. Finally, a Cajamarca restaurant with fish on the menu! (Okay, it's only sole, but it's a start.) The wine list is a bit more extensive than at most local restaurants.

Jr. Amalia Puga 589. (C) **076/340-900.** Reservations recommended. Main courses S/15–S/32. AE, DC, MC, V. Daily 9am–midnight.

La Casa de la Abuela DESSERT/INTERNATIONAL   This cute, country-kitchen-style place has wood beams, a preponderance of baskets with dried flowers, and little tables with blue-and-white-checked tablecloths and blue candles. In short, it's very unusual for Peru—one of the few small restaurants with a conscious and consistent design or look. The first thing to draw your attention will be the wide selection of desserts, including ice cream, cheesecakes, and several other colorful and delectable cakes, in the case at the entrance. But "Grandma's House" also serves a variety of items for breakfast, lunch, and dinner, such as sandwiches and hamburgers, pizzas, pastas, and a gourmet selection of meats. Plenty of people pop in just for dessert and coffee.

Jr. Cruz de Piedra 671. (C) **076/362-027.** Reservations recommended Fri–Sat. Main courses S/10–S/27. MC. Daily 8am–midnight.

La Vaca Loca ★ (Value) ITALIAN/PIZZA   If you're in need of a pizza fix, this is your place. "The Crazy Cow" is cute, and fun, and though it's inexpensive, it pays more attention to decor than any other restaurant in Cajamarca. It's brightly colored and stuffed with cows in all sorts of incarnations, from paintings, to figurines, to cartoons. Seats and booths are black-and-white faux cowhide, the walls are deep red and orange, and the ceilings are lined with rustic beams. It serves 19 different types of pizzas, from standard options to more adventurous combinations, as well as fresh salads, pastas, and lasagnas. Few people seem to order anything but the pizza, however, which is available in both personal and family size.

Jr. San Martín 320. (C) **076/828-230.** Reservations not accepted. Main courses S/8–S/18. No credit cards. Daily noon–10pm.

Om-Gri ★ (Value) ITALIAN   Eating at this tiny place is pretty much like eating in a friend's kitchen. The amiable Tito Carrera Montes prepares only pastas, topped by a dozen or so sauces which he spends 8 hours preparing—from a tiny stove tucked behind a bar and a ton of well-used pans. There are just 5 tables set up in a haphazardly decorated room with salon doors that advertise "Pastas! Lo Mejor!" (Pastas! The Best!) Tito fetches sauces from the freezer and proceeds to whip up dishes from what appears to be little more than a hot plate. Choose the pasta—fettuccine, spaghetti, lasagna—and the sauce, and watch Tito go to work. Wondering about the restaurant's odd name? It's a nod to Tito's years spent in French-speaking Europe and his full head of gray hair: a made-up, multilingual name meaning *hombre gris,* or the gray man.

Jr. San Martín 360. (C) **076/367-619.** Reservations not accepted. Main courses S/10–S/25. No credit cards. Mon–Sat 1–11pm; Sun 6:30–11pm.

Restaurant Salas (Value) PERUVIAN   From the lines at the entrance, you can expect this traditional restaurant to be good—it's packed with locals daily (even though some veterans carp that it's not as good as it used to be). Occupying the same spot on the Plaza de Armas since 1947, Salas is a huge eating hall with high ceilings and white-coated waiters scurrying about. Perhaps it's so popular because of the monstrous portions. There's a daily typed list of *platos especiales* (specials), *platos del día* (daily specials), and a set menu for about $2. The *humitas* (sweet corn tamales) are excellent. Most of the menu focuses on typical Peruvian dishes and things such as churrasco and *asado* (roasted and barbecued meats).

Amalia Puga 637. ☎ **076/362-867.** Reservations not accepted. Main courses S/6–S/25. V. Daily 9am–10pm.

CAJAMARCA AFTER DARK

For the most part, Cajamarca is a pretty quiet town, although it has at least two spots that make an evening out worthwhile.

Peña Usha Usha ★★, at Amalia Puga 142 (☎ **076/997-4514**), about 4 blocks from the Plaza de Armas, is a funky little peña bar with kerosene lamps, a smattering of tables and benches, a small altar, and graffiti everywhere. It's atmospheric and intimate, and Jamie Valera Bazán has been singing politically motivated songs here, either alone or with a couple of friends, for years. The bar, which serves simple mixed drinks only, opens at 9pm and doesn't close its doors sometimes until 6am.

The most upscale disco in town is **Los Frailones,** Av. Perú 701 (☎ **076/364-113;** at Cruz de la Piedra, at the base of Santa Apolonia hill). The cover charge is S/15 for men and S/10 for women. A slew of bars and clubs attracting nightclubs is clustered along José Galvez between Amalia Puga and Amazonas, including **Orni, Bambolé,** and **Indio Bar.**

4 MÁNCORA & PERU'S NORTHERN BEACHES

Despite its nearly 2,500 km (1,500 miles) of coastline, Peru hasn't been widely celebrated for its beaches. Peru's northern desert coast, inaccessible and poorly developed for decades, possesses the finest long, sandy beaches in the country, which have been prized by pioneering locals, travelers on their way down the coast by land from Ecuador, and especially surfers drawn to the Pacific Ocean's extraordinary swells and breaks. Only recently has the region really begun to take off with a more diverse crowd; moneyed Limeños are building chic beachside homes, and small hotel groups and entrepreneurs are descending on the region to put a stake in the market before it's too late. Accommodations previously were largely limited to thatched-roof bungalows that had the benefit of being, like the area, authentic, cool and cheap, but they weren't ideal for a wider population of national and international travelers. That has quickly changed in just the past few years, and the area is experiencing a boom.

Piura and Tumbes are the two northern departments that share the finest of Peru's beaches. **Máncora** (in Piura), 120km (75 miles) south of the Ecuadoran border and 1165km (722 miles) north of Lima, is the epicenter of the surfer and beach craze, exceedingly popular with young travelers and hippies, even if to some newcomers it may still seem rather rough around the edges. Máncora is essentially one main drag, lined end-to-end with open-air casual bars and restaurants, with the craggy desert to one side and the open sea the other. The long, sandy beaches in Máncora and extending about 25km (15 miles) north and south are excellent, even if they can't quite compete with the best sparkling white sands of Brazil or the Caribbean. But the water is warm, the sun shines virtually

all year (as opposed to further south, in and around Lima, where it seems rarely to peek **419**
through the gray haze), the seafood and ceviche are supreme, and the waves are, well,
killer. The area gets a bit crazed during the Peruvian summer and during other holiday
periods, but the rest of the year is charmingly low-key.

Two currents, the cold Humboldt from the south and Ecuatorial from the north, meet
just south of Cabo Blanco, creating vastly different water temperatures (the north being
considerably warmer year-round). For surfing fanatics, this section of the Pacific is
renowned for its excellent swells, long waves, perfect barrels, superb point breaks and
awesome lefts. The tourist zone stretches from Órganos in the south to Punta Sal and
Zorritos (part of Tumbes) north of Máncora. The top beaches for swimming and sunning
are Vichayito, Pocitas, Punta Sal, and Zorritos. To the south, Cabo Blanco, a fisherman's
village (off of which the largest black marlin on record was caught) is said by many locals
to have been the inspiration for Ernest Hemingway's *The Old Man and the Sea* (Hemingway did spend time in the area in 1956 deep-sea fishing and carousing, but I'm sure a
good many Cubans would argue the point). Top spots for surfing, some of which are for
advanced boarders only, include Cabo Blanco, Punta Ballenas, Órganos, Panic Point,
Lobitos and El Golf.

WHERE TO STAY & DINE

While budget travelers and *surfistas* congregate in occasionally raucous Máncora, my
favorite beaches for lodging are the peaceful enclaves of Las Pocitas and Vichayito. The
beaches are wide and calm, and lining them is a mix of second homes and small inns and
boutique hotels. The following boutique-style hotels along the beach are superb lodging
options; the first two count distinguished restaurants as part of their appeal, while the
third was in the process of a major property overhaul at press time that will undoubtedly
have a significant impact on the hotel's restaurant as well. There's plenty of cheap accommodation in Máncora; one of the best options is the beachside **Pink Parrot** (previously
called Del Wawa), Avenida Piura, facing el Point (© 073/258-427; www.delwawa.com).

DCO Suites, Lounge & Spa ★★★ This spectacularly chic and airy, upscale boutique hotel is unexpected in still rough-around-the-edges Máncora, but it's one of the
most stylish small hotels in Peru. Its contemporary elegance and sophistication is a first
along the northern coast. The modern, multilevel hotel, built like an ingenious architect's
townhouse, blends local stone and wood with stark white, silver and turquoise retro
accents and rises above the beach. You can see and hear the surf crashing below as you
relax in luxury at the small infinity pool, lounge terrace or the open-air, top-floor spa—
one of the finest places you'll ever get a full-body rubdown and soak in a foamy Jacuzzi.
The seven suites are hip and while not huge, have extraordinary showers and sea views.
Every detail, from iPods with special playlists given to you at check-in to colorful print
robes and the gourmet menu, which includes dishes from the star chef Pedro Miguel
Schiaffino of Lima, has been thought of. Though the hotel's name may not roll off the
tongue, this is the kind of place for which it's worth making a special trip to the northern
beaches.

Las Pocitas (3km south of Máncora). © 01/242-3961 for reservations, or 073/258-171. www.hoteldco.
com. $180 double; $280 Master Suite. AE, DC, MC, V.

Hotelier Arte y Cocina ★★ Just south of Máncora—walking distance or a short
mototaxi ride—this small (nine-room) and unpretentious three-story place has stunning
beach and sea views, friendly and knowledgeable young owners, a cool vibe, and an excellent

little beachside restaurant. Rooms are minimalist and modern, with a comfortable, beachy feel enlivened by local art and poetic graphics on the walls. Named for the mother of one of the owners, Teresa Ocampo, who is a bit of a celebrity chef in Peru, with the country's first TV cooking show, the open-air restaurant "Donde Teresa" serves the finest local seafood and specialties like "chancho al barril" (wood-fired, slow-cooked pork).

Las Pocitas (1km south of Máncora). ✆ **073/258-702.** www.hotelier.pe. S/120–S/360 double. MC, V.

Vichayito Bungalows & Carpas ★★   This formerly low-key beachside ecolodge in Vichayito has been wholly transformed since it was acquired by the Aranwa hotel group, proprietors of one of the finest hotels in Peru (See p. 248). Expanded and made more upscale and family-friendly, with paved pathways and landscaping, it fronts one of the prettiest and cleanest stretches of sandy beach in the entire region. The biggest change, though, has been the addition of a couple dozen unique luxury tents (carpas) to the already existing thatched-roof bungalows. The concept is novel, akin to "Out of Africa" or the travels of a Bedouin prince. The tents come equipped with handsome furnishings, first-quality linens, poured concrete floors and headboards, king beds, LCD TVs, and exquisite porcelain sinks and in some cases, deep clawfoot bathtubs; the only nod to "roughing it" is the tent itself, made of a tough French canvas, and the need to zips oneself in and out. It's tailor-made for the luxury-oriented adventurer. Spread out over the large property, which has 270m (710 ft.) of beachfront, are a pool, restaurant (with chandeliers under a thatched roof), game room, outdoor hot tub, and a brand-new swanky spa.

Antigua Panamericana Norte, Km 1211, Playa Vichayito (20 min southwest of Máncora). ✆ **01/436-4173** or 01/434-1452. www.vichayito.com. $81–$124 bungalow double; $140–$198 carpa double.

DINING IN MÁNCORA

Angela's Place ★   A cute little vegetarian spot, owned by an Austrian woman who passed through Máncora and never left, this is the perfect place for budget travelers who've grown "tired of chicken and rice," as Angela herself puts it. She offers instead great hummus, salads, whole-grain bread, veggie main-course options (quinoa with sautéed vegetables and vegetarian burritos), carnivore-friendly goulash, apple strudel, and a great meal deal. For S/15, you get a starter, main course and a beverage.

Av. Piura 396, Máncora. ✆ **073/258-603.** www.praiabar.com.pe. Main courses S/18–S34. No credit cards. Daily noon–10pm.

La Sirena d' Juan ★   An adorable little sliver of a place, with hip music and terrace seating, this is an excellent spot for an intimate night out in Máncora. It serves terrific seafood, including tuna sashimi and seared tuna with ginger and passion-fruit salsa (tuna is big in Máncora), and creative Novo Andino dishes. The passion-fruit cheesecake is also a winner.

Av. Piura 316, Máncora. ✆ **073/258-173.** Main courses S/15–S32. MC, V. Mon–Sat 7pm–midnight.

Praia Bar ★★   The most stylish bar in Máncora, this cool all-white cocktail lounge behind a sliding metal shop door is not only a great place for a drink, such as a tremendous maracuyá sour, it is a place to stick around for dinner. Portions are obscenely large, and the fresh tuna sashimi my wife and I had there recently—caught just hours earlier, and enough for a family of four, all for $6—was so amazing we took photographs of it and emailed them to jealous friends. Less exalted, but just as likely to hit the spot, are the

generous lomo saltado and yummy, messy cheeseburger. There are killer nightly drink **421**
specials; Monday night's three-for-one pisco drinks (superb sours of several stripes) takes
the prize.

Av. Piura 336, Máncora. (℃) **073/258-571**. www.praiabar.com.pe. Main courses S/18–S34. MC, V. Mon–Sat
7pm–midnight.

SHOPPING, SPAS & SURFING

Check out the artisans' market on the main drag, Avenida Piura, or the chic little shop
Sirena (Av. Piura 336), featuring very stylish bikinis, sundresses, *pareos* (beach wraps),
sandals and other beach apparel and accessories designed by an Argentine woman and
made in Máncora. **Soledad Surf Shop** (Av. Piura 316; (℃) **01/9983-0425**) is the go-to
place for hardcore *surfistas* and beachy types who just want to look the part.

While the terrific spa at **DCO Hotel** (see above) is also open to nonguests, another
great spa option is **Origenes Spa de Playa,** on Playa Vichayito ((℃) **073/694-460;** www.
spaorigenes.com); it offers a full menu of spa services and open-air massages, as well as a
big hot tub and attractive pool overlooking the beach.

Board rentals and surfing lessons are easily arranged in Máncora (ask at **Soledad Surf
Shop;** see above). For those interested in a full-scale surfing tour of northern Peru, contact **Octopus Surf Tours** ((℃) **19/9400-5518;** www.wavehunters.com/peru-surfing/
nperu.asp). Kite surfing is also taking off—pardon the pun—and several outfits, including **Mancora Kite Club** (www.mancorakiteclub.com) and **Máncora Kite Surf** (www.
mancorakitesurf.com), arrange lessons, gear, and trips.

GETTING THERE & GETTING AROUND

BY AIR   LAN ((℃)01/213-8200; www.lan.com) flies daily to Piura or Tumbes from
Lima. The drive to Máncora from Piura is longer (2.5 hours), but flights arrive throughout the day, giving you daylight hours to make it to your destination. Flights to Tumbes,
about an hour north of Máncora, depart daily only at 7:15pm, arriving at 9pm. Flights
start at about $115 one-way. From the airports, private taxis to Máncora run about $80
from Piura and $40 from Tumbes; buses make the trip for $6. **Máncora Travel**
((℃) **073/258-571;** www.mancoratravel.com.pe) arranges shared and private minivans
from Piura and Tumbes ($50–$150). Piura is 185km south of Máncora; Tumbes is
102km north.

BY BUS   The bus from Lima is about 16 hours (overnight is recommended); fares range
from $20 to $35. **Cruz del Sur** ((℃) **01/311-5050;** www.cruzdelsur.com.pe), **Oltursa**
((℃) **01/708-5000;** www.oltursa.com.pe) and **CIVA Transportes** ((℃) **01/418-1111;**
www.civa.com.pe) are the best options.

CAR RENTAL   Most car rental agencies are located in Piura. **Rent-a-Car San José**
((℃) **073/303-240**) has good cars ($40–$50 per day) in Piura and meets travelers at the
airport.

GETTING AROUND   Unless you have a rental car, getting around the region is almost
entirely by **mototaxis** (S/2), which are as ubiquitous as the tiny crabs on the beaches. For
a couple of *soles,* you can go about anywhere the dirt roads will take you.

INFORMATION   www.vivamancora.com is a very good site with information on
entire area, including distances, details on the best surf spots, breaks and equipment and
lessons, and fishing and diving.

5 HUARAZ & THE CORDILLERA BLANCA ★★

Rugged Peru is synonymous with the bold peaks of the Andes, and those mountains, particularly the spectacular Cordillera Blanca range 400km (250 miles) northeast of Lima, are a magnet for thousands of mountaineers and adventure-sports travelers every year. The string of dramatic snowcapped 5,000m (16,400-ft.) peaks east of the Callejón de Huaylas Valley, accessible from the main tourist hub of Huaraz (reached by bus in 7–8 hr. from Lima), is the premier spot in Peru—and perhaps the best in all of South America—for climbing and trekking. Nearly three dozen peaks soar to more than 6,000m (19,680 ft.); Huascarán, topping out at 6,768m (22,205 ft.), is Peru's highest mountain and the highest tropical mountain in the world. Nearly the entire chain is contained within the protected Huascarán National Park, a UNESCO Biosphere Reserve and World Heritage Trust site.

Not surprisingly, the region appeals above all to experienced, veteran mountaineers and adventurers. A burgeoning lineup of other adventure sports, from white-water rafting and mountain biking to hang gliding and rock climbing, have lifted off in popularity in recent years. Above all, those kinds of adventure travelers, equipped and prepared for the rigors and thrill of roughing it outdoors, get the most out of the region.

The extraordinary mountain scenery of the region, however, also appeals to those with limited time and abilities, or only passing interest in testing their physical mettle in Peru. The valley, some 20km (12 miles) wide and 180km (112 miles) long, is a superb destination for those who are more interested in day walks and village markets, too. For those who would say all play and no culture makes for a dull adventure, visitors can marry interests in adventure sports and antiquity at the marvelous ruins of Chavín de Huántar, built about 1,500 years ago, a hearty journey about 4 hours from Huaraz. However, getting to the Cordillera Blanca still requires a considerable investment of time, even though one Peruvian airline has finally begun to fly from Lima to Huaraz. Other outdoors areas in Peru (such as the Sacred Valley between Cusco and Machu Picchu, and the Colca Canyon beyond Arequipa) are easier to get to for most light adventurers.

The best months for climbing are the dry season, between May and October; of those, July and August are perhaps best. (Note that the traditional dry season has shifted a bit in recent years, with rains often lasting until the end of May but often not beginning until late November.) Mountain biking and trekking can be practiced other months as well, but the adventurous should be duly prepared for rain.

Fun Facts "La" Huascarán?

The Cordillera Blanca's El Huascarán, the namesake of the mountainous National Park in Peru's central Andes, might seem to be an eminently macho mountain: At 6,768m (22,205 ft.), it's the highest peak in Peru, the fourth highest in the Americas, and the highest tropical-zone mountain in the world. But its north peak was first climbed in 1908 by a woman, the 58-year-old American Annie Smith Peck (who 3 years later climbed Peru's Mt. Coropuna, where she proudly displayed a women's suffrage banner that read "Votes for Women").

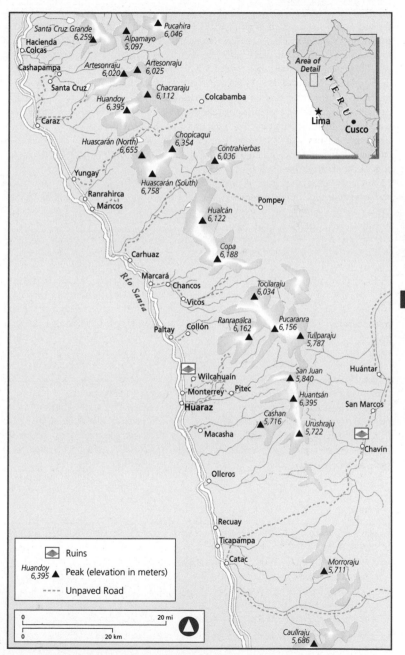

The small and bustling, ramshackle mountain city of Huaraz has few attractions besides its spectacular setting, but it serves as the base for most adventure-tour operators. With its roster of restaurants, bars, and small hotels, it's where most travelers gather to get acclimated to the altitude and get organized for their forays into the mountains. Besides Huaraz, several other small towns and villages at the base of the Cordillera mountains serve as starting points for trekking and climbing expeditions, but none is so well equipped as the capital of the Ancash department. Many expeditions to the scenic Llanganuco lakes in the Huascarán National Park begin at Yungay, while Caraz, a pleasant small mountain town known for its agreeable climate and flowers, serves as a quieter alternative to Huaraz and offers similar services required for ascents and other adventure activities.

HUARAZ
420km (261 miles) N of Lima

Huaraz is the primary base destination for most visitors keen on exploring the Callejón de Huaylas Valley that runs 200km (125 miles) right down the middle of Peru. At an altitude of 3,100m (10,170 ft.), Huaraz enjoys a spectacular setting at the foot of the Cordillera Blanca: The town is ringed by 20 snowcapped peaks, each higher than 6,000m (19,680 ft.), which rise in splendor just beyond reach of the city. Huaraz itself is a far cry from the postcard perfection of a picturesque alpine village, however. It is rough around the edges—as well as the center. Of course, it has a major earthquake to blame for its ragged look, a product of rapid and cheap concrete construction: The massive 1970 earthquake leveled nearly the entire city, eradicating half its population in the process.

Today Huaraz hums—albeit messily—with the business of mountain and adventure tourism. A wide range of facilities has sprung up to support outdoor travel; dozens of tour operators and travel agencies, restaurants and bars, and hotels and inns can be found in town, most clustered along the main drag, Avenida Luzuriaga.

Essentials
Getting There
BY PLANE Daily afternoon flights (80 min.; to Aeropuerto de Anta, 23km/14 miles north of Huaraz) are now offered from Lima on **LC Busre** (© **01/619-1313;** www. lcbusre.com.pe). Flights start at $119 one-way. Check the website for updates, as no Peruvian airline seems terribly committed to flying into Huaraz.

BY BUS Traveling by arduous bus from Lima or from other points along the north coast or the northern Andes was, until recently, the only way to get to Huaraz, though travelers now have the more comfortable option of daily flights from Lima. Most of the

---

ⓘ Tips Acute Mountain Sickness

The usual warnings about altitude in the Peruvian Andes especially apply in Huaraz and the Cordillera Blanca. Headaches and nausea are common ailments. Take several days to adequately acclimatize to the high elevation of more than 3,000m (9,840 ft.), or up to a week if you're planning to attempt a serious ascent. In the early going, don't overextend yourself physically, and drink plenty of *mate de coca* (coca-leaf tea). If symptoms persist, see a doctor. Acute mountain sickness, known locally as *soroche,* is serious business.

individual bus company terminals are along Avenida Raymondi or Avenida Fitzcarrald. For the 7- to 8-hour journey from Lima, major companies offering daily service are **CIVA Transportes** (© **01/418-1111;** www.civa.com.pe), **Cruz del Sur** (© **01/311-5050;** www.cruzdelsur.com.pe), and **Movil Tours** (© **01/433-9000;** www.moviltours.com.pe). Móvil Tours and **Transportes Línea** (© **01/424-836** or 044/297-000; www.transportes linea.com.pe) are the principal carriers to and from Trujillo (8 hr.).

Visitor Information

The **iPerú** tourist office is at Av. Luzuriaga 734 (Pasaje Atusparía, Of. 1), across from the Plaza de Armas (© **043/428-812**); it's open Monday to Friday 8am to 1pm and 4 to 7pm. General tourist information is also available during the same hours from the **tourist**

(Tips) **Safe Bus Travel**

Night bus trips departing Huaraz for Trujillo, Chiclayo, and other cities in northern Peru have earned bad reputations for theft. Some travelers have reported armed thieves boarding long-distance buses and forcibly relieving passengers of their valuables. Perhaps for this reason, the better "executive-level" services don't stop between Lima and their final destination. Be very careful with your belongings on board, even if it means threading your arms through the straps of your carry-on, if you plan to sleep.

police office between City Hall and the Post Office on Avenida Luzuriaga ((C) **043/4 21-341**). For mountaineering and trekking information, though, you're best off consulting the **Casa de Guías,** Parque Ginebra 28 ((C) **043/421-811**). The office is open Monday through Friday from 9am to 6pm, and Saturday from 9am to 1pm. The friendly folks there have up-to-date information on trails, maps, lists of certified guides, and message-board postings for those looking to form trekking and climbing groups. Mostly, though, they're there to set you up with a guide. Basic information on visiting the Huascarán National Park can be obtained from the **Parque Nacional Huascarán** office, in the Ministerio de Agricultura building on Avenida Raymondi ((C) **043/422-086**).

FAST FACTS   Most banks are found around the Plaza de Armas and along Avenida Luzuriaga. Among those that exchange traveler's checks and cash and have ATMs are **Banco de Crédito,** Av. Luzuriaga 669, at the corner of Sucre ((C) **043/421-170**); **Interbank,** Sucre 913 ((C) **044/423-015**); and **Banco Wiese,** Sucre 766 (no phone). Moneychangers can usually be found hanging around outside banks around the Plaza de Armas.

In an **emergency,** call (C) **105.** For climbing accidents and assistance, including evacuations, contact **Unidad de Salvamento de Alta Montaña (High Altitude Rescue),** Av. Arias Grazziani s/n, Yungay, at (C) **043/493-333** or 043/493-327; or **Casa de Guías,** Parque Ginebra 28 ((C) **043/421-811**). If you need the police, the **tourist police** have an office just off the Plaza de Armas ((C) **043/421-341**); see "Visitor Information," above. You can also contact the **national police,** Larrea y Loredo 720 ((C) **043/421-461**). For medical attention, go to **Hospital de Apoyo Víctor Ramos Guardia,** Av. Luzuriaga s/n ((C) **043/421-290**), or **Hospital Regional de Huaraz,** Av. Luzuriaga s/n ((C) **043/421-321**).

There are a number of Internet cabinas dotting the downtown area. Try **Avance,** Av. Luzuriaga 672, 2nd Floor ((C) **043/426-736**), which has special deals for repeat visits and is open late.

The Huaraz **post office** is at Av. Luzuriaga 702, across the street from the Plaza de Armas ((C) **043/421-030**). The **Telefónica del Perú** office is at Bolívar and Sucre, just east of the Plaza de Armas.

Getting Around

The main axis in town is Avenida Luzuriaga, which is overrun with tourist agencies, outdoor outfitters, and nearly every strolling traveler who hits Huaraz. The easiest way to get around town is by taking an inexpensive taxi—the ones incessantly honking at every pedestrian hoping for a fare—or a colectivo. Myriad bus companies serve the Cordillera Blanca region, including Chavín, Caraz, and Yungay.

BY TAXI Taxis cruise Avenida Luzuriaga in search of travelers day and night. Rides in town cost S/2, and cabs can be safely and easily hailed on the street. One operator to call is **Radio Taxi** (© **043/721-482**).

BY BUS Combis service towns in the Callejón de Huaylas around Huaraz: Chavín (4 hr.), Caraz (90 min.), and Yungay (90 min.). Most depart from the Quillcay Bridge on Alameda Fitzcarrald; others leave from Calle Caraz, a half-block east of Fitzcarrald. Fares are inexpensive, usually S/3 to S/10.

What To See & Do Around Huaraz

The emphasis on seeing and doing in Huaraz is definitely on the latter—most visitors are in town as long as it takes them to get acclimatized and organize an excursion into the mountains and valleys nearby or participate in some sort of adventure-sports activity. The town itself was hastily reconstructed after the devastating 1970 earthquake. A single street, **Jirón José Olaya** (to the right of Raymondi), gives a hint of what Huaraz looked like before it came crumbling down.

The **Museo Arqueológico de Ancash** is an interesting and well-organized small museum crammed with exhibits presenting the long history (more than 12,000 years) of the region through mummies, trepanned crania, and a terrific collection of monoliths from the Recuay and Huari cultures. There are textiles, ceramics, and other pieces from the Chavín, Huaraz, Moche, and Chimú cultures, as well as scale models of various ruins sites in the area. The museum, at Av. Luzuriaga 762 (© **043/421-551**), is open Monday through Saturday from 9am to 5pm, and Sunday from 9am to 2pm. Admission is S/5; the ticket is also good for same-day entrance to the ruins at Wilcahuaín (below).

Another diversion might be the **Museo de Miniaturas del Perú (Miniatures Museum)**. It houses dolls in traditional Peruvian dress and scale models of the ruins at Chavín de Huántar, pre-earthquake Huaraz, and the city of Yungay. The museum is in the gardens of the Gran Hotel Huascarán, Jirón Lúcar y Torre 46 (© **043/421-466**). It's open Monday through Friday from 8am to 1pm and 3 to 6pm. Admission is S/3.

But because Huaraz is almost wholly about its stunning location and getting outdoors, visitors are usually more interested in the **Mirador de Rataquenua ★**, a lookout spot on a 3,650m (12,000-ft.) mountain pass with great panoramic views; it's just less than an hour's walk southeast of downtown. The direct trail is pretty steep; there's also a less demanding dirt road with plenty of switchbacks. Go with a group during the day because the area has experienced a spate of crime in recent years and become quite dangerous; locals warn that under no circumstances should a lone traveler walk there. To get there, head south on Luzuriaga to Villón and follow the road at the end, just beyond the cemetery.

NORTHERN PERU

12

HUARAZ & THE CORDILLERA BLANCA

(Tips) Tour Operators & Travel Agencies

Guides and travel agencies are extremely useful, if not downright indispensable, for most adventure sports in the remote and often dangerous mountains. Like Cusco and Iquitos, Huaraz is chock-full of agencies and tour operators. Unfortunately, some of them are less than reliable; others are far worse. See "Trekking & Climbing in the Cordillera Blanca," later in this chapter, for a discussion of guides and agencies. It's best to check with fellow tourists (or, before arriving in Huaraz, with the South American Explorers clubs in either Lima or Cusco) to get recent reports about services.

Festival Calendar

Huaraz and the villages in the Callejón de Huaylas celebrate their Andean roots in traditional festivals that are among Peru's most spirited. If your visit coincides with a regional festival, you'll see a profusion of folk dances, costumed dances (some with extraordinary masks), and the stirring local music that accompanies them, played on exotic instruments such as *roncadoras, quenas,* and *zampoñas.* Carnaval, the Fiesta de Mayo, the Semana del Andinismo, the Patron Saint Festival, the Fiesta de las Luces, and Virgen de las Mercedes are among the most festive, but be warned that accommodations are at a premium, and prices skyrocket at these times.

Here's the complete list of regional festivals:

- **January 18 to January 21:** La Virgen de Chiquinquirá (Caraz)
- **February or March:** Carnaval Huaracino (Huaraz)
- **March or April:** Semana Santa and the steps of the pilgrimage (Huaraz and Callejón de Huaylas)
- **May 2 to May 10:** Fiesta de Mayo, celebrated with traditional dances, ski races, and a lantern procession (Huaraz)
- **June:** Semana del Andinismo, a celebration of outdoor adventure (Huaraz and Callejón de Huaylas)
- **June 22 to June 24:** San Juan Bautista, Day of the Indian (Pomabamba and the entire Sierra Andina)
- **July 6 to July 9:** La Virgen Santa Isabel (Callejón de Huaylas)
- **July 20 to July 30:** Independence Celebration (Huaraz and Caraz)
- **July 28 to July 29:** Fiestas Patrias
- **August 1 to August 6:** Patron Saint Festival (Coyllur and Huaraz)
- **August 13 to August 16:** Virgen de la Asunción (Huata and Chacas)
- **August 29 to August 30:** Fiesta Patrona (Chiquián and Santa Rosa)
- **September 14:** Fiesta de las Luces (Huaraz)
- **September 14 to September 27:** Señor de Burgos (Recuay)
- **September 23 to September 27:** Virgen de las Mercedes (Carhuaz)
- **October 5 to October 7:** Virgen del Rosario (Huari)
- **October 12:** Virgen del Pilar (Ticapampa)
- **October 28:** Fiesta Cívica (Yungay)

Located about 8km (5 miles) north of Huaraz, the **Monumento Arqueológico de Wilcahuaín** is a set of ruins from the Huari culture, which lived in the region around A.D. 1000. Two sites named for their relative size, Grande and Chico, were burial grounds and storage centers. The major temple was built around 1100. The ruins don't have established opening and closing hours, but it's certainly wisest to go during daylight. Admission is S/5 for adults and S/2 for students. To get there, take any combi marked "Wilcahuaín" from the Río Quillcay bridge. The trip takes about a half-hour and costs S/3. After visiting Chico, walk down to Grande and catch a return combi to Huaraz.

A relaxing spot to visit, perhaps after you've indulged in some trekking or other adventure sports, is the thermal baths **Baños Termales de Monterrey** (© **043/427-690**). A series of small wells and two large pools has mineral-rich waters that make the water look dark brown and rather unappealing, but your body might not be as picky as your eyes. The upper pool is the nicer of the two. The baths are open daily from 7am to 6pm, and they're usually very crowded on weekends and holidays. Admission is S/5. The baths are about 6km (3¾ miles) north of Huaraz along the road to Caraz; a colectivo from Avenida Luzuriaga drops passengers at the entrance.

Shopping

Huaraz is recognized as an *artesanía* center, and all of the usual Andean handicrafts are available at markets targeting gringos. However, the city has none of the upscale, tourist-friendly shops found in Cusco and Lima. Some of the best items are custom-made and hand-tooled leather goods, wool sweaters, ponchos, and blankets. Open-air handicrafts markets are open daily along the covered walkway (Pasaje Cáceres) off Avenida Luzuriaga and along the streets Juan de la Cruz Romero, Avenida Raymondi, and Avenida Tarapacá. A **mercado callejero** (street market) is open Monday and Thursday on Avenida Bolognesi and Confraternidad Oeste.

PeruKraft, on Jirón 28 de Julio, stocks good-quality alpaca sweaters; **Andes Souvenirs,** Parque Ginebra next to the Casa de Guías, has handicrafts, textiles, and silver jewelry. A company called **Andean Expressions** specializes in great-quality T-shirts with cool Andean designs; its products are found in several shops in town or its factory site, at Jr. Julio Arguedas 1246.

But unless you're going on a trekking excursion with all your provisions included, shopping for foodstuffs might be more important. At the **main market** on Cruz Romero, just south of Raymondi, you can find most everything you'll need to sustain yourself for a mountain climb or a trek, including canned foods, nuts, and fresh fruits and vegetables. **Ortiz,** Av. Luzuriaga 401, is a good and well-stocked supermarket. Cheese and *manjar blanco* (a caramel-like sweet) are good local items to take along on an expedition.

Where to Stay

The high season in Huaraz and the Cordillera Blanca is June through the end of September. During Easter Week and other holidays (such as the Fiestas Patrias at the end of July), hotel prices can double. The Semana del Andinismo, held annually in June, brings mountain climbers from around the world; then and throughout the dry season, climbing groups and student groups (the latter especially in Oct–Nov) often take over less inexpensive *hostales.* Locals with inexpensive accommodations in their homes as well as touts acting (sometimes independently) on behalf of inns often meet incoming buses; take what the hawkers tell you (about location, comfort, and so on) with a grain of salt. Although Huaraz is loaded with budget accommodations aimed at independent trekkers, only a few are nice enough to recommend without reservation.

Expensive

Andino Club Hotel ★★ The top choice in town, this Swiss-owned, upscale alpine lodge is the favorite of well-equipped climbers and business folks in town to visit the nearby mines. A modern, raked construction about a 10-minute uphill walk southeast of the Plaza de Armas in the Pedregal district, it boasts a great deal of comfort and amenities for scruffy Huaraz. With a friendly vibe and a very good Swiss restaurant (see the Chalet

Suisse review on p. 433), it's a fine place to prepare for or recover from rugged adventure travel. In high season, it's wise to book well in advance because it's popular with trekking and climbing groups. Accommodations are modern, spacious, and comfy, with beds with thick, striped Andean wool blankets. Some rooms have fireplaces. The best (but most expensive) rooms are on the second floor and have excellent panoramic views of the snowcapped Cordillera Blanca and Huascarán peaks from private balconies. There's climbing equipment rental, horseback riding, and free Internet access for guests.

Pedro Cochachín 357, Huaraz. (℃) **043/421-662** or (℃)/fax 01/241-5927 for reservations. www.hotel andino.com. 60 units. S/339–S/433 double; S/471–S700 suites. Rates include buffet breakfast. AE, DC, MC, V. **Amenities:** Restaurant. *In room:* TV, hair dryer.

Moderate

Edward's Inn ⟨**Value**⟩ One of Huaraz's most popular and longest-running inns, Edward's is an easygoing place that packs in trekkers during high season. Rooms are large and have good mountain views, although some detractors find the inn overpriced, given its fairly basic facilities. (The hot water, fueled by solar power, can be spotty.) The inn's also a bit removed from the action in town (about a 15-min. walk from the Plaza de Armas). Still, it's a good place to meet and hang out with fellow gringo trekkers and climbers. The eponymous owner, an experienced trekker and mountaineer, rents gear, speaks good English, and can provide good climbing and trekking information. He can also arrange tours, treks, and climbing trips. The rooftop patio is a good gathering spot.

Av. Bolognesi 121 (near the stadium), Huaraz. (℃)/fax **043/422-692.** www.huaraz.com/edwards/index. html. 14 units. $35 double. DC, MC, V. **Amenities:** Cafe; dining room. *In room:* TV.

Hotel Santa Cruz ★ ⟨**Finds**⟩ A clean, modern, three-level boutique-style inn with panoramic mountain views from massive windows and room balconies (in half the accommodations), this easygoing, well-run place (owned by Norwegians, and managed by an American) splits the difference between Huaraz's one upscale hotel and the city's numerous budget offerings. Rooms are cozy and comfortable, with a nod to Scandinavian simplicity (beds feature "eiderdown" comforters from Norway), and have clean private bathrooms. The public spaces, which include a nice terrace and dining room and lounge with large fireplaces, are great spots to relax after tiring treks and bike rides. The big breakfasts, including pancakes, eggs, fruits and more, are quite fortifying.

Jr. Gabino Uribe 255. (℃) **043/396-096.** www.santacruzperu.com. 12 units. $50 double. AE, MC, V. **Amenities:** Library; TV lounge.

Lazy Dog Inn ★★ ⟨**Finds**⟩⟨**Kids**⟩ This spectacularly sited, eco-styled inn, run by a Canadian couple in the Cordillera Blanca, 8km (5 miles) east of Huaraz, is a great place to get away and get outdoors. The adobe lodge features a main lodge with two rooms and two brand-new private cabins with fireplaces and bathtubs. Rooms are stylish, cozy, and colorfully decorated; the Condor Suite has a private balcony and great mountain views, while the Rima Rima cabin has an outdoor deck and fireplace. Cabins are perfect for families, with either extra bunk beds or an extra double bed. The inn, which operates a small NGO, Andean Alliance, that works with local communities, and recycles 90% of its waste, grows most of its own vegetables, and features an adobe outdoor sauna, outside fire pit, and has horses available for local mountain rides. Full meal plans are also available.

Km 3.1, Marian-Cachipampa Rd. (Huaraz). (℃) **043/978-9330.** www.thelazydoginn.com. 4 units. S/180–S/270 double. Rates include breakfast and dinner. AE, MC, V. **Amenities:** Horseback riding excursions; sauna. *In room:* Wi-Fi.

Tips   **More Budget Accommodations**

Huaraz can fill up with trekking groups and plenty of independent travelers between June and September. Many of the budget inns hawked by people who meet arriving buses are neither clean nor especially comfortable, though. If you arrive without a reservation and are looking for a solid, safe, and inexpensive inn, try one of the following hotels.

Alpes Andes **Value**   Huaraz's official youth hostel is modern, well run, clean, and safe. Part of the informative Casa de Guías, the hostel functions as a prime meeting place for trekkers and mountaineers looking to form groups. There are kitchen and laundry facilities. Parque Ginebra 28 G. ✆ **043/421-811.** casa_de_guias@hotmail.com. S/25 per person.

Hostal Chong Roca   This plain *hostal* has large and decent rooms that have either a full private bathroom or a toilet and sink. It's okay in a pinch. Morales 687. ✆ **043/421-154.** S/30 per person.

Hostal Virgen del Carmen   This comfortable *hostal* is run by a warm older couple who have converted their attractive house into an inn with very nice bedrooms. Cruz Romero 622. ✆ **043/421-729.** S/25 double.

Jo's Place   This relaxed, colorful and friendly inn has a cool garden terrace, excellent mountain views, and very well-maintained rooms. It's on the north side of the Río Quillcay, a 10- to 15-minute walk from the center of town, and is pretty popular with a steady stream of backpackers. Jr. Daniel Villayzán 276. ✆ **043/425-505.** www.huaraz.com/josplace. S/15–S/35 double.

Inexpensive

Albergue Churup Guest House ★ **Value**   One of the friendliest family-run inns in Huaraz, this low-key budget place plays happy host to lots of young gringo trekkers. In a quiet residential area just a short 5-block walk from the Plaza de Armas, Hostal Churup has good, clean rooms with private bathrooms for two to four people, and small dormitory rooms with shared bathrooms. The owners, the Quirós Romero family, are eager to share not only their knowledge of the area and trekking expeditions, but also their home (around the corner on Jirón Pedro Campos), where a filling and inexpensive breakfast is served with family members each morning. The lovely backyard is a good place to sit, read, and relax; the two double rooms there are the most private in the house. There's also a cool, brightly colored lounge, and guests can use the kitchen. It's a good idea to reserve in advance from June to September, when outdoors enthusiasts descend on Huaraz.

Jr. Amadeo Figueroa 1257 (near Iglesia Soledad), Huaraz. ✆ **043/422-584.** www.churup.com. 12 units. S/70–S/120 double with private bathroom; S/20–S/25 per person in dorm room with shared bathroom. MC, V. **Amenities:** Café; bar. *In room:* No phone, Wi-Fi.

Olaza's Bed & Breakfast ★ **Finds**   This small, spotless, and friendly inn, owned by one of the Olaza brothers (who have their hands in everything from mountain biking to T-shirts), is one of the best values in town. Set back from the street in the Soledad district (a 10-min. walk from Avenida Luzuriaga), it is quiet and safe, as well as very comfortable for the price. Rooms are simply equipped but large and have thick wool blankets and 24-hour hot water (often a rare commodity at the budget level). Bathrooms are impeccable. On the top floor is a terrific, sunny terrace with excellent mountain views, and there's also a fourth-floor lounge with a fireplace, DVD player, and even a fridge full of beer.

Julio Arguedas 1242 (La Soledad), Huaraz. ✆ 043/422-529. www.andeanexplorer.com/olaza. 9 units. $25–$35 double. Rates include breakfast. No credit cards. *In room:* No phone, Wi-Fi.

Where to Dine

Huaraz has plenty of pretty good, informal restaurants serving the band of Gore-Tex gringos that come to town. The main drag, Avenida Luzuriaga, is thick with restaurants offering fixed-price menus and other cheap eats. The Andean cuisine of the Cordillera includes hearty items such as Huaracino *picante de cuy* (spicy roasted guinea pig), *jaca-chasqui* (spicy guinea pig soup), *charqui* (dried pork), and *trucha* (fried river trout). For the less adventurous, there are several *chifas* and pizzerias in town where you can get a filling, inexpensive meal.

Alpes Andes INTERNATIONAL/PIZZA The food here might appear to take a back seat to the planning of mountain-climbing expeditions—as many mountain guides as eager tourists come through the doors—but this relaxing and informal cafe next door to the Casa de Guías (on Parque Ginebra) goes about its business of fortifying trekkers and adventurers for their trips to the Cordillera. Start with a breakfast of granola and yogurt, or chow down on the international trekkers' favorites: pizza and pasta (gotta load up on the carbs, you know).

Jr. Julián de Morales 753. ✆ 043/421-811. Reservations not accepted. Main courses S/10–S/24. No credit cards. Daily 7am–11pm.

Bistro de Los Andes ★ INTERNATIONAL/PERUVIAN This welcoming restaurant has long been one of the most popular places in town. It offers an interesting mix of French and Peruvian items for lunch and dinner and for Huaraz, a simple mountain town, it qualifies as upscale and almost elegant. The varied menu includes vegetarian dishes, pastas, and nicely done dishes such as *trucha a la almendra* (trout baked with almonds).

Jr. Julián de Morales 823. ✆ 043/426-249. Reservations not accepted. Main courses S/10–S/29. DC, V. Daily 5–11pm.

Huaraz's Cafe Culture

A number of cafes around town are inviting spots for good, inexpensive meals in addition to getting your coffee fix. **Café California** ★★, Av. 28 de Julio 562 (✆ 043/428-354), a favorite of gringos, has fresh-roasted coffee, a sitting lounge, fast Wi-Fi and a book exchange. **Café Andino** ★, on Av. Lucar y Torre 530 (✆ 043/421-203), is another popular hangout with good coffee (including cappuccinos and lattes) and breakfasts. It has a library book exchange with titles in several languages, board games, Wi-Fi, and a nice selection of tunes. Also worth a stop is **El Parque** (no phone), Figueroa 1025, an informal but clean and cute cafe with filling breakfasts and very cheap lunches as well as mixed drinks. Finally, the pub upstairs at the climbing agency **Monttrek,** Av. Luzuriaga 646 (✆ 043/421-121), has tasty pizza, a roaring fireplace, and strong pisco sours.

Chalet Suisse ★ FONDUE/SWISS   This upscale restaurant has a pretty simple chalet decor, but the food is some of the city's best. The restaurant is primarily occupied by those staying in the attached Andino Club Hotel, so if you're not a guest, it's best to ring for a reservation. Dishes are generally hearty. The Swiss fondues, while not cheap, are delicious, as are steaks (such as the Argentine *bife angosto* and *asado al vino tinto*). The attractive dining room is the perfect subdued spot to celebrate your big climb (if you're too weary to hit the pubs).

Pedro Cochachín 357. ⓒ 043/421-949. Reservations recommended. Main courses S/26–S/35. AE, DC, MC, V. Daily noon–2pm and 7–10pm.

Inka Pub Monte Rosa ★ ⓥalue INTERNATIONAL/PERUVIAN   Probably Huaraz's best-looking restaurant, this two-level place with an inviting bar feels, appropriately, like a mountain lodge. It has an extensive menu that's all over the board but universally pretty good. Choose from traditional *criollo* cooking, *chifa*, or pizzas; there are steaks, fondues, and pastas, too. Service is friendly, and between regular dining hours, it's a fine place to linger over a book and a beer.

Jr. José de la Mar 661. ⓒ 043/421-447. Reservations not accepted. Main courses S/10–S/35. MC, V. Tues–Sun noon–3pm and 6:30–10:30pm.

Pizza Bruno ★ ⓥalue INTERNATIONAL/PIZZA   With a French chef but a largely Italian menu, this upscale but relaxed restaurant—with a family-run Mediterranean decor and large-format photos of Paris—might appear a little confused, but it's one of the best dining options in town. The pizzas are of the authentic thin-crust type, and the pastas are excellent. If you're in the mood for experimenting, try one of the chef's specialties, which includes *"plato del diablo"* (devil's plate, or sirloin flambéed with whiskey). A French touch is delivered in the desserts, which include a tarte tatin and profiteroles. Breakfast is also offered.

Av. Luzuriaga 834. ⓒ 043/425-689. Reservations recommended. Main courses S/14–S/35. AE, MC, V. Daily 6am–11pm.

Siam de Los Andes ★ THAI   It's unusual to alight upon a Thai restaurant in Huaraz, but hungry trekkers looking for a taste of something different are really glad when they do—especially one with a fireplace. It's far from the cheapest restaurant in Huaraz, but the food is authentic and very well prepared. The stir-fries and curries are especially delicious. The amiable chef/owner Naresuan likes to greet diners, and, besides cooking, he knows a thing or two about trekking in the area.

Gamarra 419 (at the corner of Julián de Morales). ⓒ 043/428-006. Reservations not accepted. Main courses S/12–S/33. DC, V. Daily 5–10pm.

Huaraz After Dark

It's not hard to find a nightspot in Huaraz. With all the gringos gearing up for or celebrating the completion of trekking expeditions, the place hops in high season.

El Tambo ★, José de la Mar 776, about 3 blocks from Avenida Luzuriaga (ⓒ 043/423-417), is the most happening disco in town. There's plenty of drinking, dancing, and smoking until the wee hours, and the music careens between international Top 40 and more homegrown Latin sounds. There's usually a pretty good mix of locals and gringos. The cover charge ranges from S/10 to S/20. **Makondo's** (no phone), a full-throttle nightclub with food and dancing, is across from El Tambo on José de la Mar.

Other bars worth dropping in on include the intimate **Las Kenas,** Jr. Gabino Uribe 620 (ⓒ 043/428-383), which features live and recorded (often Andean) music and good pisco sours; **La Cueva del Oso,** Av. Luzuriaga 674 (no phone), a lively peña with good music and dancing; and the laid-back **Monttrek Pub,** Av. Luzuriaga 646 (© 043/421-121). Next door to Las Kenas is a slightly rowdier bar, **X-Treme** (© 043/682-115), a place to drink, listen to classic rock, and meet trekkers from around the world. Popular with backpacking types—who must feel at home with all the maps on the walls—is **Vagamundo Travelbar,** Av. Julián de Morales 753 (© 043/509-063), which has cool rock and blues music, a bar with couches, and frequent bonfires out on the patio.

Side Trips from Huaraz

Most folks who make it to Huaraz are understandably eager to get out into the country-side and up into the mountains. The point of a visit to Huaraz is really to explore some of the most stunning scenery on the planet; the entire valley is characterized by spectacu-lar snowcapped mountains, stunning alpine lakes, and tranquil meadows. For informa-tion on trekking, climbing, and other adventure sports, see "Trekking & Climbing in the Cordillera Blanca," below. Less rigorous excursions by organized tour are also possible; the most popular are the spectacular Lagunas de Llanganuco and the ancient ruins at Chavín de Huántar. The small towns of the Callejón de Huaylas, the valley that splits the middle between the mountain ranges of the Cordillera Blanca and the Cordillera Negra north of Huaraz, make good bases for hikes and are worthwhile visits in themselves.

Chavín de Huántar ★★
110km (68 miles) E of Huaraz

East of the Cordillera Blanca, Chavín de Huántar, the nearly 3,000-year-old ruins of the Chavín culture, is some 4 long hours by a largely unpaved and twisting mountain road (which is very slowly being improved) from Huaraz. The ruins, a UNESCO World Heritage Site and the best-preserved ruins of the culture, consist of a U-shaped fortress-temple with excellent stonework constructed over several centuries. The Chavín, who thrived in the region from about 1200 to 300 B.C. and whose influence was felt from Ecuador all the way to southern Peru, were the most ancient of the major cultures known to exist in Peru, and certainly one of its most sophisticated. The Chavín are considered perhaps the most influential people to have existed in the Andes until the arrival of the dynasty-building Incas (who came along a mere 2,000 years later).

However, don't expect a stunning set of Machu Picchu–like ruins. The site's archaeo-logical importance isn't nearly as transparently aesthetic. The temple comprises more than a dozen underground galleries or chambers; only a few are open to the public. Some appear as labyrinthine tunnels today because they were interred by a landslide in the 1940s. The main structure on the premises is a large pyramid, called the **Castillo,** built over well-constructed canals where water once flowed. A ways away is a large, sunken central plaza, a ceremonial gathering place. The highlight of the ruins is the **Lanzón** ★★★, a remarkable cultist carving in white granite and shaped like a prism or dagger. The monolith is found in an underground passage behind the original temple, which is much smaller than the several-times-enlarged Castillo. The huge 4.5m (15-ft.) carving depicts three figures worshiped by the Chavín culture: the serpent, the bird, and the feline, the principal deity. The Lanzón remains in its original location, at an underground crossroads, even though other important artifacts, including the famous Tello Obelisk and Raymondi Stela, were removed and are now housed at Museo de la Nación in Lima. A guide and a flashlight are needed to get the most out of the site. Once visitors could walk completely around and inspect the prized Lanzón; today, however, it can be viewed only from the side and a distance, down a cramped corridor.

The **Monumento Arqueológico Chavín de Huántar** (© 044/754-042), which **435** includes a small museum, is open daily from 8am to 4pm. The most convenient and fastest way to visit Chavín is by organized tour from Huaraz (Chavín Tours or Pablo Tours); most cost about S/45 per person (plus the S/11 entrance fee to the ruins). Virtually every agency offers the same program, a long day trip leaving Huaraz around 9am and returning around 8pm.

Nearby, the village of Chavín de Huántar is a traditional settlement. Although very few tourists stay overnight, the Lanzón has been known to exert a mystical hold on some visitors. In case you want to make a second day's visit to the ruins, there are a couple of decent inns in and near Chavín to spend the night (such as the inexpensive **Hotel La Casona,** © 044/754-020, on the Plaza de Armas; and **Koncuckos Tambo,** © 043/454-631; www.perunature.com, an upscale hotel about 10 min. outside of town).

Lagunas de Llanganuco ★★
82km (51 miles) N of Huaraz

These two brilliant turquoise alpine lakes, at nearly 4,000m (13,120 ft.) above sea level, compose a dazzling vista at the base of the Cordillera Blanca's highest snowcapped summits. The views of Chopicalqui (6,354m/20,841 ft.), Huandoy (6,395m/20,976 ft.), and hulking Huascarán (6,768m/22,199 ft.) are simply mesmerizing. If possible, wait for a clear morning to go; the sun shining on the lakes makes them shimmer and their colors change. The glacier-fed lakes within the Huascarán National Park (entry fee S/5) are a popular day trip from Huaraz, and many tour companies in Huaraz offer Llanganuco as an organized tour for about S/35 per person. Those up for more of an adventure can also organize a day trek to the lagunas (those with more time on their hands might opt for the 4- to 5-day Llanganuco–Santa Cruz trek, one of the most beautiful and popular treks on the continent; see "Trekking & Climbing in the Cordillera Blanca," below). If you're traveling independently, the lakes are easiest to get to from Yungay, which is 26km (16 miles) away; it's simple to catch a combi or truck up to the lakes from the Plaza de Armas in Yungay (about S/20 round-trip), but note that the ride can take up to 90 minutes.

Glaciar Pastoruri ★
70km (43 miles) S of Huaraz

The Cordillera Blanca is tightly packed with towering peaks that should be ascended only by skilled and properly outfitted climbers. If you're not in that camp, this relatively flat glacier, another popular day trip from Huaraz, might be a draw. Provided that you've already become acclimatized to the altitude of the area, the 45-minute trek up the glacier (5,240m/17,187 ft.) isn't difficult and can be done without special equipment, although horses and mules are frequently available to help those having a hard time trudging through the snow. Though Peruvians often ski and snowboard on the glacier, veteran skiers will be disappointed; the glacier is shrinking, the snow is icy, and the rope-tow seems to come and go. Bring sufficient cold-weather gear because it can get very frigid.

As an organized outing, the trip to Pastoruri is usually combined with a visit to the valley of **Pachacoto,** 57km (35 miles) south of Huaraz, an opportunity to see the Callejón de Huaylas's famous **Puya Raimondi** plants. The bizarre, spiky plants, like towering alien cacti, are the largest members of the bromeliad family (a relative of the pineapple). The species is thought to be one of the most ancient in the world, and it is found only in a few isolated, high-altitude parts of the Andes. The plant, which can reach a height of 12m (39 ft.), is like a tragic protagonist: It flowers but once in its life, and although it might live to be 100 years old, it dies immediately after flowering. Flowering usually happens in May, when tour groups make pilgrimages to witness the brief, beautiful sight, like a stage set against the snowy mountains. Organized Pastoruri/Puya Raymondi visits are about S/30 per person.

Carhuaz

31km (19 miles) N of Huaraz

This quiet, rather plain Andean town stands in stark contrast to the tourism hustle of Huaraz. It's becoming better known as a base in its own right for mountain-adventure travel, but it doesn't have even a fraction of the tourism infrastructure found in Huaraz. Still, it has a couple of nice *hostales* and restaurants for people looking for a more serene atmosphere. Carhuaz is locally renowned for its Virgen de las Mercedes festival, which takes place for 10 days in mid-September and is perhaps the most raucous festival in the valley.

There aren't many actual sights in town, other than the bustling Sunday market, but a few places just outside Carhuaz are worth a look. Near the small town of Mancos (a half-hour from Carhuaz by combi) is the ancient cave Cueva de Guitarreros, which some anthropologists believe to be 12,000 years old. The cave, which contains primitive rock paintings, is a nice 30-minute walk from Mancos south across the river. There are good views of Huascarán. Near Marcará, about 6.5km (4 miles) south of Carhuaz, are the Baños Termales de Chancos (hot springs).

To get to Carhuaz, take a combi from Huaraz; the trip takes about an hour and costs S/4. If you want to spend the night in Carhuaz, perhaps your best bet is one of the family-run guesthouses, or *casas de alojamiento*. Try **Las Bromelias,** Jr. Brasil 208 (© **043/394-033**), with rooms for $10 double, or, better still, **La Casa de Pocha** (© **043/363-058**), an eco-ranch outside of town, boasting a peaceful organic farm and adobe guesthouse with excellent views and opportunities for horseback riding and hiking in the forest. It runs $40 per person for a double room including meals.

Yungay

54km (33 miles) N of Huaraz

This small town is permanently marked by tragedy: It was completely buried in just a matter of minutes in a 1970 landslide, which was precipitated by the massive earthquake (7.8 on the Richter scale) that loosened tons of granite and ice from the north peak of Huascarán. The hurtling mass killed at least 20,000 people, nearly the town's entire population. Only a few children and those who, ironically, scrambled to the higher grounds of the local cemetery, survived. The rubble, called Campo Santo, is now a macabre tourist attraction. The only reminders of the life that once existed there are four palm trees that graced the Plaza de Armas and rosebushes and monuments honoring the dead. A new settlement was established about a half-mile away. Predictably, the rebuilt town isn't too easy on the eyes, save its alpine location; it's mostly a functional transportation

---

(Fun Facts) **Top of the Peaks**

Among the highest and best known of Peru's daunting pinnacles—trophies prized by climbers the world over—are Mount Huascarán, 6,768m (22,205 ft.); the Huandoy massif's three summits, all more than 6,000m (19,680 ft.) high; Chopicalqui, 6,354m (20,846 ft.); Chacraraju, 6,112m (20,052 ft.); Alpamayo, 5,957m (19,544 ft.); and Copa, 6,118m (20,072 ft.).

hub for those looking to approach the stunning lakes of Llanganuco (above). In town, there's a small museum, the **Museo de Arqueología e Historia Natural de Yungay,** Avenida Las Palmeras, Ranrahirca (✆ 043/682-322), which exhibits regional flora and fauna, ceramics, textiles, and other historical relics.

Combis leave from the Quillcay Bridge on Alameda Fitzcarrald Huaraz for Yungay. The trip, which takes about 1½ hours, costs S/3.

Caraz

68km (42 miles) N of Huaraz

Caraz is the farthest of the valley towns north of Huaraz that are accessible by public transportation. More attractive than some of the other towns that have suffered great natural disaster, and located at an elevation about 1,000m (3,280 ft.) lower than Huaraz, Caraz makes a good base for trekking and climbing in the Cordillera Blanca. The town has a pleasant plaza and a growing amount of infrastructure to serve trekkers and mountaineers, including one of the area's top outdoor-adventure agencies. Many people end up (and rest up) in Caraz after trekking the popular Llanganuco–Santa Cruz route, although nearly as many embark from here to remote treks into the northern Cordillera Blanca.

Caraz has a couple small museums: a **Museo de Arqueología,** Esquina 1 de Mayo y Manuel Cáceres (✆ 043/791-029; Tues–Sun 9am–1pm and 2–5pm; admission S/3), which has some deformed skulls and artifacts uncovered at the Cueva de Guitarreros, and the **Museo Amauta de Arte Ancashino,** Av. Noe Bazán Peralta s/n (✆ 043/791-004; daily 9am–noon and 3–5pm; admission S/3), which contains some ethnographic exhibits representing villages of the Callejón de Huaylas. Nearby are some pre-Chavín ruins, **Tunshucaiko,** about a half-mile from the center of town across the Río Llullán.

Although many people make their way to Caraz to begin some hard-core mountain excursions, several worthwhile and easier excursions make excellent day trips. Gorgeous **Laguna Parón** is a bold, bright blue lake that sits at an elevation of more than 4,000m (13,120 ft.) and is surrounded by a dozen snowcapped peaks, 30km (19 miles) east of town. Colectivos run from Santa Rosa in Caraz to Parón (90 min.). The **Cañón del Pato** is a fantastic, sheer canyon formed by the Río Santa, dividing the Cordilleras Blanca and Negra. Although it is more than 1,000m (3,280 ft.) deep, it is only 15m (49 ft.) wide. The road that knifes through the canyon, from Caraz to Huallanca, is one of the most thrilling in the country; it penetrates more than three dozen tunnels. By colectivo, it's about 2 hours to Huallanca, the far end of the canyon, from Caraz.

Caraz is a 2-hour combi ride from Huaraz. If you want to stay overnight in Caraz, try one of the following inexpensive inns that are popular with trekkers and backpackers: **Hostal Perla de los Andes,** Daniel Villar 179 (Plaza de Armas; ✆ 043/392-007; www. huaraz.com/perladelosandes; $18 double) next to the cathedral, with simple rooms overlooking the handsome Plaza de Armas; **Los Piños Lodge,** Parque San Martín 103 (✆ 043/391-140; $20 double), an attractive place with a nice cafe; or **Grand Hostal Caraz Dulzura,** Sáenz Peña 212 (✆ 043/391-523; www.huaraz.com/carazdulzura; $20 double), a pleasant, modern hotel built around a patio.

In town are **Pony Expeditions,** one of the best trekking and mountaineering agencies in the valley, with equipment rental and good guides (see "Recommended Tour Companies," below), and **Apu Expeditions,** Villar 215 (✆ 043/392-159). **Café de Rat** (✆ 043/291-642), Jr. Sucre 1286, on the Plaza de Armas above Pony Expeditions, is the place for mountaineers to hang out and fortify themselves with pizzas, pastas, crepes, good vegetarian meals, and beer. (It also has Internet access, maps, and guidebooks.)

The Cordillera Blanca, the highest tropical mountain chain in the world, is one of South America's most impressive ranges. Its glorious and imposing mountain peaks proclaim their beauty and power over a 180km (112-mile) stretch through the heart of Peru. Most visitors to the Cordillera Blanca mountain range want to view the stunning scenery of snowcapped peaks, glaciers, lakes, and rivers from up close and on high. They have one thing in mind: strapping on high-tech gear and embarking on trekking or climbing expeditions.

This section of Peru has become one of the world's mountaineering meccas. Fifty summits soar between 4,800 and 6,662m (15,748–21,857 ft.) high, and nearly the entire range forms part of the protected Parque Nacional Huascarán. Although the most challenging peaks are beacons to some of the most tested mountaineers in the world, there are plenty of trekking and climbing activities for those who haven't quite perfected their ascent techniques. And although some of the peaks are plenty daunting, access to the trail heads is fairly simple, reached by public transportation in just a few hours from Huaraz.

The 340,000-hectare (839,800-acre) Parque Nacional Huascarán was created in 1975 to protect the region's great natural resources. Within the park are the towns Recuay, Huaraz, Carhuaz, Yungay, Huaylas, Bolognesi, Huari, Asunción, Piscobamba, and Pomabamba, several of which serve as bases for explorers. The park counts 32 peaks higher than 6,000m (19,680 ft.) and includes Huascarán, Peru's highest summit, and Alpamayo, whose legendary fourth face is considered by many mountaineers as the most beautiful in the world, as well as 269 lakes and 41 rivers among its spectacular roster of natural blessings.

Most of the top climbs in the Cordillera Blanca are best done with the assistance of local guides and experts. Several climbs are not only arduous, but also extremely dangerous. Unless you're a certified member of the hard-core ilk, it's best to contract a guide or organized tour in Huaraz. There, you'll find a whole complement of services, including licensed guides, porters, climbing-gear rentals, and rescue teams. However, plenty of independent and self-reliant trekkers simply hire an *arriero* (muleteer) and set off without a proper guide.

Tips **The Cost of Trekking & Climbing**

All multiday excursions (up to 1 month) into the Huascarán National Park carry entrance fees of S/65. If you're going with a tour operator, ask whether this fee is included in your package cost. Single-day entry costs S/5.

Licensed climbing and trekking guides charge between $60 and $100 per day. *Arrieros,* local porters with mules who'll lead you on trails, charge about $15 per day, plus food. (*Arrieros* can be arranged at trail heads or at the Casa de Guías in Huaraz.) Organized treks with one of the firms listed earlier are generally around $35 to $50 per day, per person. A certified guide to lead technical mountain climbs can cost upwards of $90. Serious climbers should also factor in the cost of insurance (obtained at home) that protects against the prohibitive cost of rescue operations.

> ## (Tips) A Gear Checklist
>
> Appropriate technical gear is required for nearly all treks and climbs in the Cordillera Blanca. If you're going with an organized group, you can rent anything you need that's not provided. Independent trekkers and climbers can also rent almost anything they need in Huaraz. Some equipment is invariably dated and in less than optimal condition, so experienced mountain climbers pursuing technical climbs will surely want to bring all their own equipment. At a minimum, you'll need cold-weather and water-repellent clothing; good backpacking or climbing boots; a tent, a sleeping bag, a camping stove, and cookware; a filter and/or water-purification tablets; a compass; and topographical maps of trails.

In recent years, there has been a fair amount of grousing about the deteriorating state of the Parque Nacional Huascarán, from both trekkers and agencies; many complain that it is not being kept up as it should, with the most popular trails littered with refuse and bribes supplanting group payment of entry fees. If one of Peru's national treasures is being neglected, it will surely have a great impact not only on the local environment, but also on the local economy. So many individuals and communities depend upon the income produced by largely foreign adventure travelers who come to enjoy the remote beauty of the Peruvian Andes.

The fee to enter Huascarán National Park is S/5 for a single-day visit and S/65 for multi-day pass (valid up to 1 month). The entrance ticket to Huascarán National Park can be purchased at the Llanganuco and other entrances. You should keep a copy of your passport ready when entering and leaving the park.

Recommended Tour Companies

In Peru, it's important to pick tour operators carefully to avoid being ripped off. A good guide from a respected agency knows the routes, the weather, and the risks, and can usually steer you away from the latter. In the event of an emergency, he or she will know how to get injured parties evacuated. If you're serious about adventure sports, you don't want to skimp when it comes to the people to whom you're entrusting your safety and well-being. Locals suggest that you demand a *factura* (receipt) with an "RUC" (taxpayer registration number) from any prospective agency or guide.

The following are all recommended agencies and guides with many years of experience and good reputations in the Huaraz/Cordillera Blanca region. Even so, ask around first. Talk to people who've recently returned from treks and climbing expeditions. Contact the **South American Explorers** either in Lima, at Av. Piura 135, Miraflores (© 01/445-3306; www.saexplorers.org); or Cusco, at Choquechaca 188, no. 4 (© 084/245-484; cuscoclub@saexplorers.org). Also speak to the **Casa de Guías de Huaraz,** Parque Ginebra 28 (© 043/421-811), an excellent source of current information (although understand that its mission is primarily to hook you up with one of its guides—who generally charge about $50 per day). Don't overlook your guide's ability to speak English, which could be critical if your understanding of Spanish is poor. Even if the agency says that the guide speaks good English, don't automatically take its word for it.

Cordillera Huayhuash: The New "It" Range

As the treks in the Cordillera Blanca have become more popular in recent years, intrepid trekkers who are determined to find yet more solitude and untrammeled scenery are now setting out on extended trekking circuits of the **Cordillera Huayhuash** ★★★, which is even more pristine and remote. Although it extends only 30km (19 miles) from north to south, it, too, has phenomenal mountain vistas and sparkling lagunas—perhaps more spectacular still than the Cordillera Blanca—but only a few very isolated and primitive mountain communities.

The range, which was made a natural preserve in 2002, comprises seven peaks more than 6,000m (19,680 ft.) high and seven additional peaks higher than 5,500m (18,040 ft.). The landscape is more wide-open than that of the Cordillera Blanca, which is characterized by deep canyons. The major trekking and climbing agencies in Huaraz and Caraz offer Huayhuash treks, which usually begin in the town of Chiquián at 3,400m (11,150 ft.), 110km (68 miles) south of Huaraz. Trekking in the range is difficult, with as many as eight passes higher than 4,500m (14,760 ft.), and two main circuits are popular: One is 80km (50 miles) round-trip; the other, which covers the entire range, is as much as 165km (102 miles) and takes from 12 to 14 days.

Virtually every agency in town runs the basic and most popular little-to-no-difficulty programs to Lagunas de Llanganuco, Glaciar Pastoruri, and Chavín de Huántar (see "Side Trips from Huaraz," earlier in this chapter) for about $10 per person. Agencies often pool travelers when they can't round up enough on their own.

General Tours

- **Huaraz Chavín Tours,** Av. Luzuriaga 502, Huaraz (✆ 043/421-578 or 01/447-0024; www.chavintours.com.pe): A good company offering standard tours, including trips to Chavín de Huántar, Pastoruri Glacier, and Llanganuco lakes.
- **Pablo Tours,** Av. Luzuriaga 501, Huaraz (✆ 043/421-145; www.pablotours.com): A standard tour company, similar to Chavín Tours but offering a few more options. Also organizes good group treks.

Mountain Trekking & Climbing

- **Explorandes Peru** ★★★, Av. Centenario 489, Huaraz (✆ 043/421-960 or 01/715-2323; www.explorandes.com): This environmentally sensitive and serious agency is one of the big-name and longest-established adventure-tour operators in Peru, with fixed-departure treks in the Cordillera Blanca. It's expensive, but it's one of the best and most dependable. Explorandes offers both hard-core adventure and soft-adventure programs, and will custom-tailor a trip for small groups. Programs range from llama trekking to Chavín to 12-day treks in the Cordillera Huayhuash.
- **JM Expeditions,** Av. Luzuriaga 465, Of. 4, Huaraz (✆ 043/428-017 or 01/426-0599; www.jmexpeditions.com): Good mountain-climbing equipment and roster of guides.

- **Monttrek ★★★**, Av. Luzuriaga 646, 2nd Floor, Huaraz (℡ 043/421-124): One of the climbing and trekking pioneers in Huaraz, now going on 20 years in the area, this serious agency organizes hard-core ascents and expeditions, including ice and rock climbing. The company also offers programs for budget-conscious trekkers, as well as camping- and climbing-equipment rental, guides, mountain- and ice-climbing classes, and horseback riding, mountain biking, river rafting, and hang gliding. New programs include Overland Andino (aka World War II jeep) and excursions to Cañon del Pato and Lagunas Llanganuco. With its nice upstairs pub restaurant (which has an interior climbing wall), Monttrek is a good spot to put together a group of like-minded adventurers. Serious climbers will want to speak to the owner, Pocho, and check out his technical drawings of nearly every peak in the region.
- **Pony Expeditions ★★**, Jr. Sucre 1266, Plaza de Armas, Caraz (℡ 043/391-642; www.ponyexpeditions.com): This professional outfitter is run by a respected guide, Alberto Cafferata, with lots of different treks and climbs available. It offers an extensive program of trekking and climbing itineraries, mountain biking, and rock and ice climbing.
- **Pyramid Adventures**, Luzuriaga 530, Huaraz (℡ 043/421-864; www.pyramidadventures.net): One of the better climbing agencies, run by a family of brothers, with good service and knowledge.

Guides & Equipment Rental

- **Galaxia Mountain Shop**, Leoniza y Lescano 603 (℡ 043/422-792), and **Mount-Climb**, Mariscal Cáceres 421 (℡ 043/426-060): Both have a full range of mountain-climbing gear, including boots, sleeping bags, and crampons, for rent (about S/30 per day for full complement of equipment).
- **Montañero Aventura y Turismo**, Parque Ginebra 30B, Huaraz (℡ 043/726-386): Climbing equipment, guides, mountain bikes, and standard tours.
- **Mountain Bike Adventures ★★**, Jirón Lúcar y Torre 530, Huaraz (℡ 043/424-259; www.chakinaniperu.com): The top company for single-track riding in the Cordilleras Blanca and Negra, run by Julio Olaza. He has Trek front-suspension bikes for rent (including helmets) and offers several 4- to 7-day itineraries, as well as 1-day bike trips. The company also runs a small and enjoyable guesthouse.

Trekking

The Cordillera Blanca is blessed with some of the greatest trails and most spectacular scenery in South America, and it draws trekkers from across the world. Across gorgeous valleys and mountain passes nearly 5,000m (16,400 ft.) high, past stunning lakes, waterfalls, and rivers, the region truly earns the cliché so often accorded it: It's a mountaineer and trekker's paradise. There are terrific campsites throughout the valley and excellent guides, porters, and mules to round out your expedition.

There are some three dozen well-established treks in the Cordillera Blanca (and many dozens more that draw few tourists). Of the many treks possible from Huaraz, the classic **Llanganuco–Santa Cruz** route, one of the most beautiful on the continent, is understandably the most popular. The route across the Santa Cruz gorge begins in the village of Cashapampa and makes its way to the emerald-green lakes at the Llanganuco ravine. The 45km (28-mile) trek usually takes 4 or 5 days. Other popular circuits include **Alpamayo**, a beautiful trek among snowcapped summits that takes about 12 days; **Cedros Gorge**, which takes in mountains in the northern sector of the Huascarán Park

(4 days); and **Llanganuco** and **Portachuelo,** a less demanding trek through the Quill-cayhuanca ravine (1–2 days).

Other well-known routes are:

- **Cojup Valley** (Huaraz to Laguna Palcacucha), 20km (12 miles), 2 days (moderate)
- **Laguna Churup,** 25km (16 miles), 1 to 2 days (difficult)
- **Olleros to Chavín,** a pre-Columbian trail that ends at Chavín de Huántar, 40km (25 miles), 3 days (moderate)
- **Quebrada Quillcayhuanca to Cayesh,** 25km (16 miles), 2 to 3 days (easy to moderate)

The Casa de Guías in Huaraz has detailed information about these and other treks, and South American Explorers produces a good map of various treks in the region. Another good resource is *Peru & Bolivia: Backpacking and Trekking* (Bradt Publications, 2002), by Hilary Bradt, with descriptions of a number of treks in the Cordillera Blanca.

Even more accessible hikes in this daunting region should be undertaken only by individuals in good physical shape; tackling a mountain pass at nearly 5,000m (16,400 ft.) with gear and food is not easy for those unaccustomed to high altitudes.

Llanganuco–Santa Cruz Trek ★★★

Touted as one of the top five treks in the world by several international outdoor-oriented magazines, the 4- to 5-day Llanganuco–Santa Cruz trail is one of the most scenic in Peru. It takes in extraordinary mountain scenery of snowcapped peaks, brilliant turquoise lakes, glacier-fed rivers, sparkling waterfalls, and serene meadows. The 62km (38-mile) trail ranges from 2,900 to 4,750m (9,512–15,580 ft.) in altitude but is rated moderate to difficult, meaning that the hike can be undertaken by anyone in good physical shape who has allowed for time to acclimatize in Huaraz. In peak season, though, the trail's popularity is its enemy. It gets quite crowded, and trash is a problem. There are established campsites and pit toilets along the route.

Trekkers can walk the trail in either direction, starting at Cashapampa (2 hr. by bus from Caraz) or Vaquería (2½ hr. by bus from Carhuaz). Many independent travelers prefer to start the trail at Vaquería because the daily bus from Huaraz allows time to make it to the campsite on the first day and get a good jump on the high pass the following day.

All-inclusive treks from Santa Cruz to Llanganuco in a "pooled" service start at about $200 per person.

Mountain Climbing

Climbing in the Cordillera Blanca ranges from highly technical, multipitch ascents to rigorous but nontechnical climbs. The optimal climbing season is May through September. Huaraz serves as the principal hub for contracting qualified guides and tour operators and renting gear, but some similar infrastructure, on a smaller scale, can also be found in Caraz. The **Casa de Guías** in Huaraz (© **043/421-811**) is one of your best preclimb resources, with a list of registered guides.

For experienced climbers up to the challenge, the Cordillera Blanca is nirvana. The range includes 50 permanently snowcapped mountain peaks of more than 5,610m (18,400 ft.), amazingly packed into an area just 177km (110 miles) long and 19km (12 miles) wide. Tested mountaineers can hope to bag several 6,000m (19,680-ft.) summits in just a 2- or 3-week trip. Less experienced climbers can choose among several easier and more popular climbs. For anyone, though, acclimatization is paramount. Allow between 3 days and 1 week before attempting any serious ascent.

The snowy peaks of **Ishinca** (5,534m/18,156 ft.) and **Pisco** (5,752m/18,871 ft.)— essentially 3-day climbs—require appropriate gear, conditioning, and guides, but can be undertaken by inexperienced climbers. Peru's most beautiful mountain, **Alpamayo** (5,957m/19,544 ft.) is an appropriate climb for those with some experience. **Huascarán** (6,768m/22,205 ft.), the highest mountain in the Peruvian Andes and the tallest tropical mountain in the world, takes between 6 and 9 days and poses a very challenging climb, suitable only for those with technical knowledge and extensive experience.

Other Adventure Sports

HANG GLIDING   Yungay's hill Pan de Azúcar is the most common spot for hang gliding. For more information, contact **Monttrek** (© 043/421-124).

ICE CLIMBING   The Cordillera Blanca is a great spot to give this serious sport a try. The best mountains for ice climbing are Pisco, Ishinca, Huascarán, Alpamayo, Chopicalqui, and Artesonraju. Contact **Pony Expeditions** (© 043/391-642; www.pony expeditions.com) or **Monttrek** (© 043/421-124) for more information.

MOUNTAIN BIKING   The Callejón de Huaylas is one of Peru's top destinations for mountain bikers, with hundreds of mountain and valley horse trails cutting across fields, bridges, and creeks, and past traditional Andean villages. Dedicated cyclists can also look forward to the thrill of climbing to 5,000m (16,400 ft.) through mountain passes.

In Huaraz, you can rent mountain bikes for an hour, a day, or a week. During the annual Semana del Andinismo in June, there's a mountain-bike competition. Two of Peru's best mountain-bike agencies operate in the area: **Mountain Bike Adventures** in Huaraz (© 043/424-259; www.chakinaniperu.com) and **Pony Expeditions** in Caraz (© 043/391-642; www.ponyexpeditions.com). Both have equipment rental and excellent biking itineraries.

RIVER RAFTING   Near Carhuaz, the Río Santa, which runs the length of the Callejón de Huaylas from Laguna Conococha, is where rafting in the area is practiced. Sections differ in degree of difficulty from easy (Classes II–III) to technical (Class V). The section that's most often rafted is between Jangas and Caraz. The season is May through September, when water levels are low. **Monttrek** (© 043/421-124) and a handful of other tour operators in Huaraz offer rafting.

ROCK CLIMBING   Several agencies in Huaraz offer full-day rock-climbing tours in Caraz and Yungay, ranging from easy to moderate. Monterrey's Rocódromo and Uquia are the most popular spots. For more information, contact **Monttrek** (© 043/421-124); the agency even has an interior climbing wall at its headquarters in Huaraz.

13

Fast Facts

1 FAST FACTS: PERU

ADDRESSES "Jr." doesn't mean "junior"; it is a designation meaning *jirón*, or street, just as "Av." (sometimes "Avda.") is an abbreviation for *avenida*, or avenue. "Ctra." is the abbreviation for *carretera*, or highway; "Cdra." means *cuadra*, or block; and "Of." is used to designate office *(oficina)* number. Perhaps the most confusing element in Peruvian street addresses is "s/n," which frequently appears in place of a number after the name of the street; "s/n" means *sin número*, or no number. The house or building with such an address simply is unnumbered. At other times, a building number may appear hyphenated, such as "102–105," meaning that the building in question simply contains both address numbers (though usually only one main entrance).

AMERICAN EXPRESS See p. 112 in chapter 6 for info on American Express offices.

AREA CODES Note that even though many area codes across Peru were changed back in 2003, you many find that many published telephone numbers may still contain old area codes. The area codes for the regions covered in this book are: Lima, 01; Ica, Nasca, and Pisco, 056; Cusco and the Sacred Valley, 084; Puerto Maldonado, 082; Puno/Lake Titicaca, 051; Arequipa, 054; Huaraz, 043; Trujillo, 044; Cajamarca, 076; Chiclayo, 074; and Iquitos, 065.

BUSINESS HOURS Most stores are open from 9 or 10am to 12:30pm, and from 3 to 5 or 8pm. Banks are generally open Monday through Friday from 9:30am to 4pm, although some stay open until 6pm. In major cities, most banks are also open Saturday from 9:30am to 12:30pm. Offices are open from 8:30am to 12:30pm and 3 to 6pm, although many operate continuously from 9am to 5pm. Government offices are open Monday through Friday from 9:30am to 12:30pm and 3 to 5pm. Nightclubs in large cities often don't get going until after midnight, and many stay open until dawn.

DRUG & LIQUOR LAWS Until recently, Peru was the world's largest producer of coca leaves, the base product that is mostly shipped to Colombia for processing into cocaine. Cocaine and other illegal substances are perhaps not as ubiquitous in Peru as some might think, although in Lima and Cusco, they are commonly offered to foreigners. (This is especially dangerous; many would-be dealers also operate as police informants, and some are said to be undercover narcotics officers themselves.) Penalties for the possession and use of or trafficking in illegal drugs in Peru are strict; convicted offenders can expect long jail sentences and substantial fines. Peruvian police routinely detain drug smugglers at Lima's international airport and land-border crossings. Since 1995, more than 40 U.S. citizens have been convicted of narcotics trafficking in Peru. If you are arrested on drug charges, you will face protracted pretrial detention in poor prison conditions.

Coca leaves, either chewed or brewed for tea, are not illegal in Peru, where they're not considered a narcotic. The use of coca leaves is an ancient tradition dating back to pre-Columbian civilizations in Peru. You might very well find that *mate de coca* (coca-leaf tea) is very helpful in battling altitude sickness. However, if you attempt to take coca leaves back to your home country from Peru, you should expect them to be confiscated, and you could even find yourself prosecuted.

The hallucinogenic plants consumed in *ayahuasca* ceremonies are legal in Peru.

A legal drinking age is not strictly enforced in Peru. Anyone over the age of 16 is unlikely to have any problems ordering liquor in any bar or other establishment. Wine, beer, and alcohol are widely available—sold daily at grocery stores, liquor stores, and in all cafes, bars, and restaurants—and consumed widely, especially in public during festivals. There appears to be very little taboo associated with public inebriation at festivals.

ELECTRICITY All outlets are 220 volts, 60 cycles AC (except in Arequipa, which operates on 50 cycles), with two-prong outlets that accept both flat and round prongs. Some large hotels also have 110-volt outlets.

EMBASSIES & CONSULATES The following are all in Lima: **United States,** Avenida La Encalada, Block 17, Surco (© 01/434-3000); **Australia,** Victor A. Belaúnde 147/Vía Principal 155, Bldg. 3, Of. 1301, San Isidro (© 01/222-8281); **Canada,** Calle Bolognesi 228, Miraflores (© 01/319-3200); **United Kingdom** and **New Zealand,** Av. Jose Larco 1301, 22nd Floor, Miraflores (© 01/617-3000).

The U.S. consulate is located at Av. Pardo 845 (© **084/231-474;** CoresES@ state.gov). The honorary U.K. consulate is at Manu Expeditions, Urbanización Magisterial, G-5 Segunda Etap (© **084/239-974;** bwalker@terra.com.pe). Both are open daily from 9am to noon and 3 to 5pm.

EMERGENCIES In case of an emergency, call the 24-hour **traveler's hot line** at © **01/574-8000,** or the **tourist police** (POLTUR; © **01/460-1060** in Lima, or 01/460-0965; see "Fast Facts" in individual destination chapters for branch information). The general police emergency number is © **105.** The **Tourist Protection Service** can also assist in contacting police to report a crime; call © **01/224-7888** in Lima, or 0800/4-2579 toll-free from any private phone (the toll-free number cannot be dialed from a public pay phone).

GUIDES Officially licensed guides are available on-site at many archaeological sites and other places of interest to foreigners. They can be contracted directly, although you should verify their ability to speak English if you do not comprehend Spanish well. Establish a price beforehand. Many cities are battling a scourge of unlicensed and unscrupulous guides who provide inferior services or, worse, cheat visitors. As a general rule, do not accept unsolicited offers to arrange excursions, transportation, or hotel accommodations. See "Tipping" below for advice on tipping guides.

INSURANCE For information on traveler's insurance, trip cancelation insurance, and medical insurance while traveling please visit www.frommers.com/planning.

LANGUAGE Spanish is the official language of Peru. The Amerindian languages Quechua (recently given official status) and Aymara are spoken primarily in the highlands. (Aymara is mostly limited to the area around Lake Titicaca.) English is not widely spoken but is understood by those affiliated with the tourist industry in major cities and tourist destinations. Most people you meet on the street will have only a very rudimentary understanding of English, if that. Learning a few key phrases of Spanish will help immensely. Turn to chapter 14 for those, and consider picking up a copy of the *Frommer's Spanish Phrase-Finder & Dictionary.*

LEGAL AID If you need legal assistance, your best bets are your embassy (which, depending on the situation, might not be able to help you much) and the **Tourist Protection Service** (© **0800/4-2579** toll-free, or 01/574-8000 24-hr.), which might be able to direct you to an English-speaking attorney or legal assistance organization.

Note that bribing a police officer or public official is illegal in Peru, even if it is a relatively constant feature of traffic stops and the like. If a police officer claims to be an undercover cop, do not automatically assume that he is telling the truth. Do not get in any vehicle with such a person. Demand the assistance of your embassy or consulate, or of the Tourist Protection Service.

MAIL Peru's postal service is reasonably efficient, especially now that it is managed by a private company (**Serpost S.A.**). Post offices are open Monday through Saturday from 8am to 8pm; some are also open Sunday from 9am to 1pm. Major cities have a main post office and often several smaller branch offices. Letters and postcards to North America take between 10 days and 2 weeks, and cost S/5.50 for postcards, S/7.20 for letters; to Europe either runs S/7.80. If you are purchasing large quantities of textiles and other handicrafts, you can send packages home from post offices, but it is not inexpensive—more than $100 for 10kg (22 lb.), similar to what it costs to use DHL, where you're likely to have an easier time communicating. UPS is found in several cities, but for inexplicable reasons, its courier services cost nearly three times as much as those of DHL.

NEWSPAPERS & MAGAZINES In Lima, you will find copies (although rarely same-day publications) of the *International Herald Tribune,* the *Miami Herald,* and the odd European newspaper, as well as *Time, Newsweek,* and other special-interest publications. All might be at least several days old. Top-flight hotels sometimes offer free daily fax summations of the *New York Times* to their guests. Otherwise, your best source for timely news is likely to be checking in with news outlet websites. Outside Lima, international newspapers and magazines are hard to come by. Among local publications, look for *Rumbos,* a glossy Peruvian travel magazine in English and Spanish with excellent photography. If you read Spanish, *El Comercio* and *La República* are two of the best daily newspapers.

PASSPORTS See www.frommers.com/planning for information on how to obtain a passport. See "Embassies & Consulates," above, for whom to contact if you lose yours while traveling in the U.S. For other information, please contact the following agencies:

For Residents of Australia: Contact the **Australian Passport Information Service** at © **131-232,** or visit the government website at www.passports.gov.au.

For Residents of Canada: Contact the central **Passport Office,** Department of Foreign Affairs and International Trade, Ottawa, ON K1A 0G3 (© **800/567-6868;** www.ppt.gc.ca).

For Residents of Ireland: Contact the **Passport Office,** Setanta Centre, Molesworth Street, Dublin 2 (© **01/671-1633;** www.irlgov.ie/iveagh).

For Residents of New Zealand: Contact the **Passports Office** at © **0800/225-050** in New Zealand, or 04/474-8100; or log on to www.passports.govt.nz.

For Residents of the United Kingdom: Visit your nearest passport office, major post office, or travel agency or contact the **United Kingdom Identity & Passport Service** at © **0870/521-0410** or search its website at www.ukpa.gov.uk.

For Residents of the United States: To find your regional passport office, either check the U.S. State Department website or call the **National Passport Information Center** toll-free number (© **877/487-2778**) for automated information.

POLICE Peru has special tourist police forces (Policía Nacional de Turismo) with offices and personnel in all major tourist destinations, including Lima, Cusco, Arequipa, and Puno, as well as a dozen other cities. You are more likely to get a satisfactory response, not to mention someone who speaks at least some English, from the tourist police rather than from the regular national police (PNP). The number for the tourist police in Lima is ℂ **01/225-8698** or 01/225-8699. For other cities, see "Emergencies" above and "Fast Facts" in individual destination chapters. Tourist police officers are distinguished by their white shirts.

SAFETY Peru has not earned a great reputation for safety among travelers, although the situation is improving. Simple theft and pickpocketing remain fairly common; assaults and robbery are rare. Most thieves look for moments when travelers, laden with bags and struggling with maps, are distracted.

Although most visitors travel freely throughout Peru without incident, warnings must be heeded. In downtown Lima and the city's residential and hotel areas, the risk of street crime remains high. Carjackings, assaults, and armed robberies are not unheard of; occasional armed attacks at ATMs occur. However, in most heavily touristed places in Peru, a heightened police presence is noticeable. Use ATMs during the day, with other people present.

Street crime is prevalent in Cusco, Arequipa, and Puno, and pickpockets are known to patrol public markets. In Cusco, "strangle" muggings (in which victims are choked unconscious and then relieved of all belongings) were reported in years past, particularly on streets leading off the Plaza de Armas, the San Blas neighborhood, and near the train station. This form of violent assault seems to have subsided, but you should still not walk alone late at night on deserted streets.

In major cities, taxis hailed on the street can lead to assaults. (I highly recommend using telephone-dispatched radio taxis, especially at night.) Ask your hotel or restaurant to call a cab, or call one from the list of recommended taxi companies in the individual city sections.

Travelers should exercise extreme caution on public city transportation, where pickpockets are rife, and on long-distance buses and trains (especially at night), where thieves employ any number of strategies to relieve passengers of their bags. You need to be supremely vigilant, even to the extreme of locking backpacks and suitcases to luggage racks. Be extremely careful in all train and bus stations.

In general, do not wear expensive jewelry; keep expensive camera equipment out of view as much as possible; use a money belt worn inside your pants or shirt to safeguard cash, credit cards, and passport. Wear your daypack on your chest rather than your back when walking in crowded areas. The time to be most careful is when you have most of your belongings on your person—such as when you're in transit from airport or train or bus station to your hotel. At airports, it's best to spend a little more for official airport taxis; if in doubt, request the driver's official ID. Don't venture beyond airport grounds for a street taxi. Have your hotel call a taxi for your trip to the airport or bus station.

Large-scale terrorist activities of the local insurgency groups Sendero Luminoso (Shining Path) and MRTA (Tupac Amaru Revolutionary Movement)—which together waged a 2-decade guerrilla war against the Peruvian state, killing more than 30,000 people—were effectively stamped out in the early 1990s. However, in recent years there have been growing concerns about a possible resurgence of those groups (especially after a car bomb outside the U.S. embassy in Lima in 2002). In December 2005, a state of emergency was declared in six central

Amazon provinces after Shining Path guerrillas killed eight policemen in the remote Huanaco region—upping the total to 19 police and military officers assassinated in 2005 and again raising the specter of renewed violence across Peru. Though it remains a situation worth watching, to date the most populous (and traveled) regions of the country have not been affected, and neither group is currently active in any of the areas covered in this book.

SMOKING Smoking is common in Peru, and it is rare to find a hotel, restaurant, or bar with nonsmoking rooms. However, there are now a few hotels (usually high-end) and restaurants with designated nonsmoking rooms, and the trend is growing, albeit slowly. There are nonsmoking cars on trains, and most long-distance buses are also nonsmoking.

TAXES A general sales tax (IGV) is added automatically to most consumer bills (19%). In some upmarket hotels or restaurants, service charges of 10% are often added. At all airports, passengers must pay a departure tax: $31 for international flights, and $6 for domestic flights, payable in cash only (either U.S. dollars or Peruvian nuevos soles).

TIME Peru is 5 hours behind GMT (Greenwich Mean Time). Peru does not observe daylight saving time.

TIPPING Most people leave about a 10% tip for the waitstaff in restaurants. In nicer restaurants that add a 10% service charge, many patrons tip an additional 5% or 10% (because little, if any, of that service charge will ever make it to the waiter's pocket). Taxi drivers are not usually tipped unless they provide additional service. Bilingual tour guides on group tours should be tipped ($1–$2, per person for a short visit, and $5 or more per person for a full day). If you have a private guide, tip about $10 to $20.

TOILETS Public lavatories (baños públicos) are rarely available except in railway stations, restaurants, and theaters. Many Peruvian men choose to urinate in public, against a wall in full view, especially late at night; it's not recommended that you emulate them. Use the bathroom of a bar, cafe, or restaurant; if it feels uncomfortable to dart in and out, have a coffee at the bar. Public restrooms are labeled wc (water closet), DAMAS (Ladies), and CABALLEROS or HOMBRES (Men). Toilet paper is not always provided, and when it is, most establishments request that patrons throw it in the wastebasket rather than the toilet, to avoid clogging.

Visas For information about U.S. Visas go to **http://travel.state.gov** and click on "Visas." Or go to one of the following websites:

Australian citizens can obtain up-to-date visa information from the **U.S. Embassy Canberra,** Moonah Place, Yarralumla, ACT 2600 (© **02/6214-5600**) or by checking the U.S. Diplomatic Mission's website at **http://usembassy-australia.state.gov/consular**.

British subjects can obtain up-to-date visa information by calling the **U.S. Embassy Visa Information Line** (© **0891/200-290**) or by visiting the "Visas to the U.S." section of the American Embassy London's website at **www.usembassy.org.uk**.

Irish citizens can obtain up-to-date visa information through the **Embassy of the USA Dublin,** 42 Elgin Rd., Dublin 4, Ireland (© **353/1-668-8777;** or by checking the "Visas to the U.S." section of the website at **http://dublin.usembassy.gov**.

Citizens of **New Zealand** can obtain up-to-date visa information by contacting the **U.S. Embassy New Zealand,** 29 Fitzherbert Terrace, Thorndon, Wellington (© **644/472-2068**), or get the information directly from the website at **http://wellington.usembassy.gov**.

VISITOR INFORMATION Within Peru, there's a 24-hour tourist information line, **iPerú** (© **01/574-8000**. Peru doesn't maintain national tourism offices abroad, so your best official source of information before you go is **www.peru.info**, the website of Prom Perú (Commission for the Promotion of Peru). Other helpful trip-planning websites include **www.peruvian embassy.us**, the Embassy of Peru in Washington, D.C.; **www.traficoperu.com/ english**, the site for Traficoperu, a travel agency with information about flights, hotels, and special deals; **www.enjoyperu. com**, a similar site with good background information on specific areas; **www.peru rail.com**, the official PeruRail website with route and service information; and **www.saexplorers.org**, the South American Explorers website, which is especially good for trekking and adventure travel information. Sites with good information on specific places include **www.huaylas.com** and **www. andeanexplorer.com**, for trekking and other information on Huaraz and the Callejón de Huaylas; and **www.machupicchu. org**, for more information on the celebrated Inca ruins and other sights in the Sacred Valley of the Incas. **South American Explorers** (www.saexplorers.org), with clubhouses in Lima and Cusco, is an excellent source of information, particularly on trekking and mountaineering in Peru, with a good

selection of guides, maps, and dossiers on travel and trails, which is available to members. You can contact the group in the United States at $\textcircled{C}$ **800/274-0568** or 607/277-0488; otherwise, visit its Lima office at Piura 135, Miraflores ($\textcircled{C}$ **01/445-3306**), or the Cusco office at Choquechaca 188, no. 4 ($\textcircled{C}$ **084/245-484**).

The **Tourist Protection Bureau (Servicio de Protección al Turista),** which handles complaints and questions about consumer rights, operates a 24-hour traveler's assistance line at $\textcircled{C}$ **0800/42-579,** or 01/224-7888 in Lima. The Tourist Protection Bureau office is at La Prosa 138, San Borja, Lima ($\textcircled{C}$ **01/224-7888**) or toll-free from cities other than Lima ($\textcircled{C}$ **0800/42-579**). For local branch locations and telephone numbers of the Tourist Protection Bureau, see "Fast Facts" in individual destination chapters.

For domestic and international **flight information,** call $\textcircled{C}$ **01/575-1712** or visit www.lap.com.pe.

WATER Visitors should drink only bottled water, which is widely available. Do not drink tap water, even in major hotels. Try to avoid drinks with ice. *Agua con gas* is carbonated; *agua sin gas* is still water.

2 AIRLINE, HOTEL & CAR-RENTAL WEBSITES

MAJOR AIRLINES

Aeroméxico
www.aeromexico.com

Air France
www.airfrance.com

American Airlines
www.aa.com

Aviacsa (Mexico and southern U.S.)
www.aviacsa.com.mx

British Airways
www.british-airways.com

Continental Airlines
www.continental.com

Delta Air Lines
www.delta.com

Iberia Airlines
www.iberia.com

LAN Airlines
www.lan.com

TACA Airlines
www.taca.com

United Airlines
www.united.com

PERUVIAN AIRLINES

LC Busre
www.lcbusre.com.pe

Peruvian Airlines
www.peruvianairlines.pe

Star Perú
www.starperu.com

MAJOR HOTEL & MOTEL CHAINS

Best Western
www.bestwestern.com

Doubletree Hotels
www.doubletree.com

Hilton Hotels
www.hilton.com

Marriott
www.marriott.com

Radisson Hotels & Resorts
www.radisson.com

Ramada Worldwide
www.ramada.com

Sheraton Hotels
www.starwoodhotels.com/sheraton

Westin Hotels & Resorts
www.starwoodhotels.com/westin

Wyndham Hotels & Resorts
www.wyndham.com

CAR-RENTAL AGENCIES

Avis
www.avis.com

Budget
www.budget.com

Dollar
www.dollar.com

Enterprise
www.enterprise.com

Hertz
www.hertz.com

National
www.nationalcar.com

Thrifty
www.thrifty.com

Useful Terms & Phrases

Peruvian Spanish is, for the most part, straightforward and fairly free of the quirks and national slang that force visitors to page through their dictionaries in desperation. But if you know Spanish, some of the terms you will hear people saying are *chibolo* for *muchacho* (boy); *churro* and *papasito* for *guapo* (good-looking); *jato* instead of *casa* (house); *chapar* (literally "to grab or get"), slangier than but with the same meaning as *besar* (to kiss); *¡que paja está!* (it's great); *mi pata* to connote a dude or chick from your posse; and *papi* (or *papito*) and *mami* (or *mamita*), affectionate terms for "mother" and "father" that are also used as endearments between relatives and lovers (which can get a little confusing to the untrained outsider). The inherited Amerindian respect for nature is evident; words such as *Pachamama* (Mother Earth) tend to make it into conversation remarkably frequently.

Spanish is but one official language of Peru, though. **Quechua** (the language of the Inca Empire) was recently given official status and is still widely spoken, especially in the highlands, and there's a movement afoot to include **Aymara** as a national language. (Aymara is spoken principally in the southern highlands area around Lake Titicaca.) A couple dozen other native tongues are still spoken. A predominantly oral language (the Incas had no written texts), Quechua is full of glottal and magical, curious sounds. As it is written today, it is mystifyingly vowel-heavy and apostrophe-laden, full of q's, k's, and y's; try to wrap your tongue around *munayniykimanta* (excuse me) or *hayk' atan kubrawanki llamaykikunanmanta* (how much is it to hire a llama?). Very few people seem to agree on spellings of Quechua, as alluded to in chapter 7. Colorful phrases often mix and match Spanish and Amerindian languages: *Hacer la tutumeme* is the same as *ir a dormir,* or "to go to sleep."

In addition to these primary languages, there are dozens of Indian tongues and dialects in the Amazon region, many of which are in danger of extinction.

1 BASIC SPANISH VOCABULARY

English	Spanish	Pronunciation
Good day	**Buenos días**	*Bweh-*nohs *dee-*ahs
Hi/hello	**Hola**	*Oh-*lah
Pleasure to meet you	**Mucho gusto/Un placer**	*Moo-*choh *goos-*toh/Oon plah-*sehr*
How are you?	**¿Cómo está?**	*Koh-*moh es-*tah*
Very well	**Muy bien**	Mwee byehn
Thank you	**Gracias**	*Grah-*syahs
How's it going?	**¿Qué tal?**	Keh tahl
You're welcome	**De nada**	Deh *nah-*dah
Goodbye	**Adiós**	Ah-*dyohs*
Please	**Por favor**	Pohr fah-*bohr*

English | **Spanish** | **Pronunciation**

English	Spanish	Pronunciation
Yes	**Sí**	See
No	**No**	Noh
Excuse me (to get by someone)	**Perdóneme/ Con permiso**	Pehr-*doh*-neh-meh/ Kohn pehr-*mee*-soh
Excuse me (to begin a question)	**Disculpe**	Dees-*kool*-peh
Give me	**Déme**	*Deh*-meh
What time is it?	**¿Qué hora es?**	Keh *ohr*-ah ehs?
Where is . . . ?	**¿Dónde está . . . ?**	*Dohn*-deh eh-*stah*
the station (bus/train)	**la estación estación de ómnibus/tren**	lah eh-stah-*syohn* eh-stah-*syohn* deh *ohm*-nee-boos/trehn
a hotel	**un hotel**	oon oh-*tel*
a gas station	**una estación de servicio**	*oo*-nah eh-stah-*syohn* deh sehr-*bee*-syoh
a restaurant	**un restaurante**	oon res-tow-*rahn*-teh
the toilet	**el baño** (or **servicios**)	el *bah*-nyoh (sehr-*bee*-syohs)
a good doctor	**un buen médico**	oon bwehn *meh*-dee-coh
the road to . . .	**el camino a/hacia . . .**	el cah-*mee*-noh ah/*ah*-syah
To the right	**A la derecha**	Ah lah deh-*reh*-chah
To the left	**A la izquierda**	Ah lah ee-*skyehr*-dah
Straight ahead	**Derecho**	Deh-*reh*-choh
Is it far?	**¿Está lejos?**	Eh-*stah* *leh*-hohs?
It is close?	**¿Está cerca?**	Eh-*stah* *sehr*-kah
Open	**Abierto**	Ah-*byehr*-toh
Closed	**Cerrado**	Seh-*rah*-doh
North	**Norte**	*Nohr*-teh
South	**Sur**	Soor
East	**Este**	*Eh*-steh
West	**Oeste**	Oh-*eh*-steh
Expensive	**Caro**	*Cah*-roh
Cheap	**Barato**	Bah-*rah*-toh
I would like	**Quisiera**	Kee-*syeh*-rah
I want	**Quiero**	*Kyeh*-roh
to eat	**comer**	koh-*mehr*
a room	**una habitación**	*oo*-nah ah-bee-tah-*syohn*
Do you have . . . ?	**¿Tiene usted . . . ?**	*Tyeh*-neh oo-*stehd*
a book	**un libro**	oon *lee*-broh
a dictionary	**un diccionario**	oon deek-syoh-*na*-ryoh
change	**cambio**	kahm-byoh
How much is it?	**¿Cuánto cuesta?**	*Kwahn*-toh *kwes*-tah

USEFUL TERMS & PHRASES

BASIC SPANISH VOCABULARY

English	Spanish	Pronunciation
When?	¿Cuándo?	*Kwahn*-doh
What?	¿Qué?	Keh
There is (Is/Are there . . . ?)	(¿)Hay (. . . ?)	eye
What is there?	¿Qué hay?	Keh eye
Yesterday	Ayer	Ah-*yehr*
Today	Hoy	Oy
Tomorrow	Mañana	Mah-*nyah*-nah
Good	Bueno	*Bweh*-noh
Bad	Malo	*Mah*-loh
Better (best)	(Lo) Mejor	(Loh) Meh-*hohr*
More	Más	Mahs
Less	Menos	*Meh*-nohs
No smoking	Se prohibe fumar	Seh proh-*ee*-beh foo-*mahr*
Postcard	Tarjeta postal	Tahr-*heh*-tah pohs-*tahl*
Insect repellent	Repelente contra insectos	Reh-peh-*lehn*-teh *cohn*-trah een-*sehk*-tohs
Now	Ahora	Ah-*ohr*-ah
Right now	Ahora mismo (ahorita)	Ah-*ohr*-ah *mees*-moh (ah-ohr-*ee*-tah)
Later	Más tarde	Mahs *tahr*-deh
Never	Nunca	*Noon*-kah
Guide	Guía	*Ghee*-ah
Heat	Calor	Kah-*lohr*
It's hot!	¡Qué calor!	Keh kah-*lohr*
Cold	Frío	*Free*-oh
Rain	Lluvia	*Yoo*-byah
It's cold!	¡Qué frío!	Keh *free*-oh
Wind	Viento	*Byehn*-toh
It's windy!	¡Cuánto viento!	*Kwahn*-toh *byehn*-toh
Money-changer	Cambista	Kahm-*bee*-stah
Bank	Banco	*Bahn*-koh
Money	Dinero	Dee-*neh*-roh
Small (correct) change	Sencillo	Sehn-*see*-yoh
Credit card	Tarjeta de crédito	Tahr-*heh*-tah deh *creh*-dee-toh
ATM	Cajero automático	Kah-*heh*-roh ow-toh-*mah*-tee-koh
Tourist information office	Oficina de información turística	Oh-fee-*see*-nah deh een-for-mah-*syohn* too-*ree*-stee-kah

USEFUL TERMS & PHRASES

14

BASIC SPANISH VOCABULARY

1	**uno** (*oo*-noh)		17	**diecisiete** (dyeh-see-*syeh*-teh)
2	**dos** (dohs)		18	**dieciocho** (dyeh-*syoh*-choh)
3	**tres** (trehs)		19	**diecinueve** (dyeh-see-*nweh*-beh)
4	**cuatro** (*kwah*-troh)		20	**veinte** (*bayn*-teh)
5	**cinco** (*seen*-koh)		30	**treinta** (*trayn*-tah)
6	**seis** (sayss)		40	**cuarenta** (kwah-*ren*-tah)
7	**siete** (*syeh*-teh)		50	**cincuenta** (seen-*kwen*-tah)
8	**ocho** (*oh*-choh)		60	**sesenta** (seh-*sehn*-tah)
9	**nueve** (*nweh*-beh)		70	**setenta** (seh-*tehn*-tah)
10	**diez** (dyehs)		80	**ochenta** (oh-*chen*-tah)
11	**once** (*ohn*-seh)		90	**noventa** (noh-*ben*-tah)
12	**doce** (*doh*-seh)		100	**cien** (syehn)
13	**trece** (*treh*-seh)		200	**doscientos** (do-*syehn*-tohs)
14	**catorce** (kah-*tohr*-seh)		500	**quinientos** (kee-*nyehn*-tohs)
15	**quince** (*keen*-seh)		1,000	**mil** (meel)
16	**dieciséis** (dyeh-see-*sayss*)			

---

2 SPANISH MENU GLOSSARY

GENERAL TERMS

Beef/steak	**Lomo**	Potatoes	**Papas**
Bread	**Pan**	French fries	**Papas fritas**
Chicken	**Pollo**	Rice	**Arroz**
Dessert	**Postre**	Roast	**Asado**
Eggs	**Huevos**	Salad	**Ensalada**
Fish	**Pescado**	Seafood	**Mariscos**
Fruit	**Fruta**	Shrimp	**Camarones**
Lamb	**Cordero**	Soup	**Sopa (chupe)**
Meat	**Carne**	Sweet potato	**Camote**
Pork	**Cerdo/puerco**	Vegetables	**Verduras**

MEAT

Adobo   Meat dish in a spicy chili sauce

Alpaca   Alpaca steak

Anticuchos   Shish kebab

Cabrito   Goat

Carne de res   Beef

Chicharrones   Fried pork skins

Conejo   Rabbit

Cordero   Lamb

Empanada   Pastry turnover filled with meat, vegetables, fruit, manjar blanco, or sometimes nothing at all

Estofado   Stew

Lomo asado   Roast beef

Parrillada   Grilled meats

Pato   Duck

Pollo a la brasa   Spit-roasted chicken

Venado   Venison

SEAFOOD

Corvina Sea bass
Langosta Lobster
Langostinos Prawns
Lenguado Sole

Mero Mediterranean grouper
Paiche Large Amazon fish
Tollo Spotted dogfish

BEVERAGES

Beer **Cerveza**
Mixed fruit juice **Refresco**
Juice **Jugo**
Milk **Leche**
Soft drink **Gaseosa**

Water **Agua**
  carbonated **con gas**
  still **sin gas**
Wine **Vino**
Cocktail **Cóctel/trago**

PREPARATION

Fixed-price menu **El menu**
Spicy **Picante**
Hot (temperature) **Caliente**
Cold (temperature) **Frío**

Raw **Crudo**
Cooked **Cocido**
Fried **Frito**
Vegetarian **Vegetariano**

PERUVIAN FAVORITES

Ají de gallina Spicy/creamy chicken
Anticuchos Beef-heart brochettes
Causa Mashed potatoes with avocado, stuffed with chicken or tuna
Ceviche Marinated raw fish
Chaufa Chinese fried rice
Chicha Fermented maize beer
Chicha morada Blue-corn nonalcoholic beverage
Chifa Peruvian-Chinese food
Chupe soup or chowder (chupe de camarones, prawn chowder, is the most common)
Choclo Maize (large-kernel corn)
Cuy Guinea pig
Flan Caramel custard
Lomo saltado Strips of beef with fried potatoes, onions, and tomatoes over rice
Manjar blanco Sweetened condensed milk
Pachamanca Roast meat and potatoes, prepared underground

Paiche Amazon river fish
Palta Avocado
Palta rellena (or palta a la Reina) Stuffed avocado (with chicken or tuna salad)
Panqueque Crepe
Papa a la huancaína Boiled potatoes in a creamy and spicy cheese sauce
Papa rellena Stuffed and fried potato
Quinua Andean grain (quinoa), often in soup (sopa de quinua)
Rocoto relleno Stuffed hot pepper
Sopa a la criolla Creole soup (noodles or grain, often quinoa, vegetables, and meat)
Tamal Ground corn cooked and stuffed with chicken or pork, wrapped in banana leaves or corn husks, and then steamed
Tiradito Cevichelike strips of raw fish, marinated with ají peppers and lime but without sweet potatoes or onions, akin to Peruvian sashimi or carpaccio

3 QUECHUA & QUECHUA-DERIVED TERMS

Quechua ("*Ketch*-u-wa") was the language of the Inca Empire, and it remains widely spoken in Peru and throughout Andean nations 5 centuries after the Spaniards did so much to impose their own culture, language, and religion upon the region. It is the most widely spoken Amerindian language. Called *Runasimi* (literally, "language of the people") by Quechua speakers, the language is spoken by more than 10 million people in the highlands of South America. As much as one-third of Peru's 28 million people speak Quechua. Quechua speakers call themselves Runa—simply translated, "the people."

Quechua is an agglutinative language, meaning that words are constructed from a root word and combined with a large number of suffixes and infixes, which are added to words to change meaning and add subtlety. Linguists consider Quechua unusually poetic and expressive. Quechua is not a monolithic language, though. More than two dozen dialects are currently spoken in Peru. The one of greatest reach, not surprisingly, is the one still spoken in Cusco. Though continually threatened by Spanish, Quechua remains a vital language in the Andes.

In recent decades, however, many Andean migrants to urban areas have tried to distance themselves from their Amerindian roots, fearful that they would be marginalized by the Spanish-speaking majority in cities—many of whom regard Quechua and other native languages as the domain of the poor and uneducated. (Parents often refuse to speak Quechua with their children.) In some ways the presidency of Alejandro Toledo, himself of Amerindian descent, has led to a new valuation of Quechua (and Aymara). Toledo said he hoped to spur new interest and pride in native culture in schools and among all Peruvians, and he made a point of having the Quechua language spoken at his 2001 inaugural ceremonies at Machu Picchu. (Even Toledo's Belgian-born wife addressed the crowd in Quechua.)

Quechua has made its influence felt on Peruvian Spanish, of course, which has hundreds of Quechua words, ranging from names of plants and animals (*papa,* potato; *cuy,* guinea pig) to food (*choclo,* corn on the cob; *pachamanca,* a type of earth oven) and clothing (*chompa,* sweater; *chullu,* knitted cap). Quechua has also made its way into English. Words commonly used in English that are derived from Quechua include coca, condor, guano, gaucho, lima (as in the bean), llama, and puma.

COMMON TERMS

Altiplano   Plateau/high plains

Apu   Sacred summit/mountain spirit

Campesino   Rural worker/peasant

Chacra   Plot of land

Cocha   Lake

Huayno   Andean musical style

Inca   Inca ruler/emperor

Inti   Sun

Intiwatana   "Hitching post of the sun" (stone pillar at Inca ceremonial sites)

Mestizo   Person of mixed European and Amerindian lineage

Pachamama   Mother Earth

Pucara   Fortress

Runasimi   Quechua language

Soroche   Altitude sickness (hypoxia)

Tambo   In-transit checkpoint on Inca highway

Tawantinsuyu   Inca Empire

Tumi   Andean knife

Viracocha   Inca deity (creator god)

TRY A LITTLE QUECHUA

English	Quechua	Pronunciation
Yes	**Riki**	*Ree*-kee
No	**Mana**	*Mah*-nah
Madam	**Mama**	*Mah*-mah
Sir	**Tayta**	*Tahy*-tah
Thank you	**Añay**	Ah-*nyahy*

---

4 ETIQUETTE & CUSTOMS

APPROPRIATE ATTIRE Many travelers to Peru are dressed head-to-toe in adventure or outdoor gear (parkas, fleece wear, hiking boots, and cargo pants). This is perfectly acceptable attire for all but the fanciest restaurants, where "neat casual" would be a better solution. In churches and monasteries, err on the side of discretion (low-rise pants, midriff shirts, peekaboo thongs, and anything else that reveals a lot of skin are not usually acceptable).

AVOIDING OFFENSE In Peru, you should be tactful when discussing local politics, though open discussion of the corruption of past presidents and terrorism in Peru is perfectly acceptable and unlikely to engender heated debate. Discussion of drugs (and coca-plant cultivation) and religion should be handled with great tact. Visitors should understand that chewing coca leaves (or drinking coca tea) is not drug use but a long-standing cultural tradition in the Andes.

In a country in which nearly half the population is Amerindian, expressing respect for native peoples is important. Try to refer to them not as *indios,* which is a derogatory term, but as *indígenas.* Many Peruvians refer to foreigners as *gringos* (or *gringas*) or the generic "mister," pronounced "*mee*-ster." Neither is intended or should be received as an insult.

On the streets of Cusco and other towns across Peru, shoeshine boys and little girls selling cigarettes or postcards can be very persistent and persuasive. Others just ask directly for money (using the euphemism *propinita,* or little tip). The best way to give money to those who are obviously in need of it is to reward them for their work. I get my scruffy shoes shined on a daily basis in Peru, and I buy postcards I probably don't need. If you don't wish to be hassled, a polite but firm "*No, gracias*" is usually sufficient, but it's important to treat even these street kids with respect.

Queries about one's marital status and children are considered polite; indeed, women traveling alone or with other women should expect such questions. However, discussion of how much one earns is a generally touchy subject, especially in a poor country such as Peru. Although Peruvians might be curious and ask you directly how much you make, or how much your apartment or house or car or even clothes cost, I suggest that you deflect the question. At a minimum, explain how much higher the cost of living is in your home country, and how you're not as wealthy as you might seem. Ostentatious display of one's relative wealth is unseemly, even though Peru will be blissfully inexpensive to many budget travelers.

SHOPPING Bargaining is considered acceptable in markets and with taxi drivers, and even hotels, but only up to a point—don't overdo it. Also bear in mind that many shops in large and small towns close at midday, from 1 to 3pm or 2 to 4pm.

GESTURES Peruvians are more formal in social relations than most North Americans and Europeans. Peruvians shake hands frequently and tirelessly, and although kissing on the cheek is a common greeting for acquaintances, it is not practiced among strangers (as it is in Spain, for example). Amerindian populations are more conservative and even shy. They don't kiss to greet one another, nor do they shake hands as frequently as other Peruvians; if they do, it is a light brush of the hand rather than a firm grip. Many Indians from small villages are reluctant to look a stranger in the eye.

Using your index finger to motion a person to approach you, as practiced in the United States and other places, is considered rude. A more polite way to beckon someone is to place the palm down and gently sweep your fingers toward you.

GREETINGS When entering a shop or home, always use an appropriate oral greeting (*buenos días,* or good day; *buenas tardes,* or good afternoon; *buenas noches,* or good night). Similarly, upon leaving, it is polite to say goodbye (*Adios* or *Hasta luego*), even to shop owners with whom you've had minimal contact. Peruvians often shake hands upon leaving as well as greeting.

PHOTOGRAPHY With their vibrant dress and expressive faces and festivals, Peruvians across the country make wonderful subjects for photographs. In some heavily touristed areas, such as the Sunday market in Pisac outside of Cusco, locals have learned to offer photo ops for a price at every turn. Some foreigners hand out money and candy indiscriminately, while others grapple with the unseemliness of paying for every photo. Asking for a tip in return for being the subject of a photograph is common in many parts of Peru; in fact, some locals patrol the streets with llamas and kids in tow to pose for photographs as their main source of income. Often it's more comfortable to photograph people you have made an effort to talk to, rather than responding to those who explicitly beg to be your subject. I usually give a small tip (50 centavos to S/1, or 35¢) if it appears that my camera has been an intrusion or nuisance, or especially if I've snapped several shots.

It's not common except in very touristed places (such as the Pisac market), but some young mothers carrying adorable children in knapsacks and with flowers in their hair (and outstretched hands requesting a *propinita,* or tip) aren't actually mothers (or at least, not the mothers of the children they're carrying around); to tug at your tourist heartstrings and pockets, they have essentially "rented" the babies from real moms in remote villages. I don't think it's an especially good idea to reward this practice. If a very young woman has several children in tow, all dolled up for pictures and making the rounds all afternoon, she is very likely one of these rent-a-moms.

Photographing military, police, or airport installations is strictly forbidden. Many churches, convents, and museums also do not allow photography or video.

PUNCTUALITY Punctuality is not one of the trademarks of Peru or Latin America in general. Peruvians are customarily a half-hour late to most personal appointments, and it is not considered very bad form to leave someone hanging in a cafe for up to an hour. It is expected, so if you have a meeting scheduled, unless a strict *hora inglesa* (English hour) is specified, be prepared to wait.

INDEX